Knowledge-Guided Machine Learning

Given their tremendous success in commercial applications, machine learning (ML) models are increasingly being considered as alternatives to science-based models in many disciplines. Yet, these "black-box" ML models have found limited success due to their inability to work well in the presence of limited training data and generalize to unseen scenarios. As a result, there is a growing interest in the scientific community on creating a new generation of methods that integrate scientific knowledge in ML frameworks. This emerging field, called scientific knowledge-guided ML (KGML), seeks a distinct departure from existing "data-only" or "scientific knowledge-only" methods to use knowledge and data at an equal footing. Indeed, KGML involves diverse scientific and ML communities, where researchers and practitioners from various backgrounds and application domains are continually adding richness to the problem formulations and research methods in this emerging field.

Knowledge Guided Machine Learning: Accelerating Discovery using Scientific Knowledge and Data provides an introduction to this rapidly growing field by discussing some of the common themes of research in KGML using illustrative examples, case studies, and reviews from diverse application domains and research communities as book chapters by leading researchers.

KEY FEATURES

- First-of-its-kind book in an emerging area of research that is gaining widespread attention in the scientific and data science fields

- Accessible to a broad audience in data science and scientific and engineering fields

- Provides a coherent organizational structure to the problem formulations and research methods in the emerging field of KGML using illustrative examples from diverse application domains

- Contains chapters by leading researchers, which illustrate the cutting-edge research trends, opportunities, and challenges in KGML research from multiple perspectives

- Enables cross-pollination of KGML problem formulations and research methods across disciplines

- Highlights critical gaps that require further investigation by the broader community of researchers and practitioners to realize the full potential of KGML

Chapman & Hall/CRC

Data Mining and Knowledge Series

Series Editor: Vipin Kumar

Knowledge-Guided Machine Learning

Accelerating Discovery Using Scientific Knowledge and Data

Edited by
Anuj Karpatne
Ramakrishnan Kannan
Vipin Kumar

CRC Press
Taylor & Francis Group
Boca Raton London New York

CRC Press is an imprint of the
Taylor & Francis Group, an **informa** business
A CHAPMAN & HALL BOOK

First Edition published 2023
by CRC Press
6000 Broken Sound Parkway NW, Suite 300, Boca Raton, FL 33487-2742

and by CRC Press
4 Park Square, Milton Park, Abingdon, Oxon, OX14 4RN

CRC Press is an imprint of Taylor & Francis Group, LLC

Library of Congress Cataloging-in-Publication Data

Names: Karpatne, Anuj, editor. | Kannan, Ramakrishnan, editor. | Kumar, Vipin, 1956- editor.
Title: Knowledge guided machine learning : accelerating discovery using scientific knowledge and data / edited by Anuj Karpatne, Ramakrishnan Kannan, Vipin Kumar.
Description: First edition. | Boca Raton : CRC Press, 2022. | Series: Chapman & Hall/CRC data mining and knowledge discovery series | Includes bibliographical references and index.
Identifiers: LCCN 2021061965 | ISBN 9780367693411 (hardback) | ISBN 9780367698201 (paperback) | ISBN 9781003143376 (ebook)
Subjects: LCSH: Machine learning. | Data mining.
Classification: LCC Q325.5 .K566 2022 | DDC 006.3/1--dc23/eng20220415
LC record available at https://lccn.loc.gov/2021061965

ISBN: 978-0-367-69341-1 (hbk)
ISBN: 978-0-367-69820-1 (pbk)
ISBN: 978-1-003-14337-6 (ebk)

DOI: 10.1201/9781003143376

Typeset in CMR10 font
by KnowledgeWorks Global Ltd.

Contents

About the Editors

Anuj Karpatne is an Assistant Professor in the Department of Computer Science at Virginia Tech. His research focuses on pushing on the frontiers of knowledge-guided machine learning by combining scientific knowledge and data in the design and learning of machine learning methods to solve scientific and societally relevant problems.

Ramakrishnan Kannan is the group leader for Discrete Algorithms at Oak Ridge National Laboratory. His research expertise is in distributed machine learning and graph algorithms on HPC platforms and their application to scientific data with a specific interest for accelerating scientific discovery.

Vipin Kumar is a Regents Professor at the University of Minnesota's Computer Science and Engineering Department. His current major research focus is on knowledge-guided machine learning and its applications to understanding the impact of human-induced changes on the Earth and its environment.

List of Contributors

Aniruddha Adiga
University of Virginia
Charlottesville, Virginia

Bernhard Ahrens
Max-Planck Institute for Biogeochemistry
Jena, Germany

Alison P. Appling
U.S. Geological Survey
University Park, Pennsylvania

Thomas F. Blum
Oak Ridge National Laboratory
Oak Ridge, Tennessee

Nigel D. Browning
University of Liverpool
Liverpool, United Kingdom

Steven L. Brunton
University of Washington
Seattle, Washington

Jie Bu
Virginia Tech
Blacksburg, Virginia

Ze Cao
Virginia Tech
Blacksburg, Virginia

Gustau Camps-Valls
Universitat de Valéncia
Valéncia, Spain

Cayelan C. Carey
Virginia Tech
Blacksburg, Virginia

Nuno Carvalhais
Max-Planck Institute for Biogeochemistry
Jena, Germany

Jiangzhuo Chen
University of Virginia
Arlington, Virginia

Miaofang Chi
Oak Ridge National Laboratory
Oak Ridge, Tennessee

Souma Chowdhury
University at Buffalo, The State University
of New York
Buffalo, New York

Eric F. Darve
Stanford University
Stanford, California

Arka Daw
Virginia Tech
Blacksburg, Virginia

Matthew Farthing
US Army Engineer Research and
Development Center
Vicksburg, Mississippi

Mojtaba Forghani
Stanford University
Menlo Park, California

Fabian Gans
Max-Planck Institute for Biogeochemistry
Jena, Germany

Cristina Garcia-Cardona
Los Alamos National Laboratory,
Los Alamos, New Mexico

Nicholas Geneva
University of Notre Dame
Notre Dame, Indiana

Pierre Gentine
Columbia University
New York, New York

Jeffrey A. Graves
Oak Ridge National Laboratory
Oak Ridge, Tennessee

Long He
Virginia Tech
Blacksburg, Virginia

Tyler Hesser
US Army Engineer Research and
    Development Center
Vicksburg, Mississippi

Xiaowei Jia
University of Pittsburgh
Pittsburgh, Pennsylvania

Travis Johnston
Oak Ridge National Laboratory
Oak Ridge, Tennessee

Peter K. Kitanidis
Stanford University
Stanford, California

Basil Kraft
Max-Planck Institute for Biogeochemistry
Jena, Germany

J. Nathan Kutz
University of Washington
Seattle, Washington

Jonghyun Lee
University of Hawaii at Manoaa
Honolulu, Hawaii

Bryan Lewis
University of Virginia
Charlottesville, Virginia

Madhav V. Marathe
University of Virginia
Charlottesville, Virginia

B. Layla Mehdi
University of Liverpool
Liverpool, United Kingdom

Nikhil Muralidhar
Virginia Tech
Arlington, Virginia

Ryan Nguyen
Clemson University
Warwick, New York

Daniel Nicholls
University of Liverpool
Liverpool, United Kingdom

Paris Perdikaris
University of Pennsylvania
Philadelphia, Pennsylvania

Thomas Proffen
Oak Ridge National Laboratory
Oak Ridge, Tennessee

Yizhou Qian
Stanford University
Palo Alto, California

Rahul Rai
Clemson University
Greenville, South Carolina

Naren Ramakrishnan
Virginia Tech
Arlington, Virginia

Jordan S. Read
U.S. Geological Survey
Middleton, Wisconsin

Markus Reichstein
Max-Planck Institute for Biogeochemistry
Jena, Germany

Adam Sadilek
Google
Mountain View, California

Piyush Sao
Oak Ridge National Laboratory
Oak Ridge, Tennessee

Sudip K. Seal
Oak Ridge National Laboratory
Oak Ridge, Tennessee

Michael Steinbach
University of Minnesota
Minneapolis, Minnesota

Andrew Stevens
OptimalSensing LLC
Southlake, Texas

Danesh Tafti
Virginia Tech
Blacksburg, Virginia

R. Quinn Thomas
Virginia Tech
Blacksburg, Virginia

Chung-Yan Shih
National Energy Technology Laboratory
Pittsburgh, Pennsylvania

Alexander Y. Sun
University of Texas at Austin
Austin, Texas

Srinivasan Venkatramanan
University of Virginia
Charlottesville, Virginia

Robin Walters
Northeastern University
Boston, MA

Lijing Wang
University of Virginia
Arlington, Virginia

Rui Wang
University of California, San Diego
La Jolla, California

Sifan Wang
University of Pennsylvania
Philadelphia, Pennsylvania

William D. Watkins
U.S. Geological Survey
Davis, California

Jared D. Willard
University of Minnesota
Minneapolis, Minnesota

Alexander J. Winkler
Max-Planck Institute for Biogeochemistry
Jena, Germany

Hongkyu Yoon
Sandia National Laboratories
Albuquerque, New Mexico

Rose Yu
University of California, San Diego
La Jolla, California

Nicholas Zabaras
University of Notre Dame
Notre Dame, Indiana

Zhibo Zhang
University at Buffalo, The State University
of New York
Buffalo, New York

Zhi Zhong
University of Geosciences
Wuhan City, China

Jacob A. Zwart
U.S. Geological Survey
South Bend, Indiana

1

Introduction

Anuj Karpatne, Ramakrishnan Kannan, and Vipin Kumar

CONTENTS

Machine learning (ML) models are increasingly being used as alternatives to science-based models in many scientific disciplines. Yet, these "black-box" ML models have found limited success in scientific applications due to their inability to generalize well in the lack of training data and discover patterns consistent with existing scientific knowledge. As a result, there is a growing trend in the scientific community to integrate scientific knowledge in ML frameworks for accelerating scientific discovery, referred to as the emerging field of scientific knowledge-guided ML (KGML). This book attempts to provide a glimpse of the rapidly growing field of KGML by discussing some of the common themes of problem formulations and research methods in the space of KGML for diverse scientific applications. This introductory chapter provides an overview of the field of KGML and highlights topical problem formulations, research methods, and motivating applications of KGML.

DOI: 10.1201/9781003143376-1

This chapter also lays the structure to the invited chapters of the book prepared by leading researchers in KGML, which illustrate the state-of-the-art opportunities and challenges in KGML research from multiple perspectives. This chapter also highlights cross-cutting topics of KGML that have received recent attention and areas with critical gaps that require further investigation by the broader community of researchers and practitioners to realize the full potential of KGML.

1.1 Overview

Scientific and engineering disciplines, which have conventionally progressed through advances in domain theories, are increasingly becoming eager to harness the power of machine learning (ML) methods for accelerating scientific discovery [10, 22, 27, 34, 65, 67]. However, "black-box" ML models, which have been tremendously successful in mainstream commercial problems [43, 53], have met with limited success in scientific problems [12, 47, 50], sometimes even leading to spectacular failures [47]. This is primarily because of four main reasons. First, state-of-the-art black-box ML methods (e.g., deep learning methods) require ample supervision in the form of labeled data that is seldom available in scientific problems at the scales possible in benchmark ML problems (e.g., ImageNet has millions of labeled images [16]). Second, real-world scientific data often cover only a limited spectrum of the full range of possible data distributions. Hence, even if more accurate on labeled data used for cross-validation, a black-box ML model may perform quite poorly on out-of-sample distributions. Third, since black-box models only use supervision from data and are not tied to underlying scientific theories, they are susceptible to producing solutions that are *inconsistent* with existing scientific knowledge and thus scientifically meaningless. Finally, because of the very nature of their design, black-box models are fundamentally incapable of discovering novel scientific insights from data that can be used as building blocks in the long-standing goal of advancing our knowledge of scientific systems. These are some of the major impediments to the wider adoption of black-box ML in scientific disciplines.

In response to these pitfalls of black-box ML, there is a growing interest in the scientific community to integrate scientific knowledge in ML frameworks, so as to produce generalizable and scientifically consistent solutions even in the paucity of representative data. We refer to this emerging paradigm of research combining scientific knowledge with data in ML frameworks as **scientific knowledge-guided machine learning** (KGML) [37]. As shown in Figure 1.1, KGML seeks a distinct departure from "data-only" or "scientific knowledge-only" methods to use them at an equal footing as allies in the mutual goal of scientific discovery. The growing interest in the field of KGML is reflected in a series of recent planning reports published on this topic, including the "20-year Roadmap for Artificial Intelligence (AI) Research in the US" prepared by the Computing Community Consortium (CCC) [26, pp. 63–68] and the Report on the Department of Energy (DOE) Town Halls on "AI for Science" [67]. There is also a lot of recent activity in organizing workshops, conferences, and symposiums on topics related to KGML at leading scientific and ML venues [1,2,3,4,21,31,48]. Indeed, the field of KGML is rapidly gaining interest in diverse scientific and ML communities. Researchers and practitioners from various backgrounds and application domains are continually shaping the community by adding richness to the problem formulations and research methods in this emerging field. Given this diversity, research in the field of KGML is also referred to by several names in different communities, including "theory-guided data science", "physics-guided machine learning", "science-guided machine learning", and "physics-informed machine learning". These terms describe the

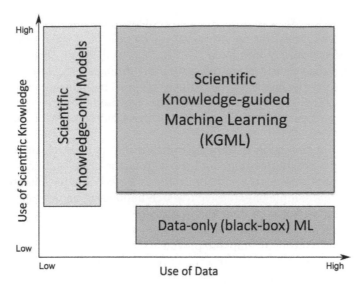

FIGURE 1.1
A pictorial description of KGML where x-axis shows the use of data while y-axis shows the use of scientific knowledge. KGML includes methods that make ample use of data while being observant of scientific knowledge.

common goal of combining scientific knowledge (or theories or physics) with data-driven machine learning methods, which we refer to as the field of KGML.

There is a long legacy of research on combining scientific knowledge with data-driven methods, spanning several research communities. For example, domain-specific knowledge is commonly used for feature construction and selection in ML frameworks. There is also a history of methods for leveraging domain knowledge in ML frameworks in the form of priors in Bayesian models [14]. Note that mainstream ML frameworks such as LSTMs and ConvNets are often considered to be prototypical examples of 'black-box' models. However, even these can be traced back to their original inspirations in leveraging domain knowledge (e.g., about the human brain and visual cortex) to inform the design of ML architectures. The evolving field of KGML encompasses, enriches, and goes significantly beyond all these efforts by exploring principled formulations for combining scientific knowledge in ML frameworks that cut across the breadth of scientific problems and ML research. Also, research in KGML is complementary to methods developed in the area of *data assimilation* where real-time data is used to update the evolution of system states without modifying the functional forms of relationships encoded in science-based models [19].

Early efforts motivating research in the field of KGML include a 2014 article that made a case for integrating scientific knowledge with data-driven methods for understanding climate change [20]. One of the first attempts to conceptualize and build the foundations of KGML includes a 2017 perspective article [37]. This article provided a roadmap for research in the field of KGML by describing several strategies (or research themes) for combining scientific knowledge and data, using illustrative examples from a wide variety of scientific disciplines. Another seminal line of work in KGML in 2017 is the formulation of a new class of neural network models termed Physics-Informed Neural Networks (PINNs) [57,58]. These networks leverage scientific supervision in physics-based partial differential equations (e.g., Navier–Stokes equations) to train neural network models for simulating physical systems. In the last few years, there has been an explosive growth in the number of papers published in the emerging field of KGML, exploring different problem formulations and research methods in the context of diverse scientific applications. As a testament to the rapid growth in KGML literature, in a recent survey article on KGML [76], Willard et al. cover more than 300 articles on integrating scientific knowledge with ML frameworks, and a majority of these have been published in the last few years. Other activities include survey articles on KGML and related topics [24, 36, 40, 62, 73], software packages and libraries on physics-informed ML [28, 39], and a recent book focusing on the practical aspects of physics-based deep learning [70].

A primary goal of this book is to bring together recent research in KGML happening in diverse scientific communities that can benefit from the cross-pollination of ideas across communities. Towards this goal, this book contains sixteen invited chapters from leading experts that provide a sample of extensive research happening on different facets of KGML in various communities. We hope that this book helps nurture the nascent field of KGML and shape the vision for future research in this growing field.

This introductory chapter attempts to provide a structure to the emerging field of KGML by presenting some of the common categories of problems and methods explored in KGML. The remainder of this chapter is organized as follows. We first discuss some of the common categories of problem formulations and research methods in the field of KGML in Sections 1.2 and 1.3, respectively. We next discuss some cross-cutting topics in KGML applicable across multiple KGML problems and methods in Section 1.4. We then place each of the sixteen invited chapters of the book in the structure of KGML problems and methods and provide short summaries for each one of them in Section 1.5. Finally, we end this chapter with concluding remarks and a discussion of future opportunities in KGML, as well as a guide to readers in Section 1.6.

1.2 Problem Formulations in KGML

To understand the variety of research problems that can be formulated in KGML, we first introduce the generic framework of science-based modeling that is commonly used in scientific and engineering disciplines. As we will see later, ML methods can serve different goals in this generic framework of science-based modeling, leading to different KGML problem formulations.

1.2.1 Generic Framework of Science-Based Modeling

A fundamental pursuit in any scientific and engineering discipline is to build *models* of a natural/physical system that are capable of predicting (or simulating) the system's behavior. In its simplest form, such a model can be viewed as an abstraction of relationships between input drivers (or causes, X) and output variables (or effects, Y) of the system. Figure 1.2

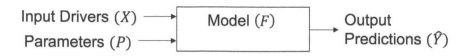

FIGURE 1.2
A generic framework for modeling natural/physical systems.

shows the generic framework of a model F mapping input drivers X to simulations of the output variables, $\widehat{Y}$. For example, in the domain of climate science, a model F can capture relationships between the current temperature and greenhouse forcings (inputs, X) and future climatic conditions (outputs, Y) [59]. A defining characteristic of **science-based** models is that their solution structure is deeply rooted in **scientific knowledge** of the system, available as governing first-principle equations, domain-specific laws, rules, heuristics, or ontological relationships. For example, scientific knowledge is available in a wide range of applications as exact forms of governing equations of mass, momentum, and energy conservation. These are commonly expressed in the language of partial differential equations (PDEs), such as Navier–Stokes equation governing the dynamics of fluids [9]. In other applications, scientific knowledge is available in the form of approximated or aggregated phenomenological rules and relationships governing real-world processes. For example, to ensure energy conservation in the problem of modeling lake temperature, the overall energy flux represented as the difference between input and output energy, should match with the change in the thermal energy [29], where each energy term is also commonly modeled (or approximated) using parameterized forms. As another example, in biology, scientific knowledge is often available in the form of ontologies (or knowledge graphs) capturing relationships between biological entities [44]. These diverse forms of knowledge are the key components of science-based models used in various application domains including fluid dynamics, epidemiology, hydrology, geoscience, subsurface science, ecology, freshwater science, climate science, and atomic imaging, as illustrated in the various chapters of this book.

The **solution structure** of science-based models may also vary widely from one application domain to another. For example, in some domains, science-based models are available as explicit computer programs (also called 'mechanistic' or process-based models) that can generate output simulations when fed with observations of input drivers. In other domains, science-based models may be implicitly obtained by solving scientific equations or making inferences using scientific rules and ontological relationships. Additionally, science-based models often involve **parameters** P for approximating the real-world relationships between X and Y. For example, state-of-the-art models in *lake modeling* [29] involve parameters P such as water clarity and salinity that can dramatically change the relationship between inputs X and outputs Y. This conventional paradigm of science-based modeling—developed over centuries of systematic research—forms the foundation of our present-day understanding of scientific systems across a broad spectrum of scientific disciplines.

1.2.2 Objectives Motivating KGML Research

Research in the field of science-based modeling is driven by several *objectives* aimed at improving our ability to explain and understand a natural/physical system or phenomenon. In particular, a fundamental objective in science-based modeling is to achieve good **predictive accuracy** of the 'forward' model simulations from X to $\widehat{Y}$, i.e., $\widehat{Y}$ is a close match to the ground-truth observations Y. However, as the proverbial saying goes, "all models are wrong, but some are useful," every science-based model is only an *approximation* of real-world phenomena that involve a number of processes unfolding at multiple scales of space and time. Hence, they are *imperfect* due to an incomplete understanding of the phenomena and/or our inability to represent real-world processes at all relevant scales. For example, in climate science, processes governing land-atmosphere interactions are not fully understood, leading to modeling imperfections. Another objective is to improve the **computational efficiency** of simulating the forward mapping from X to $\widehat{Y}$, especially in applications where the forward model F is too expensive to run at the required scales in real-world operational settings. A third fundamental objective is to **learn new scientific knowledge** from data, e.g., by discovering the governing equations of a system from observations of (X, Y), or by constructing a reduced representation of a known model F that explains most of the behavior of the system. The fourth objective in some scientific applications is to **infer parameters** of a science-based model F by learning the 'inverse' mapping from observations of (X, Y) to latent parameters P of the system. These parameters are difficult to observe directly but can be inferred from observations of (X, Y) that may be easier to obtain. For example, we can retrieve the properties of aerosols in the atmosphere, which are one of the major sources of uncertainty in climate models, from hyper-spectral measurements of solar radiation collected on the ground. Inferring parameters P in a science-based model can also help in *calibrating* (or tuning) the model to a given set of observations such that the calibrated model shows better predictive accuracy in its output predictions $\widehat{Y}$ w.r.t. ground-truth Y.

Progress in these objectives has been primarily pursued using 'scientific knowledge-only' or 'ML-only' methods. However, there are several opportunities to advance these objectives by partnering ML methods at different stages of the science-based modeling process, leading to different KGML problem formulations. In the following, we describe six key problem formulations in KGML catering to different objectives of science-based modeling. Table 1.1 provides a concise summary of these KGML problem formulations in terms of 'what is given' (data and scientific knowledge) and 'what is the objective' of each formulation. Table 1.2 provides further details of the differences between the six KGML problem formulations in terms of what is given (or available) for each formulation. Also, note that in every KGML problem formulation, data is available either in the form of *observations* of (X, Y), or in the form of *synthetic simulations* $(X, \widehat{Y})$ generated by a science-based forward model F.

1.2.3   Improved Forward Modeling

The goal of improved forward modeling is to learn an ML model that captures the forward mapping from input variables (X) to output variables (Y) *better* than state-of-the-art (or sometimes, non-existent) science-based forward models. In particular, given observations of X and Y as training data, we aim to build a KGML model that is more accurate (w.r.t. observations Y) than the available science-based model. Note that the synthetic simulations produced by a science-based model can guide the design and training of the KGML model (see Sections 1.3.3 and 1.3.4). Even in the absence of a science-based model, KGML models can be built as long as scientific knowledge is available in forms such as knowledge of the governing first-principle equations, domain-specific laws, relationships, and heuristics. One of the earliest lines of work in improved forward modeling includes research in the area of residual modeling [23, 69], where linear regression models have been developed to model the residuals (or errors) of science-based models. Some examples of recent research in improved forward modeling include the frameworks of physics-guided neural networks (PGNNs) [38] and physics-guided recurrent neural networks (PGRNNs) [32, 33]. In these models, the scientific knowledge is integrated with neural network models to improve their predictive accuracy beyond state-of-the-art science-only models. The general assumption in improved forward modeling is that the available scientific knowledge is either imperfect or incomplete in fully characterizing the ground-truth observations of Y; hence the need to 'improve' the current state of science-based models with KGML frameworks. The primary objective of improved forward modeling is to achieve better predictive accuracy in estimating the output variables, especially on unseen test scenarios coming from out-of-sample distributions, even with a limited number of training labels. Once trained, KGML models can also be more computationally efficient than science-based models that involve complex operations. This

TABLE 1.1
Categorization of KGML Problem Formulations in Terms of 'What Is Given' and 'What Is the Objective'.

KGML Problem Formulation	What Is Given?	What Is the Objective?	Additional Comments
Improved Forward Modeling	Ground-truth observations and scientific knowledge (imperfect or incomplete)	Improving predictive accuracy (i.e., $\widehat{Y}$ matches observations more closely)	We may optionally have access to science-based model simulations of $\widehat{Y}$. Additional objectives can include improving computational efficiency and discovering knowledge gaps in current science-based models
Surrogate Forward Modeling	Science-based model F	Replacing F with a computationally efficient ML-based forward model	
Reduced-Order Modeling	Science-based model F and knowledge of governing equations fully describing F	Obtaining a reduced representation of F leading to discovery of new knowledge of salient or principal relationships in F	Reduced F can also offer improvements in computational efficiency
Discovering Governing Equations	Ground-truth observations	Discovering the scientific equations and laws governing the processes of the system	
Inverse Modeling	Ground-truth observations	Inferring P given observations of (X, Y) to retrieve the latent parameters of the system	
Parameter Calibration/ Estimation	Ground-truth observations and forward model F	Inferring P such that $\widehat{Y} = F(X, P)$ becomes more accurate (i.e., $\widehat{Y}$ matches observations more closely)	

is because ML methods (e.g., deep learning methods) are very fast at making forward inferences using simple matrix operations that are amenable to modern GPU architectures. Along with achieving better accuracy and possibly improving the computational efficiency, research in this KGML problem may also "fill in" knowledge gaps in current standards of science-based models. For example, while building improved forward models, we may also be able to identify patterns of systematic bias (or deficiencies) in the outputs of F and the

TABLE 1.2

Characterizing KGML Problem Formulations on the Basis of What is Required as 'Given' in Every Formulation.

KGML Problem Formulation	Availability of Ground Truth Observations, Y	Availability of a Mechanistic Forward Model, F	Availability of Governing Equations That Fully Describe F
Improved Forward Modeling	Required	Optional	Optional
Surrogate Forward Modeling		Required	Optional
Reduced-Order Modeling			Required
Discovering Governing Equations	Required		
Inverse Modeling	Required	Optional	Optional
Parameter Calibration	Required	Required	Optional

sources of bias in the solution structure of F that can be rectified in future modeling efforts (see Jia et al. [33] for an example of this in the context of lake temperature modeling).

1.2.4 Surrogate Forward Modeling

The primary objective of surrogate forward modeling is to build computationally efficient ML-based surrogates of a science-based forward model F that is *assumed* to be perfect but too expensive to run in practical settings. Once the surrogate ML model has been trained to mimic (or emulate) the forward model, it can be applied to unseen testing scenarios for estimating output variables of interest. Thus, the problem of surrogate modeling bears some resemblance to the problem of improved forward modeling because in both problems, we aspire to learn the forward mapping from inputs X to outputs Y. However, the training data in surrogate modeling only includes synthetic simulations of $\hat{Y}$ instead of ground-truth observations of Y, and the goal is to find a 'surrogate' replacement of F that is computationally efficient. As illustrated in Table 1.2, the problem of surrogate modeling necessarily requires access to the mechanistic forward model F, that we are trying to emulate. On the other hand, in the problem of improved forward modeling, we must have access to ground-truth observations of Y. To train the ML-based surrogate of F, along with simulation data produced by F, we may optionally also leverage the governing equations that are at the basis of F to obtain surrogate models that are generalizable as well as scientifically consistent. One of the promising lines of research in KGML for surrogate modeling includes the development of physics-informed neural networks (PINNs) [56] for solving PDEs in a more computationally efficient way than existing physics-based solvers.

1.2.5 Reduced-Order Modeling

Reduced-order modeling aims to learn a reduced representation of the science-based model, F, e.g., using lower-dimensional representations of the functional forms of relationships between X and Y. Similar to surrogate modeling, the training data in this KGML problem is restricted to synthetic data generated by a high-fidelity science-based model F that is *assumed* to be perfect and complete. However, instead of simply replacing F with a computationally efficient surrogate, the goal in reduced-order modeling is also to discover a reduced set of equations or relationships between X and Y that capture most of the dynamics of the scientific system. For example, a dynamical system encountered in the study of fluids may have an intrinsic low-rank structure where a low dimensional manifold is embedded in high dimensional data. Reduced-order models may exploit this inherent low-rank structure to create more tractable models for the spatio-temporal evolution of the dynamical system. As illustrated in Table 1.2, the problem of reduced-order modeling necessarily requires complete knowledge of the governing equations that fully describe F, so that we can learn their reduced representations. This is different from the problem of surrogate forward modeling, where we only need the mechanistic forward model F, and it is not required to know the governing equations fully describing F. Thus, the objective of reduced-order modeling is two-fold: to improve the computational efficiency of the forward modeling process while also contributing to the discovery of new knowledge of the salient or principal relationships between inputs and outputs of the system. For example, researchers have developed reduced-order models that leverage linear dimensionality reduction techniques (e.g., singular value decomposition) to produce a dominant set of correlated high-energy modes as salient or principal relationships in the field of computational fluid dynamics [52, 66, 71].

1.2.6 Discovering Governing Equations

The goal in this problem formulation is to identify the governing laws or equations of a scientific system given observations of input drivers and output variables, X and Y. The basic problem setup in discovering governing equations is to feed observations of (X, Y) into an ML model that in turn extracts the governing equations of the system using a dictionary (or a basis set) of known scientific transformations (or functional forms) in the mapping from X to Y. This KGML problem formulation bears some resemblance to the area of research in *explainable machine learning* that is gaining a lot of interest in mainstream ML applications. However, instead of producing explainable theories and insights about a trained model that can be better communicated to and analyzed by end-users, the objective in this KGML problem formulation is to discover theories or equations that are consistent with our existing knowledge of scientific systems. There is a long history of work on discovering governing equations from data going back more than four decades [11, 46, 64, 72], with early works focusing on the development of Artificial Intelligence (AI) programs such as BACON [45]. A recent seminal line of research on this topic includes the framework of Sparse Identification of Non-linear Dynamics (SINDy) [11] that can select a parsimonious structure of the model of a dynamical system in an appropriate basis of feature transformations. As illustrated in Table 1.2, the KGML problem of discovering governing equations is also different from the problem of reduced-order modeling. The objective here is to discover the governing equations of a system given observations of (X, Y), rather than deriving reduced order representations of known equations of a forward model F.

1.2.7 Inverse Modeling

Inverse modeling learns the 'inverse' mapping from observations of (X, Y) to the latent parameters P of the scientific system, such that by feeding P into a science-based forward model F, we can generate simulations of outputs $\widehat{Y}$ given X that best match with the observations Y [51, 55, 68]. For example, in the problem of aerosol modeling, science-based models such as radiative transfer models simulate the solar radiation spectra reaching the ground often collected as hyperspectral measurements. Some of the parameters that are used in these models include the profiles and properties of aerosols in the atmosphere that interfere with the incoming light and change the distribution of hyperspectral values on the ground [13]. While the forward mapping from atmospheric aerosols to hyperspectral measurements is straightforward, the inverse mapping from hyperspectral measurements to aerosol profiles provides critical missing information that is difficult to observe directly. Research in the area of inverse modeling is also called scientific unmixing in some communities [41]. Note that in some inverse modeling problems, X may be unavailable, and the goal is to infer latent parameters P given observations Y [17, 35].

1.2.8 Parameter Calibration/Estimation

Given observations of (X, Y) and a science-based forward model F, parameter calibration (also known as parameter estimation) infers the latent parameters P of the forward model that results in model simulations of the output variables $\widehat{Y}$ that best match with the ground-truth observations Y.

There are three broad categories of techniques that have been commonly used for parameter calibration. The first category involves searching for the parameter setting P^* that results in the best match between $\widehat{Y}$ and Y across all potential settings of P using simple techniques such as grid search or random search [6]. Such techniques are generally employed when the number of parameters is small, and their range of values is bounded and well-defined. However, these methods can easily become computationally infeasible for large parameter spaces, especially because we need to run the forward model F to compute $\widehat{Y}$ for every parameter setting P. The second category of methods involve 'learning' the mapping from (X, Y) to P using statistical or ML models, which can be drastically more efficient in estimating P than search-based methods. These methods are related to the ones used for inverse modeling, which explore a similar objective of inferring the parameters of a science-based model given some observations. However, the critical difference here is that once the parameters P have been estimated, they are plugged back into the forward model F to improve the predictive accuracy of $\widehat{Y}$ w.r.t. observations. For example, in the problem of lake modeling, state-of-the-art science-based models such as the general lake model (GLM) [29] involve a large number of *parameters* such as water clarity and salinity. These parameters need to be custom-calibrated for each lake given some observations, such that the simulations of output variables (e.g., water temperature) match with ground-truth observations. The third category of methods involves estimating the parameters P using other sources of information as inputs (e.g., outputs of a higher-fidelity model). Such methods are commonly used in scientific applications where modeling a physical process at the required resolutions of space and time is computationally prohibitive. As a result, we are forced to run these simulations at coarser grids where finer-scale processes are approximated as subgrid parameters in the model. For example, in climate science, there is a rich body of literature on 'subgrid parameterization' of general circulation models (GCMs), where subgrid processes such as cloud formation and convective physics are approximated as parameters at aggregated scales. While subgrid parameterizations are generally performed using expensive numerical methods, recent work by Rasp et al. [60] explored the use of ML methods for learning these parameterizations directly from data. These ML methods were able to perform at par with numerical methods in terms of predictive accuracy but with an order of magnitude less computational expense. Thus, such ML methods can also be viewed as 'surrogates' for the computationally expensive subgrid parameterization techniques.

As illustrated in Table 1.2, the problem of parameter calibration necessarily requires access to ground-truth observations Y and the forward model F. Also, note that parameter calibration is different from improved forward modeling because parameter calibration aims to improve the predictive accuracy of forward models by learning better parameter settings, rather than fundamentally modifying the functional forms of relationships encoded in the forward model that is possible in improved forward modeling.

1.3 Research Methods in KGML

This section describes four common categories of KGML methods that differ in the form of scientific knowledge that they work with and the approach used for leveraging scientific knowledge in ML frameworks (see Table 1.3). These KGML methods can also be combined in various ways, as illustrated in the invited chapters of this book catering to different scientific applications. We briefly discuss these KGML methods in the following.

1.3.1 Scientific KG Learning

The primary motivation behind knowledge-guided (KG) learning is to use scientific knowledge as an *additional source of supervision* for learning generalizable ML models by jointly optimizing predictive accuracy (measured on the labeled training set) and *scientific consistency* (evaluated even on unlabeled samples) during ML training. For example, in the application domain of fluid dynamics, we can measure the scientific consistency of ML predictions of output variables (e.g., pressure and velocity fields) w.r.t. governing equations of fluid dynamics (e.g., Navier–Stokes equations) [56].

Since scientific equations and laws can be assumed to hold true across all input scenarios of X, ML models trained using KG learning procedures have been shown to generalize better even on out-of-sample distributions that haven't been observed in the labeled training set. (e.g., see [61] for an illustration in the context of lake temperature modeling).

Some examples of techniques in KG learning include the use of scientific KG priors in Bayesian modeling frameworks and scientific KG constraints in optimization problems. A recent trend in KG learning for training deep learning models is to include additional loss functions in the learning objective of neural networks, called *scientific knowledge-guided (KG) loss functions*. These loss functions measure the inconsistency of ML solutions relative to scientific equations and laws. For example, an early line of research includes

TABLE 1.3

Categorization of KGML Research Methods.

Category	Form of Knowledge
Scientific knowledge-guided (KG) Learning	Governing Equations and Laws
Scientific knowledge-guided (KG) Architecture	Mechanistic Model or Governing Equations
Scientific knowledge-guided (KG) Initialization	Mechanistic Model
Hybrid-Science-ML Modeling	Mechanistic Model (also required during testing)

the framework of physics-guided neural networks (PGNNs) [38], which balances the dual objective of minimizing the KG loss and reducing the empirical errors on the training labels. This framework is useful in many real-world applications where scientific knowledge is available in inexact or approximate forms such as high-level laws, rules, and relationships. Another early line of research on this topic is the framework of physics-informed neural networks (PINNs) [57,58], where scientific knowledge is available in exact forms of governing equations expressed in the form of PDEs of idealized systems. Since KG learning techniques use scientific knowledge to modify the ML training procedure without altering the ML architecture, they can be treated as 'softer' ways of incorporating scientific knowledge in ML frameworks.

1.3.2   Scientific KG Architecture

Another strategy for incorporating scientific knowledge in ML frameworks is to 'hard-code' or 'bake-in' scientific knowledge directly in the solution structure of ML models. For example, a common design consideration while building deep learning models is the choice of the neural network architecture, e.g., number of layers, nodes per layer, and types of connections between the layers. While such design considerations are generally treated as hyper-parameters and determined using the validation set, in KGML problems, there is an opportunity to design deep learning architectures that automatically encode our understanding of the natural/physical system. There are several possible directions for building scientific KG architectures. First, we can design ML architectures that encode known forms of invariances and symmetries in the predicted outputs of the system. Some examples of previous research in this direction include the use of equivariant neural networks for capturing various forms of symmetries while modeling dynamical systems [75] and the framework of covariant molecular neural networks for capturing the behavior and properties of many-body physical systems [8]. Second, in applications where scientific knowledge is available in the form of relationships between physical variables, KG architectures can be designed to encode such knowledge in the connectivity patterns of nodes in a neural network architecture. An example of previous research in this direction includes the framework of physics-guided architecture of LSTM (PGA-LSTM) models [15] that can encode monotonic relationships between density and depth of water as connections between LSTM node features in the illustrative application of lake temperature modeling. Third, KG architectures can be designed to simultaneously predict multiple physical variables (treated as multiple tasks) instead of predicting a single target variable. For example, in a recent work by Khandelwal et al. [42], LSTM architectures were developed to predict the target variable of streamflow along with predicting other related variables such as evapotranspiration, soil moisture, and snow depth. Fourth, KG architectures can also be constructed where the sequence of intermediate features extracted at the hidden layers of a neural network are informed by scientific knowledge. An example of previous work in this direction is the framework of PhyNet [54] developed for modeling multi-phase flow, where the features extracted at the hidden layers of the network correspond to physically meaningful intermediates in the known scientific pathway from inputs to outputs. Another example is the work by Khandelwal et al. [42] in the domain of hydrology, where useful intermediates such as evapotranspiration, soil moisture, and snow depth were expressed at the internal layers of the network for predicting streamflow at the output layer. In such problems, it is also possible to incorporate additional information about the behavior of intermediate variables (e.g., varying memory scales) in the design of KG architectures.

1.3.3 Scientific KG Initialization

Scientific knowledge can also help in finding better initialization of ML model parameters that can be further refined using a small number of ground-truth observations. One common approach in KG initialization is to use scientific simulations of output variables $\widehat{Y}$ as an imperfect but cheap approximation of gold-standard ground-truth observations of Y, which are difficult to obtain in most real-world scientific problems. An ML model pre-trained on simulation data $(X, \widehat{Y})$, generated over a diverse range of input scenarios of X, can be expected to capture generalizable patterns in the simulations of F over different possibilities of inputs that can be hard to obtain observations for. One of the first uses of science-based model simulations for pre-training deep learning models is the framework of physics-guided recurrent neural networks (PGRNNs) developed for lake temperature modeling [32, 33], which has been shown to achieve better generalization even on out-of-sample distributions in the paucity of training labels.

1.3.4 Hybrid-Science-ML Modeling

The goal here is to develop *hybrid* versions of science-based and ML models where both classes of models are jointly used to deliver better predictive performance than ML-only or science-only models. There are two major categories of approaches in hybrid-science-ML modeling. The first category of approaches, which can be referred to as *combination-based* approaches, involves concurrently running the science-based model and ML model such that their *combination* produces better estimates of output variables $\widehat{Y}$ showing improved predictive accuracy with respect to observations Y. For example, there is a long-standing tradition in the scientific community on using statistical approaches (usually, linear regression) for modeling the residuals of science-based models, referred to as *residual modeling* (or discrepancy modeling). A recent combination-based approach for hybrid modeling includes the framework of physics-guided neural network (PGNN) [38], where the outputs of science-based models are used as ancillary inputs in a neural network model. Such an approach achieves better predictive accuracy than science-only or ML-only methods. The second category is *embedding-based* approaches, where ML models are deeply embedded inside the structure of the science-based model to estimate intermediate quantities and parameters that are difficult to determine directly due to expensive computation. One example of an approach in this category is to estimate parameters in science-based models using ML components as explored by Rasp et al. [60] for subgrid parameterization in climate science. Another example in this category is where the ML methods are used to augment or replace science-based components that are currently lacking or require an involved partnership between the science-based and ML models (e.g., see Chapter 14 of this book for an illustrative example).

1.4 Cross-Cutting Topics in KGML

In this section, we discuss some cross-cutting topics. While these topics have been extensively studied in the context of data-only or science-only problems, they show unique characteristics in the context of KGML problems and hence deserve a separate discussion. These topics are frequently discussed in the invited chapters of this book.

1.4.1 Sources of Uncertainty in KGML

Quantifying the amount of uncertainty in a model's predictions and attributing its potential sources is of paramount importance in many scientific and engineering problems, especially involving real-world decision-making. For example, in the domain of climate science, quantifying the uncertainty in our forecasts of surface temperature under varying scenarios of input forcings (e.g., carbon emissions) provides vital information for devising climate change adaptation policies. There is a long history of research on uncertainty quantification spanning several decades in multiple scientific disciplines. This includes methods in statistics and ML on Bayesian modeling and variational inference, as well as methods developed in scientific modeling using ensemble methods (e.g., ensemble Kalman filters). A common way of categorizing the source of predictive uncertainty is *aleatoric* (or irreducible) uncertainty intrinsic to the system and *epistemic* (or reducible) uncertainty arising due to lack of knowledge. While both these sources of uncertainty are relevant for studying scientific systems, the problem of uncertainty quantification in KGML takes new forms. This is because KGML problems involve the use of both data and scientific knowledge through which uncertainties in model predictions can seep in, propagate, and even cascade. In the following, we discuss two primary sources of uncertainty in KGML problems.

1.4.1.1 Data Uncertainty

There are different forms of uncertainty arising in a KGML model's predictions that can be attributed to uncertainties in the input data. These uncertainties include *system stochasticity*, which is the natural variability occurring in a data distribution due to the stochastic nature inherent to the scientific system. Another form of data uncertainty is *measurement noise*, which is intrinsic to the process of collecting observations (e.g., due to errors in sensor precision). The effects of both these forms of uncertainty that are intrinsic to the input data can get compounded to affect large amounts of uncertainty in the model outputs. For example, in scientific systems exhibiting chaotic behavior (such as problems involving turbulence in fluid dynamics and climate science), small perturbations in the input conditions arising due to measurement noise at a given time can lead to large changes in the output variables that keep diverging with time. In such problems, the effect of noise on the stochastic signal in data is often captured using the signal-to-noise ratio. A related phenomenon happens in deep learning applications. For example, in computer vision, small changes in an input image can affect large differences in the predictions of deep learning models, even though these changes can be difficult to notice by humans. This is a key concern for the safety and security of deep learning models in real-world applications. However, the critical difference in these examples is that the changes to the input images are not random (e.g., because of measurement noise) but are carefully constructed using optimization techniques to fool the deep learning model, referred to as "adversarial attacks" [7, 49].

1.4.1.2 Model Uncertainty

There are two types of model uncertainty in the context of KGML, one appearing in the science-based model and the other appearing in the ML model. The uncertainty in a science-based model can either appear due to uncertainty in its latent parameters that may not be fully determined from data or due to incompleteness or inaccuracies in the science-based model. For example, in climate science problems, processes involving cloud physics or aerosol chemistry are either not fully known or intentionally simplified (sometimes even ignored) to scale the computations operationally on real-world systems. This introduces an inherent bias in the modeling form that acts as a source of uncertainty in the model predictions. On the other hand, uncertainty in ML models appears in the uncertainty of the model structures and parameters trained using data. For example, given a finite set of data samples, several choices of ML hypotheses (model structures and parameters) can fit the data, resulting in model uncertainty. This is especially true for models with higher complexity (e.g., deep learning models) that can express highly complex patterns using a large number of parameters. However, not all choices of parameters in such ML models may have the ability to yield predictions that are *consistent with scientific knowledge*, even if they fit the available data perfectly well. Eliminating such scientifically inconsistent solutions from the set of candidate hypotheses can likely help in reducing model uncertainty. Hence, in KGML problems, scientific knowledge can act as another form of supervision to reduce the uncertainty in model predictions due to the selection of ML model parameters that do not comply with existing knowledge. This type of uncertainty reduction was demonstrated in recent work by Elhamod et al. [18] for classifying fish species from image data, where the introduction of scientific supervision from biology (in the form of phylogenetic trees) helped in improving the robustness of the KGML model to adversarial attacks.

1.4.2   Generalizability in the Context of KGML

The importance of learning KGML models that can generalize to novel testing scenarios spans multiple scientific and engineering disciplines. In the following, we introduce two levels of generalization that are possible in scientific problems involving KGML models.

The first level of generalization in KGML involves testing a model on input scenarios similar but not identical to the ones observed in the training set. For example, we may test a model on unseen samples generated from the same distribution of input variables as those used while generating the training data (e.g., from the same period of time, space, or other input conditions). This level of generalization is also referred to as in-sample or in-distribution generalization since the testing samples' distribution matches the distribution of training samples. It is the most common setting for studying the generalization performance of ML models, rooted in foundations of statistical theories (e.g., bias-variance trade-off) and philosophical concepts (e.g., the Occam's razor). Note that in the absence of scientific knowledge, we can only expect our model to learn patterns from training samples that hold well on similar testing samples. Also, note that this form of generalization bears some resemblance to the problem of interpolation, where the range of input values considered during testing lies within the range of values seen during training.

The second level of generalization involves testing a KGML model on unseen input scenarios that are different from those observed during training, referred to as out-of-sample or out-of-distribution generalization (with extrapolation being a special case). One possible cause for the differences in data distributions between training and test sets is the heterogeneity (or non-stationarity) in the governing processes occurring over space, time, or other contextual attributes also referred to as the phenomenon of *distribution shift*. In such cases, bias in the sampling procedure can easily produce training and test distributions with varying properties. For example, we may have generated training samples from a subset of input scenarios that are easy to simulate or measure, but we are interested in testing over input scenarios from the entire distribution. This level of generalization is of prime importance in many scientific problems where the goal is to capture the behavior of a scientific system using generalizable and scientifically meaningful patterns that hold across multiple input scenarios. While it is unlikely for an ML model to perform well on unseen testing scenarios, the KGML paradigm provides opportunities for improving the generalization power of ML models in out-of-distribution contexts by encouraging or enforcing ML models to produce scientifically consistent predictions. In particular, given a set of scientific equations known to hold across all input scenarios universally (e.g., conversation laws), a KGML model that complies with the scientific equations while fitting the training data stands a better chance at extrapolating to unseen testing scenarios. The importance of using scientific knowledge to achieve better generalizability in different application domains is exemplified in a number of chapters in this book.

1.5   Overview of Book Chapters

Table 1.4 provides a categorization of the 16 invited chapters of this book that cover different types of KGML problems and methods in the context of various application domains. Some of these chapters provide a tutorial-style review of a broad range of literature covering a specific problem, method, or an application domain, while others present targeted case studies of recent developments in the field of KGML. In the following, we provide short summaries of each one of the 16 chapters of the book, with an emphasis on the problems, methods, and application domains that they focus upon. We subsequently present a simple guide to the readers in Figure 1.3 that pictorially depicts the six problems discussed in the book along with the illustrative application domains and methods in which they have been covered in the invited chapters.

Chapter 2. Targeted Use of Deep Learning for Physics and Engineering

This chapter by Brunton and Kutz provides an excellent review of what dynamical systems are and how they are ubiquitous to many applications of science and engineering. This chapter introduces a number of KGML problems that are relevant in the study of dynamical

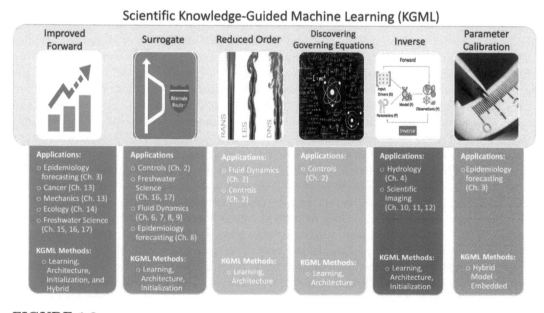

FIGURE 1.3
Guide to the readers about the coverage of the six KGML problems in the invited chapters of this book. For every KGML problem, we list the illustrative application domains and chapter numbers (in parentheses) in which they have been covered, along with the types of KGML methods explored in these chapters for every problem.

TABLE 1.4

Categorization of Chapters in the Book Based on Their KGML Problems, Methods, and Application Domains of Focus.

Chapter	KGML Problem	KGML Method	Application Domains
Ch. 2. Brunton and Kutz, "Targeted use of Deep Learning for Physics and Engineering"	Surrogate modeling of dynamical systems (review), Reduced-Order Modeling, Discovering Governing Equations		Fluid Dynamics, Control
Ch. 3. Wang et al., "Combining Theory and Data Driven Approaches for Epidemic Forecasts"	Improved Forward Modeling, Parameter Calibration	Initialization, Learning, Hybrid Modeling-Embedded	Epidemiological Forecastiing (review)
Ch. 4. Forghani et al., "Recent Advances in Machine Learning and Physics-Based Modeling in Hydrology and Geoscience"	Reduced-Order Modeling (review), Inverse Modeling		Hydrology
Ch. 5. Sun et al., "Applications of Physics-Informed Scientific Machine Learning in Subsurface Science: A Survey"			Subsurface Science (review)
Ch. 6. Wang and Perdikaris, "Adaptive Training Strategies for Physics-Informed Neural Networks"	Surrogate modeling for solving PDEs	Learning	Fluid Dynamics
Ch. 7. Geneva and Zabaras, "Modern Deep Learning for Modeling Physical Systems"	Surrogate modeling for solving PDEs, Uncertainty Quantification (review)	Learning	Fluid Dynamics
Ch. 8. Wang et al., "Physics-Guided Deep Learning for Spatiotemporal Forecasting"	Surrogate modeling of dynamical systems	Architecture	Fluid Dynamics, Climate Science, Epidemiological Forecasting
Ch. 9. Muralidhar et al., "Science-Guided Design and Evaluation of Machine Learning Models: A Case-Study on Multi-Phase Flows"	Surrogate Modeling	Architecture	Fluid Dynamics with Multi-Fidelity Simulations
Ch. 10. Browning et al., "Using the Physics of Electron Beam Interactions to Determine Optimal Sampling and Image Reconstruction Strategies for High Resolution STEM"	Inverse Modeling		Atomic Imaging (review)
Ch. 11. FUNNL: Fast Nonlinear Nonnegative Unmixing for Alternate Energy Systems	Inverse Modeling	Initialization	Scientific Imaging
Ch. 12. Structure Prediction from Scattering Profiles: A Neutron-Scattering Use-Case	Inverse Modeling	Learning, Architecture	Neutron Scattering
Ch. 13. Zhang et al., "Physics-Infused Learning: A DNN and GAN Approach"	Improved Forward Modeling	Hybrid Modeling (Combined)	Inverted Pendulum, Cancer Modeling
Ch. 14. Reichstein et al., "Combining System Modeling and Machine Learning into Hybrid Modeling"	Improved Forward Modeling	Hybrid Modeling (Embedded)	Ecology
Ch. 15. Daw et al., "Physics-Guided Neural Networks (PGNN): An Application in Lake Temperature Modeling"	Improved Forward Modeling	Learning, Hybrid Modeling (Combined)	Freshwater Science
Ch. 16. Jia et al., "Physics-Guided Recurrent Neural Networks for Predicting Lake Water Temperature"	Improved Forward Modeling	Learning, Initialization	Freshwater Science
Ch. 17. Daw et al., "Physics-Guided Architecture (PGA) of Neural Networks for Quantifying Uncertainty in Lake Temperature Modeling"	Improved Forward Modeling, Uncertainty Quantification	Architecture	Freshwater Science

systems. Specifically, this chapter discusses the problem of surrogate modeling of dynamical systems using ML methods, and how we can learn a compact representation space of the dynamical processes along the lines of reduced-order modeling. The chapter also discusses the ML framework of Sparse Identification of Nonlinear Dynamics (SINDy) [11] for discovering governing equations automatically from simulated or observational data. While the discussion of dynamical systems presented in this chapter is generically applicable to many scientific and engineering applications, they are illustrated in the context of application domains such as fluid dynamics and control in this chapter.

Chapter 3. Combining Theory and Data-Driven Approaches for Epidemic Forecasts

This chapter by Wang et al. provides an in-depth review of the state of scientific modeling in the application domain of epidemiology, spanning a long history of modeling advances in the domain ranging from science (or theory) based models to the recent use of data-driven deep learning methods. The chapter covers the problem of improved forward modeling given epidemiological data, where recent advances in the use of mechanistic causal theories to constrain graph neural network methods are described in the area of KG learning [25]. Another family of methods covered in this chapter includes KG initialization of ML models using simulation data [74]. Apart from improved forward modeling, the chapter also discusses the problem of calibrating parameters in theory-based models using ML methods trained on auxiliary data (e.g., those collected from social media) [30, 77]. This work falls in the category of 'embedding-based' approaches for hybrid modeling, where ML methods are trained to predict parameters of science-based models, which when fed into the forward models produces better estimates of the output variables.

Chapter 4. Machine Learning and Physics-Based Modeling in Hydrology and Geosciences

In this chapter, Forghani et al. present a comprehensive review of reduced-order modeling (ROM), with a focus on applications in hydrology and geoscience. This chapter bridges the gap between traditional methods for ROM that are mostly based on linear projections and deep learning methods for performing non-linear ROM, which have a lot of future potential in reduced-order modeling. The importance of deep learning-based ROMs is discussed in the context of both forward and inverse modeling problems, using an illustrative case study of modeling shallow water equations in the domain of hydrology.

Chapter 5. Applications of Physics-Informed Scientific Machine Learning in Subsurface Science: A Survey

This chapter by Sun et al. provides a systematic review of the current state of ML methodologies in the application domain of subsurface science, which is the study of geosystem processes occurring beneath the surface of the Earth. This chapter covers a wide range of ML methods relevant for the field of geosciences and application use-cases where ML methods have been explored, along with a discussion of challenges and future directions in the field of KGML for subsurface science.

Chapter 6. Adaptive Training Strategies for Physics-Informed Neural Networks.

In this chapter, Wang and Perdikaris present cutting-edge developments in surrogate modeling for solving partial differential equations (PDEs), which are commonly encountered in several scientific and engineering domains. This chapter covers recent methods developed in the seminal line of work in KG learning for solving PDEs, referred to as physics-informed neural networks (PINNs) [56]. The chapter specifically exposes the challenge of stiffness and gradient imbalance while training PINN models and presents adaptive training strategies based on ideas from Neural Tangent Kernels to mitigate these challenges.

Chapter 7. *Modern Deep Learning for Modeling Physical Systems*

This chapter by Geneva and Zabaras continues the discussion of methods in the area of KG Learning for surrogate modeling of physical systems, where scientific knowledge is available in the form of exact PDEs that fully describe the processes of the system. The chapter covers an extensive range of modern deep learning architectures that can be used to model the spatio-temporal dynamics of physical systems and their relationship with probabilitic techniques for uncertainty quantification (UQ) in the context of deep learning. The chapter also discusses methods for constraining modern deep learning architectures using the knowledge of physics (available as PDEs) in the area of scientific knowledge-guided learning. The KGML topics in this chapter are illustrated using example problems in the application domain of fluid dynamics involving the flow of fluids through porous media.

Chapter 8. *Physics-Guided Deep Learning for Spatiotemporal Forecasting*

This chapter by Wang et al. delves into the problem of surrogate modeling of dynamical systems for spatio-temporal forecasting, with illustrative applications in the domains of fluid dynamics, climate science, and epidemiology. The chapter covers methods in the area of KG Architecture, where scientific knowledge is directly embedded into the solution structure of deep learning models. In particular, for the application of turbulence modeling, this chapter explores a novel KG Architecture that embodies the solution structure of state-of-the-art physics-based models used for modeling turbulence. In the application of modeling dynamical systems for climate science and epidemiological forecasting, this chapter introduces a novel set of approaches for incorporating physics-guided symmetries in deep learning architectures, which are able to deliver improved generalizability on novel testing scenarios.

Chapter 9. *Science-Guided Design and Evaluation of Machine Learning Models: A Case-Study on Multi-Phase Flows*

In this chapter, Muralidhar et al. present a neural network approach termed PhyNet [54] for surrogate modeling in the illustrative application of modeling multi-phase flow in fluid dynamics. The goal of PhyNet is to predict high-resolution fluid forces experienced by particles suspended in a moving fluid that are simulated by high-fidelity physics-based solvers, using coarse-scale information generated by low-fidelity solvers such as the position of particles in the assembly. One of the primary innovations of PhyNet is to use a neural network design where physically meaningful intermediate quantities (e.g., pressure and velocity fields) are expressed at the hidden layers of the network. It is shown that by expressing physically meaningful quantities at the hidden layers, PhyNet can achieve better generalizability in the problem of predicting the target variable of drag force exerted by every particle on the fluid. While this chapter focuses on the motivating application of modeling multi-phase flow, the idea of using physically meaningful quantities as intermediate variables in the hidden layers of the neural network is much more general and can be applied to many scientific domains.

Chapter 10. *Using the Physics of Electron Beam Interactions to Determine Optimal Sampling and Image Reconstruction Strategies for High Resolution STEM*

In this chapter, Browning et al. discuss inpainting /machine learning methods that allow automatic recording of data in a faster-compressed form with less material damage for scanning transmission electron microscopes (STEM) images. The faster-compressed form is achieved by solving an inverse problem using the sensing matrix and the partial observations. Images from STEM are used to routinely quantify the atomic-scale structure, composition, chemistry, bonding, electron/phonon distribution, and optical properties of nanostructures, interfaces, and defects in many materials systems. However, quantitative and reproducible high-resolution observations for many materials are limited by electron beam damage. Towards this, the authors describe: (a) the basic approach for the efficient use of the electron dose (i.e., the number of electrons per unit area) that is supplied to the sample by modeling the physical interactions between them, and (b) the integration of sub-sampling/inpainting/compressive sensing and machine learning into the imaging hardware to increase the speed and reduce the damage due to decrease in the acquisition time and therefore the dose per image.

Chapter 11. FUNNL: Fast Nonlinear Nonnegative Unmixing for Alternate Energy Systems

In this chapter, Graves et al. discuss scientific unmixing, an inverse problem of extracting end-members and their associated abundance maps from a given input image, using the observed spectra at every pixel. Scientists use unmixing to understand the interaction between the catalyst palladium and the support, such as carbon, for alternate energy systems. In this chapter, the authors focus on non-negative nonlinear unmixing on Electron Energy Loss Spectrum (EELS) images using kernel methods, where the abundance maps are shared between the linear and nonlinear parts of the objective function. While such a formulation is sensitive to initialization, it is also computationally expensive in runtime and memory, making it challenging to apply to large images. Towards this, the authors propose a novel algorithm, Fast Nonlinear Nonnegative Unmixing (FUNNL), which uses scientific knowledge-guided initialization without precomputing the kernel matrix. The authors show the usefulness of the FUNNL algorithm by comparing it against baselines on a real-world dataset collected from a Scanning Transmission Electron Microscope (STEM) EELS at Oak Ridge National Laboratory (ORNL) and a pixel-wise labeled Indian Pines dataset. The FUNNL algorithm with an RBF kernel and scientific knowledge-guided initialization consistently outperforms the baselines in both of the datasets and the FUNNL algorithm, with a linear kernel, and is around 85 times faster than the nonlinear baseline, ISOMAP.

Chapter 12. Structure Prediction from Scattering Profiles: A Neutron-Scattering Use-Case

This chapter by Garcia-Cordona et al. solves an inverse problem through ML-driven methods for structure determination from neutron scattering data. One of the main goals of neutron data analysis is to determine the internal structure of materials from their neutron scattering profiles. These structures are defined by a crystallographic class label and a set of real-valued parameters specific to that class. This chapter evaluates the feasibility of using trained data-driven machine learning models as fast and accurate substitutes over existing expensive loop refinement methods. The ML models are trained on synthetically generated data and validated against experimental observations. Specifically, two categories of models are considered, called class-conditional and integrated. The first relies on a two-stage inference pipeline in which a crystallographic class label is first predicted followed by regression to predict the length/angle parameters. In the second category, the classification and regression tasks are performed as a single learning task. Finally, the chapter explains science-guided pre-processing of experimental data to match the distribution of training data.

Chapter 13. Physics-Infused Learning: A DNN and GAN Approach

This chapter by Zhang et al. introduces KGML methods in the emerging area of hybrid modeling, where the goal is to augment the simulation outputs of a physics-based model of a scientific system using ML components. The chapter covers a variety of approaches for hybrid modeling using "combination-based" strategies, where the physics-based simulations are fed into ML frameworks such as feed-forward networks or Generative Adversarial Networks (GANs) at different layers of the network. These methods are illustrated in the context of improved forward modeling in a variety of application domains including modeling the dynamics of an inverted pendulum as well as cancer modeling.

Chapter 14. Combining System Modeling and Machine Learning into Hybrid Ecosystem Modeling

This chapter by Reichstein et al. presents a novel perspective of improved forward modeling using hybrid-science-ML modeling methods, where the ML-based modeling components are deeply embedded inside and tightly integrated with the physics-based (or mechanistic) modeling components of the scientific system. This is fundamentally different from existing combination-based strategies for hybrid modeling, where the scientific model simulations are fed into the ML model that finally predicts the target variables. In contrast, this chapter proposes several strategies for embedding ML components inside the science-based modeling framework, where the outputs of ML components are fed as inputs in the mechanistic modeling components that finally simulate the target variables. These strategies are discussed in the context of illustrative examples in the application domain of ecology for modeling physical variables such as ecosystem respiration.

Chapter 15. Physics-Guided Neural Networks (PGNN): An Application in Lake Temperature Modeling.

In this chapter, Daw et al. describe the framework of physics-guided neural networks (PGNNs) for improved forward modeling in the illustrative application of lake temperature modeling for freshwater science. In this problem, scientific knowledge is available in the form of monotonic relationships between density and depth, as well as imperfect model simulations of a state-of-the-art science-based model of lake water temperature, GLM [29]. This chapter presents two key innovations. The first innovation involves the incorporation of scientific knowledge available as monotonic relationships in the training of neural network models using loss functions (in the area of KG learning). This chapter also presents another simple yet effective innovation for constructing hybrid-science-ML architectures, where the outputs of the science-based GLM model are combined with the input variables and fed into the neural network to produce predictions of target variables (i.e., temperature) that are better than a science-only GLM model or a data-only black-box neural network model. Results over multiple lake systems demonstrate the ability of the proposed PGNN framework to produce solutions that are more generalizable and scientifically consistent in comparison to baselines even in the paucity of labeled training data.

Chapter 16. Physics-Guided Recurrent Neural Networks for Predicting Lake Water Temperature

This chapter by Jia et al. describes the framework of physics-guided recurrent neural networks (PGRNN) for improved forward modeling in the illustrative application of lake temperature modeling for freshwater science. In this problem, scientific knowledge is available in the form of equations (energy conservation principle and density-depth relationships) as well as imperfect model simulations of a state-of-the-art science-based model of lake water temperature, GLM [29]. This chapter describes one of the first works to explore the idea of pre-training neural network models using scientific simulations and then fine-tune the pre-trained model on a small number of ground-truth observations, which falls in the area of KG Initialization. The proposed formulation of PGRNN also incorporates consistency with scientific knowledge as loss functions in the area of KG Learning. It is shown that by using scientific knowledge and data, the proposed KGML framework is able to generalize well even on novel testing scenarios (e.g., different seasons and lake systems) and in the paucity of labeled training samples.

Chapter 17. Physics-Guided Architecture (PGA) of LSTM Models for Uncertainty Quantification in Lake Temperature Modeling

In this chapter, Daw et al. present KGML methods for improved forward modeling in the illustrative application of lake temperature modeling in freshwater science. In this problem, scientific knowledge is available in the form of monotonic relationships between the density of a water column (estimated as a useful intermediate for predicting the target variable of temperature) and the depth of the water column. In contrast to existing KGML formulations for this problem that leverage KG Learning methods, this chapter develops a Physics-Guided Architecture of LSTM (PGA-LSTM) model, where the scientific knowledge of density-depth relationships is directly embedded in the construction of the LSTM architecture such that predictions of density (as intermediate features in the LSTM framework) monotonically increase with the sequence of depth values. An important motivation for the KG architecture presented in this chapter is to perform uncertainty quantification using Monte Carlo (MC) Dropout, such that the model outputs remain scientifically consistent even after minor perturbations in the model weights due to MC Dropout. This chapter empirically demonstrates that by hard-coding scientific knowledge in the construction of ML models, we can obtain ML predictions that are more generalizable and scientifically consistent than black-box ML methods and further result in more meaningful UQ. While this chapter focuses on lake temperature modeling as a motivating application, the idea of using KG architecture is general and can be applied in any application with known dependencies between intermediate variables.

1.6   Concluding Remarks

This introductory chapter of the book provides an overview of the emerging field of KGML. It attempts to organize research in this rapidly growing field by describing some of the common types of problem formulations and research methods explored by researchers from diverse communities. The sixteen invited chapters of the book cover multiple disciplinary perspectives, including computer science, applied mathematics, scientific modeling, and other scientific and engineering disciplines, highlighting the richness of scientific communities interested in KGML research. Since many of the problems and methods in KGML have been studied as isolated efforts in disparate communities, and it has resulted in different yet overlapping terminologies for common research topics. This introductory chapter attempted to address some of these ambiguities by clearly defining the requirements, objectives, and differentiating aspects of every KGML problem and method. For example, in the past literature, the term 'surrogate modeling' has often been used interchangeably to describe two rather distinct problems: the problem of emulating a science-based model given its simulations and the problem of improving the accuracy of a science-based model given observations. We have tried to disambiguate the differences between these two problems by referring the latter with the newly coined term 'improved forward modeling.' Similar attempts have been made to clarify differences between surrogate modeling and reduced-order modeling, as well as inverse modeling and parameter calibration.

An aspirational goal of our book is to enable researchers to look beyond their disciplinary boundaries and identify common KGML research themes that can foster the cross-pollination of ideas across diverse scientific communities. Such cross-pollination is made easier by chapters of the book that cover KGML problems and methods in the context of multiple application domains. For example, Chapter 8 by Wang et al. discusses the problem of surrogate modeling using knowledge-guided architectures in the context of fluid dynamics, climate science, and epidemiology. More generally, we hope that this book will aid in creating and nurturing new communities of scientists and practitioners to shape the future trajectory of research in the rapidly growing field of KGML. Another aspirational goal of this book is to serve as a source of challenging problems in scientific applications that fuels novel methodological research in machine learning. Unique characteristics and challenges of scientific problems (compared to their commercial counterparts) require entirely new types of ML frameworks and thus push the boundaries of mainstream ML research.

For example, there is a growing volume of work in mainstream ML research to explain ML models' outputs (e.g., in computer vision and language processing problems) using easy-to-interpret theories [5, 63]. There are tremendous opportunities to develop novel avenues of research for grounding these explanations using rich scientific knowledge. In particular, scientific knowledge-guided explainable ML can lead to new interpretable deep learning architectures. Similar to the role played by Internet-scale data in computer vision and text translation problems in revolutionizing the field of deep learning research, we anticipate the richness of challenges and opportunities encountered in KGML will influence the next major revolution in ML research.

1.6.1 Guide to Readers

This book can be used in a variety of ways by readers from diverse communities. Domain scientists and real-world practitioners can use it to identify some of the latest KGML methodological developments that may apply to their domain. Once the reader can map a problem at hand into one of the six problems in Table 1.1, they can decide on possible methods to try in Section 1.3 and then see Table 1.4 to identify representative chapters for a deep dive. Academic scholars and researchers in data science and machine learning can use this book to learn about KGML methods used in different scientific domains and look for opportunities for novel methodological advances. Readers may be interested in chapters that provide a detailed review of a particular KGML problem (Chapter 2 on dynamical systems, Chapter 4 on reduced-order modeling, or Chapter 7 on uncertainty quantification in KGML), or a particular application domain (Chapter 3 on epidemiology, Chapter 5 on subsurface science, and Chapter 10 on atomic imaging). Note that this chapter is only the first step in the long journey towards building a systematic framework of KGML problems and methods, which we hope, will be the focus of future research efforts in this emerging field. For any feedback, comments, or questions regarding the contents of this book, please contact us at kgmlbook@cs.vt.edu.

Bibliography

[1] AAAI Fall Symposium Series. 2nd Symposium on Science-guided AI to Accelerate Scientific Discovery. https://sites.google.com/vt.edu/sgai-aaai-21/.

[2] AAAI Fall Symposium Series. Symposium on Physics-guided AI to Accelerate Scientific Discovery. https://sites.google.com/vt.edu/pgai-aaai-20/.

[3] AAAI Spring Symposium Series. Symposium on Combining Artificial Intelligence and Machine Learning with Physics Sciences. https://sites.google.com/view/aaai-mlps.

[4] AAAI Spring Symposium Series. Symposium on Combining Artificial Intelligence and Machine Learning with Physics Sciences. https://sites.google.com/view/aaai-mlps.

[5] Amina Adadi and Mohammed Berrada. Peeking inside the black-box: a survey on explainable artificial intelligence (xai). *IEEE Access*, 6:52138–52160, 2018.

[6] Brian M Adams, William J Bohnhoff, Keith R Dalbey, JP Eddy, MS Eldred, DM Gay, K Haskell, Patricia D Hough, and Laura P Swiler. Dakota, a multilevel parallel object-oriented framework for design optimization, parameter estimation, uncertainty quantification, and sensitivity analysis: version 5.0 user's manual. *Sandia National Laboratories, Tech. Rep. SAND2010-2183*, 2009.

[7] Naveed Akhtar and Ajmal Mian. Threat of adversarial attacks on deep learning in computer vision: A survey. *IEEE Access*, 6:14410–14430, 2018.

[8] Brandon Anderson, Truong Son Hy, and Risi Kondor. Cormorant: Covariant molecular neural networks. *Advances in Neural Information Processing Systems*, 32:14537–14546, 2019.

[9] John David Anderson and J Wendt. *Computational Fluid Dynamics*, volume 206. Springer, 1995.

[10] Tim Appenzeller. The AI revolution in science. *Science*, 357:16–17, 2017.

[11] Steven L Brunton, Joshua L Proctor, and J Nathan Kutz. Discovering governing equations from data by sparse identification of nonlinear dynamical systems. *Proceedings of the National Academy of Sciences*, 113(15):3932–3937, 2016.

[12] P. Caldwell et al. Statistical significance of climate sensitivity predictors obtained by data mining. *Geophysical Research Letters*, 41(5):1803–1808, 2014.

[13] SA Clough, MW Shephard, EJ Mlawer, JS Delamere, MJ Iacono, K Cady-Pereira, S Boukabara, and PD Brown. Atmospheric radiative transfer modeling: A summary of the aer codes. *Journal of Quantitative Spectroscopy and Radiative Transfer*, 91(2):233–244, 2005.

[14] Peter Congdon. *Bayesian Statistical Modelling*, volume 704. John Wiley & Sons, 2007.

[15] Arka Daw, R Quinn Thomas, Cayelan C Carey, Jordan S Read, Alison P Appling, and Anuj Karpatne. Physics-guided architecture (pga) of neural networks for quantifying uncertainty in lake temperature modeling. In *Proceedings of the 2020 SIAM International Conference on Data Mining*, pages 532–540. SIAM, 2020.

[16] J Deng, W Dong, R Socher, L-J Li, K Li, and L Fei-Fei. ImageNet: A Large-Scale Hierarchical Image Database. In *CVPR09*, 2009.

[17] Nicolas Dobigeon, Yoann Altmann, Nathalie Brun, and Saïd Moussaoui. Linear and nonlinear unmixing in hyperspectral imaging. In *Data Handling in Science and Technology*, volume 30, pages 185–224. Elsevier, 2016.

[18] Mohannad Elhamod, Kelly M Diamond, A Murat Maga, Yasin Bakis, Henry L Bart, Paula Mabee, Wasila Dahdul, Jeremy Leipzig, Jane Greenberg, Brian Avants, et al. Hierarchy-guided neural networks for species classification. *bioRxiv*, 2021.

[19] Geir Evensen. *Data Assimilation: The Ensemble Kalman Filter*. Springer Science & Business Media, 2009.

[20] James H. Faghmous and Vipin Kumar. A Big Data Guide to Understanding Climate Change: The Case for Theory-Guided Data Science. *Big Data*, 3, 2014.

[21] First . First Workshop. `https://sites.google.com/view/aaai-mlps`.

[22] Nic Fleming. How artificial intelligence is changing drug discovery. *Nature*, 557(7706):S55–S55, 2018.

[23] Urban Forssell and Peter Lindskog. Combining semi-physical and neural network modeling: An example ofits usefulness. *IFAC Proceedings Volumes*, 30(11):767–770, 1997.

[24] AR Ganguly, EA Kodra, A Agrawal, A Banerjee, S Boriah, Sn Chatterjee, So Chatterjee, A Choudhary, D Das, J Faghmous, et al. Toward enhanced understanding and projections of climate extremes using physics-guided data mining techniques. *Nonlinear Processes in Geophysics*, 21(4):777–795, 2014.

[25] Junyi Gao, Rakshith Sharma, Cheng Qian, Lucas M Glass, Jeffrey Spaeder, Justin Romberg, Jimeng Sun, and Cao Xiao. Stan: spatio-temporal attention network for pandemic prediction using real-world evidence. *Journal of the American Medical Informatics Association*, 28(4):733–743, 2021.

[26] Yolanda Gil and Bart Selman. A 20-Year Community Roadmap for Artificial Intelligence Research in the US. `https://cra.org/ccc/wp-content/uploads/sites/2/2019/08/Community-Roadmap-for-AI-Research.pdf`.

[27] D Graham-Rowe, D Goldston, C Doctorow, M Waldrop, C Lynch, F Frankel, R Reid, S Nelson, D Howe, SY Rhee, et al. Big data: science in the petabyte era. *Nature*, 455(7209):8–9, 2008.

[28] Oliver Hennigh, Susheela Narasimhan, Mohammad Amin Nabian, Akshay Subramaniam, Kaustubh Tangsali, Zhiwei Fang, Max Rietmann, Wonmin Byeon, and Sanjay Choudhry. Nvidia simnet™: An ai-accelerated multi-physics simulation framework. In *International Conference on Computational Science*, pages 447–461. Springer, 2021.

[29] MR Hipsey, LC Bruce, and DP Hamilton. Glm—general lake model: Model overview and user information. *Perth (Australia): University of Western Australia Technical Manual*, 2014.

[30] Ting Hua, Chandan K Reddy, Lei Zhang, Lijing Wang, Liang Zhao, Chang-Tien Lu, and Naren Ramakrishnan. Social media based simulation models for understanding disease dynamics. In *Proceedings of the Twenty-Seventh International Joint Conference on Artificial Intelligence*, 2018.

[31] Institute for Pure and Applied Mathematics. Machine Learning for Physics and the Physics of Learning. `http://www.ipam.ucla.edu/programs/long-programs/machine-learning-for-physics-and-the-physics-of-learning/`.

[32] Xiaowei Jia, Jared Willard, Anuj Karpatne, Jordan Read, Jacob Zwart, Michael Steinbach, and Vipin Kumar. Physics guided rnns for modeling dynamical systems: A case study in simulating lake temperature profiles. In *Proceedings of the 2019 SIAM International Conference on Data Mining*, pages 558–566. SIAM, 2019.

[33] Xiaowei Jia, Jared Willard, Anuj Karpatne, Jordan S Read, Jacob A Zwart, Michael Steinbach, and Vipin Kumar. Physics-guided machine learning for scientific discovery: An application in simulating lake temperature profiles. *arXiv preprint arXiv:2001.11086*, 2020.

[34] TO Jonathan, AM Gerald, et al. Special issue: dealing with data. *Science*, 331(6018):639–806, 2011.

[35] R Kannan, AV Ievlev, N Laanait, MA Ziatdinov, RK Vasudevan, S Jesse, and SV Kalinin. Deep data analysis via physically constrained linear unmixing: universal framework, domain examples, and a community-wide platform. *Advanced Structural and Chemical Imaging*, 4(1):1–20, 2018.

[36] George Em Karniadakis, Ioannis G Kevrekidis, Lu Lu, Paris Perdikaris, Sifan Wang, and Liu Yang. Physics-informed machine learning. *Nature Reviews Physics*, 3(6):422–440, 2021.

[37] Anuj Karpatne, Gowtham Atluri, James H Faghmous, Michael Steinbach, Arindam Banerjee, Auroop Ganguly, Shashi Shekhar, Nagiza Samatova, and Vipin Kumar. Theory-guided data science: A new paradigm for scientific discovery from data. *IEEE Transactions on Knowledge and Data Engineering*, 29(10):2318–2331, 2017.

[38] Anuj Karpatne, William Watkins, Jordan Read, and Vipin Kumar. Physics-guided neural networks (pgnn): An application in lake temperature modeling. *arXiv preprint arXiv:1710.11431*, 2017.

[39] Satish Karra, Bulbul Ahmmed, and Maruti K Mudunuru. Adjointnet: Constraining machine learning models with physics-based codes. *arXiv preprint arXiv:2109.03956*, 2021.

[40] K Kashinath, M Mustafa, A Albert, JL Wu, C Jiang, S Esmaeilzadeh, K Azizzadenesheli, R Wang, A Chattopadhyay, A Singh, et al. Physics-informed machine learning: case studies for weather and climate modelling. *Philosophical Transactions of the Royal Society A*, 379(2194):20200093, 2021.

[41] Nirmal Keshava and John F Mustard. Spectral unmixing. *IEEE Signal Processing Magazine*, 19(1):44–57, 2002.

[42] Ankush Khandelwal, Shaoming Xu, Xiang Li, Xiaowei Jia, Michael Stienbach, Christopher Duffy, John Nieber, and Vipin Kumar. Physics guided machine learning methods for hydrology. *arXiv preprint arXiv:2012.02854*, 2020.

[43] Alex Krizhevsky, Ilya Sutskever, and Geoffrey E Hinton. Imagenet classification with deep convolutional neural networks. In *Advances in Neural Information Processing Systems*, pages 1097–1105, 2012.

[44] Patrick Lambrix, He Tan, Vaida Jakoniene, and Lena Strömbäck. Biological ontologies. In *Semantic Web*, pages 85–99. Springer, 2007.

[45] Pat Langley. Bacon: A production system that discovers empirical laws. In *IJCAI*, page 344. Citeseer, 1977.

[46] Pat Langley, Herbert A Simon, Gary L Bradshaw, and Jan M Zytkow. *Scientific Discovery: Computational Explorations of the Creative Processes*. 1987.

[47] David Lazer, Ryan Kennedy, Gary King, and Alessandro Vespignani. The Parable of Google Flu: Traps in Big Data Analysis. *Science (New York, N.Y.)*, 343(6176):1203–5, March 2014.

[48] Los Alamos National Laboratory. Workshop on Physics Informed Machine Learning. `http://www.cvent.com/events/3rd-physics-informed-machine-learning/` `event-summary-f98f0383e62f4bc4a68c663f7b08d22d.aspx`.

[49] Aleksander Madry, Aleksandar Makelov, Ludwig Schmidt, Dimitris Tsipras, and Adrian Vladu. Towards deep learning models resistant to adversarial attacks. *arXiv preprint arXiv:1706.06083*, 2017.

[50] Gary Marcus and Ernest Davis. Eight (no, nine!) problems with big data. *The New York Times*, 6(04):2014, 2014.

[51] TR Marsh. Doppler tomography. *Astrophysics and Space Science*, 296(1):403–415, 2005.

[52] Ariana Mendible, Steven L Brunton, Aleksandr Y Aravkin, Wes Lowrie, and J Nathan Kutz. Dimensionality reduction and reduced-order modeling for traveling wave physics. *Theoretical and Computational Fluid Dynamics*, 34(4):385–400, 2020.

[53] Volodymyr Mnih, Koray Kavukcuoglu, David Silver, Alex Graves, Ioannis Antonoglou, Daan Wierstra, and Martin Riedmiller. Playing atari with deep reinforcement learning. *arXiv preprint arXiv:1312.5602*, 2013.

[54] Nikhil Muralidhar, Jie Bu, Ze Cao, Long He, Naren Ramakrishnan, Danesh Tafti, and Anuj Karpatne. Phynet: Physics guided neural networks for particle drag force prediction in assembly. In *Proceedings of the 2020 SIAM International Conference on Data Mining*, pages 559–567. SIAM, 2020.

[55] Tamas Nemeth, Chengjun Wu, and Gerard T Schuster. Least-squares migration of incomplete reflection data. *Geophysics*, 64(1):208–221, 1999.

[56] Maziar Raissi, Paris Perdikaris, and George E Karniadakis. Physics-informed neural networks: A deep learning framework for solving forward and inverse problems involving nonlinear partial differential equations. *Journal of Computational Physics*, 378:686–707, 2019.

[57] Maziar Raissi, Paris Perdikaris, and George Em Karniadakis. Physics informed deep learning (part i): Data-driven solutions of nonlinear partial differential equations. *arXiv preprint arXiv:1711.10561*, 2017.

[58] Maziar Raissi, Paris Perdikaris, and George Em Karniadakis. Physics informed deep learning (part ii): Data-driven discovery of nonlinear partial differential equations. *arXiv preprint arXiv:1711.10566*, 2017.

[59] David A Randall, Richard A Wood, Sandrine Bony, Robert Colman, Thierry Fichefet, John Fyfe, Vladimir Kattsov, Andrew Pitman, Jagadish Shukla, Jayaraman Srinivasan, et al. Climate models and their evaluation. In *Climate Change 2007: The Physical Science Basis. Contribution of Working Group I to the Fourth Assessment Report of the IPCC (FAR)*, pages 589–662. Cambridge University Press, 2007.

[60] Stephan Rasp, Michael S Pritchard, and Pierre Gentine. Deep learning to represent subgrid processes in climate models. *Proceedings of the National Academy of Sciences*, 115(39):9684–9689, 2018.

[61] Jordan S Read, Xiaowei Jia, Jared Willard, Alison P Appling, Jacob A Zwart, Samantha K Oliver, Anuj Karpatne, Gretchen JA Hansen, Paul C Hanson, William Watkins, et al. Process-guided deep learning predictions of lake water temperature. *Water Resources Research*, 55(11):9173–9190, 2019.

[62] Markus Reichstein, Gustau Camps-Valls, Bjorn Stevens, Martin Jung, Joachim Denzler, Nuno Carvalhais, et al. Deep learning and process understanding for data-driven earth system science. *Nature*, 566(7743):195–204, 2019.

[63] Ribana Roscher, Bastian Bohn, Marco F Duarte, and Jochen Garcke. Explainable machine learning for scientific insights and discoveries. *IEEE Access*, 8:42200–42216, 2020.

[64] Michael Schmidt and Hod Lipson. Distilling free-form natural laws from experimental data. *Science*, 324(5923):81–85, 2009.

[65] Terrence J Sejnowski, Patricia S Churchland, and J Anthony Movshon. Putting big data to good use in neuroscience. *Nature Neuroscience*, 17(11):1440–1441, 2014.

[66] Lawrence Sirovich. Turbulence and the dynamics of coherent structures. i. coherent structures. *Quarterly of Applied Mathematics*, 45(3):561–571, 1987.

[67] Rick Stevens, Valerie Taylor, Jeff Nichols, Arthur Barney Maccabe, Katherine Yelick, and David Brown. Ai for science. Technical report, Argonne National Lab.(ANL), Argonne, IL (United States), 2020.

[68] Albert Tarantola. Inversion of seismic reflection data in the acoustic approximation. *Geophysics*, 49(8):1259–1266, 1984.

[69] Michael L Thompson and Mark A Kramer. Modeling chemical processes using prior knowledge and neural networks. *AIChE Journal*, 40(8):1328–1340, 1994.

[70] Nils Thuerey, Philipp Holl, Maximilian Mueller, Patrick Schnell, Felix Trost, and Kiwon Um. *Physics-based Deep Learning*. WWW, 2021.

[71] Aaron Towne, Oliver T Schmidt, and Tim Colonius. Spectral proper orthogonal decomposition and its relationship to dynamic mode decomposition and resolvent analysis. *Journal of Fluid Mechanics*, 847:821–867, 2018.

[72] Jonathan H Tu. *Dynamic Mode Decomposition: Theory and Applications*. PhD thesis, Princeton University, 2013.

[73] Laura von Rueden, Sebastian Mayer, Katharina Beckh, Bogdan Georgiev, Sven Giesselbach, Raoul Heese, Birgit Kirsch, Julius Pfrommer, Annika Pick, Rajkumar Ramamurthy, et al. Informed machine learning–a taxonomy and survey of integrating knowledge into learning systems. *arXiv preprint arXiv:1903.12394*, 2019.

[74] Lijing Wang, Jiangzhuo Chen, and Madhav Marathe. Tdefsi: Theory-guided deep learning-based epidemic forecasting with synthetic information. *ACM Transactions on Spatial Algorithms and Systems (TSAS)*, 6(3):1–39, 2020.

[75] Rui Wang, Robin Walters, and Rose Yu. Incorporating symmetry into deep dynamics models for improved generalization. *arXiv preprint arXiv:2002.03061*, 2020.

[76] Jared Willard, Xiaowei Jia, Shaoming Xu, Michael Steinbach, and Vipin Kumar. Integrating Scientific Knowledge with machine learning for Earth and Environmental Systems: A survey. *ACM Computing Survey*, 2022.

[77] Liang Zhao, Jiangzhuo Chen, Feng Chen, Wei Wang, Chang-Tien Lu, and Naren Ramakrishnan. Simnest: Social media nested epidemic simulation via online semi-supervised deep learning. In *2015 IEEE International Conference on Data Mining*, pages 639–648. IEEE, 2015.

2

Targeted Use of Deep Learning for Physics and Engineering

Steven L. Brunton and J. Nathan Kutz

CONTENTS

Deep learning represents a new mathematical architecture for representing arbitrarily complex functions, given sufficiently vast and rich training data. These deep neural networks have revolutionized many machine learning tasks, from computer vision to natural language processing. Recently, deep learning has begun to gain traction in the natural and engineering sciences, where the systems are governed by physical laws that determine how they evolve dynamically in time. This chapter will explore several targeted deep learning approaches that are being developed for physical systems, specifically those architectures that promote interpretable and generalizable models that remain *physical* by construction. Two areas will be highlighted in particular: (1) learning dynamical systems models from data and (2) learning coordinate systems in which the system is simplified. These approaches will be illustrated by several modern examples, and this chapter will also highlight pressing open challenges in the field.

2.1 Introduction

Neural networks (NNs) provide the core mathematical infrastructure for deep learning algorithms. Although NNs are more than four decades old [47], with significant mathematical advancements made in the 80s and 90s [11,54], it wasn't until deep convolutional NNs were applied to the ImageNET data set [37] in 2012 [61] that the full power of deep learning was realized. Deep learning was originally successfully applied to tasks that are fundamentally *interpolatory* in nature, i.e. computer vision and speech recognition [51], where the training data was sufficiently vast and rich that it is representative of future data. More recently, deep learning has been brought to scientific and engineering domains, which are often *extrapolatory* in nature [17, 22, 23], with interpretability and generalizability being critical concepts for advancing scientific discovery. From geophysics to lasers, deep learning methods are now being routinely developed for almost every scientific field, yielding results that often outperform existing state-of-the-art methods. *Physics-informed machine learning* methods are especially important as they constrain and target deep learning efforts to enforce known physics and learn new physics, while promoting interpretability. In what follows, we highlight the diverse and targeted use of deep learning for scientific and engineering efforts, including for applications in control, forecasting, and characterization of complex dynamics.

Physics-based models are often derived from first principles, conservation laws, and/or empirical observations. Traditional scientific computing approaches then numerically simulate these models to provide insights into dynamical behaviors, parametric dependencies, and underlying bifurcations. In contrast, deep learning algorithms aim to achieve the same level of insight and modeling accuracy in an automated fashion, directly from data acquired through sensor measurements. The ability of deep learning to perform such tasks in an interpretable and generalizable manner relies critically on constraining the NNs with known physics, thus the moniker physics-informed machine learning. For instance, Karniadakis and co-workers have pioneered a suite of algorithms centered around *physics-informed neural networks* (PINNs), which exploit various aspects of physics principles and embed them directly into the NNs [74, 98, 101, 128]. Brunton and Kutz and co-workers have similarly developed a suite of deep learning tools aimed at producing parsimonious representations of physics-based models, whether linear or nonlinear [30, 48, 75, 108, 109]. Systems for which the underlying Hamiltonian and/or Lagrangian is preserved have also been developed for large-scale, N-body interactions [6, 33, 35]. Alternatively, diffusion mappings can be used to great effect to learn geometries and manifolds on which dynamics evolve [38, 84, 127]. In each of these examples, well-known physics principles are exploited and embedded in the deep learning architecture. Indeed, these methods aim to leverage the discovery of coordinates in which advantageous representations of the dynamics are achieved.

The primary focus here is on dynamical systems, including spatio-temporal systems. In the case of standard dynamical systems, with no explicit spatial structure, time-series data is of primary interest. In such cases, one can learn how to parameterize, or *warp*, time in order to leverage advantageous representations. For instance, Lange et al. [63] show how temporal dynamics can be transformed into parsimonious and advantageous Fourier representations. This NN Koopman embedding of time-series data allows for efficient and accurate long-range forecasting, outperforming modern NNs such as LSTMs, echo state networks, etc. for time-series forecasting. Such a scheme can be modified to learn multi-scale dynamics in time [70]. For spatio-temporal systems, the discovery of coordinates and dynamics are coupled to form modern reduced-order models (ROMs) [3, 9, 43, 71, 92, 93, 104, 126] and/or coarse-grained models [5, 59]. Parish and Carlberg [93] have been especially thoughtful in comparing different NN strategies for time-stepping spatio-temporal ROMs, providing the most comprehensive comparison in the field thus far of deep learning enabled ROMs. The deep learning framework can also be ported to boundary value problems (BVPs) where coordinates and equations can once again be used to learn BVPs [112], nonlinear Green's functions [49], integrated kernel representations of solutions [65–67, 132], or constitutive models of BVPs [55]. Importantly, deep learning is revolutionizing control strategies with deep model predictive control (deep MPC) [7, 10] and deep reinforcement learning (RL) [117, 125].

The undeniable success of such a diverse range of deep learning strategies applied to physical and engineering systems shows the remarkable flexibility of NNs. Remarkably, most of these innovations have come in only the last few years, showing the extraordinary pace of progress and revealing the promise of deep learning as a transformative mathematical paradigm. Furthermore, many of the most promising methods represent a hybrid modeling strategy where traditional scientific modeling is embedded in the deep learning architecture. This empowers physics-informed machine learning, whose hallmark features are the targeted use of deep learning. In what follows, we present a number of physics-informed strategies and demonstrate how targeted deep learning is transforming the characterization, forecasting, and control of complex dynamics.

The remainder of this chapter is organized as follows. Section 2.2 provides a brief introduction to deep learning. Deep neural networks are then used to identify dynamical systems in Section 2.3 and effective coordinate systems in Section 2.4. The important topic of incorporating physics knowledge into machine learning is presented in Section 2.5. These approaches are then explored on several examples, primarily in fluid dynamics and control theory, in Section 2.6. Finally, we conclude with a discussion in Section 2.7.

2.2 Deep Learning Preliminaries

Deep learning refers to machine learning based on neural networks with a deep multi-layer structure. Deep neural networks form a core computational architecture for many modern supervised machine learning and reinforcement learning algorithms. Neural networks are particularly powerful due to their flexible representations of data and the diversity of available architectures and network topologies [17, 50]. The incredible success of deep learning is largely due to the availability of vast data sets and modern high-performance computing hardware, which have enabled the training of neural networks with millions or billions of free parameters.

The term deep refers to the number of layers in the neural network used to approximate a map from inputs to outputs; although it varies widely, five or more layers in a neural network is typically considered *deep*. The flexibility of neural networks may be formulated as the ability to approximate arbitrary functions, in the so-called universal function approximation theorem [54]. Mathematically, they assume a compositional structure

$$\mathbf{y} = \boldsymbol{\phi}_1(\boldsymbol{\phi}_2(\cdots(\boldsymbol{\phi}_n(\mathbf{x}; \boldsymbol{\theta}_n); \cdots); \boldsymbol{\theta}_2); \boldsymbol{\theta}_1). \tag{2.1}$$

The functions $\boldsymbol{\phi}_k$ $(k = 1, 2, \cdots, n)$ denote the individual layers, and the parameters $\boldsymbol{\theta}_k$ denote the neural network weights, typically the connection strengths connecting nodes from one layer to the next. This nonlinear mapping framework is incredibly flexible, making it possible to accomplish classification and regression tasks between input and output data. The neural network weights, given by the parameters $\{\boldsymbol{\theta}_k\}_{k=1}^n$, are solved via optimization to best fit the data, typically using stochastic gradient descent.

Although deep learning has traditionally been applied in commercial and industrial settings, where they have demonstrated state-of-the-art performance in image analysis and natural language processing, they are increasingly being applied to physics and engineering problems. Despite their power, there are several key limitations. Deep learning typically requires a considerable amount of labeled training data, as most tasks are supervised. Indeed, ImageNET provided approximately 15 million labeled images, which was nearly two orders of magnitude more labels than previously considered. Neural networks are also known to overfit to the training data and often result in opaque models that are hard to interpret, fail to generalize, and don't have certifiable performance guarantees. All of these issues are exacerbated in engineering applications where safety is critical, such as for self-driving cars and aerospace systems [22].

2.3   Learning Dynamical Systems

Dynamical systems provide a powerful framework to describe how a system evolves in time. In particular, given the state of a system $\mathbf{x} \in \mathbb{R}^n$, the rate of change of this state in time may be described by a system of differential equations

$$\frac{d}{dt}\mathbf{x} = \mathbf{f}(\mathbf{x}). \tag{2.2}$$

The function $\mathbf{f}$ describes the dynamics, which may be both nonlinear and highly coupled. The dynamics in $\mathbf{f}$ may come from physical law, such as $F = ma$ or the Navier–Stokes equations, or from a set of heuristic equations that are designed to fit observational data. For many complex systems of interest, as are found in neuroscience, epidemiology, and climate science, known governing equations and dynamical systems models have remained elusive. Even for systems where the governing equations are known, such as fluid dynamics, it is still beneficial to obtain reduced-order models that are more tractable for design, optimization, and control [18, 23]. Thus, there is considerable research effort focused on data-driven discovery of dynamical systems models [15, 17, 19, 62, 79, 86, 94, 98, 106, 107, 110, 111, 124, 126]. In recent years, deep neural networks have been increasingly employed to model dynamical systems, especially those that are not well-characterized from first principles, as will be discussed here.

Two simple feedforward network architectures for representing dynamical systems are shown in Figure 2.1. The first network learns the continuous-time dynamics in (2.2), while the second network learns the discrete-time dynamics

$$\mathbf{x}_{k+1} = \mathbf{F}(\mathbf{x}_k). \tag{2.3}$$

There are several examples of both networks in the literature; for example, Champion et al. [30] develop networks to identify the continuous dynamics, while Liu et al. [70] and Qin et al. [95] develop networks to identify discrete-time flow maps characterizing the dynamics. More broadly, these architectures can be used as numerical time-stepping algorithms for physics-based models [93, 104]. In general, discrete-time dynamics are more general than continuous-time dynamics, encompassing non-smooth and hybrid dynamics as well. For example, a discrete-time map $\mathbf{F}(\mathbf{x})$ might represent the flow map of the continuous-time dynamics (2.2) through some time Δt

$$\mathbf{F}(\mathbf{x}(t)) = \mathbf{x}(t + \Delta t) = \int_t^{t+\Delta t} \mathbf{f}(\mathbf{x}(\tau))\, d\tau. \tag{2.4}$$

In this case, we may consider $\mathbf{x}_k = \mathbf{x}(k\Delta t)$. However, for this reason, continuous-time dynamics will often have a simpler representation in practice. For small Δt, the flow map $\mathbf{F}$ may be approximated through a Taylor series expansion of the dynamics, such as in an Euler or Runge-Kutta numerical integration scheme. For large Δt, however, the flow map $\mathbf{F}$ may become arbitrarily complex to represent. In fact, this is a key opportunity for deep learning, where it is possible to learn maps that take larger integration steps than traditional numerical methods, which are constrained by Taylor series approximations [70].

Figure 2.2 shows another popular approach, called *reservoir* computing, which is a form of a *recurrent* neural network. In this approach, a large loosely organized processing layer,

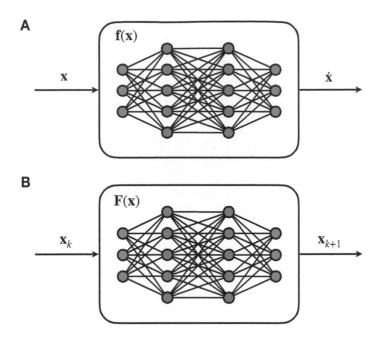

FIGURE 2.1
Two approaches for representing dynamical systems: (A) a continuous-time dynamical system $\dot{\mathbf{x}} = \mathbf{f}(\mathbf{x})$ and (B) a discrete-time dynamical system $\mathbf{x}_{k+1} = \mathbf{F}(\mathbf{x}_k)$.

called the reservoir, is used to generate nonlinear functions of the inputs. This network is not as organized as a traditional deep neural network, although chains of functions and recursions are possible, resulting in quite expressive functions. These functions are then used to construct the output. Reservoir computing has shown promise recently in the representation of chaotic systems, such as the Kuramoto–Sivashinsky equation [94].

Several other promising approaches are emerging to model dynamical systems with deep learning. Universal differential equations [97] is a deep learning framework that encompasses several types of differential equation learning problems, including stochastic, ordinary, and partial differential equations. Importantly, neural network frameworks are inherently related to automatic differentiation, which may simplify several downstream tasks, such as control, sensitivity analysis, and uncertainty quantification. Symbolic neural networks are also quite promising [6, 34, 35], providing a deep learning generalization of symbolic regression techniques that have been used to great advantage in nonlinear system identification and equation discovery [12, 111].

It is important to note that nonlinear system identification using techniques from machine learning has a rich history. For example, Bongard and Lipson [12] and Schmidt and Lipson [111] used genetic programming to obtain symbolic representations of nonlinear systems. They leveraged the principle of parsimony to pick the simplest model that describe the data out of a large family of candidate models. In subsequent work, the sparse identification of nonlinear dynamics (SINDy) algorithm [19] formulated the nonlinear system identification problem as a generalized linear regression problem, where the time derivative of a state is approximated as a linear combination of functions from a library of candidate terms that may describe the dynamics. In SINDy, sparsity-promoting regression is used to find the key terms in this candidate library that are required to describe the data, highlighting the few terms that are present in the dynamics. SINDy has since been generalized to identify partial

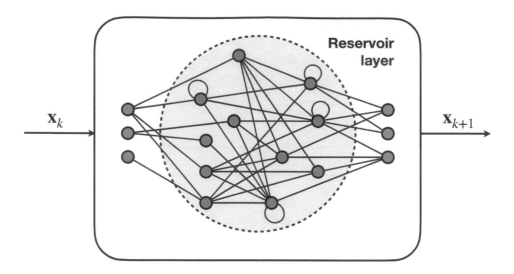

FIGURE 2.2
Schematic of reservoir computing, where a large reservoir layer is used to generate complex functions, which are then sampled for the output.

differential equations [107], stochastic systems [13, 26], rational functions [78] and hybrid dynamics [77], to identify conservative models of fluid flows [53, 72, 73] and plasmas [58], and for use in model predictive control [57]. Importantly, these nonlinear system identification techniques result in models that are highly *interpretable*, because they have only a few terms and may be analyzed using classical techniques, and that are highly *generalizable*, because they avoid overfitting to the training data. In contrast, most neural network approaches, such as the feedforward architectures in Figure 2.1 and the recurrent reservoir network in Figure 2.2, are opaque, defying straightforward analysis and interpretations. Moreover, these networks are typically useful for interpolation tasks, where they are able to *memorize* the training data, and often fail in extrapolation tasks, where they are required to generalize beyond the training data. In many applications of computer vision, the training data is so vast that interpolation is sufficient. However, when characterizing physical and engineering systems, the goal is often to build a model from limited training data, often from a limited sampling of parameter space, and have it generalize to other parameters. For example, if the model is to be used for design optimization and control, it must be valid outside of the narrow region of parameter space used to train the model. Thus, in recent years, there is a concerted effort to combine parsimonious nonlinear system identification techniques with the more modern deep learning approaches, improving the interpretability and generalizability of neural networks.

2.4   Learning Coordinate Transformations

In addition to learning dynamics, deep learning provides a tremendous opportunity to uncover effective coordinate systems in which to represent the dynamics. Figure 2.3 shows two competing neural network architectures for learning coordinates. In the first approach, a

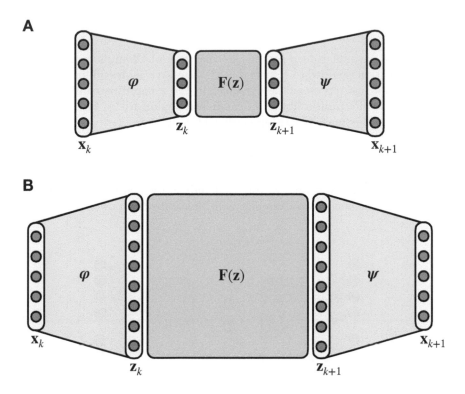

FIGURE 2.3
Two major architectures for deep learning of coordinates: (A) a deep autoencoder extracts a low-dimensional latent space **z**, and (B) an alternative approach is to lift to a much higher-dimensional space **z**.

deep autoencoder is used to uncover a low-dimensional latent space, where the dynamics are simplified. In many cases, simplified dynamics may mean *linear*, as in Koopman operator theory. In other cases, simplified dynamics will be *sparse*, having as few nonlinear terms as possible, as in the SINDy modeling procedure. In the second approach, the measured variables are lifted to a higher-dimensional space. This approach is consistent with many fields of machine learning, such as support vector machines (SVMs), where lifting to a higher dimensional space often makes tasks simpler; for example, in SVM, nonlinear classification problems often become linearly separable in higher dimensions.

Mathematically, the goal of a deep coordinate transformation is to learn a map φ from the original coordinates $\mathbf{x} \in \mathbb{R}^n$ into a new coordinate system $\mathbf{z} \in \mathbb{R}^p$,

$$\mathbf{z} = \varphi(\mathbf{x}) \tag{2.5}$$

where the dynamics become simpler in some way, e.g., the dynamics becomes linear or parsimoniuos. In the case of Figure 2.3A, the network φ is called the *encoder*. To remain physically relevant, it is often necessary to be able to recover the original state **x** from **x**:

$$\mathbf{x} = \psi(\mathbf{z}) \tag{2.6}$$

where ψ is the *decoder* network. Typically, a loss function is included in the network so that minimal information is lost when mapping through the autoencoder:

$$L = \|\psi(\varphi(\mathbf{x})) - \mathbf{x}\|_2. \tag{2.7}$$

Figure 2.4 shows a particular deep autoencoder network of Champion et al. [30], where an additional loss function is added to enforce that the latent variables admit a *sparse* nonlinear model. In particular, we represent the dynamics in the $\mathbf{z}$ coordinates in terms of a sparse combination of elements from a library of candidate nonlinearities $\boldsymbol{\Theta}(\mathbf{z})$, as in the SINDy algorithm [19, 107]. This may be written mathematically as

$$\frac{d}{dt}\mathbf{z} = \boldsymbol{\Theta}(\mathbf{z})\boldsymbol{\Xi} \tag{2.8}$$

where the columns of $\boldsymbol{\Xi}$ are sparse vectors that indicate which terms in the library $\boldsymbol{\Theta}(\mathbf{x})$ are active in the dynamics. Two examples help illustrate the power of this architecture.

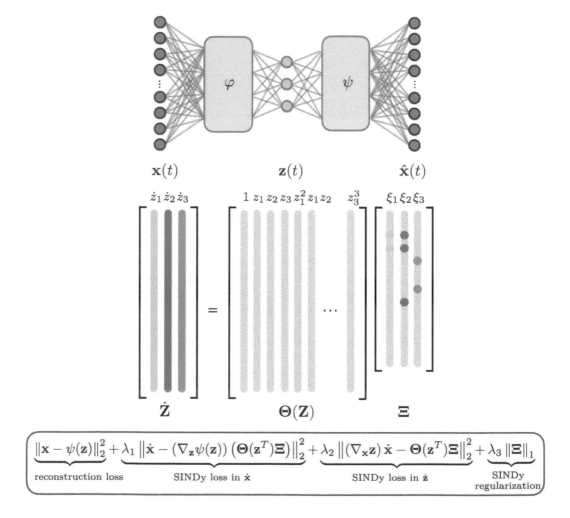

FIGURE 2.4
A deep autoencoder network is combined with the SINDy modeling procedure to design a latent space in which the dynamics are sparse. *Reproduced from Champion et al. [30].*

In the first, consider video recordings of a fully nonlinear pendulum. The above method then discovers from high-dimensional pixel space the variables of the pendulum (θ and $\dot{\theta}$) and the governing dynamics in these variables ($\ddot{\theta} = \sin(\theta)$. This example was demonstrated in [30]. Likewise, in celestial mechanics, from earth observations of the retro-grade motion of the planets, one must first learn the coordinate transformation to heliocentric coordinates before then learning $\mathbf{F} = m\mathbf{a}$ physics. Both these examples highlight critical aspects of the scientific discovery process in which coordinates and dynamics must be jointly discovered.

In principle, it is also possible to use autoencoder networks to uncover a coordinate system in which the dynamics become approximately linear. Mathematically, this is written as

$$\frac{d}{dt}\mathbf{z} = \mathbf{Kz}, \tag{2.9}$$

where $\mathbf{K}$ is a matrix. These coordinates are related to eigenfunctions of the Koopman operator [20], which is an infinite-dimensional linear operator $\mathcal{K}$ that advances measurement functions of the state, $g(\mathbf{x})$ forward in the direction of the flow of the dynamics $\mathbf{F}$, according to:

$$\mathcal{K}g(\mathbf{x}_k) = g(\mathbf{F}(\mathbf{x}_k)) = g(\mathbf{x}_{k+1}). \tag{2.10}$$

Eigenfunctions $\varphi(\mathbf{x})$ of this Koopman operator satisfy

$$\mathcal{K}\varphi(\mathbf{x}) = \lambda\varphi(\mathbf{x}) \tag{2.11}$$

and provide coordinates in which the dynamics appear linear:

$$\varphi(\mathbf{x}_{k+1}) = \mathcal{K}\varphi(\mathbf{x}_k) = \lambda\varphi(\mathbf{x}_k). \tag{2.12}$$

Figure 2.5 shows a deep autoencoder network of Lusch et al. [75] that identifies a Koopman coordinate system. This work shows that it is possible to include an auxiliary network that can parameterize the linear eigenvalues to enable the identification of systems with a continuous eigenvalue spectrum. Continuous spectrum dynamics are ubiquitous, for example as exhibited by the nonlinear pendulum, although they have been notoriously challenging to characterize with Koopman approximations.

In a sense, the Koopman autoencoder network in Figure 2.5 provides a nonlinear generalization of the *dynamic mode decomposition* (DMD) [62, 106, 110, 124]. After a Banff workshop in January 2017, several groups developed similar deep Koopman architectures [75, 79, 90, 122, 126, 129]. Obtaining finite-dimensional representations of the Koopman operator has been challenging because these representations rely on Koopman eigenfunctions, which may be irrepresentably complex [16, 20]. The universal function approximation capabilities of neural networks [54] make them ideal for representing these eigenfunctions. Recently, this framework has been extended to partial differential equations (PDEs) [48] and to establish nonlinear analogues of Green's functions [49].

2.5 Physics-Informed Learning

Physics informed learning [6, 23, 33–35, 60, 72, 73, 86, 99–101, 131] is of growing importance for scientific and engineering problems. *Physics informed* refers to our ability to constrain the

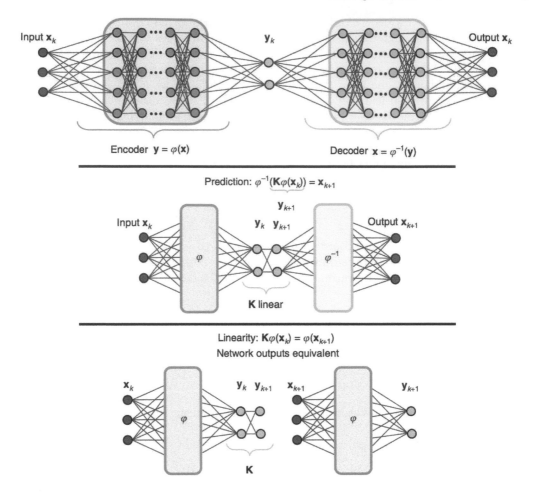

FIGURE 2.5
A deep autoencoder network is designed in which the dynamics are linear. Reproduced from
Lusch et al. [75].

learning process by known physical principles. For instance, conservation of mass, momentum, or energy may be imposed in machine learning [72], improving stability and predictive
performance while reducing the volume of data required to train the model. Physics, such as
symmetries, invariants, conservations laws, and constraints, can be incorporated into each
of the four major stages of machine learning: (1) designing the neural network architecture,
(2) crafting a loss function, (3) collecting and curating the training data, and (4) choosing the optimization strategy to train the model. Considerable effort is typically focused
on designing the learning architecture, although often collecting the data and training the
model are the most expensive stages. In images, rotational invariance is often incorporated
by augmenting the training data with rotated copies, and translational invariance is often
captured using convolutional neural networks. Additional physics and prior knowledge may
be incorporated as additional loss functions or constraints in the optimization problem.
These constraints are often enforced through the addition of regularizing terms, which are
added to the cost function. For the example of a NN model with inputs $\mathbf{x}$ and outputs $\mathbf{y}$,

this becomes

$$\text{argmin}_{\boldsymbol{\theta}_1,\boldsymbol{\theta}_2,\cdots,\boldsymbol{\theta}_n} \|\mathbf{y} - \boldsymbol{\phi}_1(\boldsymbol{\phi}_2(\cdots(\boldsymbol{\phi}_n(\mathbf{x};\boldsymbol{\theta}_n);\cdots);\boldsymbol{\theta}_2)\boldsymbol{\theta}_1)\| + \lambda g(\boldsymbol{\theta}_1,\boldsymbol{\theta}_2,\cdots,\boldsymbol{\theta}_n), \quad (2.13)$$

where the regularization $g(\cdot)$ imposes the desired physical constraint. The parameter λ is a hyper-parameter allowing the user to impose an increasingly strong regularization to enforce this constraint. Adding such physics constraints is essential for engineering and physics systems. Specifically, this is where known physics or physical constraints can be explicitly incorporated into the data-driven modeling process. Physics informed learning, often enacted with deep learning architectures, represents the state-of-the-art in ML methods for the engineering and physical sciences.

Rather than imposing physical constraints explicitly, an alternative is to learn embeddings based on physical models. This physics-guided paradigm involves learning embeddings from data produced by known first principles models of physics. The computation of these embeddings, in the context of aerospace and fluid dynamics, is often known as *modal analysis*, and has become increasingly data-driven (either from simulation or observation) in recent years [23, 119, 121]. The physical coupling between fluids and aerospace structures are particularly important, and the modes of these coupled interactions are impossible to discern by analyzing the Navier–Stokes equations and structural models alone – instead, they are determined by the boundary interactions between the coupled models. Thus, this physics-guided architecture greatly enhances the understanding and design of robust engineering systems that can withstand complex interactions, turbulence, and instabilities. Improved reduced-order models of fluid dynamics may further aid efforts in flow control [18,32] and to reduce jet noise [56]. Modern modal analysis techniques, such as POD/PCA [17], DMD [62, 110, 124], Koopman mode decomposition [20], and resolvent mode analysis [81], naturally fall under the umbrella of unsupervised learning. Furthermore, the dimensionality reduction achieved by these methods enable low-latency, efficient downstream tasks such as system identification [19], airfoil shape optimization and uncertainty quantification [105], and reduced-order modeling [4, 8, 24, 25, 27–29, 85, 115, 121].

Recently, several open-source sparse optimization software frameworks [31, 36, 130] have been developed to make it possible to enforce known physics into sparse regression problems.

2.6 Applications

There is a wide range of applications where deep learning can be used to discover dynamics and coordinates for physical and engineering systems. Much of this work has been driven by applications in fluid dynamics and control, which both have a long history in data-driven system identification and optimization.

2.6.1 Fluid Dynamics

Fluid dynamics is one of the original *big data* disciplines, and many of the algorithms predating modern machine learning find their roots in the fluid dynamics community. For example, *eigenfaces* [116] from image recognition is closely related to the proper orthogonal decomposition that is used to decompose a flow field into a low dimensional modal basis [119, 120]. Recently, there has been renewed interest in reintroducing powerful methods from machine learning to solve fluid dynamics problems [14, 21, 23, 39].

There are several areas of active development using deep learning for fluid mechanics. One of the earliest papers that connected deep learning and fluids was by Milano and Koumoutsakos [82] to analyze the boundary layer. More recently, deep neural networks are being used extensively for turbulence closure modeling [39], which is a notoriously challenging problem. For example, deep learning has been used for Reynolds averaged Navier Stokes (RANS) closures [40,69,91] and for sub-grid-scale modeling for large eddy simulation (LES) closures [80,87]. Neural networks have also been used to infer flow fields from flow visualizations [101] and for super-resolution [42,46]. Machine learning approaches have also shown great promise in accelerating computational fluid dynamics simulations [5,59,65]. Machine learning is also being used in cutting-edge flow control demonstrations [10,41,44, 45,88,96,125], as will be reviewed in the next section.

2.6.2 Control

Control theory is rapidly incorporating techniques from machine learning, and deep learning in particular. In a sense, this is a natural progression, as control theory has long used data-driven models obtained through system identification [17]. Moreover, many problems in control theory can be posed as optimization problems, constrained by the dynamics, which become nonlinear and nonconvex for nonlinear systems. Machine learning is becoming increasingly well-suited to these types of nonconvex optimization problems. Reinforcement learning (RL) [83,102,114] and model predictive control (MPC) [57,64] have seen particularly rapid growth. See Figure 2.6 and 2.7 for schematic descriptions of the use of deep learning models for model predictive control and reinforcement learning, respectively. Several problems have motivated the development of advanced deep RL and deep MPC, including games [83,114], fluid dynamics [10,44,96], nonlinear optics [7,117], robotics [52,68], and biologically inspired swimming [125] and flight [1,2,88,89,103,123].

RL [118], in particular, has seen tremendous advances in recent years due to deep learning. RL is a fundamentally biologically inspired learning paradigm, in which an agent learns from interactions with the environment with goal-oriented objectives. Modern RL is being developed for applications in autonomy and control, unlike the other two dominant paradigms of ML of supervised and unsupervised learning. An RL agent measures the state of its environment and learns advantageous actions to optimize rewards, which are often delayed. The RL agent performs actions $\mathbf{a}$ to drive the system to a desired state $\mathbf{s}$, leading to postive or negative rewards $\mathbf{r}$. The environment often evolve probabilistically, so the agent's policy must also be probabilistic. The ability to determine which actions lead to delayed rewards is one of the central challenges in RL, for example in the game of chess, where an entire game must be played before it is won or lost.

RL is often posed as an optimization problem to determine the probability of taking action $\mathbf{a}$ at a given state $\mathbf{s}$ to maximize future rewards, also known as a *policy* $\pi(\mathbf{s}, \mathbf{a})$. Given a policy π, the value function is defined as how desirable it is being in a given state in terms of expected future rewards:

$$V_\pi(\mathbf{s}) = \mathbb{E}\left(\sum_t \gamma^t \mathbf{r}_t | \mathbf{s}_0 = \mathbf{s}\right),\qquad(2.14)$$

where $\mathbb{E}$ is the expectation value and γ is a *discount rate*. Typically, the state evolves according to a Markov decision process, so the transition of a system from one state to another is probabilistic. Thus, RL often requires a very large number of trials or samples in order to determine an optimal policy. This data requirement is eased in chess and Go by self-play [113]. To deal with sporadic rewards, reward shaping is used to guide more frequent intermediate rewards. Often, in modern deep RL, a deep neural network is used to learn a *quality* function $Q(\mathbf{s}, \mathbf{a})$ that jointly describes the desirability of a given state/action pair.

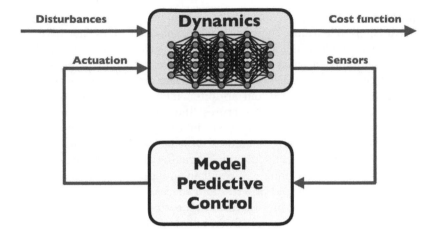

FIGURE 2.6
Schematic of deep learning a surrogate model of the complex dynamics for model predictive control.

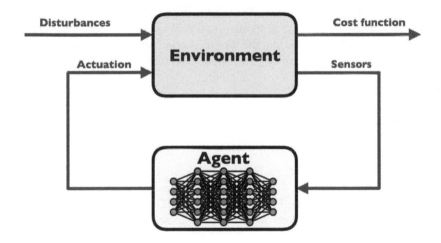

FIGURE 2.7
Schematic of deep reinforcement learning where the agent policy is parameterized by a deep neural network.

2.7 Discussion

In this chapter, we have discussed several leading approaches for the targeted use of deep learning in the physical and engineering sciences. Deep neural networks are well-suited to identifying representations of complex dynamics, along with coordinate transformations in which these dynamics may be simplified. Particular recent emphasis has been given to *physics-informed* or *physics-constrained* learning, where partial knowledge of the physics is incorporated into the learning algorithm.

Although there is a tremendous diversity of techniques that have been developed in only the last few years in deep learning, there are some canonical themes that have emerged from physics-informed machine learning. First and foremost is that coordinates and dynamics are typically paired and jointly learned for success in prediction, control, and characterization. Thus, interpretability and generalizability often emerge from this critical pairing. Second, physics constraints are instrumental and are often included by adding regularizers in the loss function of the deep learning architectures. Indeed, traditional modeling approaches can help guide and inform many applications in the physical and engineering sciences, maximally leveraging long-standing domain knowledge and expert insight into the deep learning process. As a general rule, maximally leveraging and integrating domain knowledge into the targeted use of deep learning will result in superior performance.

Despite the extraordinarily rapid progress and success of deep learning, significant challenges remain. Specifically, many physics and engineering systems are often used in applications where control and autonomy are ultimately desired. There is currently a significant challenge in providing certifiable guarantees on performance, which compromises guarantees on safety in real-world applications. Thus, there is ever-growing pressure on developing *explainable* deep learning/AI agents so as to understand how autonomous agents interact with their environment. In these applications, black-box neural networks are not sufficient for safety evaluations. Moreover, deep learning often has extraordinary data requirements as the NNs are interpolatory in nature [76], whereas many of the applications in science and engineering require some extrapolatory capabilities. Thus, there still remain significant challenges in building models that can generalize and extrapolate to new settings where little data is available. Undoubtedly, regularization and structure imposed on the deep learning process will play a critical role in solving such issues in emerging deep learning architectures.

Acknowledgments

We acknowledge funding support from the Army Research Office (ARO W911NF-17-1-0306 and W911NF-19-1-0045), the Air Force Office of Scientific Research (AFOSR FA9550-19-1-0386), and the National Science Foundation (NSF HDR award #1934292). We are also grateful for many fruitful discussions with Bethany Lusch, Kathleen Champion, and Craig Gin.

Glossary

Autoencoder: Neural network architecture that first compresses high-dimensional data with an *encoder* and then decompresses with a *decoder*. This information bottleneck uncovers key latent variables and is the nonlinear generalization of principal component analysis.

Deep learning: A neural network architecture with a deep multi-layer structure, typically containing roughly five or more layers.

Dynamic mode decomposition (DMD): A modal decomposition of high-dimensional spatiotemporal data into spatially correlated modes that are constrained to have coherent linear behavior in time.

Koopman operator: Infinite-dimensional linear operator that advances measurement functions of the state of a, possibly nonlinear, dynamical system.

Model predictive control (MPC): An iterative control optimization that determines an optimal control trajectory over a finite-time, receding horizon. The first control action in the sequence is taken, and then the optimization is reinitialized based on measurements of where the system actually went.

Physics constrained learning: Machine learning that incorporates partial physics knowledge (e.g., symmetry, conservation laws, etc.) into the learning process. Typically this is achieved through augmenting the training data, choice of custom machine learning architecture, constraining the optimization, or including additional loss functions.

Recurrent neural network (RNN): A neural network architecture that includes feedback connections, making it possible to capture temporal dynamics and time history effects.

Reinforcement learning (RL): A machine learning paradigm where an agent learns a policy for how to interact with an environment to maximize future expected rewards.

Reservoir computing: A type of recurrent network that has a large, fixed shallow layer of nonlinear functions, called the reservoir, where the inputs are mapped into and the outputs are mapped out of. Thus reservoir computing lifts the inputs to a higher dimensional space.

Sparse identification of nonlinear dynamics (SINDy): A nonlinear system identification procedure that solves for a sparse linear combination of terms from a candidate function library that best describes the time derivative of a dynamical system.

Bibliography

[1] Pieter Abbeel, Adam Coates, and Andrew Y Ng. Autonomous helicopter aerobatics through apprenticeship learning. *The International Journal of Robotics Research*, 29(13):1608–1639, 2010.

[2] Pieter Abbeel, Adam Coates, Morgan Quigley, and Andrew Y Ng. An application of reinforcement learning to aerobatic helicopter flight. In *Advances in Neural Information Processing Systems*, pages 1–8, 2007.

[3] Alessandro Alla and J Nathan Kutz. Randomized model order reduction. *Advances in Computational Mathematics*, 45(3):1251–1271, 2019.

[4] David Amsallem, Matthew Zahr, Youngsoo Choi, and Charbel Farhat. Design optimization using hyper-reduced-order models. *Structural and Multidisciplinary Optimization*, 51(4):919–940, 2015.

[5] Yohai Bar-Sinai, Stephan Hoyer, Jason Hickey, and Michael P Brenner. Learning data-driven discretizations for partial differential equations. *Proceedings of the National Academy of Sciences*, 116(31):15344–15349, 2019.

[6] Peter W Battaglia, Jessica B Hamrick, Victor Bapst, Alvaro Sanchez-Gonzalez, Vinicius Zambaldi, Mateusz Malinowski, Andrea Tacchetti, David Raposo, Adam Santoro, Ryan Faulkner, et al. Relational inductive biases, deep learning, and graph networks. *arXiv preprint arXiv:1806.01261*, 2018.

[7] Thomas Baumeister, Steven L Brunton, and J Nathan Kutz. Deep learning and model predictive control for self-tuning mode-locked lasers. *JOSA B*, 35(3):617–626, 2018.

[8] Peter Benner, Serkan Gugercin, and Karen Willcox. A survey of projection-based model reduction methods for parametric dynamical systems. *SIAM Review*, 57(4):483–531, 2015.

[9] Saakaar Bhatnagar, Yaser Afshar, Shaowu Pan, Karthik Duraisamy, and Shailendra Kaushik. Prediction of aerodynamic flow fields using convolutional neural networks. *Computational Mechanics*, 64(2):525–545, 2019.

[10] Katharina Bieker, Sebastian Peitz, Steven L Brunton, J Nathan Kutz, and Michael Dellnitz. Deep model predictive flow control with limited sensor data and online learning. *Theoretical and Computational Fluid Dynamics*, pages 1–15, 2020.

[11] Christopher M Bishop et al. *Neural Networks for Pattern Recognition*. Oxford University Press, 1995.

[12] Josh Bongard and Hod Lipson. Automated reverse engineering of nonlinear dynamical systems. *Proceedings of the National Academy of Sciences*, 104(24):9943–9948, 2007.

[13] Lorenzo Boninsegna, Feliks Nüske, and Cecilia Clementi. Sparse learning of stochastic dynamical equations. *The Journal of Chemical Physics*, 148(24):241723, 2018.

[14] MP Brenner, JD Eldredge, and JB Freund. Perspective on machine learning for advancing fluid mechanics. *Physical Review Fluids*, 4(10):100501, 2019.

[15] S L Brunton, B W Brunton, J L Proctor, E Kaiser, and J N Kutz. Chaos as an intermittently forced linear system. *Nature Communications*, 8(19):1–9, 2017.

[16] S L Brunton, B W Brunton, J L Proctor, and J N Kutz. Koopman invariant subspaces and finite linear representations of nonlinear dynamical systems for control. *PLoS ONE*, 11(2):e0150171, 2016.

[17] S L Brunton and J N Kutz. *Data-Driven Science and Engineering: Machine Learning, Dynamical Systems, and Control*. Cambridge University Press, 2019.

[18] S L Brunton and B R Noack. Closed-loop turbulence control: Progress and challenges. *Applied Mechanics Reviews*, 67:050801–1–050801–48, 2015.

[19] S L Brunton, J L Proctor, and J N Kutz. Discovering governing equations from data by sparse identification of nonlinear dynamical systems. *Proceedings of the National Academy of Sciences*, 113(15):3932–3937, 2016.

[20] Steven L Brunton, Marko Budišić, Eurika Kaiser, and J Nathan Kutz. Modern koopman theory for dynamical systems. *arXiv preprint arXiv:2102.12086*, 2021.

[21] Steven L Brunton, Maziar S Hemati, and Kunihiko Taira. Special issue on machine learning and data-driven methods in fluid dynamics. *Theoretical and Computational Fluid Dynamics*, 34(4):333–337, 2020.

[22] Steven L Brunton, J Nathan Kutz, Krithika Manohar, Aleksandr Y Aravkin, Kristi Morgansen, Jennifer Klemisch, Nicholas Goebel, James Buttrick, Jeffrey Poskin, Agnes Blom-Schieber, et al. Data-driven aerospace engineering: Reframing the industry with machine learning. *arXiv preprint arXiv:2008.10740*, 2020.

[23] Steven L Brunton, Bernd R Noack, and Petros Koumoutsakos. Machine learning for fluid mechanics. *Annual Review of Fluid Mechanics*, 52:477–508, 2020.

[24] Tan Bui-Thanh, Karen Willcox, and Omar Ghattas. Model reduction for large-scale systems with high-dimensional parametric input space. *SIAM Journal on Scientific Computing*, 30(6):3270–3288, 2008.

[25] Tan Bui-Thanh, Karen Willcox, Omar Ghattas, and Bart van Bloemen Waanders. Goal-oriented, model-constrained optimization for reduction of large-scale systems. *Journal of Computational Physics*, 224(2):880–896, 2007.

[26] Jared L Callaham, Jean-Christophe Loiseau, Georgios Rigas, and Steven L Brunton. Nonlinear stochastic modeling with Langevin regression. *arXiv preprint arXiv:2009.01006*, 2020.

[27] Kevin Carlberg, Matthew Barone, and Harbir Antil. Galerkin v. least-squares Petrov–Galerkin projection in nonlinear model reduction. *Journal of Computational Physics*, 330:693–734, 2017.

[28] Kevin Carlberg, Charbel Farhat, Julien Cortial, and David Amsallem. The GNAT method for nonlinear model reduction: effective implementation and application to computational fluid dynamics and turbulent flows. *Journal of Computational Physics*, 242:623–647, 2013.

[29] Kevin T Carlberg, Antony Jameson, Mykel J Kochenderfer, Jeremy Morton, Liqian Peng, and Freddie D Witherden. Recovering missing CFD data for high-order discretizations using deep neural networks and dynamics learning. *arXiv preprint arXiv:1812.01177*, 2018.

[30] K Champion, B Lusch, J Nathan Kutz, and Steven L Brunton. Data-driven discovery of coordinates and governing equations. *Proceedings of the National Academy of Sciences*, 116(45):22445–22451, 2019.

[31] Kathleen Champion, Peng Zheng, Aleksandr Y Aravkin, Steven L Brunton, and J Nathan Kutz. A unified sparse optimization framework to learn parsimonious physics-informed models from data. *IEEE Access*, 8:169259–169271, 2020.

[32] Tim Colonius. An overview of simulation, modeling, and active control of flow/acoustic resonance in open cavities. In *39th Aerospace Sciences Meeting and Exhibit*, page 76, 2001.

[33] Miles Cranmer, Sam Greydanus, Stephan Hoyer, Peter Battaglia, David Spergel, and Shirley Ho. Lagrangian neural networks. *arXiv preprint arXiv:2003.04630*, 2020.

[34] Miles Cranmer, Alvaro Sanchez-Gonzalez, Peter Battaglia, Rui Xu, Kyle Cranmer, David Spergel, and Shirley Ho. Discovering symbolic models from deep learning with inductive biases. *arXiv preprint arXiv:2006.11287*, 2020.

[35] Miles D Cranmer, Rui Xu, Peter Battaglia, and Shirley Ho. Learning symbolic physics with graph networks. *arXiv preprint arXiv:1909.05862*, 2019.

[36] Brian M de Silva, Kathleen Champion, Markus Quade, Jean-Christophe Loiseau, J Nathan Kutz, and Steven L Brunton. Pysindy: a python package for the sparse identification of nonlinear dynamics from data. *Journal of Open Source Software*, 5(49):2104, 2020.

[37] Jia Deng, Wei Dong, Richard Socher, Li-Jia Li, Kai Li, and Li Fei-Fei. Imagenet: A large-scale hierarchical image database. In *2009 IEEE Conference on Computer Vision and Pattern Recognition*, pages 248–255. Ieee, 2009.

[38] Carmeline J Dsilva, Ronen Talmon, Ronald R Coifman, and Ioannis G Kevrekidis. Parsimonious representation of nonlinear dynamical systems through manifold learning: A chemotaxis case study. *Applied and Computational Harmonic Analysis*, 44(3):759–773, 2018.

[39] Karthik Duraisamy, Gianluca Iaccarino, and Heng Xiao. Turbulence modeling in the age of data. *Annual Reviews of Fluid Mechanics*, 51:357–377, 2019.

[40] Karthik Duraisamy, Gianluca Iaccarino, and Heng Xiao. Turbulence modeling in the age of data. *Annual Review of Fluid Mechanics*, 51:357–377, 2019.

[41] T Duriez, S L Brunton, and B R Noack. *Machine Learning Control: Taming Nonlinear Dynamics and Turbulence*. Springer, 2016.

[42] N Benjamin Erichson, Lionel Mathelin, Zhewei Yao, Steven L Brunton, Michael W Mahoney, and J Nathan Kutz. Shallow neural networks for fluid flow reconstruction with limited sensors. *Proceedings of the Royal Society A*, 476(2238):20200097, 2020.

[43] N Benjamin Erichson, Michael Muehlebach, and Michael W Mahoney. Physics-informed autoencoders for lyapunov-stable fluid flow prediction. *arXiv preprint arXiv:1905.10866*, 2019.

[44] Dixia Fan, Liu Yang, Zhicheng Wang, Michael S Triantafyllou, and George Em Karniadakis. Reinforcement learning for bluff body active flow control in experiments and simulations. *Proceedings of the National Academy of Sciences*, 117(42):26091–26098, 2020.

[45] Nicola Fonzi, Steven L Brunton, and Urban Fasel. Data-driven nonlinear aeroelastic models of morphing wings for control. *Proceedings of the Royal Society A*, 476(2239):20200079, 2020.

[46] Kai Fukami, Koji Fukagata, and Kunihiko Taira. Super-resolution reconstruction of turbulent flows with machine learning. *Journal of Fluid Mechanics*, 870:106–120, 2019.

[47] K Fukushima. Neocognitron: A self-organizing neural network model for a mechanism of pattern recognition unaffected by shift in position. *Biological Cybernetics*, 36:193–202, 1980.

[48] Craig Gin, Bethany Lusch, Steven L Brunton, and J Nathan Kutz. Deep learning models for global coordinate transformations that linearise PDEs. *European Journal of Applied Mathematics*, pages 1–25, 2020.

[49] Craig R Gin, Daniel E Shea, Steven L Brunton, and J Nathan Kutz. Deepgreen: Deep learning of green's functions for nonlinear boundary value problems. *arXiv preprint arXiv:2101.07206*, 2020.

[50] Ian Goodfellow, Yoshua Bengio, and Aaron Courville. *Deep Learning*. MIT Press, 2016.

[51] Ian Goodfellow, Yoshua Bengio, Aaron Courville, and Yoshua Bengio. *Deep Learning*, volume 1. MIT Press, Cambridge, 2016.

[52] Shixiang Gu, Ethan Holly, Timothy Lillicrap, and Sergey Levine. Deep reinforcement learning for robotic manipulation with asynchronous off-policy updates. In *2017 IEEE International Conference on Robotics and Automation (ICRA)*, pages 3389–3396. IEEE, 2017.

[53] Yifei Guan, Steven L Brunton, and Igor Novosselov. Sparse nonlinear models of chaotic electroconvection. *arXiv preprint arXiv:2009.11862*, 2020.

[54] Kurt Hornik, Maxwell Stinchcombe, and Halbert White. Multilayer feedforward networks are universal approximators. *Neural Networks*, 2(5):359–366, 1989.

[55] Daniel Z Huang, Kailai Xu, Charbel Farhat, and Eric Darve. Learning constitutive relations from indirect observations using deep neural networks. *Journal of Computational Physics*, 416:109491, 2020.

[56] P Jordan and T Colonius. Wave packets and turbulent jet noise. *Annual Review of Fluid Mechanics*, 45:173–195, 2013.

[57] Eurika Kaiser, J Nathan Kutz, and Steven L Brunton. Sparse identification of nonlinear dynamics for model predictive control in the low-data limit. *Proceedings of the Royal Society of London A*, 474(2219), 2018.

[58] Alan A Kaptanoglu, Kyle D Morgan, Chris J Hansen, and Steven L Brunton. Physics-constrained, low-dimensional models for mhd: First-principles and data-driven approaches. *arXiv preprint arXiv:2004.10389*, 2020.

[59] Dmitrii Kochkov, Jamie A Smith, Ayya Alieva, Qing Wang, Michael P Brenner, and Stephan Hoyer. Machine learning accelerated computational fluid dynamics. *arXiv preprint arXiv:2102.01010*, 2021.

[60] Jonas Köhler, Leon Klein, and Frank Noé. Equivariant flows: sampling configurations for multi-body systems with symmetric energies. *arXiv preprint arXiv:1910.00753*, 2019.

[61] Alex Krizhevsky, Ilya Sutskever, and Geoffrey E Hinton. Imagenet classification with deep convolutional neural networks. *Advances in Neural Information Processing Systems*, 25:1097–1105, 2012.

[62] J N Kutz, S L Brunton, B W Brunton, and J L Proctor. *Dynamic Mode Decomposition: Data-Driven Modeling of Complex Systems*. SIAM, 2016.

[63] Henning Lange, Steven L Brunton, and Nathan Kutz. From Fourier to Koopman: Spectral methods for long-term time series prediction. *arXiv preprint arXiv:2004.00574*, 2020.

[64] Ian Lenz, Ross A Knepper, and Ashutosh Saxena. Deepmpc: Learning deep latent features for model predictive control. In *Robotics: Science and Systems*. Rome, Italy, 2015.

[65] Zongyi Li, Nikola Kovachki, Kamyar Azizzadenesheli, Burigede Liu, Kaushik Bhattacharya, Andrew Stuart, and Anima Anandkumar. Fourier neural operator for parametric partial differential equations. *arXiv preprint arXiv:2010.08895*, 2020.

[66] Zongyi Li, Nikola Kovachki, Kamyar Azizzadenesheli, Burigede Liu, Kaushik Bhattacharya, Andrew Stuart, and Anima Anandkumar. Multipole graph neural operator for parametric partial differential equations. *arXiv preprint arXiv:2006.09535*, 2020.

[67] Zongyi Li, Nikola Kovachki, Kamyar Azizzadenesheli, Burigede Liu, Kaushik Bhattacharya, Andrew Stuart, and Anima Anandkumar. Neural operator: Graph kernel network for partial differential equations. *arXiv preprint arXiv:2003.03485*, 2020.

[68] Timothy P Lillicrap, Jonathan J Hunt, Alexander Pritzel, Nicolas Heess, Tom Erez, Yuval Tassa, David Silver, and Daan Wierstra. Continuous control with deep reinforcement learning. *arXiv preprint arXiv:1509.02971*, 2015.

[69] Julia Ling, Andrew Kurzawski, and Jeremy Templeton. Reynolds averaged turbulence modelling using deep neural networks with embedded invariance. *Journal of Fluid Mechanics*, 807:155–166, 2016.

[70] Yuying Liu, J Nathan Kutz, and Steven L Brunton. Hierarchical deep learning of multiscale differential equation time-steppers. *arXiv preprint arXiv:2008.09768*, 2020.

[71] Yuying Liu, Colin Ponce, Steven L Brunton, and J Nathan Kutz. Multiresolution convolutional autoencoders. *arXiv preprint arXiv:2004.04946*, 2020.

[72] J-C Loiseau and S L Brunton. Constrained sparse Galerkin regression. *Journal of Fluid Mechanics*, 838:42–67, 2018.

[73] J-C Loiseau, B R Noack, and S L Brunton. Sparse reduced-order modeling: sensor-based dynamics to full-state estimation. *Journal of Fluid Mechanics*, 844:459–490, 2018.

[74] Lu Lu, Xuhui Meng, Zhiping Mao, and George E Karniadakis. Deepxde: A deep learning library for solving differential equations. *arXiv preprint arXiv:1907.04502*, 2019.

[75] Bethany Lusch, J Nathan Kutz, and Steven L Brunton. Deep learning for universal linear embeddings of nonlinear dynamics. *Nature Communications*, 9(1):4950, 2018.

[76] Stéphane Mallat. Understanding deep convolutional networks. *Philosophical Transactions of the Royal Society A*, 374(2065):20150203, 2016.

[77] Niall M Mangan, Travis Askham, Steven L Brunton, J Nathan Kutz, and Joshua L Proctor. Model selection for hybrid dynamical systems via sparse regression. *Proceedings of the Royal Society A*, 475(2223):20180534, 2019.

[78] Niall M Mangan, Steven L Brunton, Joshua L Proctor, and J Nathan Kutz. Inferring biological networks by sparse identification of nonlinear dynamics. *IEEE Transactions on Molecular, Biological, and Multi-Scale Communications*, 2(1):52–63, 2016.

[79] Andreas Mardt, Luca Pasquali, Hao Wu, and Frank Noé. VAMPnets: Deep learning of molecular kinetics. *Nature Communications*, 9(5), 2018.

[80] Romit Maulik, Omer San, Adil Rasheed, and Prakash Vedula. Subgrid modelling for two-dimensional turbulence using neural networks. *Journal of Fluid Mechanics*, 858:122–144, 2019.

[81] Beverley J McKeon and Ati S Sharma. A critical layer model for turbulent pipe flow. *Journal of Fluid Mechanics*, 658(336382), 2010.

[82] Michele Milano and Petros Koumoutsakos. Neural network modeling for near wall turbulent flow. *Journal of Computational Physics*, 182(1):1–26, 2002.

[83] Volodymyr Mnih, Koray Kavukcuoglu, David Silver, Andrei A Rusu, Joel Veness, Marc G Bellemare, Alex Graves, Martin Riedmiller, Andreas K Fidjeland, Georg Ostrovski, et al. Human-level control through deep reinforcement learning. *Nature*, 518(7540):529, 2015.

[84] Boaz Nadler, Stéphane Lafon, Ronald R Coifman, and Ioannis G Kevrekidis. Diffusion maps, spectral clustering and reaction coordinates of dynamical systems. *Applied and Computational Harmonic Analysis*, 21(1):113–127, 2006.

[85] B R Noack, K Afanasiev, M Morzynski, G Tadmor, and F Thiele. A hierarchy of low-dimensional models for the transient and post-transient cylinder wake. *Journal of Fluid Mechanics*, 497:335–363, 2003.

[86] Frank Noé, Simon Olsson, Jonas Köhler, and Hao Wu. Boltzmann generators: Sampling equilibrium states of many-body systems with deep learning. *Science*, 365(6457):eaaw1147, 2019.

[87] Guido Novati, Hugues Lascombes de Laroussilhe, and Petros Koumoutsakos. Automating turbulence modelling by multi-agent reinforcement learning. *Nature Machine Intelligence*, 3(1):87–96, 2021.

[88] Guido Novati, Lakshminarayanan Mahadevan, and Petros Koumoutsakos. Controlled gliding and perching through deep-reinforcement-learning. *Physical Review Fluids*, 4(9):093902, 2019.

[89] Melkior Ornik, Arie Israel, and Ufuk Topcu. Control-oriented learning on the fly. *arXiv preprint arXiv:1709.04889*, 2017.

[90] Samuel E Otto and Clarence W Rowley. Linearly-recurrent autoencoder networks for learning dynamics. *SIAM Journal on Applied Dynamical Systems*, 18(1):558–593, 2019.

[91] Shaowu Pan and Karthik Duraisamy. Data-driven discovery of closure models. *SIAM Journal on Applied Dynamical Systems*, 17(4):2381–2413, 2018.

[92] Shaowu Pan and Karthik Duraisamy. Long-time predictive modeling of nonlinear dynamical systems using neural networks. *Complexity*, 2018, 2018.

[93] Eric J Parish and Kevin T Carlberg. Time-series machine-learning error models for approximate solutions to parameterized dynamical systems. *Computer Methods in Applied Mechanics and Engineering*, 365:112990, 2020.

[94] Jaideep Pathak, Brian Hunt, Michelle Girvan, Zhixin Lu, and Edward Ott. Model-free prediction of large spatiotemporally chaotic systems from data: a reservoir computing approach. *Physical Review Letters*, 120(2):024102, 2018.

[95] Tong Qin, Kailiang Wu, and Dongbin Xiu. Data driven governing equations approximation using deep neural networks. *Journal of Computational Physics*, 395:620–635, 2019.

[96] Jean Rabault and Alexander Kuhnle. Deep reinforcement learning applied to active flow control. *ResearchGate Preprint https://doi. org/10.13140/RG*, 2(10482.94404), 2020.

[97] Christopher Rackauckas, Yingbo Ma, Julius Martensen, Collin Warner, Kirill Zubov, Rohit Supekar, Dominic Skinner, and Ali Ramadhan. Universal differential equations for scientific machine learning. *arXiv preprint arXiv:2001.04385*, 2020.

[98] M Raissi, P Perdikaris, and GE Karniadakis. Physics-informed neural networks: A deep learning framework for solving forward and inverse problems involving nonlinear partial differential equations. *Journal of Computational Physics*, 378:686–707, 2019.

[99] M Raissi, P Perdikaris, and GE Karniadakis. Physics-informed neural networks: A deep learning framework for solving forward and inverse problems involving nonlinear partial differential equations. *Journal of Computational Physics*, 378:686–707, 2019.

[100] Maziar Raissi and George Em Karniadakis. Hidden physics models: Machine learning of nonlinear partial differential equations. *Journal of Computational Physics*, 357:125–141, 2018.

[101] Maziar Raissi, Alireza Yazdani, and George Em Karniadakis. Hidden fluid mechanics: Learning velocity and pressure fields from flow visualizations. *Science*, 367(6481):1026–1030, 2020.

[102] Benjamin Recht. A tour of reinforcement learning: The view from continuous control. *Annual Review of Control, Robotics, and Autonomous Systems*, 2:253–279, 2019.

[103] Gautam Reddy, Antonio Celani, Terrence J Sejnowski, and Massimo Vergassola. Learning to soar in turbulent environments. *Proceedings of the National Academy of Sciences*, 113(33):E4877–E4884, 2016.

[104] Francesco Regazzoni, Luca Dede, and Alfio Quarteroni. Machine learning for fast and reliable solution of time-dependent differential equations. *Journal of Computational physics*, 397:108852, 2019.

[105] S Ashwin Renganathan. Koopman-based approach to nonintrusive reduced order modeling: Application to aerodynamic shape optimization and uncertainty propagation. *AIAA Journal*, 58(5):2221–2235, 2020.

[106] C W Rowley, I Mezic, S Bagheri, P Schlatter, and D S Henningson. Spectral analysis of nonlinear flows. *Journal of Fluid Mechanics*, 645:115–127, 2009.

[107] S H Rudy, S L Brunton, J L Proctor, and J N Kutz. Data-driven discovery of partial differential equations. *Science Advances*, 3(e1602614), 2017.

[108] S H Rudy, J N Kutz, and S L Brunton. Deep learning of dynamics and signal-noise decomposition with time-stepping constraints. *Journal of Computational Physics*, 396:483–506, 2019.

[109] Samuel H Rudy, Steven L Brunton, and J Nathan Kutz. Smoothing and parameter estimation by soft-adherence to governing equations. *Journal of Computational Physics*, 398:108860, 2019.

[110] P J Schmid. Dynamic mode decomposition of numerical and experimental data. *Journal of Fluid Mechanics*, 656:5–28, August 2010.

[111] Michael Schmidt and Hod Lipson. Distilling free-form natural laws from experimental data. *Science*, 324(5923):81–85, 2009.

[112] Daniel E Shea, Steven L Brunton, and Nathan Kutz. Sindy-bvp: Sparse identification of nonlinear dynamics for boundary value problems. *arXiv preprint arXiv:2005.10756*, 2020.

[113] David Silver, Thomas Hubert, Julian Schrittwieser, Ioannis Antonoglou, Matthew Lai, Arthur Guez, Marc Lanctot, Laurent Sifre, Dharshan Kumaran, Thore Graepel, et al. A general reinforcement learning algorithm that masters chess, shogi, and go through self-play. *Science*, 362(6419):1140–1144, 2018.

[114] David Silver, Julian Schrittwieser, Karen Simonyan, Ioannis Antonoglou, Aja Huang, Arthur Guez, Thomas Hubert, Lucas Baker, Matthew Lai, Adrian Bolton, et al. Mastering the game of go without human knowledge. *Nature*, 550(7676):354–359, 2017.

[115] Anand Pratap Singh, Shivaji Medida, and Karthik Duraisamy. Machine-learning-augmented predictive modeling of turbulent separated flows over airfoils. *AIAA Journal*, 55(7):2215–2227, 2017.

[116] L Sirovich and M Kirby. A low-dimensional procedure for the characterization of human faces. *Journal of the Optical Society of America A*, 4(3):519–524, 1987.

[117] Chang Sun, Eurika Kaiser, Steven L Brunton, and J Nathan Kutz. Deep reinforcement learning for optical systems: A case study of mode-locked lasers. *Machine Learning: Science and Technology*, 1(4):045013, 2020.

[118] Richard S Sutton and Andrew G Barto. *Reinforcement Learning: An Introduction*. MIT Press, 2018.

[119] Kunihiko Taira, Steven L Brunton, Scott Dawson, Clarence W Rowley, Tim Colonius, Beverley J McKeon, Oliver T Schmidt, Stanislav Gordeyev, Vassilios Theofilis, and Lawrence S Ukeiley. Modal analysis of fluid flows: An overview. *AIAA Journal*, 55(12):4013–4041, 2017.

[120] Kunihiko Taira, Maziar S Hemati, Steven L Brunton, Yiyang Sun, Karthik Duraisamy, Shervin Bagheri, Scott Dawson, and Chi-An Yeh. Modal analysis of fluid flows: Applications and outlook. *AIAA Journal*, 58(3):998–1022, 2020.

[121] Kunihiko Taira, Maziar S Hemati, Steven L Brunton, Yiyang Sun, Karthik Duraisamy, Shervin Bagheri, Scott TM Dawson, and Chi-An Yeh. Modal analysis of fluid flows: Applications and outlook. *AIAA Journal*, 58(3):998–1022, 2020.

[122] Naoya Takeishi, Yoshinobu Kawahara, and Takehisa Yairi. Learning Koopman invariant subspaces for dynamic mode decomposition. In *Advances in Neural Information Processing Systems*, pages 1130–1140, 2017.

[123] Russ Tedrake, Zack Jackowski, Rick Cory, John William Roberts, and Warren Hoburg. Learning to fly like a bird. In *14th International Symposium on Robotics Research*. Lucerne, Switzerland, 2009.

[124] J. H. Tu, C. W. Rowley, D. M. Luchtenburg, S. L. Brunton, and J. N. Kutz. On dynamic mode decomposition: theory and applications. *Journal of Computational Dynamics*, 1(2):391–421, 2014.

[125] Siddhartha Verma, Guido Novati, and Petros Koumoutsakos. Efficient collective swimming by harnessing vortices through deep reinforcement learning. *Proceedings of the National Academy of Sciences*, 115(23):5849–5854, 2018.

[126] Christoph Wehmeyer and Frank Noé. Time-lagged autoencoders: Deep learning of slow collective variables for molecular kinetics. *The Journal of Chemical Physics*, 148(241703):1–9, 2018.

[127] Or Yair, Ronen Talmon, Ronald R Coifman, and Ioannis G Kevrekidis. Reconstruction of normal forms by learning informed observation geometries from data. *Proceedings of the National Academy of Sciences*, 114(38):E7865–E7874, 2017.

[128] Liu Yang, Dongkun Zhang, and George Em Karniadakis. Physics-informed generative adversarial networks for stochastic differential equations. *arXiv preprint arXiv:1811.02033*, 2018.

[129] Enoch Yeung, Soumya Kundu, and Nathan Hodas. Learning deep neural network representations for Koopman operators of nonlinear dynamical systems. *arXiv preprint arXiv:1708.06850*, 2017.

[130] Peng Zheng, Travis Askham, Steven L Brunton, J Nathan Kutz, and Aleksandr Y Aravkin. Sparse relaxed regularized regression: SR3. *IEEE Access*, 7(1):1404–1423, 2019.

[131] Yaofeng Desmond Zhong and Naomi Leonard. Unsupervised learning of lagrangian dynamics from images for prediction and control. *Advances in Neural Information Processing Systems*, 33, 2020.

[132] Yinhao Zhu and Nicholas Zabaras. Bayesian deep convolutional encoder–decoder networks for surrogate modeling and uncertainty quantification. *Journal of Computational Physics*, 366:415–447, 2018.

3

Combining Theory and Data-Driven Approaches for Epidemic Forecasts

Lijing Wang, Aniruddha Adiga, Jiangzhuo Chen, Bryan Lewis, Adam Sadilek, Srinivasan Venkatramanan, and Madhav Marathe

CONTENTS

Forecasting the spatial and temporal evolution of epidemic dynamics has been an area of active research over the past couple of decades. Data-driven methods are popular since they do not need explicit knowledge of the physical behavior of the system and have been deployed successfully in multiple domains. For instance, deep learning-based predictive models have gained increasing prominence in epidemic forecasting. However, they are challenging to train

DOI: 10.1201/9781003143376-3

due to sparse and noisy training data and the limited ability to explicitly incorporate mechanisms of disease spread. In recent times, theory-based mechanistic methods have become a mainstay of epidemic forecasting due to their ability to capture the underlying causal processes through mathematical and computational representations. This chapter covers the most recent trend on combining theory-based mechanistic methods and data-driven methods for epidemic forecasting. It starts with a formal definition of an epidemic process and details the different aspects of disease spread dynamics. The problem of spatiotemporal epidemic forecasting is then formulated, and the central challenges are outlined. Subsequently, it covers major methodologies for epidemic forecasting including theory-based mechanistic methods and data-driven methods, leading to a survey of hybrid methods combining these approaches. Finally, the limitations and future directions are discussed.

3.1   Epidemic Forecasting: An Overview

In this section, we briefly introduce the terms infectious disease, an outbreak, an epidemic, and a pandemic in 3.1.1, followed by the description of disease spreading dynamics and factors impacting it in 3.1.2. In 3.1.3 spatiotemporal epidemic forecasting problem is formulated, and its challenges are discussed. Finally, in 3.1.4 we provide a brief overview of the different methodologies.

3.1.1   Definitions

Human infectious diseases are caused by pathogenic microorganisms, such as bacteria, viruses, parasites, or fungi; and can spread directly or indirectly, from one person to another. An infectious disease spread can lead to an outbreak, an epidemic, or a pandemic. While most of the chapter will be focused on diseases that can be spread directly through human contact, similar methods can be developed for environment- or vector-mediated spread.

An *outbreak* can be defined as a sudden emergence of a localized cluster of disease occurrences in a sub-population. While it usually starts in a small community or a geographical area, it may lead to case exportation to other regions or countries. It may last for a few days to weeks, or even for multiple months. Some outbreaks could be seasonal such as those caused by environmental or vector abundance-based risk factors (e.g., Lyme disease). Others could be caused by exposures to zoonotic reservoirs (e.g., Ebola) or due to incidence in undervaccinated clusters (e.g., Measles). If not quickly controlled, an outbreak can become an epidemic causing significant health burden.

An *epidemic* occurs when an infectious disease spreads rapidly to a large number of people within a community, population, or region. While they share several characteristics of an outbreak, the spatial, temporal, and social scales are usually larger in magnitude. For example, in 2003, the severe acute respiratory syndrome (SARS) epidemic spread to about 8000 confirmed cases and led to nearly 800 deaths. Likewise, the Ebola epidemic ravaged West Africa between 2014 and 2016, with 28,600 reported cases and 11,325 deaths.

A *pandemic* is an epidemic that spreads over multiple countries or continents and could last multiple years. For instance, the influenza (flu) pandemic of 1918–1919 killed between 20 and 40 million people. While more devastating pandemics have been recorded (e.g., Bubonic Plague in the 14th century), the 1918 pandemic remains the most severe one in recent history. The 2009 H1N1 influenza was a more recent global pandemic that led to an estimated 151K to 575K deaths worldwide during the first year the virus circulated. Since the 2009 H1N1 pandemic, the H1N1 flu virus along with other types has circulated seasonally in the US causing significant illnesses, hospitalizations, and deaths. As of this writing, the ongoing COVID-19 pandemic is the most acute public health emergency since the 1918 influenza pandemic. As of April 2021, it has accounted for nearly 140 million reported cases and resulted in at least 3 million deaths worldwide[1].

While these distinctions help in characterizing the scale, they also reflect the difficult in obtaining data and the various factors involved in the dynamics. For instance, the control measures may vary between these scales, and hence such adaptations might make the task of forecasting more challenging. For the purposes of this chapter, we will mainly focus on epidemics, although the techniques can be used interchangeably across the scales.

3.1.2 Disease Spread Dynamics

The spreading dynamics of an epidemic is usually characterized by: (1) when and where it started, (2) the scope and pervasiveness, (3) the duration fo spread, and (4) overall severity (how it impacts individuals, communities, countries, and the whole society). For example, the 2014–2016 West Africa Ebola epidemic is the largest Ebola outbreak in history since the virus was first discovered in 1976. The World Health Organization (WHO) reported cases of Ebola Virus Disease (EVD) in the forested rural region of southeastern Guinea on March 23, 2014. It spread between countries, starting in Guinea then moving across land borders to Sierra Leone and Liberia. The average EVD case fatality rate is around 50% and have varied from 25% to 90% in past outbreaks[2]. In Guinea, Liberia, and Sierra Leone, the Ebola epidemic resulted in devastating effects on the healthcare workforce, the provision of healthcare services, children, and the national economy[3].

Numerous factors affect the disease spreading dynamics. Human factors such as activity (mobility, daily activities, mixing patterns) and demographics (age, gender, social status, economic status, etc.) are crucial because they determine how the disease transmits in a community. Environmental factors such as sanitation facilities, water supply, food, and climate account for an estimated 24% of the global disease burden and 23% of all deaths (by WHO), which includes epidemics and sporadic outbreaks. Public health interventions are the most effective way to control the disease spreading. These interventions, both pharmaceutical (prophylactics, antivirals, vaccines) and non-pharmaceutical (stay-at-home orders, mask wearing, social distancing, safe burials) could be targeted at altering the spread dynamics. For example, during the ongoing COVID-19 pandemic, the virus is thought to spread mainly through close contact from person to person. Older adults and people of any age who have certain underlying medical conditions might be at higher risk for severe illness from COVID-19[4]. Certain jobs such as healthcare providers, school teachers, and supermarket workers are at higher risk of getting infected. The governments across the world had to rely on behavioral interventions (such as social distancing, wearing face masks in public, hand washing, monitoring and self-isolation for people exposed or symptomatic, etc.) at the beginning phase of the pandemic. With the development of multiple high efficacy vaccines that are authorized for emergency use, current measures include a combination of NPIs and vaccinations to drive down case rates, along with test/trace/isolation-based infection control.

3.1.3 Epidemic Forecasting

Infectious diseases place a heavy social and economic burden on our society. Producing timely, well-informed, and reliable spatiotemporal forecasts of the epidemic dynamics can help inform policymakers on how to provision limited healthcare resources, develop effective interventions, rapidly control outbreaks, and ensure the safety of the general public. In this section, we will first show an example of epidemic forecasting. Then we introduce the reference data used for forecasting, followed by a description of spatial and temporal epidemic forecasting. Next, we discuss the challenges of epidemic forecasting. Finally, we briefly introduce the epidemic forecasting metrics for evaluation.

3.1.3.1   Flu Forecasting – An Example of Epidemic Forecasting

A general idea of epidemic forecasting is to use observed data sources as the reference data to make spatial and temporal predictions of an epidemiological target. For instance, take the "Predict the Influenza Season Challenge" – a flu forecasting project hosted by the Centers for Disease Control and Prevention (CDC) as an example. CDC's efforts with seasonal influenza forecasting began in 2013 with a competition that encouraged outside academic and private industry researchers to forecast the timing, peak, and intensity of the flu season, along with its short-term trajectory. The CDC provides forecasting teams data, relevant public health forecasting targets, and forecast accuracy metrics evaluated against actual flu activity while each team submits their forecasts based on a variety of methods and data sources each week. The CDC has provided the Outpatient Illness Surveillance[5] report weekly at US national and U.S. Department of Health and Human Services (HHS) region[6] level since 1997 and at the state level since 2010 in FluView[7]. The historical records collected information on patient visits to healthcare providers for influenza-like illness (ILI). The CDC surveillance data is one of the reference data to make forecasts, while researchers have used other datasets such as Google Flu Trends (GFT), Google Trends, twitter data, weather data to improve forecast accuracy. The epidemiological targets being forecast included season onset, peak week, peak intensity, and short-term activity. These target definitions rely on the percent of visits to healthcare providers that are for ILI, also called ILI intensity. For instance:

- Season onset is defined as the first week when ILI intensity is at or above baseline and remains there for at least two more weeks.

- Peak week denotes the week when ILI intensity is the highest for the whole season.

- Peak intensity is the highest value of ILI intensity during the season.

- Short-term ILI activity means ILI intensity of one, two, three, and four weeks ahead of the date that they are available in FluView.

Researchers need to provide weekly predictions at national, HHS region, and state level. These are provided in a probabilistic format, thus allowing uncertainty quantification. In recent times, there have been concerted efforts to build trained ensembles of these multiple methods to provide better forecasts. This effort has led to multi-team, multi-year collaborations [57], and has become increasingly prominent in public health communication and decision making during influenza seasons. Each week during the influenza season, CDC now displays the forecasts received through the Epidemic Prediction Initiative (EPI)[8].

3.1.3.2   Reference Data

Reference data is extremely important in epidemic forecasting because it provides meaningful information about the disease spreading dynamics. In general, one could use various derived metrics, but the most common reference data is the traditional *surveillance data* which capture some measure of disease incidence for a given region over a particular time period. Examples include cases, hospitalizations or deaths on a daily resolution at the county level for COVID-19. Usually such data is generated by collecting reports from local public health laboratories and healthcare providers regularly and then aggregating the collected information to form spatial and temporal data streams. The surveillance data is just another indicator of total disease burden, and could have various lead or lag time with respect to policy goals and actions. For a well-observed disease, it is usually stable and reliable thus is used as the main reference data. However, it is delayed due to the surveillance and reporting process, and may not be at a high resolution.

Another important reference data is the *mobility data*. Infectious diseases transmit directly or indirectly from person to person via contact networks. A contact network is formed when individuals come in geographic proximity to each other for a reasonable time duration. Human mobility behavior determines the formation of a contact network thus is crucial for modeling disease spreading dynamics especially for models based on social contact networks, which will be introduced in Section 3.1.4. For example, at an aggregate level, a region's COVID-19 dynamics can potentially be affected by regions where frequent travel occurs between them. Human mobility can be modeled or estimated using mathematical models such as the gravity model[9], or real-world collected data, such as aggregate mobile phone data, air traffic data, commute data, etc.

Finally, *social media data* is often used as auxiliary information when making forecasts. Social media data is the collected information from social networks that show how users share, view, or engage with the epidemiological information, including behaviors such as searching, tweeting, or engaging in participatory surveillance (i.e., filling out surveys). There are many types of social data, such as tweets from Twitter and posts on Facebook. These data can be updated daily at finer geographic resolution but are not representative of the overall population. Furthermore, it requires large-scale data collection and curation efforts.

Other reference data pertaining to environment, policy are also used for epidemic forecasting since they can provide reference information of any of the factors discussed in Section 3.1.2.

3.1.3.3 Temporal Forecasting

In the first two decades of the 21st century, multiple public health emergencies have occurred globally, highlighting the need to understand real-time epidemic science. During these emergencies, diseases cause rapid spread within a community and invade new regions in the span of just a few weeks to months, leaving a critical window of opportunity during which real-time warning is crucial. *Real-time* forecasting is to forecast in real-time using the most recent data. Note that this does not mean forecasting only into the future, since in some cases, like seasonal influenza, the latest data available might be lagged by 1–2 weeks, thus requiring *forecasting* to the present (aka *nowcast* or even of the past (aka *hindcast*).

Retrospective forecasting is conducted by sequentially removing the data in the latest time from the full data set with the aim of evaluating and improving a model's forecasting performance retrospectively. Further, for an ongoing epidemic, the methods are often refined in real-time, and hence it is valuable to evaluate them across past data to check their out-of-sample performance.

The forecasting target as discussed above, could be short-term or long-term. While one could make forecasts of any incidence metric (say, number of K-12 outbreaks that will occur in the next 3 months), it is often useful to look at the aggregate epidemic trajectory (time series of number of cases, for example) and forecast its short-term trend and long-term characteristics. Given the process of data collection and surveillance lag, accurate statistics for epidemic warning systems are often delayed by some time, making long-term forecasting imperative without sacrificing on forecast performance.

There is no clear definition on what is short-term and long-term forecasting, but usually *short-term* forecasting refers to forecasting anywhere from one to six weeks ahead, while *long-term* forecasting is usually used to predict the long-term objectives such as time of peak, peak intensity, total number of deaths, etc.

With respect to the temporal forecasting, we'd like to introduce a commonly used definition *lead time* or *horizon*. Lead time or horizon in epidemic forecasting domain is the latency between the prediction of the epidemic dynamics (i.e., current time point) and its actual presentation (i.e., future time point). For example, we are currently at time point t when making predictions of an epidemiological target at time point $t + h$, then h is the horizon value.

3.1.3.4   Spatial Forecasting

It is well established that the aggregate characteristics of epidemic incidence are being driven by spatial aspects of transmission. Thus, accurate prediction of the spatial spread of a disease could provide valuable insights into epidemic control. Spatial epidemic forecasting can be done at multiple geographical resolutions such as national, state/province, county, and city depending on forecasting models as well as the resolution of the available data. In this chapter, we adopt terminologies defined in [75] that *flat-resolution* forecasting denotes the prediction of an epidemiological target with the same resolution as the reference data, *high-resolution* forecasting denotes the prediction with a higher geographical resolution than provided in reference data, and *coarse-resolution* forecasting denotes the prediction with a coarser geographical resolution than provided in reference data. Purely data-driven models can make flat-resolution forecasting. A coarse-resolution forecast can be obtained by (a) aggregating the flat-resolution predictions into a coarse-resolution based on their geographical attributes, or (b) aggregating the reference data to coarse resolution and running through the same forecasting methods. For theory-based mathematical models, forecasting can be made at any resolution depending on how detailed a computational model is, as long as they encode the resolution at which the forecasts are required. For example, individual-level predictions can be made if an agent-based model is used in epidemic simulations. Then the individual level incidence can be aggregated to the case count at any resolution based on the geographical location of each individual in the simulation.

3.1.3.5   Challenges of Epidemic Forecasting

Challenges with reference data. For recurring epidemics, such as seasonal influenza, the surveillance data could be at a coarse resolution and delayed in time. Other reference data is not as reliable and stable and requires extra data collecting and refining efforts. During an emerging epidemic, the forecasting problem could be particularly complicated as the training data (1) is sparse for each region (unlike seasonal flu there is no historical data); (2) noisy due to reporting bias, testing prevalence, etc.; (3) is a resultant of rapidly co-evolving dynamics of individual behavioral adaptations, government policies, and disease spread. Further such reference data could be retro-updated (referred to in the field as *backfill*) or change definitions mid-way. Difficulty obtaining real-time, reliable, and finer resolution information on disease dynamics have limited the predicting power of existing infectious disease forecasting techniques, which heavily rely on this information.

Challenges with spatial and temporal forecasting. Designing a model that can capture both spatial and temporal patterns from data is crucial yet challenging. First, real-time forecasting is challenging for systems that are compute- and data-intensive due to the need for regular and frequent updates. Thus, a model with less computational cost is more suited for real-time forecasting systems, as long as it does not sacrifice much in terms of overall accuracy. Second, a challenge in long-term epidemic forecasting is that the temporal dependency is hard to capture with short-term input data. Particularly, limited availability of reference data during emerging epidemics has resulted in failure to capture long-term patterns from the data. Models that can capture short- and long-term patterns from limited input data are required for accurate long-term forecasting. Third, as spatial data becomes available, the influence from other locations should be explored while making forecasting. However, it is difficult to investigate data from systems with models that do not represent space in some way. Models considering cross-location signals can capture spatial patterns from the data, which can lead to better forecasting performance, but could be impacted by model mis-specification biases (especially the level of connectivity). Finally, difficulty in accessing high-resolution data often fail spatial forecasting at a finer resolution.

3.1.3.6 Epidemic Forecast Evaluations

In statistics, *point estimation* involves the use of sample data to calculate a single value (known as a point estimate since it identifies a point in some parameter space) which is to serve as a "best guess" or "best estimate" of an unknown parameter. In infectious disease epidemiology, point predictions are often served as the best guess of an unknown target. More often, *probabilistic forecast* is necessary to properly reflect forecasting uncertainty. It is an estimation of the distribution of an unknown target. For example, in the CDC FluSight Challenge (see Section 3.1.3.1), for peak week forecasting, the point prediction could be the week the peak is most likely to occur during the current flu season, and the probabilistic forecast is the probabilities that the peak will occur on each week during the season (e.g., 50% peak will occur on week 1; 30% chance on week 2; 20% chance on week 3).

Evaluation of forecasting performance is crucial for model improvement. Popular metrics for evaluating point predictions in epidemic forecasting are: (1) Mean Absolute Error (MAE), (2) Mean Squared Error (MSE), (3) Root Mean Squared Error (RMSE), (4) Mean Absolute Percentage Error (MAPE). Particularly, (5) Pearson Correlation (PCORR) is used to measure the model performance on predicting disease trends. Common scoring rules to evaluate full predictive distributions in epidemic forecasting are: (6) Logarithmic Score (logS) [31] and its variation multibin logS (MBlogS) [16], (7) Continuous Ranked Probability Score (CRPS) [30]. The logS and MBlogS are used for scoring flu forecasting in the FluSight Challenge. In addition, (8) Interval Score (IS) [31] and (9) Weighted Interval Score (WIS) [31] are designed specifically for forecasts in a quantile/interval format. The IS has recently been used to evaluate forecasts of Severe Acute Respiratory Syndrome Coronavirus 1 (SARS-CoV-1) and Ebola [20] as well as SARS-CoV-2 (COVID-19) [14]. WIS has been recently widely used for COVID-19 forecasting evaluation [14]. Among these metrics, PCORR ranges in $[-1, +1]$ that larger values are better; MAE, MSE, RMSE, and MAPE range in $[0, +\infty]$ that smaller values are better; logS and MBlogS range in $[-\infty, +\infty]$ that larger values are better; CRPS, IS, and WIS are negatively oriented so that smaller values are better.

3.1.4 Methodologies for Epidemic Forecasting

Forecasting the spatial and temporal evolution of infectious disease epidemics has been an area of active research over the past couple of decades. The existing works rely on theory-based mechanistic methods and data-driven methods for forecasting. Note that in this chapter, theory-based mechanistic methods or causal methods refer to forecasting methods employing epidemic models for simulating disease transmission processes between individuals. Data-driven methods refer to forecasting methods employing statistical and time series-based methodologies without causal mechanism. In this section, we will briefly introduce these methodologies and some important related works. Refer to [57, 84, 49, 19, 53, 4, 83] for more related works.

3.1.4.1 Theory-Based Mechanistic Methods

The theory of epidemic spread is inherently tied to the progression of disease within an individual, and the processes of transmission between individuals. Historically, in epidemiology, within host disease progression has been encapsulated into compartmental models for embedding into population models. For instance, individuals get assigned various disease states such as susceptible, infectious, recovered, etc. and the host-pathogen characteristics are used to define the durations and likelihoods of various transitions in this finite state machine. These models have various extensions depending upon the disease being studied (e.g., existence of a latent phase, infectiousness after death) and the interventions being employed (e.g., hospitalization, treatments, vaccinations). See [6, 41] for some examples. Finally, to capture the transmission process, some representation of social/environmental contact is expressed in terms of mixing assumptions, contact networks, etc.

Forecasting methods employing these models are called mechanistic methods (or causal methods) because they are based on the causal mechanisms of infectious diseases. At a fairly high level, the underlying epidemic model can be either a compartmental model (CM) [28, 43, 44] or an agent-based model (ABM) [50, 17]. In a compartmental model, a population is divided into compartments (e.g., S, E, I, R), and no distinction is made among individuals within a compartment. Further, the entire population is assumed to be homogeneously mixing, a simplifying assumption, but reasonable for capturing large-scale dynamics. A differential equation system characterizes the change of the sizes of each compartment due to disease propagation and progression. Depending on the underlying assumptions, the rate of contact could be density-dependent or frequency-dependent [39]. This class of models can further be extended to the class of meta-population models where spatial connectivity is explicitly accounted for, and the disease compartments are tracked per spatial region. While these models, inspired from population ecology, are widely used in understanding human disease dynamics, they suffer from lack of fidelity to represent essential structures such as households, schools, etc. which may play a role in disease spread dynamics and control. See [7] for an overview of challenges in using such models for disease dynamics.

In an agent-based model, disease spreads among heterogeneous agents through an unstructured network [27]. Dynamics with individual behavior change exhibit significant impact on epidemic and dynamic forecast models [26], which can be implemented using a high-performance computing model [13]. The individual level details in an agent-based model can be easily aggregated to obtain epidemic data of any resolution, e.g., number of newly infected people in a county in a specific week. Such models have been used extensively to study diseases in significant detail, including Ebola [67], Influenza [47], and more recently COVID-19 [35]. There are multiple ongoing efforts to understand the relationship between these different class of models (see [5], for example). Many forecasting methods have been developed based on either CM or ABM [65, 61, 48, 81, 82, 85, 45]. Taking seasonal or pandemic influenza as an example, we list a few notable exercises that have used either of these approaches for forecasting or allied tasks. Shaman et al. [61] developed a framework for initializing real-time forecasts of seasonal influenza outbreaks, using a data assimilation technique commonly applied in numerical weather prediction. Tuite et al. [65] used an SIR CM to estimate parameters and morbidity in pandemic H1N1. Yang et al. [81] applied various filter methods to model and forecast influenza activity using an SIRS CM. In [48], the authors proposed a simulation optimization approach based on the SEIR ABM for epidemic forecasting. Venkatramanan et al. [68] factor mobility map into a metapopulation SEIR model to retrospectively forecast influenza in the USA and Australia. Causal methods are generally computationally expensive as they require the parameter estimation over a high dimensional space. As a result, the use of such methods for real-time forecasting is challenging. Furthermore, forecasting performance depends on the assumed underlying disease models.

3.1.4.2   Data-Driven Methods

The main concept of a data-driven model is to find relationships between the input and output without explicit knowledge of the physical behavior of the system. Both statistical models and deep learning models are examples of purely data-driven models. They employ statistical and time series-based methodologies to learn patterns in historical epidemic data and leverage those patterns for forecasting.

Statistical methods These methods assume that the observed data is the outcome of a random process with an unknown probability distribution, typically a parametric distribution. In addition, the observed data is considered to be a function of explanatory variables or covariates, which enables inference of distribution parameters through a likelihood function. A popular class of models are the autoregressive models (such as AR, ARMA, ARIMA) that assume that the observed time series current time step can be expressed as a linear combination of past samples and error terms. In the context of ILI forecasting, in addition to the ARIMA terms of the ILI time series, other exogenous variables such as search trends, social media data, weather data, etc. can be used as exogenous regressors to enhance nowcast performance. Yang et al. [80], Rangarajan et al. [56], Kandula et al. [37], Soebiyanto et al. [62], and Paul et al. [51] assume a Gaussian distribution on the data when modeling ILI rates and activity level. AR models for count data are modeled using Poisson [76] and negative binomial distribution [25, 54] and result in a class of generalized linear models. Owing to a large number of explanatory variables, techniques such as LASSO [63], log-likelihood ratio test [56], and block coordinate descent methods [64] are employed to select a sparse subset of most relevant variables. In the presence of sufficient seasonal data, a Bayesian weighted average of trajectories from past seasons to model current season assuming a mixture of Gaussian models is shown to perform reasonably well in the case of influenza by [70, 15] and dengue [66]. Under non-parametric models, method of analogues which attempts to find the most relevant historical segments of data or nearest neighbors with respect to the observed data and use a weighted average of the nearest neighbors to produce forecasts [70]. Exponential smoothing is another class of non-parametric regression models that employ exponentially decaying weights on historical samples (e.g., Petropoulos et al. [52]).

Deep learning based methods have gained increasing prominence in epidemic forecasting due to their ability to learn non-linear relationship between the inputs and the outputs without prior domain knowledge. Some of the common structure of such networks include: feedforward neural networks (FNNs), recurrent neural networks (RNNs), convolutional neural networks (CNNs), and graph neural networks (GNNs). A FNN is an artificial neural network wherein connections between the nodes do not form a cycle. It was the first and simplest type of artificial neural network devised [58]. Forecasting prevalence of epidemics using FNNs is a widely accepted approach. For example, dengue forecasting by Wahyunggoro et al. [72] and Aburas et al. [1], and FNNs were first applied for influenza forecasting by Xu et al. [79]. Adhikari et al. [3] propose EpiDeep for seasonal ILI forecasting by learning meaningful representations of incidence curves in a continuous feature space. The RNNs, due to their ability to inherently capture the temporal dynamics, have become a natural choice for time series forecasting. Popular RNN modules are gated recurrent unit (GRU) [21] and long-short term memory (LSTM) [33]. Volkova et al. [71] build an LSTM model for short-term ILI forecasting using CDC ILI and Twitter data. Venna et al. [69] propose an LSTM-based method that integrates the impacts of climatic factors and geographical proximity. Zhu et al. [86] propose attention-based LSTM model for epidemic forecasting. Chimmula et al. [18] use LSTM networks to predict COVID-19 transmission. The CNNs are usually used to deal with image data with regular grid data structure. The idea is to sum the neighboring node features around a center node, specified by a filter with parameterized size and learnable weight. CNNs can be used for epidemic forecasting because multivariate time series (e.g., spatial regions) of an epidemic can be treated as an image with regular grid. Wu et al. [77] construct CNNRNN-Res combining RNN and convolutional neural networks to fuse information from different sources. The GNNs are the generalized version of CNN that can work on data with non-regular structures like a graph. The basic idea is to generate node embeddings based on local network neighborhoods through message passing.

The neighborhoods are defined using an adjacency matrix. It can be any type of relationship between graph nodes. GNNs are famous for their ability to capture cross-spatial effects in dynamic environments, thus leading to an increased prominence in epidemic forecasting. Deng et al. [24] design cola-GNN, which is a cross-location attention-based graph neural network for forecasting ILI. Regarding COVID-19 forecasting, Kapoor et al. [38] and Wang et al. [74] examined graph neural networks for COVID-19 daily case prediction using mobility data. Aamchandani et al. [55] presented DeepCOVIDNet to compute equi-dimensional representations of multivariate time series.

Most statistical methods rely on the stationarity assumptions of the data. To some extent, the non-stationarity of time series data addressed through differencing and retraining over short observation windows, but performance of statistical methods is inversely related to deviation from historically observed distribution. As observed in the case of COVID-19 forecasting, most statistical methods were employed during the initial phase of the pandemic to capture exponential growth phase, but with the pandemic undergoing rapid fluctuations, these methods were not effective in accurate forecasting. Training deep learning models usually require a large training dataset, which is usually not available particularly for novel and emerging epidemics. Another well-known limitation of deep learning methods is the lack of interpretability for model predictions due to their black-box nature. Furthermore, since they are purely data-driven, they do not explicitly incorporate the underlying causal mechanisms. As a result, epidemic dynamics affected by behavioral adaptations are usually hard to capture, even for mechanistic models. However, with additional data becoming available and the surveillance systems maturing, these models are becoming more promising.

In the following section, we will present hybrid methods that combine theory-based mechanistic models and purely data-driven models for epidemic forecasting. Specifically, two frameworks that use social media mining techniques to enhance theory-based mechanistic models and one method that augments a mechanistic model with a neural network will be introduced in 3.2.1. Additional methods that use mechanistic causal theory to enhance data-driven models will be discussed in 3.2.2. We conclude the limitations and future directions of these methods in 3.3.

3.2 Hybrid Approaches for Epidemic Forecasting

Given the challenges discussed in Sections 3.1.3.5 and 3.1.4, traditional mechanistic methods have become increasingly difficult to calibrate to the spatiotemporal multivariate time series while the data-driven methods have been unable to determine the underlying causal mechanisms of disease spread and progression. A natural extension towards harnessing the benefits of both methods has been to combine theory-based mechanistic models with purely data-driven approaches. In this chapter, we explore spatiotemporal epidemic forecasting using such approaches with the aim of providing accurate predictions as well as gaining a mechanistic understanding from a learned model.

As shown in Figure 3.1, current efforts on combining theory-based mechanistic models with data-driven methods are along two lines:

- using machine learning techniques to enhance theory-based mechanistic models (① and ② marked in red arrows);

- using mechanistic causal theory to enhance data-driven models (③ and ④ marked in blue arrows).

Among many works related to the two directions, we will discuss several works respectively in the following sections with the aim of highlighting the general ideas.

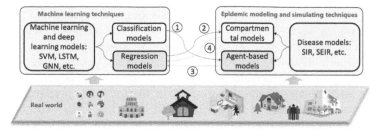

FIGURE 3.1
An overview of hybrid methods for epidemic forecasting. These methods make forecasts based on hybrid techniques, which mainly include but not limited to machine learning techniques and epidemic modeling and simulating techniques. Classification and regression models employ machine learning and deep learning models such as support vector machine (SVM), LSTM, GNN, etc. Compartmental and agent-based models employ disease models like SIR, SEIR, etc. The hybrid methods are along two lines: using machine learning techniques to enhance theory-based mechanistic models (① and ② marked in red arrows); using mechanistic causal theory to enhance data-driven models (③ and ④ marked in blue arrows).

3.2.1 Using Machine Learning Techniques to Enhance Theory-Based Mechanistic Models

Forecasting by a mechanistic model relies upon a two-stage process. First, the available reference data is used to construct and calibrate the model. Model parameters are inferred during this stage so that the model outputs of simulations are consistent with observations. Subsequently, in forecasting phase, simulations are run by projecting forward using the most recent calibrated parameters. The projected simulating outputs are used for future predictions.

There are mainly two ways to infer mechanistic model parameters. One way is to use parameters based on prior knowledge of an existing disease epidemiology which is limited particularly for new emerging epidemics. The other approach is to estimate model parameters using optimization tools. An example of such an approach is a mechanistic model calibrated using a mixed approach. In an agent-based SEIR model of seasonal influenza, the infectious and incubation distributions can be inferred directly from literature, while the disease transmissibility is estimated using an optimization algorithm. Calibrating mechanistic models is challenging as they are highly dependant on the reference data quality, which is heavily influenced by fluctuations in detection and associated processes. Another challenge is that many disease dynamic factors are difficult to quantify and hence may not be able to be described in simple functions.

We will introduce novel works that enhance model calibrating processes using social media mining techniques in Section 3.2.1.1 and using neural networks to encode model parameters in Section 3.2.1.2.

3.2.1.1 Inferring Agent-Based Model Parameters Using Social Media Mining Techniques

Traditionally, epidemiologists have relied on surveillance data to estimate the mechanistic model parameters. However, the task of calibrating these models is marred by surveillance data quality and mismatch between surveillance data and actual prevalence, as is the case for an emerging infectious diseases. The latter occurs when the observed time series is heavily influenced by fluctuations in detection and associated processes, and hence may significantly deviate from the mechanistically modeled infection process. The challenges with respect to the surveillance data are introduced in Section 3.1.3.5 and may go beyond that in the case of specific diseases and different simulating models. In the following paragraphs, we are going to introduce two works by Zhao et al. [85] and Hua et al. [36]. The two works are the first efforts to combine theory-based mechanistic models and social media mining techniques for epidemic forecasting. Both focus on influenza forecasting in the US using an agent-based SEIR model. Instead of using traditional CDC data to calibrate the model, they leverage social media data to infer disease model parameters.

The agent-based modeling allows the policymaker to define behaviors at the individual and societal level, describe the characteristics of the pathogen, and simulate the infectious disease evolution on a realistic synthetic population [27]. Thus, agent-based epidemic models are increasingly preferred to their statistical and compartmental counterparts for their representational fidelity and ability to perform complex counterfactual studies of policy relevance. In such models, each synthetic individual will be assigned geographical, social, behavioral, and demographic attributes (e.g., age and income) [13] and a set of dynamic behaviors and activities, which in turn result in social contact. Thus social contact network is simulated through assigning daily activities and locations for each node (person) in the population [13, 8]. The epidemic dynamics are then modeled as diffusion processes across the network, which enables the computation of various disease metrics equivalent to those observed in the real world. Forecasting is made by calibrating disease parameters using derivative-free simulation optimization (such as Nelder–Mead (citation needed if it is a standard method)) or Bayesian techniques (citations of some standard methods)) to match observations and then by projecting forward using the most recent calibrated values for future predictions.

Specifically, calibrating an agent-based SEIR model based on real-world data (e.g., CDC seasonal influenza surveillance) suffers from the following limitations:

(*i*) *Lack of timely multivariate data.* CDC updates surveillance data once per week with at least one week delay in flu seasons. Further, they capture the percent of visits that exhibit ILI symptoms. Given such a coarse view of disease dynamics, it is difficult to exactly match the time series without modeling the observation and detection processes (such as hospital visitation, catchment areas, etc.). In addition, interventions such as school closures and vaccinations play an important role in mitigating epidemics by changing people's infectivity and vulnerability and altering the contact network structure. But such data is not available for integration into the disease model.

(*ii*) *Lack of spatially fine-grained data.* CDC surveillance data is provided at the state-level with not much detailed information for sub-regions such as counties. However, within the agent-based model (or even a metapopulation model) there are inherent heterogeneities between the region induced by the population representation. When this is mismatched or not verifiable with the available data, it makes it difficult to tune the appropriate model parameters.

Social media data can capture timely and ubiquitous disease information from social media users who may talk about their symptoms through online posts. These posts are known to be one of the best signals for early disease detection, even before diagnoses [40]. Several attempts have been made to track disease outbreaks through including the aggregate volume of flu-related social media posts as exogenous variables in purely data-driven models [2, 32, 22, 71]. However, involving social media mining techniques into agent-based modeling and simulating process has not been explored.

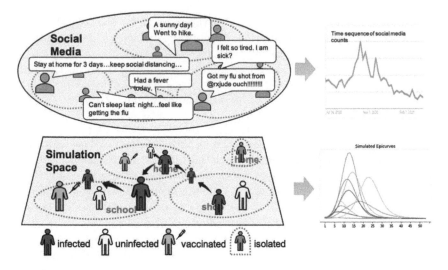

FIGURE 3.2

An abstract of the mapping between social media space and simulation space in real-world epidemics. In the social media space, based on the posts at current time point, a social media user is classified into four health states: uninfected, infected, vaccinated, and isolated, using machine learning techniques. In the simulation space, an agent-based simulation outputs individual health states with their days of being in each health state in a simulated season. In both social media space and simulation space, individuals with each health state can be aggregated to any temporal and spatial scale, such as daily (weekly) state (county) level infected case count. Mapping the aggregated statistics between the two spaces is the key idea to facilitate agent-based simulations using real-time social media data.

Given the above challenges, Zhao et al. [85] and Hua et al. [36] proposed novel frameworks that integrate the strengths of agent-based epidemic simulations and social media mining techniques. Their works are based on the same rationale: disease dynamics in the real world can be reflected by online social media users in a timely and fine-grained manner. Figure 3.2 shows an abstract of the mapping between social media space and simulation space in real world epidemics. Social media users often share posts online with geo-location enabled. Influenza-related posts are filtered and used to classify the health state of social media users. Specifically, at each day, a social media user is classified into four health states: uninfected, infected, vaccinated, and isolated based on his or her posts during the day. Users of each health state are grouped by their geographical locations shared online. Similarly, an agent-based simulation outputs individual health states with their days of being in each health state in a simulated season. Vaccine intervention can be implemented in the simulations, by specifying the quantity of vaccines applied to the population in each day or week. In both social media space and simulation space, individuals with each health state can be aggregated to any temporal and spatial scale, such as daily (weekly) state (county) level infected case count. Mapping the aggregated statistics between the two spaces is the key idea to facilitate agent-based simulations using real-time social media data.

Based on the above rationale on the effectiveness of social media data, in [85], a semi-supervised deep learning framework – SimNest – is proposed. Specifically, this framework learns the social media users' health states and intervention actions using a deep neural network model $f_{NN}(X, \Theta_1)$ in real-time, which are regularized by an agent-based simulator $f_{SIM}(\mathcal{G}, \Theta_2)$, where X is the social media user posts collected from online social media platforms, $\mathcal{G}$ is the synthetic population and contact network that is already generated and leveraged in literature, and Θ_1, Θ_2 are model parameters to be learned. $\Theta_2 = \{p_E, p_I\}$ are infectious duration and incubation duration distributions, which are both assumed to follow normal distributions, i.e., $p_E \sim \mathcal{N}(\mu_E, \sigma_E)$ and $p_I \sim \mathcal{N}(\mu_I, \sigma_I)$.

The parameters Θ_1, Θ_2 are optimized by jointly minimizing the objective function:

$$\mathcal{L}(\Theta_1, \Theta_2) = \mathcal{L}_1(f_{NN}, Y_g) + \mathcal{L}_2(f_{NN}, f_{SIM}) + \mathcal{L}_3(f_{NN}, p_I) + \mathcal{L}_4(f_{NN}, f_{NN}) \qquad (3.1)$$

where Y_g is the aggregated ground truth labels of infectious users. $\mathcal{L}_1$ is the supervised loss referring to the misclassification error. $\mathcal{L}_2$ is the bispace consistency loss which refers to the matching errors between the aggregated simulated outputs and classification predictions. $\mathcal{L}_3$ denotes the infectious duration loss which is computed as maximizing the likelihood that the predicted infectious duration of social media users follows the same distribution of infectious duration in simulations. $\mathcal{L}_4$ is the temporal proximity loss that is calculated as the difference between any two consecutive predictions of a user.

The model parameter Θ_1 and Θ_2 are optimized using stochastic gradient descent (SGD) [12] and Nelder–Mead [46] methods, respectively. Forecasting is made by running simulations using f_{SIM} by projecting forward the most recent disease parameters p_I, p_E. The outputs are individual-level infections and their infectious days at future time, which can be aggregated to any spatiotemporal resolution based on the problem formulation.

The proposed framework is tested using labeled Twitter data [42] and unlabeled Twitter posts of five states during January 1, 2011 and April 15, 2015 in the US. The forecasting lead time varies from 1 week to 20 weeks. MSE and PCORR are used to evaluate the model performance. Based on the plots and discussion of the results shown in the paper, we conclude that social media-based methods perform well with small lead time while computational epidemiology-based methods outperform others as the lead time increases. SimNest model, which combines two methods, outperforms the baselines in overall performance. Please refer to the original paper [85] for more details.

Along the lines of SimNest, Hua et al. in [36] propose a dual space framework called SMS which also combines the strength of social media mining and computational epidemiology. In social media space, individual health status (healthy, exposed, and infected) is first learned from social media data through a specially designed Bayesian graphical model. In simulation space, an agent-based SEIR model is calibrated based on the aggregated outputs from social media space. The disease model parameters, including incubation distribution and infectious distribution, are calculated and further used to compute the Gamma prior for a Dirichlet parameter of healthy status in graphical model. Forecasting is made by projecting forward the most recent calibrated disease parameters using the agent-based model for future predictions. SMS is tested on Twitter data collected in Maryland (MD) and Massachusetts (MA) from August 2012 to July 2014, and the model performance is evaluated using MSE and PCORR. The results and analysis in the paper show that SMS model is the best performer among the baselines with smallest average mean and the least variance.

Social media data is usually collected through the Application Programming Interface (API) provided by social media platforms. The collected datasets include users' information (e.g., demographics, geographical locations, and posts) which is only shared publicly by users. In the above two works, there is no discussion about how individual privacy is protected when these methods are deployed. We note that although social media users' usernames and other unwanted information can be removed to anonymize users, part of social media posts used in the above two works is labeled manually; thus, individual privacy is not fully protected. We suggest researchers to provide extra privacy guarantee when deploying these methods.

3.2.1.2 Augmenting Compartmental Models with Data-Driven Modules

During a pandemic, like COVID-19, the disease spreads worldwide and usually meets with a wide variety of interventions (the background is introduced in Section 3.1.2). The effectiveness of these responses is notoriously difficult to quantify as they interplay with other factors in changing the disease spreading dynamics without being explicitly detected. In this section, we introduce a new idea proposed by Dandekar and Barbastathis in [23] that mixed first-principles epidemiological equations and a data-driven neural network model when calibrating causal model parameters for COVID-19 forecasting. More specifically, the work augments a compartmental SIR model with a neural network that encodes the quarantine strength information into the differential equations. Compared with the existing models, the proposed model analyzes the role of the quarantine intervention in the spread of COVID-19 without using parameters based on prior knowledge of previous epidemics (e.g., SARS/MERS coronavirus epidemic). The ordinary differential equations of the augmented SIR model are described as:

$$
\begin{aligned}
\frac{dS(t)}{dt} &= -\beta S(t)\frac{I(t)}{N} \\
\frac{dI(t)}{dt} &= \beta S(t)\frac{I(t)}{N} - (\gamma + q(t))I(t) \\
\frac{dR(t)}{dt} &= \gamma I(t) + \delta T(t) \\
\frac{dT(t)}{dt} &= q(t)I(t) - \delta T(t)
\end{aligned}
\tag{3.2}
$$

where we consider a population of N individuals, each of whom can be in one of the following states: Susceptible (S), Infected (I), Recovered (R), and Quarantined (T), where $N = S(t) + I(t) + R(t) + T(t)$. β and γ are the infection and recovery rates. δ denotes the rate of recovery of the quarantined population. $q(t)$ is a time varying quarantine strength rate. Since $q(t)$ does not follow from first principles and is highly dependent on local quarantine policies, it is approximated by a neural network-based function $q(t) = f_{NN}(S(t), I(t), R(t), \Theta)$ where Θ denotes parameters of the neural network.

The parameters are optimized by minimizing the objective function:

$$
\mathcal{L}(\Theta, \beta, \gamma, \delta) = \| \log(I(t) + T(t)) - \log(I^g(t)) \|^2 + \| \log(R(t)) - \log(R^g(t)) \|^2
\tag{3.3}
$$

where $I^g(t), R^g(t)$ are ground truth. Minimization was employed using local adjoint sensitivity analysis with the ADAM optimizer.

The proposed model was used to analyze and compare the role of quarantine control policies employed in Wuhan, Italy, South Korea, and USA, in controlling spread of COVID-19 pandemic. The results show a generally strong correlation between strengthening of the quarantine controls $q(t)$; actions taken by the regions' respective governments; and decrease of the effective reproduction number. Please read the original paper for more details.

3.2.2 Using Mechanistic Causal Theory to Enhance Data-Driven Models

Unlike mechanistic methods, DNN-based models do not capture the underlying causal mechanisms due to their black-box nature. As a result, epidemic dynamics affected by behavioral adaptations are usually hard to capture. Training a deep learning model for forecasting tasks, it is crucial to answer the following questions: If one can learn a model from data, can this model not only provide the correct inferences but also some explanation for the underlying phenomenon? Can one gain a mechanistic understanding from a learned model?

In epidemiology, answering these questions is particularly important for better understanding and controlling of the disease spread. As discussed in Section 3.1.4.1, mechanistic causal models simulate infectious disease spreading process based on causal theory. Thus, incorporating causal models into deep learning framework can provide theory-based priors for the learning of data-driven models. In this section, we will introduce two related articles along the line of enhancing deep learning models using causal theory. Note that there may be other related papers or pre-prints, e.g. [73], which address a similar approach, but we choose the following two papers to highlight the general idea.

3.2.2.1   Training Deep Learning Models with Theory-Generated Data for High-Resolution Epidemic Forecasting

Disease surveillance data are usually sparse, noisy, and incomplete; thus, deep learning models trained on these data fail to capture disease dynamics at a finer scale and are incapable of generalizing for unseen data. Computational mechanistic causal models can capture the diffusion patterns of disease spread through detailed simulation using a realistic representation of the underlying social contact network formed by human mobility behavior and population demographics. The data generated by computing-based simulations can be aggregated to multi-scale spatiotemporal time series. In Wang et al. [75], a novel epidemic forecasting framework – TDEFSI – is presented. It integrates the strengths of deep neural networks and high-resolution simulations of epidemic processes over networks. Specifically, a two-branch LSTM-based model for ILI forecasting is proposed to combine within-season observations and between-season historical observations. Different from traditional deep learning models which are trained using real-world observations, in this work, the LSTM-based model is trained with theory-generated training data. The synthetic data is generated by high performance computing based simulations of well accepted causal processes that capture epidemic dynamics. Deep learning models trained with such data can capture the underlying causal processes and mathematical theory leading to an ability to make context-specific forecasts and capture the unique properties of a given region. In addition, the learned model can produce multi-resolution forecasts even though observational data might only be available at an aggregate level. The input is state-level data and the output is county-level predictions. In the loss function, two physical constraints: spatial consistency constraint and non-negative constraint are added to regularize the model. These constraints incorporate physical knowledge into deep learning models leading to more generalized models.

The TDEFSI framework (Figure 3.3) consists of three major components: (*i*) *Disease model parameter space construction*: given an existing agent-based model, a marginal distribution for each model parameter based on the surveillance data is estimated; (*ii*) *Synthetic training data generation*: a synthetic training dataset is generated at both flat-resolution and high-resolution scales by running simulations parameterized from the parameter space; and (*iii*) *Deep neural network training and forecasting*: In the training process, the LSTM-based model is trained using synthetic training data. The historical surveillance data is only used for constructing the disease model parameter space. In the predicting step, the trained model takes state-level surveillance as input and makes forecasts at both state and county levels.

TDEFSI is tested for forecasting state-level ILI case counts in Virginia and New Jersey and county-level ILI case counts in New Jersey for season 2016–2017 and season 2017–2018. The forecasting horizon is 1, 2, 3, 4, and 5 weeks ahead. The RMSE, MAPE, and PCORR are used for performance evaluation. The baselines include SARIMA [10], ARGO [80], LSTM [34], AdapLSTM [69], and EpiFast [9]. Based on the results and analysis in the paper, TDEFSI yields accurate high-resolution spatiotemporal forecasts using low-resolution time series data.

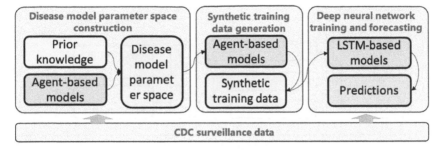

FIGURE 3.3

TDEFSI framework. In this framework, a region-specific disease parameter space for a disease model is constructed using an agent-based model based on historical surveillance data. Synthetic training data consisting of both state-level and county-level weekly ILI incidence curves is generated using the agent-based model by simulations parameterized by samples from the parameter space. An LSTM based deep neural network model is trained on the synthetic data. The trained model produces forecasts by taking surveillance data as the input.

What-if forecasts capture various what-if scenarios due to expected or unexpected public health interventions or individual-level behavioral reactions. Another highlight from the paper is that the causal model in TDEFSI enables what-if forecasting by making different assumptions in the future. Extensive experiments are conducted to demonstrate the capability of what-if forecasting. In the settings, two scenarios are investigated: (*i*) base-case is to generate synthetic training data using simulations without vaccine intervention and (*ii*) vaccine-case is the base-case with vaccine intervention applied in the simulations. Two training datasets based on the scenarios are generated and used to train TDEFSI model. The results in the paper show that vaccination-based interventions applied in the simulations to generate training datasets can significantly improve the forecasting performance. This indicates that the models learned from the vaccine-case datasets are more generalizable to unseen surveillance data.

3.2.2.2 Incorporating Causal Theory in Graph Neural Network Learning

TDEFSI combines mechanistic causal models and deep learning models in one framework, but their learning processes are not mutually dependent. Specifically, the training of deep learning models depends on causal model outputs, but not vice versa. Causal theory under this case cannot be used directly as domain knowledge for regularizing model predictions. A new emerging direction in epidemic forecasting is to integrate causal theory into deep learning models so that physical laws (i.e., epidemiological knowledge) can be used to regularize predictions of deep learning models.

Incorporating domain knowledge as physical constraints into deep learning models is an active research area and has been explored in several studies, for example, Seo et al. [59, 60] import physics into difference graph networks to handle physics-governed observations. The forecasting performance is demonstrated on graph signals on the synthetic data and the real-world weather station data. Wu et al. [78] introduce statistical constraints in loss function when training generative adversarial networks (GANs) and Beucler et al. [11] introduce methods of enforcing non-linear analytic constraints in the architecture or the loss function in neural networks.

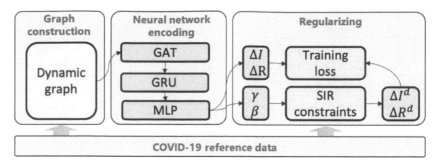

FIGURE 3.4

An overview of the STAN model. A graph is constructed that a node represents a location, and an edge is created based on geographic proximity and location population. Each node is associated with dynamic and static features, and each edge is weighted by a generated model. The graph is fed into a graph attention network (GAT) where spatiotemporal features of the graph are extracted and encoded for each node. A GRU module is used to learn the temporal pattern of the embedded graph. The hidden states of the GRU will be used to predict future number of infected ΔI and recovered cases ΔR and causal model parameters β, γ using a multi-layer perception (MLP) module. Physical laws of SIR differential equations are added to regularize the predictions. The training loss consists of prediction loss and dynamic constraint loss.

In this section, we are going to introduce the work [29] by Gao et al. where a novel framework to predict the number of COVID-19 cases is proposed to combine graph neural networks and causal theory-based models in a mutually dependent way. In the paper, a spatiotemporal graph-based attention network, called STAN, is proposed for epidemic forecasting. Figure 3.4 presents an overview of the STAN model. The COVID-19 reference data is used to construct a graph $\mathcal{G}$ where a node represents a location, and an edge is created based on geographic proximity and location population. Each node is associated with dynamic and static features, and each edge is weighted by a generated model. The graph is fed into a graph attention network (GAT) where spatiotemporal features of the graph are extracted and encoded for each node. A GRU module is used to learn the temporal pattern of the embedded graph. The hidden states of the GRU will then be fed into a multi-layer perceptron module to output disease model parameters β, γ and daily increment number of infected cases and recovered cases $\Delta I, \Delta R$ respectively. We denote the neural network modules as an encoder f_{NN}, then $\langle \beta, \gamma, \Delta I, \Delta R \rangle := f_{NN}(\mathcal{G}, \Theta)$ where Θ is the model parameters. Note that $\Delta I = \langle \Delta I_{t+1}, \ldots, \Delta I_{t+h} \rangle$ and $\Delta R = \langle \Delta R_{t+1}, \ldots, \Delta R_{t+h} \rangle$ correspond to h time steps ahead predictions. Physical laws of SIR differential equations are applied to calculate vectors of the transmission dynamics-based increment number of infected cases and recovered cases, denoted as $\Delta I^d = \langle \Delta I_{t+1}^d, \ldots, \Delta I_{t+h}^d \rangle$ and $\Delta R^d = \langle \Delta R_{t+1}^d, \ldots, \Delta R_{t+h}^d \rangle$. For time step $t + i$, ΔI_{t+i}^d is calculated as:

$$\begin{aligned} \Delta I_{t+i}^d &= \beta(N - I_{t+i-1}^d - R_{t+i-1}^d) - \gamma I_{t+i-1}^d \\ \Delta R_{t+i}^d &= \gamma I_{t+i-1}^d \end{aligned} \tag{3.4}$$

where N is the population size, I_{t+i-1}^d, R_{t+i-1}^d are cumulative number of infected cases and recovered cases calculated iteratively as $I_{t+i-1}^d = I_{t+i-2}^d + \Delta I_{t+i-1}^d$ and $R_{t+i-1}^d = R_{t+i-2}^d + \Delta R_{t+i-1}^d$. I_t^d, R_t^d are ground truth values of the most recent available data.

The loss function consists of the prediction loss $\mathcal{L}_r$ computed as the error between ground truth $\Delta I^g, \Delta R^g$ and predicted increment number of cases $\Delta I, \Delta R$ and the dynamic constraint loss $\mathcal{L}_d$ calculated as the error between the ground truth and $\Delta I^d, \Delta R^d$, described as:

$$
\begin{aligned}
\mathcal{L}(\Theta) &= \mathcal{L}_d + \mathcal{L}_r \\
&= \parallel \Delta I^d - \Delta I^g \parallel^2 + \parallel \Delta R^d - \Delta R^g \parallel^2 + \parallel \Delta I - \Delta I^g \parallel^2 + \parallel \Delta R - \Delta R^g \parallel^2
\end{aligned}
\tag{3.5}
$$

The model is trained by minimizing the loss function. In forecasting time, only $\Delta I, \Delta R$ are used to calculate the total infected cases and the transmission dynamics constraints module is used for optimizing the model in the training time.

STAN is compared with baselines SIR, SEIR, GRU, ColaGNN [24], CovidGNN [38], and two ablation variants STAN-PC and STAN-Graph. All models are tested for forecasting COVID-19 daily new confirmed cases at US county and state levels. The forecasting horizon is 5, 15, and 20 days ahead. MSE, MAE, and PCORR are used to evaluate the model performance. The results in the original paper show that STAN consistently outperforms baselines in three metrics at both state-level and county-level predictions. Please read the original paper for more details.

3.3 Conclusions

In this chapter, we give a brief overview of epidemics, epidemic forecasting, and methodologies for epidemic forecasting. We mainly focus on introducing two classes of hybrid models that effectively combine theory and data-driven methods for epidemic forecasting. These approaches, while not exhaustive, highlight the various complementary ways in which such model frameworks can be utilized for better overall performance. Recent efforts have been made towards (*i*) using machine learning techniques to enhance theory-based mechanistic models and (*ii*) using mechanistic causal theory to enhance data-driven models. Specifically, along line (*i*), novel methods that combining agent-based simulations with social media mining techniques to improve forecasting performance have been explored. Social media data provides timely and fine-grained disease dynamics, which are usually not available in traditional surveillance data. Thus, in the proposed frameworks, social media data is used instead of traditional surveillance data to infer disease model parameters which will then be used to make future predictions. We introduce these select papers with the aim of inspiring readers with new perspectives of epidemic forecasting and the rich potential of hybrid approaches in this rapidly evolving sub-discipline of immense practical importance. However, as we discussed in Section 3.1.3.5, the current forecast systems are still far from weather forecasting, due to inherent uncertainty introduced by sociopolitical heterogeneity and behavioral adaptations. Furthermore, collecting and refining such data requires extra efforts which are hard to be widely used for real-time systems. More importantly, strong privacy guarantee is essential to protect individual privacy when these methods are deployed.

Along the same direction, a new model is proposed for simulating COVID-19 dynamics. The proposed method augments a compartmental SIR model with a neural network module to encode the quarantine strength information into the differential equations. Although the forecasting performance of the augmented model is not tested and evaluated in a systematic way in the paper, the proposed method provides a new idea of formulating new mechanistic models that involve complex factors using non-linear functions as the information encoder. These factors are usually difficult to be described in an analytical formulation. However, an appropriate optimization algorithm is crucial for calibrating such models. This needs extra investigation into the problem formulation and model construction.

In direction (*ii*), a deep learning framework is proposed to train deep neural networks with theory-generated synthetic training data. The learned model can provide accurate high-resolution forecasts using low-resolution time series data. The proposed framework transfers a theory-based causal mechanism from a causal model to a deep learning model. Unlike data augmentation that are directly applied on observed data for time series classification or regression, the proposed framework generates synthetic high-resolution data which is not available or quite sparse in the real world. In addition, incorporating causal models into the framework enables what-if forecasting by deep learning models. However, it is challenging if data drift exists between synthetic data distribution and real-world observation distribution. Such data drift can be caused by the assumption error of the underlying disease model, optimization algorithm bias, and the rapidly co-evolving dynamics of disease spreading environment. Thus, a future direction is to detect and overcome the data drift in the framework.

Along direction (*ii*), a graph neural network-based framework is also discussed where SIR differential equations are incorporated into deep learning models as physical constraints to regularize model predictions so that the forecasting performance can be improved. However, the problem of how to gain mechanistic causal understanding from the learned deep learning models is not discussed. A future work is to build a framework where the causal features from mechanistic simulations and latent features from deep neural networks are fused and mutually learned in model training process, which leads to explainable AI-based epidemic systems. Another limitation of this framework is that it can only be applied for forecasting epidemics where the surveillance data of each compartments are available at each time step.

As a new emerging trend, combining theory and data-driven methods has been studied in physics, biology, geography, and many other domains. However, it is far from completely explored in epidemic forecasting. This is rightly so, given that the field is still evolving in terms of large-scale data availability due to technological advances and growing understanding of underlying processes through improved clinical studies. The aim of this chapter is to motivate the need and actual task of epidemic forecasting and provide an initial foray into the current approaches that leverage the state-of-the-art techniques being developed across the field.

Notes

[1] Source: https://covid19.who.int/

[2] Source: `https://www.who.int/health-topics/ebola/\#tab=tab_1`

[3] Source: `https://www.cdc.gov/vhf/ebola/history/2014-2016-outbreak/index.html`

[4] Source: `https://www.cdc.gov/coronavirus/2019-ncov/need-extra-precautions/index.html`

[5] Source: `https://gis.cdc.gov/grasp/fluview/fluportaldashboard.html`

[6]The 10 Regional Offices that directly serve state and local organizations are hosted by the Office of Intergovernmental and External Affairs. HHS denotes US Department of Human and Health Services.

[7]https://www.cdc.gov/flu/weekly/fluviewinteractive.htm

[8]https://predict.cdc.gov/

[9]Wikipedia: A gravity model provides an estimate of the volume of flows of, for example, goods, services, or people between two or more locations. This could be the movement of people between cities or the volume of trade between countries.

Bibliography

[1] Hani M Aburas, B Gultekin Cetiner, and Murat Sari. Dengue confirmed-cases prediction: A neural network model. *Expert Systems with Applications*, 37(6):4256–4260, 2010.

[2] Harshavardhan Achrekar, Avinash Gandhe, Ross Lazarus, Ssu-Hsin Yu, and Benyuan Liu. Online social networks flu trend tracker: a novel sensory approach to predict flu trends. In *Proceedings of the 5th International Joint Conference on Biomedical Engineering Systems and Technologies (BIOSTEC)*, pages 353–368. Springer, 2012.

[3] Bijaya Adhikari, Xinfeng Xu, Naren Ramakrishnan, and B Aditya Prakash. Epideep: Exploiting embeddings for epidemic forecasting. In *Proceedings of the 25th ACM SIGKDD International Conference on Knowledge Discovery & Data Mining*, pages 577–586, 2019.

[4] Aniruddha Adiga, Devdatt Dubhashi, Bryan Lewis, Madhav Marathe, Srinivasan Venkatramanan, and Anil Vullikanti. Mathematical models for covid-19 pandemic: a comparative analysis. *Journal of the Indian Institute of Science*, pages 1–15, 2020.

[5] Marco Ajelli, Bruno Gonçalves, Duygu Balcan, Vittoria Colizza, Hao Hu, José J Ramasco, Stefano Merler, and Alessandro Vespignani. Comparing large-scale computational approaches to epidemic modeling: agent-based versus structured metapopulation models. *BMC Infectious Diseases*, 10(1):1–13, 2010.

[6] Norman TJ Bailey et al. *The mathematical theory of infectious diseases and its applications*. Number 2nd edition. Charles Griffin & Company Ltd 5a Crendon Street, High Wycombe, Bucks HP13 6LE., 1975.

[7] Frank Ball, Tom Britton, Thomas House, Valerie Isham, Denis Mollison, Lorenzo Pellis, and Gianpaolo Scalia Tomba. Seven challenges for metapopulation models of epidemics, including households models. *Epidemics*, 10:63–67, 2015.

[8] Christopher L Barrett, Richard J Beckman, Maleq Khan, VS Anil Kumar, Madhav V Marathe, Paula E Stretz, Tridib Dutta, and Bryan Lewis. Generation and analysis of large synthetic social contact networks. In *Proceedings of the 41st Winter Simulation Conference (WSC)*, pages 1003–1014. Winter Simulation Conference, 2009.

[9] Richard Beckman, Keith R Bisset, Jiangzhuo Chen, Bryan Lewis, Madhav Marathe, and Paula Stretz. Isis: A networked-epidemiology based pervasive web app for infectious

disease pandemic planning and response. In *Proceedings of the 20th ACM SIGKDD International Conference on Knowledge Discovery and Data Mining*, pages 1847–1856. ACM, 2014.

[10] Michael A Benjamin, Robert A Rigby, and D Mikis Stasinopoulos. Generalized autoregressive moving average models. *Journal of the American Statistical Association*, 98(461):214–223, 2003.

[11] Tom Beucler, Michael Pritchard, Stephan Rasp, Jordan Ott, Pierre Baldi, and Pierre Gentine. Enforcing analytic constraints in neural networks emulating physical systems. *Physical Review Letters*, 126(9):098302, 2021.

[12] Christopher M Bishop. *Pattern Recognition and Machine Learning*. Springer, 2006.

[13] Keith R. Bisset, Jiangzhuo Chen, Xizhou Feng, V.S. Anil Kumar, and Madhav V. Marathe. EpiFast: A fast algorithm for large scale realistic epidemic simulations on distributed memory systems. In *Proceedings of the 23rd International Conference on Supercomputing*, pages 430–439. ACM, 2009.

[14] Johannes Bracher, Evan L Ray, Tilmann Gneiting, and Nicholas G Reich. Evaluating epidemic forecasts in an interval format. *PLoS Computational Biology*, 17(2):e1008618, 2021.

[15] Logan C Brooks, David C Farrow, Sangwon Hyun, Ryan J Tibshirani, and Roni Rosenfeld. Flexible modeling of epidemics with an empirical bayes framework. *PLoS Computational Biology*, 11(8):e1004382, 2015.

[16] Centers for Disease Control and Prevention. *Forecast the 2018–2019 Influenza Season Collaborative Challenge; 2018.*, Accessible online at https://predict. cdc.gov/api/v1/attachments/flusight%202018%E2%80%932019/flu_challenge_2018-19_tentativefinal_9.18.18.docx.

[17] Dennis L Chao, M Elizabeth Halloran, Valerie J Obenchain, and Ira M Longini Jr. FluTE, a publicly available stochastic influenza epidemic simulation model. *PLoS Computational Biology*, 6(1):e1000656, 2010.

[18] Vinay Kumar Reddy Chimmula and Lei Zhang. Time series forecasting of covid-19 transmission in canada using lstm networks. *Chaos, Solitons & Fractals*, page 109864, 2020.

[19] Gerardo Chowell, Lisa Sattenspiel, Shweta Bansal, and Cécile Viboud. Mathematical models to characterize early epidemic growth: A review. *Physics of Life Reviews*, 18:66–97, 2016.

[20] Gerardo Chowell, Amna Tariq, and James M Hyman. A novel sub-epidemic modeling framework for short-term forecasting epidemic waves. *BMC Medicine*, 17(1):1–18, 2019.

[21] Junyoung Chung, Caglar Gulcehre, KyungHyun Cho, and Yoshua Bengio. Empirical evaluation of gated recurrent neural networks on sequence modeling. *arXiv preprint arXiv:1412.3555*, 2014.

[22] Aron Culotta. Towards detecting influenza epidemics by analyzing twitter messages. In *Proceedings of the First Workshop on Social Media Analytics*, pages 115–122, 2010.

[23] Raj Dandekar, Chris Rackauckas, and George Barbastathis. A machine learning-aided global diagnostic and comparative tool to assess effect of quarantine control in covid-19 spread. *Patterns*, 1(9):100145, 2020.

[24] Songgaojun Deng, Shusen Wang, Huzefa Rangwala, Lijing Wang, and Yue Ning. Cola-gnn: Cross-location attention based graph neural networks for long-term ili prediction. In *Proceedings of the 29th ACM International Conference on Information & Knowledge Management*, pages 245–254, 2020.

[25] Andrea Freyer Dugas, Mehdi Jalalpour, Yulia Gel, Scott Levin, Fred Torcaso, Takeru Igusa, and Richard E Rothman. Influenza forecasting with google flu trends. *PloS One*, 8(2):e56176, 2013.

[26] Ceyhun Eksin, Keith Paarporn, and Joshua S Weitz. Systematic biases in disease forecasting-the role of behavior change. *Epidemics*, 2019.

[27] Stephen Eubank, Hasan Guclu, VS Anil Kumar, Madhav V Marathe, Aravind Srini-vasan, Zoltan Toroczkai, and Nan Wang. Modelling disease outbreaks in realistic urban social networks. *Nature*, 429(6988):180–184, 2004.

[28] Antoine Flahault, Elisabeta Vergu, Laurent Coudeville, and Rebecca F Grais. Strate-gies for containing a global influenza pandemic. *Vaccine*, 24(44):6751–6755, 2006.

[29] Junyi Gao, Rakshith Sharma, Cheng Qian, Lucas M Glass, Jeffrey Spaeder, Justin Romberg, Jimeng Sun, and Cao Xiao. Stan: spatio-temporal attention network for pandemic prediction using real-world evidence. *Journal of the American Medical In-formatics Association*, 28(4):733–743, 2021.

[30] Tilmann Gneiting, Fadoua Balabdaoui, and Adrian E Raftery. Probabilistic forecasts, calibration and sharpness. *Journal of the Royal Statistical Society: Series B (Statistical Methodology)*, 69(2):243–268, 2007.

[31] Tilmann Gneiting and Adrian E Raftery. Strictly proper scoring rules, prediction, and estimation. *Journal of the American Statistical Association*, 102(477):359–378, 2007.

[32] Hideo Hirose and Liangliang Wang. Prediction of infectious disease spread using twit-ter: A case of influenza. In *Proceedings of the 55th International Symposium on Parallel Architectures, Algorithms and Programming (PAAP)*, pages 100–105. IEEE, 2012.

[33] Sepp Hochreiter and Jürgen Schmidhuber. Long short-term memory. *Neural Compu-tation*, 9(8):1735–1780, 1997.

[34] Sepp Hochreiter and Jürgen Schmidhuber. Long short-term memory. *Neural Compu-tation*, 9(8):1735–1780, 1997.

[35] Nicolas Hoertel, Martin Blachier, Carlos Blanco, Mark Olfson, Marc Massetti, Ma-rina Sánchez Rico, Frédéric Limosin, and Henri Leleu. A stochastic agent-based model of the sars-cov-2 epidemic in france. *Nature Medicine*, 26(9):1417–1421, 2020.

[36] Ting Hua, Chandan K Reddy, Lei Zhang, Lijing Wang, Liang Zhao, Chang-Tien Lu, and Naren Ramakrishnan. Social media based simulation models for understanding disease dynamics. In *Proceedings of the Twenty-Seventh International Joint Conference on Artificial Intelligence, IJCAI-18*, pages 3797–3804. International Joint Conferences on Artificial Intelligence Organization, 7, 2018.

[37] Sasikiran Kandula, Daniel Hsu, and Jeffrey Shaman. Subregional nowcasts of seasonal influenza using search trends. *Journal of Medical Internet Research*, 19(11):e370, 2017.

[38] Amol Kapoor, Xue Ben, Luyang Liu, Bryan Perozzi, Matt Barnes, Martin Blais, and Shawn O'Banion. Examining covid-19 forecasting using spatio-temporal graph neural networks. *arXiv preprint arXiv:2007.03113*, 2020.

[39] Matt J Keeling and Pejman Rohani. Introduction to simple epidemic models. In *Modeling Infectious Diseases in Humans and Animals*, pages 15–53. Princeton University Press, 2011.

[40] Manuela Krieck, Johannes Dreesman, Lubomir Otrusina, and Kerstin Denecke. A new age of public health: Identifying disease outbreaks by analyzing tweets. In *Proceedings of Health Web-Science Workshop, ACM Web Science Conference*, 2011.

[41] Yu A Kuznetsov and Carlo Piccardi. Bifurcation analysis of periodic seir and sir epidemic models. *Journal of Mathematical Biology*, 32(2):109–121, 1994.

[42] Alex Lamb, Michael Paul, and Mark Dredze. Separating fact from fear: Tracking flu infections on twitter. In *Proceedings of the 2013 Conference of the North American Chapter of the Association for Computational Linguistics: Human Language Technologies*, pages 789–795, 2013.

[43] Jung Min Lee, Donghoon Choi, Giphil Cho, and Yongkuk Kim. The effect of public health interventions on the spread of influenza among cities. *Journal of Theoretical Biology*, 293:131–142, 2012.

[44] Antonella Lunelli, Andrea Pugliese, and Caterina Rizzo. Epidemic patch models applied to pandemic influenza: Contact matrix, stochasticity, robustness of predictions. *Mathematical Biosciences*, 220(1):24–33, 2009.

[45] Haruka Morita, Sarah Kramer, Alexandra Heaney, Harold Gil, and Jeffrey Shaman. Influenza forecast optimization when using different surveillance data types and geographic scale. *Influenza and Other Respiratory Viruses*, 12(6):755–764, 2018.

[46] John A Nelder and Roger Mead. A simplex method for function minimization. *The Computer Journal*, 7(4):308–313, 1965.

[47] Elaine Nsoesie, Madhav Mararthe, and John Brownstein. Forecasting peaks of seasonal influenza epidemics. *PLoS Currents*, 5, 2013.

[48] Elaine O Nsoesie, Richard J Beckman, Sara Shashaani, Kalyani S Nagaraj, and Madhav V Marathe. A simulation optimization approach to epidemic forecasting. *PloS One*, 8(6):e67164, 2013.

[49] Elaine O Nsoesie, John S Brownstein, Naren Ramakrishnan, and Madhav V Marathe. A systematic review of studies on forecasting the dynamics of influenza outbreaks. *Influenza and Other Respiratory Viruses*, 8(3):309–316, 2014.

[50] Jon Parker and Joshua M Epstein. A Distributed Platform for Global-Scale Agent-Based Models of Disease Transmission. *ACM Trans Model Comput Simul*, 22(1):2, 12 2011.

[51] Michael J Paul, Mark Dredze, and David Broniatowski. Twitter improves influenza forecasting. *PLoS Currents*, 6, 2014.

[52] Fotios Petropoulos and Spyros Makridakis. Forecasting the novel coronavirus covid-19. *PloS One*, 15(3):e0231236, 2020.

[53] Manliura Datilo Philemon, Zuhaimy Ismail, and Jayeola Dare. A review of epidemic forecasting using artificial neural networks. *International Journal of Epidemiologic Research*, 6(3):132–143, 2019.

[54] Jennifer M Radin, Nathan E Wineinger, Eric J Topol, and Steven R Steinhubl. Harnessing wearable device data to improve state-level real-time surveillance of influenza-like illness in the usa: a population-based study. *The Lancet Digital Health*, 2(2):e85–e93, 2020.

[55] Ankit Ramchandani, Chao Fan, and Ali Mostafavi. Deepcovidnet: An interpretable deep learning model for predictive surveillance of covid-19 using heterogeneous features and their interactions. *arXiv preprint arXiv:2008.00115*, 2020.

[56] Prashant Rangarajan, Sandeep K Mody, and Madhav Marathe. Forecasting dengue and influenza incidences using a sparse representation of google trends, electronic health records, and time series data. *PLoS Computational Biology*, 15(11):e1007518, 2019.

[57] Nicholas G. Reich, Logan C. Brooks, Spencer J. Fox, Sasikiran Kandula, Craig J. McGowan, Evan Moore, Dave Osthus, Evan L. Ray, Abhinav Tushar, Teresa K. Yamana, Matthew Biggerstaff, Michael A. Johansson, Roni Rosenfeld, and Jeffrey Shaman. A collaborative multiyear, multimodel assessment of seasonal influenza forecasting in the united states. *Proceedings of the National Academy of Sciences*, 116(8):3146–3154, 2019.

[58] Jürgen Schmidhuber. Deep learning in neural networks: An overview. *Neural Networks*, 61:85–117, 2015.

[59] Sungyong Seo and Yan Liu. Differentiable physics-informed graph networks. *arXiv preprint arXiv:1902.02950*, 2019.

[60] Sungyong Seo, Chuizheng Meng, and Yan Liu. Physics-aware difference graph networks for sparsely-observed dynamics. In *International Conference on Learning Representations*, 2019.

[61] Jeffrey Shaman and Alicia Karspeck. Forecasting seasonal outbreaks of influenza. *Proceedings of the National Academy of Sciences*, 2012.

[62] Radina P Soebiyanto, Farida Adimi, and Richard K Kiang. Modeling and predicting seasonal influenza transmission in warm regions using climatological parameters. *PloS One*, 5(3):e9450, 2010.

[63] Robert Tibshirani. Regression shrinkage and selection via the lasso. *Journal of the Royal Statistical Society: Series B (Methodological)*, 58(1):267–288, 1996.

[64] Paul Tseng. Convergence of a block coordinate descent method for nondifferentiable minimization. *Journal of Optimization Theory and Applications*, 109(3):475–494, 2001.

[65] Ashleigh R Tuite, Amy L Greer, Michael Whelan, Anne-Luise Winter, Brenda Lee, Ping Yan, Jianhong Wu, Seyed Moghadas, David Buckeridge, Babak Pourbohloul, et al. Estimated epidemiologic parameters and morbidity associated with pandemic h1n1 influenza. *Canadian Medical Association Journal*, 182(2):131–136, 2010.

[66] Willem G Van Panhuis, Sangwon Hyun, Kayleigh Blaney, Ernesto TA Marques Jr, Giovanini E Coelho, João Bosco Siqueira Jr, Ryan Tibshirani, Jarbas B da Silva Jr, and Roni Rosenfeld. Risk of dengue for tourists and teams during the world cup 2014 in brazil. *PLoS Neglected Tropical Diseases*, 8(7):e3063, 2014.

[67] Srinivasan Venkatramanan, Bryan Lewis, Jiangzhuo Chen, Dave Higdon, Anil Vullikanti, and Madhav Marathe. Using data-driven agent-based models for forecasting emerging infectious diseases. *Epidemics*, 22:43–49, 2018.

[68] Srinivasan Venkatramanan, Adam Sadilek, Arindam Fadikar, Christopher L Barrett, Matthew Biggerstaff, Jiangzhuo Chen, Xerxes Dotiwalla, Paul Eastham, Bryant Gipson, Dave Higdon, et al. Forecasting influenza activity using machine-learned mobility map. *Nature Communications*, 12(1):1–12, 2021.

[69] Siva R Venna, Amirhossein Tavanaei, Raju N Gottumukkala, Vijay V Raghavan, Anthony S Maida, and Stephen Nichols. A novel data-driven model for real-time influenza forecasting. *IEEE Access*, 7:7691–7701, 2019.

[70] Cécile Viboud, Pierre-Yves Boëlle, Fabrice Carrat, Alain-Jacques Valleron, and Antoine Flahault. Prediction of the spread of influenza epidemics by the method of analogues. *American Journal of Epidemiology*, 158(10):996–1006, 2003.

[71] Svitlana Volkova, Ellyn Ayton, Katherine Porterfield, and Courtney D Corley. Forecasting influenza-like illness dynamics for military populations using neural networks and social media. *PloS One*, 12(12):e0188941, 2017.

[72] Oyas Wahyunggoro, Adhistya Erna Permanasari, and Ahmad Chamsudin. Utilization of neural network for disease forecasting. In *59th ISI World Statistics Congress*, pages 549–554. Citeseer, 2013.

[73] Dongdong Wang, Shunpu Zhang, and Liqiang Wang. Deep epidemiological modeling by black-box knowledge distillation: An accurate deep learning model for covid-19. *arXiv preprint arXiv:2101.10280*, 2021.

[74] Lijing Wang, Xue Ben, Aniruddha Adiga, Adam Sadilek, Ashish Tendulkar, Srinivasan Venkatramanan, Anil Vullikanti, Gaurav Aggarwal, Alok Talekar, Jiangzhuo Chen, et al. Using mobility data to understand and forecast covid19 dynamics. *medRxiv*, 2020.

[75] Lijing Wang, Jiangzhuo Chen, and Madhav Marathe. Tdefsi: Theory-guided deep learning-based epidemic forecasting with synthetic information. *ACM Transactions on Spatial Algorithms and Systems (TSAS)*, 6(3):1–39, 2020.

[76] Zheng Wang, Prithwish Chakraborty, Sumiko R Mekaru, John S Brownstein, Jieping Ye, and Naren Ramakrishnan. Dynamic poisson autoregression for influenza-like-illness case count prediction. In *Proceedings of the 21th ACM SIGKDD International Conference on Knowledge Discovery and Data Mining*, pages 1285–1294. ACM, 2015.

[77] Yuexin Wu, Yiming Yang, Hiroshi Nishiura, and Masaya Saitoh. Deep learning for epidemiological predictions. In *The 41st International ACM SIGIR Conference on Research & Development in Information Retrieval*, pages 1085–1088. ACM, 2018.

[78] Zonghan Wu, Shirui Pan, Guodong Long, Jing Jiang, and Chengqi Zhang. Graph wavenet for deep spatial-temporal graph modeling. *arXiv preprint arXiv:1906.00121*, 2019.

[79] Qinneng Xu, Yulia R Gel, L Leticia Ramirez Ramirez, Kusha Nezafati, Qingpeng Zhang, and Kwok-Leung Tsui. Forecasting influenza in hong kong with google search queries and statistical model fusion. *PloS One*, 12(5):e0176690, 2017.

[80] Shihao Yang, Mauricio Santillana, and Samuel C Kou. Accurate estimation of influenza epidemics using google search data via argo. *Proceedings of the National Academy of Sciences*, 112(47):14473–14478, 2015.

[81] Wan Yang, Alicia Karspeck, and Jeffrey Shaman. Comparison of filtering methods for the modeling and retrospective forecasting of influenza epidemics. *PLoS Computational Biology*, 10(4):e1003583, 2014.

[82] Wan Yang, Marc Lipsitch, and Jeffrey Shaman. Inference of seasonal and pandemic influenza transmission dynamics. *Proceedings of the National Academy of Sciences*, 112(9):2723–2728, 2015.

[83] Abdelhafid Zeroual, Fouzi Harrou, Abdelkader Dairi, and Ying Sun. Deep learning methods for forecasting covid-19 time-series data: A comparative study. *Chaos, Solitons & Fractals*, 140:110121, 2020.

[84] Xingyu Zhang, Yuanyuan Liu, Min Yang, Tao Zhang, Alistair A Young, and Xiaosong Li. Comparative study of four time series methods in forecasting typhoid fever incidence in china. *PloS One*, 8(5):e63116, 2013.

[85] Liang Zhao, Jiangzhuo Chen, Feng Chen, Wei Wang, Chang-Tien Lu, and Naren Ramakrishnan. Simnest: Social media nested epidemic simulation via online semi-supervised deep learning. In *2015 IEEE International Conference on Data Mining*, pages 639–648. IEEE, 2015.

[86] Xianglei Zhu, Bofeng Fu, Yaodong Yang, Yu Ma, Jianye Hao, Siqi Chen, Shuang Liu, Tiegang Li, Sen Liu, Weiming Guo, et al. Attention-based recurrent neural network for influenza epidemic prediction. *BMC Bioinformatics*, 20(18):1–10, 2019.

4

Machine Learning and Projection-Based Model Reduction in Hydrology and Geosciences

Mojtaba Forghani, Yizhou Qian, Jonghyun Lee, Matthew Farthing,
Tyler Hesser, Peter K. Kitanidis, and Eric F. Darve

CONTENTS

In this chapter, we review some of the recent advances in machine learning, reduced-order modeling, and physics-based modeling in hydrology and geoscience. We address some of the challenges and how machine learning and reduced-order modeling, by relying on the available data and the known physical processes, can tackle them.

4.1   Challenges in Hydrology and Geoscience

Our world is facing a number of serious challenges, such as an increased rate of energy and water consumption, climate change, and natural hazards [9, 77, 80]. These challenges have led to very complex human-resource dynamics that require, for example, water scientists to consider an interdisciplinary approach that not only includes the water cycle dynamics, but also how it interacts with other subsystems such as bio-geochemistry, climate, vegetation dynamics, soil environments, and socio-economics [74, 75, 80]. The multi-physics and multi-disciplinary nature of these complex problems have created a number of unprecedented

DOI: 10.1201/9781003143376-4

challenges for hydrologists and geoscientists, for which the traditional approaches that are used for modeling physical processes will not work.

Many of the problems in geoscience and hydrology are inherently high-dimensional, either since many parameters are involved in their physical description, or they have a computational domain with many grid points. For instance, turbulent dynamical systems, which are common in climate, ocean, or material science, are typically high-dimensional and prone to having a large number of instabilities and high spatio-temporal variability that require fine-grid resolution of the domain in order to have accurate solutions [60, 67]. The highly heterogeneous nature of the subsurface at multiple scales also can create high-dimensional parameter spaces [18, 36]. Furthermore, the spatial extent of the problems that are studied in geoscience and hydrology are often very large, ranging from kilometers to 10s of kilometers and more, such as in the study of ocean, river or climate dynamics. This consequently leads to a very large number of computational grid points when traditional approaches such as finite difference, finite volume or finite element methods are being used [18]. The complex multi-physics and multi-disciplinary nature of modern hydrology and geoscience problems, as mentioned before, further increases the dimension of these problems. As a result, making fast prediction in these problems becomes computationally expensive and requires time and access to large-scale resources. This has consequently led to a significant interest to develop fast models that have the same level of accuracy as highly resolved models with detailed physics, but at a fraction of the computational cost. This is achievable for a class of problems where the solution can be approximated in a significantly lower-dimensional space.

Another important issue associated with hydrology and geoscience problems is that many of their processes happen in an environment that is inaccessible for direct observation or involves parameters and variables that are not directly measurable. For instance, many processes related to Earth science occur below the Earth's surface and are therefore very difficult to observe [9], e.g., study of seafloor or riverbed dynamics, earthquake, soil science. This has led to an increased attention to inverse problem modeling and inverse problem solvers. That is, the study of the methods that are used to extract the parameters and variables that generate observed quantities through a physical process. Inverse modeling in hydrology and geoscience, in particular, is very challenging because of the need to reconstruct highly detailed fields (3D fine resolution), while contending with limited and noisy experimental data. Such problems have solutions only if we are able to approximate again the solution in a low-dimensional space (in which case limited data may be sufficient to generate useful predictions) and estimate the uncertainty in our models.

Almost all fields of science and engineering have faced a large, and continuously growing, influx of data in recent decades due to advances in sensor and sensing technology. Since many problems in hydrology and geoscience, as mentioned previously, can be formulated as inverse problems, which rely on experimental and field observations, the progress in these fields has been particularly noticeable. The data gathered from satellites such as the Sentinel, Landsat, MODIS, as well as miniaturized satellites, inter-ferometric synthetic aperture radars, monitoring networks such as pressure sensors in water infrastructure, unmanned aerial vehicles (UAVs), and camera rain gauges [2, 61, 74], if used properly, can help us better understand the complex and multi-scale nature of physical and environmental processes. The main challenge, however, is that the abundance of observations in inverse modeling also result in expensive simulations because of the large amount of data that need to be assimilated. Therefore, having fast solvers of the inverse problems that can incorporate large amount of (potentially noisy) data efficiently into their structure is very essential.

In the following, we focus on how model reduction can be used to address the issues discussed above. Doing so effectively relies on two core capabilities: the ability to approximate complex multi-physics fields with a reduced-dimensional space (not necessarily a linear subspace) and provide accurate uncertainty estimates. We begin in the next section with a discussion of classical and existing reduced-order model (ROM) techniques that are based largely on linear projection methods. We then show how deep learning (DL)-based ROMs provide exciting new directions for ROMs. These methods allow developing new projection operators that are non-linear and can significantly extend the validity of traditional linear models used in ROMs. In addition, we show how techniques such as generative deep neural networks (DNNs) allow modeling complex probability distributions that extend classical models like Gaussian processes and Kriging.

4.2   Reduced-Order Modeling and Deep Learning

Reduced-order models (ROMs) are computationally efficient mathematical models that are capable of effectively approximating the main characteristics of full-order models, by replacing them with surrogates with significantly reduced dimension [19, 63]. Furthermore, they can be used to overcome the computational burden of multi-query tasks, such as uncertainty quantification (UQ), parameter estimation, risk assessment, sensitivity analysis, and model-based optimization, that are governed by large-scale partial differential equations (PDEs) [7, 18, 19]. In this section, we discuss some of the recent works in hydrology and geoscience that have attempted to tackle the challenges mentioned in Section 4.1, mostly due to existence of high-dimensional, computationally expensive, models, using ROMs.

To begin, Figure 4.1 shows a sketch of different ROM architectures and their classifications. Figure 4.1a shows a sketch of the ROM, consisting of, first, reducing the dimension of the input from high-fidelity model (the "dimension reduction" block), then a process to describe the dynamics of the low-dimensional model – temporal and/or parametric (the "low-dimensional model" block), and finally, augmenting the output of the low-dimensional model back to the space of the output of the high-fidelity model (the "dimension expansion" block). The architecture shown in Figure 4.1a is used both in the offline (training/learning) and online (prediction) stages of ROM. The offline stage (the computationally expensive stage) constitutes construction of the model describing the ROM dynamics, obtained from the high-fidelity solver, while the online stage (the computationally cheap stage) is used for prediction of new solutions for new set of parameters (inputs).

The ROMs can be categorized both based on the technique that they use to reduce the dimension of the input from the high-fidelity solver (Figure 4.1b, red), as well as the model that they use to describe the dynamics of the low-dimensional system (Figure 4.1c, blue). The dimension reduction process (Figure 4.1b) can be either linear, explained in further detail in Section 4.2.1, or non-linear (DL-based), explained in Section 4.2.2.2. The model of the low-dimensional system (Figure 4.1c, blue), similar to the categorization of dimension reduction techniques, can be either DL- or non-DL-based. Furthermore, either of these classes can be intrusive or non-intrusive, as explained briefly below: The training of the ROM parameters (the offline stage) typically requires extracting a collection of solutions obtained from the high-fidelity model, also known as snapshots, for different set of inputs. The low-dimensional models that require only snapshots to be trained are referred to as non-intrusive. On the contrary, in intrusive methods, the training of the model also requires access to the numerical solver of the differential equations describing the physics of the system under study, in order to form a reduced-order system of equations.

In Section 4.2.1, we review recent works that have used linear projection-based ROMs to solve the issues mentioned in Section 4.1, using both intrusive and non-intrusive models. In Section 4.2.2, we present some recent works that have used DL in their ROM to improve the result of linear projection-based methods, either in conjunction with linear dimension reduction techniques, or as a non-linear alternative to linear dimension reduction methods, in both intrusive and non-intrusive manner.

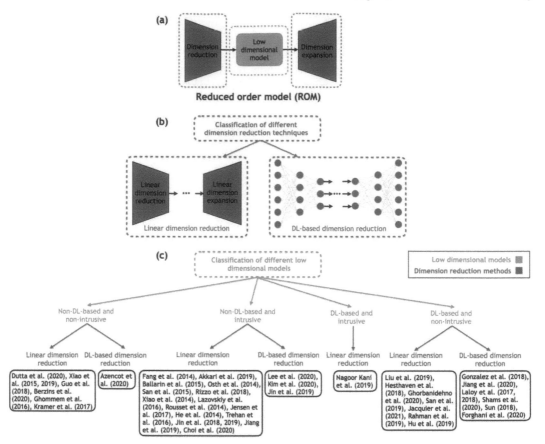

FIGURE 4.1
The ROMs (a) can be classified based on the methods being used to reduce the dimension of the high-fidelity solver (b, red), such as linear versus non-linear (DL-based) dimension reduction techniques, or based on the models being used to describe the dynamics of the low-order system (c, blue). The latter can be categorized based on DL- versus non-DL-based techniques, or intrusive versus non-intrusive techniques. DL: deep learning.

4.2.1   Linear Projection-Based Reduced-Order Modeling

Linear projection-based ROMs work in such a way that the high-dimensional complex dynamical systems will be represented with lower-dimensional surrogates that are based on linear combination of a small number of basis vectors, while keeping the solution quality within the acceptable range, thus trading in computational cost for a controlled loss of accuracy [19, 24, 67]. The reduced bases are a set of global basis functions that are able to approximate the dynamics of the high-fidelity model [19]. While there are wide array of reduced basis (RB) methods that have been proposed for parametric PDEs [18, 66], proper orthogonal decomposition (POD) and dynamic mode decomposition (DMD) are two particularly common mode decomposition approaches in linear projection-based ROMs for non-linear PDEs.

POD, also known as the principal component analysis (PCA) in other contexts, is a mathematical technique that is employed to extract the dominant statistical characteristics of a system by identifying its most energetic modes [67]. POD works via approximating the dynamics of a computationally expensive system of equations by finding its reduced-order orthogonal basis via minimization of the projection error [24]. The most energetic modes are kept to generate the reduced-order system, while the other modes are truncated [67]. DMD is another approach for mode decomposition which has emerged as an alternative to POD for the reduction of the system size, in particular, for transient, non-linear systems [11, 47]. The DMD is based on constructing linear approximations of the dynamics in the low-order model and generates modes based on their dynamics rather than just energy content. In other words, DMD spatial modes have an associated frequency and temporal dynamics based on the growth and decay of the approximated system [47, 48].

In the online stage of linear projection-based ROMs, a linear combination of the reduced-order basis modes is used in order to approximate the correct solution (the high-fidelity numerical solution) for a new set of system parameters [19]. This process can be either intrusive or non-intrusive, as it was mentioned previously. In the intrusive approach, the expansion coefficients are determined by the solution of a reduced-order system of equations, typically obtained from a Galerkin-type projection [58]. However, instability and loss of efficiency in the presence of non-linear differential equations are two important issues present in these types of projections [19]. In Section 4.2.1.1, we review some of the recent works that have used intrusive ROMs, including both Galerkin projection-based methods, as well as other techniques, collectively referred to as hyper-reduction methods, that tackle the instability and low accuracy of Galerkin-based approaches. In the second category of the linear projection-based ROMs, the non-intrusive methods, instead of solving a reduced-order system of equations, the expansion coefficients for the reduced-order solution are obtained via interpolation on the space of a reduced basis extracted from the snapshot data [19]. An important advantage of the non-intrusive methods is that they do not require modification of the source code. However, since they primarily rely on the snapshot data (instead of the governing equations), analyzing the problem-dependent properties of the solutions is generally more difficult in these types of ROMs. In Section 4.2.1.2, we review some of the recent works that have used non-intrusive ROMs in hydrology and geoscience applications.

4.2.1.1 Intrusive

A number of recent works have used *POD-Galerkin-based projections* in order to describe the dynamics of the reduced-order system, which is the most commonly used approach in intrusive linear projection-based ROMs. For instance, Fang et al. [23] used this approach to model air pollution dynamics. They validated their ROM for a range of 2D and 3D urban street canyon flow problems. In particular, they showed that the accuracy of the POD-based solutions against the solution of the high-fidelity model is maintained, where fine details of the air flows are captured, at a significantly lower computational cost. They also report that the size of the ROM is reduced by factors up to 2,400 in comparison to the high-fidelity model, while the CPU time is reduced by up to 98%.

Some recent works have proposed approaches that rely on Galerkin-based projections. However, they are equipped with techniques that aim to address the stability issues present in these methods. Akkari et al. [1] used priori enrichment of the POD modes, in a Galerkin projection-based setup, via dissipative modes associated with the gradient of the flow velocity fields, in order to tackle the stability issues present in ROMs of turbulent and incompressible Navier–Stokes equations. They report that their technique is capable of recovering very large-scale features for very long integration times in high Reynolds number flows ($Re = 45,000$). They also report speed-up of up to 10^8 times. Ballarin et al. [5] proposed a stable POD-Galerkin approximation for parameterized steady incompressible Navier–Stokes equations with low Reynolds number. Their stabilization works by adding supremizer solutions that aims at fulfilling an inf-sup condition, to the reduced velocity space. The work of Osth et al. [65] studied stabilization of the solution of turbulent flows, by analyzing a hierarchy of eddy-viscosity terms in POD-Galerkin model that account for unresolved fluctuation energy. Their method was validated on the flow around a vehicle-like bluff body.

Another class of recent works have focused on the snapshots that POD bases are constructed from. San et al. [70] proposed the principal interval decomposition (PID) approach, which works by optimizing the lengths of the time windows over which the POD is performed, and validated their ROM on the unsteady Buoyancy-driven flow. The performance of the Galerkin-based POD model with and without using the PID approach was investigated in their work. Specifically, they compared the accuracy of PID with different numbers of POD basis functions and different numbers of principal intervals (time windows), with that of Galerkin-based POD without PID. They report that the PID approach provides a significant improvement in accuracy over the standard Galerkin-POD ROM. Rizzo et al. [68] proposed an approach, referred to as Snapshot Splitting Technique (SST), which allows enriching the dimension of the POD subspace and damping the temporal increase of the modeling error, and validated their approach on the study of transport dynamics, modeled through the advection-dispersion equation. They report better performance of POD combined with SST compared to POD alone.

Intrusive, projection-based ROMs are relatively straightforward for linear problems. However, when the system is non-linear this is not the case, since direct evaluation of non-linear operators requires projection of the solution to the high-dimensional space and so destroys any online computational speedup. To address this issue, a class of techniques, commonly referred to as hyper-reduction have been introduced [8, 51]. A range of hyper-reduction methods have been proposed over the last decade [14,16,64,79], with the empirical interpolation method (EIM) [6] and its discrete counterpart, **discrete empirical interpolation method (DEIM)** [81], being perhaps the best known. DEIM, for one, enforces the reduced approximation to interpolate the original non-linear function at a specified number of sampling points, selected such that they minimize the distance between the recovered reduced basis coefficients and the optimal coefficients (obtained by projecting the non-linear snapshots onto a reduced-order subspace) [59,81]. Variations of DEIM have also appeared [64]. For example, Xiao et al. [81] used a hybrid approach for the Navier–Stokes equations. Namely, their approach applied a quadratic expansion to provide a first approximation of the non-linear operator of the equation, and then used DEIM as a corrector to improve its representation. They validated their technique by solving the incompressible Navier–Stokes equations for simulating a flow past a cylinder and gyre problems and reported significant improvement in the solution's accuracy at a very low computational cost. In the context of water resources problems, Lozovskiy et al. [59] used both DEIM and gappy POD [79] for approximation of the shallow water equations (SWE) in a stabilized finite element context. They evaluated the performance of the methods, compared to simple Galerkin-based POD, by considering their accuracy, robustness, and speed for dambreak and riverine flow problems. In this case, gappy POD, which is based on interpolation rather than collocation at sampling points, offered better robustness and efficiency than a traditional DEIM approximation for cases with shocks and strong advection [59].

Trajectory piecewise linearization (TPWL) is another hyper-reduction technique that has been used in combination with POD as a ROM strategy [69]. TPWL represents the new solutions in terms of linearizations around previously simulated (and saved) training solutions. The linearized representation is projected onto a low-dimensional space using a projection matrix constructed through the POD of solution snapshots that are generated in the training phase [69]. Rousset et al. [69] implemented a ROM based on TPWL method in which linearized representation is projected onto a low-dimensional space, with the projection matrix constructed through POD of solution snapshots, referred to as POD-TPWL. They validated their approach on primary production of oil driven by downhole heaters and a simplified model for steam-assisted gravity drainage, where water and steam are treated as a single effective phase. They reported over two orders of magnitude computational speedup for the cases considered. Jensen et al. [35] used POD-TPWL as a ROM for simulation runs of reservoir management. They report that POD-TPWL procedure has reasonable accuracy and a high degree of speedup compared to conventional approaches. POD-TPWL and its derivatives such as trajectory piecewise quadratic approximation (POD-TPWQ) have also been used to model subsurface flows [30, 78], CO_2 storage operations [38], and coupled flow-geomechanics problems [39].

Another choice in the design of a projection-based ROM is the test space onto which the high-dimensional system is projected. While Galerkin projection is by far the most common [51], the choice is less clear when the problem is non-linear [12, 13, 22]. **Gauss–Newton with approximated tensors (GNAT)** is one notable Petrov-Galerkin approach, where the test space arises from minimization of the high-dimensional residual evaluated over the low-dimensional solution space [14]. The application of GNAT in a geoscience context can be found in Jiang et al. [37], which used a POD-based GNAT for oil-water reservoir simulation. Their validation included both the evaluation of the GNAT performance on a 2D model, in which a number of different GNAT parameter combinations are considered, as well as a comparison of the method with the POD-TPWL approach. They further considered around 1,500 test cases, with varying levels of perturbation relative to training cases and report that GNAT is only slightly more accurate than POD-TPWL for cases with small perturbation, but its accuracy increases for larger perturbations. They also demonstrate the successful application of GNAT to a more realistic 3D model. Other variations of GNAT, such as the solution-based non-linear subspace (GNAT-SNS) have also been used recently [17], in order to decrease the computational cost of GNAT alone, at no loss of accuracy. Choi et al. [17] reported 20–100 times speedup of offline computational time using GNAT-SNS compared to GNAT, on different fluid flow problems.

Another approach to build intrusive models was proposed by Xu and Darve [33, 56, 85] using the ADCME (Automatic Differentiation for Computational and Mathematical Engineering) framework. ADCME is a Julia and Python library, powered by TensorFlow, which allows embedding and optimizing deep neural networks (DNNs) in complex numerical differential equation solvers (finite-element, finite-difference, etc.). These DNNs can be used to create coarse-grained models (coarse-grid resolution, sub-grid-scale models, homogenized models, etc.). They can be optimized based on noisy indirect observations of the solution at sparse locations in time and space.

4.2.1.2 Non-Intrusive

In this section, we discuss non-intrusive linear projection-based ROMs. The main advantage of non-intrusive ROMs, compared to intrusive ROMs, is that these methods do not require modifications to the source code describing the physical model, and consequently, are very beneficial when the source code is not available or easily modifiable [19]. Moreover, one of the reasons for the instability and the loss of efficiency that arise when using intrusive Galerkin-based ROMs in complex non-linear problems, is that some of the intrinsic structures present in the high-fidelity model may be lost during its transformation to low-order differential equations; non-intrusive linear ROMs can tackle these issues by avoiding any modification of the high-fidelity model [19].

Radial basis functions (RBF) is one interpolation technique, which have been used in a number of recent works in conjunction with POD [83]. For example, Dutta et al. [19] used POD-RBF to construct an efficient ROM for time-dependent problems arising in large-scale environmental flow applications. The performance of their POD-RBF is compared with a traditional non-linear Galerkin POD method by evaluating the accuracy and the robustness of the algorithms on the riverine flow problems, and higher accuracy and efficiency of

POD-RBF is verified in their test problems. Xiao et al. [82] presented a RBF-based ROM for the Navier–Stokes equations. They report that their approach avoids the stability problem of POD-Galerkin and validate the POD-RBF approach on numerical examples of a lock exchange problem and a flow past a cylinder problem using unstructured adaptive finite element ocean model. Their results show that CPU times were reduced by several orders of magnitude with negligible loss of accuracy.

Another non-intrusive approach, proposed previously in the context of non-linear structural analysis [29], combines POD with **Gaussian process regression (GPR)**, in which the GPR is used to approximate the projection coefficients. Similarly, Xiao et al. [84] developed a fast-running non-intrusive ROM for predicting the turbulent air flows found within an urban environment using POD-GPR. They employed a large eddy simulation (LES) model and solved the resulting computational model on unstructured meshes. They report that their POD-GPR was six orders of magnitude faster than the high-fidelity LES model, with insignificant loss of accuracy. Berzins et al. [10] presented a non-intrusive reduced basis method for unsteady non-linear parameterized PDE based on POD-GPR and compared it to DNNs. Their approach is validated both on the steady and time-dependent driven cavity viscous flows, as well as the flow of plastic melt inside a cross-section of a co-rotating twin-screw extruder, which is classified as a time- and temperature-dependent flow on a moving domain. They report an error of less than 3% for the predicted velocity, pressure, and temperature distributions compared to the high-fidelity model.

The **dynamic mode decomposition (DMD)** approach, as stated previously, is an alternative to using POD for finding the reduced basis. DMD can be classified as a non-intrusive approach, and it has been used in a number of recent works as an effective ROM. For example, Ghommem et al. [25] applied both an intrusive and a non-intrusive ROM in order to speed up simulations of two-phase flows in heterogeneous porous media, in the context of subsurface flow problem. In their non-intrusive approach, they used DMD, while their intrusive approach was based on POD-DEIM. They showed the effectiveness of both approaches on a benchmark permeability field problem containing two-phase flow, with DMD having the advantage of being non-intrusive and thus not requiring access to the simulation code of the physical process. Kramer et al. [47] presented a sparse sensing framework based on DMD to identify flow regimes and bifurcations in large-scale thermo-fluid systems. In their work, they applied DMD to a Direct Numerical Simulation (DNS) dataset of a 2D laterally heated cavity, where the resulting flow solutions can be divided into several regimes, ranging from steady to chaotic flow. The DMD modes and eigenvalues are expected to capture the main temporal and spatial scales in the dynamics of different regimes. In their experiments, the DMD eigenvalues allowed them to employ a short time-series of data from sensors, in order to robustly classify flow regimes, even if significant measurement noise exist in the measurement.

4.2.2   Deep Learning-Based Reduced-Order Modeling

While the hyper-reduction techniques mentioned in Section 4.2.1, as well as non-intrusive techniques, have been successful in tackling some of the issues associated with simple Galerkin-based POD, such as the low accuracy of ROMs of non-linear systems and instability of the solution, their performance may be expected to deteriorate as the system size and its complexity increase, since despite their various refinements on Galerkin POD, they build upon projection onto a linear subspace. DL, on the other hand, has emerged as a very powerful tool in many science and engineering fields for extracting complex and non-linear patterns from data, which traditional methods fail to capture. As discussed in Section 4.1 and Section 4.2.1, the success of ROMs greatly depends on their power to extract complex features from the data. This can be both their ability to project the high-fidelity solutions onto a very descriptive reduced-order representation, as well as their ability to describe the dynamics of the reduced-order system with high accuracy. In other words, DL can help to increase the efficiency and accuracy of ROMs, both through improving the dynamics of the reduced-order system, as well as replacing the linear projection with non-linear projections.

In this section, we review some of the recent works in hydrology and geoscience that have used DL in an attempt to create high-performance ROMs by either improving their dimension reduction capability, or improving the descriptive power of the dynamics of the reduced-order system. The works mentioned in this section address both surrogates for forward modeling and inverse problems. Furthermore, the DL architectures that are reviewed here are used both as the sole solver of the problem (the ROM), as well as in conjunction with other methods, some of which have been presented in Section 4.2.1 (e.g., POD). In Section 4.2.2.1, we review some of the works that have used DL combined with linear dimension reduction techniques, such as POD, as ROMs. In Section 4.2.2.2, we discuss DL-based approaches that use non-linear dimension reduction techniques in them. These methods can be intrusive, be fully based on DL, or combined with other linear or non-linear techniques that describe the evolution of the dynamics of the reduced-order system.

4.2.2.1 Linear Projection Using Deep Learning

Linear projection- and DL-based ROMs use linear dimension reduction techniques, such as POD, in combination with DL, where DL describes the dynamics of the reduced-order system (the coefficients of the reduced-order bases). Some of the recent works have combined DNNs with POD-based ROMs to improve efficiency and accuracy of using POD without DL. For example, Liu et al. [57] developed a low-dimensional parameterization based on **PCA (i.e., POD) and convolutional neural network (CNN-PCA)** to represent complex geological models. Their approach includes post-processing a PCA model to better honor complex geological features. Furthermore, a regularization involving a set of metrics for multi-point statistics is introduced in their approach. They report that data assimilation and significant uncertainty reduction can be achieved for existing wells, and physically reasonable predictions obtained for new wells. They also applied the CNN-PCA method to a complex non-stationary bimodal deltaic fan system and report high-quality realizations generated by CNN-PCA for this test case.

In another example, Hesthaven et al. [31] combined POD with DNNs as a non-intrusive ROM method for parameterized steady-state PDEs. Their method is validated on driven-cavity viscous flows, modeled through the steady incompressible Navier–Stokes equations. They also demonstrate, through several test cases, the accuracy of the **POD-NN** method and its substantial speed-up, enabled at the online stage, compared to traditional ROM strategies. Ghorbanidehno et al. [26] also developed a DL-based framework, referred to as PCA-DNN (similar to POD-NN) for riverine problems that can be trained using only a few river profiles in a computationally efficient way. Their proposed method combines a fully connected DNN with PCA to image riverbed topography using depth-averaged flow velocity observations. Their method is presented and applied to three riverine bathymetry identification problems. They report that the proposed method achieves satisfactory performance in bathymetry estimation, in terms of the prediction quality, robustness, and computational cost, while requiring a relatively small number of training samples. Similar POD-NN ROMs have also been used to model non-linear wave-propagation problem in the context of transient flows [71].

In terms of UQ, Jacquier et al. [34] used POD-NN as part of a collection of methods in the context of flood prediction. In particular, they combined POD-NN with deep ensembles and variational inference-based Bayesian neural networks, and validated them on flooding predictions in a river in the Montreal, Quebec, Canada metropolitan area. Their setup involves a set of input parameters, with a potentially noisy distribution, and accumulates the simulation data resulting from these parameters. Their purpose is to build a non-intrusive ROM that is "able to know when it does not know." Their model attempts to generate probabilistic flooding maps, which are aware of the model uncertainty. They report that the model's predictions for flooded area are broader and safer than methods that are based on regular uncertainty-uninformed surrogate models. They also presented results on the study of the time-dependent and highly non-linear case of a dam break. They show that both the ensembles and the Bayesian approach lead to reliable results for multiple smooth physical solutions, providing the correct warning when going out-of-distribution.

The **recurrent neural network (RNN)** is another widely used neural network architecture in ROMs. It is designed to operate on input information as well as previously stored observations to predict the dependencies among the temporal data sequences [67]. The connections between RNN nodes form a directed graph along a temporal sequence, allowing them to exhibit temporal dynamic behavior, thus, they are the "time series version" of DNNs. The most common kind of recurrent layers is the LSTM (long short term memory), which chooses how much past information should flow through the model. RNN or its derivatives such as the LSTM have been used in recent works to model flow problems. For example, Nagoor Kani et al. [63] used deep residual RNN (DR-DNN) in combination with POD and DEIM, in order to reduce the computational complexity associated with high-fidelity numerical simulations of the subsurface multi-phase flow problems. They also used POD to construct an optimal set of RBFs and employ DEIM to evaluate the non-linear terms, independent of the full-order model size. They show in their work that DR-RNN, combined with POD-DEIM, provides an accurate and stable ROM with a fixed computational budget that is much less than the computational cost of standard Galerkin-based POD ROM combined with DEIM for non-linear dynamical systems.

Rahman et al. [67] presented a ROM framework for large-scale quasi-stationary systems that uses LSTM. Their framework exploits the time series prediction capability of LSTM such that, in the training phase, the LSTM is trained on the modal coefficients extracted from the high-resolution data snapshots using POD, and in the testing phase, the trained model predicts the modal coefficients for the total time recursively, based on the initial time history. They consider a 2D quasi-geostrophic ocean circulation model for validation purposes. They illustrate that the conventional Galerkin projection-based POD of such systems requires a high number of POD modes to obtain stable flow physics. In addition, they show that Galerkin-based POD does not capture the intermittent bursts appearing in the dynamics of the first few most energetic modes. However, their proposed LSTM-ROM approach yields a stable solution even for a small number of POD modes and is able to capture the quasi-periodic intermittent bursts accurately. Hu et al. [32] used a similar LSTM-ROM framework to represent the spatio-temporal distribution of floods. The performance of the framework is evaluated using the Okushiri tsunami as a test case. The results obtained from the LSTM-ROM were compared with those from the full model (Fluidity). They report that the results from the full model and LSTM-ROM are in a good agreement, while the CPU cost using the LSTM-ROM is decreased by three orders of magnitude compared to full model simulations. Their results indicate that the use of LSTM-ROM can provide the flood prediction in seconds, enabling us to provide real-time predictions and inform the public in a timely manner.

4.2.2.2 Non-Linear Projection Using Deep Learning

Linear projection-based ROMs, such as the ones reviewed in Sections 4.2.1 and 4.2.2.1, can tackle the challenges that we have mentioned in Section 4.1. In particular, the computational speed-up of multi-dimensional systems, as a result of ROMs, should make it easier to run these systems repeatedly with different parameter values as part of an inverse problem framework, optimization, or UQ process. Similarly, since ROMs replace high-dimensional systems with significantly smaller ones, they enable simulations of much larger systems such as ocean, climate, or river in these contexts. Furthermore, methods such as POD that attempt to find the directions in data that account for most of their representative dynamics, allow hydrologists and geoscientists to extract meaningful patterns from the large volume of data available to the community. However, since ROMs of large-scale (in particular, noisy) systems are comparatively difficult due to instabilities, in many cases, a very large number of POD modes is required to capture their dynamics, which limits the ROM capability to efficiently represent a system [67]. Furthermore, in general, POD-based ROMs do not preserve the stability properties of the corresponding full-order model, and current POD stabilization techniques are neither cost-effective or guarantee stability of the extracted ROMs [63]. In this section, we discuss some of the recent works that have used DL, as a non-linear dimension reduction technique, to tackle these issues, which has led to more efficient and accurate ROMs in several cases.

Autoencoders (AEs) are a class of DNNs that are primarily used for non-linear dimension reduction. The AE architecture consists of two networks in series; the encoder, which projects the high-dimensional input, non-linearly, onto a low-dimensional space (the latent space), and the decoder, which augments the latent space back to the original high-dimensional data [24]. Figure 4.2(a) shows an example of an AE that projects a ten-dimensional input to a three-dimensional latent space. Autoencoders (AE) have achieved great performance in data compression, in particular, by taking advantage of the power of CNNs for detecting local spatial patterns. Figure 4.2(b) shows an encoder with CNN. Specifically, the figure shows four filters being applied to a 2D image on the left (the convolutional layer), followed by a layer that reduces the size of the images of its previous layer (the max-pooling layer), followed by two dense fully connected (FC) layers (right), the last of which is the latent space. AE has been used in conjunction with other DL methods as non-linear ROMs. For instance, Gonzalez et al. [27] proposed a DL-based ROM with application to viscous and lid-driven cavity flow, where they construct a modular model consisting of a deep convolutional AE and a modified LSTM network. The deep convolutional AE returns a low-dimensional representation in terms of coordinates on some expressive non-linear data-supporting manifold. The dynamics on this manifold are then modeled by

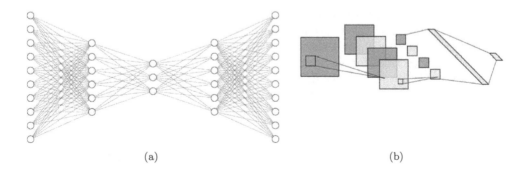

(a)   (b)

FIGURE 4.2
(a) An example of an AE architecture that projects a ten-dimensional high-fidelity model to a three-dimensional latent space and (b) an example of a convolutional encoder with four filters, a max-pool layer, and two FC layers.

the modified LSTM network in a computationally efficient manner. They tested their model on three illustrative examples, each highlighting the model's performance in prediction tasks for fluid systems with large parameter-variations and its stability in long-term prediction.

Some recent works have used AE as a non-linear dimension reduction technique in Galerkin-based projection setups. Lee et al. [55] proposed a framework for projecting dynamical systems onto non-linear manifolds using minimum-residual formulations at the time-continuous and time-discrete levels, leading to manifold Galerkin projection and manifold least-squares Petrov–Galerkin (LSPG) projection, respectively. Specifically, they propose a computationally practical approach for computing the non-linear manifold, which is based on a convolutional AE. They demonstrated the ability of the method to significantly outperform even the optimal linear-subspace ROM on a number of advection-dominated problems, demonstrating the method's ability to overcome the limitations of linear subspaces. In a similar vein, Kim et al. [44] developed a fast physics-informed DL-based ROM, namely non-linear manifold ROM (NM-ROM), which replaces the convolutional AE proposed in [55], with a shallow masked AE. A masked AE has an AE-like structure. However, some of its weights are forced to be zero (a sparse AE) in order to reflect the local connectivity, such as the Laplacian operator approximated by the central difference scheme in finite difference method [44]. They report that the choice of the shallow masked AE over the deep convolutional AE leads to a more efficient hyper-reduction technique. Their numerical results on representative advection-dominated flows show that by taking advantage of the sparsity that exists in the masked AE, they can achieve speedup of 2.6–11.7 for different fluid flow problems compared to unmasked AE.

A number of works have combined AE, as a non-linear dimension technique, with linear models that describe evolution of the dynamics of the low-dimensional system [20]. Azencot et al. [4] introduced a class of physics-based methods related to Koopman theory, offering an alternative for processing non-linear dynamical systems. In their work, they propose a consistent Koopman AE model that leverages the forward and backward dynamics. Their approach uses AE to find a low-dimensional representation of the system, and then uses linear operator on the reduced-dimension variables to describe the evolution of the dynamics of the system over time. They evaluate the method on a range of high-dimensional and short-term-dependent problems, where it achieves accurate estimates for significant prediction horizons, while also being robust to noise. Jin et al. [40] proposed a similar ROM based on an embed-to-control (E2C) framework that includes an AE as a non-linear dimension reduction technique and a linear transition model, which approximates the evolution of the system states in the low-dimension space. In addition, they also introduce a physics-based loss function that penalizes predictions that are inconsistent with the physical equations. The E2C-ROM is applied to oil-water flow in a heterogeneous reservoir, with flow driven by nine wells operating under time-varying control specifications. They report online computations speedup of three orders of magnitude relative to full-order simulations. Furthermore, they report accurate predictions for global saturation and pressure fields.

The *variational autoencoder (VAE)* is a type of AE that projects complex spatial models to a low-dimensional latent space, parameterized with simple probability density functions (e.g., Gaussian) [36]. The architecture of VAE is similar to AE, except its latent space consists of two parallel layers that provide the mean and variance of a multivariate Gaussian distribution, from which the variable that is fed into the decoder is sampled. This probabilistic structure imposes a strong regularization effect on the VAE architecture that leads to better generalization. VAE has been used in recent works for low-dimensional representation of geological patterns. Specifically, Jiang et al [36] used VAE in conjunction with stochastic gradient-based inversion methods to perform history matching on reservoir model. They present history matching results for both when the training data is based on a single as well as multiple geologic scenarios, leading to diverse features in the training data. Their comparison shows better performance of VAE compared to PCA. They report that the performance difference between the two methods becomes more significant when multiple geologic scenarios are present. Laloy et al. [50] used VAE to construct a parametric low-dimensional model of complex binary geological media. They found that their approach outperforms the PCA for unconditional geostatistical simulation of a channelized prior model. They also report achieving compression ratios of 200–500. Probabilistic inversions of 2D steady-state and 3D transient hydraulic tomography data is also used to demonstrate their inversion. For the 2D case study, they observe superior performance of VAE compared to the state-of-the-art sequential geostatistical resampling (SGR). They also report encouraging results for their 3D case study.

Generative adversarial neural networks (GANs) are a class of ROMs that have become increasingly popular in DL in recent years for low-dimensional representation of complex distributions [28]. GANs are deep networks that can be trained to stochastically generate geoscience data or natural images with similar properties as a training data set and have been tested in several hydrological applications [43, 49, 62, 73, 76]. GANs are composed of two separate neural networks, the generator and the discriminator; the generative network learns how to fool the discriminator, while the discriminator becomes better at telling the training (real) and fake data apart [73] so that an explicit loss function is not needed for training. The strength of GANs is in their ability to generate realistic examples from a latent space by achieving a (Nash) equilibrium between the discriminator and the generator, thereby, improving the network's ability to learn and produce complex spatial and temporal patterns, even in the presence of data scarcity. Therefore, GANs can be implemented to construct low-dimensional space to construct ROMs while several challenges such as vanishing gradients, mode collapse, and convergence need to be addressed during the training of GANs [3]. Example applications include Laloy et al. [49] who introduced and evaluate a training-image-based inversion approach for complex geologic media using the latent space from GANs instead of the original pixel-based parameter space. While the computation time for simulating subsurface flow and transport is still expensive since they do not use ROM simulators, generating posterior geological realizations and corresponding uncertainty quantification can be accelerated. Sun [76] presented in their study a state-parameter identification GAN (SPID-GAN) for simultaneously learning bidirectional mappings between a high-dimensional parameter space and the corresponding model state space with application to subsurface models. Approaches combined with GANs have important implications for problems that requires sampling from a high-dimensional distribution in a computationally efficient manner.

4.3 Application Example: Shallow Water Equations

Section 4.2 reviews a broad array of projection-based ROM techniques that have various strengths and weaknesses. Our ultimate goal in developing ROMs is to improve the speed and accuracy of engineering and scientific analyses. In the following, we consider a specific example, namely, the study of riverine dynamics, to show how ROMs can be integrated into both inverse problems and fast prediction in non-linear systems with indirect observations.

To be more specific, two important problems that arise when studying riverine dynamics are (a), the estimation of the riverbed profile, also known as the bathymetry, from indirect observations (e.g., flow velocity profiles) through an inverse problem framework, and (b), fast prediction of riverine flow velocities as BCs and other forcing conditions change. Because of the large scale of the riverine dynamic problems (e.g., riverine reaches of 10s of kilometers long), these problems are typically computationally expensive, and thus, can benefit significantly from ROMs.

In Section 4.3.1, we discuss the inverse problem arising in the context of the shallow water equations. In particular, in Section 4.3.1.1, we discuss the result of estimating the bathymetry of the Savannah river, GA, USA, from the observation of the riverine flow velocity (the inverse problem), using a ROM referred to as the principal component geostatistical approach (PCGA) [46, 52, 53] – a non-DL-based method. In Section 4.3.1.2, we solve the same inverse problem using a DL-based method, referred to as PCA-DNN [26], and show superior performance of it compared to the PCGA under the conditions considered. Finally, in Section 4.3.2, we use AE- and VAE-based approaches, equipped with CNN [24], to solve the forward problem (prediction of the river flow velocity given variable BCs) and show their more accurate performance compared to PCA-DNN (applied to the forward problem) and their significantly lower prediction computational cost compared to commonly used numerical solvers.

4.3.1   Inverse Problem

Despite the importance of the riverine bathymetry estimation, as discussed previously, direct high-resolution bathymetric surveys by wading or watercraft mounted multi-beam sonar equipment are rarely performed over long river reaches due to logistical and budget constraints [52]. Instead, various alternative methods have been proposed to infer bathymetry utilizing remote sensing methods such as airborne bathymetric LiDAR systems, or indirect riverine observations such as water surface elevation, and surface velocity measured from GPS drifters or estimated through particle image velocimetry with digital video camera and thermal imagery [24, 52]. Here, the surface velocity measurement is used to estimate the bathymetry. The choice of surface velocity measurement is motivated by: (1) in comparison to in-situ observations or bathymetric LiDar they are relatively easy to acquire at a low cost in all river conditions (e.g., not sensitive to high turbidity, high or low flows) and (2) surface velocities are sensitive to river depth [52]. To model riverine flow velocities in the following, the SWE are used [15]. In particular, the 2D shallow water module of the U.S. Army Corps of Engineers' Adaptive Hydraulics (AdH) model [72] is used to solve the SWE numerically. Thus, AdH is used as, (a) the numerical solver to compare computational speed of other ROM-based forward solvers with, (b) the high-fidelity solver of the SWE that generates the dataset to be used in ROMs (both inverse and forward solvers).

4.3.1.1   Inverse Problem Using Linear Projection: PCGA

In principle, the riverine bathymetry identification problem is underdetermined, i.e., there exist multiple possible configurations of bathymetry that are consistent with the limited number of measurements. The analysis must also account for uncertainties introduced by measurement error as well as imperfect representation of river hydrodynamics in the numerical SWE model. In addition to information in the data, inversion techniques utilize prior knowledge reflecting understanding of the bathymetry to weigh possible solutions among those consistent with data. These solutions can be evaluated in a probabilistic way, which is commonly treated in the Bayesian framework, by finding the probability density of feasible solutions that satisfy both model fitting and prior information [41, 45]. For example, prior information is described through the statistical model in which unknown properties are distributed randomly with prescribed mean and spatial covariance functions, which can be represented by a probabilistic density function (pdf).

The ROM that is used here to solve the inverse problem, the PCGA [46, 53], is a fast and scalable Jacobian-free inversion method with an optimal low-rank representation, *i.e.*,

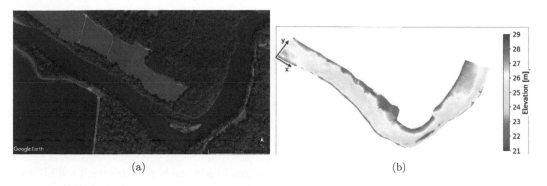

(a)　　　　　　　　　　　　　　　　(b)

FIGURE 4.3
(a) Site aerial image showing the study site on October, 2017 (Google Earth: https://www.google.com/earth/), (b) the true bathymetry of the Savannah river.

linear dimension reduction, of prior information, to data-intensive and high-dimensional riverine bathymetry estimation problems [52]. The PCGA estimates spatially distributed unknown parameters and quantifies the corresponding uncertainty rigorously in a hierarchical Bayesian framework [45]. The PCGA has also been applied successfully to other high-dimensional, data-intensive problems [21, 42, 53, 54], in which computing a Jacobian matrix is very expensive or difficult due to existence of multi-physics simulation models. The readers are referred to [53] and [46] for further algorithmic detail of the PCGA. Here, thee PCGA performance is validated on Savannah river, GA, USA. Figure 4.3 shows the true (reference) bathymetry of the Savannah river. Our model mesh of the Savannah includes 501 nodes in the along-channel direction, 41 nodes across-channel direction, and contains 40,000 triangles. The approximate nominal spacings are 2.4 m in each direction.

Figure 4.4 shows the estimated bathymetries using the PCGA with $n_{PC} = 25$, 50, and 500, where n_{PC} is the number of principal components used to represent the bathymetry distribution. The result has been observed not to be affected by the choice of prior. We observe that even 50–100 principal components are able to estimate the bathymetry with good accuracy (compare for example Figure 4.4(b) with 50 components with the true bathymetry in Figure 4.5). Note that the number of computational nodes in the high-fidelity model is $41 \times 501 = 20,541$, which is significantly larger than the number of principal components used here. Other than the high accuracy of the bathymetry reconstruction, the ROM

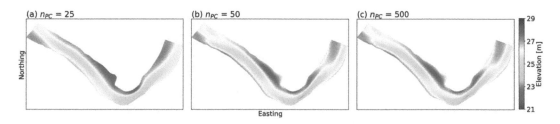

FIGURE 4.4
River bed elevation estimates obtained from the PCGA with $n_{PC} =$ (a) 25, (b) 50, and (c) 500. Measurement error of 0.025 m/s is used. Note the generated profiles are smoother than the true profile (Figure 4.3) due to Gaussian kernel assumption being used in the PCGA [53].

FIGURE 4.5
The true bathymetry of the Savannah river. The area inside the blue frame with solid lines is i-th segment from a river profile and the one inside the black frame with dashed lines is the $(i + 1)$-th segment of the river profile. The flow velocity measurements inside these frames are used as the input to the PCA-DNN, and the network estimates bathymetry profile of each segment. The subsequent frames have a large overlap area and the final output of the network for each cross-section is obtained by averaging the estimated bathymetry for segments containing that cross-section.

required only 108, 208, and 2,040 calls to the forward simulations for $n_{PC} = 25$, 50, and 500, respectively, which are very small number of forward simulations.

4.3.1.2   Inverse Problem Using Deep Learning

In this section, we present the result of using a DL-based ROM to bathymetry estimation of the Savannah river and compare its performance with PCGA. The approach used here is referred to as the PCA-DNN [26]. PCA-DNN works by using PCA, as a dimension reduction technique, in order to find the low-rank representation of the riverine bathymetry, and DNN in order to find the functional relationship between observed velocities and POD coefficients of the bathymetry. The approach also has a preprocessing step that divides the river bathymetry and velocity profiles into smaller segments, as a means to both reduce the dimension of the problem, and increase the dataset size (by turning one river bathymetry-velocity datapoint into multiple datapoints). Figure 4.5 shows the segmentation process on the computational grids of a river.

In order to generate the training data, 100 stochastic Gaussian realizations of the river profile are generated by using a Gaussian kernel of the form

$$\text{cov}(x, y) = \beta^2 \, \exp\left[-\left(\frac{\Delta x^2}{l_x^2} + \frac{\Delta y^2}{l_y^2} \right) \right] \tag{4.1}$$

where $\beta \in (1, 3)$ m, $l_x \in (20, 50)$ m and $l_y \in (80, 140)$ m. In order to have a wide variety of river profiles in the dataset, 100 stochastic Gaussian realizations of river profiles with different parabolic cross-sections are generated using similar Gaussian kernel as described above. After generating these stochastic realizations, the corresponding synthetic velocity measurements are obtained from AdH simulation using these bathymetry profiles, and then a Gaussian error with a standard deviation of 0.1 m/s is added to simulate modeling and measurement errors including the potential noise in the measurements. The generated river profiles and the corresponding flow velocities are further divided into segments consisting of 11 cross-sections, creating segments of size 41×11 (see Figure 4.5). Therefore, these 200 river profiles generated a dataset of size 98,200 ($= 491 \times 200$, where $491 = 501 - 11 + 1$ is the number of segments available in each river profile). This dataset is then shuffled and randomly split into train, validation, and test sets with ratios of 80%, 10%, and 10% respectively.

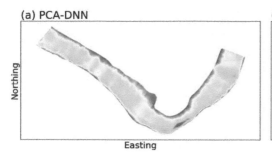
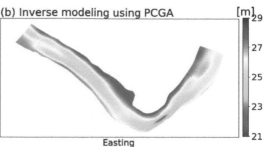

FIGURE 4.6
Comparison of the estimated river bed profile obtained by the PCA-DNN (a) and the PCGA method (b). PCA-DNN performs slightly better than PCGA. However, once the network is trained, PCA-DNN can be significantly faster than PCGA.

Figure 4.6 compares the prediction results of PCA-DNN with the PCGA results with 100 principal components. Comparing to Figure 4.5 shows that both methods provide accurate results for the Savannah river with RMSE values of 0.54 m and 0.58 m, respectively. However, the trained PCA-DNN network obtains these results in 18 seconds, while PCGA takes more than 20 hours to generate these results on the same machine. It should be noted that similar to PCA-DNN, PCGA was run in serial mode, without taking advantage of multi-processing for PCGA runs. The PCGA method can obtain the results much faster on multi-core workstations since the AdH model runs can be independently performed on different CPU processors. However, even using multi-core workstations, PCGA cannot obtain these results as fast as the PCA-DNN. This shows that the DL-based online inversion is significantly faster than even fast physics-based methods that are developed for high-dimensional problems and still can provide more accurate results. Note that the lower accuracy of the PCGA in Figure 4.6(b) compared to Figure 4.4(b) is due to the larger measurement noise that is being assumed in this section.

4.3.2 Forward Problem Using Deep Learning

In this section, we present the result of using a DL-based ROM in order to solve forward SWE problems, that is, fast prediction of the riverine flow velocity as the BCs, such as the free surface elevation and the discharge, vary [24]. The work presented here integrates the ROM, both as an inverse and forward problem solver, for flow velocity prediction. Specifically, Figure 4.7 shows the stages being used here in order to develop the ROMs. First, the bathymetry distribution is estimated via the PCGA (the same process explained in Section 4.3.1.1). Note that Figure 4.4 shows examples of the mean of this distribution for a few different number of principal components. Then this distribution is augmented, for further generalization performance of the forward solver when bathymetry changes over time, for example due to sediment deposition or erosion. In the next step, the dataset that is fed into the ROM is generated, that is, providing AdH with bathymetries sampled from the augmented distribution as well as BCs sampled from surveys of the river (e.g., United States Geological Survey (USGS)) in order to obtain their flow velocities. Finally, the bathymetry/BCs/velocity dataset is used to train the DNNs (the ROMs).

Figure 4.8 shows the different DL-based ROMs that are used here as fast forward solvers of the SWE. The PCA-DNN architecture (Figure 4.8(a)) is similar to the PCA-DNN used in Section 4.3.1.2. However, (a) the role of input and output are switched here, (b) neither

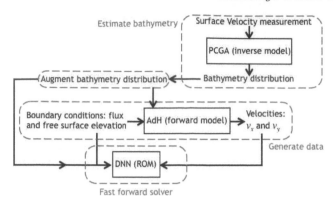

FIGURE 4.7

The schematic of the development of the forward solver. First, we estimate the posterior distribution of the bathymetry via the PCGA, then augment this distribution to a more general distribution and use AdH to generate velocities. Finally, the bathymetries, BCs, and velocities are fed to DNNs, which will be used as fast forward solvers.

input or output are riverine segments, instead, they are both profiles corresponding to the whole riverine domain (of size 41×501), and (c) the BCs are new inputs provided here, since the solution of the forward problem is BC-dependent. The SE (supervised encoder) architecture (Figure 4.8(b)) and SVE (supervised variational encoder) architecture (Figure 4.8(c)) are similar to AE and VAE, respectively, except that BCs are provided to them as additional inputs (similar to PCA-DNN), and furthermore, they are used here as supervised-learner equivalents of AE and VAE, that is, the input (bathymetry) and output (velocity) are different. We have also used CNN in SE and SVE architectures due to 2D nature of the velocity and bathymetry.

The data augmentation stage consists of first, adding a Gaussian kernel of the form presented in eq. (4.1), and then a scaling factor to generated bathymetries. Here, $\beta = 1.2$ m, $l_x = 115$ m, and $l_y = 29$ m. The scaling stage uses the Kronecker product representation of separable covariance matrices to assign the variable standard deviations in the across-the-river direction (y) with a weighting factor that linearly reduces as we get closer to shoreline. The role of this function is to capture the fact that the variations of the generated bathymetries near the shore are generally smaller than in the middle of the river. Note, the resulting set of training bathymetries is not intended to span a wide range of river types, but rather should better reflect the river in question under a wider range of possible BCs and bathymetric changes. Here, a dataset of size 5,000 is generated with the same 80%–10%–10% train-validation-test sets split as before. Once a synthetic bathymetry as well as a pair of BCs have been generated, we can use AdH to calculate the flow velocities.

Table 4.1 summarizes the root mean square errors (RMSEs) in estimating flow velocity magnitudes using different methods. In order to have a fair comparison between different methods, we use the same latent space dimension in all methods, equal to 50. The errors in Table 4.1 for SVE and SE are significantly lower than PCA-DNN, indicating that the non-linear dimension reduction contained in SVE and SE is more accurate than a linear, PCA-based approach. For example, the RMSEs of SE or SVE are on average about 2 cm/s lower than PCA-DNN, which is significant considering that the errors of PCA-based methods are on the order of 5–6 cm/s. A single prediction of the flow velocity for given bathymetries and BCs takes about 15–20 min using AdH and only one second using the DL-based approaches on a 48 core workstation that is used here [24].

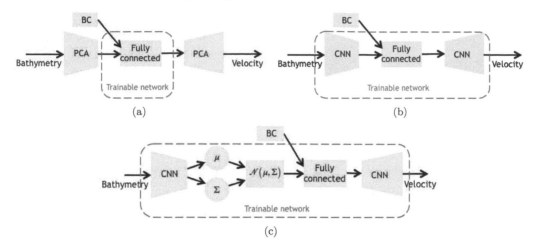

FIGURE 4.8
(a) Schematic of the PCA-DNN method. In this approach, first, dimension of inputs and outputs are reduced linearly via PCA, and then the low-dimensional data are fed to a DNN. (b) Schematic of the SE architecture. Unlike the PCA-DNN, the dimension reduction process in this method is a part of the network architecture and performed in a non-linear fashion. (c) Schematic of the SVE architecture. The difference between SVE and SE is in their bottleneck layer. In SVE, this layer generates a distribution, while in SE it is deterministic. The architecture of SVE is similar to VAE (including its probabilistic latent space), except, it is a supervised learner.

Figure 4.9 compares the performance of different methods when predicting the flow velocity magnitude (see Figure 4.3) of one of the members of the test dataset with a large BC values (free surface elevation of 34.8 m and discharge of 836.6 m^3/s). We observe that SE and SVE perform better than PCA-DNN, consistent with the result of Table 4.1. This could be due to the linear dimension reduction technique being used in this approach, which fails to capture non-linear features present in the data with 50 principal components (PCs). This type of behavior is detectable for other datapoints as well. Note also the large BC values correspond to the cases for which the discharge and free surface elevation values are high and thus, the risk of flooding is higher. Having an accurate predictor of the flow velocity that can provide results in seconds is very beneficial to assess the flooding risk and take necessary actions early enough.

TABLE 4.1

Comparison between the Error of Different Global Solvers When Predicting the Magnitude of the Flow Velocity

Fast Forward Solver RMSE (m/s)	PCA-DNN	SE	SVE
Train set RMSE (m/s)	0.0515	**0.0269**	0.0286
Validation set RMSE (m/s)	0.0570	**0.0374**	0.0398
Test set RMSE (m/s)	0.0546	**0.0381**	0.0398

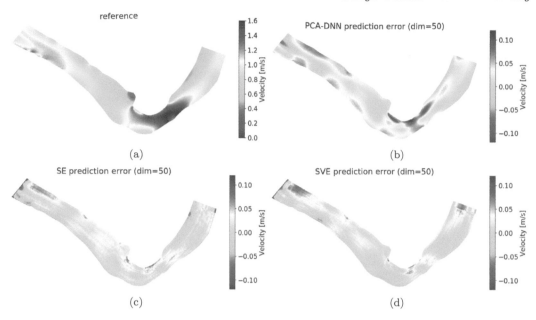

FIGURE 4.9
Examples of the error in the prediction of the velocity magnitudes for different global solvers for higher magnitude BC values ($z_f = 34.8$ m and $Q = 836.6$ m^3/s). SE and SVE outperform the PCA-DNN.

4.4   Conclusion

In this chapter, we have reviewed some of the recent ROMs used in hydrology and geo-science applications in order to tackle the high complexity of the multi-physics and multi-dimensional problems present in these fields. For example, the high computational efficiency of ROMs compared to high-fidelity numerical solvers, allows them to perform prediction of the solution of the high-dimensional multi-physics systems in a timely manner. Further, this significant speedup makes them great substitutes for computationally expensive solvers, when they are being used for inverse problems, UQ, sensitivity analysis, and model-based optimization, where a large of number of forward runs of the PDEs are required. This is an important feature, since as it was stated previously in Section 4.1, inverse problems are very common in hydrology and geoscience due to the fact that most processes in these fields occur beneath the Earth's surface. Another issue that was mentioned in Section 4.1 is the complexity of the multi-physics and multi-scale systems, which makes their physical modeling very challenging, and thus being equipped with a data-driven tool that can be combined with them in order to improve their efficiency and accuracy is very valuable. An inherent property of ROMs is their ability to extract meaningful patterns from high-dimensional and complex data, which makes them great data-driven tools to tackle the multi-physics and multi-scale issues of complex systems.

In Section 4.2.1, we reviewed some of the linear projection-based ROMs, starting from the simple Galerkin projection-based POD. We then showed how Petrov-Galerkin projections and hyper-reduction have been used in linear projection-based ROMs in order to tackle the loss of stability and efficiency that affect traditional projection-based methods when applied to non-linear problems. Then we discussed the non-intrusive linear projection-based ROMs, that have the advantage of not requiring access to the source code describing the physical model, which are consequently very beneficial when the source code is not available or easily modifiable. Then in Section 4.2.2, we discussed the ways that DL can help improve linear projection-based ROMs, both thanks to its non-linear projection technique and its ability to describe the dynamics of the reduced-order model with high accuracy. We first reviewed some of the DL techniques that are combined with linear projections in order to provide a more accurate description of the dynamics of the reduced-order system (Section 4.2.2.1), and then we showed how they can also replace linear projections in order to improve the ROM results, for instance by requiring less number of reduced-order bases compared to linear projections, or by improving the descriptive power of ROMs by extracting more meaningful patterns from high-dimensional data, such as AE or VAE (Section 4.2.2.2). Furthermore, we showed how generative DL-based ROMs such as GAN can be used to describe complex distributions via small number of basis.

In Section 4.3, we demonstrated the high efficiency and accuracy of DL-based solvers, both for forward and inverse problems, through an application example based on the SWE. Our results in this section are also consistent with observations from other researchers in their works, provided in Section 4.2.1. Namely, (a) ROMs, in general, have the capability to imitate behavior of the high-fidelity model with reasonable accuracy in a computationally efficient way, (b) combining simple linear projection-based dimension reduction techniques, e.g., POD, with a DL-based solver for the low-dimensional system, can improve the result compared to ROMs that are not equipped with DL (PCA-DNN compared to PCGA), (c) using DL as non-linear dimension reduction technique can improve the result even further (see SE or SVE compared to PCA-DNN).

Bibliography

[1] N. Akkari, F. Casenave, and V. Moureau. Time stable reduced order modeling by an enhanced reduced order basis of the turbulent and incompressible 3D Navier-Stokes equations. *Mathematical and Computational Applications*, 24:45, 2019.

[2] P. Allamano, A. Croci, and F. Laio. Toward the camera rain gauge. *Water Resources Research*, 51:1744–1757, 2015.

[3] M. Arjovsky and L. Bottou. Towards principled methods for training generative adversarial networks. *arXiv preprint arXiv:1701.04862*, 2017.

[4] O. Azencot, N.B. Erichson, V. Lin, and M.W. Mahoney. Forecasting sequential data using consistent Koopman autoencoders. In *Proceedings of the 37th International Conference on Machine Learning*, volume 2020, 2020.

[5] F. Ballarin, A. Manzoni, A. Quarteroni, and G. Rozza. Supremizer stabilization of POD-Galerkin approximation of parametrized steady incompressible Navier-Stokes equations. *International Journal for Numerical Methods in Engineering*, 102:1136–1161, 2015.

[6] M. Barrault, Y. Maday, N.C. Nguyen, and A.T. Patera. An 'empirical interpolation' method: application to efficient reduced-basis discretization of partial differential equations. *Comptes Rendus Mathematique*, 339(9):667–672, 2004.

[7] H. Bazargan, M. Christie, A.H. Elsheikh, and M. Ahmadi. Surrogate accelerated sampling of reservoir models with complex structures using sparse polynomial chaos expansion. *Advanced Water Resources*, 86:385–399, 2015.

[8] P. Benner, S. Gugercin, and K. Willcox. A survey of projection-based model reduction methods for parametric dynamical systems. *SIAM Review*, 57(4):483–531, 2015.

[9] K.J. Bergen, P.A. Johnson, M.V. de Hoop, and G.C. Beroza. Machine learning for data-driven discovery in solid Earth geoscience. *Science*, 363:eaau0323, 2019.

[10] A. Berzins, J. Helmig, F. Key, and S. Elgeti. Standardized non-intrusive reduced order modeling using different regression models with application to complex flow problems. *arXiv preprint arXiv:2006.13706*, 2020.

[11] D. Bistrian and I. Navon. An improved algorithm for the shallow water equations model reduction: Dynamic Mode Decomposition vs POD. *International Journal of Numerical Methods Fluids*, 78:552–580, 2015.

[12] K. Carlberg, M. Barone, and H. Antil. Galerkin v. least-squares Petrov–Galerkin projection in nonlinear model reduction. *Journal of Computational Physics*, 330:693–734, 2017.

[13] K. Carlberg, C. Bou-Mosleh, and C. Farhat. Efficient non-linear model reduction via a least-squares Petrov-Galerkin projection and compressive tensor approximations. *International Journal for Numerical Methods in Engineering*, 86:155–181, 2011.

[14] K. Carlberg, C. Farhat, and D. Amsallem. The GNAT method for nonlinear model reduction: effective implementation to computational fluid dynamics and turbulent flows. *Journal of Computational Physics*, 242:623–647, 2013.

[15] L. Cea and E. Blade. A simple and efficient unstructured finite volume scheme for solving the shallow water equations in overland flow applications. *Water Resources Research*, 51:5464–5486, 2015.

[16] S. Chaturantabut and D.C. Sorensen. Nonlinear model reduction via discrete empirical interpolation. *SIAM Journal on Scientific Computing*, 32(5):2737–2764, 2010.

[17] Y. Choi, D. Coombs, and R. Anderson. SNS: A solution-based nonlinear subspace method for time-dependent model order reduction. *SIAM Journal on Scientific Computing*, 42:A1116–A1146, 2020.

[18] D. Degen, K. Veroy, and F. Wellmann. Certified reduced basis method in geosciences. *Computational Geosciences*, 24:241–259, 2020.

[19] S. Dutta, M.W. Farthing, E. Perracchione, G. Savant, and M. Putti. A greedy non-intrusive reduced order model for shallow water equations. *arXiv preprint arXiv:2002.11329*, 2020.

[20] N.B. Erichson, M. Muehlebach, and M.W. Mahoney. Physics-informed autoencoders for lyapunov-stable fluid flow prediction. *arXiv preprint arXiv:1905.10866*, 2019.

[21] S. Fakhreddine, J. Lee, P. K. Kitanidis, S. Fendorf, and M. Rolle. Imaging geochemical heterogeneities using inverse reactive transport modeling: An example relevant for characterizing arsenic mobilization and distribution. *Advances in Water Resources*, 88:186–197, 2016.

[22] F. Fang, C.C. Pain, I.M. Navon, A.H. ElSheikh, J. Du, and D. Xiao. Non-linear Petrov-Galerkin methods for reduced order hyperbolic equations and discontinuous finite element methods. *Journal of Computational Physics*, 234:540–559, 2013.

[23] F. Fang, T. Zhang, D. Pavlidis, C. Pain, A. Buchan, and I. Navon. Reduced order modelling of an unstructured mesh air pollution model and application in 2D/3D urban street canyons. *Atmospheric Environment*, 96:96–106, 2014.

[24] M. Forghani, Y. Qian, H. Lee, M.W. Farthing, T. Hesser, P. Kitanidis, and Darve E.F. Application of deep learning to large scale riverine surface flow velocity estimation. *arXiv preprint arXiv:2012.02620*, 2020.

[25] M. Ghommem, E. Gildin, and M. Ghasemi. Complexity reduction of multiphase flows in heterogeneous porous media. *Society of Petroleum Engineers Journal*, 21:144–151, 2016.

[26] H. Ghorbanidehno, J. Lee, M.W. Farthing, T.J. Hesser, P.K. Kitanidis, and E.F. Darve. Deep learning technique for fast inference of large-scale riverine bathymetry. *Advances in Water Resources*, 37:103715, 2020.

[27] F.J. Gonzalez and M. Balajewicz. Deep convolutional recurrent autoencoders for learning low-dimensional feature dynamics of fluid systems. *arXiv preprint arXiv:1808.01346*, 2018.

[28] I.J. Goodfellow, J. Pouget-Abadie, M. Mirza, B. Xu, D. Warde-Farley, S. Ozair, A. Courville, and Y. Bengio. Generative Adversarial Nets. In *Proceedings of the 27th International Conference on Neural Information Processing Systems*, volume 2 of *NIPS'14*, pages 2672–2680, Cambridge, MA, 2014. MIT Press.

[29] M. Guo and J.S. Hesthaven. Reduced order modeling for nonlinear structural analysis using Gaussian process regression. *Computer Methods in Applied Mechanics and Engineering*, 341:807–826, 2018.

[30] J. He and L.J. Durlofsky. Reduced-order modeling for compositional simulation by use of trajectory piecewise linearization. *Society of Petroleum Engineers Journal*, 19:858–872, 2014.

[31] J.S. Hesthaven and S. Ubbiali. Non-intrusive reduced order modeling of nonlinear problems using neural networks. *Journal of Computational Physics*, 363:55–78, 2018.

[32] R. Hu, F. Fang, C.C. Pain, and I.M. Navon. Rapid spatio-temporal flood prediction and uncertainty quantification using a deep learning method. *Journal of Hydrology*, 575:911–920, 2019.

[33] D.Z. Huang, K. Xu, C. Farhat, and E. Darve. Learning constitutive relations from indirect observations using deep neural networks. *arXiv preprint arXiv:1905.12530*, 2019.

[34] P. Jacquier, A. Abdedou, V. Delmas, and A. Soulaimani. Non-intrusive reduced-order modeling using uncertainty-aware Deep Neural Networks and Proper Orthogonal Decomposition: Application to flood modeling. *Journal of Computational Physics*, 424:109854, 2021.

[35] J.D. Jansen and L.J. Durlofsky. Use of reduced-order models in well control optimization. *Optimization and Engineering*, 18:105–132, 2017.

[36] A. Jiang and B. Jafarpour. History matching under uncertain geologic scenarios with variational autoencoders. In *European Association of Geoscientists and Engineers*, volume 2020, pages 1–14, 2020.

[37] R. Jiang and L.J. Durlofsky. Implementation and detailed assessment of a GNAT reduced-order model for subsurface flow simulation. *Journal of Computational Physics*, 379:192–213, 2019.

[38] Z.L. Jin and L.J. Durlofsky. Reduced-order modeling of CO_2 storage operations. *International Journal of Greenhouse Gas Control*, 68:49–67, 2018.

[39] Z.L. Jin, T. Garipov, O. Volkov, and L.J. Durlofsky. Reduced-order modeling of coupled flow and quasi-statics geomechanics. In *Society of Petroleum Engineers Reservoir Simulation Conference*, volume 2019, page 193863, 2019.

[40] Z.L. Jin, Y. Liu, and L.J. Durlofsky. Deep-learning-based reduced-order modeling for subsurface flow simulation. *arXiv preprint arXiv:1906.03729*, 2019.

[41] J. Kaipio and E. Somersalo. Statistical inverse problems: Discretization, model reduction and inverse crimes. *Journal of Computational and Applied Mathematics*, 198:493–504, 2007.

[42] P.K. Kang, J. Lee, X. Fu, S. Lee, P.K. Kitanidis, and R. Juanes. Improved characterization of heterogeneous permeability in saline aquifers from transient pressure data during freshwater injection. *Water Resources Research*, 53:4444–4458, 2017.

[43] S.E. Kim, Y. Seo, J. Hwang, H. Yoon, and J. Lee. Connectivity-informed drainage network generation using deep convolution generative adversarial networks. *Scientific Reports*, 11(1):1519, 2021.

[44] Y. Kim, Y. Choi, D. Widemann, and T. Zohdi. A fast and accurate physics-informed neural network reduced order model with shallow masked autoencoder. *arXiv preprint arXiv:2009.11990*, 2020.

[45] P.K. Kitanidis. Bayesian and geostatistical approaches to inverse problems. In *Large-Scale Inverse Problems and Quantification of Uncertainty*, pages 71–85. John Wiley & Sons, Ltd, 2010.

[46] P.K. Kitanidis and J. Lee. Principal component geostatistical approach for large dimensional inverse problems. *Water Resources Research*, 50:5428–5443, 2014.

[47] B. Kramer, P. Grover, P. Boufounos, S. Nabi, and M. Benosman. Sparse sensing and DMD-based identification of flow regimes and bifurcations in complex flows. *SIAM Journal on Applied Dynamical Systems*, 16:1164–1196, 2017.

[48] J.N. Kutz, S.L. Brunton, B.W. Brunton, and J.L. Proctor. *Dynamic Mode Decomposition: Data-Driven Modeling of Complex Systems*. SIAM, Philadelphia, PA, 2016.

[49] E. Laloy, R. Herault, D. Jacques, and N. Linde. Training-image based geostatistical inversion using a spatial generative adversarial neural network. *Water Resources Research*, 54:381–406, 2018.

[50] E. Laloy, R. Herault, J. Lee, D. Jacques, and N. Linde. Inversion using a new low-dimensional representation of complex binary geological media based on a deep neural network. *Advances in Water Resources*, 110:387–405, 2017.

[51] T. Lassila, A. Manzoni., A. Quarteroni, and G. Rozza. Model order reduction in fluid dynamics: challenges and perspectives. In *Reduced Order Methods for Modeling and Computational Reduction*, volume 9 of *MS&A Series*, pages 235–274. Springer Verlag, 2014.

[52] J. Lee, H. Ghorbanidehno, M.W. Farthing, T.J. Hesser, E.F. Darve, and P.K. Kitanidis. Riverine bathymetry imaging with indirect observations. *Water Resources Research*, 54:3704–3727, 2018.

[53] J. Lee and P.K. Kitanidis. Large-scale hydraulic tomography and joint inversion of head and tracer data using the principal component geostatistical approach (PCGA). *Water Resources Research*, 50:5410–5427, 2014.

[54] J. Lee, H.K. Yoon, P.K. Kitanidis, C.J. Werth, and A.J. Valocchi. Scalable subsurface inverse modeling of huge data sets with an application to tracer concentration breakthrough data from magnetic resonance imaging. *Water Resources Research*, 52:5213–5231, 2016.

[55] K. Lee and K.T. Carlberg. Model reduction of dynamical systems on nonlinear manifolds using deep convolutional autoencoders. *Journal of Computational Physics*, 404:108973, 2020.

[56] D. Li, K. Xu, J.M. Harris, and E. Darve. Coupled time-lapse full-waveform inversion for subsurface flow problems using intrusive automatic differentiation. *Water Resources Research*, 56(8):e2019WR027032, 2020.

[57] Y. Liu, W. Sun, and L.J. Durlofsky. A deep-learning-based geological parameterization for history matching complex models. *Mathematical Geosciences*, 51:725–766, 2019.

[58] L. Lozovskiy, M.W. Farthing, and C. Kees. Evaluation of Galerkin and Petrov-Galerkin model reduction for finite element approximations of the shallow water equations. *Computer Methods in Applied Mechanics and Engineering*, 318:537–571, 2017.

[59] L. Lozovskiy, M.W. Farthing, C. Kees, and E. Gildin. POD-based model reduction for stabilized finite element approximations of shallow water flows. *Journal of Computational and Applied Mathematics*, 302:50–70, 2016.

[60] A.J. Majday and D. Qi. Strategies for reduced-order models for predicting the statistical responses and uncertainty quantification in complex turbulent dynamical systems. *SIAM Review*, 60:491–549, 2018.

[61] M.F. McCabe, M. Rodell, D.E. Alsdorf, D.G. Miralles, R. Uijlenhoet, W. Wagner, A. Lucieer, R. Houborg, N.E.C. Verhoest, T.E. Franz, J. Shi, H. Gao, and E.F. Wood. The future of Earth observation in hydrology. *Hydrology and Earth System Sciences*, 21:3879–3914, 2017.

[62] L. Mosser, O. Dubrule, and M.J. Blunt. Reconstruction of three-dimensional porous media using generative adversarial neural networks. *Physical Review E*, 96:043309, 2017.

[63] J. Nagoor Kani and A.H. ElSheikh. Reduced-order modeling of subsurface multi-phase flow models using deep residual recurrent neural networks. *Transport in Porous Media*, 126:713–741, 2019.

[64] F. Negri, A. Manzoni, and D. Amsallem. Efficient model reduction of parametrized systems by matrix discrete empirical interpolation. *Journal of Computational Physics*, 303:431–454, 2015.

[65] J. Osth, B.R. Noack, S. Krajnovic, D. Barros, and J. Boree. On the need for a nonlinear subscale turbulence term in POD models as exemplified for a high-Reynolds-number flow over an Ahmed body. *Journal of Fluid Mechanics*, 747:518–544, 2014.

[66] A. Quarteroni, A. Manzoni, and F. Negri. *Reduced Basis Methods for Partial Differential Equations - An Introduction.* Springer International Publishing, 1st edition, 2016.

[67] Sk.M. Rahman, S. Pawar, O. San, A. Rasheed, and T. Iliescu. A nonintrusive reduced order modeling framework for quasi-geostrophic turbulence. *Physical Review E*, 100:053306, 2019.

[68] C.B. Rizzo, F.P. de Barros, S. Perotto, L. Oldani, and A. Guadagnini. Adaptive POD model reduction for solute transport in heterogeneous porous media. *Computational Geosciences*, 22:297–308, 2018.

[69] M.A. Rousset, C.K. Huang, H. Klie, and L.J. Durlofsky. Reduced order modeling for thermal recovery processes. *Computational Geosciences*, 18:401–415, 2014.

[70] O. San and J. Borggaard. Principal interval decomposition framework for POD reduced-order modeling of convective Boussinesq flows. *International Journal of Numerical Methods Fluids*, 78:37–62, 2015.

[71] O. San, R. Maulik, and M. Ahmed. An artificial neural network framework for reduced order modeling of transient flows. *Communications in Nonlinear Science and Numerical Simulation*, 77:271–287, 2019.

[72] G. Savant, C. Berger, T.O. McAlpin, and J.N. Tate. Efficient implicit finite-element hydrodynamic model for dam and levee breach. *Journal of Hydraulic Engineering*, 137:1005–1018, 2010.

[73] R. Shams, M. Masihi, R. Bozorgmehry Boozarjomehry, and M.J. Blunt. Coupled generative adversarial and auto-encoder neural networks to reconstruct three-dimensional multi-scale porous media. *Journal of Petroleum Science and Engineering*, 186:106794, 2020.

[74] C. Shen. A transdisciplinary review of deep learning research and its relevance for water resources scientists. *Water Resources Research*, 54:8558–8593, 2018.

[75] M. Sivapalan and G. Bloschl. The growth of hydrological understanding: Technologies, ideas, and societal needs shape the field. *Water Resources Research*, 53:8137–8146, 2017.

[76] A.Y. Sun. Discovering state-parameter mappings in subsurface models using generative adversarial networks. *Geophysical Research Letters*, 45:11,137–11,146, 2018.

[77] P. Tahmasebi, S. Kamrava, T. Bai, and M. Sahimi. Machine learning in geo- and environmental sciences: From small to large scale. *Advances in Water Resources*, 142:103619, 2020.

[78] S. Trehan and L.J. Durlofsky. Trajectory piecewise quadratic reduced-order model for subsurface flow, with application to pde-constrained optimization. *Journal of Computational Physics*, 326:446–473, 2016.

[79] K. Willcox. Unsteady flow sensing and estimation via the gappy Proper Orthogonal Decomposition. *Computers and Fluids*, 35(2):208–226, 2006.

[80] E.F. Wood, J.K. Roundy, T.J. Troy, L.P.H. van Beek, M.F.P. Bierkens, E. Blyth, A. de Roo, P. Doll, M. Ek, J. Famiglietti, D. Gochis, N. van de Giesen, P. Houser, P.R. Jaffe, S. Kollet, B. Lehner, D.P. Lettenmaier, C. Peters-Lidard, M. Sivapalan, J. Sheffield, A. Wade, and P. Whitehead. Hyperresolution global land surface modeling: Meeting a grand challenge for monitoring Earth's terrestrial water. *Water Resources Research*, 47:W05301, 2011.

[81] D. Xiao, F. Fang, A. Buchan, C. Pain, I. Navon, J. Du, and G. Hu. Non-linear model reduction for the Navier-Stokes equations using residual DEIM method. *Journal of Computational Physics*, 263:1–18, 2014.

[82] D. Xiao, F. Fang, C. Pain, and G. Hu. Non-intrusive reduced-order modelling of the Navier-Stokes equations based on RBF interpolation. *International Journal for Numerical Methods in Fluids*, 79:580–595, 2015.

[83] D. Xiao, F. Fang, C.C. Pain, and I.M. Navon. A parameterized non-intrusive reduced order model and error analysis for general time-dependent nonlinear partial differential equations and its applications. *Computer Methods in Applied Mechanics and Engineering*, 317:868–889, 2017.

[84] D. Xiao, C.E. Heaney, L. Mottet, F. Fang, W. Lin, I.M. Navon, Y. Guo, O.K. Matar, A.G. Robins, and C.C. Pain. A reduced order model for turbulent flows in the urban environment using machine learning. *Building and Environment*, 148:323–337, 2019.

[85] K. Xu, D.Z. Huang, and E. Darve. Learning constitutive relations using symmetric positive definite neural networks. *Journal of Computational Physics*, 428:110072, 2021.

5

Applications of Physics-Informed Scientific Machine Learning in Subsurface Science: A Survey

Alexander Y. Sun, Hongkyu Yoon, Chung-Yan Shih, and Zhi Zhong

CONTENTS

Geosystems are geological formations altered by humans activities such as fossil energy exploration, waste disposal, geologic carbon sequestration, and renewable energy generation. Geosystems also represent a critical link in the global water-energy nexus, providing both the source and buffering mechanisms for enabling societal adaptation to climate variability and change. The responsible use and exploration of geosystems are thus critical to the geosystem governance, which in turn depends on the efficient monitoring, risk assessment, and decision support tools for practical implementation. Large-scale, physics-based models have long been developed and used for geosystem management by incorporating geological domain knowledge such as stratigraphy, governing equations of flow and mass transport in porous media, geological and initial/boundary constraints, and field observations. Spatial heterogeneities and the multiscale nature of geological formations, however, pose significant challenges to the conventional numerical models, especially when used in a simulation-based optimization framework for decision support. Fast advances in machine learning (ML) algorithms and novel sensing technologies in recent years have presented new opportunities for the subsurface research community to improve the efficacy and transparency of geosystem governance. Although recent studies have shown the great promise of scientific ML (SciML) models, questions remain on how to best leverage ML in the management of geosystems,

DOI: 10.1201/9781003143376-5

which are typified by multiscality, high-dimensionality, and data resolution inhomogeneity. This survey will provide a systematic review of the recent development and applications of domain-aware SciML in geosystem researches, with an emphasis on how the accuracy, interpretability, scalability, defensibility, and generalization skill of ML approaches can be improved to better serve the geoscientific community.

5.1   Introduction

Compartments of the subsurface domain (e.g., vadose zone, aquifer, and oil and gas reservoirs) have provided essential services throughout the human history. The increased exploration and utilization of the subsurface in recent decades, exemplified by the shale gas revolution, geological carbon sequestration, and enhanced geothermal energy recovery, have put the concerns over geosystem integrity and sustainability under unprecedented public scrutiny (Elsworth, Spiers, and Niemeijer, 2016; Yeo et al., 2020). In this chapter, geosystems are defined broadly as the parts of lithosphere that are modified directly or indirectly by human activities, including mining, waste disposal, groundwater pumping and energy production (National Research Council, 2013). Anthropogenic-induced changes may be irreversible and have cascading social and environmental impacts (e.g., overpumping of aquifers may cause groundwater depletion, leading to land subsidence and water quality deterioration, and increasing the cost of food production). Thus, the sustainable management of geosystems calls for integrated site characterization, risk assessment, and monitoring data analytics that can lead to better understanding, while promoting inclusive and equitable policy making. Importantly, system operators need to be able to explore and incorporate past experience and knowledge, gained either from the same site or other similar sites, to quickly identify optimal management actions, detect abnormal system signals, and to prevent catastrophic events (e.g., induced seismicity and leakage) from happening.

Fast advances in machine learning (ML) technologies have revolutionized predictive and prescriptive analytics in recent years. Significant interests exist in harnessing this new generation of ML tools for Earth system studies (Reichstein et al., 2019; Sun and Scanlon, 2019; Bergen et al., 2019). Unlike many other sectors, however, subsurface formations are often poorly characterized and scarcely monitored, thus relying extensively upon geological and geofluid modeling to generate spatially and temporally continuous "images" of the subsurface. A conventional workflow may consist of (a) geologic modeling, which seeks to provide a 3D representation of the geosystem under study by fusing qualitative interpretation of the geological structure, stratigraphy, and sedimentological facies, as well as quantitative data on geologic properties; and (b) fluid and geomechanical modeling, which describes the fluid flow, mass transport, and formation deformations through physics-based governing equations and the accompanying initial/boundary/forcing conditions. Once established, the workflow is used to generate 3D "images" of the subsurface processes for inference and/or prediction (Figure 5.1).

We argue that subsurface modeling is inherently a semisupervised generative modeling process (Chapelle, Scholkopf, and Zien, 2009), in which joint data distributions are learned via limited observations. A main difference is that in field-scale subsurface modeling, observations are always sparse and only indirectly related to data. For example, the observed quantities may be well logs, but the data of interest are fluid saturation and pore pressure (state variables); in this case, well logs are first analyzed to infer stratigraphy and parameter distributions (e.g., porosity and permeability), which are then mapped to predictions of the state variables. Physics-based modeling serves two purposes throughout this process, namely, mapping the parameter space to state space, and providing a spatiotemporal

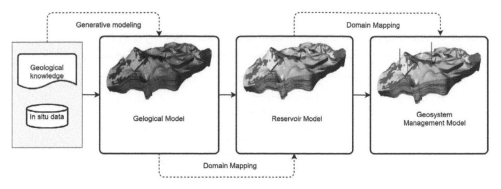

FIGURE 5.1
The conventional subsurface modeling workflow consists of (from left to right) data collection and interpretation, geological modeling, fluid modeling, and system modeling. Machine learning has potential to automate all of these steps.

interpolation/extrapolation mechanism that is guided by first principles and prior knowledge. A main issue of this traditional workflow is that a significant amount of human processing time and computational time is involved, limiting its efficiency and potentially introducing significant latency and subjectivity during the process. On the other hand, machines are good at automating processes and learning proxy models after getting trained. Tremendous opportunities now exist to integrate physics-based modeling and data-driven ML to improve the accuracy and efficacy of the geoanalytics workflow.

To help the geoscientific community better embrace and incorporate various ML methods, this chapter provides a survey of recent physics-based ML developments in geosciences, with a focus on three main aspects – a taxonomy of ML methods that have been used (Section 5.2), brief introduction to some of the commonly used ML methods (Section 5.3), the types of use cases that are amenable to physics-based ML treatment (Section 5.4 and Table 5.2), and finally challenges and future directions of ML applications in geosystem modeling (Section 5.5).

5.2   Taxonomy of GeoML Methods

Table 5.1 lists the main notations and symbols used in this survey.

Physics-based ML in the geoscientific domain (hereafter GeoML) is a type of scientific machine learning (SciML) which, in turn, may be considered a special branch of AI/ML that develops applied ML algorithms for scientific discovery, with special emphases on domain knowledge integration, data interpretation, cross-domain learning, and process automation (Baker et al., 2019). A main thrust behind the current SciML effort is to combine the strengths of physics-based models with data-driven ML methods for better transparency, interpretability, and explainability (Roscher et al., 2020). Unless otherwise specified, we shall use the terms physics-based, process-based, and mechanistic models interchangeably in this survey.

We provide three taxonomies of GeoML methods based on their design and use. First, existing GeoML methods may be classified according to the widely used ML taxonomy into unsupervised, supervised, and reinforcement learning methods. In Figure 5.2, this taxonomy

TABLE 5.1

Notations and Symbols Used in This Survey

Notations	Descriptions
$\mathbf{A}$	adjacency matrix
$\mathbf{b}$	bias vector
d	number of features
$\mathcal{D}$	discriminative network
$\mathbf{D}$	node degree matrix
$\mathbb{E}$	expectation operator
$\mathcal{E}$	graph edge set
$\mathcal{G}$	generative network
$\mathbf{I}$	identity matrix
$\mathbf{L}$	graph Laplacian
$\mathcal{I}$	prior information
n	number of samples
N	number of nodes in a graph
$p(\cdot)$	probability distribution
$\mathcal{V}$	graph node set
$\mathbf{W}$	weight matrix
$\mathbf{x} \in \mathbb{R}^d$	feature vector
$\hat{\mathbf{x}} \in \mathbb{R}^d$	estimated feature vector
$X \in \mathbb{R}^d$	feature variable
y	label, target variable, state variable
$\mathbf{d}^{obs}$	data vector
$\mathbf{z}$	latent space vector
θ	parameters

is used to group the existing GeoML applications, an exposition of which will be deferred to Section 5.4.

Another commonly used taxonomy is generative models vs. discriminative models. Generative models seek to learn the probability distributions/patterns of individual classes in a dataset, while discriminative models try to predict the boundary between different classes in a dataset (Goodfellow et al., 2016). Thus, in a supervised learning setting and for given training samples of input variables X and label y, $\{(\mathbf{x}_i, y_i)\}$, a generate model learns the joint distribution $p(X, y)$ so that new realizations can be generated, while a discriminative model learns to predict the conditional distribution $p(y \mid X)$ directly. Generative models can be used to learn from both labeled and unlabeled data in supervised, unsupervised, or supervised tasks, while discriminative models cannot learn from unlabeled data, but tend to outperform their generative counterparts in supervised tasks (Chapelle, Scholkopf, and Zien, 2009). In GeoML, generative models are particularly appealing because of the strong need for understanding the causal relationships, and because the same underlying Bayesian frameworks are also employed in many physics-based frameworks. In the classic Bayesian inversion framework, for example, the parameter inference problem may be cast as (Sun and Sun, 2015),

$$p(\theta \mid \mathbf{d}^{obs}, \mathcal{I}) = \frac{p(\theta \mid \mathcal{I})p(\mathbf{d}^{obs} \mid \theta, \mathcal{I})}{p(\mathbf{d}^{obs} \mid \mathcal{I})}, \tag{5.1}$$

where the posterior distribution of model parameters θ are inferred from the state observations $\mathbf{d}^{obs}$ and prior knowledge $\mathcal{I}$. Many physics-based ML applications exploit the use of

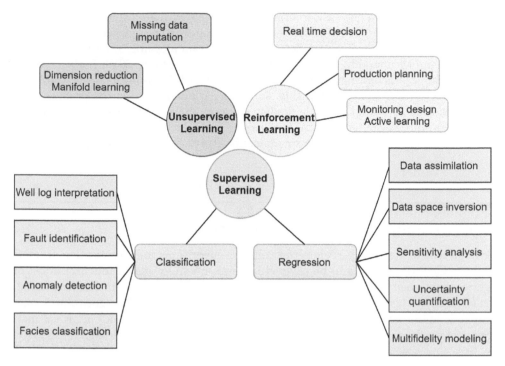

FIGURE 5.2
Common ML applications in geosciences may be grouped under unsupervised, supervised, and reinforcement learning.

ML models for estimating the same distributions, but by fusing domain knowledge to form priors and constraints.

On the basis of how physical laws and domain knowledge are incorporated, existing GeoML methods fall into pre-training, physics-informed training, residual modeling, and hybrid learning methods.

In pre-training methods, which are widely used in ML-based surrogate modeling, prior knowledge and process-based models are mainly used to generate training samples for ML from limited real information. The physics is implicitly embedded in the training samples. After the samples are generated, an ML method is then used to learn the unknown mappings between parameters and model states through solving a regression problem. In physics-informed training, physics laws and constraints are utilized explicitly to formulate the learning problem, such that ML models can reach a fidelity on par to PDE-based solvers. Residual modeling methods use ML as a fine-tuning, post-processing step, under the assumption that the process-based models reasonably capture the large-scale "picture" but have certain missing processes, due to either conceptual errors or unresolved/unmodeled processes (e.g., subgrid processes). ML models are then trained to learn the mapping between model inputs and error residuals (e.g., between model outputs and observations), which are used to correct the effect of missing processes on model outputs (Sun et al., 2019a; Reichstein et al., 2019). A main caveat of the existing ML paradigm is that models are trained offline using historical data, and then deployed in operations, in the hope that the future environment stays more or less under the same conditions. This is referred to as the closed-world assumption, namely, classes of all new test instances have already been seen during training (Chen and Liu, 2018). In some situations, new classes of data may appear or the environment itself may drift over time; in other situations, it is desirable to adapt a model trained on one task to other similar tasks without training separate models. Hybrid learning methods focus on continual or lifelong learning, in which ML models and process-based models co-evolve to reflect new information available. The past knowledge is accumulated and then used to help future learning (Chen and Liu, 2018; Parisi et al., 2019). Hybrid learning methods thus have elements of multitask learning, transfer learning, and reinforcement learning from the ML side, and data assimilation from the process modeling side. Understandably hybrid learning models are more difficult to formulate and train, but they represent important steps toward the "real" AI, in which agents learn to act reasonably well not in a single domain but in many domains (Bostrom and Yudkowsky, 2014).

5.3   Commonly Used GeoML Algorithms

For completeness, we briefly review the common algorithms and application frameworks behind the GeoML use cases to be covered in Section 5.4 (see also Table 5.2). Most of the categories mentioned herein are not exclusive. Autoencoders, the generative adversarial networks (GANs), and graph neural networks (GNNs) are high-level ML algorithmic categories that include many variants, while spatial-temporal methods and physics-informed methods are application frameworks that may be implemented using any of the ML methods.

5.3.1   Autoencoders

A main premise of the modern AI/ML is in representation learning, which seeks to extract the low-dimensional features or to disentangle the underlying factors of variation from learning subjects that can support generic and effective learning (Bengio, Courville, and Vincent, 2013). An important class of methods for representation learning is autoencoders, which are unsupervised learning methods that encode unlabeled input data into low-dimensional embeddings (latent space variables) and then reconstruct the original data from the encoded information. For input data $\mathbf{x}$, the encoder maps it to a latent space vector, $\mathbf{z} = f(\mathbf{x}; \mathbf{W}_e)$, while the decoder reconstructs the input data, $\hat{\mathbf{x}} = g(\mathbf{z}; \mathbf{W}_d)$, where $\mathbf{W}_e$ and $\mathbf{W}_d$ are weight matrices of the encoder and decoder, respectively. The standard autoencoder is trained by minimizing the reconstruction error, which implies a good representation should keep the information of the input data well. Once trained, the autoencoder may serve as a generative model (prior) for generating new samples, clustering, or for dimension reduction. Variants of autoencoders include variational autoencoder (VAE) and restricted Boltzmann machine (RBM) (Goodfellow et al., 2016; Doersch, 2016).

It is worth pointing out that the notion of representation learning has long been investigated in the context of parameterization and inversion of physics-based models, although the primary goal there is to make the inversion process less ill-posed by reducing the degree of unknowns. In geosciences, autoencoders are closely related to stochastic geological modeling, which is the main subject of study in geostatistics (Journel and Huijbregts, 1978). In stochastic geological modeling, the real geological formation is considered one realization of a generative stochastic process that can only be "anchored" through a limited set of measurements. The classic principle component analysis (PCA) may be used to encode statistically stationary random processes, while other algorithms, such as the multipoint statistics simulators, have been commonly used to simulate more complex depositional environments (Caers and Zhang, 2004; Mariethoz, Renard, and Straubhaar, 2010). Autoencoders, when implemented using the deep convolutional neural nets (CNNs) (Chan and Elsheikh, 2017; Yoon, Melander, and Verzi, 2019), provide a more flexible tool for parameterizing the complex geological processes and for generating (synthetic) training samples for the downstream tasks, such as surrogate modeling. From this sense, autoencoders fall in the category of pre-training methods.

5.3.2 Generative Adversarial Networks (GANs)

GANs, introduced originally in (Goodfellow et al., 2014), have spurred strong interests in geosciences. The vanilla GAN (Goodfellow et al., 2014) trains a generative model (or generator) and a discriminator model (discriminator) in a game theoretic setting. The generator $\hat{\mathbf{x}} = \mathcal{G}(\mathbf{z}; \mathbf{W}_g)$ learns the data distribution and generates fake samples, while the discriminator $\mathcal{D}(\mathbf{x}; \mathbf{W}_d)$ predicts the probability of fake samples being from the true data distribution, where $\mathbf{W}_g$ and $\mathbf{W}_d$ are trainable weight matrices. A minimax optimization problem is formulated, in which the generator is trained to minimize the reconstruction loss to generate more genuine samples, while the discriminator is trained to maximize its probability of distinguishing true samples from the fake samples,

$$\underset{\mathcal{G}}{\operatorname{argmin}}\underset{\mathcal{D}}{\operatorname{max}}\mathbb{E}_{\mathbf{x}\sim p_{data}(\mathbf{x})} \log[\mathcal{D}(\mathbf{x}; \mathbf{W}_d)] + \mathbb{E}_{\mathbf{z}\sim p(\mathbf{z})} \log[1 - \mathcal{D}(\mathcal{G}(\mathbf{z}; \mathbf{W}_g); \mathbf{W}_d)], \tag{5.2}$$

where $p_{data}(\cdot)$ and $p_{\mathbf{z}}(\cdot)$ are data and latent variable distributions. In practice, the generator and discriminator are trained in alternating loops, the weights of one model is frozen when the weights of the other are updated. It has been shown that if the discriminator is trained to optimality before each generator update, minimizing the loss function is equivalent to minimizing the Jensen-Shannon divergence between data $p_{data}(\cdot)$ and generator $p_{\hat{\mathbf{x}}}(\cdot)$ distributions (Goodfellow et al., 2016).

Many variants of the vanilla GAN have been proposed, such as the deep convolutional GAN (DCGAN)(Radford, Metz, and Chintala, 2015), superresolution GAN (SR-GAN) (Ledig et al., 2017), Cycle-GAN (Zhu et al., 2017), StarGAN (Choi et al., 2018), and missing data imputation GAN (GAIN) (Yoon, Jordon, and Van Der Schaar, 2018). Recent surveys of GANs are provided in (Creswell et al., 2018; Pan et al., 2019). So far, GANs have demonstrated superb performance in generating photo-realistic images and learning cross-domain mappings. Training of the GANs, however, are known to be challenging due to (a) larger-size networks, especially those involving a long chain of CNN blocks and multiple pairs of generators/discriminators, (b) the nonconvex cost functions used in GAN formulations, (c) diminished gradient issue, namely, the discriminator is trained so well early on in training that the generator's gradient vanishes and learns nothing, and (d) the "mode collapse" problem, namely, the generator only returns samples from a small number of modes of a mutimodal distribution (Goodfellow et al., 2016). In the literature, different strategies have been proposed to alleviate some of the aforementioned issues. For example, to adopt and modify deep CNNs for improving training stability, the DCGAN architecture (Radford, Metz, and Chintala, 2015) was proposed by including stride convolutions and ReLu/LeakyRelu activation functions in the convolution layers. To ameliorate stability issues with the GAN loss function, the Wasserstein distance was introduced in the Wasserstein GAN (WGAN) (Arjovsky, Chintala, and Bottou, 2017; Gulrajani et al., 2017) to measure the distance between generated and real data samples, which was then used as the training criterion in a critic model. To remedy the mode collapse problem, the multimodal GAN (Huang et al., 2018) was introduced, in which the latent space is assumed to consist of domain-invariant (called content code) and domain specific (called style code) parts; the former is shared by all domains, while the latter is only specific to one domain. The multimodal GAN is trained by minimizing the image space reconstruction loss, and the latent space reconstruction loss. In the context of continual learning, the memory replay GAN (Wu et al., 2018) was proposed to learn from a sequence of disjoint tasks. Like the autoencoders, GAN represents a general formulation for supervised and semi-supervised learning, thus its implementation is not restricted to certain types of network models.

5.3.3 Graph Neural Networks (GNNs)

ML methods originating from the computer vision typically assume the data has a Euclidean structure (i.e., grid like) or can be reasonably made so through resampling. In many geoscience applications, data naturally exhibits a non-Euclidean structure, such as the data related to natural fracture networks and environmental sensor networks, or the point cloud data obtained by lidar. These unstructured data types are naturally represented using graphs. A graph $\mathcal{G}$ consists of a set of nodes $\mathcal{V}$ and edges $\mathcal{E}$, $\mathcal{G} = (\mathcal{V}, \mathcal{E})$. Each node $v_i \in \mathcal{V}$ is characterized by its attributes and has a varying number of neighbors, while each edge $e_{ij} \in \mathcal{E}$ denotes a link from node v_j to v_i. The binary adjacency matrix $\mathbf{A}$ is used to define graph connections, with its elements $a_{ij} = 1$ if there is edge between i and j and $a_{ij} = 0$ otherwise.

Various GNNs have been introduced in recent years to perform ML tasks on graphs, a problem known as "geometric learning" (Bronstein et al., 2017). The success (e.g., efficiency over deep learning problems) of CNN is owed to several nice properties in its design, such as shift-invariance and local connectivity, which lead to shared parameters and scalable networks (Goodfellow et al., 2016). A significant endeavor in the GNN development has been related to extending these CNN properties to graphs using various clever tricks.

The graph convolutional neural networks (GCNN) extend CNN operations to non-Euclidean domains and consist of two main classes of methods, the spectral-based methods and the spatial-based methods. In spectral-based methods, the convolution operation is defined in the spectral domain through the normalized graph Laplacian, $\mathbf{L}$, defined as

$$\mathbf{L} = \mathbf{I} - \mathbf{D}^{-1/2}\mathbf{A}\mathbf{D}^{-1/2} = \mathbf{U}\Lambda\mathbf{U}^{\mathbf{T}}, \tag{5.3}$$

where $\mathbf{A}$ is adjacency matrix, $\mathbf{I}$ is identify matrix, $\mathbf{D}$ is the node degree matrix (i.e, $d_{ii} = \sum_j a_{ij}$), and $\mathbf{U}$ and Λ are eigenvector matrix and diagonal eigenvalue matrix of the normalized Laplacian. Utilizing $\mathbf{U}$ and Λ, the spectral graph convolution on input $\mathbf{x}$ is defined by a graph filter $\mathbf{g}_\theta$ (Bruna et al., 2013)

$$\mathbf{g}_\theta * \mathbf{x} = \mathbf{U}\mathbf{g}_\theta(\Lambda)\mathbf{U}^T\mathbf{x}, \tag{5.4}$$

where $*$ denotes the graph convolution operator and the graph filter $\mathbf{g}_\theta(\Lambda)$ is parameterized by the learnable parameters θ_{ij}. Main limitations of the original graph filter given in Eqn. 5.4 are it is non-local, only applicable to a single domain (i.e., fixed graph topology), and involves the computationally expensive eigendecomposition ($O(N^3)$ time complexity) (Bronstein et al., 2017; Wu et al., 2020). Later works proposed to make the graph filter less computationally demanding by approximating $\mathbf{g}_\theta(\Lambda)$ using the Chebychev polynomials of Λ, which led to ChebNet (Defferrard, Bresson, and Vandergheynst, 2016) and Graph Convolutional Net (GCN) (Kipf and Welling, 2016). It can be shown these newer constructs lead to spatially localized filters, such that the number of learnable parameters per layer does not depend upon the size of the input (Bronstein et al., 2017). In the case of GCN, for example, the following graph convolution operator was proposed (Kipf and Welling, 2016),

$$\mathbf{g}_\theta * \mathbf{x} \approx \theta \left(\mathbf{I} + \mathbf{D}^{-1/2}\mathbf{A}\mathbf{D}^{-1/2} \right) \mathbf{x} = \theta \left(\tilde{\mathbf{D}}^{-1/2}\tilde{\mathbf{A}}\tilde{\mathbf{D}}^{-1/2} \right) \mathbf{x}, \tag{5.5}$$

where θ is a set of filter parameters, and a renormalization trick was applied in the second equality in Eqn. 5.5 to improve the numerical stability, $\tilde{\mathbf{A}} = \mathbf{A} + \mathbf{I}$ and $\tilde{d}_{ii} = \sum_j \tilde{a}_{ij}$.

The above graph convolutional operation can be generalized to multichannel inputs $\mathbf{X} \in \mathbb{R}^{N \times C}$, such that the output is given by $\tilde{\mathbf{D}}^{-1/2} \tilde{\mathbf{A}} \tilde{\mathbf{D}}^{-1/2} \mathbf{X} \Theta$, where Θ is a matrix of filter parameters.

In spatial-based methods, graph convolution is defined directly over a node's local neighborhood, instead via the eigendecomposition of Laplacian. In diffusion CNN (DCNN), information propagation on a graph is modeled as a diffusion process that goes from one node to its neighboring node according to a transition probability (Atwood and Towsley, 2016). The graph convolution in DCNN is defined as

$$\mathbf{H}^{(k)} = \sigma \left(\mathbf{W}^{(k)} \circ \mathbf{P}^k \mathbf{X} \right), \quad k = 1, \dots, K, \tag{5.6}$$

where $\mathbf{X}$ is input matrix, $\mathbf{P} = \mathbf{D}^{-1}\mathbf{A}$ is transition probability matrix, k defines the power of $\mathbf{P}$, K is the total number of power terms used (i.e., the number of hops or diffusion steps) in the hidden state extraction, and $\mathbf{W}$ and $\mathbf{H}$ are the weight and hidden state matrices, respectively. The final output is obtained by concatenating the hiddden state matrices and then passing to an output layer. In GraphSAGE (Hamilton, Ying, and Leskovec, 2017) and message passing neural network (MPNN) (Gilmer et al., 2017), a set of aggregator functions are trained to learn to aggregate feature information from a node's local neighborhood. In general, these networks consist of three stages, message passing, node update, and readout. That is, for each node v and at the k-th iteration, the aggregation function f_k combines the node's hidden representation with those from its local neighbors $\mathcal{N}(v)$, which is then passed to update functions to generate the hidden states for the next iteration,

$$\mathbf{h}_v^{(k)} = \sigma \left(\mathbf{W}^{(k)}, f_k \left(\mathbf{h}_v^{(k-1)}, \left\{ \mathbf{h}_u^{(k-1)}, u \in \mathcal{N}(v) \right\} \right) \right), \tag{5.7}$$

where $\mathbf{h}$ denotes a hidden-state vector. Finally, in the readout stage, a fixed-length feature vector is computed by a readout function and then passed to a fully connected layer to generate the outputs.

In general, spatial-based methods are more scalable and efficient than the spectral methods because they do not involve the expensive matrix factorization, the computation can be performed in mini-batches and, more importantly, the local nature indicates that the weights can be shared across nodes and structures (Wu et al., 2020). Counterpart implementations of all well-established ML architectures (e.g., GAN, autoencoder, and RNN) can now be found in GNNs. Recent reviews on GNNs can be found in (Zhou et al., 2018; Wu et al., 2020).

For subsurface applications, a main challenge is related to graph formulation, namely, given a set of spatially discrete data, how to connect the nodes. Common measures calculate certain pairwise distances (e.g., correlation, Euclidean, city block), while other methods incorporate the underlying physics (e.g., discrete fracture networks (Hyman et al., 2018)) to identify the graphs.

5.3.4   Spatiotemporal ML Methods

In this and the next subsection, we review two methodology categories that use one or more of the aforementioned methods as construction blocks. Spatiotemporal processes are omnipresent in geosystems and represent an important area of study (Kyriakidis and Journel, 1999). For gridded image-like data, the problem bears similarity to the video processing problem in computer vision. In general, two classes of ML methods have been applied, those involving only CNN blocks and those combining with recurrent neural nets (RNNs).

Fully-connected CNNs can be used to model temporal dependencies by stacking the most recent sequence of images/frames in a video stream. In the simplest case, the channel dimension of the input tensor is used to hold the sequence of images and CNN kernels are used to extract features like in a typical CNN-based model (i.e., 2D kernels for a stack of 2D images). In other methods, for example, C3D (Tran et al., 2015) and temporal shift module (TSM) (Lin, Gan, and Han, 2019), an extra dimension is added to the tensor variable to help extract temporal patterns. C3D uses 3D CNN operators, which generally leads to much larger networks. TSM was designed to shift part of the channels along the temporal dimension, thus facilitating information extraction from neighboring frames, while adding almost no extra computational costs compared to the 2D CNN methods (Lin, Gan, and Han, 2019).

The hybrid methods use a combination of RNNs with CNNs, using the former to learn long-range temporal dependencies and the latter to extract hierarchical features from each image. The convolutional long short-term memory (ConvLSTM) network (Shi et al., 2015) represents one the most well known methods under this category. In ConvLSTM, features from convolution operations are embedded in the LSTM cells, as described by the following series of operations (Shi et al., 2015)

$$
\begin{aligned}
\mathbf{i}_t &= \sigma\left(\mathbf{W}_{xi} * \mathbf{X}_t + \mathbf{W}_{hi} * \mathbf{H}_{t-1} + \mathbf{W}_{ci} \circ \mathbf{C}_{t-1} + \mathbf{b}_i\right), \\
\mathbf{f}_t &= \sigma\left(\mathbf{W}_{xf} * \mathbf{X}_t + \mathbf{W}_{hf} * \mathbf{H}_{t-1} + \mathbf{W}_{cf} \circ \mathbf{C}_{t-1} + \mathbf{b}_f\right), \\
\mathbf{C}_t &= \mathbf{f}_t \circ \mathbf{C}_{t-1} + \mathbf{i}_t \circ \tanh\left(\mathbf{W}_{xc} * \mathbf{X}_t + \mathbf{W}_{hc} * \mathbf{H}_{t-1} + \mathbf{b}_c\right), \\
\mathbf{o}_t &= \sigma\left(\mathbf{W}_{xo} * \mathbf{X}_t + \mathbf{W}_{ho} * \mathbf{H}_{t-1} + \mathbf{W}_{co} * \mathbf{C}_t + \mathbf{b}_o\right), \\
\mathbf{H}_t &= \mathbf{o}_t \circ \tanh(\mathbf{C}_t),
\end{aligned}
\tag{5.8}
$$

where $\mathbf{X}$, $\mathbf{H}$, and $\mathbf{C}$ are input, hidden, and cell output matrices, $\mathbf{W}$ and $\mathbf{b}$ represent learnable weights and biases, σ and tanh denote activation functions, and $\mathbf{i}$, $\mathbf{f}$, and $\mathbf{o}$ are the input, forget, and output gates. The symbols $*$ and $\circ$ denote the convolution operator and Hadamard (element-wise) product, respectively. Because of its complexity and size, ConvLSTM networks may be more difficult to train than the CNN-only methods.

Geological processes are known to exhibit certain correlation in space and time. The convolution operations are like a local filter and not good at catching large scale features, which is especially the case for relatively shallow CNN-based models. In recent years, attention mechanisms have been introduced to better capture the long-range dependencies in space and time, and to give higher weight to most relevant information (Vaswani et al., 2017). In the location-based attention mechanism, for example, input feature maps are transformed and used to calculate a location-dependent attention map (Wang et al., 2018; Zhang et al., 2019)

$$
\mathbf{F} = \mathbf{W}_f * \mathbf{X}_i, \ \mathbf{G} = \mathbf{W}_g * \mathbf{X}_j,
\tag{5.9}
$$

$$
\alpha_{ji} = \frac{\exp(s_{ij})}{\sum_{i=1}^{N} \exp(s_{ij})}, \ s_{ij} = \mathbf{F}^T \mathbf{G}
\tag{5.10}
$$

$$
\mathbf{O}_j = \sum_{i=1}^{N} \alpha_{ji}(\mathbf{W}_h * \mathbf{X}_i),
\tag{5.11}
$$

where $\mathbf{X} \in \mathbb{R}^{C \times H \times W}$ are the input feature maps, C, H, and W are the channel and spatial dimensions of the input feature map, $N = CW$ is the total number of features in the feature map, $\mathbf{F}$ and $\mathbf{G}$ are two transformed feature maps obtained by passing the inputs to separate 1×1 convolutional layers, and the attention weights α_{ji} measure the influence of remote location i on region j. The resulting attention map is then concatenated with the input feature maps to give the final outputs from the attention block. A similar attention mechanism may be defined for the temporal dimension to catch the temporal correlation

(Zhu et al., 2018). The attention-based ML models thus offer attractive alternatives to many parametric geostatistical methods for 4D geoprocess modeling.

For unstructured data, GNNs can be used to learn spatial and temporal relationships. For example, spatiotemporal graph convolution network (ST-GCN) and spatiotemporal multi-graph convolution network (Geng et al., 2019) were used for skeleton-based action recognition and for ride share forecast, respectively. The spatial-based GNNs may also be suitable for the missing data problem, where the neighborhood information can be used to estimate missing nodal values. For problems that can be treated using GNNs, the resulting learnable parameter sizes are generally much smaller.

5.3.5 Physics-Informed Methods

As mentioned in the last subsection, all GeoML applications that incorporate certain domain knowledge or use process-based models in the workflow may be considered physics informed. Recently, a number of SciML frameworks have been developed to incorporate the governing equations in a more principled way. In general, these methods may be divided into finite-dimensional mapping methods, neural solver methods, and neural integral operator methods (Li et al., 2020). All these methods seek to either parameterize the solution of a PDE, $u = \mathcal{M}(a)$, where $\mathcal{M}$ is model operator, $u \in \mathcal{U}$ is the solution and $a \in \mathcal{A}$ are parameters, or to approximate the model operator itself.

Finite-dimensional methods learn mappings between finite-dimensional Euclidean spaces (e.g., the discretized parameter space and solution space), which is similar to many use cases in computer vision. The main difference is that additional PDE loss terms related to the PDE being solved are incorporated. For example, Zhu et al. (2019) considered the steady-state flow problem in porous media (an elliptic PDE) and used the variational form of the PDE residual as a loss term, in addition to the data mismatch term. Many of the existing methods (e.g., U-Net) from the computer vision can be directly applied in these methods. A main limitation of the finite-dimensional methods is they are grid specific (without resampling) and problem specific.

In neural solver methods, such as physics-informed neural networks (PINNs) (Raissi, Perdikaris, and Karniadakis, 2019; Zhu et al., 2019; Lu et al., 2019), universal differential equation (UDE) (Rackauckas et al., 2020), and PDE-Net (Long, Lu, and Dong, 2019), the neural networks (differentiable functions by design) are used to approximate the solution and the PDE residual is derived for the given PDE by leveraging auto differentiation and neural symbolic computing. In general, these approaches assume the PDE forms/classes are known a priori, although some approaches (e.g., PDE-Net) can help to identify whether certain terms are present in a PDE or not under relatively simple settings.

The neural integral operator methods (Fan et al., 2019; Winovich, Ramani, and Lin, 2019; Li et al., 2020) parameterize the differential operators (e.g., Green's function, Fourier transform) resulting from the solution of certain types of PDEs. These methods are mesh independent and learn mappings between infinite-dimensional spaces. In other words, a trained model has the "super-resolution" capability to map from a low-dimensional grid to a high-dimensional grid.

All the physics-informed methods may provide accurate proxy models. The advantages of these differential equation oriented methods are (a) smooth solutions, by enforcing derivatives as constraints they effectively impose smoothness in the solution, (b) extrapolation, by forcing the NN to replicate the underlying differential equations these methods also inherit the extrapolation capability of physics-based models, which is lacking in purely data-driven methods, (c) closure approximations, by parameterizing the closure terms using hidden neurons they allow the unresolved processes to be represented and "discovered" in the solution process, and (d) less data requirements, which comes as the result of the extensive constraints used in those frameworks. On the other hand, the starting point of many methods are differential equations, which means extensive knowledge and analysis are still required to select and formulate the equations, a process that is well known for its equifinality issue (Beven and Freer, 2001). Future works are still required to make the physics-informed methods less PDE-class specific and be able to handle flexible initial/boundary conditions and forcing terms.

5.4 Applications

The number of GeoML publications has grown exponentially in recent years. Here we review a selected set of recent GeoML applications according to the taxonomy discussed under Section 5.2, and plotted in Figure 5.2. The list of publications is also summarized in Table 5.2, according to their ML model class, model type, use case, and the way physics was incorporated. In making the list, we mainly focused on reservoir-scale studies. Reviews of porous flow ML applications in other disciplines (e.g., material science and chemistry) can be found in (Alber et al., 2019; Brunton, Noack, and Koumoutsakos, 2020).

Early works adopting the deep learning methods explored their strong generative modeling capability for geologic simulation. In (Chan and Elsheikh, 2017), WGAN was used to generate binary facies realizations (bimodal). Training samples were generated using a training image, which has long been used in multipoint geostatistics as a geology-informed guide for constraining image styles (Strebelle, 2002). WGAN was trained to learn the latent space encoding of the bimodal facies field. The authors showed that WGAN achieved much better performance than PCA, which is a linear feature extractor that works best on single-modal, Gaussian-like distributions. In (Liu, Sun, and Durlofsky, 2019), a convolutional encoder was trained to reconstruct a complex geologic model from its PCA parameterization. A key idea there was to learn the mismatch between the naïve PCA representations and the original high-fidelity counterparts such that new high-resolution realizations can be generated using latent variables obtained from PCA. Recently, DCGANs have been applied to generate drainage networks by transforming the training network images to directional information of flow on each node of the network (Kim et al., 2020). The generated network has been dramatically improved by optimal decomposition of the drainage connectivity information into multiple binary layers with the connectivity constraints stored.

A large number of GeoML applications fall under surrogate modeling, which is not surprising given that the geocommunity has long been utilizing surrogate models in model-based optimization, sensitivity analysis, and uncertainty quantification (Forrester and Keane, 2009; Razavi, Tolson, and Burn, 2012). Because reservoir models are 2D or 3D distributed models, many ML studies entailed some type of end-to-end, cross-domain learning architecture, which translates an image of input parameter to state variable maps. In general, these methods utilize physics-based porous flow models to generate training samples. In (Mo et al., 2019b), a convolutional autoencoder was trained to learn the cross-domain mapping between permeability maps and reservoir states (pressure and saturation distributions) at different times. In (Zhong, Sun, and Jeong, 2019; Zhong et al., 2020), a U-Net based convolutional GAN was trained to solve a similar problem. Both studies also demonstrated the strong skill of ML-based models in uncertainty quantification. In Tang, Liu, and Durlofsky (2020), a hybrid U-Net and ConvLSTM model was trained to learn the dynamic mappings in multiphase reservoir simulations. In (Mo et al., 2020), multi-level residual learning blocks were used to implement a GAN model for surrogate modeling. ML techniques have also been combined with model reduction techniques (e.g., proper

TABLE 5.2
List of Physics-Informed GeoML Applications

Model Class	Model Name	Use Case	Physics Used	Citation
Autoencoder	Conv-VAE	Geologic simulation	Geology	(Laloy et al., 2018), (Canchumuni, Emerick, and Pacheco, 2019)
	CNN-PCA	Geologic simulation	Geology, reservoir model	(Liu, Sun, and Durlofsky, 2019)
	Conv-AE	Surrogate modeling	Reservoir model outputs	(Mo et al., 2019b), (Mo et al., 2019a)
	CNN	Model reduction, surrogate modeling	Multiphase flow model	(Wang and Lin, 2020)
Generative adversarial networks	WGAN	Unconditional geologic simulation	Geology	(Chan and Elsheikh, 2017)
	DiscoGAN	Bidirectional parameter-state mapping	Groundwater model outputs	(Sun, 2018)
	Conditional GAN	Surrogate modeling	Reservoir model outputs	(Zhong, Sun, and Jeong, 2019), (Zhong et al., 2020)
	ConvGAN	Inversion	Geology, groundwater model	(Mo et al., 2020)
	CycleGAN	Tridirectional parameter-state mapping	Multiphase flow, petrophysics	(Zhong, Sun, and Wu, 2020)
	CycleGAN	Bidirectional parameter-state mapping	Full waver inversion	(Wu and Lin, 2019), (Wang et al., 2019)
	DCGAN	Drainage networks	Hydraulic connectivity	(Kim et al., 2020)
Graph neural nets	Diffusion GNN	Discrete fracture modeling	Fracture connectivity	(Schwarzer et al., 2019), (Sidorov and Yngve Hardeberg, 2019)
Spatiotemporal	Unet-LSTM	Surrogate modeling	Reservoir model outputs	(Tang, Liu, and Durlofsky, 2020)
	CNN only	Surrogate modeling	Reservoir model	(Zhong, Sun, and Jeong, 2019), (Mo et al., 2019b)
PDE-informed	DNN	Parameter estimation	Soil physics	(Tartakovsky et al., 2020)
	DNN	Forward modeling and inversion	Soil physics	(Bekele, 2020)
	Conv-AE	Surrogate modeling	Flow equation	(Zhu et al., 2019)
	DNN	Immsicible flow modeling	Reservoir flow equation	(Fuks and Tchelepi, 2020)
	Neural operator	Surrogate modeling	Darcy flow equation	(Li et al., 2020)

orthogonal decomposition or POD) to first reduce the dimension of models states before applying ML (Jin, Liu, and Durlofsky, 2020). The Darcy's flow problem has also been used as a classic test case in many physics-informed studies, but generally under relatively simple settings (Zhu et al., 2019; Winovich, Ramani, and Lin, 2019; Li et al., 2020)

Model calibration and parameter estimation represent an integral component of the closed-loop geologic modeling workflow. A general strategy has been using autoencoders to parameterize the model parameters as random fields, the resulting latent variables are then "calibrated" using observation data in an outer-loop optimization, such as Markov chain Monte Carlo (Laloy et al., 2018) and ensemble smoothers (Canchumuni, Emerick, and Pacheco, 2019; Liu, Sun, and Durlofsky, 2019; Mo et al., 2020; Liu and Grana, 2020). In Bayesian terms, this workflow yields the so-called conditional realizations of the uncertain parameters, which are simply samples of a posterior distribution informed by observations and priors (see Eqn 5.1). Other studies approached the inversion problem directly using cross-domain mapping. For example, DiscoGAN and CycleGAN were used to learn bidirectional (Sun, 2018; Wu and Lin, 2019) and tri-directional mappings (Zhong, Sun, and Wu, 2020).

Many process-based models are high-dimensional and expensive to run, prohibiting the direct use of cross-domain surrogate modeling. ML-based multifidelity modeling offers an intermediate step. The general idea is to reduce the requirements on high-fidelity model runs by utilizing cheaper-to-run, lower fidelity models. Towards this goal, in (Perdikaris et al., 2017), a recursive Gaussian process was trained sequentially using data from multiple model fidelity levels, reducing the number of high-fidelity model runs. In (Meng and Karniadakis, 2020), a multifidelity PINN was introduced to learn mappings (cross-correlations) between low- and high-fidelity models, by assuming the mapping function can be decomposed into a linear and a nonlinear part. Their method was expanded using Bayesian neural networks to not only learn the correlation between low- and high-fidelity data, but also give uncertainty quantification (Meng, Babaee, and Karniadakis, 2020).

Fractures and faults are extensively studied in geosystem modeling for risk assessment and production planning. In (Schwarzer et al., 2019), a recurrent GNN was used to predict the fracture propagation, using simulation samples from high-fidelity discrete fracture network models. In (Sidorov and Yngve Hardeberg, 2019), GNN was used to extract crack patterns directly from high-resolution images, which may have a significant implication to a wide range of geological applications.

Ultimately, the goal of geosystem modeling is to train ML agents to quickly identify optimal solutions and/or policies, which is a challenging problem that requires integrating many pieces in the current ML ecosystems. The recently advanced deep reinforcement learning algorithms offer a new paradigm for exploiting past experiences, while exploring new solutions (Mnih et al., 2013). In general, model-based deep reinforcement learning frameworks solve a sequential decision making problem. At any time, the agent chooses a trajectory that maximizes the future rewards. Doing so would require hopping many system states in the system space, which is challenging for high-dimensional systems. In Sun (2020), the deep Q learning (DQL) algorithm was used to identify the optimal injection schedule in a geologic carbon sequestration planning. A deep surrogate, autoregressive model was trained using U-Net to facilitate state transition prediction. A discrete planning horizon was assumed to reduce the total computational cost. In Ma et al. (2019), a set of deep reinforcement learning algorithms were applied to maximize the net present value of water flooding rates in oil reservoirs. It remains a challenge to generate the surrogate models for arbitrary state transitions, such as that is encountered in well placement problems where both the number and locations of new wells need to be optimized.

5.5 Challenges and Future Directions

Our survey shows that GeoML has opened a new window for tackling longstanding problems in geological modeling and geosystem management. Nevertheless, a number of challenges remain, which are described below.

5.5.1 Training Data Availability

GeoML tasks require datasets for training, validation, and testing. In the subsurface domain, data acquisition can be costly. For example, to acquire 3D seismic data, an operator may spend at least $1M before seeing results. The costs of drilling new exploration wells are on the same order of magnitudes. Thus, data augmentation using synthetic datasets will play an important role in improving the current generalization capability of ML models. A main challenge is related to generating realistic datasets that also meet unseen field conditions. In addition, generating simulation data for subsurface applications can also be time consuming if the parameter search space is large and requires substantial computational resources.

Efforts from the public and private sectors have started to make data available. Government agencies encourage or require oil and gas operators to regularly report well information (e.g., drilling, completion, plugging, production, etc.) and make the data available to the public. Standing on the foundation, companies integrate the data and added proprietary assessments for commercial licenses. The U.S. Energy Information Administration (EIA) implements multiple approaches to facilitate data access (`https://www.eia.gov/opendata`). Over the last decade, the National Energy Technology Laboratory (NETL) has developed a data repository and laboratory, called Energy Data eXchange (EDX), to curate and preserve data for reuse and collaboration that supports the entire life cycle of data (`https://edx.netl.doe.gov/`). Open Energy Information (`https://openei.org`) represents an example of community-driven platform for sharing energy data. However, challenges related to data Findability, Accessibility, Interoperability, and Reuse (FAIR) remain to be solved. For example, government agencies or data publishers may have different definitions and data capturing processes. Comparing data on the same basis requires additional processing and deciphering (Lackey et al., 2021).

Because of the high cost of acquiring data, proprietary, and other reasons, companies often are hesitant to share their data to form a unified or centralized dataset for ML training. A new approach, federated learning, is emerging to address the data privacy issue (Konečný et al., 2016). The approach trains an algorithm across decentralized models with their local datasets. Instead of sending the data to form a unified dataset, federated learning exchanges parameters among local models to generate a global model. This approach shows one way to solve the data issues in the subsurface fields to promote collaboration.

5.5.2 Model Scalibility

Geosystems are a type of high-dimensional dynamic systems. Image-based, deep learning algorithms originating from computer vision were developed for fixed, small-sized training images. Large-scale models (e.g., hyperresolution groundwater model) are thus too big to use without resampling, a procedure that inevitably loses fine details. There is a strong need for developing multi-resolution, multi-fidelity ML models that are suitable for uncovering multiscale geological patterns. We are beginning to see new developments in this direction from the applied mathematics (Park et al., 2020; Meng, Babaee, and Karniadakis, 2020;

Li et al., 2020; Fan et al., 2019). However, the feasibility of these approaches on field-scale problems in geosciences needs to be tested.

From the cyber-infrastructure side, next-generation AI/ML acceleration hardware continuously evolve to tackle the scalability issue. For example, a recent pilot study in computational fluid dynamics showed that it could be more than 200 times faster than the same workload on an optimized number of cores on the NETL's supercomputer JOULE 2.0 (Rocki et al., 2020). Similar scaling performance has been reported on other exascale computing clusters involving hundreds of GPU's (Byna et al., 2020).

5.5.3   Domain Transferrability

Even though geologic properties are largely static, the boundary and forcing conditions of geosystems are dynamic. A significant challenge is related to adapting ML models trained for one set of conditions or a single site (single domain) to other conditions (multiple domains), with potentially different geometries and boundary/forcing conditions. This problem has been tackled under lifelong learning (see Section 5.2). In recent year, few-shot meta-learning algorithms (Finn, Abbeel, and Levine, 2017; Sun et al., 2019b) have been developed to enable domain transferrability. The goal of meta-learning is to train a model on a variety of learning tasks such that the trained model can discover the common structure among tasks (i.e., learning to learn), which is then used to solve new learning tasks using only a small number of training samples (Finn, Abbeel, and Levine, 2017). Future GeoML research needs to adapt these new developments to enhance transfer learning across geoscience domains.

5.6   Conclusions

Geosystems play an important role in the current societal adaptation to climate change. Tremendous opportunities exist in applying AI/ML to manage the geosystems in transparent, fair, and sustainable ways. This chapter provided a review of the current applications and practices of ML in the geosystem management. Significant progress has been made in recent years to incorporate deep learning algorithms and physics-based learning. Nevertheless, many of the current approaches/models are limited by their generalization capability because of data limitations, domain specificity, and/or resolution limitation. In addition, many of the current models were demonstrated over simplistic toy problems. Future efforts should focus on mitigating these aspects to make GeoML models more generalizable and trustworthy.

Acknowledgments

A. Sun was partly supported by the U.S. Department of Energy, National Energy Technology Laboratory (NETL) under grants DE-FE0026515, DE-FE0031544, and the Science-informed Machine Learning for Accelerating Real-Time Decisions in Subsurface Applications (SMART) Initiative. This work was also supported by the Laboratory Directed Research and Development LDRD program at Sandia National Laboratories (213008). Sandia National Laboratories is a multimission laboratory managed and operated by National Technology and Engineering Solutions of Sandia, LLC., a wholly owned subsidiary of Honeywell International, Inc., for the U.S. Department of Energy's National Nuclear

Security Administration under contract DE-NA-0003525. This paper describes objective technical results and analysis. Any subjective views or opinions that might be expressed in the paper do not necessarily represent the views of the U.S. Department of Energy or the United States Government.

Bibliography

[1] Mark Alber et al. "Integrating machine learning and multiscale modeling—perspectives, challenges, and opportunities in the biological, biomedical, and behavioral sciences". In: *NPJ digital medicine* 2.1 (2019), pp. 1–11.

[2] Martin Arjovsky, Soumith Chintala, and Léon Bottou. "Wasserstein gan". In: *arXiv preprint arXiv:1701.07875* (2017).

[3] James Atwood and Don Towsley. "Diffusion-convolutional neural networks". In: *Advances in neural information processing systems*. 2016, pp. 1993–2001.

[4] Nathan Baker et al. *Workshop report on basic research needs for scientific machine learning: Core technologies for artificial intelligence*. Tech. rep. USDOE Office of Science (SC), Washington, DC (United States), 2019.

[5] Yared W Bekele. "Physics-informed deep learning for one-dimensional consolidation". In: *Journal of Rock Mechanics and Geotechnical Engineering* (2020).

[6] Yoshua Bengio, Aaron Courville, and Pascal Vincent. "Representation learning: A review and new perspectives". In: *IEEE transactions on pattern analysis and machine intelligence* 35.8 (2013), pp. 1798–1828.

[7] Karianne J Bergen et al. "Machine learning for data-driven discovery in solid Earth geoscience". In: *Science* 363.6433 (2019).

[8] Keith Beven and Jim Freer. "Equifinality, data assimilation, and uncertainty estimation in mechanistic modelling of complex environmental systems using the GLUE methodology". In: *Journal of hydrology* 249.1-4 (2001), pp. 11–29.

[9] Nick Bostrom and Eliezer Yudkowsky. "The ethics of artificial intelligence". In: *The Cambridge handbook of artificial intelligence* 1 (2014), pp. 316–334.

[10] Michael M Bronstein et al. "Geometric deep learning: going beyond euclidean data". In: *IEEE Signal Processing Magazine* 34.4 (2017), pp. 18–42.

[11] Joan Bruna et al. "Spectral networks and locally connected networks on graphs". In: *arXiv preprint arXiv:1312.6203* (2013).

[12] Steven L Brunton, Bernd R Noack, and Petros Koumoutsakos. "Machine learning for fluid mechanics". In: *Annual Review of Fluid Mechanics* 52 (2020), pp. 477–508.

[13] Suren Byna et al. "ExaHDF5: Delivering Efficient Parallel I/O on Exascale Computing Systems". In: *Journal of Computer Science and Technology* 35.1 (2020), pp. 145–160.

[14] Jef Caers and Tuanfeng Zhang. "Multiple-point geostatistics: a quantitative vehicle for integrating geologic analogs into multiple reservoir models". In: (2004).

[15] Smith WA Canchumuni, Alexandre A Emerick, and Marco Aurelio C Pacheco. "Towards a robust parameterization for conditioning facies models using deep variational autoencoders and ensemble smoother". In: *Computers & Geosciences* 128 (2019), pp. 87–102.

[16]   Shing Chan and Ahmed H Elsheikh. "Parametrization and generation of geological models with generative adversarial networks". In: *arXiv preprint arXiv:1708.01810* (2017).

[17]   Olivier Chapelle, Bernhard Scholkopf, and Alexander Zien. *Semi-supervised learning.* MIT Press, Cambridge, 2009.

[18]   Zhiyuan Chen and Bing Liu. "Lifelong machine learning". In: *Synthesis Lectures on Artificial Intelligence and Machine Learning* 12.3 (2018), pp. 1–207.

[19]   Yunjey Choi et al. "Stargan: Unified generative adversarial networks for multi-domain image-to-image translation". In: *Proceedings of the IEEE conference on computer vision and pattern recognition.* 2018, pp. 8789–8797.

[20]   Antonia Creswell et al. "Generative adversarial networks: An overview". In: *IEEE Signal Processing Magazine* 35.1 (2018), pp. 53–65.

[21]   Michaël Defferrard, Xavier Bresson, and Pierre Vandergheynst. "Convolutional neural networks on graphs with fast localized spectral filtering". In: *Advances in neural information processing systems* 29 (2016), pp. 3844–3852.

[22]   Carl Doersch. "Tutorial on variational autoencoders". In: *arXiv preprint arXiv:1606.05908* (2016).

[23]   Derek Elsworth, Christopher J Spiers, and Andre R Niemeijer. "Understanding induced seismicity". In: *Science* 354.6318 (2016), pp. 1380–1381.

[24]   Yuwei Fan et al. "A multiscale neural network based on hierarchical matrices". In: *Multiscale Modeling & Simulation* 17.4 (2019), pp. 1189–1213.

[25]   Chelsea Finn, Pieter Abbeel, and Sergey Levine. "Model-agnostic meta-learning for fast adaptation of deep networks". In: *arXiv preprint arXiv:1703.03400* (2017).

[26]   Alexander IJ Forrester and Andy J Keane. "Recent advances in surrogate-based optimization". In: *Progress in aerospace sciences* 45.1-3 (2009), pp. 50–79.

[27]   Olga Fuks and Hamdi A Tchelepi. "Limitations of physics informed machine learning for nonlinear two-phase transport in porous media". In: *Journal of Machine Learning for Modeling and Computing* 1.1 (2020).

[28]   Xu Geng et al. "Spatiotemporal multi-graph convolution network for ride-hailing demand forecasting". In: *Proceedings of the AAAI Conference on Artificial Intelligence.* Vol. 33. 2019, pp. 3656–3663.

[29]   Justin Gilmer et al. "Neural message passing for quantum chemistry". In: *arXiv preprint arXiv:1704.01212* (2017).

[30]   Ian Goodfellow et al. *Deep learning.* MIT press Cambridge, 2016.

[31]   Ian Goodfellow et al. "Generative adversarial nets". In: *Advances in neural information processing systems* 27 (2014), pp. 2672–2680.

[32]   Ishaan Gulrajani et al. "Improved training of wasserstein gans". In: *Advances in neural information processing systems.* 2017, pp. 5767–5777.

[33]   Will Hamilton, Zhitao Ying, and Jure Leskovec. "Inductive representation learning on large graphs". In: *Advances in neural information processing systems.* 2017, pp. 1024–1034.

[34]   Xun Huang et al. "Multimodal unsupervised image-to-image translation". In: *Proceedings of the European Conference on Computer Vision (ECCV).* 2018, pp. 172–189.

[35] Jeffrey D Hyman et al. "Identifying backbones in three-dimensional discrete fracture networks: A bipartite graph-based approach". In: *Multiscale Modeling & Simulation* 16.4 (2018), pp. 1948–1968.

[36] Zhaoyang Larry Jin, Yimin Liu, and Louis J Durlofsky. "Deep-learning-based surrogate model for reservoir simulation with time-varying well controls". In: *Journal of Petroleum Science and Engineering* (2020), p. 107273.

[37] Andre G Journel and Charles J Huijbregts. *Mining geostatistics*. Vol. 600. Academic press London, 1978.

[38] Sung Eun Kim et al. "Connectivity-informed Drainage Network Generation using Deep Convolution Generative Adversarial Networks". In: *arXiv preprint arXiv:2006.13304* (2020).

[39] Thomas N Kipf and Max Welling. "Semi-supervised classification with graph convolutional networks". In: *arXiv preprint arXiv:1609.02907* (2016).

[40] Jakub Konečný et al. "Federated learning: Strategies for improving communication efficiency". In: *arXiv preprint arXiv:1610.05492* (2016).

[41] Phaedon C Kyriakidis and André G Journel. "Geostatistical space–time models: a review". In: *Mathematical geology* 31.6 (1999), pp. 651–684.

[42] G. Lackey et al. "Public data from three US states provides new insights into well integrity". In: *Under review* (2021).

[43] Eric Laloy et al. "Training-image based geostatistical inversion using a spatial generative adversarial neural network". In: *Water Resources Research* 54.1 (2018), pp. 381–406.

[44] Christian Ledig et al. "Photo-realistic single image super-resolution using a generative adversarial network". In: *Proceedings of the IEEE conference on computer vision and pattern recognition*. 2017, pp. 4681–4690.

[45] Zongyi Li et al. "Fourier neural operator for parametric partial differential equations". In: *arXiv preprint arXiv:2010.08895* (2020).

[46] Ji Lin, Chuang Gan, and Song Han. "Tsm: Temporal shift module for efficient video understanding". In: *Proceedings of the IEEE International Conference on Computer Vision*. 2019, pp. 7083–7093.

[47] Mingliang Liu and Dario Grana. "Time-lapse seismic history matching with an iterative ensemble smoother and deep convolutional autoencoder". In: *Geophysics* 85.1 (2020), pp. M15–M31.

[48] Yimin Liu, Wenyue Sun, and Louis J Durlofsky. "A deep-learning-based geological parameterization for history matching complex models". In: *Mathematical Geosciences* 51.6 (2019), pp. 725–766.

[49] Zichao Long, Yiping Lu, and Bin Dong. "PDE-Net 2.0: Learning PDEs from data with a numeric-symbolic hybrid deep network". In: *Journal of Computational Physics* 399 (2019), p. 108925.

[50] Lu Lu et al. "DeepXDE: A deep learning library for solving differential equations". In: *arXiv preprint arXiv:1907.04502* (2019).

[51] Hongze Ma et al. "Waterflooding Optimization under Geological Uncertainties by Using Deep Reinforcement Learning Algorithms". In: *SPE Annual Technical Conference and Exhibition*. Society of Petroleum Engineers. 2019.

[52] Gregoire Mariethoz, Philippe Renard, and Julien Straubhaar. "The direct sampling method to perform multiple-point geostatistical simulations". In: *Water Resources Research* 46.11 (2010).

[53] Xuhui Meng, Hessam Babaee, and George Em Karniadakis. "Multi-fidelity Bayesian Neural Networks: Algorithms and Applications". In: *arXiv preprint arXiv:2012.13294* (2020).

[54] Xuhui Meng and George Em Karniadakis. "A composite neural network that learns from multi-fidelity data: Application to function approximation and inverse PDE problems". In: *Journal of Computational Physics* 401 (2020), p. 109020.

[55] Volodymyr Mnih et al. "Playing atari with deep reinforcement learning". In: *arXiv preprint arXiv:1312.5602* (2013).

[56] Shaoxing Mo et al. "Deep autoregressive neural networks for high-dimensional inverse problems in groundwater contaminant source identification". In: *Water Resources Research* 55.5 (2019), pp. 3856–3881.

[57] Shaoxing Mo et al. "Deep convolutional encoder-decoder networks for uncertainty quantification of dynamic multiphase flow in heterogeneous media". In: *Water Resources Research* 55.1 (2019), pp. 703–728.

[58] Shaoxing Mo et al. "Integration of adversarial autoencoders with residual dense convolutional networks for estimation of non-Gaussian hydraulic conductivities". In: *Water Resources Research* 56.2 (2020), e2019WR026082.

[59] National Research Council. *Induced seismicity potential in energy technologies*. National Academies Press, Washington, D. C., 2013, p. 225.

[60] Zhaoqing Pan et al. "Recent progress on generative adversarial networks (GANs): A survey". In: *IEEE Access* 7 (2019), pp. 36322–36333.

[61] German I Parisi et al. "Continual lifelong learning with neural networks: A review". In: *Neural Networks* 113 (2019), pp. 54–71.

[62] Jung Yeon Park et al. "Multiresolution Tensor Learning for Efficient and Interpretable Spatial Analysis". In: *arXiv preprint arXiv:2002.05578* (2020).

[63] Paris Perdikaris et al. "Nonlinear information fusion algorithms for data-efficient multi-fidelity modelling". In: *Proceedings of the Royal Society A: Mathematical, Physical and Engineering Sciences* 473.2198 (2017), p. 20160751.

[64] Christopher Rackauckas et al. "Universal differential equations for scientific machine learning". In: *arXiv preprint arXiv:2001.04385* (2020).

[65] Alec Radford, Luke Metz, and Soumith Chintala. "Unsupervised representation learning with deep convolutional generative adversarial networks". In: *arXiv preprint arXiv:1511.06434* (2015).

[66] Maziar Raissi, Paris Perdikaris, and George E Karniadakis. "Physics-informed neural networks: A deep learning framework for solving forward and inverse problems involving nonlinear partial differential equations". In: *Journal of Computational Physics* 378 (2019), pp. 686–707.

[67] Saman Razavi, Bryan A Tolson, and Donald H Burn. "Review of surrogate modeling in water resources". In: *Water Resources Research* 48.7 (2012).

[68] Markus Reichstein et al. "Deep learning and process understanding for data-driven Earth system science". In: *Nature* 566.7743 (2019), pp. 195–204.

[69] Kamil Rocki et al. "Fast stencil-code computation on a wafer-scale processor". In: *arXiv preprint arXiv:2010.03660* (2020).

[70] Ribana Roscher et al. "Explainable machine learning for scientific insights and discoveries". In: *IEEE Access* 8 (2020), pp. 42200–42216.

[71] Max Schwarzer et al. "Learning to fail: Predicting fracture evolution in brittle material models using recurrent graph convolutional neural networks". In: *Computational Materials Science* 162 (2019), pp. 322–332.

[72] Xingjian Shi et al. "Convolutional LSTM network: A machine learning approach for precipitation nowcasting". In: *Advances in neural information processing systems* 28 (2015), pp. 802–810.

[73] Oleksii Sidorov and Jon Yngve Hardeberg. "Craquelure as a Graph: Application of Image Processing and Graph Neural Networks to the Description of Fracture Patterns". In: *Proceedings of the IEEE/CVF International Conference on Computer Vision (ICCV) Workshops*. 2019.

[74] Sebastien Strebelle. "Conditional simulation of complex geological structures using multiple-point statistics". In: *Mathematical geology* 34.1 (2002), pp. 1–21.

[75] Alexander Y Sun. "Discovering State-Parameter Mappings in Subsurface Models Using Generative Adversarial Networks". In: *Geophysical Research Letters* 45.20 (2018), pp. 11–137.

[76] Alexander Y Sun. "Optimal carbon storage reservoir management through deep reinforcement learning". In: *Applied Energy* 278 (2020), p. 115660.

[77] Alexander Y Sun and Bridget R Scanlon. "How can Big Data and machine learning benefit environment and water management: a survey of methods, applications, and future directions". In: *Environmental Research Letters* 14.7 (2019), p. 073001.

[78] Alexander Y Sun et al. "Combining Physically Based Modeling and Deep Learning for Fusing GRACE Satellite Data: Can We Learn From Mismatch?" In: *Water Resources Research* 55.2 (2019), pp. 1179–1195.

[79] Ne-Zheng Sun and Alexander Sun. *Model calibration and parameter estimation: for environmental and water resource systems*. Springer, 2015.

[80] Qianru Sun et al. "Meta-transfer learning for few-shot learning". In: *Proceedings of the IEEE conference on computer vision and pattern recognition*. 2019, pp. 403–412.

[81] Meng Tang, Yimin Liu, and Louis J Durlofsky. "A deep-learning-based surrogate model for data assimilation in dynamic subsurface flow problems". In: *Journal of Computational Physics* (2020), p. 109456.

[82] Alexandre M Tartakovsky et al. "Physics-Informed Deep Neural Networks for Learning Parameters and Constitutive Relationships in Subsurface Flow Problems". In: *Water Resources Research* 56.5 (2020), e2019WR026731.

[83] Du Tran et al. "Learning spatiotemporal features with 3d convolutional networks". In: *Proceedings of the IEEE international conference on computer vision*. 2015, pp. 4489–4497.

[84] Ashish Vaswani et al. "Attention is all you need". In: *Advances in neural information processing systems*. 2017, pp. 5998–6008.

[85] Xiaolong Wang et al. "Non-local neural networks". In: *Proceedings of the IEEE conference on computer vision and pattern recognition*. 2018, pp. 7794–7803.

[86] Yating Wang and Guang Lin. "Efficient deep learning techniques for multiphase flow simulation in heterogeneous porousc media". In: *Journal of Computational Physics* 401 (2020), p. 108968.

[87]   Yuqing Wang et al. "Seismic impedance inversion based on cycle-consistent gener-
       ative adversarial network". In: *SEG Technical Program Expanded Abstracts 2019*.
       Society of Exploration Geophysicists, 2019, pp. 2498–2502.

[88]   Nick Winovich, Karthik Ramani, and Guang Lin. "ConvPDE-UQ: Convolutional
       neural networks with quantified uncertainty for heterogeneous elliptic partial dif-
       ferential equations on varied domains". In: *Journal of Computational Physics* 394
       (2019), pp. 263–279.

[89]   Chenshen Wu et al. "Memory replay gans: Learning to generate new categories
       without forgetting". In: *Advances in Neural Information Processing Systems*. 2018,
       pp. 5962–5972.

[90]   Yue Wu and Youzuo Lin. "InversionNet: An Efficient and Accurate Data-Driven Full
       Waveform Inversion". In: *IEEE Transactions on Computational Imaging* 6 (2019),
       pp. 419–433.

[91]   Zonghan Wu et al. "A comprehensive survey on graph neural networks". In: *IEEE
       Transactions on Neural Networks and Learning Systems* (2020).

[92]   IW Yeo et al. "Causal mechanism of injection-induced earthquakes through the M w
       5.5 Pohang earthquake case study". In: *Nature communications* 11.1 (2020), pp. 1–
       12.

[93]   Hongkyu Yoon, Darryl J Melander, and Stephen Joseph Verzi. *Permeability Predic-
       tion of Porous Media using Convolutional Neural Networks with Physical Properties*.
       Tech. rep. Sandia National Lab.(SNL-NM), Albuquerque, NM (United States), 2019.

[94]   Jinsung Yoon, James Jordon, and Mihaela Van Der Schaar. "Gain: Missing data
       imputation using generative adversarial nets". In: *arXiv preprint arXiv:1806.02920*
       (2018).

[95]   Han Zhang et al. "Self-attention generative adversarial networks". In: *International
       conference on machine learning*. PMLR. 2019, pp. 7354–7363.

[96]   Zhi Zhong, Alexander Y Sun, and Hoonyoung Jeong. "Predicting co2 plume mi-
       gration in heterogeneous formations using conditional deep convolutional generative
       adversarial network". In: *Water Resources Research* 55.7 (2019), pp. 5830–5851.

[97]   Zhi Zhong, Alexander Y Sun, and Xinming Wu. "Inversion of Time-lapse Seismic
       Reservoir Monitoring Data Using CycleGAN: A Deep Learning Based Approach
       for Estimating Dynamic Reservoir Property Changes". In: *Journal of Geophysical
       Research: Solid Earth* (2020), e2019JB018408. DOI: doi:10.1029/2019JB018408.

[98]   Zhi Zhong et al. "Predicting field production rates for waterflooding using a machine
       learning-based proxy model". In: *Journal of Petroleum Science and Engineering* 194
       (2020), p. 107574.

[99]   Jie Zhou et al. "Graph neural networks: A review of methods and applications". In:
       arXiv preprint arXiv:1812.08434 (2018).

[100] Jun-Yan Zhu et al. "Unpaired image-to-image translation using cycle-consistent ad-
       versarial networks". In: *Proceedings of the IEEE international conference on com-
       puter vision*. 2017, pp. 2223–2232.

[101] Yinhao Zhu et al. "Physics-constrained deep learning for high-dimensional surro-
       gate modeling and uncertainty quantification without labeled data". In: *Journal of
       Computational Physics* 394 (2019), pp. 56–81.

[102] Zheng Zhu et al. "End-to-end flow correlation tracking with spatial-temporal at-
       tention". In: *Proceedings of the IEEE conference on computer vision and pattern
       recognition*. 2018, pp. 548–557.

6

Adaptive Training Strategies for Physics-Informed Neural Networks

Sifan Wang and Paris Perdikaris

CONTENTS

Physics-informed neural networks (PINNs) are defining a new emerging paradigm for seamlessly integrating physical models with gappy and noisy observational data. However, despite their towering empirical success, little is known about how such constrained neural networks behave during their training via gradient descent, and under which conditions they may fail. In this chapter we discuss recent advances towards elucidating the training dynamics of PINNs, with a specific focus on the design of adaptive training strategies for enhancing the trainability and generalization performance of PINNs. Specifically, we will review the recently developed Neural Tangent Kernel (NTK) theory for PINNs, and illustrate how it can motivate the development of new optimization algorithms for physics-informed learning. The effectiveness of these methods will be demonstrated across a diverse collection of benchmark problems in computational physics.

6.1 Introduction

Thanks to breakthrough results across a diverse range of scientific disciplines [1, 3, 9, 24, 52], deep learning is currently influencing the way we process data, recognize patterns, and build

DOI: 10.1201/9781003143376-6

predictive models of complex systems. Many of these predictive tasks are currently being tackled using over-parameterized, black-box, discriminative models such as deep neural networks, in which interpretability and robustness is often sacrificed in favor of flexibility in representation and scalability in computation. Such models have yielded remarkable results in data-rich domains [10, 24, 40], and its application is currently reaching all corners of science and engineering.

Deep learning tools are also introducing a new trend in tackling forward and inverse problems in computational mechanics. Under this emerging paradigm, unknown quantities of interest are typically parametrized by deep neural networks, and a multi-task learning problem is posed with the dual goal of fitting observational data and approximately satisfying a given physical law, mathematically expressed via systems of partial differential equations (PDEs). Since the early studies of Psichogios *et al.* [39] and Lagaris *et al.* [25], and their modern re-incarnation via the framework of PINNs [44], the use of neural networks to represent PDE solutions has undergone rapid growth, both in terms of theory [33,50,51,62] and diverse applications in computational science and engineering [29, 55, 61, 70]. PINNs in particular, have demonstrated remarkable power in applications including fluid dynamics [20,45,46], biomedical engineering [23,49,68], meta-material design [7,12], free boundary problems [58], Bayesian networks and uncertainty quantification [64,66], high dimensional PDEs [16,21,43], stochastic differential equations [67], and beyond [13,31]. However, despite this early empirical success, we are still lacking a concrete mathematical understanding of the mechanisms that render such constrained neural network models effective, and, more importantly, the reasons why these models can oftentimes fail. In fact, more often than not, PINNs can be notoriously hard to train, especially for forward problems exhibiting high-frequency or multi-scale behavior.

Recent work by Wang *et al.* [59, 62] has identified two fundamental weaknesses in conventional PINNs formulations. The first is related to spectral bias [6, 41, 47]; a commonly observed pathology of deep fully-connected networks that prevents them from learning high-frequency functions. As analyzed in [62] using NTK theory [2, 19, 27], spectral bias indeed exists in PINN models and is the leading reason that prevents them from accurately approximating solutions of multi-scale PDEs. To this end, recent work in [28, 30, 57], attempts to empirically address this pathology by introducing appropriate input scaling factors to convert the problem of approximating high frequency components of the target function to one of approximating lower frequencies. In another line of work, Tancik *et al.* [56] introduced Fourier feature networks that use a simple Fourier feature mapping to enhance the ability of fully-connected networks to learn high-frequency functions. Although these techniques can be effective in some cases, in general, they still lack a concrete mathematical justification in relation to how they potentially address spectral bias.

The second fundamental weakness of PINNs is related to a remarkable discrepancy of convergence rate between the different terms that define a PINN loss function. As demonstrated by Wang *et al.* [59], the gradient flow of PINN models becomes increasingly stiff for PDE solutions exhibiting high-frequency or multi-scale behavior, often leading to imbalanced gradients during back-propagation. A subsequent analysis using the recently developed NTK theory [62], has revealed how different terms in a PINNs loss may dominate one another, leading to models that cannot simultaneously fit the observed data and minimize the PDE residual. These findings have motivated the development of novel optimization schemes and adaptive learning rate annealing strategies that are demonstrated to be very effective in minimizing multi-task loss functions, such as the ones routinely encountered in PINNs [59, 62].

Building on these recent findings, this chapter attempts to summarize the reasoning and implementation of different adaptive training strategies for constrained neural networks, with a particular focus on resolving stiff gradient flows that often hamper the trainability and performance of PINNs. To this end, we we present two effective algorithms for automatically balancing the interplay between different terms in a PINNs loss function. The first method discussed in Section 6.3.1 draws motivation from the adaptive moment estimation ideas employed in Adam; perhaps the most celebrated stochastic gradient descent method for training deep learning models [22]. The purely empirical nature of this approach motivates us to further study the training dynamics of PINNs using NTK theory [19] – a recently developed framework for analyzing deep neural networks through the lens of kernel methods. The insights gained from this analysis lead us to propose a second effective algorithm for training PINNs that is theoretical grounded and yields state-of-the-art results across a collection of benchmarks.

The remaining of this paper is organized as follows. In Section 6.2, we present a brief overview of PINNs with a particular focus on stiffness and imbalanced gradient pathologies that commonly arise during their training. In Section 6.3, we present two effective algorithms for training PINNs, and discuss their motivation, theoretical foundations, and implementation. In Section 6.4, we present a collection of numerical studies that highlights how conventional PINN models can fail in practice, and illustrates the effectiveness of the proposed algorithms in solving both forward and inverse problems. Finally, in Section 6.5, we summarize our findings and provide a discussion on lingering open questions and promising directions for future research.

6.2 Physics-Informed Neural Networks

PINNs [44] define a class of deep learning models that aim to seamlessly integrate observational data and PDEs by embedding the PDEs into the loss function of a neural network using automatic differentiation (AD) [4]. The PDEs could be integer-order PDEs [44], integro-differential equations [32], fractional PDEs [38], or stochastic PDEs [65, 69].

6.2.1 General Formulation

In this work, we consider PDEs of the following form

$$\mathcal{N}[\boldsymbol{u}](\boldsymbol{x}) = \boldsymbol{f}(\boldsymbol{x}), \quad \boldsymbol{x} \in \Omega, \tag{6.1}$$

$$[\boldsymbol{u}](\boldsymbol{x}) = \boldsymbol{g}(\boldsymbol{x}), \quad \boldsymbol{x} \in \partial\Omega, \tag{6.2}$$

where $\mathcal{N}[\cdot]$ is a differential operator and $[\cdot]$ corresponds to Dirichlet, Neumann, Robin, or periodic boundary conditions [11]. In addition, $\boldsymbol{u} : \overline{\Omega} \to \mathbb{R}$ describes the unknown latent quantity of interest that is governed by the PDE system of Equation 6.1. For time-dependent problems, we consider time t as a special component of $\boldsymbol{x}$, and Ω then also contains the temporal domain. In that case, initial conditions can be simply treated as a special type of boundary condition on the spatio-temporal domain.

Following the original formulation of Raissi *et al.* [44], we proceed by approximating $\boldsymbol{u}(\boldsymbol{x})$ by a deep neural network $\boldsymbol{u}_{\boldsymbol{\theta}}(\boldsymbol{x})$, where $\boldsymbol{\theta}$ denotes all tunable parameters of the network (e.g., weights and biases). Then, a physics-informed model can be trained by minimizing the following composite loss function

$$\mathcal{L}(\boldsymbol{\theta}) = \lambda_r \mathcal{L}_r(\boldsymbol{\theta}) + \lambda_b \mathcal{L}_b(\boldsymbol{\theta}), \tag{6.3}$$

where

$$\mathcal{L}_r(\boldsymbol{\theta}) = \frac{1}{N_r} \sum_{i=1}^{N_r} \left| \mathcal{N}[\boldsymbol{u_\theta}](\boldsymbol{x}_r^i) - \boldsymbol{f}(\boldsymbol{x}_r^i) \right|^2, \tag{6.4}$$

$$\mathcal{L}_b(\boldsymbol{\theta}) = \frac{1}{N_b} \sum_{i=1}^{N_b} \left| [\boldsymbol{u_\theta}](\boldsymbol{x}_b^i) - \boldsymbol{g}(\boldsymbol{x}_b^i) \right|^2, \tag{6.5}$$

and N_r and N_b denote the batch-sizes of training data $\{\boldsymbol{x}_b^i, \boldsymbol{g}(\boldsymbol{x}_b^i)\}_{i=1}^{N_b}$ and $\{\boldsymbol{x}_r^i, \boldsymbol{f}(\boldsymbol{x}_r^i)\}_{i=1}^{N_r}$, respectively, which can be randomly sampled in the computational domain at each iteration of a gradient descent algorithm. Notice that all required gradients with respect to input variables $\boldsymbol{x}$ or parameters $\boldsymbol{\theta}$ can be efficiently computed via AD [4]. Moreover, the parameters $\{\lambda_r, \lambda_b\}$ correspond to weight coefficients in the loss function that can effectively assign a different learning rate to each individual loss term. These weights may be user-specified or tuned automatically during network training [35, 59, 62].

6.2.2   Stiffness and Imbalanced Gradients

Despite a series of promising results [23, 42, 45, 53, 54, 67], the original formulation of Raissi *et al.* [44] often has difficulties in constructing an accurate approximation to the exact latent solution $\boldsymbol{u}(\boldsymbol{x}, t)$ for reasons that yet remain poorly understood. In fact, training pathologies can manifest themselves even in the simplest possible setting corresponding to solving classical linear elliptic PDEs. As an example, let us consider the one-dimensional Poisson's equation

$$\Delta u(x) = f(x), \quad x \in (0, 1), \tag{6.6}$$

subject to the boundary condition

$$u(0) = u(1) = 0.$$

The fabricated solution we consider is

$$u(x) = \sin(C\pi x),$$

where C is a parameter used to modulate the frequency of the target solution, and $f(x)$ can be derived using Equation 6.6.

In the following, we draw motivation from the seminal work of Glorot and Bengio [15] and investigate the behavior of a PINNs model by monitoring the distribution of its back-propagated gradients during training. Rather than tracking the gradients of the aggregate loss $\mathcal{L}(\theta)$ with respect to the trainable parameters θ, we track the gradients of each individual terms $\mathcal{L}_b(\theta)$ and $\mathcal{L}_r(\theta)$ with respect to the weights in each hidden layer of the neural network. A snapshot of the gradients histogram at the end of training is presented in Figure 6.1. One can observe that the gradients of the boundary loss term $\mathcal{L}_b(\theta)$ in each layer are sharply concentrated at the origin and overall attain significantly smaller values than the gradients of the PDE residual loss $\mathcal{L}_r(\theta)$. This implies that minimizing the PDE residual may dominate the total training process and consequently our trained model is heavily biased towards returning a solution with a small PDE residual, while a large error is present in fitting the boundary conditions. As we know, a PDE system may have infinitely many solutions if no proper boundary or initial conditions are specified [11]. Therefore, we may conclude that the gradients of the boundary loss $\nabla_\theta \mathcal{L}_b(\theta)$ and the residual loss $\nabla_\theta \mathcal{L}_r(\theta)$ should match to each other in magnitude otherwise the network ultimately tends to learn

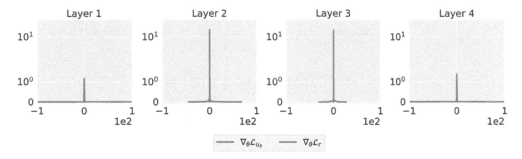

FIGURE 6.1
Histograms of back-propagated gradients $\nabla_\theta \mathcal{L}_r(\theta)$ and $\nabla_\theta \mathcal{L}_b(\theta)$ of each layer for $C = 4$ at initialization.

any solutions that satisfy the equation and thus is prone to return erroneous predictions. In conventional neural networks, the work of Glorot and Bengio [15] has addressed issues related to vanishing gradients by designing an appropriate initialization scheme that balances the variance of inputs, outputs and intermediate network activation. However, designing a similarly appropriate initialization mechanism for PINNs is not possible as the target output function $u(\boldsymbol{x})$ is latent, and no observations of it are available, except for boundary or initial conditions.

To provide further insight into this pathology of imbalanced gradients, let us consider the continuous limit of the learning dynamics for calibrating the neural network parameters θ, as governed by the gradient flow system

$$\frac{d\boldsymbol{\theta}}{dt} = -\nabla_\theta \mathcal{L}_r(\boldsymbol{\theta}) - \sum_{i=1}^{M} \nabla_\theta \mathcal{L}_i(\boldsymbol{\theta}). \tag{6.7}$$

Starting from an initial guess, one can integrate over the gradient flow to obtain a local equilibrium of the total loss $\mathcal{L}(\theta)$. It is straightforward to see that gradient descent updates of Equation 6.24 correspond to a forward Euler discretization [18] of Equation 6.7. It is also well understood that the stability of this explicit, first-order discretization strategy is severely limited by the choice of the step-size/learning rate, especially for cases in which the governing gradient flow dynamics are stiff. We believe that such cases arise routinely in the context of PINNs in which the different terms in their loss have inherently different nature and often correspond to competing objectives (e.g., fitting a set of noisy data versus enforcing a zero PDE residual).

To obtain a quantitative assessment of stiffness in the gradient flow dynamics of a neural network one can compute and monitor the largest eigenvalue $\sigma_{\max}(\nabla_\theta^2 \mathcal{L}(\theta))$ of the Hessian matrix $\nabla_\theta^2 \mathcal{L}(\theta)$ during model training [37, 48], as shown in Figure 6.2. This immediately follows from performing a stability analysis for the linearized system

$$\frac{d}{dt}\tilde{\theta}(t) = -\nabla_\theta^2 \mathcal{L}(\tilde{\theta}(t)) \cdot \tilde{\theta}(t). \tag{6.8}$$

It is well known that the largest eigenvalue of the Hessian dictates the fastest time-scale of the system and directly imposes a restriction on the learning rate that one needs to employ to ensure stability in the forward Euler discretization, as reflected by the gradient descent update rule of Equation 6.24. In fact, a classical result in numerical analysis on the conditional stability of the forward Euler method requires bounding the learning rate as $\eta < 2/\sigma_{\max}(\nabla_\theta^2 \mathcal{L}(\theta))$ [18]. We can also see in Figure 6.2 that different values of the control

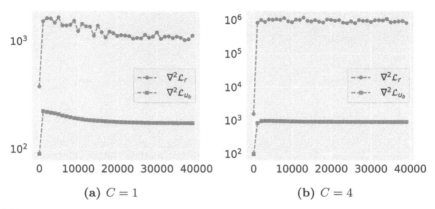

(a) $C = 1$ **(b)** $C = 4$

FIGURE 6.2
Largest eigenvalue of the Hessians $\nabla_\theta^2 \mathcal{L}_\nabla(\theta)$ and $\nabla_\theta^2 \mathcal{L}_\lfloor(\theta)$ during training of a PINNs model for approximating the solution of the one-dimensional Poisson problem (see Equation 6.6), for different values of the control parameter C.

parameter C result in different amounts of stiffness in gradients. Figure 6.3 shows the effect of the control parameter C on the imbalance in gradients at initialization.

6.2.3   Training Dynamics and the Neural Tangent Kernel

While the imbalanced gradient pathologies discussed in the previous section reveal the practical difficulties introduced by stiff gradient flows, a clear mathematical justification of when and why the training dynamics of PINNs become stiff is still missing. In this section, we will attempt to answer this questions by investigating the training dynamics of fully-connected neural networks in the infinite-width limit. Let us start by formally defining the forward pass of a scalar valued fully-connected network with L hidden layers, with the input and output dimensions denoted as $d_0 = d$, and $d_{L+1} = 1$, respectively. For inputs $\boldsymbol{x} \in \mathbb{R}^d$ we also denote the input layer of the network as $\boldsymbol{f}^{(0)}(\boldsymbol{x}) = \boldsymbol{x}$ for convenience. Then a fully-connected neural network with L hidden layers is defined recursively as

$$\boldsymbol{f}^{(h)}(\boldsymbol{x}) = \frac{1}{\sqrt{d_h}} \boldsymbol{W}^{(h)} \cdot \boldsymbol{g}^{(h)} +^{(h)} \in \mathbb{R}^{d_{h+1}}, \tag{6.9}$$

$$\boldsymbol{g}^{(h)}(\boldsymbol{x}) = \sigma(\boldsymbol{W}^{(h-1)} \boldsymbol{f}^{(h-1)}(\boldsymbol{x}) +^{(h-1)}), \tag{6.10}$$

for $h = 1, \ldots, L$, where $\boldsymbol{W}^{(h)} \in \mathbb{R}^{d_{h+1} \times d_h}$ are weight matrices and $^{(h)} \in \mathbb{R}^{d_{h+1}}$ are bias vectors in the h-th hidden layer, and $\sigma : \mathbb{R} \to \mathbb{R}$ is a coordinate-wise smooth activation function. The final output of the neural network is given by

$$f(\boldsymbol{x}, \boldsymbol{\theta}) = \boldsymbol{f}^{(L)}(\boldsymbol{x}) = \frac{1}{\sqrt{d_L}} \boldsymbol{W}^{(L)} \cdot \boldsymbol{g}^{(L)}(\boldsymbol{x}) +^{(L)}, \tag{6.11}$$

where $\boldsymbol{W}^{(L)} \in \mathbb{R}^{1 \times d_L}$ and $^{(L)} \in \mathbb{R}$ are the weight and bias parameters of the last layer. Here, $\boldsymbol{\theta} = \{\boldsymbol{W}^{(0)}, ^{(0)}, \ldots, \boldsymbol{W}^{(L)}, ^{(L)}\}$ represents all parameters of the neural network. We remark that such a parameterization is known as the "NTK parameterization" following the original work of Jacot *et al.* [19].

We initialize all the weights and biases to be independent and identically distributed (i.i.d.) as standard normal $\mathcal{N}(0, 1)$ random variables, and consider the sequential limit of hidden widths $d_1, d_2, \ldots, d_L \to \infty$. As described in [19, 26, 34], all coordinates of $\boldsymbol{f}^{(h)}$ at each hidden layer asymptotically converge to an i.i.d centered Gaussian process with covariance

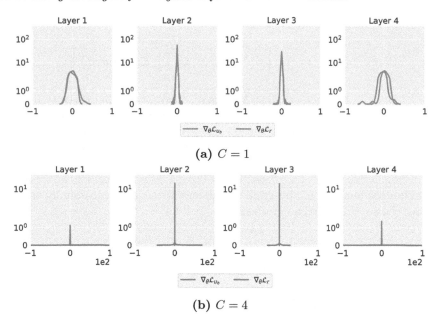

(a) $C = 1$

(b) $C = 4$

FIGURE 6.3
Histograms of back-propagated gradients $\nabla_\theta \mathcal{L}_r(\theta)$ and $\nabla_\theta \mathcal{L}_b(\theta)$ of each layer for different values of the constant C at initialization.

$\Sigma^{h-1} : \mathbb{R}^{d_{h-1}} \times \mathbb{R}^{d_{h-1}} \to \mathbb{R}$ defined recursively as

$$\Sigma^{(0)}(\boldsymbol{x}, \boldsymbol{x}') = \boldsymbol{x}^T \boldsymbol{x}' + 1,$$

$$\boldsymbol{\Lambda}^{(h)}(\boldsymbol{x}, \boldsymbol{x}') = \begin{pmatrix} \Sigma^{(h-1)}(\boldsymbol{x}, \boldsymbol{x}) & \Sigma^{(h-1)}(\boldsymbol{x}, \boldsymbol{x}') \\ \Sigma^{(h-1)}(\boldsymbol{x}', \boldsymbol{x}) & \Sigma^{(h-1)}(\boldsymbol{x}', \boldsymbol{x}') \end{pmatrix} \in \mathbb{R}^{2\times2}, \qquad (6.12)$$

$$\Sigma^{(h)}(\boldsymbol{x}, \boldsymbol{x}') = \mathop{\mathbb{E}}_{(u,v)\sim\mathcal{N}(0,\Lambda^{(h)})} [\sigma(u)\sigma(v)] + 1,$$

for $h = 1, 2, \ldots, L$.

To introduce the NTK, we also need to define

$$\dot{\Sigma}^{(h)}(\boldsymbol{x}, \boldsymbol{x}') = \mathop{\mathbb{E}}_{(u,v)\sim\mathcal{N}(0,\Lambda^{(h)})} [\dot{\sigma}(u)\dot{\sigma}(v)] \qquad (6.13)$$

where $\dot{\sigma}$ denotes the derivative of the activation function σ.

Following the derivation of [2, 19], the NTK can be generally defined at any time t, as the neural network parameters $\theta(t)$ are changing during model training by gradient descent. This definition takes the form

$$Ker_t(\boldsymbol{x}, \boldsymbol{x}') = \left\langle \frac{\partial f(\boldsymbol{x}, \boldsymbol{\theta}(t))}{\partial \boldsymbol{\theta}}, \frac{\partial f(\boldsymbol{x}', \boldsymbol{\theta}(t))}{\partial \boldsymbol{\theta}} \right\rangle, \qquad (6.14)$$

and this kernel converges in probability to a deterministic kernel $\Theta^{(L)}(\boldsymbol{x}, \boldsymbol{x}')$ at random initialization as the width of hidden layers goes to infinity [19]. Specifically,

$$\lim_{d_L \to \infty} \cdots \lim_{d_1 \to \infty} Ker_0(\boldsymbol{x}, \boldsymbol{x}') = \lim_{d_L \to \infty} \cdots \lim_{d_1 \to \infty} \left\langle \frac{\partial f(\boldsymbol{x}, \boldsymbol{\theta}(0))}{\partial \boldsymbol{\theta}}, \frac{\partial f(\boldsymbol{x}', \boldsymbol{\theta}(0))}{\partial \boldsymbol{\theta}} \right\rangle = \Theta^{(L)}(\boldsymbol{x}, \boldsymbol{x}').$$

$$(6.15)$$

Here $\Theta^{(L)}(\boldsymbol{x}, \boldsymbol{x}')$ is recursively defined by

$$\Theta^{(L)}(\boldsymbol{x}, \boldsymbol{x}') = \sum_{h=1}^{L+1}\left(\Sigma^{(h-1)}(\boldsymbol{x}, \boldsymbol{x}') \cdot \prod_{h'=h}^{L+1}\dot{\Sigma}^{(h')}(\boldsymbol{x}, \boldsymbol{x}')\right), \tag{6.16}$$

where $\dot{\Sigma}^{(L+1)}(\boldsymbol{x}, \boldsymbol{x}') = 1$ for convenience. Moreover, Jacot *et al.* [19] proved that, under some suitable conditions and training time T fixed, Ker_t converges to $\Theta^{(L)}$ for all $0 \leq t \leq T$, as the width goes to infinity. As a consequence, a properly randomly initialized and sufficiently wide deep neural network trained by gradient descent is equivalent to a kernel regression with a deterministic kernel.

Now we can derive the NTK of a PINNs. To this end, consider $\lambda_r = \lambda_b = 1$ and minimizing the loss function 6.3 by gradient descent with an infinitesimally small learning rate, yielding the continuous-time gradient flow system

$$\frac{d\boldsymbol{\theta}}{dt} = -\nabla\mathcal{L}(\boldsymbol{\theta}), \tag{6.17}$$

and let $[\boldsymbol{u}](t) = [\boldsymbol{u}](\boldsymbol{x}_b, \boldsymbol{\theta}(t)) = \{u(\boldsymbol{x}_b^i, \boldsymbol{\theta}(t))\}_{i=1}^{N_b}$ and $\mathcal{N}[\boldsymbol{u}](t) = \mathcal{N}[\boldsymbol{u}](\boldsymbol{x}_r, \boldsymbol{\theta}(t)) = \mathcal{N}[\boldsymbol{u}](\boldsymbol{x}_r, \boldsymbol{\theta}(t))\}_{i=1}^{N_r}$. Then the following lemma characterizes how $[\boldsymbol{u}](t)$ and $\mathcal{N}[\boldsymbol{u}](t)$ evolve during training by gradient descent [62].

Lemma 6.1 *Given the data points $\{\boldsymbol{x}_b^i, g(\boldsymbol{x}_b^i)\}_{i=1}^{N_b}, \{\boldsymbol{x}_r^i, f(\boldsymbol{x}_r^i)\}_{i=1}^{N_r}$ and the gradient flow 6.17, $[\boldsymbol{u}](t)$ and $\mathcal{N}[\boldsymbol{u}](t)$ obey the following evolution*

$$\begin{bmatrix} \frac{d[\boldsymbol{u}](\boldsymbol{x}_b, \boldsymbol{\theta}(t))}{dt} \\ \frac{d\mathcal{N}[\boldsymbol{u}](\boldsymbol{x}_r, \boldsymbol{\theta}(t))}{dt} \end{bmatrix} = -\begin{bmatrix} \boldsymbol{K}_{uu}(t) & \boldsymbol{K}_{ur}(t) \\ \boldsymbol{K}_{ru}(t) & \boldsymbol{K}_{rr}(t) \end{bmatrix} \cdot \begin{bmatrix} [\boldsymbol{u}](\boldsymbol{x}_b, \boldsymbol{\theta}(t)) - g(\boldsymbol{x}_b) \\ \mathcal{N}[\boldsymbol{u}](\boldsymbol{x}_r, \boldsymbol{\theta}(t)) - f(\boldsymbol{x}_r) \end{bmatrix}, \tag{6.18}$$

where $\boldsymbol{K}_{ru}(t) = \boldsymbol{K}_{ur}^T(t)$ and $\boldsymbol{K}_{uu}(t) \in \mathbb{R}^{N_b \times N_b}, \boldsymbol{K}_{ur}(t) \in \mathbb{R}^{N_b \times N_r}, and \boldsymbol{K}_{rr}(t) \in \mathbb{R}^{N_r \times N_r}$ whose (i, j)-th entry is given by

$$\begin{aligned} (\boldsymbol{K}_{uu})_{ij}(t) &= \left\langle \frac{d[\boldsymbol{u}](\boldsymbol{x}_b^i, \boldsymbol{\theta}(t))}{d\boldsymbol{\theta}}, \frac{d[\boldsymbol{u}](\boldsymbol{x}_b^j, \boldsymbol{\theta}(t))}{d\boldsymbol{\theta}} \right\rangle \\ (\boldsymbol{K}_{ur})_{ij}(t) &= \left\langle \frac{d[\boldsymbol{u}](\boldsymbol{x}_b^i, \boldsymbol{\theta}(t))}{d\boldsymbol{\theta}}, \frac{d\mathcal{N}[\boldsymbol{u}](\boldsymbol{x}_r^j, \boldsymbol{\theta}(t))}{d\boldsymbol{\theta}} \right\rangle \\ (\boldsymbol{K}_{rr})_{ij}(t) &= \left\langle \frac{d\mathcal{N}[\boldsymbol{u}](\boldsymbol{x}_r^i, \boldsymbol{\theta}(t))}{d\boldsymbol{\theta}}, \frac{d\mathcal{N}[\boldsymbol{u}](\boldsymbol{x}_r^j, \boldsymbol{\theta}(t))}{d\boldsymbol{\theta}} \right\rangle. \end{aligned} \tag{6.19}$$

Remark 6.1 *$\langle \cdot, \cdot \rangle$ here denotes the inner product over all neural network parameters in $\boldsymbol{\theta}$. For example,*

$$(\boldsymbol{K}_{uu})_{ij}(t) = \sum_{\theta \in \boldsymbol{\theta}} \frac{du(\boldsymbol{x}_b^i, \boldsymbol{\theta}(t))}{d\theta} \cdot \frac{du(\boldsymbol{x}_b^j, \boldsymbol{\theta}(t))}{d\theta}.$$

Remark 6.2 *We will denote the matrix $\begin{bmatrix} \boldsymbol{K}_{uu}(t) & \boldsymbol{K}_{ur}(t) \\ \boldsymbol{K}_{ru}(t) & \boldsymbol{K}_{rr}(t) \end{bmatrix}$ by $\boldsymbol{K}(t)$ in the following sections. It is easy to see that $\boldsymbol{K}_{uu}(t), \boldsymbol{K}_{rr}(t)$ and $\boldsymbol{K}(t)$ are all positive semi-definite matrices. Figure 6.4 shows the imbalance among the eigenvalues of $\boldsymbol{K}, \boldsymbol{K}_{uu}$ and $\boldsymbol{K}_r$ at initialization for $u(x) = \sin(C\pi x)$ where $C = 4$. Indeed, let $\boldsymbol{J}_u(t)$ and $\boldsymbol{J}_r(t)$ be the Jacobian matrices of $u(t)$ and $\mathcal{N}u(t)$ with respect to $\boldsymbol{\theta}$ respectively. Then, we can observe that*

$$\boldsymbol{K}_{uu}(t) = \boldsymbol{J}_u(t)\boldsymbol{J}_u^T(t), \quad \boldsymbol{K}_{rr}(t) = \boldsymbol{J}_r(t)\boldsymbol{J}_r^T(t), \quad \boldsymbol{K}(t) = \begin{bmatrix} \boldsymbol{J}_u(t) \\ \boldsymbol{J}_r(t) \end{bmatrix}[\boldsymbol{J}_u^T(t), \boldsymbol{J}_r^T(t)].$$

Remark 6.3 *It is worth pointing out that Equation 6.18 holds for any differential operator $\mathcal{N}$ and any neural network architecture [62].*

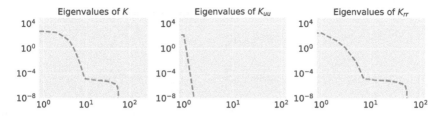

FIGURE 6.4
1D Poisson equation: The eigenvalues of K, K_{uu} and K_{rr} at initialization in descending order for different fabricated solutions $u(x) = \sin(C\pi x)$ where $C = 4$.

6.3 Adaptive Training Strategies

In this section we present a collection of remarks and insights that motivate the developed of adaptive training training algorithms for PINNs. Specifically, we present two distinct approaches for automatically balancing the interplay between different terms in a PINNs loss function, comment on their motivation, and highlight their main implementation aspects. A detailed performance comparison will then be presented in Section 6.4.

6.3.1 Balancing the Statistics of Back-Propagated Gradients

It is straightforward to see that minimizing the training loss of PINNs via gradient descent essentially corresponds to a forward Euler discretization [18] of Equation 6.7. It is also well understood that the stability of this explicit, first-order discretization strategy is severely limited by the choice of the step-size/learning rate, especially for cases in which the governing gradient flow dynamics are stiff. We believe that such cases arise routinely in the context of PINNs in which the different terms in their loss have inherently different nature and often correspond to competing objectives (e.g., fitting a set of noisy data versus enforcing a zero PDE residual).

Having identified this common mode of failure leading to imbalanced gradients during back-propagation, we can investigate potential remedies for overcoming this pathology. To do so, let us re-examine the general form of a PINNs loss function

$$\mathcal{L}(\theta) := \mathcal{L}_r(\theta) + \sum_{i=1}^{M} \mathcal{L}_i(\theta), \tag{6.20}$$

the minimization of which is typically performed according to the following gradient descent update

$$\theta_{n+1} = \theta_n - \eta \nabla_\theta \mathcal{L}(\theta_n)$$
$$= \theta_n - \eta[\nabla_\theta \mathcal{L}_r(\theta_n) + \sum_{i=1}^{M} \nabla_\theta \mathcal{L}_i(\theta_n)], \tag{6.21}$$

where η is a learning rate parameter. To balance the interplay between the different terms in this loss, a straightforward way is to multiply a constant λ_i to each $\mathcal{L}_i(\theta)$ term. More specifically, we consider minimizing the following loss in which the weights λ resemble the role of penalty coefficients in constrained optimization [5] or multi-rate integrators in numerical analysis, [14]

$$\mathcal{L}(\theta) := \mathcal{L}_r(\theta) + \sum_{i=1}^{M} \lambda_i \mathcal{L}_i(\theta). \tag{6.22}$$

Consequently, the corresponding gradient descent updates now take the form

$$\theta_{n+1} = \theta_n - \eta \nabla_\theta \mathcal{L}(\theta_n) \tag{6.23}$$

$$= \theta_n - \eta \nabla_\theta \mathcal{L}_r(\theta_n) - \eta \sum_{i=1}^{M} \lambda_i \nabla_\theta \mathcal{L}_i(\theta_n), \tag{6.24}$$

where we see how the constants λ_i can effectively introduce a re-scaling of the learning rate corresponding to each loss term. Obviously, the next question that needs to be answered is how those weights λ_i should be chosen? It is straightforward to see that choosing λ_i arbitrarily following a trial and error procedure is extremely tedious and may not produce satisfying results. Moreover, the optimal constants may vary greatly for different problems, which means we cannot find a fixed empirical recipe that is transferable across different PDEs. Most importantly, the loss function always consists of various parts that serve to provide restrictions on the equation. It is impractical to give different weights to different parts of the loss function manually.

Here we draw motivation from Adam [22] – one the most widely used adaptive learning rate optimizers in the deep learning literature – to derive an adaptive rule for choosing the λ_i weights online during model training. The basic idea behind Adam is to keep track of the first- and second-order moments of the back-propagated gradients during training, and utilize this information to adaptively scale the learning rate associated with each parameter in the θ vector. In a similar spirit, our proposed learning rate annealing procedure, as summarized in Algorithm 6.1, is designed to automatically tune the λ_i weights by utilizing the back-propagated gradient statistics during model training, such that the interplay between all terms in Equation 6.22 is appropriately balanced.

The intuition behind the proposed algorithm is fairly straightforward. Recall that our goal is to assign appropriate weight to each term in the loss function such that theirs gradients during back propagation are similar in magnitude. According to our analysis in previous sections, we may conclude that the gradients of the residual loss generally dominate the gradients of the others. Based on this observation, our goal can be stated as follows: for any given loss term $\mathcal{L}_i$, find λ_i such that

$$\lambda_i \overline{|\nabla_\theta \mathcal{L}_i(\theta)|} = \max_{\theta_n}\{|\nabla_\theta \mathcal{L}_r(\theta_n)|\},$$

which follows

$$\lambda_i = \frac{\max_{\theta_n}\{|\nabla_\theta \mathcal{L}_r(\theta_n)|\}}{|\nabla_\theta \mathcal{L}_i(\theta_n)|}, \quad i = 1, \ldots, M.$$

As these instantaneous values are expected to exhibit high variance due to the stochastic nature of the gradient descent updates, the actual weights λ_i are computed as a running average of their previous values, as shown in Equation 6.25, 6.26. Here, we remark that the updates in Equations 6.25 and 6.26 can either take place at every iteration of the gradient descent loop, or at a frequency specified by the user (e.g., every 10 gradient descent steps). Finally, a gradient descent step is performed to update the neural network parameters θ using the current weight values stored in λ_i, see Equation 6.27. The key benefits of the proposed automated procedure is that this adaptive method can be easily generalized to loss functions consisting of multiple terms (e.g., multi-variate problems with multiple boundary conditions on different variables), while the extra computational overhead associated with computing the gradient statistics in Equation 6.25 is small, especially in the case of infrequent updates. Moreover, our computational studies confirm very low sensitivity on the additional hyper-parameter α, as the accuracy of our results does not exhibit any significant variance when this parameter take values within a reasonable range (e.g., $\alpha \in [0.05, 0.2]$).

Algorithm 6.1 Learning rate annealing for PINNs

Consider a PINN $f_\theta(x)$ with parameters θ and a loss function

$$\mathcal{L}(\theta) := \mathcal{L}_r(\theta) + \sum_{i=1}^{M} \lambda_i \mathcal{L}_i(\theta),$$

where $\mathcal{L}_r(\theta)$ denotes the PDE residual loss, the $\mathcal{L}_i(\theta)$ correspond to data-fit terms (e.g., measurements, initial or boundary conditions, etc.), and $\lambda_i = 1$, $i = 1, \ldots, M$ are free parameters used to balance the interplay between the different loss terms. Then use S steps of a gradient descent algorithm to update the parameters θ as:

for $n = 1, \ldots, S$ **do**

(a) Compute $\hat{\lambda}_i$ by

$$\hat{\lambda}_i = \frac{\max_{\theta_n}\{|\nabla_\theta \mathcal{L}_r(\theta_n)|\}}{\overline{|\nabla_\theta \lambda_i \mathcal{L}_i(\theta_n)|}}, \quad i = 1, \ldots, M, \tag{6.25}$$

where θ_n denotes the values of the parameters θ at n-th iteration, $|\cdot|$ denotes the element-wise absolute value and $\overline{|\nabla_\theta \mathcal{L}_i(\theta_n)|}$ the mean of $|\nabla_\theta \mathcal{L}_i(\cdot)|$ evaluated at θ_n.

(b) Update the weights λ_i using a moving average of the form

$$\lambda_i = (1 - \alpha)\lambda_i + \alpha\hat{\lambda}_i, \quad i = 1, \ldots, M. \tag{6.26}$$

(c) Update the parameters θ via gradient descent

$$\theta_{n+1} = \theta_n - \eta \nabla_\theta \mathcal{L}_r(\theta_n) - \eta \sum_{i=1}^{M} \lambda_i \nabla_\theta \mathcal{L}_i(\theta_n) \tag{6.27}$$

end for

The recommended hyper-parameter values are: $\eta = 10^{-3}$ and $\alpha = 0.1$ [59].

6.3.2   Resolving Discrepancies in Convergence Rate

While the aforementioned adaptive training procedure (Algorithm 6.1) has been demonstrated to be effective in practice [59], its formulation is largely empirical and lacks a theoretical justification. In this section, we will further investigate the effectiveness of adaptive weight strategies through the lens of NTK theory discussed in Section 6.2.3. Specifically, let us consider general PDEs of the form 6.1–6.2, and approximate the latent solution $u(x)$ by a fully-connected neural network $u(x, \theta)$ with multiple hidden layers. As before, we seek to train the parameters θ by minimizing the following composite loss function

$$\mathcal{L}(\theta) = \mathcal{L}_b(\theta) + \mathcal{L}_r(\theta) \tag{6.28}$$

$$= \frac{\lambda_b}{2N_b} \sum_{i=1}^{N_b} |u(x_b^i, \theta) - g(x_b^i)|^2 + \frac{\lambda_r}{2N_r} \sum_{i=1}^{N_r} |r(x_r^i, \theta)|^2, \tag{6.29}$$

where λ_b and λ_r are some hyper-parameters, which may be tuned manually or automatically by utilizing the back-propagated gradient statistics during training [59]. Here, the training data $\{x_b^i, g(x_b^i)\}_{i=1}^{N_b}$ and $\{x_r^i, f(x_b^i)\}$ may correspond to the full data-batch or mini-batches that are randomly sampled at each iteration of gradient descent.

Similar to the proof of Lemma 6.1 (see [62] for the detailed proof), we can derive the joint dynamics of the outputs $u(x, \theta)$ and the PDE residual $\mathcal{L}u(x, \theta)$ corresponding to the above loss function as

$$
\begin{bmatrix} \frac{du(\boldsymbol{x}_b, \boldsymbol{\theta}(t))}{dt} \\ \frac{d\mathcal{L}u(\boldsymbol{x}_r, \boldsymbol{\theta}(t))}{dt} \end{bmatrix} = - \begin{bmatrix} \frac{\lambda_b}{N_b}\boldsymbol{K}_{uu}(t) & \frac{\lambda_r}{N_r}\boldsymbol{K}_{ur}(t) \\ \frac{\lambda_b}{N_b}\boldsymbol{K}_{ru}(t) & \frac{\lambda_r}{N_r}\boldsymbol{K}_{rr}(t) \end{bmatrix} \cdot \begin{bmatrix} u(\boldsymbol{x}_b, \boldsymbol{\theta}(t)) - g(\boldsymbol{x}_b) \\ \mathcal{L}u(\boldsymbol{x}_r, \boldsymbol{\theta}(t)) - f(\boldsymbol{x}_r) \end{bmatrix} \tag{6.30}
$$

$$
:= -\boldsymbol{K}(t) \cdot \begin{bmatrix} u(\boldsymbol{x}_b, \boldsymbol{\theta}(t)) - g(\boldsymbol{x}_b) \\ \mathcal{L}u(\boldsymbol{x}_r, \boldsymbol{\theta}(t)) - f(\boldsymbol{x}_r) \end{bmatrix}, \tag{6.31}
$$

where $\boldsymbol{K}_{uu}, \boldsymbol{K}_{ur}$, and $\boldsymbol{K}_{rr}$ are defined to be the same as in Equation 6.19. From a simple stability analysis of gradient descent (i.e., forward Euler [36]) discretization of above ODE system, the maximum learning rate should be less than or equal to $2/\lambda_{\max}(\boldsymbol{K}(t))$. Also note that an alternative mechanism for controlling stability is to increase the batch size, which effectively corresponds to decreasing the learning rate.

Recall that the current setup in the main theorems put forth in this work holds for the model problem in Equation 6.6 and fully-connected networks of one hidden layer with an NTK parameterization. This implies that, for general nonlinear PDEs, the NTK of PINNs may not remain fixed during training. Nevertheless, as mentioned in Remark 6.3, we emphasize that, given an infinitesimal learning rate, Equation 6.30 holds for any network architecture and any differential operator. Similarly, the singular values of NTK $\boldsymbol{K}(t)$ determine the convergence rate of the training error using singular value decomposition, since $\boldsymbol{K}(t)$ may not necessarily be semi-positive definite. Therefore, we can still understand the training dynamics of PINNs by tracking their NTK $\boldsymbol{K}(t)$ during training, even for general nonlinear PDE problems [62].

A key observation here is that the magnitude of λ_b, λ_r, as well as the size of mini-batch would have a crucial impact on the singular values of $\boldsymbol{K}(t)$, and, thus, the convergence rate of the training error of $u(\boldsymbol{x}_b, \boldsymbol{\theta})$ and $\mathcal{L}u(\boldsymbol{x}_r, \boldsymbol{\theta})$. For instance, if we increase λ_b and fix the batch size N_b, N_r and the weight λ_r, then this will improve the convergence rate of $u(\boldsymbol{x}_b, \boldsymbol{\theta})$. Furthermore, in the sense of convergence rate, changing the weights λ_b or λ_r is equivalent to changing the corresponding batch size N_b, N_r. Based on these observations, we can overcome the discrepancy between $\boldsymbol{K}_{uu}$ and $\boldsymbol{K}_{rr}$ by calibrating the weights or the batch-size such that each component of of $u(\boldsymbol{x}_r, \boldsymbol{\theta})$ and $\mathcal{L}u(\boldsymbol{x}_r, \boldsymbol{\theta})$ has similar convergence rate in magnitude. Since manipulating the batch-size may involve extra computational costs (e.g., it may result to prohibitively large batches), here we fix the batch size and just consider adjusting the weights λ_b or λ_r according to Algorithm 6.2.

First, we remark that the updates in Equations 6.32 and 6.33 can either take place at every iteration of the gradient descent loop, or at a frequency specified by the user (e.g., every 10 gradient descent steps). To compute the sum of eigenvalues, it suffices to compute the trace of the corresponding NTK matrices, which can save some computational resources. Besides, we point out that the computation of the NTK $\boldsymbol{K}(t)$ is associated with the training data points fed to the network at each iteration, which means that the values of the kernel are not necessarily the same at each iteration. However, if we assume that all training data points are sampled from the same distribution and the change of NTK at each iteration is negligible [19], then the computed kernel should be approximately equal up to a permutation matrix. As a result, the change of eigenvalues of $\boldsymbol{K}(t)$ at each iteration is also negligible and, therefore, the training process of Algorithm 6.2 should be stable. In Section 6.4, we performed detailed numerical experiments to validate the effectiveness of the proposed algorithm.

In contrast to the empirical formulation leading to Algorithm 6.1, the approach presented in this section follows naturally from the NTK theory presented in Section 6.2.3, and aims to trace and tackle the pathological convergence behavior of PINNs at its root.

Algorithm 6.2 Adaptive weights for PINNs

Consider a PINN $u(\boldsymbol{x}, \boldsymbol{\theta})$ with parameters $\boldsymbol{\theta}$ and a loss function

$$\mathcal{L}(\boldsymbol{\theta}) := \lambda_b \mathcal{L}_b(\boldsymbol{\theta}) + \lambda_r \mathcal{L}_r(\boldsymbol{\theta}),$$

where $\mathcal{L}_r(\boldsymbol{\theta})$ denotes the PDE residual loss and $\mathcal{L}_b(\boldsymbol{\theta})$ corresponds to the boundary loss. $\lambda_b = \lambda_r = 1$ are free parameters used to overcome the discrepancy between $\boldsymbol{K}_{uu}$ and $\boldsymbol{K}_{rr}$. Then use S steps of a gradient descent algorithm to update the parameters $\boldsymbol{\theta}$ as:
for $n = 1, \ldots, S$ **do**
  (a) Compute λ_b and λ_r by

$$\lambda_b = \frac{\sum_{i=1}^{N_r+N_b} \lambda_i(n)}{\sum_{i=1}^{N_b} \lambda_i^{uu}(n)} = \frac{Tr(\boldsymbol{K}(n))}{Tr(\boldsymbol{K}_{uu}(n))} \tag{6.32}$$

$$\lambda_r = \frac{\sum_{i=1}^{N_r+N_b} \lambda_i(n)}{\sum_{i=1}^{N_r} \lambda_i^{rr}(n)} = \frac{Tr(\boldsymbol{K}(n))}{Tr(\boldsymbol{K}_{rr}(n))} \tag{6.33}$$

where $\lambda_i(n), \lambda_i^{uu}$ and $\lambda_i^{rr}(n)$ are eigenvalues of $\boldsymbol{K}(n), \boldsymbol{K}_{uu}(n), \boldsymbol{K}_{rr}(n)$ at n-th iteration.
  (b) Update the parameters θ via gradient descent

$$\boldsymbol{\theta}_{n+1} = \boldsymbol{\theta}_n - \eta \nabla_{\boldsymbol{\theta}} \mathcal{L}(\boldsymbol{\theta}_n) \tag{6.34}$$

end for

6.4 Numerical Studies

In this section we present a collection of numerical studies that aim to highlight the performance and effectiveness of the adaptive training algorithms described in Section 6.3. Specifically, we present two benchmarks covering both forward and inverse problems for which conventional PINNs models [44] fail to train.

6.4.1 One-Dimensional Wave Equation

Here we present a comparative study that demonstrates the effectiveness of Algorithm 6.1 and Algorithm 6.2 in a practical problem for which conventional PINNs models face severe difficulties. To this end, we consider a one-dimensional wave equation in the domain $\Omega = [0,1] \times [0,1]$ taking the form

$$u_{tt}(x,t) - 4u_{xx}(x,t) = 0, \quad (x,t) \in (0,1) \times (0,1) \tag{6.35}$$

$$u(0,t) = u(1,t) = 0, \quad t \in [0,1] \tag{6.36}$$

$$u(x,0) = \sin(\pi x) + \frac{1}{2}\sin(4\pi x), \quad x \in [0,1] \tag{6.37}$$

$$u_t(x,0) = 0, \quad x \in [0,1]. \tag{6.38}$$

First, by d'Alembert's formula [11], the solution $u(x,t)$ is given by

$$u(x,t) = \sin(\pi x)\cos(2\pi t) + \frac{1}{2}\sin(4\pi x)\cos(8\pi t). \tag{6.39}$$

Here we treat the temporal coordinate t as an additional spatial coordinate in $\boldsymbol{x}$, and the initial condition 6.37 can be included in the boundary condition 6.36, namely

$$u(\boldsymbol{x}) = g(\boldsymbol{x}), \quad x \in \partial\Omega.$$

We proceed by approximating the solution $u(\boldsymbol{x})$ by a 5-layer deep fully-connected network $u(\boldsymbol{x}, \boldsymbol{\theta})$ with 500 neurons per hidden layer, where $\boldsymbol{x} = (x, t)$. Then we can formulate a "physics-informed" loss function as

$$\mathcal{L}(\boldsymbol{\theta}) = \lambda_u \mathcal{L}_u(\boldsymbol{\theta}) + \lambda_{u_t} \mathcal{L}_{u_t}(\boldsymbol{\theta}) + \lambda_r \mathcal{L}_r(\boldsymbol{\theta}) \tag{6.40}$$

$$= \frac{\lambda_u}{2N_u} \sum_{i=1}^{N_u} |u(\boldsymbol{x}_u^i, \boldsymbol{\theta}) - g(\boldsymbol{x}_u^i)|^2 + \frac{\lambda_{u_t}}{2N_{u_t}} \sum_{i=1}^{N_{u_t}} |u_t(\boldsymbol{x}_{u_t}^i, \boldsymbol{\theta})|^2 + \frac{\lambda_r}{2N_r} \sum_{i=1}^{N_r} |\mathcal{L}u(\boldsymbol{x}_r^i, \boldsymbol{\theta})|^2, \tag{6.41}$$

where the hyper-parameters $\lambda_u, \lambda_{u_t}, \lambda_r$ are initialized to 1, the batch sizes are set to $N_u = N_{u_t} = N_r = 300$, and $\mathcal{N} = \partial_{tt} - 4\partial_{xx}$. Here, all training data are uniformly sampling inside the computational domain at each gradient descent iteration. The network $u(\boldsymbol{x}, \boldsymbol{\theta})$ is initialized using the standard Glorot scheme [15], and subsequently trained by minimizing the above loss function via stochastic gradient descent using the Adam optimizer with default settings [22] and learning rate schedule with a decay rate of 0.9 every 1,000 iterations. Figure 6.5a provides a comparison between the predicted solution against the ground truth obtained after $80,000$ training iterations. Clearly, the original PINN model fails to approximate the ground truth solution and the relative L^2 error is above 40%.

To explore the reason behind the PINN model's failure for this example, we first track the back-propagated gradients at initialization. As shown in Figure 6.6, there exists a large discrepancy among the gradients distributions of $\mathcal{L}_r, \mathcal{L}_u, \mathcal{L}_{u_t}$, respectively. This is a clear manifestation of the imbalanced gradient pathology described in Section 6.3.1. Besides, we also compute its NTK and track it during training. In particular, the corresponding NTK can be derived from the loss function 6.40

$$\begin{bmatrix} \frac{du(\boldsymbol{x}_u, \boldsymbol{\theta}(t))}{dt} \\ \frac{du_t(\boldsymbol{x}_{u_t}, \boldsymbol{\theta}(t))}{dt} \\ \frac{d\mathcal{L}u(\boldsymbol{x}_r, \boldsymbol{\theta}(t))}{dt} \end{bmatrix} := \boldsymbol{K}(t) \cdot \begin{bmatrix} u(\boldsymbol{x}_b, \boldsymbol{\theta}(t)) - g(\boldsymbol{x}_b) \\ u_t(\boldsymbol{x}_{u_t}, \boldsymbol{\theta}(t)) \\ \mathcal{N}u(\boldsymbol{x}_r, \boldsymbol{\theta}(t)) \end{bmatrix}, \tag{6.42}$$

where

$$\boldsymbol{K}(t) = \begin{bmatrix} \frac{\lambda_u}{N_u} \boldsymbol{J}_u(t) \\ \frac{\lambda_{u_t}}{N_{u_t}} \boldsymbol{J}_{u_t}(t) \\ \frac{\lambda_r}{N_r} \boldsymbol{J}_r(t) \end{bmatrix} \cdot \left[\boldsymbol{J}_u^T(t), \boldsymbol{J}_{u_t}^T(t), \boldsymbol{J}_r^T(t) \right],$$

$$[\boldsymbol{K}_u(t)]_{ij} = \left[\boldsymbol{J}_u(t)\boldsymbol{J}_u^T(t) \right]_{ij} = \left\langle \frac{du(\boldsymbol{x}_u^i, \boldsymbol{\theta}(t))}{d\boldsymbol{\theta}}, \frac{du(\boldsymbol{x}_u^j, \boldsymbol{\theta}(t))}{d\boldsymbol{\theta}} \right\rangle$$

$$[\boldsymbol{K}_{u_t}(t)]_{ij} = \left[\boldsymbol{J}_{u_t}(t)\boldsymbol{J}_{u_t}^T(t) \right]_{ij} = \left\langle \frac{du_t(\boldsymbol{x}_{u_t}^i, \boldsymbol{\theta}(t))}{d\boldsymbol{\theta}}, \frac{du(\boldsymbol{x}_{u_t}^j, \boldsymbol{\theta}(t))}{d\boldsymbol{\theta}} \right\rangle$$

$$[\boldsymbol{K}_r(t)]_{ij} = \left[\boldsymbol{J}_r(t)\boldsymbol{J}_r^T(t) \right]_{ij} = \left\langle \frac{d\mathcal{N}u(\boldsymbol{x}_r^i, \boldsymbol{\theta}(t))}{d\boldsymbol{\theta}}, \frac{d\mathcal{N}u(\boldsymbol{x}_r^j, \boldsymbol{\theta}(t))}{d\boldsymbol{\theta}} \right\rangle.$$

A visual assessment of the eigenvalues of $\boldsymbol{K}_u, \boldsymbol{K}_{u_t}$, and $\boldsymbol{K}_r$ for different snapshots of the gradient descent are presented in Figure 6.7. It can be observed that the NTK does not remain fixed and all eigenvalues move "outward" in the beginning of the training, and then remain almost static such that $\boldsymbol{K}_r$ and $\boldsymbol{K}_{u_t}$ dominate $\boldsymbol{K}_u$ during training. Consequently, the

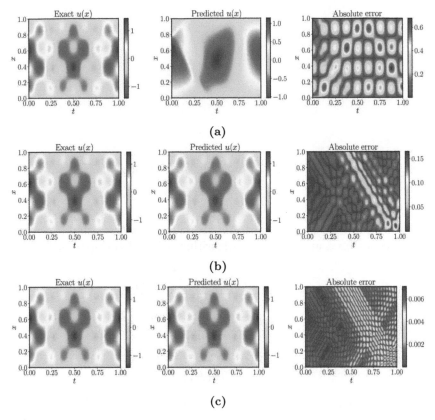

FIGURE 6.5

One-dimensional wave equation: (a) The predicted solution versus the exact solution by training a fully-connected neural network with five hidden layers and 500 neurons per layer using the Adam optimizer with default settings [22] after 80,000 iterations. The relative L^2 error is $4.518e-01$. (b) The predicted solution versus the exact solution by training the same network using Algorithm 6.1 after 80,000 iterations. The relative L^2 error is $7.025e-02$. (c) The predicted solution versus the exact solution by training the same network using Algorithm 6.2 after 80,000 iterations. The relative L^2 error is $1.728e-03$.

components of $u_t(\boldsymbol{x}_{u_t}, \boldsymbol{\theta})$ and $\mathcal{N}u(\boldsymbol{x}_r, \boldsymbol{\theta})$) converge much faster than the loss of boundary conditions, and, therefore, introduce a severe discrepancy in the convergence rate of each different term in the loss, causing this standard PINNs model to collapse.

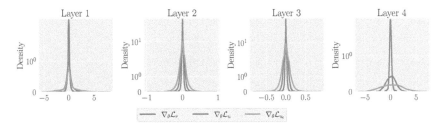

FIGURE 6.6

One-dimensional wave equation: Histograms of back-propagated gradients $\nabla_\theta \mathcal{L}_r(\theta)$, $\nabla_\theta \mathcal{L}_u(\theta)$, and $\nabla_\theta \mathcal{L}_{u_t}(\theta)$ at each hidden layer.

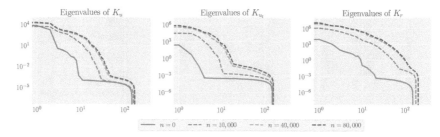

FIGURE 6.7

One-dimensional wave equation: Evolution of the spectra of $\boldsymbol{K}_u, \boldsymbol{K}_{u_t}$, and $\boldsymbol{K}_r$ during gradient descent.

Next, we train the same network with Algorithm 6.1 and Algorithm 6.2, respectively. In particular, the generalized update rule of Algorithm 6.2 for hyper-parameters $\lambda_u, \lambda_{u_t}, \lambda_r$ is modified by

$$\lambda_u = \frac{Tr(\boldsymbol{K}_u) + Tr(\boldsymbol{K}_{u_t}) + Tr(\boldsymbol{K}_r)}{Tr(\boldsymbol{K}_u)} \tag{6.43}$$

$$\lambda_{u_t} = \frac{Tr(\boldsymbol{K}_u) + Tr(\boldsymbol{K}_{u_t}) + Tr(\boldsymbol{K}_r)}{Tr(\boldsymbol{K}_{u_t})} \tag{6.44}$$

$$\lambda_r = \frac{Tr(\boldsymbol{K}_u) + Tr(\boldsymbol{K}_{u_t}) + Tr(\boldsymbol{K}_r)}{Tr(\boldsymbol{K}_r)}. \tag{6.45}$$

In particular, we update these weights every 1,000 training iterations, hence the extra computational costs compared to a standard PINNs approach is negligible. The predicted solutions are visualized in Figures 6.5b and 6.5c, from which one can easily see that both proposed adaptive training schemes lead to much more accurate predicted solutions than the original PINNs. We also observe that Algorithm 6.2 outperforms Algorithm 6.1, with a resulting relative L^2 error of $1.73e - 3$. In addition, we also compare the evolution of the assigned hyper-parameters λ_u, λ_{u_t} and λ_r of Algorithm 6.1 Algorithm 6.2 during training. As it can be seen in Figure 6.8, the updated hyper-parameters by Algorithm 6.1 exhibit high oscillations and do not converge. On the other hand, the updated λ_u, λ_{u_t} by Algorithm 6.2 increase rapidly and then remain almost fixed, while λ_r is near 1 for all time. So we may conclude that the overall training process using Algorithm 6.2 is stable.

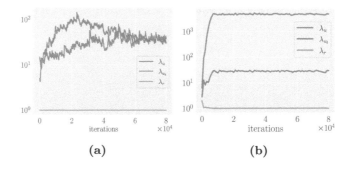

FIGURE 6.8

One-dimensional wave equation: (a) Evolution of adaptive weights under Algorithm 6.1. (b) Evolution of adaptive weights under Algorithm 6.2.

6.4.2 Two-Dimensional Navier–Stokes Equation

In this example we aim to demonstrate the effectiveness of proposed algorithms in a more challenging setting. To this end, we focus on applying Algorithm 6.2 to an inverse problem involving a two-dimensional steady-state flow in a idealized aneurysm, which can be described by the incompressible Navier–Stokes equations as follows

$$
\begin{aligned}
\boldsymbol{u} \cdot \nabla \boldsymbol{u} + \nabla p - \tfrac{1}{Re}\Delta \boldsymbol{u} = 0, \quad \boldsymbol{x} \in \Omega, \\
\nabla \cdot \boldsymbol{u} = 0, \quad \boldsymbol{x} \in \Omega,
\end{aligned}
\tag{6.46}
$$

subject to a no-slip boundary condition

$$
\boldsymbol{u} = 0, \quad \boldsymbol{x} \in \partial\Omega,
\tag{6.47}
$$

where $\boldsymbol{x} = (x, y)$ denotes the spatial coordinates, $\boldsymbol{u}(\boldsymbol{x}) = (u(\boldsymbol{x}), v(\boldsymbol{x}))$ is a velocity vector field, and $p = p(\boldsymbol{x})$ is a scalar pressure field. The aneurysm vessel is idealized as an asymmetric tube with a varying cross-section radius, which is parameterized by the following function

$$
R(x) = R_0 - A \frac{1}{\sqrt{(2\pi\sigma^2)}} \exp\left(-\frac{(x-\mu)^2}{2\sigma^2}\right),
\tag{6.48}
$$

where R_0 is the radius of the inlet, while A, μ, and σ define the shape of the idealized aneurysm geometry. Parameter μ defines the stream-wise location of the minimum (maximum) radius of the aneurysm, and σ affects the steepness of the geometric variation. In this example, we choose a relatively simple case corresponding to a Reynolds number of $Re = 1{,}000$ for which it is well understood that the flow quickly converges to an incompressible steady-state solution. We also set $R_0 = 0.05, A = -0.019, \mu = 0.5, \sigma = 0.1$. Visualizations of the reference velocity field are shown in Figure 6.9a.

Now, suppose that the geometry of the vessel is unknown except for the position of the inlet and the outlet, and our goal is to simultaneously reconstruct the velocity field u in the computational domain and identify the vessel geometry, assuming that some sparse measurements of $\boldsymbol{u}$ are given inside the domain. To this end, we can first introduce a neural network representation with parameters $\boldsymbol{\theta}$ that aims to learn how to map spatial coordinates (x, y) to the latent scalar functions $u(x, y), v(x, y), p(x, y)$, i.e.,

$$
[x, y] \xrightarrow{f_\theta} [u_\theta(x, y), v_\theta(x, y), p_\theta(x, y)].
\tag{6.49}
$$

Next, following the methodology of Wang *et al.* [58], we can introduce another network s_β to approximate the unknown vessel geometry. Then, we can define the PDE residual as

$$
R_\theta^u(x, y) := u_\theta \frac{\partial u_\theta}{\partial x} + v_\theta \frac{\partial u_\theta}{\partial y} + \frac{\partial p_\theta}{\partial x} - \frac{1}{Re}\left(\frac{\partial^2 u_\theta}{\partial x^2} + \frac{\partial^2 u_\theta}{\partial y^2}\right),
\tag{6.50}
$$

$$
R_\theta^v(x, y) := u_\theta \frac{\partial v_\theta}{\partial x} + v_\theta \frac{\partial v_\theta}{\partial y} + \frac{\partial p_\theta}{\partial y} - \frac{1}{Re}\left(\frac{\partial^2 v_\theta}{\partial x^2} + \frac{\partial^2 v_\theta}{\partial y^2}\right),
\tag{6.51}
$$

$$
R_\theta^c(x, y) := \frac{\partial u_\theta}{\partial x} + \frac{\partial v_\theta}{\partial y}.
\tag{6.52}
$$

We hypothesize that a PINN model $f_\theta(x, y)$ with a parametrized boundary $s_\beta(x)$ can now be trained to approximate the unknown velocity field as well as the unknown boundary $s(x)$ by minimizing the following composite loss

$$
\mathcal{L}(\boldsymbol{\theta}, \boldsymbol{\beta}) = \lambda_u \mathcal{L}_u(\boldsymbol{\theta}) + \lambda_v \mathcal{L}_v(\boldsymbol{\theta}) + \lambda_{R_u}\mathcal{L}_{R_u}(\boldsymbol{\theta}) + \lambda_{R_v}\mathcal{L}_{R_v}(\boldsymbol{\theta}) + \lambda_{R_c}\mathcal{L}_{r_c}(\boldsymbol{\theta}) + \lambda_{\mathcal{L}_b}(\boldsymbol{\theta}, \boldsymbol{\beta}),
\tag{6.53}
$$

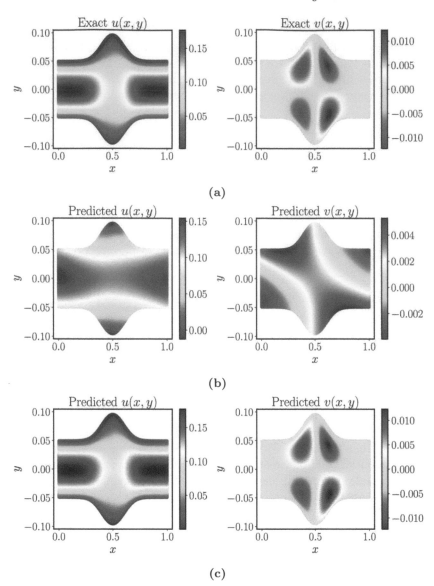

FIGURE 6.9
Two-dimensional Navier–Stokes equation: (a) Exact velocity field. (b) Reconstructed velocity field of a trained conventional PINN model. (c) Reconstructed velocity field of a PINN model trained using Algorithm 6.2.

where $\lambda_u, \lambda_v, \lambda_{R_u}, \lambda_{R_v}, \lambda_{R_c}, \lambda_{\mathcal{L}_b}$ are some hyper-parameters that can be updated during training, and

$$\mathcal{L}_u(\boldsymbol{\theta}) = \frac{1}{N} \sum_{i=1}^{N} [u_{\boldsymbol{\theta}}(x^i, y^i) - u^i]^2, \qquad (6.54)$$

$$\mathcal{L}_v(\boldsymbol{\theta}) = \frac{1}{N} \sum_{i=1}^{N} [v_{\boldsymbol{\theta}}(x^i, y^i) - v^i]^2, \qquad (6.55)$$

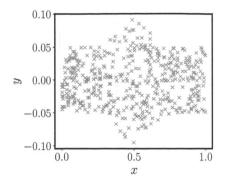

FIGURE 6.10
Two-dimensional Navier–Stokes equation: An illustration of the location of velocity measurements.

$$\mathcal{L}_{R_u}(\boldsymbol{\theta}) = \frac{1}{N_r} \sum_{i=1}^{N_r} [R_{\boldsymbol{\theta}}^u(x_r^i, y_r^i)]^2, \tag{6.56}$$

$$\mathcal{L}_{R_v}(\boldsymbol{\theta}) = \frac{1}{N_r} \sum_{i=1}^{N_r} [R_{\boldsymbol{\theta}}^v(x_r^i, y_r^i)]^2, \tag{6.57}$$

$$\mathcal{L}_{R_c}(\boldsymbol{\theta}) = \frac{1}{N_r} \sum_{i=1}^{N_r} [R_{\boldsymbol{\theta}}^c(x_r^i, y_r^i)]^2 \tag{6.58}$$

$$\mathcal{L}_b(\boldsymbol{\theta}, \boldsymbol{\beta}) = \frac{1}{N_r} \sum_{i=1}^{N_r} \left[|u_{\boldsymbol{\theta}}(s_{\boldsymbol{\beta}}(x_r^i))|^2 + |u_{\boldsymbol{\theta}}(-s_{\boldsymbol{\beta}}(x_r^i))|^2 + |v_{\boldsymbol{\theta}}(s_{\boldsymbol{\beta}}(x_r^i))|^2 |v_{\boldsymbol{\theta}}(-s_{\boldsymbol{\beta}}(x_r^i))|^2 \right], \tag{6.59}$$

where $\{x^i, y^i, u^i, v^i\}_{i=1}^N$ are some spare measurements of the velocity field, and $\{x_r^i, y_r^i\}_{i=1}^{N_r}$ are collocation points that are randomly sampled inside the computational domain at each iteration.

Specifically, we represent the latent variables u, v, p and the unknown vessel geometry by two 5-layer fully-connected neural networks with 100 units per hidden layer, respectively. In particular, both networks are equipped with tanh activation functions. As visualized in Figure 6.10, we randomly select $N = 500$ measurements of the velocity field as our training data-set. We let $\lambda_u = \lambda_v, \lambda_{R_u} = \lambda_{R_v} = \lambda_{R_c} = \lambda_{\mathcal{L}_b} = 1$ and train our physics-informed model by minimizing the loss function 6.53 for 40,000 iterations using the Adam optimizer with default settings. The reconstructed velocity field and the vessel geometry are shown in Figures 6.9b and 6.11a, respectively. Apparently, this conventional PINNs approach is not able to yield correct predictions.

Before applying Algorithm 6.2 to PINNs, we need to derive the corresponding NTK over the parameter space $\boldsymbol{\theta}$, which is given by

$$\begin{bmatrix} \frac{du_{\boldsymbol{\theta}}(\boldsymbol{x}, \boldsymbol{y})}{dt} \\ \frac{dv_{\boldsymbol{\theta}}(\boldsymbol{x}, \boldsymbol{y})}{dt} \\ \frac{dR_{\boldsymbol{\theta}}^u(\boldsymbol{x}_r, \boldsymbol{y}_r)}{dt} \\ \frac{dR_{\boldsymbol{\theta}}^v(\boldsymbol{x}_r, \boldsymbol{y}_r)}{dt} \\ \frac{dR_{\boldsymbol{\theta}}^c(\boldsymbol{x}_r, \boldsymbol{y}_r)}{dt} \end{bmatrix} := \boldsymbol{K}(t) \cdot \begin{bmatrix} u_{\boldsymbol{\theta}}(\boldsymbol{x}, \boldsymbol{y}) - \boldsymbol{u} \\ v_{\boldsymbol{\theta}}(\boldsymbol{x}, \boldsymbol{y}) - \boldsymbol{v} \\ R_{\boldsymbol{\theta}}^u(\boldsymbol{x}_r, \boldsymbol{y}_r) \\ R_{\boldsymbol{\theta}}^v(\boldsymbol{x}_r, \boldsymbol{y}_r) \\ R_{\boldsymbol{\theta}}^c(\boldsymbol{x}_r, \boldsymbol{y}_r) \end{bmatrix}, \tag{6.60}$$

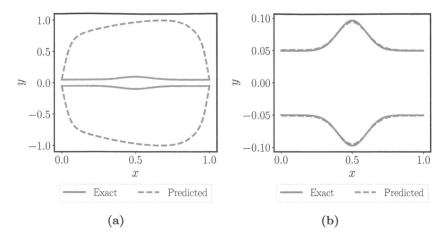

FIGURE 6.11
Two-dimensional Navier–Stokes equation: (a)(b) Exact vessel geometry versus the identified vessel geometry obtained by a trained PINN model with or without Algorithm 6.2.

where

$$\boldsymbol{K}(t) = \begin{bmatrix} \boldsymbol{J}_u(t) \\ \boldsymbol{J}_v(t) \\ \boldsymbol{J}_{R_u}(t) \\ \boldsymbol{J}_{R_v}(t) \\ \boldsymbol{J}_{R_c}(t) \end{bmatrix} \cdot \left[\boldsymbol{J}_u^T(t), \boldsymbol{J}_v^T(t), \boldsymbol{J}_{R_u}^T(t), \boldsymbol{J}_{R_v}^T(t), \boldsymbol{J}_{R_c}^T(t) \right],$$

$$[\boldsymbol{K}_u(t)]_{ij} = \left[\boldsymbol{J}_u(t)\boldsymbol{J}_u^T(t) \right]_{ij} = \left\langle \frac{du_{\boldsymbol{\theta}}(x^i, y^i)}{d\boldsymbol{\theta}}, \frac{du_{\boldsymbol{\theta}}(x^j, y^j)}{d\boldsymbol{\theta}} \right\rangle$$

$$[\boldsymbol{K}_v(t)]_{ij} = \left[\boldsymbol{J}_v(t)\boldsymbol{J}_v^T(t) \right]_{ij} = \left\langle \frac{dv_{\boldsymbol{\theta}}(x^i, y^i)}{d\boldsymbol{\theta}}, \frac{dv_{\boldsymbol{\theta}}(x^j, y^j)}{d\boldsymbol{\theta}} \right\rangle$$

$$[\boldsymbol{K}_{R_u}(t)]_{ij} = \left[\boldsymbol{J}_{R_u}(t)\boldsymbol{J}_{R_u}^T(t) \right]_{ij} = \left\langle \frac{dR_{\boldsymbol{\theta}}^u(x_r^i, y_r^i)}{d\boldsymbol{\theta}}, \frac{dR_{\boldsymbol{\theta}}^u(x_r^j, y_r^j)}{d\boldsymbol{\theta}} \right\rangle$$

$$[\boldsymbol{K}_{R_v}(t)]_{ij} = \left[\boldsymbol{J}_{R_v}(t)\boldsymbol{J}_{R_v}^T(t) \right]_{ij} = \left\langle \frac{dR_{\boldsymbol{\theta}}^v(x_r^i, y_r^i)}{d\boldsymbol{\theta}}, \frac{dR_{\boldsymbol{\theta}}^v(x_r^j, y_r^j)}{d\boldsymbol{\theta}} \right\rangle$$

$$[\boldsymbol{K}_{R_c}(t)]_{ij} = \left[\boldsymbol{J}_{R_c}(t)\boldsymbol{J}_{R_c}^T(t) \right]_{ij} = \left\langle \frac{dR_{\boldsymbol{\theta}}^c(x_r^i, y_r^i)}{d\boldsymbol{\theta}}, \frac{dR_{\boldsymbol{\theta}}^c(x_r^j, y_r^j)}{d\boldsymbol{\theta}} \right\rangle.$$

Then, the update rule for the weights in Equation 6.53 can be derived as

$$\lambda_u = \frac{Tr(\boldsymbol{K}_u) + Tr(\boldsymbol{K}_v) + Tr(\boldsymbol{K}_{R_u}) + Tr(\boldsymbol{K}_{R_v}) + Tr(\boldsymbol{K}_{R_c})}{Tr(\boldsymbol{K}_u)} \tag{6.61}$$

$$\lambda_v = \frac{Tr(\boldsymbol{K}_u) + Tr(\boldsymbol{K}_v) + Tr(\boldsymbol{K}_{R_u}) + Tr(\boldsymbol{K}_{R_v}) + Tr(\boldsymbol{K}_{R_c})}{Tr(\boldsymbol{K}_v)} \tag{6.62}$$

$$\lambda_{R_u} = \frac{Tr(\boldsymbol{K}_u) + Tr(\boldsymbol{K}_v) + Tr(\boldsymbol{K}_{R_u}) + Tr(\boldsymbol{K}_{R_v}) + Tr(\boldsymbol{K}_{R_c})}{Tr(\boldsymbol{K}_{R_u})} \tag{6.63}$$

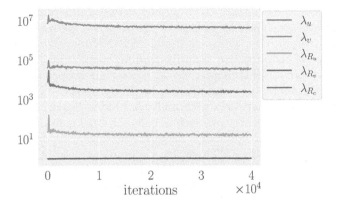

FIGURE 6.12
Two-dimensional Navier–Stokes equation: Evolution of adaptive weights under Algorithm 6.2 during training.

$$\lambda_{R_v} = \frac{Tr(\boldsymbol{K}_u) + Tr(\boldsymbol{K}_v) + Tr(\boldsymbol{K}_{R_u}) + Tr(\boldsymbol{K}_{R_v}) + Tr(\boldsymbol{K}_{R_c})}{Tr(\boldsymbol{K}_{R_v})} \qquad (6.64)$$

$$\lambda_{R_c} = \frac{Tr(\boldsymbol{K}_u) + Tr(\boldsymbol{K}_v) + Tr(\boldsymbol{K}_{R_u}) + Tr(\boldsymbol{K}_{R_v}) + Tr(\boldsymbol{K}_{R_c})}{Tr(\boldsymbol{K}_{R_c})}. \qquad (6.65)$$

Now we can train the network with the Algorithm 6.2 for 40,000 iterations of gradient descent using the Adam optimizer under exactly the same hyper-parameter settings described above. The predicted velocity field of the trained model are shown in Figure 6.9c, from which one can observe that an excellent agreement can be achieved between the model predictions and the ground truth. Moreover, as visualized in Figure 6.11b, we see that the reconstructed vessel geometry agrees with the exact one well with the relative L^2 error of $1.19e-2$. These observations indicate the necessity of assigning appropriate weights in training PINNs. As shown in Figure 6.12, these weights may span different orders of magnitude, hence tuning them by hand or via simple hyper-parameter optimization and meta-learning techniques may be infeasible. This further illustrates the merit of the adaptive schemes discussed in this work.

6.5   Discussion

As physics-informed deep learning tools are introducing a new paradigm in synthesizing governing physical laws and observational data, several open questions arise related to the trainability, robustness and accuracy of such models. Specific to the framework of PINNs [44], a need arises for stochastic optimization tools that can be effective in minimizing composite multi-task loss functions. In this chapter we review recent developments in adaptive training strategies for PINNs [59,60,62] with the goal of shedding light into the mechanisms that may trigger training instabilities, subsequently motivating the development of novel optimization schemes. Specifically, we demonstrate how PINNs suffer from a remarkable discrepancy in the convergence rate between different components in their loss, ultimately leading to stiff gradient flows and vanishing gradients during training. We employ NTK theory to elucidate the training dynamics of PINNs under gradient descent, and design novel optimization schemes that can effectively balance the interplay between different terms in the loss and lead to robust convergence. The effectiveness of the proposed algorithms is demonstrated in two representative scenarios for which conventional PINN models fail, thus indicating the practical importance of the propsoed adaptive training algorithms.

The findings presented in this chapter also give rise to new open questions worth exploring in future work. From a theory point of view, can the proposed NTK theory for PINNs be extended to fully-connected networks with multiple hidden layers, nonlinear equations, as well as the neural network architectures such as convolutional neural networks, residual networks, etc.? Going beyond vanilla gradient descent dynamics, how do the training dynamics of PINNs and their corresponding NTK evolve via gradient descent with momentum (e.g., Adam [22])? From a practical point of view, does the proposed NTK theory hold for general multi-task learning problems? Can other heuristic methods for multi-task learning [8,17,63] be analyzed and improved under this setting? We believe that answering these questions not only paves a new way to better understand PINNs and its training dynamics, but also opens a new door for developing scientific machine learning algorithms with provable convergence guarantees, as needed for many critical applications in computational science and engineering.

Acknowledgments

This work received support from DOE grant DE-SC0019116, AFOSR grant FA9550-20-1-0060, and DOE-ARPA grant DE-AR0001201.

Bibliography

[1] Babak Alipanahi, Andrew Delong, Matthew T Weirauch, and Brendan J Frey. Predicting the sequence specificities of dna-and rna-binding proteins by deep learning. *Nature Biotechnology*, 33(8):831, 2015.

[2] Sanjeev Arora, Simon S Du, Wei Hu, Zhiyuan Li, Russ R Salakhutdinov, and Ruosong Wang. On exact computation with an infinitely wide neural net. In *Advances in Neural Information Processing Systems*, pages 8141–8150, 2019.

[3] Pierre Baldi, Peter Sadowski, and Daniel Whiteson. Searching for exotic particles in high-energy physics with deep learning. *Nature Communications*, 5:4308, 2014.

[4] Atılım Güneş Baydin, Barak A Pearlmutter, Alexey Andreyevich Radul, and Jeffrey Mark Siskind. Automatic differentiation in machine learning: a survey. *The Journal of Machine Learning Research*, 18(1):5595–5637, 2017.

[5] Dimitri P Bertsekas. *Constrained Optimization and Lagrange Multiplier Methods*. Academic Press, 2014.

[6] Yuan Cao, Zhiying Fang, Yue Wu, Ding-Xuan Zhou, and Quanquan Gu. Towards understanding the spectral bias of deep learning. *arXiv preprint arXiv:1912.01198*, 2019.

[7] Yuyao Chen, Lu Lu, George Em Karniadakis, and Luca Dal Negro. Physics-informed neural networks for inverse problems in nano-optics and metamaterials. *Optics Express*, 28(8):11618–11633, 2020.

[8] Zhao Chen, Vijay Badrinarayanan, Chen-Yu Lee, and Andrew Rabinovich. Gradnorm: Gradient normalization for adaptive loss balancing in deep multitask networks. In *International Conference on Machine Learning*, pages 794–803. PMLR, 2018.

[9] Kyunghyun Cho, Bart Van Merriënboer, Caglar Gulcehre, Dzmitry Bahdanau, Fethi Bougares, Holger Schwenk, and Yoshua Bengio. Learning phrase representations using rnn encoder-decoder for statistical machine translation. *arXiv preprint arXiv:1406.1078*, 2014.

[10] Jeffrey Donahue, Lisa Anne Hendricks, Sergio Guadarrama, Marcus Rohrbach, Subhashini Venugopalan, Kate Saenko, and Trevor Darrell. Long-term recurrent convolutional networks for visual recognition and description. In *Proceedings of the IEEE Conference on Computer Vision and Pattern Recognition*, pages 2625–2634, 2015.

[11] LC Evans and American Mathematical Society. *Partial Differential Equations*. Graduate studies in mathematics. American Mathematical Society, 1998.

[12] Zhiwei Fang and Justin Zhan. Deep physical informed neural networks for metamaterial design. *IEEE Access*, 8:24506–24513, 2019.

[13] Han Gao, Luning Sun, and Jian-Xun Wang. PhyGeoNet: Physics-informed geometry-adaptive convolutional neural networks for solving parametric PDEs on irregular domain. *arXiv preprint arXiv:2004.13145*, 2020.

[14] Charles William Gear and DR Wells. Multirate linear multistep methods. *BIT Numerical Mathematics*, 24(4):484–502, 1984.

[15] Xavier Glorot and Yoshua Bengio. Understanding the difficulty of training deep feedforward neural networks. In *Proceedings of the Thirteenth International Conference on Artificial Intelligence and Statistics*, pages 249–256, 2010.

[16] Jiequn Han, Arnulf Jentzen, and E Weinan. Solving high-dimensional partial differential equations using deep learning. *Proceedings of the National Academy of Sciences*, 115(34):8505–8510, 2018.

[17] A Ali Heydari, Craig A Thompson, and Asif Mehmood. Softadapt: Techniques for adaptive loss weighting of neural networks with multi-part loss functions. *arXiv preprint arXiv:1912.12355*, 2019.

[18] Arieh Iserles. *A First Course in the Numerical Analysis of Differential Equations*. Number 44. Cambridge University Press, 2009.

[19] Arthur Jacot, Franck Gabriel, and Clément Hongler. Neural tangent kernel: Convergence and generalization in neural networks. In *Advances in Neural Information Processing Systems*, pages 8571–8580, 2018.

[20] Xiaowei Jin, Shengze Cai, Hui Li, and George Em Karniadakis. Nsfnets (Navier-Stokes flow nets): Physics-informed neural networks for the incompressible Navier-Stokes equations. *arXiv preprint arXiv:2003.06496*, 2020.

[21] Sharmila Karumuri, Rohit Tripathy, Ilias Bilionis, and Jitesh Panchal. Simulator-free solution of high-dimensional stochastic elliptic partial differential equations using deep neural networks. *Journal of Computational Physics*, 404:109120, 2020.

[22] Diederik P Kingma and Jimmy Ba. Adam: A method for stochastic optimization. *arXiv preprint arXiv:1412.6980*, 2014.

[23] Georgios Kissas, Yibo Yang, Eileen Hwuang, Walter R Witschey, John A Detre, and Paris Perdikaris. Machine learning in cardiovascular flows modeling: Predicting arterial blood pressure from non-invasive 4D flow MRI data using physics-informed neural networks. *Computer Methods in Applied Mechanics and Engineering*, 358:112623, 2020.

[24] Alex Krizhevsky, Ilya Sutskever, and Geoffrey E Hinton. Imagenet classification with deep convolutional neural networks. In *Advances in Neural Information Processing Systems*, pages 1097–1105, 2012.

[25] Isaac E Lagaris, Aristidis Likas, and Dimitrios I Fotiadis. Artificial neural networks for solving ordinary and partial differential equations. *IEEE Transactions on Neural Networks*, 9(5):987–1000, 1998.

[26] Jaehoon Lee, Yasaman Bahri, Roman Novak, Samuel S Schoenholz, Jeffrey Pennington, and Jascha Sohl-Dickstein. Deep neural networks as Gaussian processes. *arXiv preprint arXiv:1711.00165*, 2017.

[27] Jaehoon Lee, Lechao Xiao, Samuel Schoenholz, Yasaman Bahri, Roman Novak, Jascha Sohl-Dickstein, and Jeffrey Pennington. Wide neural networks of any depth evolve as linear models under gradient descent. In *Advances in Neural Information Processing Systems*, pages 8572–8583, 2019.

[28] Xi-An Li, Zhi-Qin John Xu, and Lei Zhang. A DNN-based algorithm for multi-scale elliptic problems. *arXiv preprint arXiv:2009.14597*, 2020.

[29] Zongyi Li, Nikola Kovachki, Kamyar Azizzadenesheli, Burigede Liu, Kaushik Bhattacharya, Andrew Stuart, and Anima Anandkumar. Fourier neural operator for parametric partial differential equations. *arXiv preprint arXiv:2010.08895*, 2020.

[30] Ziqi Liu, Wei Cai, and Zhi-Qin John Xu. Multi-scale deep neural network (MscaleDNN) for solving Poisson-Boltzmann equation in complex domains. *arXiv preprint arXiv:2007.11207*, 2020.

[31] Lu Lu, Pengzhan Jin, and George Em Karniadakis. DeepONet: Learning nonlinear operators for identifying differential equations based on the universal approximation theorem of operators. *arXiv preprint arXiv:1910.03193*, 2019.

[32] Lu Lu, Xuhui Meng, Zhiping Mao, and George E Karniadakis. DeepXDE: A deep learning library for solving differential equations. *arXiv preprint arXiv:1907.04502*, 2019.

[33] Tao Luo and Haizhao Yang. Two-layer neural networks for partial differential equations: Optimization and generalization theory. *arXiv preprint arXiv:2006.15733*, 2020.

[34] Alexander G de G Matthews, Mark Rowland, Jiri Hron, Richard E Turner, and Zoubin Ghahramani. Gaussian process behaviour in wide deep neural networks. *arXiv preprint arXiv:1804.11271*, 2018.

[35] Levi McClenny and Ulisses Braga-Neto. Self-adaptive physics-informed neural networks using a soft attention mechanism. *arXiv preprint arXiv:2009.04544*, 2020.

[36] Parviz Moin. *Fundamentals of Engineering Numerical Analysis*. Cambridge University Press, 2010.

[37] Geir K Nilsen, Antonella Z Munthe-Kaas, Hans J Skaug, and Morten Brun. Efficient computation of hessian matrices in tensorflow. *arXiv preprint arXiv:1905.05559*, 2019.

[38] Guofei Pang, Lu Lu, and George Em Karniadakis. fpinns: Fractional physics-informed neural networks. *SIAM Journal on Scientific Computing*, 41(4):A2603–A2626, 2019.

[39] Dimitris C Psichogios and Lyle H Ungar. A hybrid neural network-first principles approach to process modeling. *AIChE Journal*, 38(10):1499–1511, 1992.

[40] Alec Radford, Luke Metz, and Soumith Chintala. Unsupervised representation learning with deep convolutional generative adversarial networks. *arXiv preprint arXiv:1511.06434*, 2015.

[41] Nasim Rahaman, Aristide Baratin, Devansh Arpit, Felix Draxler, Min Lin, Fred Hamprecht, Yoshua Bengio, and Aaron Courville. On the spectral bias of neural networks. In *International Conference on Machine Learning*, pages 5301–5310, 2019.

[42] Maziar Raissi. Deep hidden physics models: Deep learning of nonlinear partial differential equations. *The Journal of Machine Learning Research*, 19(1):932–955, 2018.

[43] Maziar Raissi. Forward-backward stochastic neural networks: Deep learning of high-dimensional partial differential equations. *arXiv preprint arXiv:1804.07010*, 2018.

[44] Maziar Raissi, Paris Perdikaris, and George E Karniadakis. Physics-informed neural networks: A deep learning framework for solving forward and inverse problems involving nonlinear partial differential equations. *Journal of Computational Physics*, 378:686–707, 2019.

[45] Maziar Raissi, Alireza Yazdani, and George Em Karniadakis. Hidden fluid mechanics: Learning velocity and pressure fields from flow visualizations. *Science*, 367(6481):1026–1030, 2020.

[46] Brandon Reyes, Amanda A Howard, Paris Perdikaris, and Alexandre M Tartakovsky. Learning unknown physics of non-Newtonian fluids. *arXiv preprint arXiv:2009.01658*, 2020.

[47] Basri Ronen, David Jacobs, Yoni Kasten, and Shira Kritchman. The convergence rate of neural networks for learned functions of different frequencies. In *Advances in Neural Information Processing Systems*, pages 4761–4771, 2019.

[48] Levent Sagun, Leon Bottou, and Yann LeCun. Eigenvalues of the hessian in deep learning: Singularity and beyond. *arXiv preprint arXiv:1611.07476*, 2016.

[49] Francisco Sahli Costabal, Yibo Yang, Paris Perdikaris, Daniel E Hurtado, and Ellen Kuhl. Physics-informed neural networks for cardiac activation mapping. *Frontiers in Physics*, 8:42, 2020.

[50] Yeonjong Shin, Jérôme Darbon, and George Em Karniadakis. On the convergence of physics informed neural networks for linear second-order elliptic and parabolic type PDEs. 2020.

[51] Yeonjong Shin, Zhongqiang Zhang, and George Em Karniadakis. Error estimates of residual minimization using neural networks for linear PDEs. *arXiv preprint arXiv:2010.08019*, 2020.

[52] David Silver, Julian Schrittwieser, Karen Simonyan, Ioannis Antonoglou, Aja Huang, Arthur Guez, Thomas Hubert, Lucas Baker, Matthew Lai, Adrian Bolton, et al. Mastering the game of go without human knowledge. *Nature*, 550(7676):354–359, 2017.

[53] Justin Sirignano and Konstantinos Spiliopoulos. DGM: A deep learning algorithm for solving partial differential equations. *Journal of Computational Physics*, 375:1339–1364, 2018.

[54] Luning Sun, Han Gao, Shaowu Pan, and Jian-Xun Wang. Surrogate modeling for fluid flows based on physics-constrained deep learning without simulation data. *arXiv preprint arXiv:1906.02382*, 2019.

[55] Luning Sun, Han Gao, Shaowu Pan, and Jian-Xun Wang. Surrogate modeling for fluid flows based on physics-constrained deep learning without simulation data. *Computer Methods in Applied Mechanics and Engineering*, 361:112732, 2020.

[56] Matthew Tancik, Pratul P Srinivasan, Ben Mildenhall, Sara Fridovich-Keil, Nithin Raghavan, Utkarsh Singhal, Ravi Ramamoorthi, Jonathan T Barron, and Ren Ng. Fourier features let networks learn high frequency functions in low dimensional domains. *arXiv preprint arXiv:2006.10739*, 2020.

[57] Bo Wang, Wenzhong Zhang, and Wei Cai. Multi-scale deep neural network (MscaleDNN) methods for oscillatory stokes flows in complex domains. *arXiv preprint arXiv:2009.12729*, 2020.

[58] Sifan Wang and Paris Perdikaris. Deep learning of free boundary and Stefan problems. *arXiv preprint arXiv:2006.05311*, 2020.

[59] Sifan Wang, Yujun Teng, and Paris Perdikaris. Understanding and mitigating gradient pathologies in physics-informed neural networks. *arXiv preprint arXiv:2001.04536*, 2020.

[60] Sifan Wang, Hanwen Wang, and Paris Perdikaris. On the eigenvector bias of fourier feature networks: From regression to solving multi-scale pdes with physics-informed neural networks. *arXiv preprint arXiv:2012.10047*, 2020.

[61] Sifan Wang, Hanwen Wang, and Paris Perdikaris. Learning the solution operator of parametric partial differential equations with physics-informed deeponets. *arXiv preprint arXiv:2103.10974*, 2021.

[62] Sifan Wang, Xinling Yu, and Paris Perdikaris. When and why PINNs fail to train: A neural tangent kernel perspective. *arXiv preprint arXiv:2007.14527*, 2020.

[63] Haowen Xu, Hao Zhang, Zhiting Hu, Xiaodan Liang, Ruslan Salakhutdinov, and Eric Xing. Autoloss: Learning discrete schedules for alternate optimization. *arXiv preprint arXiv:1810.02442*, 2018.

[64] Liu Yang, Xuhui Meng, and George Em Karniadakis. B-pinns: Bayesian physics-informed neural networks for forward and inverse pde problems with noisy data. *arXiv preprint arXiv:2003.06097*, 2020.

[65] Liu Yang, Dongkun Zhang, and George Em Karniadakis. Physics-informed generative adversarial networks for stochastic differential equations. *SIAM Journal on Scientific Computing*, 42(1):A292–A317, 2020.

[66] Yibo Yang, Mohamed Aziz Bhouri, and Paris Perdikaris. Bayesian differential programming for robust systems identification under uncertainty. *Proceedings of the Royal Society A: Mathematical, Physical and Engineering Sciences*, 476(2243):20200290, November 2020.

[67] Yibo Yang and Paris Perdikaris. Adversarial uncertainty quantification in physics-informed neural networks. *Journal of Computational Physics*, 394:136–152, 2019.

[68] Alireza Yazdani, Lu Lu, Maziar Raissi, and George Em Karniadakis. Systems biology informed deep learning for inferring parameters and hidden dynamics. *PLoS Computational Biology*, 16(11):e1007575, 2020.

[69] Dongkun Zhang, Ling Guo, and George Em Karniadakis. Learning in modal space: Solving time-dependent stochastic PDEs using physics-informed neural networks. *SIAM Journal on Scientific Computing*, 42(2):A639–A665, 2020.

[70] Yinhao Zhu, Nicholas Zabaras, Phaedon-Stelios Koutsourelakis, and Paris Perdikaris. Physics-constrained deep learning for high-dimensional surrogate modeling and uncertainty quantification without labeled data. *Journal of Computational Physics*, 394:56–81, 2019.

7

Modern Deep Learning for Modeling Physical Systems

Nicholas Geneva and Nicholas Zabaras

CONTENTS

Advances in deep learning have made constructing, training and deploying deep neural networks (DNNs) more accessible than ever before. Due to their flexibility and predictive accuracy, DNNs have ushered in a new wave of data-driven modeling for physical phenomena. With several key research breakthroughs in the deep learning field, modern deep learning architectures are now more accurate and generalizable than their predecessors developed over two decades ago. This chapter is a review of several core modern DNN architectures discussed in the context of learning physical phenomena. It provides a concise introduction to surrogate modeling with state-of-the-art deep learning. Probabilistic frameworks are also reviewed including Bayesian neural networks and deep generative models to facilitate uncertainty quantification of deep learning surrogate models. Leveraging these recent DNN advancements allows for the development of powerful models of physical systems that can predict complex mutli-scale features.

DOI: 10.1201/9781003143376-7

7.1   Introduction

In recent years, machine learning and deep learning have entered a renaissance in which groundbreaking findings have made deep learning models widely successful for a vast number of applications. One such application is surrogate modeling in which a deep learning model can be used as a black box method to approximate a physical system. Among the most popular deep learning models is DNNs due to their superior accuracy for big data problems. A DNN can show unique generalization properties yielding accurate predictions for distributions of physical systems rather than a single solution. These are typically over-parameterized models (hundreds and thousands of times more parameters than training data), but well-designed DNNs tend not to overfit, i.e. the test error does not grow as the network parameters increase. This can be achieved through multiple means such as selecting a DNN architecture that leverages inductive bias well suited for the data set of interest. Weight decay terms and probabilistic frameworks can be used to enforce sparsity on the model's learnable weights as well as further prevent over-fitting. Loss functions that integrate prior knowledge such as physical constraints, invariances or conservation properties allow DNNs to further increase generalization even in out of sample test cases. These techniques make it feasible to use deep neural networks for surrogate modeling physics. As shown in recent literature, DNNs are capable of capturing the complex nonlinear mapping between high-dimensional inputs and outputs due to their expressiveness.

DNNs have already proven to be effective for modeling a wide spectrum of physical systems such as flow through porous media, Navier–Stokes equations, turbulence modeling, molecular dynamics and more. With an ever growing interest in the application of DNNs for modeling physics, the volume of literature surrounding this topic is daunting. This particular chapter aims to provide a selection of several modern deep learning methods for learning physics in a concise high-level overview. The rest of this chapter is structured into two parts: Section 7.2 discusses deterministic aspects of DNN models for learning physical systems. Following in Section 7.3, probabilistic methods for DNNs are discussed covering how a probabilistic framework can be used for uncertainty quantification.

7.2   Modern Neural Networks for Physical Systems

With the resurgence of interest in deep learning, particularly DNNs, a significant amount of research has been performed studying and improving neural network architectures in the machine learning community. These interdisciplinary advancements have allowed DNN models to increase predictive accuracy, convergence and generalization. Taking advantage of these advances for constructing physical models is frequently neglected by the scientific machine learning community in favor of traditional, typically fully-connected models developed over two decades ago. While at a cost of increased design complexity, modern DNN architectures have significant potential for building data-driven surrogates of physical systems with unprecedented accuracy and speed.

7.2.1   Deep Convolutional Neural Networks

Convolutional neural networks have become a foundational part of modern machine learning. While originally proposed several decades ago, convolutional operations are at the

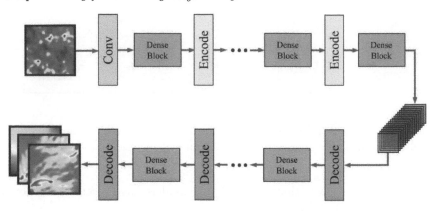

FIGURE 7.1
Dense convolutional encoder–decoder network for the prediction of high-dimensional stochastic PDEs [28].

core of modern deep learning present in landmark models such as AlexNet [15], VGG [25], ResNet [11], etc. Convolutional neural networks require significantly less learnable weights than fully-connected networks due to parameter sharing which allows for faster predictions. Recently, convolutional neural networks have been shown to yield faster convergence and better predictive capability for physics-constrained training compared to fully-connected networks [28, 29].

A common model design pattern for semantic segmentation or depth regression is the encoder–decoder architecture. The intuition is to learn regression between two high-dimensional objects through a coarse-refine process, i.e. to extract high-level coarse features from the input images using an encoder network, and then refine the coarse features to output images through a decoder network. The convolutional encoder–decoder can be parameterized as the function composition:

$$f_{\mathbf{w}}\left(\boldsymbol{x}\right) = decoder \circ encoder(\boldsymbol{x}), \tag{7.1}$$

$$\boldsymbol{y} = decoder\left(\boldsymbol{z}, \mathbf{w}_d\right), \quad \boldsymbol{z} = encoder\left(\boldsymbol{x}, \mathbf{w}_e\right), \tag{7.2}$$

where $\{\mathbf{w}_e, \mathbf{w}_d\} = \mathbf{w}$ are the encoder and decoder learnable parameters, respectively. $\boldsymbol{z}$ are latent variables that are of lower-dimensionality than the input $\boldsymbol{x}$. Encoder–decoder models have been successfully implemented for modeling a spectrum of physical systems. Zhu and Zabaras [28] use a densely connected encoder–decoder for surrogate modeling elliptic PDEs. Similar to many models in deep learning, this model uses residual connections in the encoder–decoder structure to improve predictive performance. The model, illustrated in Figure 7.1, takes a property field of the system as an input and outputs the corresponding state-variables of the system we are interested in.

The convolutional encoder–decoder's applicability extends beyond that of just elliptic PDEs. This general architecture has been used as a foundation for building auto-regressive models of dynamical systems [7, 20] as well as generative models [8, 19]. For multi-scale systems, an encoder–decoder model is well suited since the features in the model are intrinsically of different scaling at each convolutional level [8]. Note that the use of standard convolutions relies on the data being discretized on a structured Euclidean representation akin to that of pixels on an image. This can pose a problem for modeling physical systems where an unstructured domain may be needed. Extensions of convolutional neural networks to unstructured and non-Euclidean domains can be achieved through geometric deep learning [2], an emerging field that focuses on extending convolutional operators past structured data. Although geometric deep learning tends to be more computationally expensive

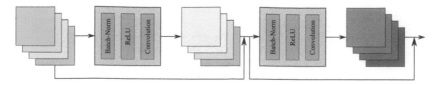

FIGURE 7.2
Dense block with a growth rate and length of 2. Residual connections between convolutions progressively stack feature maps resulting in 12 output channels in this schematic [7].

compared to standard convolutions, graph-based models have recently been explored for modeling physical systems with success.

7.2.2 Residual Blocks

One of the key components of most modern deep neural network architectures is the presence of residual blocks. As discovered in the landmark ResNet paper [11], residual connections allow models to be deeper and increase predictive accuracy. Prior to this work, the depth of neural networks were fairly limited due to saturation and eventual degradation of the models accuracy as the number of layers increased. Models such as U-Net [23] and DenseNet [12] both take advantage of residual connections on all layers of their encoder–decoder architecture. Illustrated in Figure 7.2, these dense blocks contain a set of residual connections between convolutional operations allowing information to easily flow to different levels. As illustrated in Figure 7.1, the model from Zhu and Zabaras [28] uses dense blocks. When designing neural network for a physical surrogate, residual blocks should be prioritized as an essential ingredient in the model.

7.2.3 Deep Neural Networks for Dynamics

Dynamical systems account for a large portion of physical models that are of academic and industrial interest. When designing deep neural networks for predicting dynamical systems, there are multiple methods to accurately model temporal dependencies. The simplest methodology is to simply introduce time as an additional input feature [20]. While this has proven to be effective for physical systems within a fixed time range, explicit dependence on time is not ideal since such models cannot extrapolate. Another simple approach is to implement an auto-regressive model that can integrate itself forward in time such as the one illustrated in Figure 7.3. Such models have a unique advantage to extrapolate beyond their initial time range [7]. In a similar spirit, deep neural networks can be directly integrated with classical numerical time-integration methods. This concept is the foundation behind neural ODE models [4] which have gained increased attention over recent years due to the connections they offer between deep learning and classical numerical analysis methods.

DNNs with recurrent connections allow models to learn latent temporal dependencies which can increase predictive accuracy for dynamical systems as illustrated in Figure 7.4. This includes methods such as gated recurrent models and long short-term memory (LSTM) models. With the recent advances of convolutional models in deep learning literature, a particularly useful approach is the convolutional LSTM [24]. Convolutional LSTM is a variation of the traditional LSTM structure that employs convolutional operations, retaining the advantages of traditional LSTM while using significantly less learnable parameters. The combination of recurrent blocks with the multi-scale structure of a convolutional encoder–decoder can result in complex multi-scale temporal features such as the model used in

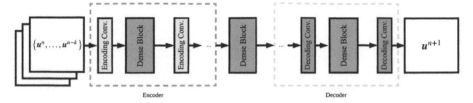

FIGURE 7.3

Schematic of the auto-regressive dense encoder–decoder for predicting dynamic PDEs [7]. The encoding-decoding process is interleaved with dense blocks that contain multiple densely connected layers in which the dimensionality of the feature maps is held constant.

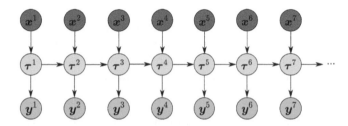

FIGURE 7.4

Unfolded computational graph of a recurrent neural network model for which the arrows show functional dependence [8]. The input and output at time-step n are denoted by $\boldsymbol{x}^n$ and $\boldsymbol{y}^n$, respectively. $\boldsymbol{\tau}^n$ are the recurrent temporal features passed forward in time each time-step.

Geneva and Zabaras [8]. A dimensionality schematic of this model is illustrated in Figure 7.5, where the multi-scale structure can clearly be seen between the output of the model $\boldsymbol{y}^n$ and its latent variables $\boldsymbol{z}^{(i),n}$. The multi-scale LSTM features, $\boldsymbol{\tau}^n$, allow the model to learn temporal dynamics of both high-dimensional features near $\boldsymbol{y}^n$ as well as the coarse-grained features deeper in the model.

7.2.4 Physics-Constrained Learning

While DNNs have been proven to be both accurate and computationally efficient for physical modeling, it is commonly known that training such models may require a significant amount of data. Depending on the system of interest, training data may either be sparse, extremely expensive to obtain or not available at all. Considering that the underlying governing equations are known, physics-constrained loss functions can allow significant reduction or complete removal of training data (e.g. without having to solve the equations governing the system of interest). The PDE solutions are represented as an optimization problem by either minimizing an energy functional [29] or alternatively the square of the PDE residual [7] using the model's prediction.

As an example consider a DNN, $\hat{u} = f_{\mathbf{w}}(K, f)$, modeling the fluid flow through a porous medium governed by Darcy's law:

$$-\nabla \cdot (K\nabla u) = f, \quad K, u, f \in \Omega, \tag{7.3}$$

with the conductivity K and source f fields being an input to the model defined in a domain

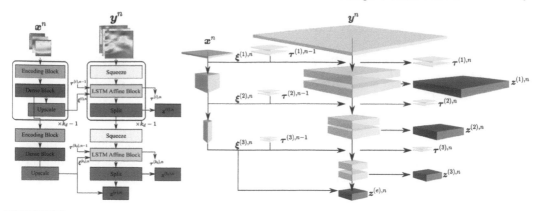

FIGURE 7.5
Invertible neural network for modeling turbulent fluid flow schematic (left) and dimensionality diagram (right). This model is comprised of a low-fidelity encoder that conditions a generative flow model to produce samples of high-fidelity fluid snapshots. LSTM blocks are introduced to pass information between time-steps using recurrent connections [8].

Ω with a boundary Γ. This DNN can be trained using one of the physics-constrained losses:

$$V_{PDE}(\hat{u}, K) = \int_{\Omega} \left(\nabla \cdot (K \nabla \hat{u}) + f \right)^2 ds, \tag{7.4}$$

$$V_{PDE}(\hat{u}, K) = \int_{\Omega} \left(\frac{1}{2} K \nabla \hat{u} \cdot \nabla \hat{u} - f \hat{u} \right)^2 ds - \int_{\Gamma} g \hat{u} \, ds \tag{7.5}$$

which are the strong residual and energy functional losses, respectively. Using the DNN's predictions to evaluate the PDE provides an optimization objective for training.

The philosophy of learning ordinary or partial differential equations through constraint-based loss functions has related works reaching back over two decades ago. These early works focused on solving initial/boundary value problems in which the solution is parameterized by a fully-connected network which allows for a fully-differentiable and closed analytic form [16]. With the resurgence of interest in neural networks, such techniques have been rediscovered by multiple works in recent years where this core idea has been expanded upon [7, 22, 29]. Using modern convolutional models, gradient terms of the loss can be efficiently evaluated using convolutional filters that approximate gradients through well-known finite difference based formulations [7,8,29]. This approach not only allows for training physical models with no training data, but also allows physical constraints or invariances to be enforced. For example, the divergence free condition, $\nabla \cdot \boldsymbol{u} = 0$, can be used as part of the loss function when training a model for incompressible fluid flow [8].

7.3   Probabilistic Deep Learning for Uncertainty Quantification

When developing models of physical systems, uncertainty quantification (UQ) is essential for characterizing and reducing uncertainty in the model's predictions. UQ becomes increasingly important when a surrogate is deployed on extrapolative test cases, containing phenomena not present in the training data. Historically speaking, methods such as Gaussian processes or polynomial chaos expansions have been popularized for surrogate modeling largely in part to their built-in probabilistic frameworks that allow for UQ despite their known limitations for high-dimensional data. Although the deterministic models discussed in Section 7.2 can model high-dimensional data easily, these DNNs do not intrinsically have the probabilistic framework for UQ. Given DNN's black-box nature, limited training data and finite model capacity, quantifying their predictive accuracy is desired particularly for systems of increased dimensionality and complexity. Even with a fairly large data-set, there is no guarantee that a DNN surrogate will generalize well to all test cases.

Fortunately, with probabilistics being a fundamental aspect of all machine learning, integrating uncertainty estimation into DNNs is a large on-going research effort which can be applied to UQ. Stochastic components can be added into pre-existing deterministic architectures or complete probabilistic frameworks can encapsulate modern deterministic DNNs. Generally speaking there are two schools of thoughts when approaching modern probabilistic machine learning: Bayesian approaches and generative approaches. Bayesian DNNs provide interpretable uncertainty bounds with direct control over the probabilistic formulation at a cost of implementation and optimization complications. Generative models on the other hand provide increased flexibility with an ability to learn a complex distribution but lack complete interpretability and can require a significant amount of training data.

7.3.1 Bayesian Deep Neural Networks

With the Bayesian paradigm being fundamental for the fields of machine learning and data-science, Bayesian DNNs are a popular approach for developing probablistic neural networks. The crucial property of Bayesian deep learning is that predictions are the result of marginalization of a distribution of models rather than relying on a single optimized neural network. This process known as Bayesian model averaging is the core driver behind Bayesian DNN's increased accuracy and generalization capabilities even in the small data regime. Bayesian inference is well suited for neural networks [27] and recent advances have made Bayesian DNNs more accessible and scalable than ever before.

There are two foundational sources of uncertainty that are typically of interest: epistemic and aleatoric uncertainty of the neural network. Aleatoric uncertainty is uncertainty that is present within the training data, $\mathcal{D}$, provided to the model. In applied machine learning this may be noise from sensors, numerical error in simulators, discretization error, etc. On the other hand, epistemic uncertainty, also typically referred to as model uncertainty, describes the uncertainty in the neural network's learnable parameters capturing the limited predictive capacity of a DNN [13]. In the Bayesian paradigm, the likelihood of the model's predictions, $p(\boldsymbol{y}|f_{\mathbf{w}}(\boldsymbol{x}), \beta)$ captures the aleatoric uncertainty where $f_{\mathbf{w}}(\cdot)$ denotes the DNN forward pass and β is the noise parameter. Epistemic uncertainty is addressed by the model's weights being random variables, resulting in a prior on the DNN's learnable parameters $p(\mathbf{w})$. The result of the Bayesian neural network formulation is an optimization objective centered around the posterior of the model:

$$p(\mathbf{w}, \beta) \sim p(\boldsymbol{y}|f_{\mathbf{w}}(\boldsymbol{x}), \beta)p(\mathbf{w})p(\beta). \tag{7.6}$$

Once learned the final goal of Bayesian neural networks is to sample the predictive distribution:

$$p(\boldsymbol{y}^*|\boldsymbol{x}^*, \mathcal{D}) = \int p(\boldsymbol{y}^*|f_{\mathbf{w}}(\boldsymbol{x}^*), \beta)p(\mathbf{w}, \beta)d\mathbf{w}d\beta, \tag{7.7}$$

with the marginalization typically approximated with Monte Carlo. This requires samples from the posterior of the model, which is the main challenge of Bayesian neural networks. Older techniques for obtaining Bayesian statistics include the placement of distributions over network weights and direct sampling with Monte Carlo methods to approximate statistical bounds as well as ensemble methods. But these approaches fail to scale to the size of modern DNNs. More recently, methods involving stochastic variational inference have brought a new wave a Bayesian neural network techniques. Here we discuss three examples of Bayesian inference approaches of increasing complexity for DNNs.

7.3.1.1   Bayesian Dropout

Dropout variational inference is one of the most widely known and most practical approximate inference algorithm for modern Bayesian DNNs [5, 13]. The weights of neural network are assigned a Gaussian prior, which is reparameterized by an approximate Bernoulli distribution that is precisely what deterministic dropout regularization uses [26]. During training optimization is posed as performing variational inference between the approximate dropout distribution $q(\mathbf{w})$ and the model's true posterior by minimizing the Kullback–Leibler (KL) divergence. The resulting loss for variational dropout is as follows:

$$\mathcal{L} = -\frac{1}{N} \sum_{i=1}^{N} \log p(\boldsymbol{y}_i | f_{\hat{\mathbf{w}}_i}(\boldsymbol{x}_i), \beta) + \frac{1-p}{2N} \left(\|\mathbf{w}\|^2 + \|\beta\|^2 \right), \tag{7.8}$$

with N data points where the model's samples $\hat{\mathbf{w}}_i \sim q(\mathbf{w})$ are from the dropout procedure with drop rate p. Typically, the likelihood is defined as a Gaussian such that:

$$-\log p(\boldsymbol{y}_i | f_{\hat{\mathbf{w}}_i}(x_i), \beta) \propto \frac{1}{2\beta^2} \|\boldsymbol{y}_i - f_{\hat{\mathbf{w}}_i}(\boldsymbol{x}_i)\|^2 + \frac{1}{2} \log \beta^2, \tag{7.9}$$

in which the noise term β captures the uncertainty in the training data. During test time, the model weights are simply sampled using dropout and the predictive statistics are approximated through Monte Carlo. While variational dropout remains one of the most simple inference methods, it is highly approximate and lacks full control over the specified posterior form. Hence, it should be regarded as a simple base line but not an ideal probabilistic approach.

7.3.1.2   Stochastic Weight Averaging Gaussian

Another method for Bayesian DNNs is stochastic weight averaging Gaussian (SWAG) [18]. In this approach, a Laplace approximation is used to approximate the final posterior of the DNN allowing for predictive model averaging. Given a posterior in the form of Eq. 7.6, SWAG approximates this posterior in two phases:

1. The model of interest is first trained using traditional machine learning methods to minimize the negative log of the posterior (equivalent to solving for the maximum a posteriori (MAP) estimate).

2. Once the model has been trained, gradient descent is ran again at a constant learning rate. During this process, samples of the model's parameters are collected. The core idea is to explore the local support region of the MAP estimate and construct an approximate local distribution.

The posterior over the DNN's parameters is approximated as a Gaussian distribution with S samples:

$$p(\boldsymbol{\theta}|\mathcal{S}) \sim \mathcal{N}\left(\boldsymbol{\theta}_{SWA}, \boldsymbol{\Sigma}_{SWA}\right), \quad \boldsymbol{\theta} \equiv \{\mathbf{w}, ln(\beta)\}. \tag{7.10}$$

We note that the noise precision, β, has a log-normal posterior approximation to ensure that it is positive. The mean and the covariance are approximated using the model parameters collected while running gradient descent:

$$\boldsymbol{\theta}_{SWA} = \frac{1}{S}\sum_{i=1}^{S}\boldsymbol{\theta}_i, \quad \boldsymbol{\Sigma}_{SWA} = \frac{1}{2}\left(\boldsymbol{\Sigma}_{Diag} + \boldsymbol{\Sigma}_{lr}\right), \qquad (7.11)$$

$$\bar{\boldsymbol{\theta}}^2 = \frac{1}{S}\sum_{i=1}^{S}\boldsymbol{\theta}_i^2, \quad \boldsymbol{\Sigma}_{Diag} = \mathrm{Diag}\left(\bar{\boldsymbol{\theta}}^2 - \boldsymbol{\theta}_{SWA}^2\right), \qquad (7.12)$$

$$\boldsymbol{\Sigma}_{lr} = \frac{1}{K-1}\boldsymbol{D}\boldsymbol{D}^T, \quad \boldsymbol{D}_i = \left(\boldsymbol{\theta}_i - \boldsymbol{\theta}_{SWA}\right), \qquad (7.13)$$

where $\boldsymbol{\theta}_i$ are the model parameters at epoch i, and $\boldsymbol{D} \in \mathbb{R}^{K \times H}$ is a deviation matrix consisting of the H most recent parameter samples forming a low-rank approximation. $\boldsymbol{D}_i \in \mathbb{R}^K$ is a column of this deviation matrix. With this explicit Gaussian approximation, sampling from the posterior of the model's parameters is trivial allowing for predictive statistics to be calculated.

SWAG offers another simple approach for Bayesian inference with explicit designing of the model's posterior. Additionally, due to its use of weight samples from the SGD optimization, SWAG is not invasive to the training process unlike variational dropout. However, this inference approach still relies on the approximation of the posterior form as a Gaussian essentially being a gradient powered Laplace approximation [1]. This means that SWAG assumes the posterior is unimodal, which may not always be the case. Despite its drawbacks, SWAG has been successfully implemented for various problems including surrogate modeling physical systems [7]. In Figure 7.6, SWAG is used for UQ of an auto-regressive DNN surrogate modeling of a 2D PDE.

7.3.1.3 Stein Variational Gradient Descent

Stein variational gradient descent (SVGD) [17] is a method that approximates a variational distribution through a set of particles. SVGD is a non-parametric algorithm of similar

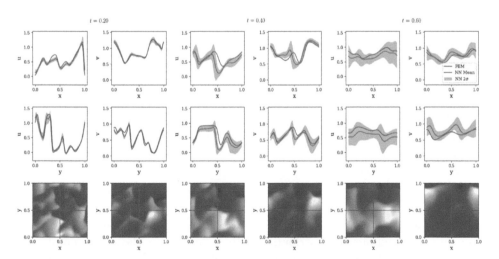

FIGURE 7.6
Instantaneous profiles with two sigma confidence intervals of an Bayesian auto-regressive model using SWAG [7] predicting the dynamical 2D Burgers' equation [3]. (Top to bottom) Horizontal profile at $y = 0.5$, vertical profile at $x = 0.5$ and target contour with blue lines to show the profile locations. (Left to right) x-velocity and y-velocity profiles at $t = 0.2$, 0.4, and 0.6.

form as standard gradient descent. To optimize the parameters in the neural network, SVGD minimizes the KL divergence between the true parameter posterior, $p(\mathbf{w}, \beta | \mathcal{D})$, given the training data set $\mathcal{D}$, with the variational distribution $q(\mathbf{w}, \beta)$ that lies in some set of distributions $\mathcal{Q}$:

$$q^*(\mathbf{w}, \beta) = \min_{q \in \mathcal{Q}} \{ \mathrm{KL} \left(q || p \right) \equiv \mathbb{E}_q(\log q(\mathbf{w}, \beta)) - \mathbb{E}_q(\log \tilde{p}(\mathbf{w}, \beta | \mathcal{D})) + \mathcal{K} \}, \tag{7.14}$$

for which $\tilde{p}(\mathbf{w}, \beta | \mathcal{D})$ is the unnormalized posterior and $\mathcal{K}$ is the log normalization constant that is not required to be computed during optimization. Rather than attempting to recover a parametric form of the variational distribution, SVGD describes $q(\mathbf{w}, \beta)$ by a particle approximation. Namely, a set of M deterministic neural networks each representing a particle $\{ \boldsymbol{\theta}_i \}_{i=1}^M$, $\boldsymbol{\theta}_i = \{ \mathbf{w}_i, \beta_i \}$, leads to an empirical measure $q_M(\mathbf{w}', \beta') = q_M(\boldsymbol{\theta}') = \frac{1}{M} \sum_{i=1}^M \delta(\boldsymbol{\theta}_i - \boldsymbol{\theta}')$. The objective is now for the empirical probability measure, μ_M, to converge in distribution towards the true measure of the posterior ν,

$$\mu_N(d\boldsymbol{\theta}) = \frac{1}{M} \sum_{i=1}^M \delta(\boldsymbol{\theta}_i - \boldsymbol{\theta}) d\boldsymbol{\theta} = \frac{1}{M} \sum_{i=1}^M \boldsymbol{\theta}_i, \tag{7.15}$$

$$\nu(d\boldsymbol{\theta}) = p(\boldsymbol{\theta} | \mathcal{D}) d\boldsymbol{\theta}. \tag{7.16}$$

To minimize the KL divergence, we assume that $q(\mathbf{w}, \beta)$ is from a class of distributions that can be obtained through a set of smooth transforms. A small perturbation function, resembling that of standard gradient descent, is used to update the particles:

$$\boldsymbol{\theta}_i^{t+1} = \boldsymbol{T}(\boldsymbol{\theta}_i^t) = \boldsymbol{\theta}_i^t + \eta^t \boldsymbol{\phi}(\boldsymbol{\theta}_i^t), \tag{7.17}$$

where η is the step size and $\boldsymbol{\phi}(\boldsymbol{\theta}_i^t)$ is the direction of the update that lies in a function space $\mathcal{F}$ for the t-th iteration. It is now a matter of finding the optimal direction to permute the particles which should be chosen such that the gradient of the KL divergence is maximized,

$$\boldsymbol{\phi}^* = \max_{\boldsymbol{\phi} \in \mathcal{F}} \left(-\frac{d}{d\eta} \mathcal{KL}(\boldsymbol{T}\mu_N || \nu)|_{\eta=0} \right), \tag{7.18}$$

where $\boldsymbol{T}\mu$ denotes the updated empirical measure of the particles. Liu *et al.* [17] identify connections between the function $\boldsymbol{\phi}$ and Stein's method and show that:

$$\frac{\partial}{\partial \eta} KL(\boldsymbol{T}\mu_N || \nu)|_{\eta=0} = \mathbb{E}_\mu \left(\mathcal{T}_p \boldsymbol{\phi} \right), \quad \mathcal{T}_p \boldsymbol{\phi} = (\nabla \log p(\boldsymbol{\theta} | \mathcal{D})) \cdot \boldsymbol{\phi} + \nabla \cdot \boldsymbol{\phi}, \tag{7.19}$$

in which $\mathcal{T}_p$ is known as the Stein's operator. Assuming that this function space $\mathcal{F}$ lies within a reproducing kernel Hilbert space $\mathcal{H}$ with positive kernel $k(\boldsymbol{\theta}, \boldsymbol{\theta}')$, the optimal direction to use during gradient descent has the closed form:

$$\boldsymbol{\phi}^*(\boldsymbol{\theta}) \propto \mathbb{E}_{\boldsymbol{\theta}' \sim \mu} \left[(\nabla \log p(\boldsymbol{\theta}' | \mathcal{D})) k(\boldsymbol{\theta}, \boldsymbol{\theta}') + \nabla_{\boldsymbol{\theta}'} k(\boldsymbol{\theta}, \boldsymbol{\theta}') \right]. \tag{7.20}$$

A simple example of SVGD is illustrated in Figure 7.7, where a set of particles are optimized to approximate a multimodal distribution. When applied to Bayesian neural networks, each particle is an independent neural network which must all be trained in parallel. Each converged DNN can be considered a sample from the posterior and predictive statistics can be calculated once again using Monte Carlo.

Of the inference algorithms discussed, SVGD is the most rigorous with the only limitation on its accuracy being the number of particles used to approximate its posterior. However, the drawback of this method is clear: one must train N neural networks simultaneously for N posterior samples. This makes SVGD unsuitable for models that are extremely

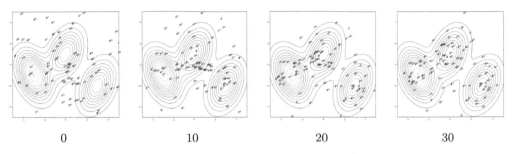

| 0 | 10 | 20 | 30 |

FIGURE 7.7
30 steps of SVGD optimizing a set of particles to a target distribution defined as a multi-modal Gaussian distribution.

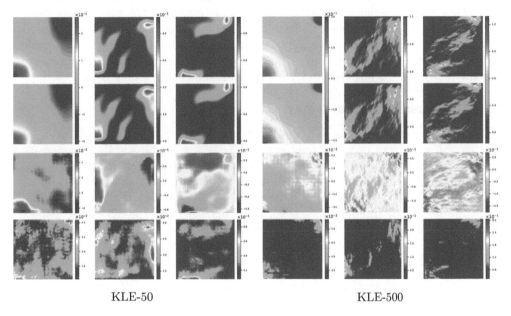

KLE-50   KLE-500

FIGURE 7.8
Prediction of stochastic elliptic system modeling flow through porous media using a Bayesian DNN with SVGD [28]. The rows from top to bottom show the simulation output fields (ground truth), the predictive mean, the error of the above two, and two standard deviation of the predictive output distribution per pixel. The three columns from left to right correspond to the pressure field p, and the two velocity fields u_x, u_y, respectively.

large in size which will result in a memory bottle neck on the computer hardware used for training. Despite its drawbacks, SVGD has been used in multiple surrogate settings including predicting subterranean flow [28] as well as turbulence modeling [6]. In Figure 7.8, SVGD is used to quantify uncertainty of a DNN surrogate for predicting the Darcy equation which generalizes well between problems of varying dimensionality quantified by the Karhunen–Loève expansion (KLE).

7.3.2 Deep Generative Neural Networks

Deep generative models provide a flexible framework for building probablistic DNNs due to their ability to learn complex distributions. Generative models are centered around the use of random latent variables, z, in a deep learning model allowing the likelihood of the model's output, y, to be expressed as the following marginal:

$$p_{\mathbf{w}}(y) = \int p_{\mathbf{w}}(y|z) \, p_{\mathbf{w}}(z) \, dz, \tag{7.21}$$

in which $\mathbf{w}$ denotes the model's parameters. The latent variables are specifically designed such that their distribution is simple for sampling. However, this marginal is typically not practical to train due to the large number of samples needed from $p_{\mathbf{w}}(z)$ to approximate the marginalization. Hence, generative models such as variational auto-encoders [14] as well as generative adversarial networks [10] approximate this likelihood through variational inference or by a min-max adversarial game, respectively.

Since generative models learn the distribution of the training data directly through latent parameters, generative DNNs generally have greater freedom over architecture and optimization than Bayesian approaches. However, interpreting the uncertainty bounds of generative model predictions is not as clear. Deep generative models lack the structured form of the posterior present in the Bayesian paradigm, eliminating the ability to determine the contribution of different sources of uncertainty. Despite this, deep generative approaches are promising for UQ of high-dimensional systems with sufficient training data.

7.3.2.1 Adversarial Neural Networks

Generative adversarial networks (GANs) [10] is considered one of the most important breakthroughs of the modern deep learning era. GANs is a machine learning framework that establishes an adversarial game between two neural networks: a generative neural network that learns the distribution over the training data and a discrimative network that computes the probability that a sample is from the data-set versus the generator. To learn the distribution of the training data, $p(y)$, the generator maps the low-dimensional latent vector, z, from the latent distribution, $p(z)$, to the data space. The discriminator is trained to maximize the probability of distinguishing the real samples from the generated (fake) samples. Mathematically, the adversarial game can be posed as the following min-max loss:

$$\mathcal{L} = \min_{\mathcal{G}} \max_{\mathcal{D}} \mathbb{E}_{y \sim p(y)} \left[\log \mathcal{D}(y) \right] + \mathbb{E}_{z \sim p(z)} \left[\log \left(1 - \mathcal{D}(\mathcal{G}(z)) \right) \right]. \tag{7.22}$$

in which $\mathcal{G}$ and $\mathcal{D}$ are the generative and discrimative network, respectively.

The adversarial training in GANs results in significantly improved predictions compared to alternative generative models such as variational auto-encoders. This can be adventitious for modeling physical systems with high-dimensional fields with sharp gradients/features. Additionally, the generative aspect of GANs allows for a distribution of predictions to be sampled, effortlessly enabling UQ of the physical surrogate. However, GANs and similar methods are not without their issues. It is well-documented that GANs can be very difficult to train and typically suffer from mode collapse. While there has been significant literature working on improving GANs training, the reliability of adversarial models is an open issue.

As an example, the work of Mo *et al.* [19] uses adversarial learning with an encoder-decoder model for multiphase flow field inversion in subterranean flow. As illustrated in Figure 7.9, this model combines GANs with the dense encoder–decoder model where the deepest features of the model are random latent variables. Coupling the adversarial encoder-decoder with traditional inversion algorithms, this surrogate can recover high-dimensional hydraulic conductivity/solute fields from a sparse set of sensors as seen in Figure 7.10.

7.3.2.2 Invertible Neural Networks

A recent generative approach for DNNs are invertible neural networks (INNs), which are based on normalizing flows. Generative normalizing flows provide a bijective mapping

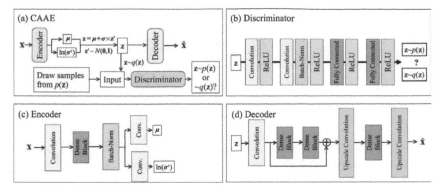

FIGURE 7.9
Illustration of a convolutional adversarial autoencoder (CAAE), which is composed of a discriminator (b), an encoder/generator (c), and a decoder (d) [19]. The encoder decoder use dense blocks, regular convolutions and upscaling convolutions. The discriminator is comprised of convolutions and fully-connected layers.

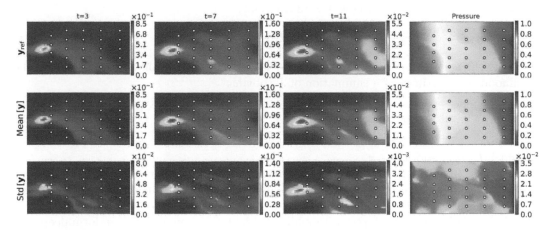

FIGURE 7.10
Inversion of 2D solute conductivity fields from an array of sparse sensors denoted by the white dots on each contour. (Top to bottom) Plotted are the ground truth, recovered ensemble mean and standard deviation of the concentration fields at times (left to right) $t = 3, 7, 11$ and hydraulic pressure fields of the 2D model obtained using the CAAE surrogate [19].

between an unknown likelihood density of the observations $p_{\mathbf{w}}(\mathbf{y})$ and a known latent density $p_{\mathbf{w}}(\mathbf{z})$. Typically, $p_{\mathbf{w}}(\mathbf{y})$ can be viewed as the unknown likelihood of a system for which we have a finite number of observations, i.e. training data. Let us consider a mapping with a tractable Jacobian determinant, allowing for the likelihood to be expressed as:

$$p_{\mathbf{w}}(\mathbf{y}) = p_{\mathbf{w}}(\mathbf{z}) \left| \det \left(\frac{\partial \mathbf{z}}{\partial \mathbf{y}} \right) \right|, \qquad (7.23)$$

which is nothing more than the change of variables formula. This implies that the model can be trained by maximizing the likelihood of $p_{\mathbf{w}}(\mathbf{y})$ (unknown) through the latent variables assigned a simple distribution *a-priori* (typically Gaussian). As depicted in Figure 7.11a, we use $f_{\mathbf{w}}(\cdot)$ to denote the learnable function, with a tractable Jacobian, that transforms

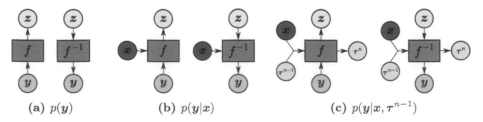

(a) $p(\boldsymbol{y})$ (b) $p(\boldsymbol{y}|\boldsymbol{x})$ (c) $p(\boldsymbol{y}|\boldsymbol{x}, \boldsymbol{\tau}^{n-1})$

FIGURE 7.11
Comparison of the forward and backward passes of various INN structures including (a) the standard INN, (b) conditional INN [29] and (c) recurrent conditional INN [8].

an observation to a set of latent variables. To generate samples of $\boldsymbol{y}_i \sim p_{\mathbf{w}}(\boldsymbol{y})$, samples are drawn from the latent distribution $\boldsymbol{z}_i \sim p_{\mathbf{w}}(\boldsymbol{z})$, which are then transformed using the inverse of the model $f_{\mathbf{w}}^{-1}(\cdot)$.

However, the requirement for a tractable Jacobian as well as a function that can efficiently be inverted for sampling is not trivial. Normalizing flows address this challenge by using a series of change of variable transformations,

$$\boldsymbol{y} \xleftrightarrow{f_{\mathbf{w}_1}} \boldsymbol{h}_1 \xleftrightarrow{f_{\mathbf{w}_2}} \boldsymbol{h}_2 \ldots \xleftrightarrow{f_{\mathbf{w}_K}} \boldsymbol{z}, \tag{7.24}$$

each of which has a tractable Jacobian and is invertible. This allows for the log of the likelihood to be written as a summation of Jacobians:

$$\log p_{\mathbf{w}}(\boldsymbol{y}) = \log p_{\mathbf{w}}(\boldsymbol{z}) + \sum_{k=1}^{K} \log \left| \det \left(\frac{\partial \boldsymbol{h}_k}{\partial \boldsymbol{h}_{k-1}} \right) \right|, \tag{7.25}$$

in which $\boldsymbol{h}_0 \equiv \boldsymbol{y}$ and $\boldsymbol{h}_K \equiv \boldsymbol{z}$.

In INNs, each change of variables is a layer in the neural network allowing the model to learn the likelihood *exactly*. One approach for building INNs is using affine coupling layers: carefully designed functions such that the inverse mapping and the Jacobian can be easily calculated. Affine coupling layers with additional invertable operations can form deep networks that are competitive with other generative approaches. Such flow-based models do not require a discriminator, greatly simplifying the hyper-parameter search and increasing robustness against mode collapse. The vanilla INN can be modified for learning conditional distributions such $p_{\mathbf{w}}(\boldsymbol{y}|\boldsymbol{x})$ as well as temporal features $p_{\mathbf{w}}(\boldsymbol{y}|\boldsymbol{x}, \boldsymbol{\tau}^{n-1})$ depicted in Figures 7.11b and 7.11c, respectively.

Since INNs are able to learn the likelihood of the data exactly, they are an ideal generative model class for UQ. In the presence of data, training INNs is straight forward using the log-likelihood in Eq. 7.25. However, INNs can also be used with physics-constrained learning discussed in Section 7.2.4 where only a potential is available [8,29]. This is achieved through the use of the reverse KL-divergence as a loss function:

$$\mathcal{L} = \sum_{i=1}^{N} D_{KL}\left(p_{\mathbf{w}}(\boldsymbol{y}_i) \| p_\beta(\boldsymbol{y}_i)\right) = \sum_{i=1}^{N} \mathbb{E}_{p_{\mathbf{w}}} \left[\log \frac{p_{\mathbf{w}}(\boldsymbol{y}_i)}{p_\beta(\boldsymbol{y}_i)} \right], \tag{7.26}$$

for N data points in which $p_{\mathbf{w}}(\boldsymbol{y})$ is the log-likelihood of the INN. $p_\beta(\boldsymbol{y})$ is an energy-based density function with a controllable parameter β that accounts for a physical potential. This energy density can be parameterized as the Boltzmann distribution $p_\beta(\boldsymbol{y}) = \exp\left(-\beta V_{PDE}(\cdot)\right)/Z_\beta$ where V_{PDE} is the energy functional or PDE residual. Note that both are evaluated using samples from the model $\boldsymbol{y}_i \sim p_{\mathbf{w}}(\boldsymbol{y})$, training the model in the inverse direction.

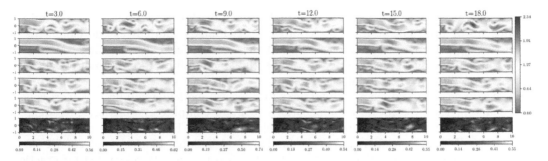

FIGURE 7.12

Generative prediction of turbulent flows from a low-fidelity simulation using a conditional INN model. (Top to bottom) Velocity magnitude of the high-fidelity target, low-fidelity input, 3 INN samples and standard deviation for two test flows [8].

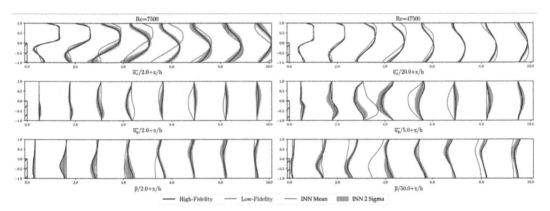

FIGURE 7.13

(Top to bottom) Time averaged x-velocity, y-velocity and pressure profiles for two different test cases at (left to right) $Re = 7500$ and $Re = 47500$. The INN expectation and confidence interval are computed using 20 time-series samples [8].

INNs have been demonstrated to be effective for UQ of multiple physical systems such as surrogate modeling elliptic PDEs [29], conductivity field inversion [21] and turbulent flow models [8]. In Geneva and Zabaras [8], INNs are used for predicting turbulent fluid flow given an inexpensive low-fidelity solution. This model, illustrated previously in Figure 7.5, is a generative model capable of capturing multi-scale phenomena in the spatial and temporal domains. The INN can produce diverse samples of turbulent fluid flow illustrated in Figure 7.12 which can then be used to yield acceptable confidence intervals of fluid flow statistics seen in Figure 7.13.

7.4 Outlook

The progression of deep learning for modeling physical systems will require modern approaches for predicting phenomena beyond the trivial benchmarks. Deep learning researchers in engineering, chemistry and physical sciences will need better synergy with the core deep learning communities in computer vision, language processing, neural science, etc. Common challenges such as learning high-dimensional features, complex temporal dependencies or probabilistic frameworks are interdisciplinary and current developments in deep learning literature can dramatically aid the scientific machine learning community. This will become increasingly necessary as the fundamental limitations of more traditional machine learning models are fully realized.

Developing improved DNN architectures for physical modeling will become increasingly important in the near future as applications to more complex systems are investigated. The design of such deep learning models should be inspired by the physics of the problem of interest. While one should expect the fundamental building blocks of current DNNs to remain relevant, modern methods will need to be used to scale deep learning for practical applications. The integration of physical constraints or invariances into DNNs will also continue to be a major area of study. Whether this be through the loss functions or explicitly in the model's architecture, using known properties of the physics governing the system will be essential. Graph neural networks have gained increased interest in molecular dynamics due to the graphical structure of atomistic systems. The potential of GNNs for learning systems with unstructured domains such as solid or fluid mechanics on non-uniform meshes is significant. Recently, self-attention models originally designed for learning temporal dependencies in natural language processing have been proven to be effective for learning physical dynamics [9]. Given their success in other fields, models using graph neural networks or self-attention will likely be in the state-of-the-art physical deep learning surrogates of tomorrow.

Improving the generalization of machine learning models for physics will become an increasingly large research focus in the near future. Unlike the computer vision or language processing fields, having a surplus of data for training a DNN is rare for physical systems. This research area may include development of hybrid models that integrate traditional numerical solvers with deep learning for increased generalization. This includes conditioning models on cheap low-fidelity simulations [8], learning PDE closure models [6] or learning other components of numerical solvers such as interpolation or time-integration schemes. Additional promising areas of interest include pre-training, transfer-learning, or meta-learning, which are training frameworks for generalizing DNNs between distinct problems. Given that many natural phenomena share physical characteristics, a DNN surrogate for one system could be fine tuned to another system with very little training data. For systems where data may be sparse or extremely expensive to acquire, these approaches will be essential.

Lastly, the need to verify and validate physical surrogates will continue to be a pressing issue for the field. Quantifying the uncertainty will be a fundamental part of certifying deep learning models to predict critical systems. Both Bayesian neural networks as well as deep generative models offer unique approaches for obtaining predictive uncertainty bounds. As the field matures, the demand of UQ of DNN based physical models will dramatically increase akin to the UQ demand for traditional numerical methods. Improvements in Bayesian deep learning and generative models made in the deep learning community will play an important role for deep UQ in the future.

Bibliography

[1] Christopher M Bishop. *Pattern Recognition and Machine Learning*. Information science and statistics. Springer, New York, NY, 2006. Softcover published in 2016.

[2] MM Bronstein, J Bruna, Y LeCun, A Szlam, and P Vandergheynst. Geometric deep learning: Going beyond Euclidean data. *IEEE Signal Processing Magazine*, 34(4):18–42, 2017.

[3] JM Burgers. A mathematical model illustrating the theory of turbulence. Volume 1 of *Advances in Applied Mechanics*, pages 171–199. Elsevier, 1948.

[4] Ricky TQ Chen, Yulia Rubanova, Jesse Bettencourt, and David Duvenaud. Neural ordinary differential equations. *arXiv preprint arXiv:1806.07366*, 2018.

[5] Yarin Gal and Zoubin Ghahramani. Dropout as a Bayesian approximation: Representing model uncertainty in deep learning. In *International Conference on Machine Learning*, pages 1050–1059. PMLR, 2016.

[6] Nicholas Geneva and Nicholas Zabaras. Quantifying model form uncertainty in Reynolds-averaged turbulence models with Bayesian deep neural networks. *Journal of Computational Physics*, 383:125–147, 2019.

[7] Nicholas Geneva and Nicholas Zabaras. Modeling the dynamics of pde systems with physics-constrained deep auto-regressive networks. *Journal of Computational Physics*, 403:109056, 2020.

[8] Nicholas Geneva and Nicholas Zabaras. Multi-fidelity generative deep learning turbulent flows. *Foundations of Data Science*, 2(2639-8001_2020_4_391):391, 2020.

[9] Nicholas Geneva and Nicholas Zabaras. Transformers for modeling physical systems. *arXiv preprint arXiv:2010.03957*, 2020.

[10] Ian Goodfellow, Jean Pouget-Abadie, Mehdi Mirza, Bing Xu, David Warde-Farley, Sherjil Ozair, Aaron Courville, and Yoshua Bengio. Generative adversarial nets. In *Advances in Neural Information Processing Systems*, pages 2672–2680, 2014.

[11] Kaiming He, Xiangyu Zhang, Shaoqing Ren, and Jian Sun. Deep residual learning for image recognition. In *Proceedings of the IEEE Conference on Computer Vision and Pattern Recognition*, pages 770–778, 2016.

[12] Gao Huang, Zhuang Liu, Laurens van der Maaten, and Kilian Q. Weinberger. Densely connected convolutional networks. In *The IEEE Conference on Computer Vision and Pattern Recognition (CVPR)*, July 2017.

[13] Alex Kendall and Yarin Gal. What uncertainties do we need in Bayesian deep learning for computer vision? In *Proceedings of the 31st International Conference on Neural Information Processing Systems*, NIPS'17, page 5580–5590. Curran Associates Inc., 2017.

[14] Diederik P Kingma and Max Welling. Auto-encoding variational bayes. *arXiv preprint arXiv:1312.6114*, 2013.

[15] Alex Krizhevsky, Ilya Sutskever, and Geoffrey E Hinton. Imagenet classification with deep convolutional neural networks. In F. Pereira, C. J. C. Burges, L. Bottou, and K. Q. Weinberger, editors, *Advances in Neural Information Processing Systems*, volume 25. Curran Associates, Inc., 2012.

[16] Isaac E Lagaris, Aristidis Likas, and Dimitrios I Fotiadis. Artificial neural networks for solving ordinary and partial differential equations. *IEEE Transactions on Neural Networks*, 9(5):987–1000, 1998.

[17] Qiang Liu and Dilin Wang. Stein variational gradient descent: A general purpose Bayesian inference algorithm. In D. D. Lee, M. Sugiyama, U. V. Luxburg, I. Guyon, and R. Garnett, editors, *Advances in Neural Information Processing Systems 29*, pages 2378–2386. Curran Associates, Inc., 2016.

[18] Wesley Maddox, Timur Garipov, Pavel Izmailov, Dmitry P. Vetrov, and Andrew Gordon Wilson. A simple baseline for Bayesian uncertainty in deep learning. *CoRR*, abs/1902.02476, 2019.

[19] Shaoxing Mo, Nicholas Zabaras, Xiaoqing Shi, and Jichun Wu. Integration of adversarial autoencoders with residual dense convolutional networks for estimation of nongaussian hydraulic conductivities. *Water Resources Research*, 56(2):e2019WR026082, 2020. e2019WR026082 10.1029/2019WR026082.

[20] Shaoxing Mo, Yinhao Zhu, Nicholas Zabaras, Xiaoqing Shi, and Jichun Wu. Deep convolutional encoder-decoder networks for uncertainty quantification of dynamic multiphase flow in heterogeneous media. *Water Resources Research*, 55(1):703–728, 2019.

[21] Govinda Anantha Padmanabha and Nicholas Zabaras. Solving inverse problems using conditional invertible neural networks. *Journal of Computational Physics*, page 110194, 2021.

[22] M Raissi, P Perdikaris, and GE Karniadakis. Physics-informed neural networks: A deep learning framework for solving forward and inverse problems involving nonlinear partial differential equations. *Journal of Computational Physics*, 378:686–707, 2019.

[23] Olaf Ronneberger, Philipp Fischer, and Thomas Brox. U-net: Convolutional networks for biomedical image segmentation. In Nassir Navab, Joachim Hornegger, William M. Wells, and Alejandro F. Frangi, editors, *Medical Image Computing and Computer-Assisted Intervention – MICCAI 2015*, pages 234–241, Cham, 2015. Springer International Publishing.

[24] Xingjian SHI, Zhourong Chen, Hao Wang, Dit-Yan Yeung, Wai-kin Wong, and Wang-chun WOO. Convolutional LSTM network: A machine learning approach for precipitation nowcasting. In *Advances in Neural Information Processing Systems 28*, pages 802–810. Curran Associates, Inc., 2015.

[25] Karen Simonyan and Andrew Zisserman. Very deep convolutional networks for large-scale image recognition. *arXiv preprint arXiv:1409.1556*, 2014.

[26] Nitish Srivastava, Geoffrey Hinton, Alex Krizhevsky, Ilya Sutskever, and Ruslan Salakhutdinov. Dropout: A simple way to prevent neural networks from overfitting. *The Journal of Machine Learning Research*, 15(1):1929–1958, 2014.

[27] Andrew Gordon Wilson. The case for Bayesian deep learning. *arXiv preprint arXiv:2001.10995*, 2020.

[28] Yinhao Zhu and Nicholas Zabaras. Bayesian deep convolutional encoder–decoder networks for surrogate modeling and uncertainty quantification. *Journal of Computational Physics*, 366:415–447, 2018.

[29] Yinhao Zhu, Nicholas Zabaras, Phaedon-Stelios Koutsourelakis, and Paris Perdikaris. Physics-constrained deep learning for high-dimensional surrogate modeling and uncertainty quantification without labeled data. *Journal of Computational Physics*, 394:56–81, 2019.

8

Physics-Guided Deep Learning for Spatiotemporal Forecasting

Rui Wang, Robin Walters, and Rose Yu

CONTENTS

DOI: 10.1201/9781003143376-8

8.1 Introduction

8.1.1 Background

Modeling the evolution of large-scale spatiotemporal data over a wide range of spatial and temporal scales is a fundamental task in science and engineering. Numerical methods for simulating complex dynamics are computationally-intensive, requiring significant computational resources and expertise. Deep learning (DL) provides an efficient alternative to approximate high-dimensional spatiotemporal dynamics by directly forecasting the future states and bypassing numerical integration. Recent works have shown DL can significantly accelerate the prediction of physical dynamics relative to numerical solvers, from turbulence modeling to weather prediction. This opens up new opportunities at the intersection of machine learning and physical sciences.

Despite the tremendous progress, it remains a grand challenge to incorporate physical principles in a systematic manner to the design, training, and inference of such models. Purely data-driven DL models still adhere to the fundamental rules of statistical inference. Without explicit constraints, DL models are prone to make physically implausible forecasts, violating the governing laws of physical systems. Additionally, DL models often struggle with generalization: models trained on one dataset cannot adapt properly to unseen scenarios with different distributions. Generalization is even more complex for spatiotemporal forecasting. Distribution shift occurs not only because the dynamics are non-stationary and non-linear, but also due to the changes in system parameters including initial and boundary conditions.

Physics-guided DL is an emerging area to principally integrate physical laws into DL models and algorithms. Physics as a discipline, has a long tradition of using first-principled models to describe spatiotemporal dynamics. The laws of physics, manifested by the profound concepts of symmetry, have greatly improved our understanding of the physical world. Physics-guided DL offers a set of tools to blend these physical concepts such as differential equation and symmetry with deep neural networks. On one hand, these hybrid models offer great computational benefits over traditional numerical solvers. On the other hand, these models impose appropriate inductive biases on the DL models, leading to scientific valid predictions, reduced sample complexity, and guaranteed improvement in generalization. We also note that constraining DL models with domain knowledge is not new, with a plethora of research in constrained optimization and Bayesian inference. Our focus, however, is on spatiotemporal forecasting. Besides incorporating physical principles, our research also generate novel insights for the broader machine learning community regarding modeling continuous-valued, sequential, and highly dynamic data.

8.1.2 Chapter Overview

There is a growing need for integrating traditional physics-based approaches with DL models so that we can take the best of both types of approaches. We first define formally the spatiotemporal forecasting problem, followed by several examples of dynamical systems. We present three physics-guided DL approaches for spatiotemporal forecasting. In 8.3, we review a physics-guided model, `TF-Net`, which demonstrate the benefits of integrating traditional physics-based approaches with DL models for spatiotemporal dynamics forecasting. `TF-Net` marries the numerical techniques with custom-designed neural networks, and predict accurate physical fields that obey desirable physical characteristics. In 8.4, we then investigates the generalization problem in forecasting, which is a key challenge of DL for dynamics forecasting. We found that DL models fail to forecast under shifted distributions either in the data domain or the parameter domain that naturally happens in dynamical systems. This calls attention to rethink generalization especially for learning dynamical systems. In 8.5, we provide one way to improve generalization by incorporating symmetries into deep dynamics models. Specifically, we employ a variety of methods each tailored to enforce a different symmetry into convolutional neural networks (CNN). The equivariant deep dynamics models are both theoretically and experimentally robust to distributional shift by the symmetry group transformations and enjoy favorable sample complexity.

8.1.3 Problem Definition

Dynamical systems [60] describe the evolution of phenomena occurring in nature. A dynamical system is governed by a set of differential equations:

$$\{\xi^i(\mathbf{x}, \dot{\mathbf{x}}, \ddot{\mathbf{x}}, \dots; \psi) = 0\} \tag{8.1}$$

where $\mathbf{x} \in \mathbb{R}^d$ is a d-dimensional state of the system, $\dot{\mathbf{x}} = \partial \mathbf{x}/\partial t$ is the derivative over time, and ψ are the parameters. Oftentimes, the dynamics parameter ψ can represent different system coefficients, external forces or boundary conditions.

The problem of dynamic forecasting is that given a set of series from the system in Equation 8.1 $\{(\mathbf{x}_1, \mathbf{x}_2, \dots, \mathbf{x}_t)^{(i)}\}_{i=1}^n$, we want to learn a map f such that:

$$f : (\mathbf{x}_{t-l+1}, \dots, \mathbf{x}_t) \longrightarrow (\mathbf{x}_{t+1}, \dots \mathbf{x}_{t+h}) \tag{8.2}$$

Here l is the length of the input series and h is the forecasting horizon in the output. Spatiotemporal forecasting is more general than dynamic forecasting. The state of the system $\mathbf{x} \in \mathbb{R}^{d \times d}$ is structured, representing for example a frame in the video. A second example is for time-evolving graphs, the spatial information of $\mathbf{x} \in \mathbb{R}^d$ can also be represented as an adjacent matrix $\mathbf{A} \in \mathbb{R}^{d \times d}$.

8.1.4 Examples of Dynamical Systems

We describe a few examples of dynamical systems that we investigate in this chapter.

8.1.4.1 Turbulent Flows (Navier–Stokes Equations)

Turbulent convection is a major feature of the dynamics of the oceans, the atmosphere, as well as engineering and industrial processes, which has motivated numerous experimental

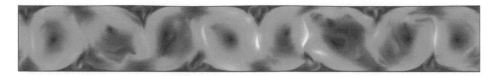

FIGURE 8.1
A snapshot of the velocity norm ($\sqrt{v_x^2 + v_y^2}$) fields of the 2D RBC flow [10]. The spatial resolution is 1792 x 256 pixels.

and theoretical studies for many years. Turbulent fluctuations occur over a wide range of length and time scales with high correlations between these scales. Turbulent flows are characterized by chaotic motions and intermittency, which are difficult to predict.

Let $\boldsymbol{w}(t)$ be the vector velocity field of the flow with two components $(u(t), v(t))$, velocities along x and y directions, the governing equations for divergence-free turbulence are:

$$\nabla \cdot \boldsymbol{w} = 0 \qquad\qquad \text{Continuity Equation}$$

$$\frac{\partial \boldsymbol{w}}{\partial t} + (\boldsymbol{w} \cdot \nabla)\boldsymbol{w} = -\frac{1}{\rho_0}\nabla p + \nu\nabla^2\boldsymbol{w} + f \qquad \text{Momentum Equation}$$

$$\frac{\partial T}{\partial t} + (\boldsymbol{w} \cdot \nabla)T = \kappa\nabla^2 T \qquad\qquad \text{Temperature Equation}$$

where p and T are pressure and temperature respectively, κ is the coefficient of heat conductivity, ρ_0 is the uniform density, α is the coefficient of thermal expansion, ν is the kinematic viscosity, f the body force that is due to gravity.

One of the physical systems we investigate in this chapter is 2-dimensional Rayleigh–Bénard convection (RBC), a model for turbulent convection. RBC results from a horizontal layer of fluid heated from below so that the lower surface is at a higher temperature than the upper surface. The RBC system serves as an idealized model for turbulent convection that exhibits the full range of dynamics of turbulent convection for sufficiently large temperature gradients. Figure 8.1 shows a snapshot in our RBC flow dataset.

8.1.4.2   Lotka–Volterra (LV)

Lotka–Volterra system [1] of Equation 8.3 describes the dynamics of biological systems in which predators and preys interact, where d denotes the number of species interacting and p_i denotes the population size of species i at time t. The unknown parameters $r_i \geq 0$, $k_i \geq 0$ and A_{ij} denote the intrinsic growth rate of species i, the carrying capacity of species i when the other species are absent, and the interspecies competition between two different species, respectively. The LV equations can also be used to model online activities [42].

$$\frac{dp_i}{dt} = r_i p_i\left(1 - \frac{\sum_{j=1}^{d} A_{ij}p_j}{k_i}\right),$$
$$i = 1, 2, \ldots, d. \qquad (8.3)$$

8.1.4.3   FitzHugh–Nagumo (FHN)

Richard FitzHugh [21] and J. Nagumo [46] independently derived the Equation 8.4 to qualitatively describe the behavior of spike potentials in the giant axon of squid neurons. The system describes the reciprocal dependencies of the voltage x across an axon membrane and a recovery variable y summarizing outward currents. The unknown parameters a, b, and

c are dimensionless and positive, and c determines how fast y changes relative to x.

$$\left\{ \begin{array}{l} \dfrac{dx}{dt} = c(x + y - \dfrac{x^3}{3}), \\[2ex] \dfrac{dy}{dt} = -\dfrac{1}{c}(x + by - a). \end{array} \right. \tag{8.4}$$

8.1.4.4   SEIR

SEIR system of Equation 8.5 models the spread of infectious diseases [25]. It has four compartments: Susceptible (S) denotes those who potentially have the disease, Exposed (E) models the incubation period, Infected (I) denotes the infectious who currently have the disease, and Removed/Recovered (R) denotes those who have recovered from the disease or have died. The total population N is assumed to be constant and the sum of these four states. The unknown parameters β, σ and γ denote the transmission, incubation, and recovery rates, respectively.

$$\left\{ \begin{array}{l} dS/dt = -\beta SI/N, \\ dE/dt = \beta SI/N - \sigma E, \\ dI/dt = \sigma E - \gamma I, \\ dR/dt = \gamma I, \\ N = S + E + I + R. \end{array} \right. \tag{8.5}$$

8.2   Related Work

Our chapter is related to many fields in machine learning, applied mathematics and scientific domains. Here we highlight a few most relevant areas.

8.2.1   Dynamical System Modeling

Modeling the spatiotemporal dynamics of a system in order to forecast the future is of critical importance in fields as diverse as physics, economics, and neuroscience [60]. Methods in dynamical system literature from physics [27] to neuroscience [65] describe the spatiotemporal dynamics with differential equations and are *physics-based*. The seminal work by [59] proposed to solve ODEs by creating a dictionary of possible terms and applying sparse regression to select appropriate terms. But it assumes that the chosen library is sufficient. Local methods, such as ARIMA and Gaussian SSMs [17, 53, 56] learn the parameters individually for each time series. Deep sequence models have been widely used for learning dynamical systems. Most work has been purely *data-driven*, where complex DL models are learned directly from data without explicitly enforcing physical constraints, e.g., [36, 77, 79, 80]. Sequence to sequence models and the Transformer, have an encoder-decoder structure that can directly map input sequences to output sequences with different lengths [22, 35, 52, 62, 74]. Fully connected neural networks can also be used autoregressively to produce multiple time-step forecasts [5, 37]. Neural ODE [8] is based on the assumption that the data is governed by an ODE system and able to generate continuous predictions. When the data is spatially correlated, deep graph models, such as graph convolution networks and graph attention networks [63], have also been used.

8.2.2   Physics-Informed Deep Learning

DL models have been used often to model physical dynamics. For example, [31] studied unsupervised generative modeling of turbulent flows but the model is not able to make real-time future predictions given the historic data. [2, 43, 58] directly solves differential equations with neural nets given space x and time t as input. This type of methods cannot be used for forecasting since future t would always lie outside of the training domain and neural nets cannot extrapolate to unseen domain [3, 33]. [45] incorporated Koopman theory into a encoder-decoder architecture but did not study the symmetry of fluid dynamics. [19, 38] studied tensor invariant neural networks to learn the Reynolds stress tensor while preserving Galilean invariance, but Galilean invariance only applies to flows without external forces. [6, 28, 29, 73] tried to incorporate physical knowledge into DL by explicitly regularising the loss function with physical constraints. Still, regularization is quite ad-hoc, and it is difficult to tune the hyper-parameters of the regularizer. Hybrid DL models, e.g., [4, 8, 68, 81] integrate differential equations in DL for temporal dynamics forecasting.

8.2.3   Video Prediction

Our work is also related to future video prediction. Conditioning on the observed frames, video prediction models are trained to predict future frames, e.g., [20, 20, 41, 47, 64, 78]. Many of these models are trained on natural videos with complex noisy data from unknown physical processes. Therefore, it is difficult to explicitly incorporate physical principles into these models. Our work is substantially different because we do not attempt to predict object or camera motions. Instead, our approach aims to emulate numerical simulations given noiseless observations from known governing equations. Hence, some of these techniques are perhaps under-suited for our application.

8.2.4   Fluid Animation

In parallel, the computer graphics community has also investigated using DL to speed up numerical simulations for generating realistic animations of fluids such as water and smoke. For example, [61] used an incompressible Euler's equation with a customized CNN to predict velocity update within a finite difference method solver. [11] propose double CNN networks to synthesize high-resolution flow simulation based on reusable space-time regions. [75] and [61] developed DL models in the context of fluid flow animation, where physical consistency is less critical. [71] proposed a method for the data-driven inference of temporal evolutions of physical functions with DL. However, fluid animation emphases on the realism of the simulation rather than the physical consistency of the predictions or physics metrics and diagnostics of relevance to scientists.

8.2.5   Epidemic Forecasting

Compartmental models are commonly used for modeling epidemics. [9] proposes a time-dependent SIR model that uses ridge regression to predict the transmission and recovery rates over time. A potential limitation with this method is that it does not consider the incubation period and unreported cases. [48] modified the compartments in the SEIR model into the subpopulation commuting among different places, and estimated the model parameters using iterated filtering methods. [66] proposes a population-level survival-convolution method to model the number of infectious people as a convolution of newly infected cases and the proportion of individuals remaining infectious over time. [82] proposes the SuEIR model that incorporates the unreported cases, and the effect of the exposed group on susceptibles. [15] shows the importance of simultaneously modeling the transmission rate among the fifty U.S. states since transmission between states is significant.

8.3 Learning Trainable Operators for Dynamical Systems

We first introduce a physics-guided DL model architecture for turbulent flow prediction, which we call `Turbulent-Flow Net` (TF-Net). We adopt a hybrid approach by marrying two well-established turbulent flow simulation techniques with custom-designed U-net. The global idea behind our method is to decompose the turbulent flow into components of different scales, and parameterize the convolutional operators with trainable weights for each component. We call this type of approach to parameterize mathematical operators "learning trainable operators". First, we provide a brief introduction of the CFD techniques, which are foundations for our idea.

8.3.1 Brief Introduction of Computational Fluid Dynamics

Computational techniques are at the core of present-day turbulence investigations. Direct Numerical Simulation (DNS) are accurate but not computationally feasible for practical applications. Great emphasis was placed on the alternative approaches including Large-Eddy Simulation (LES) and Reynolds-averaged Navier–Stokes (RANS). See the book on turbulence [44] for details.

RANS decomposes the turbulent flow w into two separable time scales: a time-averaged mean flow $\bar{w}$ and a fluctuating quantity w'. The resulting RANS equations contain a closure term, the Reynolds stresses, that require modeling, the classic closure problem of turbulence modeling. While this approach is a good first approximation to solving a turbulent flow, RANS does not account for broadband unsteadiness and intermittency, characteristic of most turbulent flows. Further, closure models for the unresolved scales are often inadequate, making RANS solutions to be less accurate. n here is the moving average window size.

$$w(\boldsymbol{x}, t) = \bar{w}(\boldsymbol{x}, t) + w'(\boldsymbol{x}, t), \quad \bar{w}(\boldsymbol{x}, t) = \frac{1}{n} \int_{t-n}^{t} T(s) w(\boldsymbol{x}, s) ds \qquad (8.6)$$

LES is an alternative approach based on low-pass filtering of the Navier–Stokes equations that solves a part of the multi-scale turbulent flow corresponding to the most energetic scales. In LES, the large-scale component is a spatially filtered variable $\tilde{w}$, which is usually expressed as a convolution product by the filter kernel S. The kernel S is often taken to be a Gaussian kernel. Ω_i is a subdomain of the solution and depends on the filter size [55].

$$w(\boldsymbol{x}, t) = \tilde{w}(\boldsymbol{x}, t) + w'(\boldsymbol{x}, t), \quad \tilde{w}(\boldsymbol{x}, t) = \int_{\Omega_i} S(\boldsymbol{x}|\boldsymbol{\xi}) w(\boldsymbol{\xi}, t) d\boldsymbol{\xi} \qquad (8.7)$$

The key difference between RANS and LES is that RANS is based on time averaging, leading to simpler steady equations, whereas LES is based on a spatial filtering process, which is more accurate but also computationally more expensive.

Hybrid RANS-LES Coupling combines both RANS and LES approaches in order to take advantage of both methods [7, 18]. It decomposes the flow variables into three parts: mean flow, resolved fluctuations and unresolved (subgrid) fluctuations. RANS-LES coupling applies the spatial filtering operator S and the temporal average operator T sequentially. We can define $\bar{w}$ in discrete form with using w^* as an intermediate term,

$$w^*(\boldsymbol{x}, t) = S * w = \sum_{\boldsymbol{\xi}} S(\boldsymbol{x}|\boldsymbol{\xi}) w(\boldsymbol{\xi}, t) \qquad (8.8)$$

$$\bar{w}(\boldsymbol{x}, t) = T * w^* = \frac{1}{n} \sum_{s=t-n}^{t} T(s) w^*(\boldsymbol{x}, s) \qquad (8.9)$$

then $\tilde{w}$ can be defined as the difference between w^* and $\bar{w}$:

$$\tilde{w} = w^* - \bar{w}, \quad w' = w - w^* \tag{8.10}$$

Finally, we can have the three-level decomposition of the velocity field.

$$w = \bar{w} + \tilde{w} + w' \tag{8.11}$$

This hybrid approach combines computational efficiency of RANS with the resolving power of LES to provide a technique that is less expensive and more tractable than pure LES.

8.3.2   Turbulent-Flow Net

Inspired by techniques used in hybrid RANS-LES Coupling to separate scales of a multi-scale system, we propose a hybrid DL framework, TF-Net, based on the multi-level spectral decomposition of the turbulent flow.

Specifically, we decompose the velocity field into three components of different scales using two scale separation operators, the spatial filter S and the temporal filter T. In traditional CFD, these filters are usually pre-defined, such as the Gaussian spatial filter. In TF-Net, both filters are *trainable* neural networks. The spatial filtering process is instantiated as one layer CNN with a single 5×5 filter to each input image. The temporal filter is also implemented as a convolutional layer with a single 1×1 filter applied to every T images. The motivation for this design is to explicitly guide the DL model to learn the non-linear dynamics of both large and small eddies as relevant to the task of spatio-temporal prediction.

We design three identical encoders to encode the three scale components separately. We use a shared decoder to learn the interactions among these three components and generate the final prediction. Each encoder and the decoder can be viewed as a U-net without duplicate layers and middle layer in the original architecture [54]. The encoder consists of four convolutional layers with double the number of feature channels of the previous layer and stride 2 for down-sampling. The decoder consists of one output layer and four deconvolutional layers with summation of the corresponding feature channels from the three encoders and the output of the previous layer as input.

To generate multi-step forecasts, we perform one-step ahead prediction and roll out the predictions autoregressively. Furthermore, we also consider a variant of TF-Net by explicitly adding physical constraint to the loss function. Since the turbulent flow under investigation has zero divergence ($\nabla \cdot w$ should be zero everywhere), we include $||\nabla \cdot w||^2$ as a regularizer to constrain the predictions, leading to a constrained TF-Net, or Con TF-Net.

8.3.3   Experiments on Forecasting Rayleigh–Bénard Convection

8.3.3.1   Rayleigh–Bénard Convection Data

The dataset for our experiments comes from 2-dimensional turbulent flow simulated using the Lattice Boltzmann Method [10]. We use only the velocity vector fields, where the spatial resolution of each image (snapshots in time) is 1792 x 256. Each image has two channels, one is the turbulent flow velocity along x direction and the other one is the velocity along y direction. The physics parameters relevant to this numerical simulation are: Prandtl number = 0.71, Rayleigh number = 2.5×10^8 and the maximum Mach number = 0.1. We use 1500 images for our experiments. The task is to predict the spatiotemporal velocity fields up to 60 steps ahead given 10 initial frames.

We divided each 1792 by 256 image into 7 square sub-regions of size 256 x 256, then downsample them into 64 x 64 pixels sized images. We use a sliding window approach to generate 9,870 samples of sequences of velocity fields: 6,000 training samples, 1,700 validation samples and 2,170 test samples. The DL model is trained using back-propagation through prediction errors accumulated over multiple steps. We use a validation set for hyper-parameters tuning based on the average error of predictions up to six steps ahead. All results are averaged over three runs with random initialization.

8.3.3.2 Evaluation Metrics

Even though Root Mean Square Error (RMSE) is a widely accepted metric for quantifying the prediction performance, it only measures pixel differences. We need to check whether the predictions are physically meaningful and preserve desired physical quantities, such as Turbulence Kinetic Energy, Divergence and Energy Spectrum. Therefore, we include a set of additional metrics for evaluation.

- RMSE: We calculate the RMSE of all predicted values from the ground truth for each pixel.

- Divergence: Since we investigate incompressible turbulent flows in this work, which means the divergence, $\nabla \cdot \mathbf{w}$, at each pixel should be zero, we use the average of absolute divergence over all pixels at each prediction step as an additional evaluation metric.

- Turbulence Kinetic Energy: In fluid dynamics, turbulence kinetic energy is the mean kinetic energy per unit mass associated with eddies in turbulent flow. Physically, the turbulence kinetic energy is characterised by measured root mean square velocity fluctuations,

$$(\overline{(u')^2} + \overline{(v')^2})/2, \quad \overline{(u')^2} = \frac{1}{T} \sum_{t=0}^{T} (u(t) - \bar{u})^2 \tag{8.12}$$

where t is the time step. We calculate the turbulence kinetic energy for each predicted sample of 60 velocity fields.

- Energy Spectrum: The energy spectrum of turbulence, $E(k)$, is related to the mean turbulence kinetic energy as

$$\int_0^\infty E(k)dk = (\overline{(u')^2} + \overline{(v')^2}), \tag{8.13}$$

where k is the wavenumber, the spatial frequency in 2D Fourier domain. We calculate the Energy Spectrum on the Fourier transformation of the turbulence kinetic energy fields. The large eddies have low wavenumbers and the small eddies correspond to high wavenumbers. The spectrum indicates how much kinetic energy is contained in eddies with wavenumber k. Figure 8.2 shows a theoretical turbulence kinetic energy spectrum plot. The spectrum can describe the transfer of energy from large scales of motion to the small scales and provides a representation of the dependence of energy on frequency. Thus, the Energy Spectrum Error (ESE) can indicate whether the predictions preserve the correct statistical distribution and obey the energy conservation law. A trivial example that can illustrate why we need ESE is that if a model simply outputs moving averages of input frames, the accumulated RMSE of predictions might not be high but the ESE would be really big because all the small or even medium eddies are smoothed out.

8.3.3.3 Experimental Results

TF-Net is compared against four purely data-driven models: ResNet [24], ConvLSTM [76], U-Net [54] and GAN and against two physics-guided models: SST [16] and DHPM [51]. All

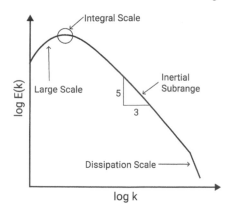

FIGURE 8.2
Theoretical turbulence energy spectrum plot.

models are tested on the task of forecasting velocity fields of RBC flow as shown in Figure 8.1. Figure 8.3 shows `TF-Net` consistently outperforms all baselines on RMSE, physically relevant metrics (Divergence and Energy Spectrum) as well as Average time to produce single velocity field. Constraining it with divergence free regularizer can further reduce the RMSE and Divergence. Thus, `TF-Net` is able to generate both accurate and physically meaningful predictions of the velocity fields that preserve critical quantities of relevance. Furthermore, `TFNet` has a significantly smaller number of parameters than most baselines, and hence is a compact and efficient model. For more details, please refer to [67].

We see that incorporating prior physics knowledge or physics-based models can guide DL models to better learn complex patterns that are consistent with the physics laws from

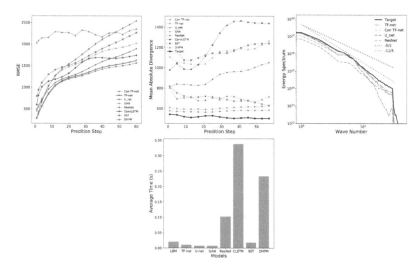

FIGURE 8.3
Top row from left to right: RMSEs of different models' predictions at varying forecasting horizon; Mean absolute divergence of different models' predictions at varying forecasting horizon; The Energy Spectrum of target, `TF-Net`, `U-net` and `ResNet` on the leftmost square sub-region; Bottom row: Average time to produce one 64 × 448 2D velocity field for all models on single V100 GPU.

data, thus more accurate and physically consistent. However, most current physics-guided DL models for dynamics modeling still struggle with generalization and are still trained to model a specific system. Generalization is a fundamental problem in machine learning. A trustworthy and reliable model for learning physical dynamics should be able to generalize across systems with various parameters, external forces, or boundary conditions while preserve high accuracy. Thus, further research into generalization of DL models for learning dynamical system is needed. And we will study the generalization of DL models in dynamics forecasting setting in the next section.

8.4 Learning Dynamical Systems Requires Rethinking Generalization

Previous section has shown that DL can accelerate the simulation and prediction of complex spatiotemporal dynamics such as turbulent flow. However, generalization remains a fundamental problem in machine learning. A model's performance often degrades quickly when the test domain is different from the training domain. In this section, we study the generalization ability of DL models in the dynamics forecasting setting. We compare DL models and physics-based approaches on learning *Sine*, *SEIR*, *Lotka–Volterra*, and *FitzHugh–Nagumo*. We experimentally explore the two cases, distribution shift in the data, where the observations range changes; and parameter domains, where the parameter range of the system in training and test differs.

8.4.1 Data-Driven vs. Physics-Based Approaches

We start by defining the general problem for learning dynamical systems.

8.4.1.1 Problem Formulation

Consider the dynamical system in the form of Equation 8.14. We denote $\boldsymbol{y} \in \mathbb{R}^d$ as observed variables and $\boldsymbol{u} \in \mathbb{R}^p$ as the unobserved variables:

$$
\begin{cases}
\dfrac{d\boldsymbol{y}}{dt} = f_{\boldsymbol{\theta}}(t, \boldsymbol{y}, \boldsymbol{u}) \\[2mm]
\dfrac{d\boldsymbol{u}}{dt} = g_{\boldsymbol{\theta}}(t, \boldsymbol{y}, \boldsymbol{u}) \\[2mm]
\boldsymbol{y}(t_0) = \boldsymbol{y}_0 \\[1mm]
\boldsymbol{u}(t_0) = \boldsymbol{u}_0.
\end{cases}
\tag{8.14}
$$

where $\boldsymbol{y}_0, \boldsymbol{u}_0$ specify the initial conditions. Given observations $(\boldsymbol{y}_0, \boldsymbol{y}_1, ..., \boldsymbol{y}_{k-1})$ as inputs, the task of learning dynamical systems is to learn $f_{\boldsymbol{\theta}}$ and $g_{\boldsymbol{\theta}}$, and produce accurate forecasts $(\boldsymbol{y}_k, ..., \boldsymbol{y}_{k+q-1})$, where q is called the forecasting horizon.

A plethora of work has been devoted to learning dynamical systems. When $\boldsymbol{f}_{\boldsymbol{\theta}}$ is known, physics-based methods based on numerical integration are commonly used for parameter estimation [26]. [2, 43, 58] propose to directly solve $\boldsymbol{y}$ by approximating $\boldsymbol{f}$ with neural networks that take the coordinates and time as input. When $\boldsymbol{f}_{\boldsymbol{\theta}}$ is unknown and the data is abundant, data-driven methods are preferred. For example, DL, especially deep sequence models [5, 22, 52, 57] have demonstrated success in time series forecasting. In addition, [4, 8, 67, 68] have developed hybrid DL models based on differential equations for spatiotemporal dynamics forecasting.

Next, we provide an overview of both data-driven modeling and physics-based modeling methods for learning dynamical systems.

8.4.1.2 Data-Driven Modeling

For data-driven models, we assume both f and g are unknown. We are given training and test samples either as sliced sub-sequences from a long sequence (same parameters, different initial conditions) or independent samples from the system (different parameters, same initial conditions). In particular, let p_S be the training data distribution and p_T be the test data distribution. DL seeks a hypothesis $h \in \mathcal{H} : \mathbb{R}^{d \times k} \mapsto \mathbb{R}^{d \times q}$ that maps a sequence of past values to future values:

$$h(\boldsymbol{y}_0^{(i)}, ..., \boldsymbol{y}_{k-1}^{(i)}) = \hat{\boldsymbol{y}}_k^{(i)}, ..., \hat{\boldsymbol{y}}_{k+q-1}^{(i)} \tag{8.15}$$

where (i) denotes individual sample, k is the input length and q is the output length.

Following the standard statistical learning setting, a deep sequence model minimizes the training loss $\hat{L}_1(h) = \frac{1}{n} \sum_{i=1}^n l(\boldsymbol{y}^{(i)}, h)$, where $\boldsymbol{y}^{(i)} = (\boldsymbol{y}_0^{(i)}, ..., \boldsymbol{y}_{k+q-1}^{(i)}) \sim p_S$ is the ith training sample, l is a loss function. For example, for square loss, we have

$$l(\boldsymbol{y}^{(i)}, h) = ||h(\boldsymbol{y}_0^{(i)}, ..., \boldsymbol{y}_{k-1}^{(i)}) - (\boldsymbol{y}_k^{(i)}, ..., \boldsymbol{y}_{k+q-1}^{(i)})||_2^2$$

The test error is given as $L_1(h) = \mathbb{E}_{\boldsymbol{y} \sim p_T}[l(\boldsymbol{y}, h)]$. The goal is to achieve small test error $L_1(h)$ and small $|\hat{L}_1(h) - L_1(h)|$ indicates good generalization ability.

A fundamental difficulty of forecasting in dynamical system is the distributional shift that naturally occur in learning dynamical systems [3,33]. In forecasting, the data in the future p_T often lie outside the training domain p_S, and requires methods to extrapolate to the unseen domain. This is in contrast to classical machine learning theory, where generalization refers to model adapting to unseen data drawn from the same distribution [23,49].

8.4.1.3 Physics-Based Modeling

Physics-based modeling assumes we already have an appropriate system of ODEs to describe the underlying dynamics. We know the function f and g, but not the parameters. We can use automatic differentiation to estimate the unknown parameters $\boldsymbol{\theta}$ and the initial values $\boldsymbol{u}_0$. We coin this procedure as `AutoODE`. Similar approaches have been used in other papers [50,82] but have not been well formalized. The main procedure is described in the Algorithm 8.1. In the meanwhile, we need to ensure $\boldsymbol{u}$ and $\boldsymbol{y}$ have enough correlation that `AutoODE` can correctly learn all the parameters based on the observable $\boldsymbol{y}$ only. If $\boldsymbol{u}$ and $\boldsymbol{y}$ are not correlated or loosely correlated, we may be not able to estimate $\boldsymbol{u}$ solely based on the observations of $\boldsymbol{y}$.

Algorithm 8.1: `AutoODE`

0: Initialize the unknown parameters $\boldsymbol{\theta}, \boldsymbol{u}_0$ in Eqn. 8.14 randomly.
1: Discretize Eqn. 8.14 and apply 4-th order Runge Kutta (RK4) Method.
2: Generate estimation for $\boldsymbol{y}$: $(\hat{\boldsymbol{y}}_0, ..., \hat{\boldsymbol{y}}_k)$
3: Minimize the forecasting loss with the Adam optimizer,
$L_2(\boldsymbol{\theta}, \boldsymbol{u}_0) = \frac{1}{k} \sum_{i=0}^{k-1} ||\hat{\boldsymbol{y}}_i(\boldsymbol{\theta}, \boldsymbol{u}, t) - \boldsymbol{y}_i(\boldsymbol{\theta}, \boldsymbol{u}, t)||^2$.
4: After convergence, use estimated $\hat{\boldsymbol{\theta}}, \hat{\boldsymbol{u}}_0$ and 4-th order Runge Kutta Method to generate final prediction, $(\boldsymbol{y}_k, ..., \boldsymbol{y}_{t+q-1})$.

NeuralODE [8] uses the adjoint method to differentiate through the numerical solver. Adjoint methods are more efficient in higher-dimensional neural network models which require complex numerical integration. In our case, since we are dealing with low dimension ordinary differential equations and the RK4 is sufficient to generate accurate predictions. We can directly implement the RK4 in Pytorch and make it fully differentiable.

In order to understand the generalization abilities of various model for dynamic forecasting, we design two type of forecasting tasks based on the parameter ranges in training and testing.

8.4.2 Interpolation and Extrapolation Tasks

We define p_S and p_T as the training and the test data distributions. And the θ_S and θ_T denote *parameter* distributions of training and test sets, where the *parameter* here refers to the coefficients and the initial values of dynamical systems. A distribution is a function that map a sample space to the interval $[0,1]$ if it a continuous distribution, or a subset of that interval if it is a discrete distribution. The domain of a distribution p, i.e., $\text{Dom}(p)$, refers to the set of values (sample space) for which that distribution is defined.

We define two types of interpolation and extrapolation tasks. Regarding the data domain, we define a task as an interpolation task when the data domain of the test data is a subset of the domain of the training data, i.e., $\text{Dom}(p_T) \subseteq \text{Dom}(p_S)$, and then extrapolation occurs $\text{Dom}(p_T) \nsubseteq \text{Dom}(p_S)$. Regarding the *parameter* domain, an interpolation task indicates that $\text{Dom}(\theta_T) \subseteq \text{Dom}(\theta_S)$, and an extrapolation task indicates that $\text{Dom}(\theta_T) \nsubseteq \text{Dom}(\theta_S)$.

8.4.3 Generalization in Dynamical Systems: Unseen Data in the Different Data Domain

Through a simple experiment on learning the *Sine* curves, we show deep sequence models have poor generalization on extrapolation tasks regarding the data domain, i.e., $\text{Dom}(p_T) \nsubseteq \text{Dom}(p_S)$. Specifically, we generate 2k *Sine* samples of length 60 with different frequencies and phases, and randomly split them into training, validation and interpolation-test sets. The extrapolation-test set is the interpolation-test set shifted up by 1. We investigate four models, including Seq2Seq (sequence to sequence with LSTMs), Transformer, FC (autoregressive fully connected neural nets) and NeuralODE. All models are trained to make 30 steps ahead prediction given the previous 30 steps.

Table 8.1 shows that all models have substantially larger errors on the extrapolation test set. Figure 8.4 shows Seq2Seq predictions on an interpolation (left) and an extrapolation (right) test samples. We can see that Seq2Seq makes accurate predictions on the interpolation-test sample, while it fails to generalize when the same samples are shifted up only by 1.

TABLE 8.1

RMSEs of the Interpolation and Extrapolation Tasks of Sine Dynamics.

RMSE	Inter	Extra
Seq2Seq	0.012	1.242
Auto-FC	0.009	1.554
Transformer	0.016	1.088
NeuralODE	0.012	1.214

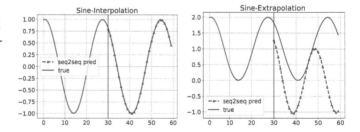

FIGURE 8.4

Seq2Seq predictions on an interpolation (left) and an extrapolation (right) test samples of Sine dynamics, the vertical black line in the plots separates the input and forecasting period.

TABLE 8.2
The Initial Values and System Parameters Ranges of Interpolation and Extrapolation Test Sets.

	System Parameters		Initial Values	
	Interpolation	Extrapolation	Interpolation	Extrapolation
LV	$k \sim U(0, 250)^4$	$k \sim U(250, 300)^4$	$p_0 \sim U(30, 200)^4$	$p_0 \sim U(0, 30)^4$
FHN	$c \sim U(1.5, 5)$	$c \sim U(0.5, 1.5)$	$x_0 \sim U(2, 10)$	$x_0 \sim U(0, 2)$
SEIR	$\beta \sim U(0.45, 0.9)$	$\beta \sim U(0.3, 0.45)$	$I_0 \sim U(30, 100)$	$I_0 \sim U(10, 30)$

8.4.4 Generalization in Dynamical Systems: Unseen Data with Different System Parameters

Even when $\text{Dom}(p_{\mathcal{T}}) \subseteq \text{Dom}(p_{\mathcal{S}})$, deep sequence models can still fail to learn the correct dynamics if there is a distributional shift in the parameter domain, i.e., $\text{Dom}(\theta_{\mathcal{T}}) \not\subseteq \text{Dom}(\theta_{\mathcal{S}})$.

For each of the three dynamics in Section 8.1.4, we generate 6k synthetic time series samples with different system parameters and initial values. The training/validation/interpolation-test sets for each dataset have the same range of system parameters while the extrapolation-test set contains samples from a different range. Table 8.2 shows the *parameter* distribution of test sets. For each dynamics, we perform two experiments to evaluate the models' extrapolation generalization ability on initial values and system parameters. All samples are normalized so that $\text{Dom}(p_{\mathcal{T}}) = \text{Dom}(p_{\mathcal{S}})$.

Table 8.3 shows the prediction RMSEs of the models on initial values and system parameter interpolation and extrapolation test sets. We observe that the models' prediction errors on extrapolation test sets are much larger than the error on interpolation test sets. Figures 8.5 and 8.6 show that `Seq2Seq` and `FC` fail to make accurate prediction when tested outside of the parameter distribution even though these models are powerful enough to memorize the training data, and perform well on the interpolation tasks.

`AutoODE` always obtains the lowest errors as it would be not affected by the range of parameters or the initial values. However, it is a local method and we need to train one model for each sample. In contrast, DL models can only mimic the behaviors of SEIR, LV and FHN dynamics rather than understanding the underlying mechanisms.

In conclusion, we experimentally show that four DL models fail to generalize under shifted distributions in both the data and the parameter domains. Even though these models are powerful enough to memorize the training data, and perform well on the interpolation tasks.

TABLE 8.3
RMSEs on Initial Values and System Parameter Interpolation and Extrapolation Test Sets.

RMSE	LV				FHN				SEIR			
	k		p_0		c		x_0		β		I_0	
	Int	Ext	Int	Ext	Int	Ext	Int	Ext	Int	Ext	Int	Ext
Seq2Seq	0.050	0.215	0.028	0.119	0.093	0.738	0.079	0.152	1.12	4.14	2.58	7.89
FC	0.078	0.227	0.044	0.131	0.057	0.402	0.057	0.120	1.04	3.20	1.82	5.85
Transformer	0.074	0.231	0.067	0.142	0.102	0.548	0.111	0.208	1.09	4.23	2.01	6.13
NeuralODE	0.091	0.196	0.050	0.127	0.163	0.689	0.124	0.371	1.25	3.27	2.01	5.82
AutoODE	0.057	0.054	0.018	0.028	0.059	0.058	0.066	0.069	0.89	0.91	0.96	1.02

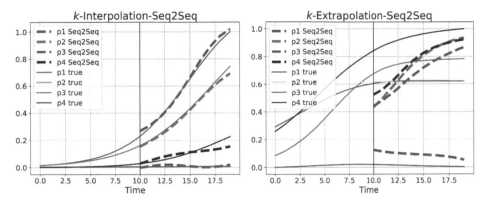

FIGURE 8.5

Seq2Seq predictions on a k-interpolation and a k-extrapolation test samples of LV dynamics, the vertical black line separates the input and forecasting period.

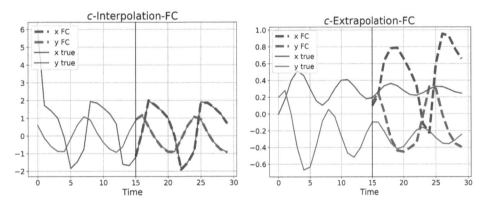

FIGURE 8.6

FC predictions on a c-interpolation and a c-extrapolation test samples of FHN dynamics, the vertical black line in the plots separates the input and forecasting period.

Our study provides important insights on learning real-world dynamical systems: to achieve accurate forecasts with DL, we need to ensure that both the data and dynamical system parameters in the training set are sufficient enough to cover the domains of the test set.

8.5 Incorporating Symmetry into Deep Dynamics Model for Improved Generalization

In this section, we provide one way to improve the generalization DL models for physical dynamics by incorporating symmetries into the deep dynamics model. We propose to improve the generalization and physical accuracy of DL models for physical dynamics by incorporating symmetries into the forecasting model. In physics, Noether's Law gives a correspondence between conserved quantities and groups of symmetries. By designing a model that is inherently equivariant to transformations of its input, we can guarantee that our model generalizes automatically across these transformations, making it robust to distributional shift.

Research into equivariant neural networks has mostly been applied to tasks such as image classification and segmentation [32, 69, 70]. In contrast, we design equivariant networks in a completely different context, that of a time series representing a physical process. Forecasting high-dimensional turbulence is a significant step for equivariant neural networks compared to the low-dimensional physics examples and computer vision problems treated in other works.

The symmetries we consider, translation, rotation, uniform motion, and scale, have different properties, and thus we tailor our methods for incorporating each symmetry. Specifically, for scale equivariance, we replace the convolution operation with group correlation over the group G generated by translations *and* rescalings. Our method builds on [72], with significant novel adaptations to the physics domain: scaling affecting time, space, and magnitude; both up and down scaling; and scaling by any real number. For rotational symmetries, we leverage the key insight of [13] that the input, output, and hidden layers of the network are all acted upon by the symmetry group and thus should be treated as representations of the symmetry group. Our rotation-equivariant model is built using the flexible E(2)-CNN framework developed by [69]. In the case of a uniform motion, or Galilean transformation, we show the above methods are too constrained. We use the simple but effective technique of convolutions conjugated by averaging operations.

We test on a simulated turbulent convection dataset and on real-world ocean current and temperature data. Ocean currents are difficult to predict using numerical methods due to unknown external forces and complex dynamics not fully captured by simplified mathematical models. These domains are chosen as examples, but since the symmetries we focus on are pervasive in almost all physics problems, we expect our techniques will be widely applicable.

8.5.1 Mathematical Preliminaries

8.5.1.1 Symmetry Groups and Equivariant Functions

A **group of symmetries** or simply **group** consists of a set G together with a composition map $\circ\colon G \times G \to G$. The composition map is required to be associative and have an identity $1 \in G$. Most importantly, composition with any element of G is required to be invertible.

Groups are abstract objects, but they become concrete when we let them act. A group G has an **action** on a set S if there is an action map $\cdot\colon G \times S \to S$ which is compatible with the composition law. We say further that S is a G-**representation** if the set S is a vector space and the group acts on S by linear transformations. for a more formal treatment see [34]

Definition 8.1 (invariant, equivariant) *Let $f\colon X \to Y$ be a function and G be a group. Assume G acts on X and Y. The function f is G-**equivariant** if $f(gx) = gf(x)$ for all $x \in X$ and $g \in G$. The function f is G-**invariant** if $f(gx) = f(x)$ for all $x \in X$ and $g \in G$.*

See Figure 8.7 for an illustration. In the setting of forecasting, f approximates the underlying dynamical system. The set of valid transformations g is called the symmetry group of the system.

8.5.1.2 Symmetries of Differential Equations

By classifying the symmetries of a system of differential equations, the task of finding solutions is made far simpler, since the space of solutions will exhibit those same symmetries. Let G be a group equipped with an action on 2-dimensional space $X = \mathbb{R}^2$ and 3-dimensional spacetime $\hat{X} = \mathbb{R}^3$. Let $V = \mathbb{R}^d$ be a G-representation. Denote the set of all V-**fields** on $\hat{X}$ as $\hat{\mathcal{F}}_V = \{\boldsymbol{w}\colon \hat{X} \to V : \boldsymbol{w} \text{ smooth}\}$. Define $\mathcal{F}_V$ similarly to be V-fields on X. Then G has an induced action on $\hat{\mathcal{F}}_V$ by $(g\boldsymbol{w})(x,t) = g(\boldsymbol{w}(g^{-1}x, g^{-1}t))$ and on $\mathcal{F}_V$ analogously.

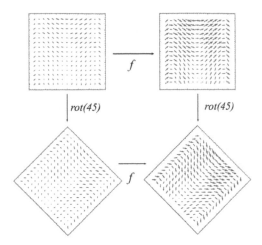

FIGURE 8.7
Illustration of equivariance of, e.g., $f(x) = 2x$ with respect to $T = \text{rot}(\pi/4)$.

Consider a system of differential operators $\mathcal{D}$ acting on $\hat{\mathcal{F}}_V$. Denote the set of solutions $\text{Sol}(\mathcal{D}) \subseteq \hat{\mathcal{F}}_V$. We say G is a symmetry group of $\mathcal{D}$ if G preserves $\text{Sol}(\mathcal{D})$. That is, if φ is a solution of $\mathcal{D}$, then for all $g \in G$, $g(\varphi)$ is also. In order to forecast the evolution of a system $\mathcal{D}$, we model the forward prediction function f. Let $\boldsymbol{w} \in \text{Sol}(\mathcal{D})$. The input to f is a collection of k snapshots at times $t - k, \ldots, t - 1$ denoted $\boldsymbol{w}_{t-i} \in \mathcal{F}_d$. The prediction function $f \colon \mathcal{F}_d^k \to \mathcal{F}_d$ is defined $f(\boldsymbol{w}_{t-k}, \ldots, \boldsymbol{w}_{t-1}) = \boldsymbol{w}_t$. It predicts the solution at a time t based on the solution in the past. Let G be a symmetry group of $\mathcal{D}$. Then for $g \in G$, $g(\boldsymbol{w})$ is also a solution of $\mathcal{D}$. Thus, $f(g\boldsymbol{w}_{t-k}, \ldots, g\boldsymbol{w}_{t-1}) = g\boldsymbol{w}_t$. Consequently, f is G-equivariant.

8.5.1.3 Symmetries of Navier–Stokes Equations

We investigate two dynamical systems: RBC and real-world ocean current and temperature. These systems are governed by Navier–Stokes equations. The Navier–Stokes equations are invariant under the following five different transformations. Individually each of these types of transformations generates a group of symmetries of the system.

- Space translation: $\quad T_{\boldsymbol{c}}^{\text{sp}} \boldsymbol{w}(\boldsymbol{x}, t) = \boldsymbol{w}(\boldsymbol{x} - \boldsymbol{c}, t), \quad \boldsymbol{c} \in \mathbb{R}^2,$
- Time translation: $\quad T_{\tau}^{\text{time}} \boldsymbol{w}(\boldsymbol{x}, t) = \boldsymbol{w}(\boldsymbol{x}, t - \tau), \quad \tau \in \mathbb{R},$
- Uniform motion: $\quad T_{\boldsymbol{c}}^{\text{um}} \boldsymbol{w}(\boldsymbol{x}, t) = \boldsymbol{w}(\boldsymbol{x}, t) + \boldsymbol{c}, \quad \boldsymbol{c} \in \mathbb{R}^2,$
- Rotation/Reflection: $\quad T_R^{\text{rot}} \boldsymbol{w}(\boldsymbol{x}, t) = R\boldsymbol{w}(R^{-1}\boldsymbol{x}, t), R \in O(2),$
- Scaling: $\quad T_{\lambda}^{\text{sc}} \boldsymbol{w}(\boldsymbol{x}, t) = \lambda \boldsymbol{w}(\lambda \boldsymbol{x}, \lambda^2 t), \quad \lambda \in \mathbb{R}_{>0}.$

where $O(2)$ is the group of $2{\times}2$ orthogonal matrices.

8.5.1.4 Equivariant Networks

The key to building equivariant networks is that the composition of equivariant functions is equivariant. Hence, if the maps between layers of a neural network are equivariant, then the whole network will be equivariant. Note that both the linear maps and activation functions must be equivariant. An important consequence of this principle is that the hidden layers must also carry a G-action.

8.5.1.4.1 Equivariant Convolutions. Consider a convolutional layer $\mathcal{F}_{\mathbb{R}^{d_{in}}} \to \mathcal{F}_{\mathbb{R}^{d_{out}}}$ with kernel K from a $\mathbb{R}^{d_{in}}$-field to a $\mathbb{R}^{d_{out}}$-field. Let $\mathbb{R}^{d_{in}}$ and $\mathbb{R}^{d_{out}}$ be G-representations with action maps ρ_{in} and ρ_{out} respectively. [12] prove the network is G-equivariant if and only if

$$K(gv) = \rho_{out}^{-1}(g)K(v)\rho_{in}(g) \qquad \text{for all } g \in G. \tag{8.16}$$

A network composed of such equivariant convolutions is called a *steerable CNN*.

Equivariant `ResNet` and `U-net`. Equivariant `ResNet` architectures appear in [13, 14], and equivariant transposed convolution, a feature of `U-net`, is implemented in [69]. We prove in general that adding skip connections to a network does not affect its equivariance with respect to linear actions. Define $f^{(ij)}$ as the functional mapping between layer i and layer j.

Proposition 8.1 *Let the layer $V^{(i)}$ be a G-representations for $0 \leq i \leq n$. Let $f^{(ij)}: V^{(i)} \to V^{(j)}$ be G-equivariant for $i < j$. Define recursively $\boldsymbol{x}^{(j)} = \sum_{0 \leq i < j} f^{(ij)}(\boldsymbol{x}^{(i)})$. Then $\boldsymbol{x}^{(n)} = f(\boldsymbol{x}^{(0)})$ is G-equivariant.*

Proof 8.1 *Assume $\boldsymbol{x}^{(i)}$ is an equivariant function of $\boldsymbol{x}^{(0)}$ for $i < j$. Then by equivariance of $f^{(ij)}$ and by linearity of the G-action,*

$$\sum_{0 \leq i < j} f^{(ij)}(g\boldsymbol{x}^{(i)}) = \sum_{0 \leq i < j} g f^{(ij)}(\boldsymbol{x}^{(i)}) = g\boldsymbol{x}^{(j)},$$

for $g \in G$. By induction, $\boldsymbol{x}^{(n)} = f(\boldsymbol{x}^{(0)})$ is equivariant with respect to G.

8.5.1.4.2 Relation to Data Augmentation. A classic strategy for dealing with distributional shift by transformations in a group G is to augment the training set $\mathcal{S}$ by adding samples transformed under G. That is, using the new training set $\mathcal{S}' = \bigcup_{g \in G} g(S)$. We show that data augmentation has no advantage for a perfectly equivariant parameterized function $f_\theta(x)$ since training samples (x, y) and (gx, gy) are equivalent. That is, f_θ learns the same from (x, y) as from (gx, gy) but with only possibly different sample weight.

Proposition 8.2 *Let G act on X and Y. Let $f_\theta: X \to Y$ be a parameterized class of G-equivariant functions differentiable with respect to θ. Let $\mathcal{L}: Y \times Y \to \mathbb{R}$ be a G-equivariant loss function, where G acts on $\mathbb{R}$ by χ, we have,*

$$\chi(g)\nabla_\theta \mathcal{L}(f_\theta(x), y) = \nabla_\theta \mathcal{L}(f_\theta(gx), gy).$$

Proof 8.2 *Equality of the gradients follows equality of the functions $\mathcal{L}(f_\theta(gx), gy) = \chi(g)\mathcal{L}(g^{-1}f_\theta(gx), y) = \chi(g)\mathcal{L}(f_\theta(x), y)$.*

In the case of RMSE and rotation or uniform motion, the loss function is invariant. That is, equivariant with $\chi(g) = 1$. Thus, the gradient for sample (x, y) and (gx, gy) is equal. In the case of scale, the loss function is equivariant with $G = (\mathbb{R}_{>0}, \cdot)$ and $\chi(\lambda) = \lambda$. In that case, the sample (gx, gy) is the same as the sample (x, y) but with sample weight $\chi(g)$.

8.5.2   Equivariant Deep Dynamics Models

We prescribe equivariance by training within function classes containing only equivariant functions. Our models can thus be theoretically guaranteed to be equivariant up to discretization error. We incorporate equivariance into two state-of-the-art architectures for dynamics prediction, `ResNet` and `U-net` [67]. Below, we describe how we modify the convolution operation in these models for different symmetries G to form four Equ_G-`ResNet` and four Equ_G-`Unet` models.

8.5.2.1 Time and Space Translation Equivariance

CNNs are time translation-equivariant as long as we predict in an autoregressive manner. Convolutional layers are also naturally space translation-equivariant (if cropping is ignored). Any activation function which acts identically pixel-by-pixel is equivariant.

8.5.2.2 Rotational Equivariance

To incorporate rotational symmetry, we model f using SO(2)-equivariant convolutions and activations within the `E(2)-CNN` framework of [69]. In practice, we use the cyclic group $G = C_n$ instead of $G = $ SO(2) as for large enough n the difference is practically indistinguishable due to space discretization. We use powers of the regular representation $\rho = \mathbb{R}[C_n]^m$ for hidden layers. The representation $\mathbb{R}[C_n]$ has basis given by elements of C_n and C_n-action by permutation matrices. It has good descriptivity since it contains all irreducible representations of C_n, and it is compatible with any activation function applied channel-wise.

8.5.2.3 Uniform Motion Equivariance

Uniform motion is part of Galilean invariance and is relevant to all non-relativistic physics modeling. For a vector field $X \colon \mathbb{R}^2 \to \mathbb{R}^2$ and vector $c \in \mathbb{R}^2$, uniform motion transformation is adding a constant vector field to the vector field $X(v)$, $T_c^{\mathrm{um}}(X)(v) = X(v) + c, c \in \mathbb{R}^2$. By the following corollary, enforcing uniform motion equivariance as above by requiring all layers of the `CNN` to be equivariant severely limits the model.

We prove that for the combined convolution-activation layers of a CNN to be uniform motion equivariant, the CNN must be an affine function. We assume that the activation function is applied pointwise. That is, the same activation function is applied to every 1-dimensional channel independently.

Proposition 8.3 *Let $\boldsymbol{X}$ be a tensor of shape $h \times w \times c$ and K be convolutional kernel of shape $k \times k \times c$. Let $f(\boldsymbol{X}) = \boldsymbol{X} * K$ be a convolutional layer, which is equivariant with respect to arbitrary uniform motion $\boldsymbol{X} \mapsto \boldsymbol{X} + \boldsymbol{C}$ for $\boldsymbol{C}$ a constant tensor of the same shape as $\boldsymbol{X}$. That is $C_{ijk} = c$ for all i, j, k for some fixed $c \in \mathbb{R}$. Then the sum of the weights of K is 1.*

Proof 8.3 *Since f is equivariant, $\boldsymbol{X} * K + \boldsymbol{C} = (\boldsymbol{X} + \boldsymbol{C}) * K$. By linearity, $\boldsymbol{C} * K = \boldsymbol{C}$. Then because $\boldsymbol{C}$ is a constant vector field, $\boldsymbol{C} * K = \boldsymbol{C}(\sum_v K(v))$. As $\boldsymbol{C}$ is arbitrary, $\sum_v K(v) = 1$.*

For an activation function to be uniform motion equivariant, it must be a translation.

Proposition 8.4 *Let $\sigma \colon \mathbb{R} \to \mathbb{R}$ be a function satisfying $\sigma(x + c) = \sigma(x) + c$. Then σ is a translation.*

Proof 8.4 *Let $a = \sigma(0)$. Then $\sigma(x) = \sigma(x + c) - c$. Choosing $c = -x$ gives $\sigma(x) = a + x$.*

Proposition 8.5 *Let $\boldsymbol{X}$ and K be as in Prop 8.3. Let f be a convolutional layer with kernel K and σ an activation function. Assume $\sigma \colon \mathbb{R} \to \mathbb{R}$ is piecewise differentiable. Then if the composition $\varphi = \sigma \circ f$ is equivariant with respect to arbitrary uniform motions, it is an affine map of the form $\varphi(\boldsymbol{X}) = K' * \boldsymbol{X} + b$, where b is a real number and $\sum_v K'(v) = 1$.*

Proof 8.5 *If f is non-zero, then we can choose a tensor X, and constant tensor C full of $c \in \mathbb{R}$, and $p \in \mathbb{Z}^2$ such that c and $\beta = (f(X))_p$ are any two real numbers. Let $\lambda = \sum_v K(v)$. As before $f(C) = \lambda C$. Equivariance thus implies*

$$\sigma(\beta + c\lambda) = \sigma(\beta) + c.$$

Note $\lambda \neq 0$, since if $\lambda = 0$, then $\sigma(\beta) = \sigma(\beta) + c$ implies $c = 0$. However, c is arbitrary. Let $h = c\lambda$. Then

$$\frac{\sigma(\beta + h) - \sigma(\beta)}{h} = \frac{1}{\lambda}.$$

This holds for arbitrary β and h, and thus we find σ is everywhere differentiable with slope λ^{-1}. So $\sigma(x) = x/\lambda + b$ for some $b \in \mathbb{R}$. We can then rescale the convolution kernel $K' = K/\lambda$ to get $\varphi(\boldsymbol{X}) = K' * \boldsymbol{X} + b$.

Corollary 8.1 *If f is a CNN alternating between convolutions f_i and pointwise activations σ_i and the combined layers $\sigma_i \circ f_i$ are uniform motion equivariant, then f is affine.*

Proof 8.6 *This follows from Proposition 8.4 and the fact that composition of affine functions is affine.*

To overcome this limitation, we relax the requirement by conjugating the model with shifted input distribution. For each sliding local block in each convolutional layer, we shift the mean of input tensor to zero and shift the output back after convolution and activation function per sample. In other words, if the input is $\boldsymbol{P}_{b \times d_{in} \times s \times s}$ and the output is $\boldsymbol{Q}_{b \times d_{out}} = \sigma(\boldsymbol{P} \cdot K)$ for one sliding local block, where b is batch size, d is number of channels, s is the kernel size, and K is the kernel, then

$$\boldsymbol{\mu}_i = \text{Mean}_{jkl}\left(\boldsymbol{P}_{ijkl}\right); \quad \boldsymbol{P}_{ijkl} \mapsto \boldsymbol{P}_{ijkl} - \boldsymbol{\mu}_i; \quad \boldsymbol{Q}_{ij} \mapsto \boldsymbol{Q}_{ij} + \boldsymbol{\mu}_i. \tag{8.17}$$

This will allow the convolution layer to be equivariant with respect to uniform motion. If the input is a vector field, we apply this operation to each element.

Proposition 8.6 *A residual block $f(\boldsymbol{x}) + \boldsymbol{x}$ is uniform motion equivariant if the residual connection f is uniform motion invariant.*

Proof 8.7 *We denote the uniform motion transformation by $\boldsymbol{c}$ by $T_{\boldsymbol{c}}^{\text{um}}(\boldsymbol{w}) = \boldsymbol{w} + \boldsymbol{c}$. Let f be an invariant residual connection, which is a composition of convolution layers and activation functions. Then we compute*

$$\begin{aligned} f(T_{\boldsymbol{c}}^{\text{um}}(\boldsymbol{w})) + T_{\boldsymbol{c}}^{\text{um}}(\boldsymbol{w}) &= f(\boldsymbol{w}) + \boldsymbol{w} + \boldsymbol{c} \\ &= (f(\boldsymbol{w}) + \boldsymbol{w}) + \boldsymbol{c} \\ &= T_{\boldsymbol{c}}^{\text{um}}(f(\boldsymbol{w}) + \boldsymbol{w}). \end{aligned}$$

as desired.

Within `ResNet`, residual mappings should be *invariant*, not equivariant, to uniform motion. That is, the skip connection $f^{(i,i+2)} = I$ is equivariant and the residual function $f^{(i,i+1)}$ should be invariant. Hence, for the first layer in each residual block, we omit adding the mean back to the output $\boldsymbol{Q}_{ij}$. In the case of `Unet`, when upscaling, we pad with the mean to preserve the overall mean.

8.5.2.4 Scale Equivariance

Scale equivariance in dynamics is unique as the physical law dictates the scaling of magnitude, space and time simultaneously. This is very different from scaling in images regarding resolutions [72]. For example, the Navier–Stokes equations are preserved under a specific scaling ratio of time, space, and velocity given by the transformation

$$T_\lambda : \boldsymbol{w}(\boldsymbol{x}, t) \mapsto \lambda \boldsymbol{w}(\lambda \boldsymbol{x}, \lambda^2 t), \tag{8.18}$$

where $\lambda \in \mathbb{R}_{>0}$. We implement two different approaches for scale equivariance, depending on whether we tie the physical scale with the resolution of the data.

8.5.2.4.1 Resolution Independent Scaling. We fix the resolution and scale the magnitude of the input by varying the discretization step size. An input $w \in \mathcal{F}_{\mathbb{R}^2}^k$ with step size $\Delta_x(w)$ and $\Delta_t(w)$ can be scaled $w' = T_\lambda^{sc}(w) = \lambda w$ by scaling the magnitude of vector alone, provided the discretization constants are now assumed to be $\Delta_x(w') = 1/\lambda \Delta_x(w)$ and $\Delta_t(w') = 1/\lambda^2 \Delta_t(w)$.

We refer to this as *magnitude* equvariance hereafter.

To obtain magnitude equivariance, we divide the input tensor by the MinMax scaler (the maximum of the tensor minus the minimum) and scale the output back after convolution and activation per sliding block. We found that the standard deviation and mean L2 norm may work as well but are not as stable as the MinMax scaler. Specifically, using the same notation as in Section 8.5.2.3,

$$\boldsymbol{\sigma}_i = \mathrm{MinMax}_{jkl}\left(\boldsymbol{\mathcal{P}}_{ijkl}\right); \quad \boldsymbol{\mathcal{P}}_{ijkl} \mapsto \boldsymbol{\mathcal{P}}_{ijkl}/\boldsymbol{\sigma}_i; \quad \boldsymbol{\mathcal{Q}}_{ij} \mapsto \boldsymbol{\mathcal{Q}}_{ij} \cdot \boldsymbol{\sigma}_i. \qquad (8.19)$$

8.5.2.4.2 Resolution Dependent Scaling. If the physical scale of the data is fixed, then scaling corresponds to a change in resolution and time step size.

To achieve this, we replace the convolution layers with group correlation layers over the group $G = (\mathbb{R}_{>0}, \cdot) \ltimes (\mathbb{R}^2, +)$ of scaling and translations. In convolution, we translate a kernel K across an input w as such $v(p) = \sum_{q \in \mathbb{Z}^2} w(p + q)K(q)$. The G-correlation upgrades this operation by both translating *and* scaling the kernel relative to the input,

$$v(p, s, \mu) = \sum_{\lambda \in \mathbb{R}_{>0}, t \in \mathbb{R}, q \in \mathbb{Z}^2} \mu w(p + \mu q, \mu^2 t, \lambda) K(q, s, t, \lambda), \qquad (8.20)$$

where s and t denote the indices of output and input channels respectively. We add an axis to the tensors corresponding the scale factor μ. Note that we treat the channel as a time dimension both with respective to our input and scaling action. As a consequence, as the number of channels increases in the lower layers of Unet and ResNet, the temporal resolution increases, which is analogous to temporal refinement in numerical methods [30, 39]. For the input $\tilde{w}$ of first layer, where $\tilde{w}$ has no levels originally, $w(p, s, \lambda) = \lambda \tilde{w}(\lambda p, \lambda^2 s)$.

Our model builds on the methods of [72], but with important adaptations for the physical domain. Our implementation of group correlation Equation 8.20 directly incorporates the physical scaling law Equation 8.18 of the Navier–Stokes Equations. This affects time, space, and magnitude. (For heat, we drop the magnitude scaling.) The physical scaling law dictates our model should be equivariant to both up and down scaling and by any $\lambda \in \mathbb{R}_{>0}$.

Practically, the sum is truncated to 7 different $1/3 \leq \lambda \leq 3$ and discrete data is continuously indexed using interpolation. Note Equation 8.18 demands we scale *anisotropically*, i.e., differently across time and space.

8.5.3 Experiments

We test our models on simulated RBC and real-world ocean dynamics.

8.5.3.1 Experimental Setup

Our goal is to show that adding symmetry improves both the accuracy and physical consistency of predictions. For accuracy, we use RMSE of forward predictions from the ground truth over all pixels. For physical consistency, we calculate the ESE which is the RMSE regarding the log of energy spectrum. ESE can indicate whether the predictions preserve the correct statistical distribution and obey the energy conservation law, which is a critical metric for physical consistency.

As shown in Section 8.3, ResNet and U-net are the best-performing models for our tasks [67] and well-suited for our equivariance techniques. Thus, we implemented these

TABLE 8.4

Equivariance Errors of `ResNet(Unets)` and `Equ-ResNet(Unets)`.

EE	Uniform	Magnitude	Rotation	Scale
Equ-ResNets	0.0	0.0	1190.1	578.9
ResNets	2009.8	1884.6	5895.1	1658.3
Equ-Unets	0.0	0.0	794.2	480.6
Unets	1070.1	200.4	1548.3	1809.1

two convolutional architectures equipped with four different symmetries, which we name `Equ-ResNet(U-net)`. We use rolling windows to generate sequences with step size 1 for RBC data and step size 3 for ocean data. All models predict raw velocity/temperature fields up to 10 steps autoregressively using the MSE loss function that accumulates the forecasting errors. We use 60%-20%-20% training-validation-test split across time and report the averages of prediction errors over five runs.

8.5.3.2 Equivariance Errors

The equivariance errors can be defined as $\text{EE}_T(x) = |T(f(x)) - f(T(x))|$, where x is an input, f is a neural net, T is a transformation from a symmetry group. We empirically measure the equivariance errors of all equivariant models we have designed. Table 8.4 shows the equivariance Errors of `ResNet` and `Equ-ResNet`. The transformation T is sampled in the same way as we generated the transformed RBC test sets.

8.5.3.3 Experiments on Rayleigh–Bénard Convection

8.5.3.3.1 Data Description We use same RBC dataset as in 8.3.3. We divide each 1792×256 image into 7 square subregions of size 256×256, then downsample to 64×64 pixels. To test the models' generalization ability, we generate additional four test sets : 1) *UM*: added random vectors drawn from $U(-1,1)$; 2) *Mag*: multiplied by random values sampled from $U(0,2)$; 3) *Rot*: randomly rotated by the multiples of $\pi/2$; 4) *Scale*: scaled by λ sampled from $U(1/5,2)$. Due to lack of a fixed reference frame, real-world data would be transformed relative to training data. We use transformed data to mimic this scenario.

8.5.3.3.2 Prediction Performance Table 8.5 shows the RMSE and ESE of predictions on the original and four transformed test sets by the non-equivariant `ResNet(Unet)` and four `Equ-ResNets(Unets)`. `Augm` is `ResNet(Unet)` trained on the augmented training set with additional samples with random transformations applied from the relevant symmetry group. The augmented training set contains additional transformed samples twice as many samples in the original training set. So the Augmented training set is three times as big as the original training set. Each column contains the prediction errors by the non-equivariant and equivariant models on each test set. On the original test set, all models have similar RMSE, yet the equivariant models have lower ESE. This demonstrates that incorporating symmetries into convolutional layers preserves the representation powers of CNNs and even improves models' physical consistency.

On the transformed test sets, we can see that `ResNet(Unet)` fails, while `Equ-ResNets (Unets)` performs even much better than `Augm-ResNets(Unets)`. This demonstrates the value of equivariant models over data augmentation for improving generalization. Figure 8.8 shows the ground truth and the predicted velocity fields at time step 1, 5 and 10 by the `ResNet` and four `Equ-ResNets` on the four transformed test samples.

TABLE 8.5

The RMSE and ESE of the ResNet (Unet) and Four Equ-ResNets (Unets) Predictions on the Original and Four Transformed Test Sets of RBC. Augm is ResNet (Unet) Trained on the Augmented Training Set with Additional Samples Applied with Random Transformations from the Relevant Symmetry Group. Each Column Contains all Models' Prediction Errors on the Original Test Set and Four Different Transformed Test Sets.

	Root Mean Square Error (10^3)					Energy Spectrum Errors				
	Orig	UM	Mag	Rot	Scale	Orig	UM	Mag	Rot	Scale
ResNet	0.67 ± 0.24	2.94 ± 0.84	4.30 ± 1.27	3.46 ± 0.39	1.96 ± 0.16	0.46 ± 0.19	0.56 ± 0.29	0.26 ± 0.14	1.59 ± 0.42	4.32 ± 2.33
Augm	0.71 ± 0.26	1.10 ± 0.20	1.54 ± 0.12	0.92 ± 0.09	1.01 ± 0.11		1.37 ± 0.02	1.14 ± 0.32	1.92 ± 0.21	1.55 ± 0.14
Equ$_{UM}$	**0.71 ± 0.26**	**0.71 ± 0.26**				**0.33 ± 0.11**	**0.33 ± 0.11**			
Equ$_{Mag}$	0.69 ± 0.24		**0.67 ± 0.14**			0.34 ± 0.09		**0.19 ± 0.02**		
Equ$_{Rot}$	**0.65 ± 0.26**			**0.76 ± 0.02**		0.31 ± 0.06			**1.23 ± 0.04**	
Equ$_{Scal}$	0.70 ± 0.02				**0.85 ± 0.09**	0.44 ± 0.22				**0.68 ± 0.26**
U-net	0.64 ± 0.24	2.27 ± 0.82	3.59 ± 1.04	2.78 ± 0.83	1.65 ± 0.17	0.50 ± 0.04	0.34 ± 0.10	0.55 ± 0.05	0.91 ± 0.27	4.25 ± 0.57
Augm	0.68 ± 0.26	0.75 ± 0.28	1.33 ± 0.33	0.86 ± 0.04	1.11 ± 0.07		0.96 ± 0.23	0.44 ± 0.21	1.24 ± 0.04	1.47 ± 0.11
Equ$_{UM}$	0.67 ± 0.11	**0.71 ± 0.24**				0.23 ± 0.06	**0.14 ± 0.05**			
Equ$_{Mag}$	0.67 ± 0.11		**0.68 ± 0.14**			0.42 ± 0.04		**0.34 ± 0.06**		
Equ$_{Rot}$	0.68 ± 0.25			**0.74 ± 0.01**		**0.11 ± 0.02**			**1.16 ± 0.05**	
Equ$_{Scal}$	0.69 ± 0.13				**0.90 ± 0.25**	0.45 ± 0.32				**0.89 ± 0.29**

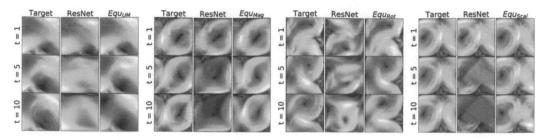

FIGURE 8.8

The ground truth and the predicted velocity norm fields $\|w\|_2$ at time step 1, 5 and 10 by the `ResNet` and four `Equ-ResNets` on the four transformed test samples. The first column is the target, the second is `ResNet` predictions, and the third is predictions by `Equ-ResNets`.

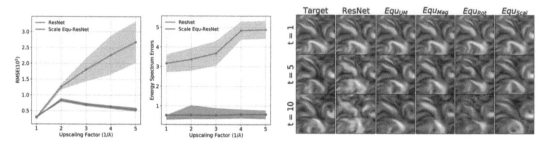

FIGURE 8.9

Left: Prediction RMSE and ESE over five runs of `ResNet` and `Equ_Scal-ResNet` on the RBC test set upscaled by different factors. Right: The ground truth and predicted ocean currents $\|w\|_2$ by `ResNet` and four `Equ-ResNets` on the test set of future time.

In order to evaluate models' generalization ability with respect to the extent of distributional shift, we created additional test sets with different scale factors from $\frac{1}{5}$ to 1. Figure 8.9 shows `ResNet` and `Equ_Scal-ResNet` prediction RMSEs (left) and ESEs (right) on the test sets upscaled by different factors. We observed that `Equ_Scal-ResNet` is very robust across various scaling factors while `ResNet` does not generalize. We also compare `ResNet` and `Equ-ResNet` when both train and test sets have random transformations from the relevant symmetry group applied to each sample. This mimics real-world data in which each sample has unknown reference frame. `Equ-ResNet` is more sample efficient as it does not require data augmentation.

8.5.3.4 Experiments on Real-World Ocean Dynamics

8.5.3.4.1 Data Description We use reanalysis ocean current velocity data generated by the NEMO ocean engine [40].[1] We selected an area from each of the Atlantic, Indian and North Pacific Oceans from 01/01/2016 to 08/18/2017 and extracted 64×64 sub-regions for our experiments. The corresponding latitude and longitude ranges for the selected regions are (-44∼-23, 25∼46), (55∼76, -39∼-18) and (-174∼-153, 5∼26) respectively. We not only test all models on the future data but also on a different domain (-180∼-159, -40∼-59) in South Pacific Ocean from 01/01/2016 to 12/15/2016.

8.5.3.4.2 Prediction Performance Table 8.6 shows the RMSE and ESE of `ResNets(Unets)`, `Augm ResNets(Unets)` and `Equ-ResNets (Unets)` on the test sets with different time range

TABLE 8.6

The prediction RMSEs and ESEs Comparison on the two ocean currents test sets.

	RMSE		ESE	
	$Test_{time}$	$Test_{domain}$	$Test_{time}$	$Test_{domain}$
ResNet	0.71 ± 0.07	0.72 ± 0.04	0.83 ± 0.06	0.75 ± 0.11
Augm$_{UM}$	0.70 ± 0.01	0.70 ± 0.07	1.06 ± 0.06	1.06 ± 0.04
Augm$_{Mag}$	0.76 ± 0.02	0.71 ± 0.01	1.08 ± 0.08	1.05 ± 0.8
Augm$_{Rot}$	0.73 ± 0.01	0.69 ± 0.01	0.94 ± 0.01	0.86 ± 0.01
Augm$_{Scal}$	0.97 ± 0.06	0.92 ± 0.04	0.85 ± 0.03	0.95 ± 0.11
Equ$_{UM}$	0.68 ± 0.06	0.68 ± 0.16	0.75 ± 0.06	0.73 ± 0.08
Equ$_{Mag}$	0.66 ± 0.14	$\mathbf{0.68 \pm 0.11}$	0.84 ± 0.04	0.85 ± 0.14
Equ$_{Rot}$	0.69 ± 0.01	0.70 ± 0.08	$\mathbf{0.43 \pm 0.15}$	$\mathbf{0.28 \pm 0.20}$
Equ$_{Scal}$	$\mathbf{0.63 \pm 0.02}$	0.68 ± 0.21	0.44 ± 0.05	0.42 ± 0.12
U-net	0.70 ± 0.13	0.73 ± 0.10	0.77 ± 0.12	0.73 ± 0.07
Augm$_{UM}$	0.68 ± 0.02	0.68 ± 0.01	0.85 ± 0.04	0.83 ± 0.04
Augm$_{Mag}$	0.69 ± 0.02	0.67 ± 0.10	0.78 ± 0.03	0.86 ± 0.02
Augm$_{Rot}$	0.79 ± 0.01	0.70 ± 0.01	0.79 ± 0.01	0.78 ± 0.02
Augm$_{Scal}$	0.71 ± 0.01	0.77 ± 0.02	0.84 ± 0.01	0.77 ± 0.02
Equ$_{UM}$	0.66 ± 0.10	0.67 ± 0.03	0.73 ± 0.03	0.82 ± 0.13
Equ$_{Mag}$	$\mathbf{0.63 \pm 0.08}$	$\mathbf{0.66 \pm 0.09}$	0.74 ± 0.05	0.79 ± 0.04
Equ$_{Rot}$	0.68 ± 0.05	0.69 ± 0.02	$\mathbf{0.42 \pm 0.02}$	0.47 ± 0.07
Equ$_{Scal}$	0.65 ± 0.09	0.69 ± 0.05	0.45 ± 0.13	$\mathbf{0.43 \pm 0.05}$

and domain from the training set. All the equivariant models outperform the non-equivariant baseline on RMSE, and Equ$_{Scal}$-ResNet achieves the lowest RMSE. For ESE, only the Equ$_{Mag}$-ResNet(Unet) is worse than the baseline. Also, it is remarkable that the Equ$_{Rot}$ models have significantly lower ESE than others, suggesting they correctly learn the statistical distribution of ocean currents. In all cases equivariant models outperforms baselines trained with data augmentation. We find data augmentation sometimes improves slightly on RMSE but not as much as the equivariant models. And, in fact, ESE is uniformly worse for models trained with data augmentation than even the baselines. In contrast, the equivariant models have much better ESE than the baselines with or without augmentation. We believe data augmentation presents a trade-off in learning. Though the model may be less sensitive to the various transformations we consider, we need to train bigger models longer on many more samples. The models may not have enough complexity to learn equivariance from augmented data and the details of the fluid dynamics at the same time. In contrast, equivariant architectures do not have this trade-off.

Figure 8.9 shows the ground truth and the predicted ocean currents at time step 1, 5 and 10 by the non-equivariant ResNet(Unet) and Equ-ResNets(Unets). We see that equivariant models' predictions are more accurate and contain more details than the baselines. Thus, incorporating symmetry into DL models can improve prediction accuracy of ocean currents.

8.6 Discussion and Future Work

Through the development of TF-Net, we show that DL can accelerate the prediction of physical dynamics relative to numerical solvers and incorporating prior physical knowledge improves the model's physical accuracy. Our study in generalization empirically shows DL models fail to forecast under shifted distributions either in the data domain or the parameter domain. This calls attention to rethink generalization especially for learning dynamical systems. We show that embedding symmetries into DL models is one way to improve generalization. And we demonstrated that encoding of rotation, scaling and uniform motion symmetries into DL models greatly improves generalization on forecasting turbulence. Future work includes extending these techniques to very high-resolution, 3D turbulent flows and developing generalizable physics-guided DL models by incorporating additional physical constraints, like symmetry and conservation of momentum.

Note

[1]The data are available at `https://resources.marine.copernicus.eu/?option=com_csw&view=details&product_id=GLOBAL_ANALYSIS_FORECAST_PHY_001_024`

Bibliography

[1] S Ahmad. On the nonautonomous Volterra-Lotka competition equations. In *Proceedings of the American Mathematical Society*, 1993.

[2] Ali Al-Aradi, Adolfo Correia, Danilo Naiff, Gabriel Jardim, and Yuri Saporito. Solving nonlinear and high-dimensional partial differential equations via deep learning. *arXiv preprint arXiv:1811.08782*, 2018.

[3] Dario Amodei, Chris Olah, Jacob Steinhardt, Paul Christiano, John Schulman, and Dan Mané. Concrete problems in ai safety. *arXiv preprint arXiv:1606.06565*, 2019.

[4] Ibrahim Ayed, Emmanuel De Bézenac, Arthur Pajot, and Patrick Gallinari. Learning partially observed PDE dynamics with neural networks, 2019.

[5] Konstantinos Benidis, Syama Sundar Rangapuram, V Flunkert, Bernie Wang, Danielle C Maddix, A Türkmen, Jan Gasthaus, Michael Bohlke-Schneider, David Salinas, L Stella, L Callot, and Tim Januschowski. Neural forecasting: Introduction and literature overview. *ArXiv*, abs/2004.10240, 2020.

[6] Tom Beucler, Michael Pritchard, Stephan Rasp, Pierre Gentine, Jordan Ott, and Pierre Baldi. Enforcing analytic constraints in neural-networks emulating physical systems. *arXiv preprint arXiv:1909.00912*, 2019.

[7] Bruno Chaoua. The state of the art of hybrid rans/les modeling for the simulation of turbulent flows. *Springer Netherlands*, 99:279–327, 2017.

[8] Ricky TQ Chen, Yulia Rubanova, Jesse Bettencourt, and David Duvenaud. Neural ordinary differential equations. In S. Bengio, H. Wallach, H. Larochelle, K. Grauman, N. Cesa-Bianchi, and R. Garnett, editors, *Advances in Neural Information Processing Systems 31*, pages 6571–6583. Curran Associates, Inc., 2018.

[9] Yi-Cheng Chen, Ping-En Lu, Cheng-Shang Chang, and Tzu-Hsuan Liu. A time-dependent sir model for covid-19 with undetectable infected persons. *arXiv preprint arXiv:2003.00122*, 2020.

[10] Dragos Bogdan Chirila. *Towards lattice Boltzmann models for climate sciences: The GeLB programming language with applications*. PhD thesis, University of Bremen, 2018.

[11] Mengyu Chu and Nils Thuerey. Data-driven synthesis of smoke flows with cnn-based feature descriptors. *ACM Transactions on Graphics (TOG)*, 36(4):69, 2017.

[12] Taco S Cohen, Mario Geiger, and Maurice Weiler. A general theory of equivariant cnns on homogeneous spaces. In *Advances in Neural Information Processing Systems*, pages 9142–9153, 2019.

[13] Taco S Cohen and Max Welling. Group equivariant convolutional networks. In *International Conference on Machine Learning (ICML)*, pages 2990–2999, 2016.

[14] Taco S Cohen and Max Welling. Steerable CNNs. *arXiv preprint arXiv:1612.08498*, 2016.

[15] Jessica T Davis, Matteo Chinazzi, Nicola Perra, Kunpeng Mu, Ana Pastore y Piontti, Marco Ajelli, Natalie E Dean, Corrado Gioannini, Maria Litvinova, Stefano Merler, Luca Rossi, Kaiyuan Sun, Xinyue Xiong, M Elizabeth Halloran, Ira M Longini Jr., Cécile Viboud, and Alessandro Vespignani. Estimating the establishment of local transmission and the cryptic phase of the covid-19 pandemic in the USA. *medRXiv preprint https://doi.org/10.1101/2020.07.06.20140285*, 2020.

[16] Emmanuel de Bezenac, Arthur Pajot, and Patrick Gallinari. Deep learning for physical processes: Incorporating prior scientific knowledge. In *International Conference on Learning Representations*, 2018.

[17] Nan Du, Hanjun Dai, Rakshit Trivedi, Utkarsh Upadhyay, Manuel Gomez-Rodriguez, and Le Song. Recurrent marked temporal point processes: Embedding event history to vector. In *the 22nd ACM SIGKDD International Conference on Knowledge Discovery and Data Mining*, 2016.

[18] P Sagaut and E Labourasse. Advance in rans-les coupling, a review and an insight on the nlde approach. *Archives of Computational Methods in Engineering*, 11:199–256, 2004.

[19] Rui Fang, David Sondak, Pavlos Protopapas, and Sauro Succi. Deep learning for turbulent channel flow. *arXiv preprint arXiv:1812.02241*, 2018.

[20] Chelsea Finn, Ian Goodfellow, and Sergey Levine. Unsupervised learning for physical interaction through video prediction. In *Advances in Neural Information Processing Systems*, pages 64–72, 2016.

[21] Richard FitzHugh. Impulses and physiological states in theoretical models of nerve membrane. *Biophyiscal Journal*, 1:445–466, 1961.

[22] V. Flunkert, David Salinas, and Jan Gasthaus. Deepar: Probabilistic forecasting with autoregressive recurrent networks. *ArXiv*, abs/1704.04110, 2017.

[23] Trevor Hastie, Robert Tibshirani, and Jerome Friedman. Springer, 2009.

[24] Kaiming He, Xiangyu Zhang, Shaoqing Ren, and Jian Sun. Deep residual learning for image recognition. In *Proceedings of the IEEE Conference on Computer Vision and Pattern Recognition*, pages 770–778, 2016.

[25] Tillett HE. Infectious diseases of humans; dynamics and control. *Epidemiol Infect*, 1992.

[26] B Houska, F Logist, M Diehl, and J Van Impe. A tutorial on numerical methods for state and parameter estimation in nonlinear dynamic systems. In D. Alberer, H. Hjalmarsson, and L. Del Re, editors, *Identification for Automotive Systems, Volume 418, Lecture Notes in Control and Information Sciences*, pages 67–88. Springer, 2012.

[27] Eugene M Izhikevich. *Dynamical Systems in Neuroscience*. MIT Press, 2007.

[28] Xiaowei Jia, Jared Willard, Anuj Karpatne, Jordan Read, Jacob Zwart, Michael Steinbach, and Vipin Kumar. Physics guided rnns for modeling dynamical systems: A case study in simulating lake temperature profiles. In *Proceedings of the 2019 SIAM International Conference on Data Mining*, pages 558–566. SIAM, 2019.

[29] Anuj Karpatne, William Watkins, Jordan Read, and Vipin Kumar. Physics-guided neural networks (pgnn): An application in lake temperature modeling. *arXiv Preprint arXiv:1710.11431*, 2017.

[30] Ihn S Kim and Wolfgang JR Hoefer. A local mesh refinement algorithm for the time domain-finite difference method using maxwell's curl equations. *IEEE Transactions on Microwave Theory and Techniques*, 38(6):812–815, 1990.

[31] Junhyuk Kim and Changhoon Lee. Deep unsupervised learning of turbulence for inflow generation at various Reynolds numbers. *Journal of Computational Physics*, page 109216, 2020.

[32] Risi Kondor and Shubhendu Trivedi. On the generalization of equivariance and convolution in neural networks to the action of compact groups. In *Proceedings of the 35th International Conference on Machine Learning (ICML)*, volume 80, pages 2747–2755, 2018.

[33] Wouter M Kouw and Marco Loog. An introduction to domain adaptation and transfer learning. *arXiv preprint arXiv:1812.11806*, 2018.

[34] Serge Lang. *Algebra*. Springer, Berlin, 3rd edition, 2002.

[35] Shiyang Li, Xiaoyong Jin, Yao Xuan, Xiyou Zhou, Wenhu Chen, Yu-Xiang Wang, and Xifeng Yan. Enhancing the locality and breaking the memory bottleneck of transformer on time series forecasting. *arXiv preprint arXiv:1907.00235*, 2020.

[36] Yaguang Li, Rose Yu, Cyrus Shahabi, and Yan Liu. Diffusion convolutional recurrent neural network: Data-driven traffic forecasting. In *International Conference on Learning Representations (ICLR)*, 2018.

[37] Bryan Lim and Stefan Zohren. Time series forecasting with deep learning: A survey. *ArXiv*, abs/2004.13408, 2020.

[38] Julia Ling, Andrew Kurzawski, and Jeremy Templeton. Reynolds averaged turbulence modeling using deep neural networks with embedded invariance. *Journal of Fluid Mechanics*, 807:155–166, 2016.

[39] Vadim Lisitsa, Galina Reshetova, and Vladimir Tcheverda. Finite-difference algorithm with local time-space grid refinement for simulation of waves. *Computational Geosciences*, 16(1):39–54, 2012.

[40] Gurvan Madec et al. NEMO ocean engine, 2015. Technical Note. Institut Pierre-Simon Laplace (IPSL), France. `https://epic.awi.de/id/eprint/39698/1/NEMO_book_v6039.pdf`.

[41] Michael Mathieu, Camille Couprie, and Yann LeCun. Deep multi-scale video prediction beyond mean square error. *arXiv preprint arXiv:1511.05440*, 2015.

[42] Yasuko Matsubara, Yasushi Sakurai, and Christos Faloutsos. The web as a jungle: Non-linear dynamical systems for co-evolving online activities. In *WWW' 15 Proceedings of the 14th International Conference on World Wide Web*, pages 721–731, 2015.

[43] George Em Karniadakis Maziar Raissi. Hidden physics models: Machine learning of nonlinear partial differential equations. *Journal of Computational Physics*, 357:125–141, 2018.

[44] JM McDonough. *Introductory Lectures on Turbulence*. Mechanical Engineering Textbook Gallery, 2007.

[45] Jeremy Morton, Antony Jameson, Mykel J Kochenderfer, and Freddie Witherden. Deep dynamical modeling and control of unsteady fluid flows. In *Advances in Neural Information Processing Systems (NeurIPS)*, 2018.

[46] Jinichi Nagumo, Suguru Arimoto, and Shuji Yoshizawa. An active pulse transmission line simulating nerve axon. *Proceedings of the IRE*, 50(10):2061–2070, 1962.

[47] Sergiu Oprea, P Martinez-Gonzalez, A Garcia-Garcia, John Alejandro Castro-Vargas, S Orts Escolano, J Garcia-Rodriguez, and Antonis A Argyros. A review on deep learning techniques for video prediction. *ArXiv*, abs/2004.05214, 2020.

[48] Sen Pei and Jeffrey Shaman. Initial simulation of sars-cov2 spread and intervention effects in the continental us. *medRXiv preprint https://doi.org/10.1101/2020.03.21.20040303*, 2020.

[49] Tomaso Poggio, Lorenzo Rosasco, Charlie Frogner, and Guille D. Canas. Statistical learning theory and applications. 2012.

[50] Christopher Rackauckas, Y Ma, Julius Martensen, Collin Warner, K Zubov, Rohit Supekar, D Skinner, and Ali Ramadhan. Universal differential equations for scientific machine learning. *ArXiv*, abs/2001.04385, 2020.

[51] Maziar Raissi. Deep hidden physics models: Deep learning of nonlinear partial differential equations. *The Journal of Machine Learning Research*, 19(1):932–955, 2018.

[52] Syama Sundar Rangapuram, Matthias W Seeger, Jan Gasthaus, L Stella, Y Wang, and Tim Januschowski. Deep state space models for time series forecasting. In *NeurIPS*, 2018.

[53] Carl Edward Rasmussen and Christopher KI Williams. *Gaussian Process for Machine Learning*. MIT Press, 2006.

[54] Olaf Ronneberger, Philipp Fischer, and Thomas Brox. U-net: Convolutional networks for biomedical image segmentation. In *International Conference on Medical Image Computing and Computer-Assisted Intervention*, pages 234–241. Springer, 2015.

[55] Pierre Sagaut. *Large Eddy Simulation for Incompressible Flows.* Springer-Verlag Berlin Heidelberg, 2001.

[56] David Salinas, Michael Bohlke-Schneider, Laurent Callot, Roberto Medico, and Jan Gasthaus. High-dimensional multivariate forecasting with low-rank gaussian copula processe. In *Advances in Neural Information Processing Systems 32*, 2019.

[57] Omer Berat Sezer, Mehmet Ugur Gudelek, and Ahmet Murat Ozbayoglu. Financial time series forecasting with deep learning : A systematic literature review: 2005-2019. *arXiv preprint arXiv:1911.13288*, 2019.

[58] Justin Sirignano and Konstantinos Spiliopoulos. Dgm: A deep learning algorithm for solving partial differential equations. *arXiv preprint arXiv:1708.07469*, 2018.

[59] J Nathan Kutz, Steven L Brunton, and Joshua L Proctor. Discovering governing equations from data: Sparse identification of nonlinear dynamical systems. *arXiv preprint arXiv:1509.03580*, 2015.

[60] Steven H. Strogatz. *Nonlinear Dynamics and Chaos: With Applications to Physics, Biology, Chemistry, and Engineering.* CRC Press, 2018.

[61] Jonathan Tompson, Kristofer Schlachter, Pablo Sprechmann, and Ken Perlin. Accelerating eulerian fluid simulation with convolutional networks. In *Proceedings of the 34th International Conference on Machine Learning-Volume 70*, pages 3424–3433. JMLR. org, 2017.

[62] Ashish Vaswani, Noam Shazeer, Niki Parmar, Jakob Uszkoreit, Llion Jones, Aidan N. Gomez, Lukasz Kaiser, and Illia Polosukhin. Attention is all you need. *ArXiv*, 2017.

[63] Petar Velickovic, Guille mCucurull, Arantxa Casanova, Adriana Romero, Pietro Lio, and Yoshua Bengio. Graph attention networks. *arXiv preprint arXiv:1710.10903*, 2017.

[64] Ruben Villegas, Jimei Yang, Seunghoon Hong, Xunyu Lin, and Honglak Lee. Decomposing motion and content for natural video sequence prediction. In *International Conference on Learning Representations (ICLR)*, 2017.

[65] John Wainwright and George Francis Rayner Ellis. *Dynamical Systems in Cosmology.* Cambridge University Press, 2005.

[66] Qinxia Wang, Shanghong Xie, Yuanjia Wang, and Donglin Zeng. Survival-convolution models for predicting covid-19 cases and assessing effects of mitigation strategies. *medRXiv preprint https://doi.org/10.1101/2020.04.16.20067306*, 2020.

[67] Rui Wang, Karthik Kashinath, Mustafa Mustafa, Adrian Albert, and Rose Yu. Towards physics-informed deep learning for turbulent flow prediction. *Proceedings of the 26th ACM SIGKDD International Conference on Knowledge Discovery and Data Mining*, 2020.

[68] Rui Wang, Robin Walters, and Rose Yu. Incorporating symmetry into deep dynamics models for improved generalization. 2021.

[69] Maurice Weiler and Gabriele Cesa. General E(2)-equivariant steerable CNNs. In *Advances in Neural Information Processing Systems (NeurIPS)*, pages 14334–14345, 2019.

[70] Maurice Weiler, Fred A. Hamprecht, and Martin Storath. Learning steerable filters for rotation equivariant CNNs. *Computer Vision and Pattern Recognition (CVPR)*, 2018.

[71] Steffen Wiewel, Moritz Becher, and Nils Thuerey. Latent space physics: Towards learning the temporal evolution of fluid flow. In *Computer Graphics Forum*, volume 38, pages 71–82, 2019.

[72] Daniel Worrall and Max Welling. Deep scale-spaces: Equivariance over scale. In *Advances in Neural Information Processing Systems (NeurIPS)*, pages 7364–7376, 2019.

[73] Jin-Long Wu, Karthik Kashinath, Adrian Albert, Dragos Chirila, Prabhat, and Heng Xiao. Enforcing statistical constraints in generative adversarial networks for modeling chaotic dynamical systems. *arXiv e-prints*, May 2019.

[74] Neo Wu, Bradley Green, Xue Ben, and Shawn O'Banion. Deep transformer models for time series forecasting: The influenza prevalence case. *arXiv preprint arXiv:2001.08317*, 2020.

[75] You Xie, Erik Franz, Mengyu Chu, and Nils Thuerey. tempogan: A temporally coherent, volumetric gan for super-resolution fluid flow. *ACM Transactions on Graphics (TOG)*, 37(4):95, 2018.

[76] Shi Xingjian, Zhourong Chen, Hao Wang, Dit-Yan Yeung, Wai-Kin Wong, and Wang chun Woo. Convolutional lstm network: A machine learning approach for precipitation nowcasting. In *Advances in Neural Information Processing Systems (NeurIPS)*, pages 802–810, 2015.

[77] SHI Xingjian, Zhourong Chen, Hao Wang, Dit-Yan Yeung, Wai-Kin Wong, and Wang-chun Woo. Convolutional lstm network: A machine learning approach for precipitation nowcasting. In *Advances in Neural Information Processing Systems*, pages 802–810, 2015.

[78] Tianfan Xue, Jiajun Wu, Katherine Bouman, and Bill Freeman. Visual dynamics: Probabilistic future frame synthesis via cross convolutional networks. In *Advances in Neural Information Processing Systems*, pages 91–99, 2016.

[79] Huaxiu Yao, Fei Wu, Jintao Ke, Xianfeng Tang, Yitian Jia, Siyu Lu, Pinghua Gong, Jieping Ye, and Zhenhui Li. Deep multi-view spatial-temporal network for taxi demand prediction. In *Thirty-Second AAAI Conference on Artificial Intelligence*, 2018.

[80] Xiuwen Yi, Junbo Zhang, Zhaoyuan Wang, Tianrui Li, and Yu Zheng. Deep distributed fusion network for air quality prediction. In *Proceedings of the 24th ACM SIGKDD International Conference on Knowledge Discovery & Data Mining*, pages 965–973, 2018.

[81] Saibal Mukhopadhyay Yun Long, Xueyuan She. Hybridnet: Integrating model-based and data-driven learning to predict evolution of dynamical systems. *ArXiv Preprint arXiv:1806.07439*, 2019.

[82] Difan Zou, Lingxiao Wang, Pan Xu, Jinghui Chen, Weitong Zhang, and Quanquan Gu. Epidemic model guided machine learning for covid-19 forecasts in the United States. *medRXiv preprint https://doi.org/10.1101/2020.05.24.20111989*, 2020.

9

Science-Guided Design and Evaluation of Machine Learning Models: A Case-Study on Multi-Phase Flows

Nikhil Muralidhar, Jie Bu, Ze Cao, Long He, Naren Ramakrishnan, Danesh Tafti, and Anuj Karpatne

CONTENTS

This chapter presents recent developments in science-guided machine learning for a problem in fluid dynamics on predicting the drag forces on individual particles suspended in a moving fluid. We present PhyNet, a deep learning model using *physics-guided structural priors* in the architecture of neural networks and *physics-guided aggregate supervision* for training neural networks informed by physics knowledge of multiphase flow. We empirically demonstrate the usefulness of including physics knowledge in deep learning formulations by comparing PhyNet with state-of-the-art models on experiments with varying flow settings.

DOI: 10.1201/9781003143376-9

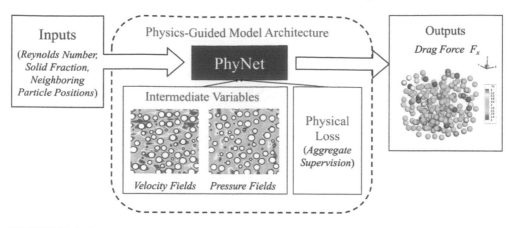

FIGURE 9.1
Our proposed PhyNet Model [26, 27].

We also conduct experiments to demonstrate the extrapolation abilities of baseline models on unseen particle assemblies. All the code used in this study has been made available on this link `https://github.com/nmuralid1/PhyNet.git`.

9.1 Introduction

In today's rapidly evolving technological landscape, machine learning (ML) has become ubiquitous across several disciplines and has an ever expanding reach, leading to ML models being continuously exposed to new challenges and paradigms. Many of these new applications treat ML models as black-box predictors. In such contexts, despite the existence of a rich corpus of scientific knowledge governing the processes being modeled, the ML models are trained in a manner agnostic to this knowledge. Such domain-agnostic training practices may have unintended effects like the ML model learning spurious correlations between covariates (i.e., input features) and target (i.e., variable being modeled). Another consequence may be that the ML models may learn representations that aren't readily verifiable to be consistent with the accepted physical understanding of the target process. It is also the case that in many scientific disciplines, training data generation is costly due to the requirement of executing expensive simulations or due to the nature of data collection processes. For example, generating a large amount of data for training ML models is impractical in computational fluid dynamics (CFD) because CFD simulations are expensive to perform. Thus, it is one of our primary goals in this chapter to develop a science-guided machine learning (SGML) model capable of performing effectively under data paucity. This science-guided nature of the model also helps improve the explainability of the result and allows physics domain experts to verify the consistency of model predictions with prior physics knowledge.

In this chapter, we bridge the gap between science-based models and ML models by discussing methods of incorporating scientific domain knowledge into the design and learning of ML models. Specifically, we present three ways for incorporating domain knowledge in neural networks: (1) Science-guided design of neural network architectures, (2) Science-guided aggregate supervision of neural network training and (3) Science-guided post facto consistency verification. We present and evaluate our model for applications in modeling multi-phase flow phenomena. Specifically, we train an SGML model to model the drag forces acting on particles immersed in a fluid. Details about the system are presented in Section 9.3.

Our proposed science-guided model PhyNet [26, 27], leverages prior physics theory for improved representation learning of the drag forces affecting different particles in assemblies in the context of multi-phase flows. Specifically, we develop PhyNet to have a physics-aware neural network architecture, which is designed such that each layer in the network learns one of the various physical properties that interact to produce the drag force on a particle. The aforementioned physics-informed architecture design follows a sequential pattern wherein representations learned in earlier layers are made to correspond to physical intermediates which have a direct effect on physical phenomena described by later layers. This deliberate introduction of physics knowledge in the sequential model design of neural networks allows the system to learn physically consistent representations at the hidden layers. In conjunction with the aforementioned physics-guided architecture design, we introduce physics-aware statistical constraints during model training which we term *science-guided aggregate supervision*. The goal of aggregate supervision is to enable PhyNet to learn physically consistent representations of the pressure and velocity fields (both of which follow complex and multi-modal distributions) in the vicinity of each particle in the assembly.

This chapter is organized as follows. Section 9.2 describes relevant literature on employing physics domain knowledge to augment machine learning pipelines for better and/or more physically consistent model performance. Section 9.3 details background knowledge for the target application of multi-phase fluid-particle systems. Section 9.4 presents details of the proposed PhyNet model. We further detail in Section 9.5, the data and experimental setup employed by PhyNet followed by detailed results in Section 9.6 & concluding remarks in Section 9.7.

9.2 Related Work on SGML

There have been many previous lines of research that try to leverage domain knowledge to increase the performance of ML models by employing physically based priors in probabilistic frameworks [6, 37, 38], physically motivated regularizers [4, 22], constraining optimization methods [23, 24], and rules in expert systems [1, 36]. Popular deep learning architectures like residual networks and recurrent neural networks have been adapted to represent discrete approximations of ordinary differential equations (ODEs) by recent lines of research [5, 39].

Previous work such as [15] have also explored the direction of incorporating prior domain knowledge to regularize the training loss in neural networks and have demonstrated good generalization. In [1], a 'learning-from-examples' paradigm is employed to incorporate prior domain knowledge into the learning pipeline. An approach without training labels was adopted in [33, 34] where a customized loss function was formed to directly incorporate domain knowledge as a source of weak supervision. Physics-informed neural networks (PINN) [31, 32] are yet another recent line of research in the same domain of direct modeling with domain knowledge, wherein specific Partial Differential Equation (PDE) constraints are used in the loss functions of neural networks as sources of domain-based supervision. Other efforts like [16, 28] have explored the idea of incorporating physics-based loss functions to capture monotonic constraints while yet others [14] incorporated the principles of energy conservation as physics-based loss terms in the learning pipeline.

Complementary to the practice of incorporating loss function-based domain supervision, there have also been efforts toward incorporating prior domain knowledge into model architecture design. Low rank *structural priors* were incorporated into design of convolutional filters in [13]. In the application of complex many-body systems, [2] is an effort wherein the authors develop a neural network model comprising of each individual neuron learning "laws" similar to physics laws. [18] puts forth theoretical details for the design of neural network architectures in contexts of the data comprising of non-trivial symmetries. In this work, we are interested in modeling the drag force acting on a particle (part of a random assembly of particles) suspended in a fluid. Specifically, we are interested in a setting where the physics domain knowledge governing the relationships between the input variables (i.e., neighboring particle distances around the candidate particles) and the target variable (i.e., drag force acting on the candidate particle), is unavailable in explicit form and other 'softer' forms of domain knowledge have to be incorporated into the learning pipeline.

9.3   Multiphase Fluid-Particle Systems

Many scientific applications like propulsion, energy, pharmaceuticals, food processing and various other environmental applications comprise fluid-particle systems as a cricial component. There exist many methodologies for simulating dense mixtures of fluids and particles ranging from fine-grained high-fidelity simulations (like particle resolved simulations – PRS) to coarse-grained simulations (like Discrete Element Method simulations – DEM). PRS simulations are costly and can only simulate systems with a few thousand particles [7] while DEM simulations can support millions of particles in the simulation [20]. In PRS, each particle is defined by its shape and explicitly resolved as an independent entity in the calculation. This explicit resolution allows the flow and pressure fields that result from the presence of a particle to be readily available from the PRS simulation. Contrary to PRS, in the DEM-based coarse-grained simulations, particles are not explicitly resolved and are instead treated as point mass proxies. Due to this reason, the resolution scale at which the pressure and velocity fields are resolved is much larger than the size of a single particle. The transition from high-fidelity (PRS) to lower-fidelity simulations (like DEM) allows increased scalability at the cost of decreased simulation accuracy. The overarching goal is to attain high prediction accuracy in large particle systems simulated using DEM while minimizing the high cost of employing the expensive PRS simulation. We may consider each thousand particle simulation performed using PRS as a microcosm of a corresponding million particle (DEM simulation) system. This allows us to employ the fine-grained high-fidelity results obtained from PRS to inform the construction of models of sub-scale phenomena in large (potentially million particle) systems leading to improved prediction accuracy. One of the most important forces that has a significant influence on the dynamics of the fluid-particulate system is the *drag force* applied by the fluid on the particles [21] and that applied by the particles on the fluid. The drag force from fluid forces acting on the particle surface, can be calculated (directly) from PRS with high accuracy by directly integrating the pressure and velocity fields surrounding a particle, which is directly available from PRS. In coarse-grained simulations like DEM, since the particle is not explicitly resolved and instead represented as a 'point mass', the pressure and velocity fields are also only resolved at a much coarser scale and thus the drag forces acting on each particle have to be approximated by models and cannot be directly (and precisely) calculated as in PRS.

The drag force acting on an isolated spherical particle (although we consider spherical particles in this chapter, the proposed methods are agnostic to particle shape and may be applied to non-spherical particles as well) is a function of *the approach velocity U, particle diameter D, fluid density ρ* and *viscosity μ*. The Reynolds number is a function of the aforementioned quantities $\left(Re = \frac{\varrho U D}{\mu} \right)$. However, when we consider particle assemblies (i.e., when a set of many particles are present as in a suspension of particles), the drag force acting on each particle is also influenced by all the other particles. In low-fidelity simulations, the current state-of-the-art is to employ the mean drag force (which is a zeroth order approximation of the actual drag force acting on a particle in suspension) based on the local Re and ϕ of the experiment. The mean drag force is employed because the velocity and pressure fields surrounding the particle of interest (which are required to calculate the drag force acting on the particle) are absent in the CFD-DEM (i.e., DEM in the context of CFD) at the required (i.e., at the particle) scale.

The mean drag force is a crude estimate of forces acting on any particle in a suspension [10–12]. Owing to the highly non-linear and variable characteristics of drag forces acting on individual particles in a particle suspension, this chapter explores techniques in SGML to advance the current state-of-the-art for particle drag force prediction in CFD-DEM by learning from a small amount of PRS data. The PRS simulations (conducted in a fully-periodic cubic domain simulating an unbounded suspension, with flow along the x-direction) are performed using the immersed boundary method (IBM) [29]. A random arrangement consisting of 7260 spherical particles suspended in a fluid is simulated for each solid fraction and Reynolds number.

After obtaining the flow solution using the PRS simulation, the drag force acting on the particles by the fluid, is obtained by directly integrating the pressure and velocity fields (calculated by PRS) over the particle surface. The drag force acting on each particle comprises of viscous shear forces and pressure forces, which are individually calculated for each particle and the total drag acting on each particle is obtained by integrating the corresponding shear and pressure drag forces on the particle.

9.4 Proposed Method

The field of knowledge discovery and data mining involves a well-established multi-step pipeline [8, 9] involving unprocessed (raw) data at the outset followed by *Data Processing & Transformation → Model Design → Model Training → Inference → Model Decision Evaluation*. Prior knowledge about the scientific domain under consideration may be incorporated into this ML pipeline as *inductive bias*. Note that the use of inductive bias is common in many standard deep learning frameworks such as convolutional neural networks (CNNs) that assumes a special type of spatial structure in the data [25] and also encodes many desirable properties like parameter sharing and translation equivariance [17]. In particular, each step of the ML pipeline may be augmented according to scientific principles known about an application domain of interest being modeled. Figure 9.2 depicts a general SGML pipeline that we detail in this chapter. The pipeline consists of a dataset $\mathbf{X}$, which may be a result of some experiment or scientific simulation.

The first stage of the learning process involves transforming each instance $\mathbf{x} \in \mathbf{X}$ appropriately for ingestion by a learning model. $T(\mathbf{x})$ may represent a transformation function involving feature engineering or dimensionality reduction [35]. In this step, we may employ domain knowledge about our process being modeled to restrict the space of transformations to obey certain symmetries or conservation phenomena. The second stage in the pipeline involves development of the model architecture. In Figure 9.2, we depict a neural network architecture, where the design of the neural architecture may be chosen to reflect the nature of phenomenological dependencies in the process being modeled. For example, the NN model described in Section 9.4.2 has been so designed keeping in mind a hierarchical task

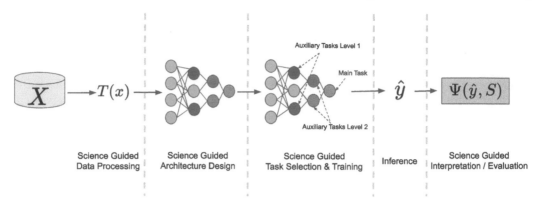

FIGURE 9.2
SGML Learning & Inference Pipeline.

dependence structure of various phenomena in the process of interest. The third stage of the SGML pipeline involves selecting appropriate learning tasks (indicated by the red, pink, light and dark purple neurons) in Figure 9.2, related to the task of interest and also selection of a training curriculum. Both these aspects may be influenced by scientific knowledge to better model the dependent variable y of interest by leveraging other phenomena related to y. Specifically in this case, the training curriculum chosen is joint training using multi-task learning of the hierarchical set of related tasks. Once the model is trained, we may seek model responses on unseen experimental settings (i.e., stage four, *inference*). In this step, given a known set of scientific phenomena S, we may employ consistency functions $\Psi(\hat{y}, S)$ to verify consistency of the model predictions $\hat{y}$ (obtained in the inference step) with known scientific knowledge. We now leverage the proposed SGML pipeline to develop a solution for particle drag force predictions in 3D multi-phase fluid flows.

9.4.1   Problem Background

We study SGML in the context of predicting the drag forces acting on a collection of N particles randomly suspended in a moving fluid. The drag force acting on the ith particle (denoted as F_i) due to the fluid, measured along the x-direction is of interest as this is the primary flow direction. The task may be formulated as a supervised regression task in ML where the dependent variable F_i is predicted as a function of co-variates (i.e., input features) which comprise the spatial arrangement of the nearest neighbors of the candidate particle (i.e., particle i). The input features also include the Reynolds number (Re) and the solid fraction (ϕ - the fraction of unit volume occupied by the particles in a given experimental setting) for a holistic representation of the experimental and spatial context of the candidate particle.

Hence, the co-variates we employ as inputs comprise the relative distances (along the x,y,z direction) of the candidate particle p_i w.r.t. its 15 nearest neighboring particles. These relative distances are represented as a flat 45-dimensional vector, which is then concatenated with (Re,ϕ) corresponding to the experimental setting. Hence, the total input feature set for the ith particle comprises a 47-dimensional vector $\mathbf{A}_i$.

Learning to predict drag forces acting on particles based on the spatial orientation and the experimental context likely involves learning highly non-linear relationships [11]. In recent times, deep neural networks have been shown to being effective at learning highly non-linear functions. We hence employ deep feed-forward neural network (DNN) models to learn the transformation function from $\mathbf{A}_i$ to F_i, i.e., to learn the mapping from inputs for a candidate particle i, to the drag force (in the x-direction) acting on that particle. However, most neural network architectures are black-box (with arbitrary architecture design considerations) wherein the model learning and decision-making is opaque to the end user. Since our goal is to design and train a DNN model that learns physically consistent representations and is able to perform well with limited data, we employ a novel *physics-guided* DNN model PhyNet, which employs knowledge from the PRS simulation process in model design and learning of the DNN model, as detailed in Sections 9.4.2–9.4.5.

9.4.2 Science-Guided Architecture Design

We derive inspiration from the known physical pathway starting from co-variates $\mathbf{A}_i$ to the model output drag force F_i to develop the architecture of PhyNet. This physical pathway is similar to the pipeline at the core of physics simulations like the Particle Resolved Simulation (PRS). In particular, we make use of the following three forms of scientific guidance in the design of PhyNet.

Science Guidance 1: The drag force F_i of a particle can be directly calculated from the pressure field ($\mathbf{P}_i$) and velocity field ($\mathbf{V}_i$) in the vicinity of the candidate particle p_i. Hence $\mathbf{P}_i, \mathbf{V}_i$ at the particle surface serve as two key physical intermediate variables which encompass the entire information required to determine the drag force acting on a candidate particle p_i.

Science Guidance 2: The total drag force F_i is a composition of two components of drag acting on p_i, namely, the drag force due to pressure F_i^P (pressure component) and the drag force due to velocity F_i^S (shear component). Hence, the total drag may be calculated as $F_i = F_i^P + F_i^S$.

Science Guidance 3: It is further known that the shear component of drag F_i^S is directly affected by the gradient of velocity field $\mathbf{V}_i$ on the particle surface and the pressure component of drag F_i^P is directly affected by the pressure field $\mathbf{P}_i$ on the particle surface.

We employ all three forms of scientific guidance about the properties and dependencies of the drag force of p_i to develop our science-guided architecture of PhyNet detailed in figure 9.3. The design of PhyNet encompasses the modeling of physically meaningful intermediate variables like the pressure field, velocity field, and the components of the drag force acting on p_i, in the effort to transform $\mathbf{A}_i$ to F_i. Figure 9.3 also includes details about the number of layers in the architecture, the types of activation functions used, and the input and output dimensions of each block of layers employed in PhyNet. Specifically, the input layer accepts a 47-dimensional input vectors $\mathbf{A}_i$ of co-variates, transformed and passed to a set of *Shared Layers* that learn a common hidden representation to be employed by

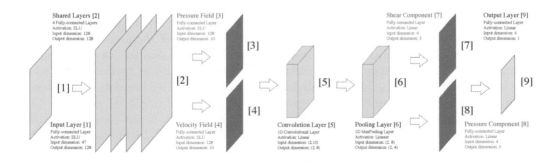

FIGURE 9.3
PhyNet Architecture.

subsequent branches in the network. The representation learned by the *Shared Layers* is passed separately to the *Pressure Field Layer* and the *Velocity Field Layer*, which are tasked with predicting the pressure field ($\mathbf{P}_i$) and velocity field ($\mathbf{V}_i$), respectively, on the surface of particle p_i as 10-dimensional vectors. These layers learn physically meaningful intermediate representations of the pressure and velocity fields at discrete uniformly sampled intervals around the particle surface (we consider them as 10-dimensional vectors unless otherwise stated). It is well known that the pressure and velocity fields each exhibit spatial correlation and hence to exploit this fact, we pass the pressure field and velocity field predictions into a 1D convolutional layer that extracts the relevant spatial representations present in the $\mathbf{P}_i$ and $\mathbf{V}_i$ vectors. This is followed by a pooling layer which processes the output of the 1D convolutional layer to produce a 4-dimensional hidden representation each of the predicted pressure field and velocity field.

The output of the convolutional and pooling layers results in a two-channel 4-dimensional output vector where one channel corresponds to the representation of the pressure field and the other to the representation of the velocity field. The convolved and pooled pressure field representation is operated upon by the *Pressure Component Layer*, which is tasked with predicting the pressure component of drag $\mathbf{F}_i^P$, while the convolved and pooled velocity field representation is operated upon by the *Shear Component Layer* that is tasked with predicting the shear (i.e., velocity) component of drag $\mathbf{F}_i^S$. This *decomposed* drag prediction step also represents an opportunity for post-facto interpretability of model predictions to be demonstrated in later sections. The decomposed drag predictions are then passed to the final layer which yields the total drag prediction F_i acting on p_i. The aforementioned architecture design of PhyNet is deliberately chosen so that each layer (or set of layers) in the pipeline is able to learn a specific concept on which the total drag force F_i of the candidate particle p_i depends. The sequential nature of PhyNet also reflects the physical task dependence similar to popular simulation methods like PRS. The various science guided auxiliary tasks that are solved en-route to addressing the main task of predicting the total drag force allows PhyNet to be more interpretable and less of a black-box than traditional DNN-based learning architectures because the model learns specific physics concepts per layer instead of arbitrarily complex representations. It also allows explicit verification of the consistency of the learned representation with known scientific phenomena as demonstrated in later sections.

9.4.3   Learning with Physical Intermediates

As outlined in Section 9.4.2, the PhyNet model architecture not only models the total drag force acting on a particle p_i but also produces estimates of several other related auxiliary variables like the pressure field $\mathbf{P}_i$, velocity field $\mathbf{V}_i$, the pressure drag F_i^P, and the shear drag F_i^S. Each of these auxiliary variables that PhyNet predicts are actually produced as by-products of PRS simulations. Hence, each one of the auxiliary estimates that PhyNet predicts is explicitly supervised by values from PRS simulations during model training. Hence, the science-guided architecture of PhyNet enables us to learn with additional supervision by making full use of all data available from a PRS simulation as opposed to simply learning direct transformations from $\mathbf{A}_i$ to F_i as in traditional ML pipelines. Our science-guided architecture consisting of auxiliary tasks in addition to the main task of drag force prediction can be trained by minimizing the following empirical training loss:

$$Loss_{MSE} = \lambda_P\,MSE(\mathbf{P}, \widehat{\mathbf{P}}) + \lambda_V\,MSE(\mathbf{V}, \widehat{\mathbf{V}}) +$$
$$\lambda_{FP}MSE(\mathbf{F^P}, \widehat{\mathbf{F^P}}) + \lambda_{FS}MSE(\mathbf{F^S}, \widehat{\mathbf{F^S}}) + MSE(F, \widehat{F})$$

where MSE represents mean squared error (MSE), $\hat{x}$ represents the estimate of x, and λ_P, λ_V, λ_{FP}, and λ_{FS} represent the trade-off parameters in miniming the errors on the intermediate variables. Optimizing the above equation will help to constrain PhyNet with loss terms not only at the output layer but also at intermediate layers (i.e., intermediate layer supervision similar to Lee et al. [19]) thereby grounding the PhyNet to learn more physically consistent representations. We adopt a multi-task learning [3] approach to solve $Loss_{MSE}$. The prediction of total drag F_i may be considered the primary task of interest while all the other tasks may be considered auxiliary tasks related to the main task through science-guided connections as outlined in Section 9.4.2.

9.4.4 Science-Guided Training with Aggregate Supervision

In addition to minimizing the aforementioned loss, we also know that the pressure and velocity fields for various (Re,ϕ) exhibit multi-modal behavior. Only training our PhyNet model in a traditional inductive learning sense on the full pressure and velocity field data will lead to the model learning only a small subset of the pressure and velocity field distributions and hence cause a majority of the distributions to be underrepresented. To avoid this occurrence, we enforce that the mean of the pressure field predictions $\widehat{\mathbf{P}}_{(Re,\phi)}$, and mean of the velocity field predictions $\widehat{\mathbf{V}}_{(Re,\phi)}$ made by PhyNet around the surface of a particle for a given (Re,ϕ) setting be similar to the overall mean pressure field $\overline{P}_{(Re,\phi)}$ and mean velocity field $\overline{V}_{(Re,\phi)}$ for each (Re,ϕ) setting. This additional science-guided loss termed *aggregate supervision* enables alignment of the overall statistics of the predicted pressure and velocity fields around p_i with that of the corresponding ground truth field distributions. Specifically, we consider minimizing the following science-guided loss:

$$Loss_{PHY} = \sum_{Re} \sum_{\phi} MSE(\mu(\widehat{\mathbf{P}}_{(\mathbf{Re},\phi)}), \overline{P}_{(Re,\phi)})$$
$$+ MSE(\mu(\widehat{\mathbf{V}}_{(\mathbf{Re},\phi)}), \overline{V}_{(Re,\phi)})$$

The function $\mu(\cdot) : R \to R$ is a *mean* function. The total loss considered for learning the proposed PhyNet model is hence $Loss_{MSE} + Loss_{PHY}$.

9.4.5 Inference & Science-Guided Consistency Verification

Scientific applications commonly have properties that a particular quantity or set of quantities are known to exhibit. In Section 9.4 (specifically Figure 9.2), we assumed the existence of a set S of such known properties and a consistency function $\Psi(\hat{y}, S)$ capable of verifying or quantifying the degree of consistency exhibited by the model predictions $\hat{y}$ in satisfying the known properties S. In the case of PhyNet, the inference procedure is carried out on unseen data and our *science-guided architecture design* and *training* allows us access to the pressure and shear drag forces ($\mathbf{F}_i^P$, $\mathbf{F}_i^S$ respectively. We employ the predictions of the pressure and shear drag to verify an established evolutionary characteristic about the ratio of pressure to shear drag across different (Re,ϕ) settings, detailed in Section 9.6.6.

9.5 Data & Experiment Details

In this chapter, the data we have employed consists of an arrangement of 7260 particles randomly dispersed in a fluid. The input features for each candidate particle (i.e., particle

TABLE 9.1

The ML models receive 47 input features per candidate particle for which drag force is to be estimated. The input features are enumerated in the table. $\mathbf{X}, \mathbf{Y}, \mathbf{Z}$ correspond to the relative distances in the x, y, z directions respectively of the nearest neighboring particles of a particular particle of interest. Re is the Reynolds numbers. ϕ is the global solid fraction for the particular experimental setting.

Features	Range of Data
$\mathbf{X} \in \mathbb{R}^{15 \times 1}$	$-5 \sim 5$
$\mathbf{Y} \in \mathbb{R}^{15 \times 1}$	$-5 \sim 5$
$\mathbf{Z} \in \mathbb{R}^{15 \times 1}$	$-5 \sim 5$
$Re \in \mathbb{R}^{1 \times 1}$	$\{10, 50, 100, 200\}$
$\phi \in \mathbb{R}^{1 \times 1}$	$\{0.1, 0.2, 0.3, 0.35\}$

of interest for which the drag force is to be predicted by the ML model) consist of (i) 3-dimensional relative distances to its 15 nearest neighboring particles (i.e., relative distance along the x,y,z dimensions for each of 15 nearest neighboring particles), (ii) the Reynolds number (Re) of the experimental setting (iii) the solid fraction (ϕ) of the experimental setting. Feature sets (i),(ii),(iii) constitute a total of 47 input features to the ML model for each candidate particle (see Table 9.1). There are a total of 16 experimental settings with different (Re, ϕ) combinations. Target labels for each candidate particle are the total drag force acting on it in the X-direction $F_i \in \mathbb{R}^{1 \times 1}$ along with the auxiliary training variables, i.e., velocity fields ($\mathbf{V_i} \in \mathbb{R}^{k \times 1}$), pressure fields ($\mathbf{P_i} \in \mathbb{R}^{k \times 1}$), shear components ($\mathbf{F_i^S} \in \mathbb{R}^{3 \times 1}$) and pressure components of the drag force ($\mathbf{F_i^P} \in \mathbb{R}^{3 \times 1}$). The dimension k of $\mathbf{P_i}$, $\mathbf{V_i}$ is a hyperparameter which governs the number of samples around the particle vicinity at which the pressure and velocity field values are sampled ($k = 100$ in our case unless stated otherwise). The value of k thus governs the granularity of the field representation used to train the PhyNet models.

9.5.1   Pressure & Velocity Field Sampling Methodology

As the drag force acting on a particle is significantly influenced by the pressure and velocity fields around it, the PhyNet model is trained to predict the pressure and velocity fields around the candidate particle in addition to the total drag force acting on it. To supervise this pressure and velocity field prediction task in PhyNet, we employ samples of these fields in the vicinity of the candidate particle. The discrete sampling procedure we employ to obtain pressure ($\mathbf{P_i}$) and velocity field ($\mathbf{V_i}$) samples around a particle p_i, is detailed in Eq. 9.1.

$$\mathbf{q_j^x} = p_i.x + \epsilon \cdot cos(t)$$
$$\mathbf{q_j^y} = p_i.y + \epsilon \cdot sin(t) \tag{9.1}$$
$$\mathbf{q_j^z} = p_i.z$$

Let $\mathbf{Q_i} \in R^{k \times 3}$ represent the sampling field locations around p_i and let the x,y and z coordinates of the particle p_i's center be represented by $p_i.x$, $p_i.y$, $p_i.z$ respectively. Then, $\mathbf{Q_i} = \{\mathbf{q_1}^T, ..., \mathbf{q_k}^T\}$ where $\mathbf{q_j} \in \mathbb{R}^{3 \times 1}$ and $\mathbf{q_j} = \{q_j^x, q_j^y, q_j^z\}$. At each location $\mathbf{q_j} \in \mathbf{Q_i}$, we record the pressure field and velocity field value. ϵ (constant throughout our experiments) is a distance 0.15 units away from the particle surface. Unlike pressure, the velocity field samples are a 3-dimensional vector value and we calculate magnitude of the velocity field vector at each point q_j and use that as the discrete representation of V_i for each particle p_i.

9.5.2 Experimental Setup

All neural network models employed in our experiments have 5 hidden layers, and hidden size of 128 in each layer. Each model was trained for 500 epochs with a batch size of 100. Unless otherwise stated, we employ 55% of the dataset for training and the remaining data for testing and evaluation. Standardization was applied to all the input features and labels in the data preprocessing step.

Baselines: PhyNet performance is compared with several state-of-the-art regression baselines and a few close variants of PhyNet.

1. Linear Regression (Linear Reg.), Random Forest Regression (RF Reg.), Gradient Boosting Regression (GB Reg.) [30]. We employed an ensemble of 100 estimators for RF, GB Reg. models and left all other parameters unchanged.

2. DNN: A standard feed-forward neural network model for predicting the scalar valued particle drag force F_i.

3. DNN-MT-Pres: A DNN model which predicts the pressure field around a particle ($\mathbf{P_i}$) in addition to F_i. The pressure and drag force tasks are modeled in a multi-task manner with a set of disjoint layers for each of the two tasks and a separate set of shared layers.

4. DNN-MT-Vel: Similar to DNN-MT-Pres except in this case the auxiliary task models the velocity field around the particle ($\mathbf{V_i}$) in addition to drag force (F_i).

We employ three metrics for model evaluation:

MSE & MRE: We employ the mean squared error (MSE) and mean relative error (MRE) [11] metrics to evaluate model performance. Though MSE can capture the absolute deviation of model prediction from the ground truth values, it can vary a lot for different scales of the label values, e.g., for higher drag force values, MSE is prone to be higher, vice versa. Thus, the need for a metric that is invariant to the scale of the label values brings in the MRE as an important supplemental metric in addition to MSE.

$$MRE = \frac{1}{m} \sum_{i=1}^{m} \frac{|\widehat{F_i} - F_i|}{\overline{F}_{(Re,\phi)}}$$

$\overline{F}_{(Re,\phi)}$ is the mean drag force for (Re, ϕ) setting and $\widehat{F_i}$ the predicted drag force for particle i.

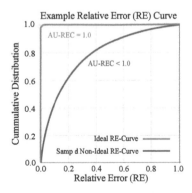

AU-REC: The third metric we employ is the *area under the relative error curve* (AU-REC). The relative error curve represents the cumulative distribution of relative error between the predicted drag force values and the ground truth PRS drag force data. AU-REC calculates the area under this curve. The AU-REC metric ranges between [0,1] and higher AU-REC values indicate superior performance.

9.6   Results & Discussion

Multiple experiments are conducted to characterize and evaluate the model performance of PhyNet with *physics-guided architecture* and *physics-guided aggregate supervision*. Due to the high cost of generating particle drag force data, we shall focus on evaluating models in context of low volume (i.e., paucity) of labeled training data. Our main goals are as follows: (i) We wish to develop a model to generate effective drag force predictions under low data volume and (ii) characterize the consistency of the trained prediction model with respect to known prior domain knowledge. To that end, we conduct several experiments to verify consistency of intermediate predictions of our model with known physics phenomena, thus ensuring explainability of model predictions. We finally also address the challenging problem of extrapolation and characterize the ability of the proposed PhyNet model to extrapolate to unseen settings.

9.6.1   Physics-Guided Auxiliary Task Selection

Many learning pipelines are confronted with the challenge of low volumes of training data. In such cases where data about the target task is limited, exogenous inputs corresponding to processes that have an indirect influence over the target process may be leveraged to alleviate the effects of data paucity during model training. Multi-task learning [3] is an effective methodology to achieve this goal. We evaluated several multi-task and single task architectures in the context of particle drag force prediction and the results are detailed in Table 9.2. In physics, it is widely accepted that the pressure and velocity fields acting on an assembly of particles have a significant influence over the drag force acting upon each particle in the assembly [11]. Hence, in addition to modeling the main task of particle drag force prediction, we also wish to additionally model the pressure and velocity fields around a particle. To this end (as described in Section 9.5.2), we developed DNN-MT-Pres, DNN-MT-Vel, each a multi-task model which predicts the pressure and velocity respectively in addition to the drag force around the candidate particle of interest. We notice that both DNN-MT-Pres and DNN-MT-Vel show inferior performance compared to the DNN model. However, the PhyNet model, which is a combination of both the auxiliary tasks (i.e., pressure field and velocity field prediction) outperforms all models as shown in Table 9.2, including the DNN. This performance improvement as seen in the case of PhyNet, may be attributed to (i) carefully selected auxiliary tasks (i.e., physics guided auxiliary task selection) (ii) model architecture design to aid in learning the representation of the main task.

9.6.2   Physics-Guided Learning Architecture

In Section 9.6.1, we detailed the effectiveness of multi-task learning employed in conjunction with *physics-guided auxiliary task selection* in the context of PhyNet models and demonstrated how this lead to learning improved representations of particle drag force.

We shall now delve deeper and inspect the effects of expanding the realm of auxiliary tasks. Additionally, we also leverage prior domain knowledge regarding the physics of entities affecting the drag force acting on each particle to influence PhyNet model architecture through *physics-guided structural priors*. As mentioned in Section 9.4, PhyNet has four carefully and deliberately chosen auxiliary tasks (pressure field prediction, velocity field prediction, predicting the pressure component(s) of drag, predicting the shear components of drag) aiding the main task of particle drag force prediction. In addition to this, the auxiliary tasks are arranged in a sequential manner to incorporate physical inter-dependencies

TABLE 9.2

The performance of PhyNet and its variant PhyNet-$F_x^P F_x^S$ (only x-components of pressure and shear drag are modeled) are compared with several state-of-the-art regression baselines. We showcase that PhyNet yields a significant performance improvement over all other models for the particle drag force prediction task. The model performance is evaluated in the context of three specific metrics described in Section 9.5.2. In the last column, we report the AU-REC metric while the center column reports the MRE metric. In both these columns, percentage improvement of the best performing model (i.e PhyNet) w.r.t all other models in the context of the specific metric (AU-REC & MRE) is also quantified. PhyNet models achieve lower errors across all metrics relative to other models.

Model	MSE	MRE (%IMP)	AU-REC (%IMP)
Linear Reg.	49.80	38.48 (-68.58%)	0.731 (-19.9%)
RF Reg.	32.58	19.38 (-37.62%)	0.819 (-8.08%)
GB Reg.	28.70	18.04 (-32.98%)	0.832 (-6.62%)
DNN	20.77	13.91 (-13.1%)	0.874 (-2.0%)
DNN-MT-Pres	20.83	15.01 (-19.45%)	0.864 (-3.03%)
DNN-MT-Vel	21.02	14.79 (-18.26%)	0.865 (-2.92%)
PhyNet-$F_x^P F_x^S$	**15.01**	12.46 (-2.96%)	0.888 (-0.34%)
PhyNet	15.78	**12.09** (–)	**0.891** (–)

among them leading up to the main task of particle drag force prediction. This deliberately chosen physics-guided architecture allows intermediate layer supervision, a practice that has been deemed effective for representation learning, especially in low data volume settings [19]. The effect of this carefully chosen physics-guided architecture and auxiliary tasks is demonstrated in Table 9.2 by the superior performance of PhyNet architectures. We now inspect each component of this physics-guided architecture of the PhyNet model.

First, we evaluate PhyNet model performance with respect to the DNN and mean baseline. In Figure 9.4, we showcase the cumulative distribution of relative error of the predicted drag forces with respect to the PRS ground truth drag force data. From the figure, we see that PhyNet and DNN models yield lower relative errors than the mean baseline which predicts the mean value per (Re,ϕ) combination. We may further infer that PhyNet outperforms the DNN (current state-of-the-art [11]) model to yield the best overall performance. In addition to the DNN model, we also evaluated the performance of DNN variants which included dropout and L_2 regularization as part of the architecture but found degrading model performance. Figure 9.4 also showcases that over 80% of the predictions of the PhyNet model have lower than a 20% error with respect to PRS-based drag force estimates. This percentage (i.e., the percentage of predictions with lower than 20% error w.r.t PRS-based drag force estimates) is significantly lower in the case of the DNN and *Mean* models.

9.6.3   Performance with Limited Data

Due to high data generation costs of the PRS simulation, we now evaluate another important property of the PhyNet model, namely, its ability to learn effective representations for drag force prediction under a paucity of training data. Thus, we create different experimental settings by continually reducing the fraction of data available for model training and evaluate the performance of PhyNet as well as other single task and multi-task DNN models in each experimental setting. The training fraction was reduced from 0.85 (i.e., 85% of the data used for training) to 0.35 (i.e., 35% of the data used for training) in the aforementioned experiments.

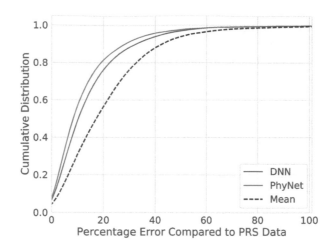

FIGURE 9.4

Cumulative distribution function of relative error for all (Re, ϕ) combinations. Overall, the PhyNet model outperforms the DNN model and the Mean baseline (dotted line).

In Figure 9.5 which characterizes the performance of models under data paucity, we see that PhyNet significantly outperforms all other models in most settings (sparse and dense). PhyNet outperforms all other models even for the setting with highest data paucity i.e., training fraction 0.35. All other regression models (except the DNN model) fail to capture useful information with increase in the proportion of training data. Another important takeaway is that PhyNet outperforms the DNN for all of the evaluated settings although it must be noted that the performance of the DNN and the PhyNet model is comparable for the setting with the highest volume of data i.e., 0.85 training fraction.

9.6.4 Characterizing PhyNet Performance For Different (Re, ϕ) Settings

To gauge model behavior holistically, qualitative inspection of model predictions is imperative in conjunction with quantitative evaluation of model performance. A qualitative

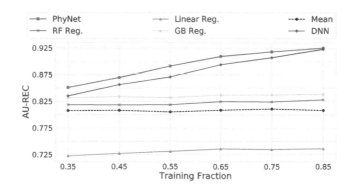

FIGURE 9.5

Model performance comparison of popular regression baselines (and PhyNet) for different levels of data paucity in the context of the drag force prediction task. We can see that PhyNet outperforms all other models for all training fractions.

analysis of model predictions is detailed in Figure 9.6, detailing particle drag force predictions by the PhyNet model for different (Re,ϕ) combinations. We notice that the PhyNet model yields accurate predictions (i.e red and blue curves are aligned). This is indicative of PhyNet being able to capture sophisticated particle interactions and also the consequent effect of said interactions on drag forces of interacting particles. At high (Re,ϕ) settings, like the one indicated in Figure 9.6, we notice that the PRS curve (red) is non-linear in nature and that the magnitude is also higher than for lower (Re,ϕ) settings. Such differing scales of drag force and the differing nature of the drag force characteristics across (Re,ϕ) settings can also complicate the drag force prediction problem as it is non-trivial for a single model to effectively learn such multi-modal target distributions. However, we find that the PhyNet model is effective in this setting.

We have thus far only evaluated the per (Re,ϕ) performance of PhyNet model. However, in order to gain a deeper understanding of PhyNet performance, we compare it to other baselines in different (Re,ϕ) settings. To this end, we show percentage improvement for the AUREC metric of PhyNet model and three other models (DNN, DNN-MT-Pres, DNN-MT-Vel) in Figures 9.7(a)-(c). Figure 9.7 showcases that PhyNet outperforms the other models in most of the (Re,ϕ) settings. When compared with the DNN model, PhyNet achieves especially good performance for low solid fraction (ϕ) settings. This behavior may be attributed to the inability of the DNN model to learn effectively with low data volumes (in contrast to PhyNet model behavior observed so far) as lower solid fractions have fewer training instances. PhyNet significantly outperforms the multi-task deep network models (i.e., DNN-MT-*), for low and high (Re,ϕ) cases. This indicates that PhyNet is able to perform well in the most complicated scenarios (high Re, high ϕ) as well as under data paucity (low ϕ). We notice that PhyNet achieves superior performance in 14 out of the 16 (Re, ϕ) settings across all three models.

9.6.5 Verifying Consistency with Domain Knowledge

In addition to the performance improvements, another advantage of the *physics-guided multi-task architecture design* is the increased interpretability provided by the resulting architecture. As noted previously, each component of PhyNet has been designed and included based on sound domain theory. In addition to architecture design, we can also employ this theoretical understanding to verify through experimentation that the resulting behavior of each auxiliary component in PhyNet is indeed consistent with known theory. First, we verify that performance of the pressure and shear drag component prediction tasks in PhyNet is consistent with known domain knowledge. We specifically leverage the well known result in theory that for high Reynolds (Re) numbers, the contribution of shear drag components ($\mathbf{F^S}$) to the total drag decreases relative to the contribution of the pressure drag components ($\mathbf{F^P}$) [11]. This is evaluated by calculating the ratio of the magnitude of predicted pressure components in the x-direction ($F_x^P \in \mathbf{F^P}$) to magnitude of predicted shear components in the x-direction ($F_x^S \in \mathbf{F^S}$) for every (Re, ϕ) setting[1]. Figure 9.8 shows a heatmap depicting comparison of the ratio of predicted pressure components to predicted shear components to a similar ratio derived from the ground truth pressure and shear components. We notice a good agreement between the two figures for the corresponding (Re,ϕ) settings. We can also see that in the case of the predicted setting (left figure in Figure 9.8), the behavior is indeed consistent with known domain theory because of the noticeable decrease in the ratio (due to the decrease in proportion of the shear components) as we move toward high Re and high solid fraction ϕ settings.

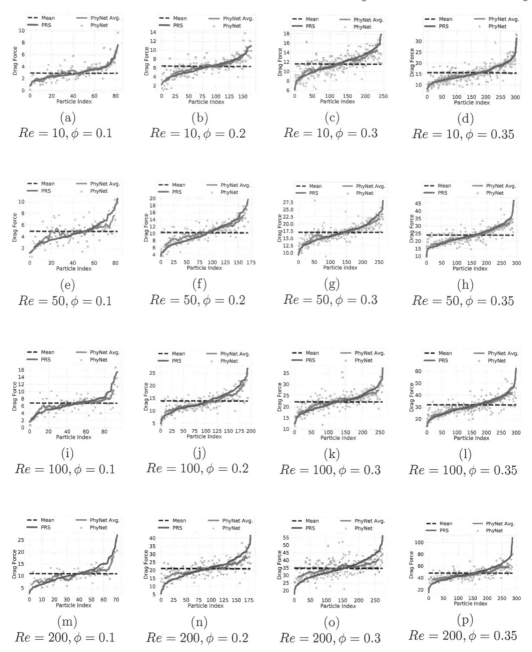

FIGURE 9.6

Each figure (a-p) presents a comparison between avg. PhyNet predictions (blue curve) and ground truth drag force data (red curve), for different (Re, ϕ) cases. In each figure, the particle index on the x-axis indicates unique particle IDs assigned in increasing order of predicted drag force per particle. PhyNet Avg. is a rolling average (window size 10) over the individual PhyNet predictions (blue dots) ordered by particle index. We also showcase the mean drag force value for each (Re, ϕ) case (black). The top row of figures indicates experiments conducted with low Re i.e Re=10 and different ϕ values. Notice that as ϕ increases, the number of samples is higher and hence the model is able to achieve a better representation of the corresponding PRS data curve (yellow). We also notice that as Re and ϕ increase, the degree of non-linearity of the system increases due to the increase in complexity of the interactions between the particles. The magnitude of drag forces is also higher at higher Re and ϕ values.

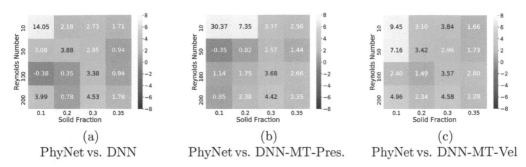

(a)
PhyNet vs. DNN

(b)
PhyNet vs. DNN-MT-Pres.

(c)
PhyNet vs. DNN-MT-Vel

FIGURE 9.7

In each figure, the percentage improvement in the context of the AU-REC metric of the PhyNet model over the DNN (a), DNN-MT-Pres (b) and DNN-MT-Vel (c) is shown. Red squares show that PhyNet does better and blue squares indicate that PhyNet is outperformed by other models. The figures show that PhyNet yields significant performance improvement over other models. In settings corresponding to low solid fractions, (i.e low number of particles), we notice significant performance improvement of PhyNet over all other models. It is to be noted that the percentage improvement is at least 1.76% over other models even in the most complex modeling setting of Re=200 and $\phi = 0.35$.

9.6.6 Auxiliary Representation Learning with Physics-Guided Statistical Constraints

Leveraging prior domain knowledge that the pressure and velocity fields influence the drag force of a particle, we hypothesize that modeling these fields explicitly should help the model learn improved representations of the main task of particle drag force prediction. Hence, two of the auxiliary prediction tasks (i.e., in addition to the auxiliary tasks of pressure and shear drag force components evaluated previously) involve predicting the pressure and velocity field samples around each particle. Figure 9.9 showcases that the ground-truth pressure

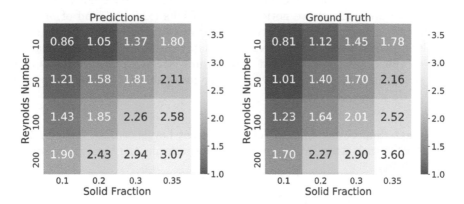

FIGURE 9.8

In each figure, a heatmap with ratio of absolute value of pressure drag (F_x^P) x-component to shear drag (F_x^S) x-component i.e ($\frac{|F_x^P|}{|F_x^S|}$) is depicted for each of the (Re,ϕ) settings. In the left figure, ratio for PhyNet predictions is shows while the right figure shows the same ratio for ground truth data. We notice that both figures have an almost identical distribution of ratios.

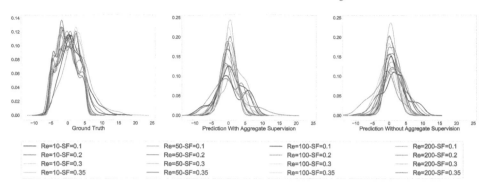

FIGURE 9.9
The figure depicts the densities of the ground truth (left) and predicted (center, right) pressure fields of the PhyNet model for each (Re,ϕ). Specifically, we wish to highlight the effect of aggregate supervision (physics-guided statistical prior) on the predicted pressure field. Notice that the PDFs of the pressure fields predicted with aggregate supervision (center figure) are relatively more distributed and similar to the ground truth distribution of pressure field PDFs whereas the plot on the right representing predicted pressure field PDFs without aggregate supervision incorrectly depicts a some what unimodal (grouped) behavior for all the PDFs of different (Re,ϕ) cases.

field PDFs exhibit a grouped structure wherein the PDFs can be divided into three distinct groups with all pressure fields with $\phi = 0.2$ being grouped to the left of the plot, pressure fields with $\phi = 0.1$ grouped toward the bottom, right of the plot and the rest forming a core (highly dense) group in the center. This indicates that solid fraction has a significant influence on the pressure field. Such multi-modal behavior is non-trivial for learning pipelines to automatically replicate. Hence, we introduce *physics-guided statistical priors* through aggregate supervision during model training to enable PhyNet to better replicate the ground-truth grouped structure of the pressure distributions. The learned distribution with aggregate supervision (Figure 9.9 (center)) shows a similar grouped structure to the ground truth PDF pressure field. Predicted pressure field PDFs in PhyNet trained without aggregate supervision (result is depicted in Figure 9.9 (right)) does not showcase the required group structure. Instead, we notice that the PDFs exhibit a kind of *mode collapse* behavior and are not similar to ground truth pressure field PDFs. The predicted velocity fields were also learned with a similar aggregate supervision and we found that incorporating physics-guided aggregate supervision to ensure learning representations consistent with theory, significantly improved model performance. Table 9.3, where the performance

TABLE 9.3
Effect of Aggregate Supervision on PhyNet for Different Levels of Data Paucity. The Table Shows That PhyNet with Aggregate Supervision Outperforms the Variant without It.

Training Fraction	No Aggregate Supervision (AUREC)	Aggregate Supervision (AUREC)
0.35	0.83265	**0.85096**
0.45	0.85874	**0.86969**
0.55	0.85635	**0.89138**
0.65	0.9005	**0.91**
0.75	0.86516	**0.918016**
0.85	0.90869	**0.92495**

TABLE 9.4

The Results for Extrapolation to two Unseen Particle Assemblies Using Different Neighborhood Sizes Depict That PhyNet Outperforms the DNN Model for Higher Neighborhood Sizes (10,15 Neighbors). PhyNet Achieves an Average of **2%** Improvement Over DNN in Terms of MRE, Measured Across all the Extrapolation Settings.

Neighborhood Size	Model	MSE	MRE
5	DNN	41.64	**22.89**
	PhyNet	**39.563**	22.95
10	DNN	32.613	21.42
	PhyNet	**29.67**	**21.15**
15	DNN	28.447	19.72
	PhyNet	**24.79**	**18.88**

of PhyNet with and without aggregate supervision is evaluated for different training fractions (0.35–0.85) as before. We notice that in all settings PhyNet with aggregate supervision performs better than the variant without aggregate supervision. Once again the evaluation is on the particle drag force prediction task.

9.6.7 Effect of Neighborhood Size & Extrapolation to Unseen Assemblies

Extrapolation which is the ultimate test of generalizability of a learned representation is one of the most challenging context for ML models. We conduct extrapolation experiments to evaluate the generalization capability of our PhyNet model by evaluating model performance for predicting drag forces of unseen particle assemblies. A particle assembly indicates a certain spatial arrangement of particles for a particular (Re, ϕ) case used to perform a CFD experiment. The arrangement of particles around a particle of interest significantly affects the drag force acting on it and hence different particle arrangements during training and testing will yield different drag force profiles and distributions thereby forming a challenging setting to test model generalization ability.

Three separate particle assemblies (each with 16 combinations of the same range of (Re, ϕ) settings) were generated and we used 55% of one of the particle assemblies for training while the entirety of the other two particle assemblies were held out and used to evaluate model extrapolation performance. In Table 9.4 we see that both PhyNet model and the DNN model yield improved performance with larger particle neighborhoods indicating that larger neighborhoods enable learning of richer particle interaction information. However, even in the extrapolation context, we see that the PhyNet model outperforms the DNN model for higher particle neighborhoods (i.e., cases when 10 ,15 neighboring particles considered as inputs), while the DNN slightly outperforms the PhyNet model for the case with very few (5) neighbors.

9.7 Conclusion

In this chapter, we introduced and discussed various ways of leveraging prior scientific domain knowledge to augment the ML process. Specifically, we introduced PhyNet , a physics inspired deep learning model developed to incorporate fluid mechanical theory into the model architecture and propose physics informed auxiliary task selection to aid with training under data paucity. We also showcase the effectiveness of our proposed ideas with rigorous analyses to test PhyNet performance in settings with limited training data and find that PhyNet significantly outperforms all state-of-the-art baselines for the task of particle drag force prediction. We verify the consistency of the presented physics informed auxiliary tasks of PhyNet with existing physics theory, thereby yielding greater model interpretability. Thereafter we also detailed a sampling procedure consistent with the periodic boundary condition of the underlying simulation domain for obtaining a granular sample of the pressure and velocity fields (employed in modeling two of the auxiliary tasks in PhyNet) around the particle surface. We also characterize the effect of augmenting PhyNet with physics-guided aggregate supervision to constrain auxiliary tasks to be consistent with ground truth training data. Additionally, we present results relating to the effect the size of a particle's neighborhood considered, has on modeling its drag force. In this experiment, we notice that larger particle neighborhoods enable better modeling of drag forces acting on the candidate particle (i.e., particle of interest). Finally, we test the effectiveness of PhyNet in the context of generalization to unseen particle assemblies. We shall conduct additional experiments further characterizing extrapolation ability in yet other settings moving forward. In the future, properties like the effect that upstream and downstream particles have on the pressure, velocity fields and drag force of a particle of interest may be interesting problems to characterize. In conclusion, this chapter details a general framework for incorporating physics into ML models through intermediaries which influence the quantity being modeled but are not available during model deployment; a frequently encountered situation in computational science and engineering when highly resolved simulations are used to develop models to be deployed as "subgrid" models in low resolution calculations. While in this chapter, we have demonstrated the PhyNet framework in the context of predicting particle drag in a suspension, the same framework may be leveraged for other CFD-based model development efforts in a variety of fields like atmospheric, geological sciences and various engineering applications.

Note

[1]Similar behavior was observed when ratios were taken for all three pressure and shear drag components.

Bibliography

[1] Yaser S Abu-Mostafa. Learning from hints in neural networks. *Journal of Complexity*, 6(2), 1990.

[2] Brandon Anderson et al. Cormorant: Covariant molecular neural networks. *arXiv:1906.04015*, 2019.

[3] Rich Caruana. Multitask learning. In *Learning to Learn*. Springer, 1998.

[4] Soumyadeep Chatterjee et al. Sparse group lasso: Consistency and climate applications. In *SDM12'*. SIAM, 2012.

[5] Tian Qi Chen et al. Neural ordinary differential equations. In *NeurIPS*, 2018.

[6] Huseyin Denli et al. Multi-scale graphical models for spatio-temporal processes. In *NeurIPS*, 2014.

[7] A Eshghinejadfard, S A Hosseini, and D Thevenin. Effect of particle density in turbulent channel flows with resolved oblate spheroids. *Computers and Fluids*, 184:29—39, 2019.

[8] Usama Fayyad, Gregory Piatetsky-Shapiro, and Padhraic Smyth. From data mining to knowledge discovery in databases. *AI Magazine*, 17(3):37–37, 1996.

[9] Usama Fayyad, Gregory Piatetsky-Shapiro, and Padhraic Smyth. The kdd process for extracting useful knowledge from volumes of data. *Communications of the ACM*, 39(11):27–34, 1996.

[10] Long He and Danesh Tafti. Variation of drag, lift and torque in a suspension of ellipsoidal particles. *Powder Technology*, 335, 2018.

[11] Long He and Danesh K Tafti. A supervised machine learning approach for predicting variable drag forces on spherical particles in suspension. *Powder Technology*, 345, 2019.

[12] Long He, Danesh K Tafti, and Krishnamurthy Nagendra. Evaluation of drag correlations using particle resolved simulations of spheres and ellipsoids in assembly. *Powder Technology*, 313, 2017.

[13] Yani Andrew Ioannou. *Structural Priors in Deep Neural Networks*. PhD thesis, University of Cambridge, 2018.

[14] Xiaowei Jia et al. Physics guided rnns for modeling dynamical systems: A case study in simulating lake temperature profiles. In *SDM19'*. SIAM, 2019.

[15] Anuj Karpatne et al. Theory-guided data science: A new paradigm for scientific discovery from data. *IEEE TKDE*, 29(10), 2017.

[16] Anuj Karpatne, William Watkins, Jordan Read, and Vipin Kumar. Physics-guided neural networks (pgnn): An application in lake temperature modeling. *arXiv preprint arXiv:1710.11431*, 2017.

[17] Osman Semih Kayhan and Jan C van Gemert. On translation invariance in cnns: Convolutional layers can exploit absolute spatial location. In *Proceedings of the IEEE/CVF Conference on Computer Vision and Pattern Recognition*, pages 14274–14285, 2020.

[18] Risi Kondor and Shubhendu Trivedi. On the generalization of equivariance and convolution in neural networks to the action of compact groups. *arXiv:1802.03690*, 2018.

[19] Chen-Yu Lee, Saining Xie, Patrick Gallagher, Zhengyou Zhang, and Zhuowen Tu. Deeply-supervised nets. In *Artificial Intelligence and Statistics*, pages 562–570. PMLR, 2015.

[20] F Li, F Song, S Benyahia, W Wang, and J Li. Mp-pic simulation of cfb riser with emms-based drag model. *Chem. Eng. Sci.*, 82(12):104–113, 2012.

[21] Jie Li and JAM Kuipers. Gas-particle interactions in dense gas-fluidized beds. *Chemical Engineering Science*, 58(3-6), 2003.

[22] Jin Liu et al. Accounting for linkage disequilibrium in genome-wide association studies: a penalized regression method. *Statistics and Its Interface*, 6(1), 2013.

[23] Andrew J Majda and John Harlim. Physics constrained nonlinear regression models for time series. *Nonlinearity*, 26(1), 2012.

[24] Andrew J Majda and Yuan Yuan. Fundamental limitations of ad hoc linear and quadratic multi-level regression models for physical systems. *Discrete and Continuous Dynamical Systems B*, 17(4), 2012.

[25] Benjamin R Mitchell et al. *The Spatial Inductive Bias of Deep Learning*. PhD thesis, Johns Hopkins University, 2017.

[26] Nikhil Muralidhar, Jie Bu, Ze Cao, Long He, Naren Ramakrishnan, Danesh Tafti, and Anuj Karpatne. Phynet: Physics guided neural networks for particle drag force prediction in assembly. In *Proceedings of the 2020 SIAM International Conference on Data Mining*, pages 559–567. SIAM, 2020.

[27] Nikhil Muralidhar, Jie Bu, Ze Cao, Long He, Naren Ramakrishnan, Danesh Tafti, and Anuj Karpatne. Physics-guided deep learning for drag force prediction in dense fluid-particulate systems. *Big Data*, 8(5):431–449, 2020.

[28] Nikhil Muralidhar et al. Incorporating prior domain knowledge into deep neural networks. In *Big Data*. IEEE, 2018.

[29] K Nagendra, D K Tafti, and K Viswanath. A new approach for conjugate heat transfer problems using immersed boundary method for curvilinear grid based solvers. *Journal of Comptuational Physics*, 267:225–246, 2014.

[30] F. Pedregosa et al. Scikit-learn: Machine learning in Python. *JMLR*, 12, 2011.

[31] Maziar Raissi, Paris Perdikaris, and G Karniadakis. Physics informed deep learning (part i): Data-driven solutions of nonlinear partial differential equations. *arXiv preprint arXiv:1711.10561*, 2017.

[32] Maziar Raissi, Paris Perdikaris, and George Em Karniadakis. Physics informed deep learning (part ii): Data-driven discovery of nonlinear partial differential equations. *arXiv preprint arXiv:1711.10566*, 2017.

[33] Hongyu Ren et al. Learning with weak supervision from physics and data-driven constraints. *AI Magazine*, 39(1), 2018.

[34] Russell Stewart and Stefano Ermon. Label-free supervision of neural networks with physics and domain knowledge. In *AAAI*, 2017.

[35] Laurens Van Der Maaten, Eric Postma, and Jaap Van den Herik. Dimensionality reduction: a comparative. *Journal of Machine Learning Research*, 10(66-71):13, 2009.

[36] Donald Waterman. A guide to expert systems. 1986.

[37] Ken CL Wong, Linwei Wang, and Pengcheng Shi. Active model with orthotropic hyperelastic material for cardiac image analysis. In *Functional Imaging and Modeling of the Heart*. Springer, 2009.

[38] Jingjia Xu et al. Robust transmural electrophysiological imaging: Integrating sparse and dynamic physiological models into ecg-based inference. In *MICCAI*. Springer, 2015.

[39] Mai Zhu, Bo Chang, and Chong Fu. Convolutional neural networks combined with runge-kutta methods. *arXiv:1802.08831*, 2018.

10

<hr>

Using the Physics of Electron Beam Interactions to Determine Optimal Sampling and Image Reconstruction Strategies for High Resolution STEM

<hr>

Nigel D. Browning, B. Layla Mehdi, Daniel Nicholls, and Andrew Stevens

CONTENTS

<hr>

10.1 Introduction

The concept that we will discuss in this chapter is that we can use the advanced mathematical concepts of compressive sensing (CS) and artificial intelligence (AI)/machine learning (ML) based on the incomplete sampling of images (i.e. sub-sampling) to optimize the manner by which we acquire and interpret images and spectra that are obtained from a scanning transmission electron microscope (STEM). This approach will implement key insights from how AI/ML is used to make interpretations from "big data" to determine and obtain the smallest possible set of most important "targeted images" that can then be used to achieve a higher overall spatial/temporal resolution and quantified precision from the experimental process. In a world where the majority of people have a camera in their cell phone, we tend to think of images (which are a designated form of data) as being "free" – we can just take more and more of them as we please. Many demonstrations of AI have made use of this concept of "free/big data", using data that has been stored in varied formats over the years to provide, for example, new medical treatments, optimized supply chains for businesses, or new materials discoveries (Figure 10.1). However, scientific images obtained from expensive and scarce experimental resources typically do have a "penalty or cost" associated with them, even if it is simply in storage and transmission (with cell phones, this is why

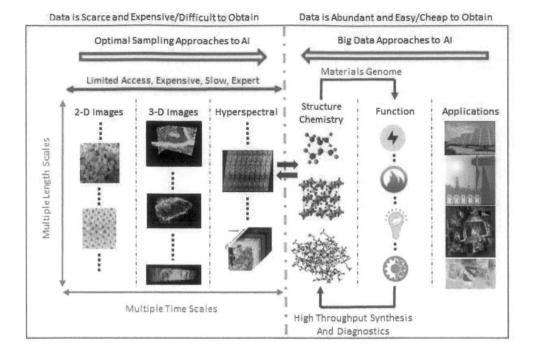

FIGURE 10.1

Current AI approaches typically use existing data to identify hidden phenomena. This avoids specialized and expensive data acquisition by using free datasets and therefore tends to uncover new trends by serendipity. In the most advanced scientific imaging methods, data is not free and is designated for specific tasks. *The goal in using physical processes to drive the use of AI is to integrate the acquisition and analysis process to identify optimal imaging strategies, greatly reducing the amount of data needed while expanding the potential for targeted discoveries.*

images are compressed as much as possible). For advanced characterization techniques that use ionizing radiation, such as the STEM, the main penalty/cost is damage to the sample during imaging, and this can severely limit the resolution and precision of images to a value that is significantly below what the hardware should be able to deliver (Figure 10.1). More importantly, this penalty/cost means that some types of samples are simply impossible to image in the STEM at all. This means that the extensive benefits of atomic-scale STEM imaging (Pennycook and Nellist 2011) that have previously fuelled transformative developments in semiconductors, complex oxides, and structural materials are now unavailable to provide the unique insights that could drive advancements in metastable materials and new clean energy technologies.

Here we will evaluate and apply the best-integrated hardware/software approaches available to seamlessly embed AI/ML concepts into wide-ranging applications of STEM imaging. Over the last few years, improvements in electron microscope hardware alone have actually reduced the range of materials that can be analyzed by STEM, although for the few samples that can withstand the higher dose levels (i.e., the number of electrons per unit area), they are now imaged with much higher resolution/sensitivity. Overcoming this limitation in the types of samples that can be studied by atomic-resolution STEM is exactly where the AI for STEM (AI4STEM) approach will have the most impact, changing the characterization paradigm and making atomic-scale images accessible a wide range of "beam sensitive" samples. The success of this approach will have significant implications in the use of STEM for materials characterization and discovery. For example, we would be able to observe diffusion in next-generation batteries on the atomic scale, leading to the design of new energy storage systems for electrical vehicles and grid applications (Goodenough and Kim 2010). It would be possible to observe the electron and phonon interactions and dynamics in solar materials (Lee et al. 2012) and thermoelectrics (Biswas et al. 2012) by electron energy loss spectroscopy imaging (EELSI), leading to more efficient clean energy generation. In the case of catalysts, the atomic and molecular processes in the catalyst that cause the conversion of molecules can be observed on the fundamental length and time scales (Melzer et al. 2019), leading to improvements in efficiency and selectivity of reactions and much reduced environmental effects for many industrial processes. For biology, the need to freeze the sample for cryo-EM will be removed, as the speed and precision of the imaging process will allow structures to be observed in their natural liquid environment (de Jonge and Ross 2011), opening up the potential to study protein dynamics in-situ (de Jonge et al. 2009). In all of these cases (and many others), electron beam damage caused during image acquisition is the only thing limiting microscopy from uncovering new materials and processes. We will show here that by incorporating the physical understanding of the mechanism by which an electron microscope forms an image (and the sample damages), we can determine an optimal approach to sampling and the use of ML to generate the most efficient image.

10.2   Basic Concepts of Scanning Transmission Electron Microscopy (STEM)

The STEM forms images by scanning the electron beam over the surface of the specimen and collecting the transmitted scattering on a series of detectors as a function of the probe position (Figure 10.2) (Pennycook and Nellist 2011). Atomic structure determination, i.e., the method requiring images with the highest spatial resolution, is usually made with the Z-contrast imaging technique. Z-contrast images (Pennycook and Boatner 1988; Jesson et al. 1993; Nellist and Pennycook 1999) are formed by collecting the high-angle scattering on an annular detector and synchronously displaying its integrated output on a screen while the electron probe is scanned across the specimen. Detecting the scattered intensity at high-angles and over a large angular range effectively averages coherent effects between atomic columns in the specimen, allowing each atom to be considered to scatter independently with a cross-section approaching a Z^2 dependence on atomic number. This cross-section forms an object function that is strongly peaked at the atom sites. The detected intensity is, to a first approximation, a convolution of this object function with the probe *intensity* profile. The small width of the object function ($\sim$0.1 Å) means that the spatial resolution is limited only by the probe size of the microscope. For a crystalline material in a zone-axis orientation, where the atomic spacing is greater than the probe size (probe size is now typically $\sim$0.1 nm or less for aberration-corrected STEM (Haider et al. 1998; Batson et al. 2002; Erni et al. 2009; Muller et al. 2008)), the atomic columns can be illuminated individually. Therefore, as the probe is scanned over the specimen, an atomic resolution compositional map is generated in which the intensity depends on the average atomic number of the atoms in the column. An important feature of this method is that changes in focus and thickness do not cause contrast reversals in the image, so that atomic sites can be identified unambiguously during the experiment. Since the initial development of Z-contrast imaging technique, there have been many studies that have confirmed the general concept of incoherent imaging.

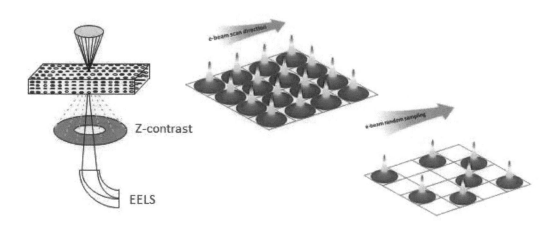

FIGURE 10.2
(left) STEM configuration for signal acquisition, (center) regularly sampled scan, and (right) sub-sampled scan (Nicholls et al. 2020).

However, interpretation of the intensities within the atomic columns seen in the images can be a little more complicated than the simple incoherent model suggests under certain conditions (LeBeau et al. 2008; LeBeau et al. 2009; Dwyer et al. 2008; Oxley et al. 2007). There are also methods such as annular bright field imaging (ABF) (Ishikawa et al. 2011; Findlay et al. 2010), low angle annular dark-field imaging (LAADF) (Yu et al. 2004), where contrast again becomes a little more complicated, but the general principle of scattering arising from a particular beam location holds here too. It should also be noted that electron energy loss spectroscopy (EELS) (Browning et al. 1993; Batson 1993; Muller et al. 1993; Kimoto et al. 2007) and energy dispersive X-ray spectroscopy (EDS) (Yang et al. 2015) can also be performed and atomic composition/bonding maps can be generated with atomic spatial resolution (Figure 10.1).

In a standard STEM, the way the scan works is that it moves the beam from left to right across a single row with a dwell time (typically ∼5 μs) for each pixel in that row (Figure 10.2). At the end of the row, the beam flies back to the left-hand side, moves down one pixel, and then completes a row again (this is like the way a traditional typewriter used to work or an older cathode ray tube (CRT) television). After the flyback to the left-hand side, the beam typically has a longer dwell time at the edge to allow for any hysteresis in the scan to damp out and the left-hand edge of the scan to be aligned at the same location for each row. In the STEM mode of operation, the beam size is the same regardless of the magnification of the image, which is ∼0.1 nm for an aberration-corrected STEM. In a low magnification image, the area of the scan is large, and the pixel size is therefore much larger than the size of the beam. For example, in a 1000 × 1000 pixel scan covering 1 mm × 1 mm of sample, the pixel size is 1 μm, i.e., 1000 × the size of the beam. To achieve atomic resolution, the magnification of the microscope is increased to the point where the pixel size approaches the atomic separation, i.e., ∼0.1–0.5 nm. For many of the most impressive atomic resolution images that have been obtained from beam stable samples, the magnification is turned up to a level where the pixel size is actually much smaller than the probe size, leading to an oversampling of the image. When the microscope is running at low-magnification, beam damage is not an issue as the distance between the beam locations is large, and the likelihood that the scan hits exactly the same location in successive sweeps is very small. It is only when the beam and pixel size starts to overlap that the damage becomes serious, and this is, of course, the condition that the microscope aims to achieve. If we think about the problem from the perspective of the beam overlap, then if we can increase the spacing of the beam positions at high magnification, then we will be able to avoid the beam damage problem (Figure 10.2). The problem with this sparse sampling approach is, of course, that we would then need a means to reconstruct the full image from this sub-sampled image. As the quality of the image then would obviously depend on how much sampling was included, the best or optimal sampling would be the one where the physics of the beam damage process was minimized and the ability to reconstruct the image was maximized. This optimal sampling approach is the physics-driven compressed sensing and ML that will be discussed in the rest of this chapter.

10.3   Defining the Physical Constraints for Optimal Sampling

While aberration-corrected STEM has led to an unprecedented increase in the achievable spatial resolution from all forms of imaging (Z-contrast, Annular Bright Field, etc.), it has also been accompanied by a simultaneous increase in the operational probe current under typical imaging conditions. Although the increased current is advantageous for observations of atomic-scale dopants in some samples, typical electron doses are now several orders of magnitude higher than many materials can withstand. Dose considerations are now the most critical experimental parameters when imaging beam sensitive materials or performing in-situ experiments, which usually leads to a reduction in the electron dose and dose rate at the cost of decreased signal-to-noise ratios and a poorer spatial resolution than the microscope is capable of delivering at the higher dose/rate levels. The two main types of damage that samples experience in an electron microscope are knock-on (Gu et al. 2017) (cascade displacement effects) and radiolysis (Egerton 2013) (cleavage of chemical bonds) damage. These damage processes have sample and microscope parameter dependant critical thresholds (Egerton et al. 2004) – if the microscope parameters are maintained below this threshold (voltage, beam current, sample temperature) for a given sample, minimal damage will take place. To generalize these effects here we introduce the concept of beam influence (Figure 10.3) (Nicholls et al. 2020). Beam influence is the change in the sample that is a result of the beam-sample interactions, and similar to dose rate, beam damage will happen at a point in a sample when the beam influence exceeds a critical threshold. This allows us to discuss beam damage on a fundamental level without needing the specifics of process (for any given sample, the mechanism of damage will always be the same, the only difference will be how we put the beam into the specimen and the interactions that follow).

In using the concept of the beam influence, we can now examine how the delivery of the electron dose/rate to the sample affects damage. A simple example of this concept of beam influence is the difference between imaging a sample in either STEM or TEM mode. A TEM and a STEM experiment can have the same integrated dose and dose rate, but the TEM mode illuminates a defined area for the entire image duration, whereas the STEM mode illuminates smaller areas of the sample sequentially during the same acquisition time. In this example, the peak dose/rate in STEM is higher than for TEM, but the TEM area experiences the dose for a longer period of time, and the influence of the beam on the sample will be different for each case. In typical STEM operation, the electron beam performs a raster scan over the sample. At each position in the scan, beam influence is generated during the spot "dwell time" and the "diffusion time" of the interactions that progresses after the

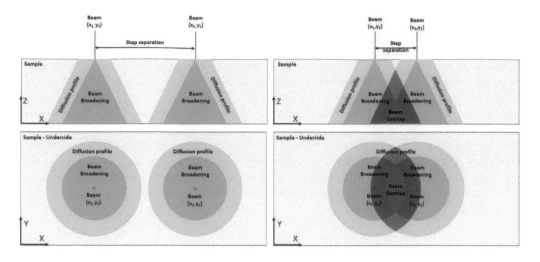

FIGURE 10.3
Small step separations between successive sampling points causes beam overlap due to beam broadening and/or diffusion effects. Increasing the step separation beyond a certain value reduces the effects of beam overlap.

beam illumination starts and finishes, increasing the beam influence beyond the area of the initial beam location and affecting neighboring positions (Figure 10.3). While individual scan positions may not produce enough beam influence to exceed the critical threshold, in a linear scan, every successive scan position may also experience "diffusion" interactions (Figure 10.3). This phenomenon is effectively a diffusion profile overlap, and we note here that beam broadening in thick samples will exacerbate this effect. Therefore, the results are normalized by the mean free path (mfp) (Williams and Carter 2009).

Equation 10.1 shows how the change in beam influence per time step can be calculated for every pixel in a scan. The first term of the equation, $D\nabla^2\varphi$, calculates the amount of beam influence that is diffusing, and the second term, f, is the amount of beam influence deposited at that pixel, which is generated via the scanning pattern and beam broadening, which is governed by Equation 10.2. If the pixel is within the area of irradiation, beam influence is added.

$$\frac{\partial\varphi}{\partial t} = D\nabla^2\varphi + f \tag{10.1}$$

where D is the diffusion constant associated with the beam influence and $\varphi(x,y,z,t)$ is defined as the beam influence per unit volume. The source term, f, is analogous to the STEM probe that adds beam influence to the system. The beam broadening, defined by Goldstein and later by Jones (Joy et al. 1986) is given by

$$b = 8 \times 10^{-12} \tfrac{Z}{E_0}(N_v)^{1/2} \, T^{3/2} \tag{10.2}$$

where b is the amount of beam broadening and T is the sample thickness, both in m, Z is the atomic number, E_0 is the beam energy, and N_v is the number of atoms/m^3.

To investigate diffusion overlap independently from beam broadening, a standard sample can be used, and for proof of principle here a thin homogenous copper film was used. For the simulation, the material under consideration must have the following parameters defined; thickness, atomic number, lattice constant, and the number of atoms per unit cell. By choosing the thickness to be small, such that the thickness is much less than the mfp,

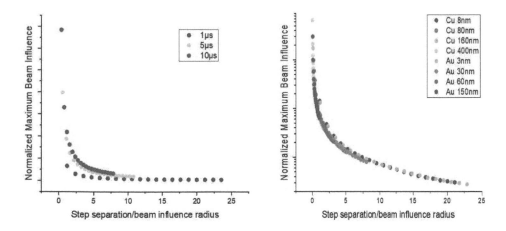

FIGURE 10.4

(left) Increasing dwell time causes an increase in the step separation required to avoid beam overlap in a thin sample. The reduction in beam influence is predominantly controlled by the step separation rather than the reduced dose. (right) Increasing sample thickness causes an increase in the step separation required to avoid beam overlap. In these plots, the separation of the beam is normalized by the beam profile radius, making the interpretation independent of instrument resolution. The beam influence is normalized to the effect of a single isolated beam location and is therefore plotted in arbitrary units.

the beam broadening is negligible, and the focus can be placed on the diffusion-based phenomenon. Figure 10.4 shows the effective beam influence as a function of the separation between beam positions. What is clear from these normalized plots is that as the scan puts the beam positions closer together, i.e., magnification is increased, the beam influence increases significantly (a similar response occurs if the is held in each position longer).

Another parameter that affects the step separation is the diffusion coefficient of the damage products. Beam influence is used in this study in order to generalize the damage mechanisms at play, and it can be considered that each mechanism of beam damage exists as a cross-section of the beam influence, such that if a critical beam influence value is exceeded, then that damage type occurs. If we simplify the system and assume there is only one damage mechanism that occurs, such as vacancy migration, then the physical principles can be studied using this model, and the step separation required to minimize this phenomenon can be calculated. In the more realistic case that many damage phenomena occur, then setting the beam influence diffusion rate to the quickest of the diffusing mechanisms would give the step separation required to produce the least damage overall – if overlap for a quick phenomenon is avoided, it must be avoided for slow phenomena as well. Figure 10.5 shows the step separations required to minimize the maximum beam influence for a range of coefficients. In this figure, the diffusion coefficient of vacancy migration, D_v, can be calculated from (Nastasi et al. 1996).

$$D_v = \frac{\Gamma_v d^2}{6} \tag{10.3}$$

where d is the atomic jump distance, and Γ_v is the vacancy jump frequency;

$$\Gamma_v = Ce^{-\frac{E_m^v}{k_B T}} \tag{10.4}$$

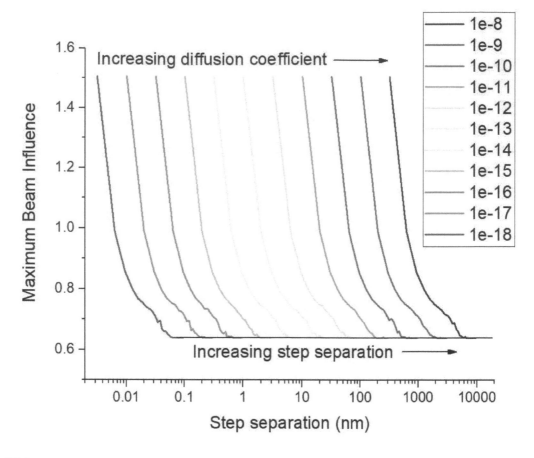

FIGURE 10.5
Increasing the speed of diffusion increases the step separation required to minimize the beam influence. The beam influence is normalized to the effect of a single isolated beam location and is therefore plotted in arbitrary units.

where E_m^v is the vacancy migration energy, k_B is the Boltzmann constant, T is the temperature in kelvin, and C is a proportionality constant assumed to be 1. Values of E_m^v have been calculated (Wynblatt 1968) and experimentally measured (Stevens et al. 2014) for many elements and typically lie in the region of 0.5–2.5 eV. With $E_m^v = 0.8$eV and d = 0.4 nm, D_v = 4.36E-17 and for a thin specimen with a $1\mu s$ dwell time at ambient temperature, a step separation of 0.355 nm would be required to reduce the beam overlap, and the resulting damage to the specimen.

10.4   Practical Implementation of Sampling Strategies

As STEM is a serial imaging technique, it can in theory be readily adapted for sparse sampling, leading to an immediate lowering of the beam influence effects. The expected reduction of dose will depend on the type of sparse sampling, the reconstruction algorithms, and the acceptable image quality, which we will discuss in detail later. In the original theoretical STEM paper by Stevens et al. (Stevens et al. 2014), it was shown in image simulations that inpainting reconstructions using Bayesian dictionary learning (Zhou et al. 2012) could provide suitable reconstructions with better than an order of magnitude sub-sampling. Practical realization of this sparse sampling in STEM can be achieved either directly with the scan coils (by steering the beam to the sparse pixel locations) or by applying beam blanking on top of a conventional scan (blanking the beam at all but a few randomly selected pixels). Directly controlling the beam, rather than using the beam blanker, is a very attractive option since it offers improvement in acquisition time in addition to dose reduction. However, for a typical STEM image with a pixel dwell time of only few microseconds, electron beam controlled sampling may not be easily adopted due to the dynamic response of the scan causing significant delays between desired and current positions.

A viable approach has been previously proposed and demonstrated for SEM, where the scan coil dynamics were characterized, thus allowing a post-acquisition correction of the positional assignments (Anderson et al. 2013). The beam-blanking approach eliminates the positional uncertainties, but only permits reduction of dose. Possibly a more important issue, however, is the fact that beam-blanking approach will also be associated with extra dose and time due to the beam blanking itself. As the beam is moved on and off the sample (blanking), a finite time for stabilization has to be accounted for, leading to additional dose and acquisition time. The experimental demonstration of sparse acquisition based on an electromagnetic blanker was demonstrated in the recent work of Béché et al. 2016 and a faster electrostatic blanker was demonstrated by Muecke-Herzberg et al. (2016). In this current work, we pursue an approach to sparse sampling that directly controls the scan coils and eliminates the uncertainties with beam position assignment (it also offers several additional advantageous as compared to the previously applied scan-coils controlled sparse sampling) (Kovarik et al. 2016).

A "fully random" or 2D Bernoulli pixel sampling, as shown in Figure 10.6, represents one of the most advantageous strategies for sparse sampling and inpainting. This sampling has the lowest degree of coherence and permits the highest degree of under-sampling without the introduction of reconstruction distortions. One can easily envision that Bernoulli sampling could be accomplished by randomly changing the pixel step size during image acquisition. However, in order to practically implement sparse sampling by changing the step size, it has to be assured that the beam steps can be realized in a much shorter time than the dwell time. To assess the viability of beam-controlled sparse sampling on the JEOL ARM200CF STEM at the Pacific Northwest National Laboratory (PNNL), we evaluated the dynamic response of the beam by measuring the beam rise time, which represents the response time for the beam to reach a desired set location. The rise time was evaluated from a pair of images acquired in interlaced fashion under different dwell times (a detailed explanation of the derivation of the beam rise time will be presented elsewhere). As shown in Figure 10.6, we find that the time required for the beam to reach 90% of the desired location is approximately 60 microseconds, which is significantly higher than the dwell time used for conventional STEM imaging. Given this relatively long time and the complex response of the scan coils, it is clear that even for relatively long dwell times (~tens of microseconds), performing sparse sampling by changing the step size would lead to an uncontrollable build-up of hysteresis induced random probe positions. It should be noted that in a regular full scan (all pixels), a dwell time of only a few microseconds will not cause any image distortions because after the initial acceleration, which can take few pixels, the beam inevitably reaches a steady-state speed with the desired pixel size/dwell time (This is without any other additional corrections applied to the scan generator).

To overcome the issue of slow beam response, we developed an approach where the sparse sampling is accomplished by a continuous lateral scan that imposes a random vertical

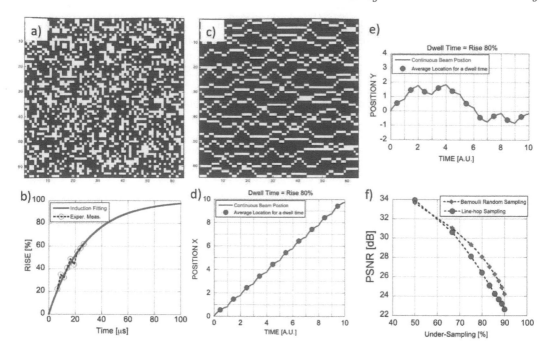

FIGURE 10.6

(a) Bernoulli sparse sampling. (b) Experimentally derived rise time for scan coils in JEOL ARM 200 based on the assumption that the beam movement is dictated by induction in scan coils (c) line-hopping sparse sampling (d, e). Simulated position of the electron beam along X and Y direction for dwell time corresponding to 80% of rise. (f) Theoretically obtained PSNR from digitally sparsely sampled Au gold standard images, considering Bernoulli random sampling and line hop sampling[40].

perturbation. In this sparse sampling approach, as shown in Figure 10.6, the beam moves at constant speed along horizontal (x) direction, while sampling a range of pixels along the vertical (y) direction. The step size is kept constant and each step corresponds to only a one-pixel jump along x and y-direction. Since the movement of the beam is constant along the x-direction, just as in the case of regular scan, the average beam position along x is well defined. For the y-direction, the beam randomly hops up and down within a pre-defined range of pixels. To assure that the beam positions can be reliably driven and assigned to underlying pixel grid (along the y direction), the dwell time has to be restricted to a predefined range, as dictated by the rise time of the scan coils. It can be shown that the dwell times corresponding to $\sim$70–90% of rise are adequate for implementation of this sparse line-hopping approach. The simulated beam positions for the movement along the y-direction (as well as the x-direction) for a dwell time of 80% of the rise are shown in Figure 10.6. The average position of the beam along the y-direction is well within the center of the periodic grid, thus enabling a reliable pixel assignment. A 70% dwell time translates to just over 30 microseconds on the JEOL 200kV ARM, which is higher than the conventional dwell time, but still results in a time reduction when sparse sampling is employed, and it allows the total acquisition time to be relevant for high-resolution applications. Figure 10.7 shows how the line hop and random sampling schemes discussed above compare with each other in terms of beam influence. Most notably at low sampling percentages, the line hop sampling that is used to overcome the hysteresis in the scan coils actually performs better than the purely random sampling in terms of its damage effect on the sample.

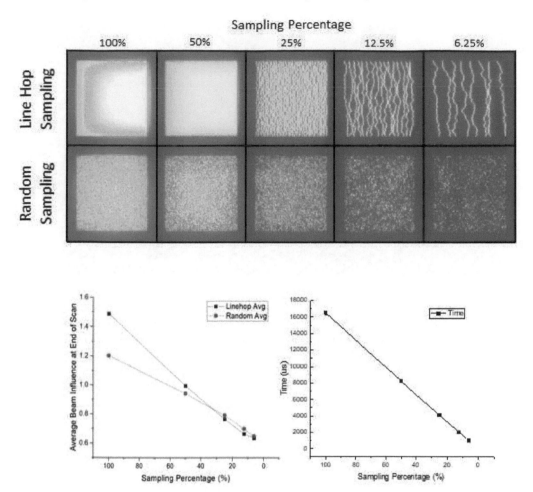

FIGURE 10.7

(top) Line hop sampling provides an approximately equivalent distribution to random sampling at the same sampling percentage. The irradiated area is 128 × 128 pixels. (bottom) (Left) Reducing sampling percentage reduces the beam influence for line hop and random scans differently. (Right) Reducing the sampling reduces the scan time as less pixels are sampled[27].

10.5 Spatial and Temporal Resolution Expectations from the Optimal Sampling Approach

To determine the optimum approach to compressive sensing (i.e., the level of dose and/or sub-sampling that produces the best images) we first compare the results of sub-sampling with a fully sampled low-dose image under precisely controlled conditions for high-resolution imaging (Stevens et al. 2013, Stevens et al. 2017). Figure 10.8 and Table 10.1 shows simulations of Z-contrast images for ZnSe, which is a standard test sample for atomic resolution STEM. These images were simulated using the multi-slice frozen phonon image simulation method in the QSTEM software package (Koch 2002). A specimen thickness of 10nm was used. The primary beam energy of the microscope was set to 200 keV. The probe-forming

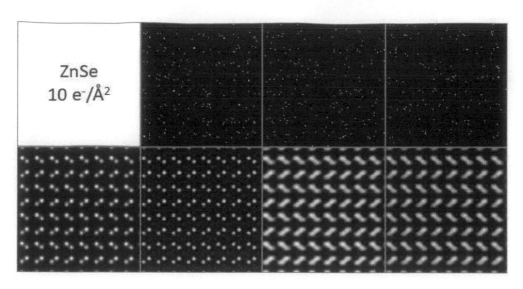

FIGURE 10.8
Representative reconstructions for a dose of 10 e$^-$/Å^2. Top row: white pixels represent locations where the number of detected electrons is greater than 1. Bottom row: Simulated, Adaptive, Jittered, and Low-dose reconstructions from the image above. Resolution and contrast metrics are shown in Table 10.1. The jittered and adaptive reconstructions use 10% of the pixel locations. It is apparent that uniform dose reduction causes a subsampling effect, thus most of the dose is wasted in regions producing zero electron detections.

convergence semi-angle was 22 mrad, and the annular dark field (ADF) detector collection angle was 75–300 mrad. A probe source size of 0.6 Å was used, and the image pixel size was 0.2 × 0.2 Å. To simulate low-dose imaging conditions, each pixel is corrupted with Poisson noise consistent with the mean value predicted by the simulation at the corresponding dose. The first is adaptive sampling, which begins with an initial Cartesian jittered random sub-sampling (shown in Figure 10.6), and then subsequent new scans are adapted to sample the regional maxima identified in the previous scan (to fill in missing information). Each subsequent scan collects pixels that have not been previously collected, but as the acquisition is in a completely new scan, the time between sampling adjacent pixels is much longer than the diffusion constant. Such an adaptive approach has the effect of putting the dose in the expected atom column locations. The second strategy uses a jittered (non-adaptive) random sub-sampling (as shown in Figure 10.6, this produces a similar dose strategy to the

TABLE 10.1
Resolution and contrast metrics reconstructions of various sampling schemes (10%) applied to atomic resolution images of GaAs and ZnSe. For ZnSe, jittered and conventional resolutions are inter-dumbbell (not atomic). Stevens et al. 2018.

Material	GaAs 10 e$^-$/Å^2		ZnSe 10 e$^-$/Å^2	
Method	Res. (Å)	Contrast	Res. (Å)	Contrast
Simulated	0.6115	1.115	0.6414	1.237
Adaptive	0.4083	1.138	0.556	1.33
Jiittered	0.5886	1.119	0.8	1.114
Conventional	0.5892	1.02	0.8	1.188

line-hopping mode). In the sub-sampling approaches, 10% of the pixels are used, and the dose is kept consistent with the fully sampled images by increasing the Poisson mean in each sampled pixel by the fraction of sub-sampling (i.e., the sub-sampled dose in a pixel is 10 × the dose in a pixel of the fully sampled image, making the total dose the same). Third is conventional "low-dose" strategy, whereby the intensity of the image is lowered uniformly in each pixel (in microscopy terms, this is the case when the beam current or dwell time is lowered to reduce the dose). Exemplar reconstructions are shown in Figure 10.8. Notably, at extremely low-dose, the traditional low-dose sensing produces a de-facto sub-sampling. To allow for a direct comparison between the methods, reconstructed images for each sampling strategy use the same algorithm. First, the Fourier transform is computed. Next, a punctured median filter is used to find and filter the peaks in the magnitude image. Finally, the magnitude beyond a maximum spatial frequency is set to zero, and the inverse transform gives the reconstructed image. In the adaptive setting, this reconstruction is used for each adaptive step. It should be noted here that the algorithm chosen for this reconstruction is based on the application to highly periodic high-resolution images (Stevens et al. 2014). However, similar algorithms could be chosen for other applications, such as in-situ microscopy (Mehdi et al. 2019).

A summary of these simulations is shown in Figure 10.9, which provides us with an intuitive understanding of how exactly the sub-sampling approach helps to improve low-dose imaging. In the comparison between the jittered sampling and full low-dose sampling, the sensitivity and resolution is essentially the same. This means that however the random application of the dose is applied (either by picking the pixels or lowering the dose uniformly), the images are the same quality. However, sub-sampling does provide a significant increase in image acquisition speed. Accompanied by this increase of speed, the system also generates less data, so the data transfer and storage involved with imaging is also reduced by an order of magnitude. The adaptive sampling approach has all the speed and data transfer/storage advantages of the sub-sampling approach but can also improve the resolution. The reason for this is that the sub-sampled dose can be used initially to recover a lower resolution image, and then this image can be used to sample pixels in a second sub-sampled scan to provide more of the missing information (i.e., by estimating the atomic column locations). By adapting to the structure being imaged, the dose can be lowered significantly for the same resolution, or the resolution can be extended for the same dose. The reconstructed images show the same traits in terms of resolution. As dose decreases, it is harder to resolve the atomic dumbbells and to obtain the correct contrast. The exception to this appears to be the case of the adaptive sensing. In this case, the basic adaptive approach adopted, i.e., sampling more in the areas of the highest intensity, causes a higher Z-contrast than expected. Combining crystallographic information in the reconstruction in the future would help rectify this issue. Crystallographic image processing was not used here to maintain the simplicity of the reconstruction approach (i.e., Fourier peak-finding).

The results shown so far do not take into account the effect of the line-hopping scan. The effect of sub-sampling and inpainting a line-hop acquisition is shown in Figure 10.10. As stated above, the line-hopping approach is a mechanism to approach the random sub-sampling without exceeding the hysteresis limits of the electromagnetic scan coils of the STEM used to acquire the images. This hysteresis limit means that it is not possible in most (if not all) commercial systems to randomly jump to any point in the image. Instead, the scan moves uniformly in the x direction while randomly moving over a defined pixel range randomly in the y-direction (for example, to get 10% scanning the beam can move randomly −1,0,+1 pixels over a 10-pixel range). As can be seen in Figure 10.10, the sub-sampling approach again produces an equivalent sampling to the low-dose method. Importantly, however, the image shows a "missing wedge" of data in the Fourier transform caused by the inability to sample completely randomly in the y-direction. This constrained

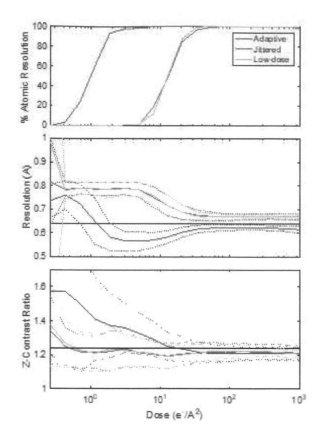

FIGURE 10.9

The plots show quantitative metrics from 200 simulations at each dose comparing the three-dose fractioning methods. The first row shows a phase transition for obtaining atomic resolution – this is the probability that the dumbbells in the reconstructed image pass the Rayleigh criterion. The middle and bottom rows show the mean (solid) plus/minus 1 standard deviation (dotted) for resolution and contrast, and the simulated metric is solid black. A trough can be seen on the Adaptive sampling resolution curve, which occurs because the method adapts so strongly to the peaks that it is super resolving the image. It can also be seen that this superresolution effect also changes the contrast since it prefers taller peaks[40].

y-movement limits the resolution in this case since the pixel size (i.e., random movement) is the same order of magnitude as the structural feature being imaged (it is not possible to increase the magnification to decrease pixel size, or oversample the atom locations as both would increase the dose beyond stability conditions). These results demonstrate that the sub-sampling method can have a significant effect on the reconstruction of the result. Ideally, a fast electrostatic scan generator for a microscope would permit scanning any pixel location and quickly adapting the scan with negligible hysteresis.

10.6   Application to In-Situ Imaging

The recent development of in-situ liquid stages for high-resolution (scanning) transmission electron microscopes (STEM) has provided a direct means to observe nucleation and growth phenomena in materials under various driving forces (Woehl et al. 2012;

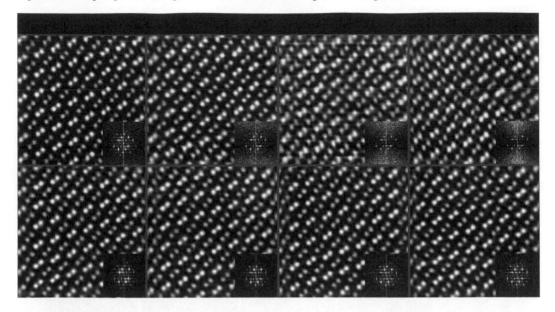

FIGURE 10.10
Reconstruction of real acquisitions of NiTi showing agreement with the low-dose vs. sub-sampling simulations for ZnSe. The Fourier magnitude of the acquisition is inset. The top row images are subsampled using the line-hop method at 50%, 25%, 12.5%, 6.25% with a pixel dwell time of 60 μs. The bottom row images are sampled at 100% with pixel dwell times of 30, 15, 7.5, and 3.75 μs.

Woehl et al. 2014; Evans et al. 2011). For example, in the studies of silver (Ag) metal nanoparticles nucleating in aqueous solution by Woehl et al. 2012, 2014 it was found that individual nanoparticles follow an Ostwald ripening mechanism consistent with classical nucleation theory. However, as growth continues, the particle size distribution is dominated by a Smoluchowski agglomeration mechanism. Further work in this area by Welch et al. 2016, identified that particles going beyond agglomeration to coalesce are dominated by an oriented attachment effect where the effect of the solvent shield around the nanoparticles promotes tip-to-tip attachment. In these studies (and all observations using *in-situ* liquid cells generated by the TEM community so far), the resolution of the images that have been obtained has been limited by the effect of the electron beam changing the local chemistry of the solution. While nucleation and growth are typically triggered by the electron beam, if the electron dose is too high, then the liquid breaks down forming radicals and eventually extensive gas bubbles (Grogan et al. 2014). To increase the spatial and temporal resolution of these *in-situ* observations in the liquid stage, it is therefore imperative to use imaging methodologies that extract the most information from the least amount of electron dose put into the cell.

To investigate how optimal-sampling also affects in-situ imaging, a 0.1 mM AgNO$_3$ solution was prepared following the recipe of Woehl et al. 2012, and illuminated with a wide range of electron doses and sub-sampling rates to induce nucleation and growth. Figure 10.11 shows frames from the reconstructed videos (videos are included in the supplementary information as is a full description of the subsampling and inpainting process) at 100%, 25%, 12%, and 3% of the pixels acquired. The electron beam current remains constant across each sampling-level, meaning that the electron dose in each acquisition is scaled down by the degree of sub-sampling from the full sampled image dose. As can be seen from the raw acquisitions, the reduction in dose significantly changes the rate of growth. Moreover,

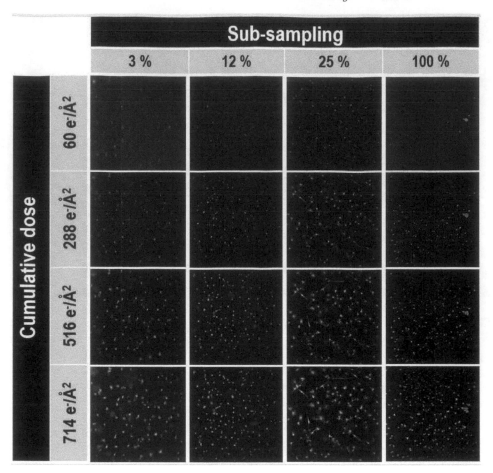

FIGURE 10.11
A set of sub-sampled images taken from different cumulative doses (i.e., time stamps) in the *in-situ* nucleation and growth of Ag nanoparticles. For each of the images, the cumulative dose is controlled by both the magnification, scan speed and sub-sampling of the images.

there are 3 distinct structural forms of the precipitates that exist in these experiments – each for is clearly visible in the video frames (Figure 10.12). The first type of shape visible in the images is a uniform almost spherical or facetted square structure, which has uniform contrast across the majority of the nanoparticle – which we term as a "regular" particle here. As we are using Z-contrast imaging to form the image, this means that this type of nanoparticle must have uniform thickness, and it is likely that these nanoparticles are as thick as they are wide. The second type of nanoparticle observed is one that is larger than the first in terms of area but has much less contrast in the image indicating that it is a flat structure or "raft". The third and final type of particle is a thin needle-looking structure that has a very high intensity compared to the others, which we term as a "pillar". The pillars and rafts both appear to be 2-D in nature but grow at 90 degrees to each other.

From the segmentation of the images shown in Figure 10.12, we can track the nucleation and growth of the 3 types of particles as a function of the sampling. All particles are found to fit to a Finke-Watzky model for nucleation and growth (Finney et al. 2009). The regular particles appear to show similar nucleation and growth rates for each sampling-level, indicating that the conditions for the formation of these particles (i.e., both the nucleation

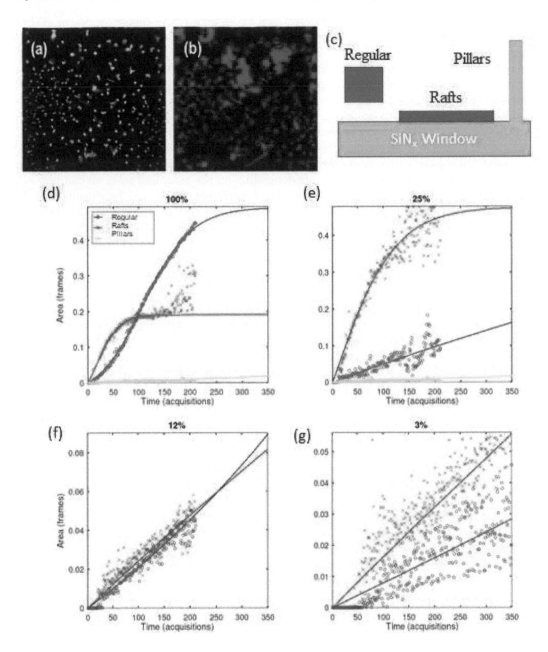

FIGURE 10.12
(a) The reconstructed image can be segmented (b) to track the development of the 3 types of nanoparticles unambiguously identified from the mass-thickness contrast in the Z-contrast image as regular, raft, and pillar. (c) Analysis of the nucleation and growth rate for the 3 nanoparticle types using the F-W model in Equation 10.1 (A full description of the segmentation and tracking process is given in the supplementary information) for (d) 100% sampling (e) 25% sampling, (f) 12% sampling, and (g) 100% sampling. For the lower doses, the particles are still growing at the end of the experiment, whereas for the higher sampling the particles are constant by the end of the experiment. There is a clear separation between the modes for higher sampling rates that reduces significantly for the lower sampling rates.

energy-barrier and the Ag-ion flux) are relatively constant across each experiment. While there is no difference in the incubation time of the raft structures (which nucleate almost immediately), the growth rate for raft structures is faster at higher sampling-levels. This suggests that the nucleation barrier is similar for each experiment, but that there is a larger flux of Ag ions for the growth of these raft structures in the highly-sampled experiments. The dendrites also have an incubation time that scales with the sampling rate, but in this case, they are only seen to occur for the highest levels of sampling (both 100% and 25%) and appear to grow after and between the rafts.

Given that we have unambiguously identified 3 different nanoparticle structures that are nucleated during the experiment, and that the fit to the F-W model shows that each one has different nucleation/growth constants depending on the sampling rate, we can now ask the question as to what is it about the *in-situ* experiment that could be causing this. In this regard, a recent paper by Jiang 2017, showed that when the high energy electron beam passes through an insulator such as the SiN_x window, it can create secondary electrons, which in turn creates an electric field at the surface of that insulator. For the in-situ cell, of course, one of the surfaces of the insulating window is the interface between the window and the nominally conducting aqueous solution, and the presence of a field at this interface should change the distribution of the charged ions in solution. An example of the type of field created in the region of the STEM probe is shown in Figure 10.13, where an increased gradient of the electric field is formed at both the upper and lower SiN_x windows of the *in-situ* liquid STEM cell. In any real microscopy experiment, the upper window would experience more primary electrons, making the field higher than at the bottom window. We can estimate what effect this has on the ions that are created in the reaction solution using the Nernst-Planck equation, with the results shown in Figure 10.13.

Figure 10.13 shows a COMSOL finite element simulations of the distribution of ions in solution under different illumination conditions. While it is very difficult to calculate exactly how many secondary electrons are produced in each experiment, and the cross-section for radiolysis is not known, we can model the effects of a high beam dose concentration vs low beam dose concentration and high initial solution concentration vs low initial solution concentration to understand the differences in these *in-situ* experiments. The results show that at a given concentration of the $AgNO_3$ solution, the effect of the electron beam always causes an increase in the concentration of the reactants directly in the window area. As the field depends on the integrated dose, the only way to reduce this effect is to minimize the spatio-temporal distribution of the dose. This has an additional effect on the reaction process by reducing the number of Ag ions that are released from solution – the creation of Ag ions is also a function of the beam dose concentration. For controlled formation of nanoparticles, we can see that the low dose concentration regime of the sub-sampling has multiple benefits.

Having established that the liquid-window interface is important during these *in-situ* experiments, we can now interpret our observations of the formation of regular, raft, and pillar structures in terms of the presence of this interface. For the regular particles, the fact that they have an incubation time longer than the rafts and are essentially unchanged in growth rate with sampling, strongly suggests that these are particles nucleated outside of the increased concentration zone around the window shown in Figure 10.13 and are homogeneously nucleated. Since the raft structures nucleate first, appear to be 2-D in nature, and have a growth rate that is proportional to the sampling, it can be concluded that these particles arise from heterogeneous nucleation on the windows. When the sub-sampling reaches a high enough level, the doping of the interface is such that it is energetically more favorable for the Ag atoms to form a raft than it is for them to form homogeneous particles. Such an effect would be consistent with classical nucleation theory where the interaction with the support decreases the surface energy and promotes more rapid growth of 2-D structures

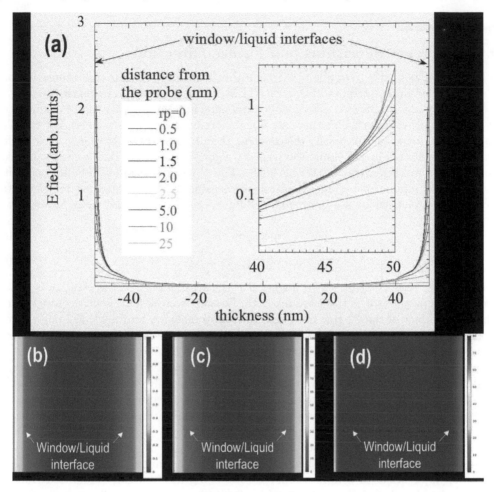

FIGURE 10.13

(a) Simulations of the electric field increase at the windows caused by illumination by the electron beam. The amount of increase is directly related to dose (dose rate) – the higher the electron dose (dose rate) the larger the build-up of secondary electrons, and the larger the field. COMSOL finite element simulation for the increase in concentration at the interface for (b) a low field (0.2V) and low starting concentration (0.1M), (c) a low field (0.2V) and high starting concentration (10M) and (d) a high field (2V) and higher starting concentration (1M). In all cases, the effect of the field is to increase the concentration of reactants at the windows.

rather than 3-D structures. In the case of the pillars, they only form towards the end of the most highly-sampled experiments. Obviously, in the case of the fully-sampled acquisition, there is a high super-saturation of reactants in the vicinity of a very high electric field at the liquid-window interface. Under these circumstances, the precipitation and a "dendritic growth" mechanism are not surprising and are completely consistent with the pillar growth that is observed here.

10.7   Current Algorithms and Future Directions

We have so far not talked yet about the algorithms that are used for the reconstruction of the sub-sampled images acquired from the STEM, as our goal was to demonstrate what the use of recovery algorithms means for low-dose imaging in STEM rather than to demonstrate how to do the process (for which there are many more publications available). For completeness, however, here we will briefly discuss how the process works for the images we have shown. As a first step in discussing the recovery algorithms, we will define the image acquisition problem mathematically (Stevens 2018). The 4 major categories of image acquisition are Direct-, Computational-, and Compressive-Sensing, and Subsampling for Inpainting. Figure 10.14 depicts each case mathematically and visually, and all 4 cases have the basic form

$$y = Hx + e \qquad\qquad (10.5)$$

$$y_i = \sum_j H_{ij} x_j + e_i \qquad\qquad (10.6)$$

where x is the vectorized (flattened) image, H is the sensing matrix, the e-vector is additive noise/error, and y-vector is the acquired data. In other words, first, each acquired pixel y_i is the dot product of the ith row of H and the entire image x, and next, the noise/error is added. There are sensing strategies that consider other noise forms, such as Poisson noise, but these follow a similar approach to the case we discuss here. In the case of direct-sensing, each pixel is acquired individually and with the same intensity, this means that the sensing matrix H is the identity matrix. All that remains in this setting is to remove the noise (i.e., image denoising) if it cannot be tolerated. Written mathematically, direct sensing reveals itself to be inefficient, since we have so many zeros being multiplied. If the zeros elements could be for sensing we could boost the signal to noise ratio (if e is readout noise) and/by acquiring multiple pixels simultaneously.

Parallel acquisition is exactly the approach taken in computational-sensing, with one of the first applications of computational-sensing being the (optical) Hadamard transform spectrometer (Harwit and Sloane 1979). Using 2 slits in succession for direct-sensing, greatly reduced the amount of light at the detector and made scanning all the energy levels very time-consuming. By using a full matrix for H rather than the identity, the spectrometer was able to keep the number of photons at the detector high and collect multiple energy levels simultaneously. The catch is that now the image x must be recovered. The main assumption in direct sensing is that the H matrix is full-rank, so finding the solution is straightforward and by using techniques such as penalized least-squares regression the image can be denoised and recovered simultaneously.

Computational sensing (CS) can give a dramatic increase in efficiency compared to direct sensing, but how can maximum efficiency be achieved? This is where CS enters. The (mathematical) theory of CS seeks to categorize sensing matrices by the probability that the original data can be recovered. The parameter that is optimized is the number of rows in H, the sensing matrix. To contrast, computational- and direct-sensing have the same number of measurements as pixels, while CS has fewer measurements than pixels. This means that, without any constraints on the image, there will be an infinite number of solutions. A typical constraint is that x is sparse (there are many other possible restrictions). At face value, forcing x to be sparse is a problem since many interesting images are not sparse. Sparsity is not limiting though, since images can be transformed into a sparse representation (as can almost all interesting data). By inserting this "sparsifying transform" D into the sensing

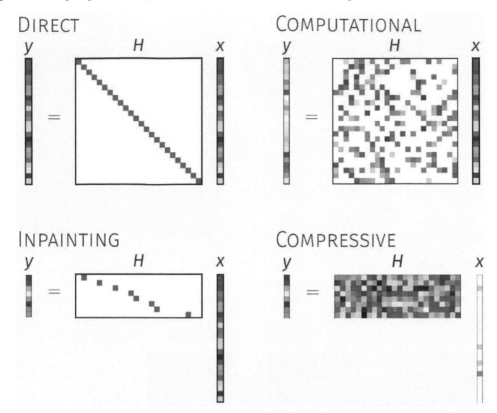

FIGURE 10.14

Schematic illustrations of the mathematics of sensing. Direct-sensing uses an identity matrix, which is fast and simple, but it can be inefficient. Computational-sensing uses parallel acquisition (multiple pixels simultaneously) to increase efficiency and robustness to noise, but the cost is that now x must be solved for (this is simple since there is a measurement for each pixel, i.e. H is full rank). Compressive-sensing (CS) takes another step toward maximum efficiency, by acquiring fewer measurements than pixels. CS has a much higher computational cost and assumptions, such as sparsity, must be placed on the data. Inpainting, the approach discussed in this chapter, takes a different step towards efficiency by directly sensing a subset of the pixels (sub-sampling). The assumption made in inpainting is that the subset of acquired data contains enough information to recover missing neighbor pixels.

equation, we have:

$$y = HDw + e$$
$$y = Gw + e \tag{10.7}$$

where the image $x = Dw$, and D have been combined (i.e., multiplied) with H to form a new sensing matrix G, which recovers the original form of the sensing equation. Common sparsifying transforms include Fourier, Wavelet, and learned (data-driven) dictionary transforms. The addition of the sparsifying transform is depicted in Figure 10.15.

In order to obtain the image x from compressively sensed data, w must first be recovered. This is a difficult problem since w must be sparse and H is low rank. Testing all possible combinations of zeros for w is infeasible even in small problems. One approach to solve the

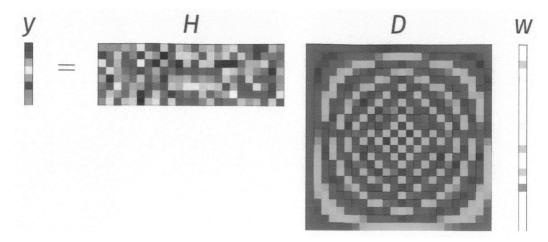

FIGURE 10.15
An illustration of CS with a sparsifying transform D and sparse representation w. When the image x is not sparse it can be replaced by Dw, this ensures that the CS problem meets the sparsity requirement.

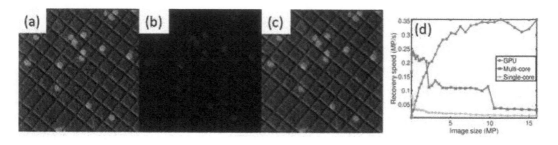

FIGURE 10.16
An inpainting example and recovery speed results using STEM data with the Fourier-l1 method. (a) Original; (b) 33% Subsampled; (c) Reconstruction; and (d) Plot of recovery speed in Millions of pixels (MP) per second versus image size. The image shown in (c) was resized to produce images with sizes between 128 × 128 and 4096 × 4096 pixels. The test was performed using a random 25% of the pixels on a laptop with a Nvidia Quadro P2000 Mobile GPU and a 12-core Intel i9-8950HK CPU

problem in a reasonable amount of time is to use approximate sparsity as a proxy. Instead of enforcing that there are exact zeros in w, the sum of the absolute values of the elements of w must be small. This approach, l1-regularized regression, can be formulated a few different ways, but the most famous is due to Tibshirani 1996. The algorithm is called lasso and it minimizes the following objective:

$$\min \sum_i \left(y_i - \sum_j H_{ij} x_i \right)^2 \quad \text{subject to} \quad \sum_i |x_i| < \tau \qquad (10.8)$$

where τ is a threshold that affects sparsity and noise removal. This simply says we want the x that most accurately matches the data with the given sensing matrix, and x should also have an absolute value less than τ. Optimizing the lasso objective is an iterative process with each iteration (minimally) solving the simple least-squares problem.

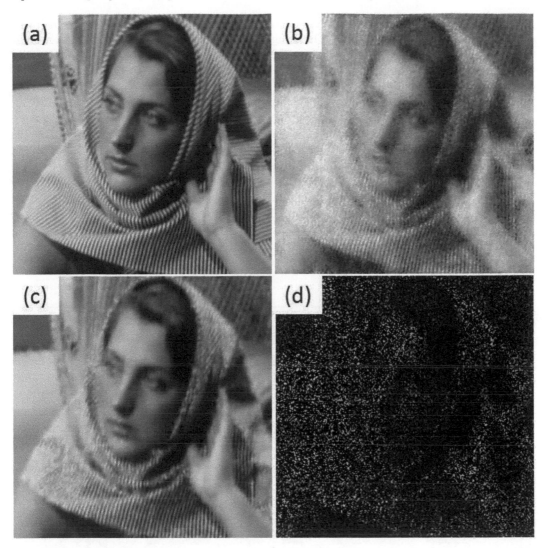

FIGURE 10.17

A comparison of Bayesian factor analysis and Fourier-l1 for inpainting the 256×256 Barbara image from 20% of the pixels. (a) Original; (b) Fourier-l1 reconstruction; (c) Bayesian factor analysis reconstruction; and (d) subsampled image. The Fourier-l1 reconstruction can be computed in 1 second, but the quality is low, even though the image is recognizable. The factor analysis reconstruction is relatively higher quality, but this method takes about 2 minutes to reconstruct this (tiny) image (the algorithm scales quadratically in the number of pixels, so a 512×512 can take up to 30 minutes).

Another approach to increasing efficiency during acquisition is to subsample the pixels—the approach that has been exemplified in the previous sections of this chapter. This leads to the inpainting problem, which is to paint the missing pixels. Mathematically this is direct sensing, but a large portion of the data is skipped. The missing data can be inpainted because it is missing at random locations not correlated with the image data, and the image has high spatial correlation (both nearby and long-range patterns can be used as templates for missing pixels). The lasso algorithm can be used for inpainting with a slight modification to include the Fourier transform.. This Fourier-l1 approach works very well for images with periodic structures and can be used when speed is more important than quality. The image recovery speed is shown in Figure 10.16 using a STEM image of latex beads across a range of image sizes and in 3 computing regimes (single-core, multi-core, and GPU).

Another algorithm for image inpainting is dictionary learning. Dictionary learning attempts to simultaneously learn a dictionary (i.e., sparsifying transform) and the sparse representation. The dictionary can be thought of as a summary of different patterns/textures in the image, and the sparse representation encodes how the patterns are combined to build the image. Algorithms for dictionary learning typically alternate between optimizing the dictionary and the "sparse codes". Some algorithms use the lasso during the sparse coding step. Most dictionary learning algorithms depend on having all of the pixels, so they typically train on similar datasets, then use the learned dictionary with an algorithm like the lasso for inpainting. This is impractical in STEM where data collection is expensive, and dose issues prevent acquisition of full images. Bayesian Factor Analysis (Stevens 2018; Zhou et al. 2011) solves this by allowing simultaneous dictionary learning and inpainting (and CS recovery). A comparison of Bayesian factor analysis and the Fourier-L1 method are shown in Figure 10.17.

10.8   Conclusions

The results discussed in this chapter demonstrate that it is possible to use a physical understanding of the mechanism by which an electron microscope forms an image to determine an optimal approach to forming the most efficient image. By moving beyond hardware only defined solutions for imaging beam sensitive samples and employing CS/inpainting/ML methods to reconstruct images that are sub-sampled, we can increase the spatial and temporal resolution of images. This approach opens up a wide range of materials and dynamic processes that can now be studied by electron microscopy. As the analysis so far has only

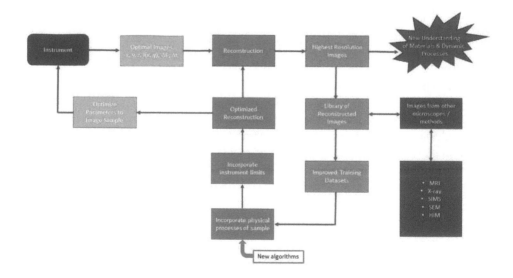

FIGURE 10.18
The physics of beam interactions can be incorporated into sampling strategies for many experimental methods, optimizing the use of each method individually and enhancing the scientific information obtained from the methods used together to solve materials challenges.

focused on employing these AI methods to the analysis of single images and sets of images from a single sample, there is potential to extend the resolution limits for imaging even further in the future as more images of different samples are included in the training data set. In addition to increasing the efficiency of the algorithms for the analysis of particular image/scattering processes in electron microscopy, we can develop an overall workflow that will improve imaging capabilities across multiple techniques. Figure 10.18 shows how the incorporation of different imaging methods into the workflow can bring multi-scale, hyperspectral measurements into the training datasets, and these complete analyses can then be used to improve the resolution of wide-ranging expensive, difficult to use and over-subscribed scientific instrumentation that is the bedrock of the development of new advanced materials.

Acknowledgment

The application of the CS methods to the STEM images was supported by the Chemical Imaging, Signature Discovery and Analytics in Motion Laboratory Directed Research and Development (LDRD) Initiatives at PNNL. PNNL is a multi-program national laboratory operated by Battelle for the US Department of Energy (DOE) under Contract DE-AC05-76RL01830. A portion of the research was performed using the Environmental Molecular Sciences Laboratory (EMSL), a national scientific user facility sponsored by the Department of Energy's Office of Biological and Environmental Research and located at PNNL. The initial development of these methods for the liquid stage and the nucleation and growth experiments were supported by the Department of Energy, Office of Science, Basic Energy Sciences under grant number DE-FG02-03ER46057 and by the PNNL LDRD program. The electrochemistry experiments were initially supported by the Joint Center for Energy Storage Research (JCESR), an Energy Innovation Hub funded by the Department of Energy, Office of Science, Basic Energy Sciences, and more recently by the UK Faraday Institution (EP/S003053/1) project FIRG013 "characterization".

Bibliography

[1] Anderson, H. S., J. Ilic-Helms, B. Rohrer, J. Wheeler, and K. Larson. 2013. Sparse Imaging for fast electron microscopy. In *IS&T/SPIE Electronic Imaging*, ed. C.A. Bouman, I. Pollak, and P.J. Wolfe, SPIE.

[2] Batson P. E., N. Dellby, and O. L. Krivanek. 2002. Sub-angstrom resolution using aberration corrected electron optics. *Nature* 418: 617–620.

[3] Batson, P. E. 1993. Simultaneous STEM imaging and electron-energy-loss spectroscopy with atomic-column sensitivity. *Nature* 366: 727–728.

[4] Béché, A., B. Goris, B. Freitag, and J. Verbeeck. 2016. Development of a fast electromagnetic beam blanker for compressed sensing in STEM. *Applied Physics Letters* 108: 093103.

[5] Biswas, K., J. Q. He, I. D. Blum, C. I. Wu, T. P. HoganD. N. Seidman, V. P. Dravid, and M. G. Kanatzidis. 2012. High performance bulk thermoelectrics with all-sacle hierarchical architectures. *Nature* 489: 414–418.

[6] Browning, N. D., M. F. Chisholm, and S. J. Pennycook. 1993. Atomic resolution chemical analysis using a STEM. *Nature* 366: 143–146.

[7] de Jonge N. and F. M. Ross. 2011. Electron microscopy of specimens in liquid. *Nature Nanotechnology* 6: 695–704.

[8] de Jonge N., D. B. Peckys, G. J. Kremers, and D. W. Piston. 2009. Electron microscopy of whole cells in liquid with nanometer resolution. *Proceedings of the National Academy of Sciences of the United States of America* 106: 2159–2164.

[9] Dwyer, C., S. D. Findlay, and L. J. Allen. 2008. Multiple elastic scattering of core-loss electrons in atomic resolution imaging. *Physical Review B* 77: 184107.

[10] Egerton, R. F. 2013. Control of radiation damage in TEM. *Ultramicroscopy* 127: 100–108.

[11] Egerton, R. F., P. Li, and M. Malac. 2004. Radiation damage in the TEM and SEM. *Micron* 35: 399–409.

[12] Erni R., M. D. Rossell, C. Kisielowski, and U. Dahmen. 2009. Atomic-resolution imaging with a sub-50-pm electron probe. *Physical Review Letters* 102: 096101.

[13] Evans J. E., K. L. Jungjohann, N. D. Browning, and I. Arslan. 2011. Controlled growth of nanoparticles from solution with in situ liquid transmission electron microscopy. *Nano Letters* 11: 2809–2813.

[14] Findlay S. D., N. Shibata, H. Sawada, E. Okunishi, Y. Kondo, and Y. Ikuhara. 2010. Dynamics of annular bright field imaging in scanning transmission electron microscopy. *Ultramicroscopy* 110: 903–923.

[15] Finney, E. E. and R. G. Finke. 2009. Fitting and interpreting transition-metal nanocluster formation and other sigmoidal-appearing kinetic data: A more thorough testing of dispersive kinetic vs chemical-mechanism-based equations and treatments for 4-step type kinetic data. *Chemistry of Materials* 21: 4692–4705.

[16] Goodenough, J. B. and Y. Kim. 2010. Challenges for rechargeable Li batteries. *Chemistry of Materials* 22: 587-603.

[17] Grogan, J. M., N. M. Schneider, F. M. Ross, and H. H. Bau. 2014. Bubble and pattern formation in liquid induced by an electron beam. *Nano Letters* 14: 359–364.

[18] Gu, H. G. Li, C. Liu, F. Yuan, F. Han, L. Zhang, and S. Wu. 2017. Considerable knock-on displacement of metal atoms under a low energy electron beam. *Scientific Reports* 7: 184.

[19] Haider M., S. Uhlemann, E. Schwan, H. Rose, B. Kabius, and K. Urban. 1998. Electron microscopy image enhanced. *Nature* 392: 768–769.

[20] Harwit M. and N. J. Sloane. 1979. *Hadamard Transform Optics*. Academic Press.

[21] Ishikawa R., E. Okunishi, H. Sawada, Y. Kondo, F. Hosokawa, and E. Abe. 2011. Direct imaging of hydrogen-atom columns in a crystal by annular bright-field electron microscopy. *Nature Materials* 10: 278–281.

[22] Jesson D. E., S. J. Pennycook, J. M. Baribeau, and D. C. Houghton. 1993. Direct imaging of surface cusp evolution during strained-layer epitaxy and implications for strain relaxation. *Physical Review Letters* 71: 1744–1747.

[23] Jiang, N. 2017. Note on in situ (scanning) transmission electron microscopy study of liquid samples. *Ultramicroscopy* 179: 81–83.

[24] Joy, D. C., A. D. Romig. Jr., and J.I. Goldstein. 1986. *Principles of Analytical Electron Microscopy.* Springer.

[25] Kimoto K., T. Asaka, T. Nagai, M. Saito, Y. Matsui, and K. Ishizuka K. 2007. Element-selective imaging of atomic columns in a crystal using STEM and EELS. *Nature* 450: 702–704.

[26] Koch, C. T. 2002. PhD Thesis Determination of core structure periodicity and point defect density along dislocations. PhD thesis, Arizona State University.

[27] Kovarik L., A. Stevens, A. Liyu, and N. D. Browning. 2016. Implementing an accurate and rapid sparse sampling approach for low-dose atomic resolution STEM imaging of electron beam sensitive materials. *Applied Physics Letters* 109: 164102.

[28] LeBeau, J. M., S. D. Findlay, L. J. Allen, and S. Stemmer. 2008. Quantitative atomic resolution STEM. *Physical Review Letters* 100: 206101.

[29] LeBeau, J. M., S. D. Findlay, X. Q. Wang, A. J. Jacobson, L. J. Allen, and S. Stemmer. 2009. High angle scattering of fast electrons from crystals containing heavy elements: Simulation and experiment. *Physical Review B* 79: 214110.

[30] Lee, M. M., J. Teuscher, T. Miyasaka, T. N. Murakami, and H. J. Snaith. 2012. Efficient hybrid solar cells based on meso-superstructured organometal halide perovskites. *Science* 338: 643–647.

[31] Mehdi B. L., Stevens A., Kovarik L., Jiang, N., Mehta, H., Liyu, A., Reehl, S., Stanfill, B., Luzzi, L., MacPhee, K., Bramer, L., and Brownming, N. D. 2019. Controlling and observing the kinetics of nucleation and growth by sub-sampling and inpainting dynamic *in-situ* STEM images. *Applied Physics Letters* 115, 063102.

[32] Melzer, D., G. Mestl, K. Wanninger, Y. Y. Zhu, N. D. Browning, M. Sanchez-Sanchez, and J. A. Lercher. 2019. Design and synthesis of highly active MoVTeNb-oxides for ethane oxidative dehydrogenation. *Nature Communications* 10: 4012.

[33] Muecke-Herzberg, D., P. Abellan, M. Sarahan, I. Godfrey, Z. Zaghi, J. Ma, R. Leary, A. Stevens, P. A. Midgley, N. D. Browning, and Q. M. Ramasse. 2016. Practical implementation of compressive sensing for high resolution STEM. *Microsc. Microanal.* 22:558–559.

[34] Muller D. A., L. F. Kourkoutis, M. Murfitt, J. H. Song, H. Y. Hwang, J. Silcox, N. Dellby, and O. L. Krivanek. 2008. Atomic-scale chemical imaging of composition and bonding by aberration-corrected microscopy. *Science* 319: 1073–1076.

[35] Muller, D. A., Y. Tzou, R. Ray, and J. Silcox. 1993. Mapping SP2 and SP3 states of carbon at subnanometer spatial resolution. *Nature* 366: 725–727.

[36] Nastasi, N., J. W. Mayer, and J. K. Hirvonen. 1996. *Ion-solid Interactions: Fundamentals and Applications.* Cambridge University Press.

[37] Nellist P. D. and S. J. Pennycook. 1999. Incoherent imaging using dynamically scattered coherent electrons. *Ultramicroscopy* 78: 111–124.

[38] Nicholls, D., J. Lee, H. Amari, A. Stevens, B. L. Mehdi, and N. D. Browning. 2020. Minimising damage in high resolution STEM images of nanoscale structures and processes. *Nanoscale* 12: 21248–21254.

[39] Oxley, M. P., M. Varela, T. J. Pennycook, K. van Benthem, S. D. Findlay, A. J. D'Alfonso, L. J. Allen, and S. J. Pennycook. 2007. Interpreting atomic resolution spectroscopic images. *Physical Review B* 76: 064303.

[40] Pennycook S. J. and L. A. Boatner. 1988. Chemically sensitive structure-imaging with a scanning-transmission electron-microscope. *Nature* 336: 565–567.

[41] Pennycook, S. J. and P. D. Nellist. 2011. *Scanning Transmission Electron Microscopy – Imaging and Analysis.* Springer.

[42] Stevens A., H. Yang, L. Carin, I. Arslan, and N. D. Browning. 2013. The potential for Bayesian compressive sensing to significantly reduce electron dose in high-resolution STEM images. *Microscopy* 63: 41–51.

[43] Stevens A., H. Yang, L. Luzzi, L. Kovarik, B. L. Mehdi, A. Liyu, M. E. Gehm, and N. D. Browning. 2018. Sub-sampled approaches for extremely low-dose scanning transmission electron microscopy. *Applied Physics Letters* 112: 043104.

[44] Stevens, A. 2018. Compressive sensing in transmission electron microscopy. PhD thesis, Duke University.

[45] Tibishrani, R. 1996. Regression Shrinkage and selection via the lasso. *Journal of Royal Statistical Society Series B (Methodological)* 58: 267–288.

[46] Welch, D. A., T. J. Woehl, C. Park, R. Faller, J. E. Evans, and N. D. Browning. 2016. Understanding the role of solvation forces on the preferential attachment of nanoparticles in liquid. *ACS Nano* 10: 181–187.

[47] Williams D. B. and C. B. Carter. 2009. *Transmission Electron Microscopy*, 2nd ed. Springer.

[48] Woehl T. J., C. Park, J. E. Evans, I. Arslan, W. D. Ristenpart, and N. D. Browning. 2014. Direct observation of aggregative nanoparticle growth: Kinetic modeling of the size distribution and growth rate. *Nano Letters* 14: 373–378.

[49] Woehl T. J., J. E. Evans, I. Arslan, W. D. Ristenpart, and N. D. Browning. 2012. Direct in situ determination of the mechanisms controlling nanoparticle nucleation and growth. *ACS Nano* 6: 8599–8610.

[50] Wynblatt, P. 1968. Calculation of the vacancy migration energy in cubic crystals. *Journal of Physics and Chemistry of Solids* 29: 215–224.

[51] Yang H., H. S. Lee, P. G. Kotula, Y. Sato, Y. Ikuhara, and N. D. Browning. 2015. Amphoteric doping of praseodymium Pr^{3+} in $SrTiO_3$ grain boundaries. *Applied Physics Letters* 106: 121904.

[52] Yu, Z. H., D. A. Muller, and J. Silcox. 2004. Study of strain fields at a a-Si/SiC interface. *Journal of Applied Physics* 95: 3362–3371.

[53] Zhou, M., H. Chen, J. Paisley, L. Ren, L. Li, Z. Xing, and L. Carin. 2012. Nonparametric Bayesian dictionary learning for analysis of noisy and incomplete images. *IEEE Transactions on Image Processing* 21: 130–144.

[54] Zhou, M., H. Chen, J. Paisley, L. Ren, L. Li, Z. Xing, and L. Carin. 2011. Nonparametric Bayesian dictionary learning for analysis of noisy and incomplete images. *IEEE Transactions on Image Processing* 21: 130–144.

11

FUNNL: Fast Nonlinear Nonnegative Unmixing for Alternate Energy Systems

Jeffrey A. Graves, Thomas F. Blum, Piyush Sao, Miaofang Chi, and Ramakrishnan Kannan

CONTENTS

11.1 Introduction

Palladium is an important catalyst useful for the conversion of carbon monoxide to methane, a critical step in the process of alternative fuel production. Palladium is also used as a catalyst in automotive catalytic converters and fuel cells. The effectiveness of palladium and other catalysts is strongly dependent upon the conditions at their surface [1,22,38]. Electron energy loss spectrum (EELS) scanning is a helpful technique that allows scientists to analyze the chemical interactions on a nanometer scale and map chemical distributions, as well as other sub-nanometer phenomena, which is useful for uncovering knowledge about the conditions at the catalyst surface. Carbon is a common support layer used in catalytic reactions and electron microscopy samples, and the carbon EELS signal (the K-edge) overlaps

DOI: 10.1201/9781003143376-11

with the palladium signal (the M_4,5-edge). These overlapping signals along with nonlinear interactions between the atomic elements can make interpreting EELS images challenging.

Spectral unmixing is a general image analysis technique that has been applied to a wide range of spectral images, both in terms of spatial and spectral resolution, as well as across many different domains [28]. Unmixing has been used to help identify and characterize complex biological mechanisms at the cellular level [39,57] and aid in karyotyping analysis of chromosomes within cells [42] using images obtained with fluorescence microscopy. In an effort to develop more cost-effective ways of monitoring coral reef health, unmixing has been applied to satellite imagery to estimate the distribution of coral reef substrates (living corals, dead corals, bleached corals, and forms of algae) [23]. At its core, unmixing is the problem of decomposing the pixels of a spectral image into their constituent spectra (*endmembers*), along with their corresponding proportions (*abundances*) within each pixel. Spectral unmixing remains a challenging problem because individual pixels within a spectral image can be composed of multiple endmembers, as is common in low spacial resolution imagery (e.g., satellite imagery). This problem can not be solved by simply increasing the spatial resolution because the constitute enmembers may reside as part of a homogenous mixture or be physically overlapping.

Unlike the pixels in the more familiar digital images, which consist of a few channels (e.g., RGB – red, green, blue), the pixels in spectral images consist of many channels. In the case of satellite imagery, these channels often represent narrow bands across the electromagnetic spectrum. In EELS imagery, the channels represent electron energy loss with their values being counts of electrons. While the endmembers obtained from unmixing represent the basic components of the image, their interpretation is highly dependent upon the domain the technique is being applied to. For instance, given a hyperspectral image (HSI) obtained from airborne or spaceborne remote sensors, the endmembers obtained from unmixing may represent different parts of land cover, such as mountains, rivers, forests, and croplands [3,4, 41]. For the EELS data obtained from a scanning transmission electron microscope (STEM) used as part of our case study, the endmembers represent atomic elements (i.e., palladium and carbon).

In recent years there has been a growing interest in using data mining and machine learning techniques for unmixing. One of the defacto techniques for performing data-mining-based unmixing is to cast the spectral data as a matrix to obtain the endmembers and abundance maps from non-negative matrix factorization (NMF) [28]. For example, as shown in Figure 11.1, a spectral image of width w and height h having $p = w \cdot h$ pixels and c spectral channels can be represented as $\mathbf{A} \in \mathbb{R}_+^{c \times p}$ matrix. Assuming the presence of k endmembers, the non-negative factor matrices $\mathbf{W} \in \mathbb{R}_+^{c \times k}$ and $\mathbf{H} \in \mathbb{R}_+^{p \times k}$ from NMF can be interpreted as endmembers and abundance map, respectively. The notations used in this chapter are introduced in Table 11.1. Typically, the number of spectral channels c will be in the order of hundreds or thousands, while the number of pixels p will be in the order of tens or hundreds of thousands. Formally, NMF attempts to identify matrices $\mathbf{W}$ and $\mathbf{H}$ such that

$$\underset{\mathbf{W} \geqslant 0, \mathbf{H} \geqslant 0}{\arg \min} \left\| \mathbf{A} - \mathbf{W} \mathbf{H}^T \right\|_F^2 . \tag{11.1}$$

The factors matrices, $\mathbf{W}$ and $\mathbf{H}$, are normally found by first randomly initializing these matrices and then applying iterative algorithms to update $\mathbf{W}$ and $\mathbf{H}$ until some convergence criteria is met [33]. Even though NMF is good at capturing global macroscopic information, it cannot characterize local information and can fail miserably due to nonlinear interactions between endmembers within the pixels.

One advantage of kernel-based methods is that they allow the casting of linear unmixing algorithms on an implicitly formulated high-dimensional feature space, which can effectively

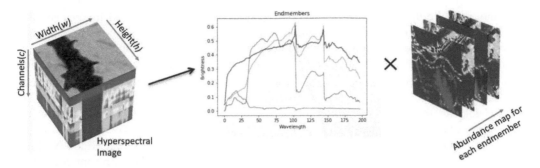

FIGURE 11.1
Decomposing a spectral image cube into endmembers $\mathbf{W}$ and abundances $\mathbf{H}$ (matrix $\mathbf{A}$ not depicted).

capture the nonlinearities in the original data. Towards this, the community has been exploring Symmetric NMF (SymNMF) for kernel matrices [35, 36], as the Mercer kernel matrices are symmetric positive semi-definite. Given a kernel matrix $\mathbf{S} \in \mathbb{R}^{p \times p}$, SymNMF attempts to identify a matrix $\mathbf{H}$ such that

$$\underset{\mathbf{H} \geqslant 0}{\arg\min} \left\| \mathbf{S} - \mathbf{H}\mathbf{H}^{T} \right\|_{F}^{2} . \tag{11.2}$$

The above formulation gives the abundance maps $\mathbf{H}$, but it does not provide the endmembers $\mathbf{W}$. Typically, we have to solve a least-squares problem with constraints (e.g., non-negativity, sum-to-one) to recover the endmembers $\mathbf{W}$ [24, 54]. Nevertheless, for the recovered endmembers, the abundance maps are not necessarily an optimal outcome. And so, in the case of nonlinear approaches with kernel tricks, recovering stationery endmembers and abundance maps can be a problem. ISOMAP is an example of this and is used as a baseline for the experiments presented in Section 11.4. To address this problem, recent work [20, 56] has focused on the joint optimization (Joint NMF (JointNMF)) of the linear (11.1) and nonlinear (11.2) approaches above:

$$\underset{\mathbf{W} \geqslant 0, \mathbf{H} \geqslant 0}{\arg\min} \left\| \mathbf{A} - \mathbf{W}\mathbf{H}^{T} \right\|_{F}^{2} + \left\| \mathbf{S} - \mathbf{H}\mathbf{H}^{T} \right\|_{F}^{2} . \tag{11.3}$$

While the above formulation works well for sparse data, there are two main challenges that make the use of JointNMF for unmixing Scanning transmission electron microscope (STEM) images difficult:

(a) First, the joint formulation (11.3) is much more restrictive and has a smaller solution space over the individual formulations (11.1) and (11.2). And so, in most cases, the amount of change in $\mathbf{H}$ from the random initialization will be small and may not converge to a meaningful stationery point. That is to say, JointNMF is very sensitive to initialization. Consequently, if we were to start at a meaningful point, it is much more likely that JointNMF will yield a solution with meaningful endmembers and abundance maps.

(b) Second, obtaining the kernel matrix $\mathbf{S}$ can be difficult. Typically, STEM data represented as a matrix $\mathbf{A} \in \mathbb{R}_{+}^{c \times p}$ is small and fat, with the number of channels c in the order hundreds or thousands and total pixels p in the order of tens to hundreds of thousands (i.e., $c \ll p$). For most practical applications, when the number of endmembers k is in the tens or hundreds, a good approximation of the input matrix can be obtained. Given these values, $\mathbf{S}$ is very expensive to compute, with a runtime complexity in $\Omega(2cp^2)$ and a memory complexity in $\Omega(p^2)$. Because of the complexity, JointNMF cannot handle large data, and it can even be difficult to produce timely results on moderately sized images containing around 10,000 pixels. Talwalkar, Kumar, and Rowley [46] proposed a Nyström-based approximation to scale such manifold techniques for unconstrained problems. However, no known approaches can scale on large scientific data with constraints such as non-negativity.

In this chapter, we propose a novel algorithm, fast nonlinear nonnegative unmixing (FUNNL), that addresses the problems of (a) initialization and (b) utilization of the kernel matrix $\mathbf{S}$ for the JointNMF formulation given in (11.3). With this introduction, we would like to highlight the key contribution of our work. As a case study, we show the usefulness of the proposed FUNNL algorithm on STEM images collected at Oak Ridge National Laboratory (ORNL) over linear and nonlinear unmixing baselines. We present a science-guided initialization technique, inspired by the pure pixel assumption (which is common in the literature [52]), but based upon a "pure channel" perspective. The proposed initialization scheme is computationally less expensive, works well on STEM and real-world image data, and provides better results (in terms of both endmembers and abundance maps) over random initialization. Our algorithm updates the factor matrices $\mathbf{W}$ and $\mathbf{H}$ without pre-computing the kernel matrix $\mathbf{S}$; the computationally expensive matrix multiplications involving $\mathbf{S}$ are replaced with products or sums of products of smaller matrices. We have shown that popular kernels, such as linear and euclidean kernels, can exploit this solution. Under the mild assumption that $p > 2c$, we show that FUNNL is always faster than pre-computing $\mathbf{S}$. For the Radial Basis Function (RBF) kernel, we represent $\mathbf{S}$ as a sparse matrix, reducing the memory and the computation in the order of the number of non-zeros. Our experiments show that our algorithm runs considerably faster than ISOMAP (2 minutes vs. 3 hours) while achieving higher accuracy (i.e., a lower reconstruction error).

Relevant background relating to STEM EELS data and a brief review of the literature is presented in Section 11.2. Subsequently, we discuss the technical details of our core contribution in Section 11.3, and finally, we compare our proposed FUNNL algorithm with representative baselines on real-world STEM dataset and the Indian Pine dataset [3] in Section 11.4. We show that FUNNL consistently outperforms the baselines in both accuracy and running time.

TABLE 11.1
Notations

Notations	Description
h	Image Height in Pixels
w	Image Width in Pixels
c	Number of Spectral Channels
$p = h \times w$	Total Number of Pixels
$\mathbf{A} \in \mathbb{R}_+^{c \times p}$	Image Matrix Where Every Column
	Represents One Pixel
k	Low Rank/Number of Endmembers
$\mathbf{W} \in \mathbb{R}_+^{c \times k}$	Endmember Matrix
$\mathbf{H} \in \mathbb{R}_+^{p \times k}$	Abundances Matrix
$\kappa(\mathbf{a}_i, \mathbf{a}_j) \in \mathbb{R}$	Kernel Function
$\mathbf{S} \in \mathbb{R}^{p \times p}$	Kernel Matrix of $\mathbf{A}$, where
	$s_{i,j} = \kappa(\mathbf{a}_i, \mathbf{a}_j)$
$\mathbf{G} \in \mathbb{R}_+^{c \times c}$	Gram Matrix – $\mathbf{A}\mathbf{A}^T$
P	Set of r Pure Channel Indices
$\mathbf{C} \in \mathbb{R}_+^{k \times k}$	Pure Channel Rows of $\mathbf{W}$
$\mathbf{N} \in \mathbb{R}_+^{(c-k) \times k}$	Impure Channel Rows of $\mathbf{W}$
$\mathbf{G}_h \in \mathbb{R}_+^{k \times k}$	Gram Matrix – $\mathbf{H}^T \mathbf{H}$
$\mathbf{I}_n \in \mathbb{R}_+^{n \times n}$	Identity Matrix of Order n

11.2   Background and Related Works

In this section, we would like to briefly introduce the readers with the scientific application — image analysis for alternate fuels using EELS data gathered from an STEM at ORNL. In addition, we briefly present work related to the spectral unmixing problem.

11.2.1   STEM EELS Measurements for Alternate Fuels

A STEM taking EELS measurements will focus a beam of electrons to a fine point and raster across a sample, typically in a high vacuum environment. The electrons in the beam will lose some of their energy as they interact with the electronic structure of the chemicals in the sample; depending on the thickness of the sample, a significant number of these electrons may be scattered multiple times as they pass through the sample. These transmitted electrons then pass through a magnetic prism that separates the electrons by their kinetic energies, which are then detected with a 2D charge-coupled device (CCD) array and binned to form a 1D spectrum. The spectral intensities represent the number of transmitted electrons and the energy they have lost while interacting with the sample as they pass through. This process is illustrated in Figure 11.2.

Palladium is a critical catalyst used to help reduce toxic car emissions, and it is also being used in fuel cells as an alternative to fossil-fuel-based energy [45] and is highly valuable due to its scarcity. As previously mentioned, the effectiveness of palladium as a catalyst is strongly dependent upon the conditions at its surface. Leveraging STEM EELS data, we can gain better insight into the conditions of palladium within nanoscale materials. However, STEM EELS data poses some interesting challenges when it comes to unmixing: (i) interactions between endmembers tend to be nonlinear due to multiple scattering effects, and (ii) some

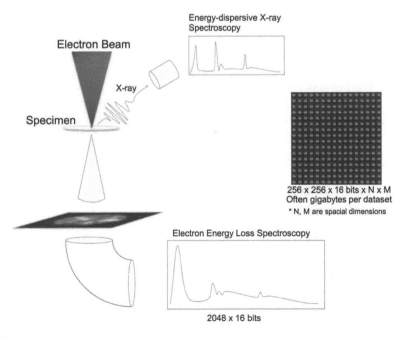

FIGURE 11.2
Hyperspectral EELS imaging in STEMs.

endmembers are always found in the presence of others (e.g., palladium resting on top of the carbon support).

11.2.2   Spectral Unmixing

The problem of unmixing has been approached using many different techniques from several diverse communities [5,25,32,43,51]. Geometric approaches, mostly based on convex spaces, have been developed by several researchers [6,12,14,26]; examples include the ATGP [44], N-FINDR [52], PPI [7], FIPPI [13], SGA [11], and VCA [40] algorithms. Physics-based models, developed mostly for hyperspectral imagery, take inspiration from infinite reflections [8] and ray tracing [21]. Some of these physics-based models only provide endmembers, and the corresponding abundances must be obtained via other methods, such as solving a least-squares problem with appropriate constraints. However, this comes with the implicit assumption that interactions between endmembers are linear. Approaches based on Bayesian techniques [18,19,48,53] and sparse regression [27,50,55] have also been developed.

11.2.2.1   Geometric-Based Methods

One common approach to spectral unmixing is to first identify the basis spectral signatures corresponding to the materials (i.e., endmembers) found in the image. Once these signatures are determined, each pixel in the image cube can then be 'unmixed' to obtain the fractional abundances of each endmember. Several techniques exist for determining the endmembers, and most of them require the help of a trained domain specialist. Some unmixing approaches assume that the spectral image contains at least one pure pixel (a pixel whose corresponding spectrum is formed from a single endmember) for each endmember; this is referred to as the *pure pixel assumption*. In geometric-based methods, these pure pixels correspond to the vertices of a convex space in higher dimensions.

One of the difficulties in applying endmember extraction methods is that they do not yield the corresponding abundance maps. These abundances can be retrieved by solving a least-squares problem with appropriate constraints. However, this imposes an implicitly assumption that the interactions between endmembers are linear; due to the multiple scattering effects in EELS data, this is most likely not the case. The use of nonlinear unmixing methods enables the detection of signals that may otherwise be overlooked and provides disambiguation. For instance, the distinctions between metallic palladium and oxidized palladium are subtle. Moreover, their spectral signatures may not be distinctive enough for convex methods to distinguish between them. While there are several geometric-based algorithms for determining endmembers, we focus on two for use as baselines in our experiments:

- N-FINDR [52] – this algorithm leverages the observation that the volume of a simplex formed by the endmembers (purest pixels) is larger than any other volume defined by any other combination of pixels.

- ATGP [44] – this algorithm searches for the most distinctive pixels by using an orthogonal subspace projection (OSP) approach.

11.2.2.2   Matrix Factorization-Based Methods

The most standard linear unmixing techniques based on matrix factorization are singular value decomposition (SVD) and NMF [31]. In the case of SVD, we obtain orthogonal (i.e., independent or perpendicular) endmembers and abundance maps. The challenge with SVD is that the endmembers have no physical interpretation because of the possible presence of negative values. NMF [28] solves this problem and produces meaningful endmembers and abundance maps.

Even though linear unmixing techniques, such as NMF and SVD, are good at capturing the global macroscopic information, they often fail to capture intrinsic microscopic information due to nonlinearities in the data. Most approaches found in the literature that attempt to address this will focus on running linear unmixing techniques on transformed data using Mercer kernels [10]. Broadwater, Chellappa, Banerjee, and Burlina [9] proposed an algorithm that estimates abundances in the kernel feature space, while enforcing the non-negativity and sum-to-one constraints, on Airborne Visible/Infrared Imaging Spectrometer (AVIRIS) and Cuprite datasets with RBF kernels.

Chen, Richard, and Honeine [15, 16] explored kernel-based unmixing approaches using a linear mixing part and a nonlinear fluctuation for the endmembers, where the nonlinear function was defined through kernel methods. These joint functions with constraints, such as non-negativity, resulted in different algorithms, and the usefulness of these novel methods using Gaussian kernels was shown on real-world HSI data and compared against physical models.

The JointNMF formulation, seen in Equation (11.3), has appeared in other applications. The observation of the inability to obtain endmembers for nonlinear dimensionality reduction using kernel matrices was made by Zhu and Honeine [56]. Independently, Du, Drake, and Park [20] were exploring similar formulations in social network contexts (e.g., Twitter and bibliographic data), where both the network data (represented as an adjacency matrix $\mathbf{S}$) and text (represented as a bag of word matrix $\mathbf{A}$) were available. These contexts differ only in the properties of the symmetric matrix $\mathbf{S}$. The bi-objective optimization problem performs NMF in both input and feature spaces by combining linear and kernel-based models with a shared factor matrix $\mathbf{H}$ between them. The first objective function stems from the conventional linear NMF, while the second objective function, defined in the feature space, is derived from the kernel-based NMF model. This is what leads to the JointNMF formulation

$$\underset{\mathbf{W} \geqslant 0, \mathbf{H} \geqslant 0}{\arg\min} \left\| \mathbf{A} - \mathbf{W}\mathbf{H}^T \right\|_F^2 + \left\| \mathbf{S} - \mathbf{H}\mathbf{H}^T \right\|_F^2$$

at the core of FUNNL.

11.3   Fast Nonlinear Nonnegative Unmixing

Solving the JointNMF formulation, given in Equation (11.3), can be done in many different ways. In order to apply standard block coordinate descent (BCD) techniques [33], and leverage scalable frameworks such as MPIFAUN [29, 30], we reformulate the problem as follows:

$$\underset{\mathbf{W} \geqslant 0, \mathbf{H} \geqslant 0, \widehat{\mathbf{H}} \geqslant 0}{\arg\min} \left\| \mathbf{A} - \mathbf{W}\mathbf{H}^T \right\|_F^2 + \alpha \left\| \mathbf{S} - \mathbf{H}\widehat{\mathbf{H}}^T \right\|_F^2 + \beta \left\| \widehat{\mathbf{H}} - \mathbf{H} \right\|_F^2 \tag{11.4}$$

In the above equation, we are introducing a surrogate variable $\widehat{\mathbf{H}}$ and defining it to be close to the abundance map matrix $\mathbf{H}$. With such a formulation, we now have a three-block BCD ($\mathbf{W}$, $\mathbf{H}$ and $\widehat{\mathbf{H}}$) and can leverage the ANLS-BPP algorithm [34] to cyclically solve each block. Note that α and β are positive scalars, which serve as regularization hyperparameters. They are used to control the importance of different parts of the objective function. For instance, if $\alpha > \beta$, then more importance is placed on making $\mathbf{H}\widehat{\mathbf{H}}^T$ a good approximation of $\mathbf{S}$ than

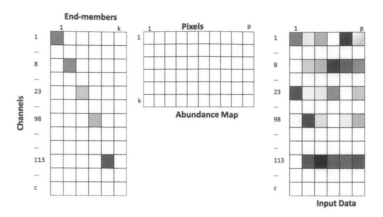

FIGURE 11.3

Pure channels on scientific images.

making $\mathbf{H}$ and $\widehat{\mathbf{H}}$ close. In the remainder of this section, we address two important building blocks for FUNNL: (a) initialization and (b) utilization of the kernel matrix $\mathbf{S}$.

11.3.1   Science Guided Initialization of FUNNL

There is a large amount of local information in STEM EELS data that can be leveraged to obtain a good initialization for the endmember matrix $\mathbf{H}$. The interior pixels of a particular class can be completely identified by a single endmember. However, due to spatial resolution and multi-scattering effects, the pixels near the edges of a class will be nonlinear mixtures of endmembers from neighboring classes. Our objective is to obtain a good representative from each of these distinct classes.

In the reduced dimension endmember representation, a high reflectance in certain wavelengths (represented by spectral channels) will most likely belong to a single endmember. That is to say, in the $\mathbf{W}$ endmember matrix, there exists a positive real-number γ such that $w_{i,j} > \gamma$ and $w_{i,j'} < \gamma$ and for all $j' \neq j$; only one entry in every row of the $\mathbf{W}$ matrix is greater than γ. Let us call such wavelengths *pure channels*. The remaining wavelengths, other than pure channels, may contribute to more than one endmember. Also, there can be more than one row that serves as a pure channel for a given endmember. The initialization primarily consists of (i) determining the indices of these pure channels and (ii) using the indices of the pure channels along with $\mathbf{A}$ to obtain a good initialization of $\mathbf{H}$. Figure 11.3 pictorially presents the notion of pure channels and their impact on the input data. We can see that pure channels on the input image will be a scaled copy across the pixels. Remember that, on some pixels, the pure channels need not participate and their value can be near zero.

To obtain a small number of representatives for use as pure channels for each class, we begin by taking the Gram matrix $\mathbf{G} = \mathbf{A}^T\mathbf{A}$ of $\mathbf{A}$. The matrix $\mathbf{G}$ represents the sample similarity between the c channels, and selecting outlying vectors from $\mathbf{G}$ will obtain candidates for the pure channels; the indices of the outlying vectors correspond to spectral channels, which are taken to be the pure channels. The selection of the outlying vectors is accomplished by iteratively applying the Gram-Schmidt orthogonalization process, as seen in Algorithm 11.1. The pure channel candidates, along with the matrices $\mathbf{G}$ and $\mathbf{A}$, are then used to initialize the endmember matrix $\mathbf{W}$. Let us assume that the rows and the columns of the Gram matrix are permuted so that the rows and columns of the pure channels are in

---

Algorithm 11.1 Pure Channels Representative Extraction

Input: Matrix $\mathbf{G} \in \mathbb{R}_+^{c \times c}$, number of candidates r
Output: Candidate list as set P
 1: **Algorithm** CANDIDATES($\mathbf{G}$, r)
 2:     $P \leftarrow \{\emptyset\}$
     // *find the farthest point from origin*
 3:     $v \leftarrow \{k \mid \|\mathbf{g}_k\|_2^2 \geqslant \|\mathbf{g}_i\|_2^2, \forall i \in 1, \cdots, c\}$
 4:     $P \leftarrow P \cup \{v\}$
     // *Shift $\mathbf{G}$'s origin to $\mathbf{g}_v$*
 5:     $\tilde{\mathbf{G}} \leftarrow \mathbf{G} - \mathbf{g}_v$
     // *calculate the first index*
 6:     $v \leftarrow \{k \mid \|\tilde{\mathbf{g}}_k\|_2^2 \geqslant \|\tilde{\mathbf{g}}_i\|_2^2, \forall i \in 1, \cdots, c\}$
 7:     $P \leftarrow P \cup \{v\}$
 8:     $\mathbf{B}[:, 0] \leftarrow \mathbf{g}_v$
     // *calculate the rest of the candidates*
 9:     **for** $j = 1$ to $r - 1$ **do**
10:         $\tilde{\mathbf{G}} \leftarrow \tilde{\mathbf{G}} - \mathbf{b}_{j-1}(\mathbf{b}_{j-1}^T \tilde{G})$
11:         $v \leftarrow \{k \mid \|\tilde{\mathbf{g}}_k\|_2^2 \geqslant \|\tilde{\mathbf{g}}_i\|_2^2, \forall i \in 1, \cdots, c\}$
12:         $P \leftarrow P \cup \{v\}$
13:         $\mathbf{B}[:, j] \leftarrow \mathbf{g}_v$
14:     **end for**
15:     **return** P
16: **end Algorithm**

---

the top left portion of the matrix. The recovery of $\mathbf{W}$ from this top left permuted $\mathbf{G}$ matrix is pictorially represented in Figure 11.4, and the pseudocode (motivated by Arora, Ge, and Moitra [2]) is given in Algorithm 11.2.

Algorithm 11.2 Initialization of $\mathbf{W}$ from $\mathbf{G}$

Input: Matrix $\mathbf{G} \in \mathbb{R}_+^{c \times c}$, low rank k, candidate list P
Output: Matrix $\mathbf{W} \in \mathbb{R}_+^{c \times k}$
 1: **Algorithm** INITIALIZATION($\mathbf{G}$, k, P)
 2:     ASSERT($k = |P|$)
     // *Permute $\mathbf{G}$ so P rows and columns are on top left*
 3:     $\mathbf{G} \leftarrow$ PERMUTE(P, $\mathbf{G}$)
     // *Extract top left $k \times k$ matrix of $\mathbf{G}$*
 4:     $CGhC \leftarrow \mathbf{G}[1:k, 1:k]$
     // *Extract the first k rows of $\mathbf{G}$ of size $k \times c$*
 5:     $CGhWt \leftarrow \mathbf{G}[1:k, :]$
     // *Compute the row sum of $CGhWt$*
 6:     $CGhWt_{r\_sum} \leftarrow$ SUM($CGhWt, axis = 1$)
     // *$\mathbf{z} \in \mathbb{R}^k$ that minimizes the following relation*
 7:     $\mathbf{z} \leftarrow \arg\min_{\mathbf{z}} \|CGhC\, \mathbf{z} - CGhWt_{r\_sum}\|_2^2$
     // *Find the sparse non-negative projection*
 8:     $\mathbf{W}^T \leftarrow \arg\min_{\mathbf{W} \geqslant 0} \|CGhC\, \text{diag}(\mathbf{z})\mathbf{W} - CGhWt\|_F^2$
 9:     $\mathbf{W}^T \leftarrow \mathbf{W}^T + \lambda \|\mathbf{W}\|_{\ell 1}$
     // *Reverse the permuted index on $\mathbf{W}$ to align correct indices*
10:     $\mathbf{W} \leftarrow$ REVERSEPERMUTE(P, $\mathbf{W}$)
11:     **return** $\mathbf{W}$
12: **end Algorithm**

We discuss briefly the details of Algorithm 11.2. Our objective is to recover $\mathbf{W}$ given $\mathbf{G}$ and a k candidate list of pure channels obtained from Algorithm 11.1. According to Lemma 11.1 (see below), we know that $\mathbf{CG}_h$ is equal to the row sum of $\mathbf{CG}_h \mathbf{W}^T$, where $\mathbf{W}$ is column normalized to sum to 1, as computed in Line 6 of Algorithm 11.2. Remember, we assume $\mathbf{C}$ is a diagonally dominant matrix with the entries in the diagonal no less than γ. Hence, $\mathbf{CG}_h \mathbf{C}$ is invertible. Since $\mathbf{z} = (\mathbf{CG}_h \mathbf{C})^{-1} \mathbf{CG}_h \mathbf{1} = \mathbf{C}^{-1} \mathbf{1}$ (Line 7), we can also

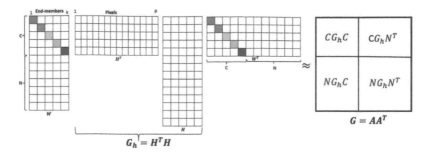

FIGURE 11.4
Initialization of **W** from **G**.

infer that $\mathbf{Cz} = 1$ and $\mathbf{C}\operatorname{diag}(\mathbf{z})$ will be the identity matrix. Finally, we can obtain **W** by solving $(\mathbf{CG}_h\mathbf{C}\operatorname{diag}(\mathbf{z}))^{-1}\mathbf{CG}_h\mathbf{W}^T = (\mathbf{CG}_h)^{-1}\mathbf{CG}_h\mathbf{W}^T$. We should mention here that, in the case of numerical linear algebra, we never compute an inverse directed (as it tends to be numerically unstable) but instead rely on numerical methods.

Lemma 11.1. *If* **A** *and* **B** *are matrices such that the columns of* **B** *sum to 1, then the row sums of* **A** *are equal to the row sums of* $\mathbf{AB}^T$.

Proof. Let **A** and **B** be matrices such that the columns of **B** sum to 1. Observe that the row sums of **A** and $\mathbf{AB}^T$ are given, respectively, by $\mathbf{A}\mathbf{1}$ and $\mathbf{AB}^T\mathbf{1}$, where $\mathbf{1} \in \mathbb{R}^n$ is a column vector of ones. Since the columns of **B** sum to 1, the rows of $\mathbf{B}^T$ sum to 1, whence $\mathbf{B}^T\mathbf{1} = 1$. That is to say, $\mathbf{AB}^T\mathbf{1} = \mathbf{A}\mathbf{1}$, and the row sums of **A** are equal to the row sums of $\mathbf{AB}^T$, as desired. $\square$

Now that we have a good starting point for initializing the endmember matrix **W**, we proceed to the discussion on solving the JointNMF formulation given in Equation (11.4).

11.3.2   Utilization of the Kernel Matrix

Let us begin by reviewing the JointNMF optimization problem we want to solve: given positive real-numbers α and β, and non-negative matrices **A** and **S**, we wish to find non-negative matrices **W**, **H**, and $\widehat{\mathbf{H}}$ such that

$$\underset{\mathbf{W}\geqslant 0,\mathbf{H}\geqslant 0,\widehat{\mathbf{H}}\geqslant 0}{\arg\min} \left\|\mathbf{A} - \mathbf{WH}^T\right\|_F^2 + \alpha\left\|\mathbf{S} - \mathbf{H}\widehat{\mathbf{H}}^T\right\|_F^2 + \beta\left\|\widehat{\mathbf{H}} - \mathbf{H}\right\|_F^2.$$

Just like for any NMF algorithm, we start by randomly initializing **H** and $\widehat{\mathbf{H}}$ (**W** is initialized using Algorithm 11.2. Then, **W**, **H**, and $\widehat{\mathbf{H}}$ are cynically updated using Equation (11.5) until some termination criteria are met; in our case, we specify a fixed number of iterations as our termination criteria.

$$\mathbf{W} \leftarrow \underset{\mathbf{W}\geqslant 0}{\arg\min}\left\|\mathbf{HW}^T - \mathbf{A}^T\right\|_F^2 \tag{11.5a}$$

$$\widehat{\mathbf{H}} \leftarrow \underset{\widehat{\mathbf{H}}\geqslant 0}{\arg\min}\left\|\begin{bmatrix}\sqrt{\alpha}\mathbf{H}\\\sqrt{\beta}\mathbf{I}_k\end{bmatrix}\widehat{\mathbf{H}}^T - \begin{bmatrix}\sqrt{\alpha}\mathbf{S}\\\sqrt{\beta}\mathbf{H}^T\end{bmatrix}\right\|_F^2 \tag{11.5b}$$

$$\mathbf{H} \leftarrow \underset{\mathbf{H}\geqslant 0}{\arg\min}\left\|\begin{bmatrix}\mathbf{W}\\\sqrt{\alpha}\widehat{\mathbf{H}}\\\sqrt{\beta}\mathbf{I}_k\end{bmatrix}\mathbf{H}^T - \begin{bmatrix}\mathbf{A}\\\sqrt{\alpha}\mathbf{S}\\\sqrt{\beta}\widehat{\mathbf{H}}^T\end{bmatrix}\right\|_F^2 \tag{11.5c}$$

Here we would like to provide a brief explanation for solving a Non-Negative Least Squares (NLS) problem, which is a building block for many NMF frameworks, such as MPI-FAUN [29,30]. Consider the equation

$$\min_{\mathbf{x} \geqslant 0} \|\mathbf{C}\mathbf{x} - \mathbf{b}\|_2. \tag{11.6}$$

The Karush–Kuhn–Tucker (KKT) optimality conditions for Equation (11.6) are as follows:

$$\mathbf{y} = \mathbf{C}^T\mathbf{C}\mathbf{x} - \mathbf{C}^T\mathbf{b}, \tag{11.7a}$$

$$\mathbf{x}, \mathbf{y} \geqslant 0, \tag{11.7b}$$

$$x_i y_i = 0 \text{ for all } i. \tag{11.7c}$$

These conditions state that, at optimality, the support sets (i.e., the non-zero elements) of $\mathbf{x}$ and $\mathbf{y}$ are complementary to each other (i.e., $\mathbf{x}^T\mathbf{y} = 0$). Therefore, Equation (11.7) is an instance of the Linear Complementarity Problem (LCP), which arises frequently in quadratic programming. The use of active-set and active-set-like methods are very suitable when $k \ll \min(m, n)$, because most computations involve matrices of sizes $c \times k$, $p \times k$, and $k \times k$, which are small and easy to handle. Thus, if we can formulate the computations of Equation (11.5) as matrix multiplications of lower dimensions, we can leverage these computationally efficient frameworks for large data.

For convenience, let us define NLS($\mathbf{C}, \mathbf{B}$), where $\mathbf{C} \in \mathbb{R}_+^{k \times k}$ and $\mathbf{B} \in \mathbb{R}_+^{k \times n}$, to return a non-negative solution $\mathbf{X} \in \mathbb{R}_+^{k \times n}$ to the NLS problem. In our work, we are using the ANLS-BPP [33] algorithm for solving the NLS subproblems. General frameworks, like MPI-FAUN offer many alternatives for solving NLS problems, such as MU [37] and HALS [17], to obtain $\mathbf{X}$.

The biggest bottleneck to scaling a JointNMF solver for large data, in the case of Equation (11.5), is the kernel matrix $\mathbf{S}$ and its use in computations with other factor matrices. Typically $\mathbf{S}$ is a kernel matrix, where $s_{i,j} = \kappa(\mathbf{a}_i, \mathbf{a}_j)$, for some kernel function κ. Calculating $\mathbf{S}$ is expensive, both in terms of computation and memory, which are in the order of $\Omega(p^2)$. While $\Omega(p^2)$ is tractable and may not seem like an issue, it can be preventative in practice. Consider, for example, a 500×500 spectral image containing $500^2 = 250,000$ pixels. This image, represented by a $\mathbf{A} \in \mathbb{R}_+^{c \times 250,000}$ matrix, will result in a kernel matrix $\mathbf{S} \in \mathbb{R}_+^{250,000 \times 250,000}$ containing $250,000^2$ entries. It would require 500GB of memory to hold $\mathbf{S}$ if it were stored using full 64-bit precision. Furthermore, any updates found in Equation (11.5) involving $\mathbf{S}$ will be embarrassingly slow due to computational requirements.

There are two potential optimizations for dealing with $\mathbf{S}$: (i) In the case of the RBF kernel, we can represent $\mathbf{S}$ as a sparse matrix, reducing the memory and the computation in the order of the number of non-zeros. (ii) In the case of the linear kernel, instead of pre-computing $\mathbf{S}$, we show that $\mathbf{S}$ can be represented as a product, or sums of products, of matrices in dimensions much smaller than $p \times p$. Leveraging the associativity of matrix multiplication, we can always order the multiplication of the low-rank factors $\mathbf{H}$ and $\widehat{\mathbf{H}}$ so that we never have to compute or store the full $p \times p$ matrix.

We will now demonstrate how the FUNNL algorithm can be implemented with a linear kernel function $\kappa(\mathbf{a}_i, \mathbf{a}_j) = \mathbf{a}_i^T\mathbf{a}_j$ without pre-computing the $\mathbf{S}$ matrix.

Theorem 11.1. *For the linear kernel, $\kappa(\mathbf{a}_i, \mathbf{a}_j) = \mathbf{a}_i^T\mathbf{a}_j$, the update function for $\widehat{\mathbf{H}}$ in equation (11.5b), without pre-computing $\mathbf{S}$, becomes*

$$\widehat{\mathbf{H}} \leftarrow \text{NLS}\left(\alpha\mathbf{H}^T\mathbf{H} + \beta\mathbf{I}_k, \, \alpha(\mathbf{H}^T\mathbf{A}^T)\mathbf{A} + \beta\mathbf{H}^T\right). \tag{11.8}$$

Proof. Observe that

$$
\begin{aligned}
\underset{\widehat{\mathbf{H}} \geqslant 0}{\arg\min} & \left\| \begin{bmatrix} \sqrt{\alpha}\mathbf{H} \\ \sqrt{\beta}\mathbf{I}_k \end{bmatrix} \widehat{\mathbf{H}}^T - \begin{bmatrix} \sqrt{\alpha}\mathbf{S} \\ \sqrt{\beta}\mathbf{H}^T \end{bmatrix} \right\|_F^2 \\
&= \mathrm{NLS}\left(\begin{bmatrix} \sqrt{\alpha}\mathbf{H}^T & \sqrt{\beta}\mathbf{I}_k \end{bmatrix} \begin{bmatrix} \sqrt{\alpha}\mathbf{H} \\ \sqrt{\beta}\mathbf{I}_k \end{bmatrix}, \begin{bmatrix} \sqrt{\alpha}\mathbf{H}^T & \sqrt{\beta}\mathbf{I}_k \end{bmatrix} \begin{bmatrix} \sqrt{\alpha}\mathbf{A}^T\mathbf{A} \\ \sqrt{\beta}\mathbf{H}^T \end{bmatrix} \right) \\
&= \mathrm{NLS}(\alpha\mathbf{H}^T\mathbf{H} + \beta\mathbf{I}_k, \ \alpha(\mathbf{H}^T\mathbf{A}^T)\mathbf{A} + \beta\mathbf{H}^T),
\end{aligned}
\tag{11.9}
$$

as desired.   □

Theorem 11.2. *For the linear kernel,* $\kappa(\mathbf{a}_i, \mathbf{a}_j) = \mathbf{a}_i^T\mathbf{a}_j$, *the update function for* $\mathbf{H}$ *in equation (11.5c), without pre-computing* $\mathbf{S}$, *becomes* $\mathrm{NLS}(\mathbf{W}^T\mathbf{W} + \alpha\widehat{\mathbf{H}}^T\widehat{\mathbf{H}} + \beta\mathbf{I}_k, \mathbf{W}^TA + \alpha(\widehat{\mathbf{H}}^T\mathbf{A}^T)\mathbf{A} + \beta\widehat{\mathbf{H}}^T)$.

Proof. Observe that

$$
\begin{aligned}
\underset{\mathbf{H} \geqslant 0}{\arg\min} & \left\| \begin{bmatrix} \mathbf{W} \\ \sqrt{\alpha}\widehat{\mathbf{H}} \\ \sqrt{\beta}\mathbf{I}_k \end{bmatrix} \mathbf{H}^T - \begin{bmatrix} \mathbf{A} \\ \sqrt{\alpha}\mathbf{S} \\ \sqrt{\beta}\widehat{\mathbf{H}}^T \end{bmatrix} \right\|_F^2 \\
&= \mathrm{NLS}\left(\begin{bmatrix} \mathbf{W}^T & \sqrt{\alpha}\widehat{\mathbf{H}}^T & \sqrt{\beta}\mathbf{I}_k \end{bmatrix} \begin{bmatrix} \mathbf{W} \\ \sqrt{\alpha}\widehat{\mathbf{H}} \\ \sqrt{\beta}\mathbf{I}_k \end{bmatrix}, \begin{bmatrix} \mathbf{W}^T & \sqrt{\alpha}\widehat{\mathbf{H}}^T & \sqrt{\beta}\mathbf{I}_k \end{bmatrix} \begin{bmatrix} \mathbf{A} \\ \sqrt{\alpha}\mathbf{A}^T\mathbf{A} \\ \sqrt{\beta}\widehat{\mathbf{H}}^T \end{bmatrix} \right) \\
&= \mathrm{NLS}\left(\mathbf{W}^T\mathbf{W} + \alpha\widehat{\mathbf{H}}^T\widehat{\mathbf{H}} + \beta\mathbf{I}_k, \mathbf{W}^T\mathbf{A} + \alpha\left(\widehat{\mathbf{H}}^T\mathbf{A}^T\right)\mathbf{A} + \beta\widehat{\mathbf{H}}^T \right),
\end{aligned}
$$

$$\tag{11.10}$$

as desired.   □

In the case of the euclidean kernel, where $\kappa(\mathbf{a}_i, \mathbf{a}_j) = \|\mathbf{a}_i - \mathbf{a}_j\|_2^2$, we have that

$$
\begin{aligned}
s_{i,j} &= \|\mathbf{a}_i - \mathbf{a}_j\|_2^2 \\
&= (\mathbf{a}_i - \mathbf{a}_j)^T(\mathbf{a}_i - \mathbf{a}_j) \\
&= \|\mathbf{a}_i\|_2^2 - 2 * \mathbf{a}_i^T\mathbf{a}_j + \|\mathbf{a}_j\|_2^2,
\end{aligned}
\tag{11.11}
$$

and so,

$$
\mathbf{S} = \begin{bmatrix} \|\mathbf{a}_1\|_2^2 \\ \|\mathbf{a}_2\|_2^2 \\ \vdots \\ \|\mathbf{a}_p\|_2^2 \end{bmatrix} \mathbf{1}^T - 2\mathbf{A}^T\mathbf{A} + \mathbf{1} \begin{bmatrix} \|\mathbf{a}_1\|_2^2 & \|\mathbf{a}_2\|_2^2 & \cdots & \|\mathbf{a}_p\|_2^2 \end{bmatrix},
\tag{11.12}
$$

where $\mathbf{1} \in \mathbb{R}^p$ is a column vector of ones, and $\mathbf{1}^T$ is a row vector of ones. The update rules for $\widehat{\mathbf{H}}$ and $\mathbf{H}$ on Theorems 11.1 and 11.2 for linear kernel can be easily modified to accommodate the euclidean kernel.

Having now established all of the necessary building blocks, we present the linear version of our FUNNL algorithm with the linear kernel (see Algorithm 11.3).

11.3.3 Fast Nonlinear Nonnegative Unmixing

We will briefly address the computational complexity of our Linear FUNNL algorithm and establish the bounds under which it will be faster than the classical algorithm; we refer to the classical algorithm as the one that pre-computes the linear kernel matrix $\mathbf{S}$ and naively

---

Algorithm 11.3 fast nonlinear nonnegative unmixing (FUNNL)

Input: Matrix $\mathbf{A} \in \mathbb{R}_+^{c \times p}$, low rank k

Output: Endmembers matrix $\mathbf{W} \in \mathbb{R}_+^{c \times k}$

Output: Abundances matrix $\mathbf{H} \in \mathbb{R}_+^{p \times k}$

  1: **Algorithm** INITIALIZATION($\mathbf{A}, k$)

  2:     $\mathbf{G} \leftarrow \mathbf{A}^T \mathbf{A}$

      // *get a k candidate list of pure channels*

  3:     $P \leftarrow$ CANDIDATES($\mathbf{G}, k$)

      // *get a representative* $\mathbf{H}$

  4:     $\mathbf{W} \leftarrow$ CANDIDATES($\mathbf{G}, k, P$)

      // *Use* $\mathbf{W}$ *to estimate an* $\mathbf{H}$

  5:     $\mathbf{H} \leftarrow$ NLS($\mathbf{W}^T \mathbf{W}, \mathbf{W}^T \mathbf{A}$)

  6:     **while** stopping criteria not met **do**

  7:         **if** RBF kernel **then**

  8:             $\widehat{\mathbf{H}} \leftarrow$ NLS($\alpha \mathbf{H}^T \mathbf{H} + \beta \mathbf{I}_k, \ \alpha \mathbf{H}^T \mathbf{S} + \beta \mathbf{H}^T$)

  9:             $\mathbf{H} \leftarrow$ NLS($\mathbf{W}^T \mathbf{W} + \alpha \widehat{\mathbf{H}}^T \widehat{\mathbf{H}} + \beta \mathbf{I}_k, \ \mathbf{W}^T \mathbf{A} + \alpha \widehat{\mathbf{H}}^T \mathbf{S} + \beta \widehat{\mathbf{H}}^T$)

10:         **else**

11:             $\widehat{\mathbf{H}} \leftarrow$ NLS($\alpha \mathbf{H}^T \mathbf{H} + \beta \mathbf{I}_k, \ \alpha (\mathbf{H}^T \mathbf{A}^T) \mathbf{A} + \beta \mathbf{H}^T$)

12:             $\mathbf{H} \leftarrow$ NLS($\mathbf{W}^T \mathbf{W} + \alpha \widehat{\mathbf{H}}^T \widehat{\mathbf{H}} + \beta \mathbf{I}_k, \ \mathbf{W}^T \mathbf{A} + \alpha (\widehat{\mathbf{H}}^T \mathbf{A}^T) \mathbf{A} + \beta \widehat{\mathbf{H}}^T$)

13:         **end if**

14:         $\mathbf{W} \leftarrow$ NLS($\mathbf{H}^T \mathbf{H}, \mathbf{H}^T \mathbf{A}^T$)

15:     **end while**

16:     **return** $\mathbf{W}, \mathbf{H}$

17: **end Algorithm**

---

updates the factor matrices using Equation (11.5) directly. The proposed Linear FUNNL algorithm will be faster than the classical algorithm, based on update Equation (11.5), when $p > 2c$.

The major difference between the classical algorithm and the proposed Linear FUNNL algorithm is the computation of (i) $\widehat{\mathbf{H}}^T \mathbf{S}$ as $(\widehat{\mathbf{H}}^T \mathbf{A}^T) \mathbf{A}$ and (ii) $\mathbf{H}^T \mathbf{S}$ as $(\mathbf{H}^T \mathbf{A}^T) \mathbf{A}$ based upon Theorems 11.1 and 11.2, respectively. Recall that

$$\mathbf{A} \in \mathbb{R}_+^{c \times p}, \quad \mathbf{H}, \widehat{\mathbf{H}} \in \mathbb{R}_+^{p \times k}, \quad \mathbf{S} \in \mathbb{R}^{p \times p}.$$

The cost of computing $\widehat{\mathbf{H}}^T \mathbf{S}$ or $\mathbf{H}^T \mathbf{S}$ directly is $2kp^2$. However, the cost of computing $(\widehat{\mathbf{H}}^T \mathbf{A}^T) \mathbf{A}$ or $(\mathbf{H}^T \mathbf{A}^T) \mathbf{A}$ is $4ckp$. And so — since $c, k, p > 0$ — we have that $2kp^2 > 4ckp$ precisely when $p > 2c$. This implies that each iteration of Linear FUNNL will have a lower computational cost than the classical algorithm. Given that the classical algorithm incurs the additional cost of $2cp^2$ for pre-computing and storing the $\mathbf{S}$ matrix, Linear FUNNL will require less computation than the classical algorithm whenever $p > 2c$. A similar analysis can be performed for other kernels, such as the euclidean kernel $\kappa(\mathbf{a}_i, \mathbf{a}_j) = \|\mathbf{a}_i - \mathbf{a}_j\|_2^2$.

11.4   A Case Study

In this section, we present a case study in which we apply the proposed FUNNL algorithm on two real-world datasets with different characteristics. In the following sections, we outline the baseline algorithms chosen for comparison and describe the hardware testbed used for the experiments. We provide details for the two datasets along with a summary of the results and some observations.

11.4.1 Baselines

We have selected three machine learning algorithms to serve as baselines for comparison against the linear and RBF variants of FUNNL. Both SVD and NMF are linear solutions, while ISOMAP is a nonlinear solution [47]. In addition, we have selected the N-FINDR and ATGP algorithms, as they were developed specifically to solve the unmixing problem.

11.4.2 Experimental Setup

Python 2.7 was selected to implement FUNNL, and the matrix operations were linked with the OpenBLAS library. Baseline implementations of SVD, NMF, and ISOMAP were taken from scikit-learn, and PySptools [49] was used for implementations of N-FINDR and ATGP. All of the experiments were performed on machines in the Rhea cluster at Oak Ridge Leadership Computing Facility (OLCF). The first 512 nodes of the cluster make up the Rhea compute partition, and each node contains two 8-core 2.0 GHz Intel Xeon processors with Intel's Hyper-Threading (HT) Technology and 128GB of main memory. Each CPU features 8 physical cores, for a total of 16 physical cores per node. With Intel Hyper-Threading Technology enabled, each node has 32 logical cores capable of executing 32 hardware threads for increased parallelism.

11.4.3 Indian Pines Dataset

The Indian Pine Test Site 3 dataset (or simply the Indian Pine dataset) is an airborne image taken over the Purdue University Agronomy farm and surrounding area. The HSI covers a two-mile by two-mile area and was collected using an AVIRIS hyperspectral sensor. The data consists of 21024 (145 by 145) pixels with 220 spectral reflectance bands ranging in wavelength from $0.4e^{-6}$ to $2.5e^{-6}$; bands corresponding to regions of water absorption (i.e., bands 104-108, 150-163, and 220) were removed. Ground-truth labels are provided with this dataset, and every pixel has been assigned to one of sixteen classes (e.g., alfalfa, corn, oats, wheat, grass/pasture, grass/trees, etc.) [3]. This dataset was selected partially because it provides ground-truth information. It was also selected due to the spatial challenges it poses to the unmixing task. The low spatial resolution of the image, in which every pixel represents a 70-foot by 70-foot area of farmland, virtually guarantees that multiple endmembers will be present in every pixel.

11.4.3.1 Evaluation Metrics

Since every pixel is labeled as one of sixteen classes, the Indian Pines dataset poses a classification task. The various algorithms were used to extract pixel-wise features. For JointNMF, the factor matrices were randomly initialized . The features obtained from the various algorithms were then used to perform k-NN classification using the 5 nearest neighbors. To estimate the performance of the various algorithms, 10-fold cross-validation was performed and the results were averaged across then 10 folds. The following performance metrics were calculated on the holdout fold:

Accuracy – percentage of correctly classified pixels

Mean Accuracy – average of accuracy on each of the 16 classes

Mean Precision – average of precision for each of the 16 classes

$$\text{Precision} = \frac{\text{True Positive}}{\text{True Positive} + \text{False Positives}}$$

Mean Recall – the average of recall for each of the 16 classes

$$\text{Recall} = \frac{\text{True Positive}}{\text{True Positive} + \text{False Negatives}}$$

Mean F1 – the average of F1-Score for each of the 16 classes

$$\text{F1-Score} = 2 \cdot \frac{\text{Precision} \cdot \text{Recall}}{\text{Precision} + \text{Recall}}$$

11.4.3.2 Results

SVD, NMF, JointNMF (with random initialization), and Linear/RBF FUNNL were used to extract pixel-wise features and reduce the dimension of every pixel to 10, 20, 30, 40, and 50. On the obtained features, we used k-NN classification with 5 nearest neighbors over 10-fold cross-validation, and the performance results (averaged across the 10 folds) can be seen in Figure 11.5. The results for a low rank k of 40 and 50 are also presented in Tables 11.2 and 11.3, which include runtime. We can see that RBF FUNNL clearly outperforms the other baselines across all metrics, while Linear FUNNL outperforms all baselines in terms of every metric except overall accuracy. We can also see that JointNMF performs poorly over the linear counterparts NMF and SVD. This demonstrates the advantage of FUNNL over JointNMF thanks to the science-guided initialization proposed in Algorithm 11.2. The RBF FUNNL is faster than the nonlinear ISOMAP but slower than the other linear techniques SVD and NMF. This is partially due to the fact that scikit-learn implementations of SVD and NMF rely on fast binaries, while FUNNL is implemented using a mixture of Python and OpenBLAS. While we are currently working on further optimizing FUNNL, we do not expect that it will never be faster than NMF because of the additional factor matrices involved.

11.4.4 Palladium

The Palladium dataset is a nanoscale dataset in which a solution of palladium (Pd) nanocubes was dispersed on a lacy carbon substrate supported by an etched copper grid. The HSI was acquired with a FEI Titan 300kV transmission electron microscope operating in the scanning spectrum imaging mode. The dataset consists of 19500 (156 by 125) pixels and 2048 channels, resulting in a 19500 by 2048 data matrix. The Palladium dataset is of particular interest due to the nonlinear interactions between the endmembers due to multiple scattering effects. In addition, the image contains no pure palladium pixels as they are always resting upon the carbon substrate.

Unlike the previous dataset, there is no ground-truth provided as part of this dataset. To determine the number of endmembers present, we used the explained variance ratio of the singular values, depicted in Figure 11.6, and found that three or four endmembers should encompass the variance of the signal in the data. Here we present the endmembers and abundance maps for both three and four endmembers.

Figures 11.7 and 11.8 show the endmembers and abundance maps for three components. The last of the NMF components appears dominated by noise, while RBF FUNNL appears to have identified the abundance of the palladium particle the best. NMF and Linear FUNNL both appear to have left the carbon support and the palladium particle components mixed.

Figures 11.9 and 11.10 show the endmembers and abundance maps for four components. Here it can be seen that the fourth NMF component has captured the palladium cube in the abundance maps while the first component has captured the carbon support. RBF

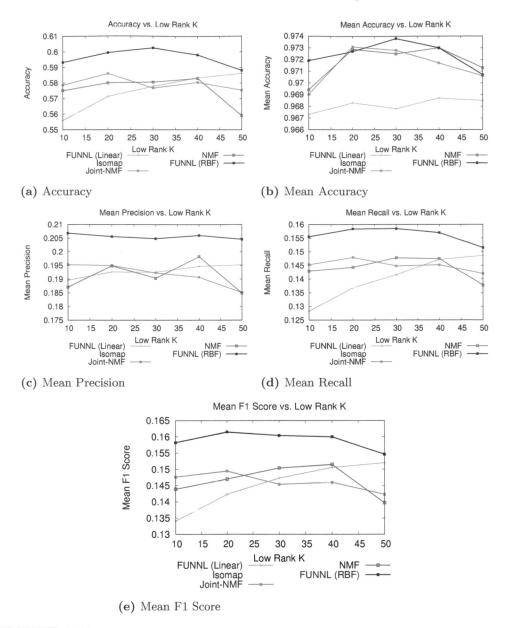

(a) Accuracy

(b) Mean Accuracy

(c) Mean Precision

(d) Mean Recall

(e) Mean F1 Score

FIGURE 11.5
Performance evaluation as a function of low rank K on Indian pines.

FUNNL has also captured the palladium particle and the carbon support while segregating the noise to the last component. With four components, the shape of the palladium spectral component has also become more clear for RBF FUNNL. Linear FUNNL has not separated the components as clearly as NMF and RBF FUNNL, as is evident by the similarity in the last two components of the abundance maps (see Figure 11.10.A.III and Figure 11.10.A.IV).

When the number of components is limited to just three, RBF FUNNL is still able to identify the palladium and carbon support while NMF struggles to separate the palladium and carbon support. Increasing, unmixing with four endmembers produced more

TABLE 11.2

Performance Estimation ($K = 40$)

	Accuracy	Mean Accuracy	Mean Precision	Mean Recall	Mean F1 Score	Runtime
SVD	0.5823	0.9509	0.1950	0.1501	0.1497	0:00:49
NMF	0.5829	0.9509	0.1982	0.1475	0.1515	0:00:20
ISOMAP	0.5648	0.9488	0.1886	0.1376	0.1417	1:58:35
Linear FUNNL	0.5834	0.9510	0.1947	0.1472	0.1506	0:01:46
RBF FUNNL	0.5981	0.9527	0.2060	0.1570	0.1600	0:00:48

TABLE 11.3

Performance Estimation ($K = 50$)

	Accuracy	Mean Accuracy	Mean Precision	Mean Recall	Mean F1 Score	Runtime
SVD	0.5787	0.9504	0.1888	0.1475	0.1475	0:00:50
NMF	0.5590	0.9481	0.1849	0.1378	0.1378	0:00:26
ISOMAP	0.5607	0.9483	0.1812	0.1370	0.1370	2:53:10
Linear FUNNL	0.5862	0.9513	0.1952	0.1486	0.1486	0:02:12
RBF FUNNL	0.5881	0.9515	0.2046	0.1515	0.1515	0:00:54

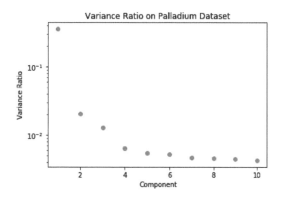

FIGURE 11.6

SVD variance ratio on palladium dataset. This technique determines the number of potential end-members.

interpretable spectra due to the segregation of noise in the data to the fourth endmember for RBF FUNNL, as seen in Figure 11.10.B.IV.

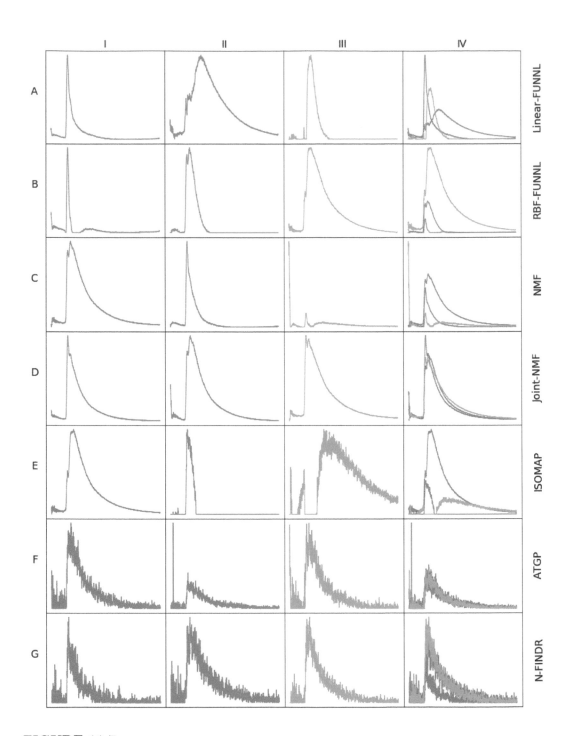

FIGURE 11.7
Palladium unmixed with three endmembers.

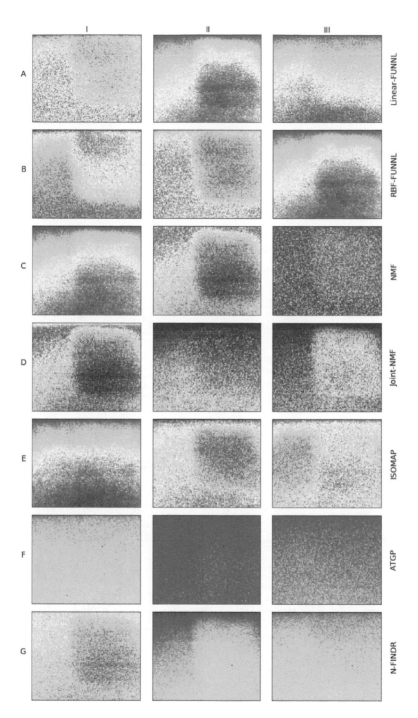

FIGURE 11.8
Palladium abundance maps for three endmembers.

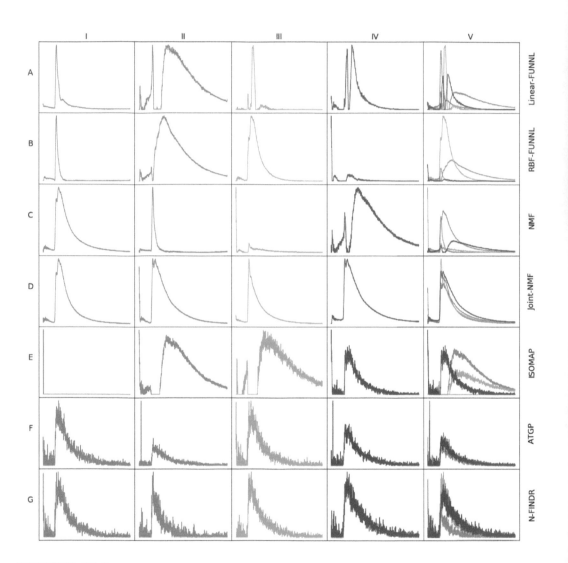

FIGURE 11.9
Palladium unmixed with four endmembers.

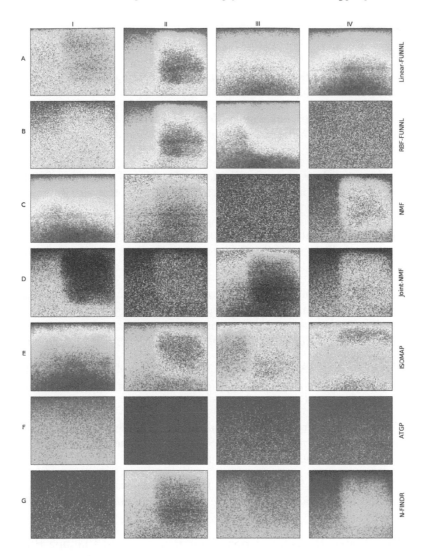

FIGURE 11.10
Palladium abundance maps for four endmembers.

11.5   Conclusion and Future Work

In this chapter, we proposed a novel FUNNL algorithm for non-negative nonlinear unmixing, which leveraged a science-guided initialization technique along with algebraic tricks to reduce computational and memory requirements of JointNMF. The advantages afforded by FUNNL were demonstrated on real-world spectral images and compared against common linear and nonlinear methods, both from the spectral unmixing domain as well as machine learning. Our future work involves optimizing the use of the RBF kernel used in FUNNL with a focus on the distributed and high-performance implementations.

Bibliography

[1] Ermete Antolini. Palladium in fuel cell catalysis. *Energy & Environmental Sciencetal Science*, 2(9):915–931, September 2009.

[2] Sanjeev Arora, Rong Ge, and Ankur Moitra. Learning topic models – going beyond SVD. In *2012 IEEE 53rd Annual Symposium on Foundations of Computer Science*, October 2012.

[3] Marion F. Baumgardner, Larry L. Biehl, and David A. Landgrebe. 220 band AVIRIS hyperspectral image data set: June 12, 1992 indian pine test site 3, September 2015.

[4] José M Bioucas-Dias, Antonio Plaza, Gustavo Camps-Valls, Paul Scheunders, Nasser M. Nasrabadi, and Jocelyn Chanussot. Hyperspectral remote sensing data analysis and future challenges. *IEEE Geoscience and remote sensing magazine*, 1(2):6–36, June 2013.

[5] José M Bioucas-Dias, Antonio Plaza, Nicolas Dobigeon, Mario Parente, Qian Du, Paul Gader, and Jocelyn Chanussot. Hyperspectral unmixing overview: Geometrical, statistical, and sparse regression-based approaches. *IEEE Journal of Selected Topics in Applied Earth Observations and Remote Sensing*, 5(2):354–379, April 2012.

[6] Joseph W. Boardman. Automating spectral unmixing of aviris data using convex geometry concepts. In *Summaries of the 4th Annual JPL Airborne Geoscience Workshop*, volume 1, pages 11–14, October 1993.

[7] Joseph W. Boardman, Fred A. Kruse, and Robert O. Green. Mapping target signatures via partial unmixing of aviris data. In *Summaries of the Fifth Annual JPL Airborne Earth Science Workshop*, volume 1, January 1995.

[8] Christoph C. Borel and Siegfried A. W. Gerstl. Nonlinear spectral mixing models for vegetative and soil surfaces. *Remote Sensing of Environment*, 47(3):403–416, March 1994.

[9] Joshua Broadwater, Rama Chellappa, Amit Banerjee, and Philippe Burlina. Kernel fully constrained least squares abundance estimates. In *2007 IEEE International Geoscience and Remote Sensing Symposium*, pages 4041–4044, July 2007.

[10] Gustavo Camps-Valls, Luis Gomez-Chova, Jordi Muñoz-Marú, Joan Vila-Francés, and Javier Calpe-Maravilla. Composite kernels for hyperspectral image classification. *IEEE Geoscience and Remote Sensing Letters*, 3(1):93–97, January 2006.

[11] C-I Chang, C-C Wu, Weimin Liu, and Y-C Ouyang. A new growing method for simplex-based endmember extraction algorithm. *IEEE Transactions on Geoscience and Remote Sensing*, 44(10):2804–2819, 2006.

[12] Chein-I Chang, Shih-Yu Chen, Hsiao-Chi Li, Hsian-Min Chen, and Chia-Hsien Wen. Comparative study and analysis among ATGP, VCA, and SGA for finding endmembers in hyperspectral imagery. *IEEE Journal of Selected Topics in Applied Earth Observations and Remote Sensing*, 9(9):4280–4306, September 2016.

[13] Chein-I Chang and Antonio Plaza. A fast iterative algorithm for implementation of pixel purity index. *IEEE Geoscience and Remote Sensing Letters*, 3(1):63–67, January 2006.

[14] Chein-I Chang, Chia-Hsien Wen, and Chao-Cheng Wu. Relationship exploration among PPI, ATGP and VCA via theoretical analysis. *International Journal of Computational Science and Engineering (IJCSE)*, 8(4):361–367, October 2013.

[15] Jie Chen, Cédric Richard, and Paul Honeine. Nonlinear unmixing of hyperspectral images based on multi-kernel learning. In *2012 4th Workshop on Hyperspectral Image and Signal Processing: Evolution in Remote Sensing (WHISPERS)*, June 2012.

[16] Jie Chen, Cédric Richard, and Paul Honeine. Nonlinear unmixing of hyperspectral data based on a linear-mixture/nonlinear-fluctuation model. *IEEE Transactions on Signal Processing*, 61(2), January 2013.

[17] Andrzej Cichocki and Phan Anh-Huy. Fast local algorithms for large scale nonnegative matrix and tensor factorizations. *IEICE Transactions on Fundamentals of Electronics, Communications and Computer Sciences*, E92.A(3):708–721, March 2009.

[18] Nicolas Dobigeon, Saïd Moussaoui, Martial Coulon, Jean-Yves Tourneret, and Alfred O. Hero. Joint Bayesian endmember extraction and linear unmixing for hyperspectral imagery. *IEEE Transactions on Signal Processing*, 57(11):4355–4368, November 2009.

[19] Nicolas Dobigeon, Jean-Yves Tourneret, and Chein-I Chang. Semi-supervised linear spectral unmixing using a hierarchical bayesian model for hyperspectral imagery. *IEEE Transactions on Signal Processing*, 56(7):2684–2695, July 2008.

[20] Rundong Du, Barry Drake, and Haesun Park. Hybrid clustering based on content and connection structure using joint nonnegative matrix factorization. *Journal of Global Optimization*, 74(4):861–877, August 2019.

[21] W. M. Grundy, S. Douté, and B. Schmitt. A monte carlo ray-tracing model for scattering and polarization by large particles with complex shapes. *Journal of Geophysical Research: Planets*, 105(E12):29291–29314, December 2000.

[22] Gary L. Haller and Daniel E. Resasco. Metal-support interaction: Group viii metals and reducible oxides. *Advances in Catalysis*, 36, 1989.

[23] John D. Hedley, P. J. Mumby, K. E. Joyce, and S. R. Phinn. Spectral unmixing of coral reef benthos under ideal conditions. *Coral Reefs*, 23(1):60–73, April 2004.

[24] Daniel C. Heinz and Chein-I Chang. Fully constrained least squares linear spectral mixture analysis method for material quantification in hyperspectral imagery. *IEEE Transactions on Geoscience and Remote Sensing*, 39(3):529–545, March 2001.

[25] Rob Heylen, Mario Parente, and Paul Gader. A review of nonlinear hyperspectral unmixing methods. *IEEE Journal of Selected Topics in Applied Earth Observations and Remote Sensing*, 7(6):1844–1868, June 2014.

[26] Paul Honeine and Cédric Richard. Geometric unmixing of large hyperspectral images: A barycentric coordinate approach. *IEEE Transactions on Geoscience and Remote Sensing*, 50(6):2185–2195, June 2011.

[27] Marian-Daniel Iordache, José M. Bioucas-Dias, and Antonio Plaza. Collaborative sparse regression for hyperspectral unmixing. *IEEE Transactions on Geoscience and Remote Sensing*, 52(1):341–354, January 2013.

[28] R. Kannan, A. V. Ievlev, N. Laanait, M. A. Ziatdinov, R. K. Vasudevan, S. Jesse, and S. V. Kalinin. Deep data analysis via physically constrained linear unmixing: universal framework, domain examples, and a community-wide platform. *Advanced Structural and Chemical Imaging*, 4(6), December 2018.

[29] Ramakrishnan Kannan, Grey Ballard, and Haesun Park. A high-performance parallel algorithm for nonnegative matrix factorization. In *Proceedings of the 21st ACM SIGPLAN Symposium on PPoPP*, volume 51, pages 1–11, August 2016.

[30] Ramakrishnan Kannan, Grey Ballard, and Haesun Park. MPI-FAUN: An MPI-based framework for alternating-updating nonnegative matrix factorization. *IEEE Transactions on Knowledge and Data Engineering*, 30(3):544–558, March 2018.

[31] Nirmal Keshava. A survey of spectral unmixing algorithms. *Lincoln Laboratory Journal*, 14(1):55–78, 2003.

[32] Nirmal Keshava and John F Mustard. Spectral unmixing. *IEEE Signal Processing Magazine*, 19(1):44–57, January 2002.

[33] Jingu Kim, Yunlong He, and Haesun Park. Algorithms for nonnegative matrix and tensor factorizations: a unified view based on block coordinate descent framework. *Journal of Global Optimization*, 58:285–319, February 2014.

[34] Jingu Kim and Haesun Park. Fast nonnegative matrix factorization: An active-set-like method and comparisons. *SIAM Journal on Scientific Computing*, 33(6):3261–3281, November 2011.

[35] Da Kuang, Chris Ding, and Haesun Park. Symmetric nonnegative matrix factorization for graph clustering. In *Proceedings of the 2012 SIAM International Conference on Data Mining (SDM)*, April 2012.

[36] Da Kuang, Sangwoon Yun, and Haesun Park. SymNMF: Nonnegative low-rank approximation of a similarity matrix for graph clustering. *Journal of Global Optimization*, 62:545–574, July 2015.

[37] Daniel D. Lee and H. Sebastian Seung. Algorithms for non-negative matrix factorization. *Advances in Neural Information Processing Systems 13 (NIPS 2000)*, May 2001.

[38] Jingyue Liu. Advanced electron microscopy of metal-support interactions in supported metal catalysts. *ChemCatChem*, 3(6):934–948, June 2011.

[39] Tristan D. McRae, David Oleksyn, Jim Miller, and Yu-Rong Gao. Robust blind spectral unmixing for fluorescence microscopy using unsupervised learning. *Plos One*, 14(12): 12: 2019.

[40] José M. P. Nascimento and José M. Bioucas Dias. Vertex component analysis: A fast algorithm to unmix hyperspectral data. *IEEE Transactions on Geoscience and Remote Sensing*, 43(4):898–910, April 2005.

[41] Ravdeep S. Pasricha, Pravallika Devineni, Evangelos E. Papalexakis, and Ramakrishnan Kannan. Tensorized feature spaces for feature explosion. In *2020 25th International Conference on Pattern Recognition (ICPR)*, pages 6298–6304, January 2021.

[42] Tamara A. Potapova, Jay R. Unruh, Andrew C. Box, William D. Bradford, Christopher W. Seidel, Brian D. Slaughter, Shamilene Sivagnanam, Yuping Wu, and Rong Li. Karyotyping human and mouse cells using probes from single-sorted chromosomes and open source software. *BioTechniques*, 59(6):335–346, December 2015.

[43] Carmen Quintano, Alfonso Fernández-Manso, Yosio E. Shimabukuro, and Gabriel Pereira. Spectral unmixing. *International Journal of Remote Sensing*, 33(17):5307–5340, February 2012.

[44] Hsuan Ren and Chein-I Chang. Automatic spectral target recognition in hyperspectral imagery. *IEEE Transactions on Aerospace and Electronic Systems*, 39(4):1232–1249, October 2003.

[45] Alan J. Stephen, Neil V. Rees, Iryna Mikheenko, and Lynne E. Macaskie. Platinum and palladium bio-synthesized nanoparticles as sustainable fuel cell catalysts. *Frontiers in Energy Research*, 7(66), July 2019.

[46] Ameet Talwalkar, Sanjiv Kumar, and Henry Rowley. Large-scale manifold learning. In *2008 IEEE Conference on Computer Vision and Pattern Recognition*, June 2008.

[47] Joshua B. Tenenbaum, Vin de Silva, and John C. Langford. A global geometric framework for nonlinear dimensionality reduction. *Science*, 290(5500):2319–2323, December 2000.

[48] Konstantinos E. Themelis, Athanasios A. Rontogiannis, and Konstantinos D. Koutroumbas. A novel hierarchical bayesian approach for sparse semisupervised hyperspectral unmixing. *IEEE Transactions on Signal Processing*, 60(2):585–599, February 2011.

[49] C. Therien. Welcome to the pysptools documentation. https://pysptools.source forge.io/, 2020.

[50] Rui Wang, Heng-Chao Li, Aleksandra Pizurica, Jun Li, Antonio Plaza, and William J. Emery. Hyperspectral unmixing using double reweighted sparse regression and total variation. *IIEEE Geoscience and Remote Sensing Letters*, 14(7):1146–1150, July 2017.

[51] Jiaojiao Wei and Xiaofei Wang. An overview on linear unmixing of hyperspectral data. *Mathematical Problems in Engineering*, 2020, August 2020.

[52] Michael E. Winter. N-FINDR: An algorithm for fast autonomous spectral end-member determination in hyperspectral data. In *Imaging Spectrometry V*, volume 3753, pages 266–275, July 1999.

[53] Jie Xue, Yee Leung, and Tung Fung. An unmixing-based bayesian model for spatio-temporal satellite image fusion in heterogeneous landscapes. *Remote Sensing*, 11(3):324, February 2019.

[54] L. Zhang, B. Wu, B. Huang, and P. Li. Nonlinear estimation of subpixel proportion via kernel least square regression. *International Journal of Remote Sensing*, 28(18):4157–4172, August 2007.

[55] Shaoquan Zhang, Jun Li, Heng-Chao Li, Chengzhi Deng, and Antonio Plaza. Spectral-spatial weighted sparse regression for hyperspectral image unmixing. *IIEEE Transactions on Geoscience and Remote Sensing*, 56(6):3265–3276, June 2018.

[56] Fei Zhu and Paul Honeine. Biobjective nonnegative matrix factorization: Linear versus kernel-based models. *IEEE Transactions on Geoscience and Remote Sensing*, 54(7):4012–4022, July 2016.

[57] Timo Zimmermann, Jens Rietdorf, and Rainer Pepperkok. Spectral imaging and its applications in live cell microscopy. *FEBS Letters*, 546(1):87–92, July 2003.

12

Structure Prediction from Scattering Profiles: A Neutron-Scattering Use-Case

Cristina Garcia-Cardona, Ramakrishnan Kannan, Travis Johnston, Thomas Proffen, and Sudip K. Seal

CONTENTS

DOI: 10.1201/9781003143376-12

12.1 Introduction

Crystallographic structure determination and refinement has been the cornerstone of materials science and our understanding of the atomic structure for many decades. The ability to design customized material with targeted mechanical and chemical properties relies on their internal structure. Neutron scattering is a state-of-the-art experimental technique that allows scientists to probe material structures with atomic resolutions by scattering beams of neutrons from them. While calculating the scattering intensities of a given crystal structure is straight forward, obtaining the atomic structure from the scattering intensities is not due to the so-called "crystallographic phase problem". In a nutshell, the scattering intensities we measure only give us the amplitude of the structure factor F but not the phase value .

Solving and refining the atomic structure of materials using neutron and x-ray scattering is one of the main driving forces behind understanding materials and their properties. Figure 12.1 illustrates a typical experiment related to the work in this chapter. The scientific sample is placed in a neutron beam and the arrangement of atoms gives raise to Bragg reflections, where waves show positive interference giving raise to the diffraction pattern. Here we deal with powder diffraction resulting in a one-dimensional pattern with Bragg peaks overlapping. While calculating a diffraction pattern from an atomic model is straight forward (e.g., using GSAS-II), the reverse is a classical inverse problem, which is the main motivation for the work presented. Hence, one of the major tasks in neutron data analysis is to solve the inverse problem of determining the internal structure of the target material based on its observed Bragg profile.

12.1.1 Motivation

Currently, it is common in the literature to solve these inverse problems using loop refinement techniques. That is, solve a forward physics-based model using an initial guess of the internal structure to generate a scattering Bragg profile and compare this generated Bragg

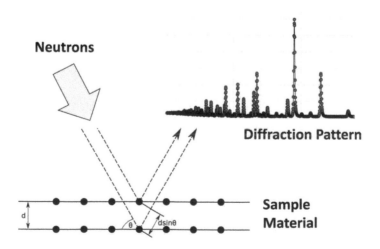

FIGURE 12.1
Illustration of neutron and X-scattering experiment for solving and refining atomic structure of materials.

profile with the observed experimental pattern. If both of these patterns are similar, the initial guess is a good representation of the material's internal structure. Otherwise, repeat this process with a different initial guess. This iterative loop refinement technique is like finding a needle in a haystack type of search problem. In practice, this loop refinement technique is very time-consuming as the number of iterations required to converge to an acceptable level of similarity between the computed and observed Bragg profiles vary widely between samples. It is common in practice that it can take many days, even weeks, to perform these hundreds and thousands of iterations till convergence. The overall time-to-solution and the quality of results from loop refinement methods also depend on the fidelity of the forward model used to generate the Bragg profiles within the loop iterations. There is a trade-off between fidelity, quality, and time. Higher fidelity usually results in a better quality of solutions but requires longer time-to-solution. On the other hand, shorter time-to-solutions with low-fidelity forward models compromise the quality of solutions. The main motivation of the work presented here is to evaluate alternative data-driven approaches to accelerate this discovery process while circumventing these trade-offs inherent in loop refinement methods.

12.1.2 Definitions

Crystalline materials belong 14 Bravais lattices [8] build from the seven crystallographic classes and shown in Figure 12.2. Each crystal class is characterized by a set of unit cell lengths, denoted by the parameter set $\{a, b, c\}$, and unit cell angles, denoted by the parameter set $\{\alpha, \beta, \gamma\}$. Depending on the crystallographic class of the material, these parameters satisfy unique constraint relations, as shown in Figure 12.2. Therefore, given the Bragg profile of a material sample, a trained ML model needs to predict the crystallographic class to which it belongs as well as the unit cell lengths and angles that satisfy the relations conditioned on that class.

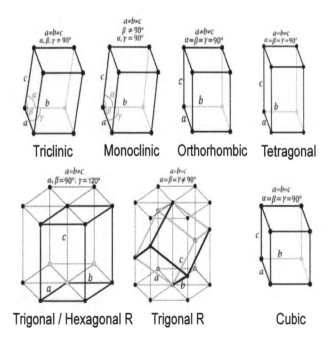

FIGURE 12.2
Figure shows the seven crystal classes.

12.1.3   Challenges

In order to replace these archaic loop refinement methods, this chapter explores pre-trained inverse machine learning (ML) models as inference engines for predictions of the structure parameters of material samples based on the information embedded in their Bragg profiles. However, data-driven ML approaches for this problem encounter a host of challenges.

- One of the major challenges in adopting an ML approach is the paucity of labeled neutron data with which to train ML models. Since neutron experiments are extremely resource-intensive and cannot be carried out on-demand, the amount of observed experimental data (Bragg profiles) that are reliably labeled are very limited. The quality of ML models is dependent on a large amount of training data.

- Another challenge is that the number and kinds of parameters to be predicted differ from one material to another depending on its crystallographic class. Thus, an ML model should not only be able to predict the class of the material but also the correct set of cell length/angle parameters that correspond to that class.

- Additionally, experimental observations collected from neutron detectors are mixed in with background noise that is unique to each detector experiment. Identifying the signal from the noise and using this information to wrangle the data for more accurate model training poses yet another challenge.

- Finally, the sampling space spanned by the structural parameters $\{a, b, c\}$ and $\{\alpha, \beta, \gamma\}$ grows exponentially with the number of parameters that define each symmetry class.

12.1.4   Related Work

ML-driven methods for structure determination from neutron scattering data is an emerging area of research. Recently, auto-encoders have been demonstrated to be effective in extracting spin Hamiltonians from neutron scattering data [12]. Principal component analysis with an artificial neural network was shown to predict neutron scattering cross-sections to constrain the parameters of a pre-existing model Hamiltonian in [15]. An unsupervised ML approach to study phase transitions in single crystal x-ray diffraction data was reported in [16]. An ML-based approach to classify the local chemical environment of specific metal families from the simulated K-edge XANES of a large number of compounds was reported in [10]. The use of ML in understanding neutron physics is beginning to gain greater acceptance as highlighted recently in [14]. To our knowledge, the results reported here represent one of the first efforts in this direction and makes multiple advances beyond the findings based on shallow ML models presented by the authors in [3].

12.1.5   Contributions

The work presented here makes multiple advances in the application of ML models to scientific knowledge discovery in the neutron sciences. Specific contributions are the following:

- We demonstrate that deep learning models perform significantly better than shallow learning models [3] in predicting structure parameters from neutron scattering data.

- We show that transfer learning techniques can be gainfully leveraged to build unified deep learning models that predict both the class labels and the class-dependent parameters from Bragg profiles with acceptable levels of accuracy.

- We present new heuristic methodologies to control the effects of background noise in the learning task.

- We conclusively demonstrate that an integrated model that predicts the class as well as the class-specific parameters in a single learning task performs better than class-conditional models which learn to predict the class and the class-dependent parameters as separate learning tasks.

Use of ML models for structure prediction from neutron scattering data is a very nascent field and, to the best of our knowledge, the methodology and results presented here have not been reported before. The rest of the chapter is organized as follows. Section 12.2 provides a brief overview of the type of ML models used in this study. Section 12.3 describes the data generation methods and specifications. In Section 12.4, the class-conditional and integrated models are described followed by the results of our experiments in Section 12.5. We draw some conclusion in Section 12.6.

12.2 Preliminaries

In this section, the network models used in the remainder of the chapter are briefly described.

12.2.1 Random Forest

Random forest (RF) is a type of ensemble predictor that aggregates results of distinct decision trees to solve classification or regression problems [2]. The aggregation of individual results improves the performance of the model reducing the variance in the predictions and leading to good generalization over data not used for training. More about RFs and their implementation can be found in [1–4].

12.2.2 Convolutional Neural Network

A convolutional neural network (CNN) [9] is a feed-forward neural network composed of convolution and pooling layers. Each node n in a convolutional layer i computes the following operation:

$$y_n^i = \sigma_{i,n} \left(\sum_m^{M^i} \mathbf{w}_{n,m}^i * \mathbf{x}_m^i + b_n^i \right)$$

where $\mathbf{x}_m^i$ represents the m-th input map at layer i; $\mathbf{w}_{n,m}^i$, b_n^i and $\sigma_{i,n}$ represent node parameters, namely, the m-th convolutional kernel, the bias and the activation function, respectively; M^i are the number of input maps at layer i (which correspond to the output maps at layer $i-1$, i.e., the number of nodes at layer $i-1$); and $*$ denotes a convolutional operation. The activation function is usually a rectified linear unit (ReLU) that corresponds to the following operation $\text{ReLU}(\nu) = \max(0, \nu)$. The pooling layer i reduces the dimensionality of the input pattern by averaging (or taking the maximum) over a fixed neighborhood structure in the input pattern, while sweeping the pattern with a consistent stride, and making the model more robust to local variations in the input. Note that the size of the stride used determines the extent of dimensionality reduction, e.g., if the pooling uses a stride of 2 the dimensionality is reduced to half and so on.

As any other neural network (NN) model, the CNN network is trained to produce a desired output by minimizing a loss function over the training data set. The minimization determines a set of model parameters, corresponding to the values of the convolutional kernels and the biases, that better approximate the desired output. However, since the node operations are based on convolutions that take into account the entire signal, and since the convolutional kernels are compactly supported kernels of low dimensionality (typically 3-11 components in 1D), CNNs are able to capture local invariant patterns in the data, which are optimal throughout the input signal. This also implies that the number of parameters is much less than it would be required if the layer was a regular (i.e., densely) connected layer, thereby yielding a more compact representation. In summary, CNN models capture local correlations using a much lower number of parameters than regular densely connected NNs.

12.2.3 Auto-Encoder

An auto-encoder consist of two parts: an encoder and a decoder [5,17]. The encoder maps the input into a hidden (latent) representation. The decoder is able to use the hidden representation and map it back to the input space. Auto-encoders are used for many applications. One possible application is dimensionality reduction: the encoder maps the input pattern to a latent representation with a smaller dimensionality than the input space, while the decoder tries to minimize the error in reconstructing the original pattern when mapping the latent representation back to the input space. Thus, an auto-encoder is a type of unsupervised model that can be trained by minimizing the error between input and output patterns. Since the error of reconstruction from a latent representation is minimized, it is deemed that the latent representation captures the essential features of the pattern, and since the latent representation has a smaller dimensionality than the input space, the auto-encoder trained in this way can be regarded as a dimensionality-reduction model. A convolutional auto-encoder (CAE) uses CNNs to build the encoder, the decoder, or both [6].

12.3 Data Generation

To address the challenge of scarcity of labeled data, the six-dimensional parameter space, collectively denoted by Y, where Y represents the set $\{a, b, c, \alpha, \beta, \gamma\}$ of unit cell parameters, is uniformly sampled (within appropriate ranges established from domain knowledge) and a Bragg profile is computed at each sampled point using the generalized structure analysis system (GSAS), a widely used structure refinement software in the neutron and X-ray crystallography community [13]. GSAS-II requires two sets of input specifications to simulate a diffraction pattern – (1) the crystallographic class information and (2) the instrument description. The first allows determination of the appropriate physics-driven constraint equations corresponding to the symmetry class, while the second allows modelling of the diffractometer physics used to generate the diffraction profile.

In this preliminary work, we limit the scope of our study to a perovskite material called *barium titanate* $(BaTiO_3)$. Since barium titanate, without doping, exists only in three of the seven symmetric classes labeled training data sets are generated only for the tetragonal, trigonal and cubic crystallographic symmetry classes using GSAS-II. The instrument specification used was for the NOMAD instrument [11] to maintain consistency with the NOMAD-generated experimental data against which the model predictions are subsequently validated.

Diffraction patterns from barium titanate in cubic, trigonal and tetragonal crystallographic classes were generated to build the labeled training set. For cubic class, a was

TABLE 12.1

Training Data Set of Labeled Neutron Diffractions

Class	Parameters	Samples (n)	Size (in GB)	Cell Length (step=10^{-3})	Cell Angle (step=$0.5°$)
Cubic (predict a)	$a = b = c$	1,000	0.043	[3.5, 4.5]	90°
Trigonal (predict a, α)	$a = b = c$ $\alpha = \beta = \gamma \neq 90°$	47,719	2	[3.8, 4.2]	[60°, 89.8°] [90.5°, 120°]
Tetragonal (predict a, c)	$a = b \neq c$ $\alpha = \beta = \gamma = 90°$	160,400	6.8	[3.8, 4.2]	90°

sampled in the range [3.5, 4.5] with step 10^{-3}. For the trigonal class, a was sampled in the range [3.8, 4.2] with step 10^{-3}, while α in the ranges [60°, 89.8°] and [90.5°, 120°] with step 0.5°. For the tetragonal class, a, c were sampled in the range [3.8, 4.2] with step 10^{-3}. We used a time-of-flight (ToF), in the range [1,360μs, 18,919μs] with step 0.0009381μs. Sweeping over these ranges yields a collection of diffraction patterns. Each diffraction pattern X is a set of 2807 2-tuples $(x, I(x))$, where x is the time-of-flight (ToF) and $I(x)$ is the GSAS-generated scattering profile. Table 12.1 lists the relations for the three symmetry classes used in this study.

Depending on the particular combination of crystallographic symmetry and structural parameters, each labeled sample in the training sets required between 2s to 30s to compute. An MPI-based parallel framework [3] was developed to generate the diffraction patterns in a concurrent and distributed manner.

12.4 Models

Recall that the cumulative task of predicting the structural parameters consists of predicting a class label as well as the unit cell parameters corresponding to that class. The first is a classification task while the second a regression task. As mentioned in Section 12.1, the number of cell parameters to be predicted varies with the predicted class. To address this challenge of conditional predictions, two categories of models were tested and their accuracies compared. In the first category, called *class-conditional models* (denoted by **C**), the overall prediction is carried out in a sequence of two independent learning tasks. In the first task, a classifier predicts the crystallographic symmetry and, in the second, a regressor predicts the cell lengths/angles. The second category, called *integrated* or *multi-task models* (denoted by **I**), are designed to predict the symmetry class and the cell lengths/angles in a single ML task. Central to both categories of models is the classifier that predicts the crystallographic class. This is described next.

12.4.1 Classifier for Crystallographic Symmetry

A 1D CNN was trained on data generated by GSAS-II (described in Section 12.3) to distinguish training samples belonging to the tetragonal, trigonal and cubic classes. Specifically, the CNN was designed to accept an input vector of length 2,807 representing the normalized intensities of each curve and predict (classify) the crystallographic symmetry group it belongs to. An example of an intensity vs. time of flight (ToF) curve (Bragg profile) is shown in Figure 12.3. The NN structure that was trained is as follows:

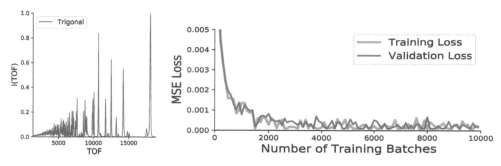

(a) Example of training data   (b) Training and Validation losses

FIGURE 12.3
Example of intensity vs time of flight curves (Bragg profile) used as training data and training and validation losses of the classifier.

- Feature Learner

  - 1D Convolution (16 learned filters, kernel width=3, stride=1)
  - 1D Max Pooling (kernel width=2, stride=2)
  - 1D Convolution (32 learned filters, kernel width=4, stride=2)
  - 1D Max Pooling (kernel width=2, stride=2)
  - Fully Connected (256 hidden neurons, w/ReLU activation)

- Fully Connected (3 output neurons, w/Softmax)

Training used stochastic gradient descent with a fixed learning rate of 0.001, weight decay of .005, momentum of 0.9, and a batch size of 90. Since the number of examples in each of the three groups is not balanced (128K Tetragonal examples, 38K Trigonal examples, and only 800 cubic examples) each mini-batch was constructed by randomly sampling an equal number of examples from each class, i.e., 30 examples from each class. The training and validation losses during training is shown in Figure 12.3(b).

12.4.2   Class-Conditional Models

12.4.2.1   Class-Conditional Random Forest, C_1

As in Figure 12.4(a), three different class-conditional RF models were trained. Each model was trained independently to predict the unit cell parameters for cubic, tetragonal and trigonal symmetries, respectively. Hence, given an input corresponding to a diffraction pattern and given the corresponding symmetry classification, the appropriate regression model is trained and used afterwards for prediction. The cubic model is trained to predict a, the tetragonal model is trained to predict a and c and the trigonal model is trained to predict a and α. In order to control the complexity of the RF and to prevent the models from overfitting, we limited the depth of the individual trees and set a maximum number of individual trees in the forest.

12.4.2.2   Transfer Learner, C_2

It is clear from Figure 12.3(b) that the fine-tuned classifier discussed in Section 12.4.1 classifies the cubic, tetragonal and trigonal classes with high accuracy in the synthetic data set. The class-conditional model discussed here, called the *transfer learner*, leverages the

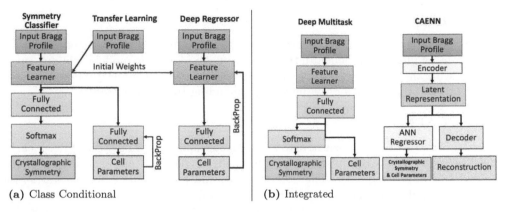

(a) Class Conditional | **(b)** Integrated

FIGURE 12.4
(a) Class-conditional models (C_2 and C_3) first predict a crystallographic symmetric class followed by a regression to predict the cell lengths and angles and (b) integrated models (I_1 and I_3) are trained to perform classification and regression as a single learning task.

features (learnt with high accuracy) by the classifier to regress the continuous parameters Y. Note that for the tetragonal class, $Y = \{a, c, 90°\}$; for the trigonal class, $Y = \{a, a, \alpha\}$; and for cubic, $Y = \{a, a, 90°\}$. For each Bragg profile (training sample), the trained classifier from Section 12.4.1 is run and 256 features learned by the first fully connected layer is used as the input features of a fully connected regressor model to estimate the continuous parameter set Y updating only the weights of this fully connected during back propagation. Note that the regressor still trains separately conditioned on the predicted class.

12.4.2.3   Deep Regressor, C_3

As a natural extension to the transfer learner model, a second class-conditional model is evaluated in which the last layer is replaced with a linear layer to produce continuous outputs Y using mean square error to compute the loss and update the weights of *all* the layers during back-propagation and not just the weight of the linear regressor. Note that this too is a class-conditional model, which we refer to as *deep regressor*. In this model, the weights from the classifier are only used to initialize the corresponding layers in Deep Regressor.

12.4.3   Integrated Models

Recall that integrated models predict both the class labels and the regression values of the unit cell lengths/angles in a single prediction task. Accordingly, as in Figure 12.4(b), the integrated models predict four outputs, namely, the class label, S (0: cubic, 1: tetragonal and 2: trigonal), the lattice parameter a, the lattice parameter c and the angle parameter α. Note that these four predictions form the minimal set of parameters necessary to determine the structures of the three crystal symmetries studied here (see Table 12.1).

12.4.3.1   Deep MultiTask, I_1

This multitask network, referred to as *Deep MultiTask*, uses the output from the first fully connected layer of the classifier from Section 12.4.1 to train both a regressor (using softmax) in addition to the original classification task. The classifier updates the weights using the error obtained from cross entropy loss while the regressor uses MSE loss for every batch.

12.4.3.2   Random Forest, I_2

Instead of building a class-conditional regression model for each of the symmetries, RF were used to train an integrated model. In this case a unique regression model with four outputs is trained with the goal of predicting the class of the crystal symmetry and the unit cell parameters (a, c and α) for a given input corresponding to a Bragg profile.

12.4.3.3   CAENN, I_3

In order to construct features sensitive to local correlations in Bragg profiles, a deep learning model based on CNN was implemented. Specifically, a 1D CNN auto-encoder (CAE) was combined with a NN regressor. The CAE helps to find a good latent representation for a given Bragg profile. This latent representation is used as the input to an integrated NN-based regressor that predicts the crystal symmetry and the unit cell parameters. Since all the Bragg profiles share the same x component (ToF), each profile, though two-dimensional, can be regarded as a one-dimensional pattern with the understanding that the first dimension is common to all the samples. As such, a 1D symmetrical bottle-neck CAE suffices. The CAE is designed with a symmetrical bottle-neck architecture of 4 layers (total), the thin part of which corresponds to a latent representation. Note that some symmetrical bottle-neck auto-encoders are built with tied weights, but in our case, we learned different (not-tied) weights for encoder and decoder. Finally, an integrated NN regressor with 4 densely connected layers and ReLU activations is built to predict simultaneously the crystal symmetry and unit cell parameters (a, c and α) for a given Bragg profile.

12.5   Results

The models described above were trained using data generated by GSAS-II, as described in Section 12.3. These trained models were then used as inference engines to predict the structure parameters using experimental Bragg profiles collected using the NOMAD diffractometer for barium titanate samples. The predicted parameters were then used as inputs to the GSAS-II simulator and the resulting simulated Bragg profile was compared with the experimental Bragg profile for validation. The remainder of this section presents the results of these experiments using models described in the previous section.

12.5.1   Metrics

Since we evaluate the performance of class conditional and integrated models on the parameters a, c and α, we use mean squared error (MSE).

$$\mathrm{MSE}(Y, \hat{Y}) = \frac{1}{n} \sum_{i=1}^{3} ||Y_i - \hat{Y}_i||_2^2 \,, \tag{12.1}$$

The vectors $Y_i, \hat{Y}_i \in \mathrm{R}^n$ represent the ground truth and predicted value of the parameters a, c and α, respectively. The mean squared error reported on class conditional models and integrated models are different with respect to the number of samples n. In the case of class conditional models, $Y \in \mathrm{R}^{n \times 3}$, where n is the total test samples for each of the class as detailed in Section 12.3. For an integrated model, however, $n = 41,824$ includes samples from all three symmetric classes, viz., cubic, trigonal and tetragonal.

12.5.2   Synthetic Data

The simulated diffraction patterns were split into two sets: 80% for training and 20% for testing. This corresponds to the following sizes:

- Cubic: 800 diffraction patterns for training and 200 for testing.

- Trigonal: 38,175 diffraction patterns for training and 9,544 for testing.

- Tetragonal: 128,320 diffraction patterns for training and 32,080 for testing.

- Integrated: 167,295 diffraction patterns for training and 41,824 for testing.

All the data were pre-processed in the same way. Specifically, each histogram was vertically shifted to the minimum value of 0 and then scaled appropriately to the maximum value of 1. The following subsections describe the different models that were trained and the results of evaluating them on the test sets (samples not seen during training).

12.5.2.1   Random Forest

The following parameters were used to train the RF models. Cubic: a RF of 150 trees with maximum depth of 50, trigonal: a RF of 200 trees with maximum depth of 50 and tetragonal: a RF of 200 trees with maximum depth of 50. The integrated model corresponds to a RF of 250 trees with maximum depth of 50.

For training a random subsample over the training set was used (cubic: 792; trigonal: 6,500; tetragonal: 20,500 and integrated: 27,800 diffraction patterns). Note that to reduce the noise, the left-most and the right-most ends of the diffraction patterns were discarded, specifically 256 and 55 pairs of $(x, I(x))$ values at the low and the high TOF (x) ends, respectively, resulting in training patterns of dimensionality 2,496. This heuristic is an ad hoc attempt motivated by the experimental patterns available, which exhibit rapid oscillations at the low TOF end and a saturated zero-signal at the high TOF end. Evaluation of other strategies to reduce noise at pre-processing stages will be part of future work.

12.5.2.2   Transfer Learning

Note that the two class-conditional models, C_2 and C_3, and the integrated model, I_1, are all variants of transfer learning approaches. These three models were trained using a batch size of 512 and trained for 500 epochs. In order to produce balanced classes, 800 cubic samples were used with replacement in every epoch. We used ADAM optimizer with learning of 10^{-3} for backpropogation.

12.5.2.3   CAENN

The following parameters were used to train the CAENN model. Note that the tails of the Bragg profiles are discarded yielding a 2,496 dimensionality for the input patterns like in the RF model.

CNN Auto-Encoder: The 1D CAE is designed with a symmetrical bottle-neck architecture of 4 layers total: 2 for the encoder and 2 for the decoder. The structure that was trained for the encoder is the following:

- 1D Convolution (9 learned filters, kernel width = 15, stride = 1) followed by ReLU activation.

- 1D Max Pooling (kernel width = 2, stride = 2)

- 1D Convolution (2 learned filters, kernel width = 7, stride = 1) followed by ReLU activation.

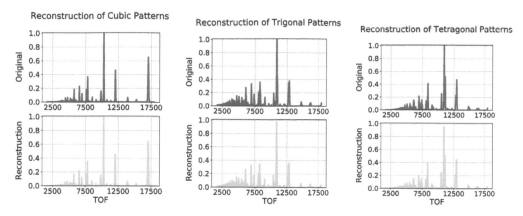

FIGURE 12.5
Examples of CAE reconstruction for test samples. For each class, one random sample was reconstructed.

- 1D Max Pooling (kernel width = 2, stride = 2)

The decoder is a symmetrical reflection of this structure, with weights that are also learned during CAE training.

A total of 34,100 diffraction patterns from the three different symmetries were used for training. This is about 20% of the tetragonal and trigonal training sets and 800 diffraction patterns of the cubic symmetry. The CAE was trained for 250 epochs, to minimize the mean absolute error function, using an Adaptive Moment Estimation (ADAM) [7] optimizer with a learning rate of 10^{-3} and a batch size of 20. The best model over five-fold cross validation evaluated over the testing set is selected as the CAE model. The testing MSE for this CAE is 85.34. Randomly selected examples of reconstructions for samples in the test set for each of the three crystal symmetries cubic, trigonal and tetragonal evaluated using the best CAE model are shown in Figure 12.5.

NN Regressor: The integrated NN regressor has a four-layer structure with 150, 70 and 20 nodes in the intermediate layers and 4 outputs. The random subsample of 34,100 diffraction patterns that was used for training the CAE is also used to train the NN. The regressor was trained to minimize an ℓ_2-regularized MSE function with 10^{-4} regularization weight, during 500 epochs, using an ADAM optimizer with an initial learning rate of 10^{-3} and a decaying factor of 0.1 on epochs 100, 250 and 400, and a batch size of 20.

12.5.2.4   Model Performance

Tables 12.2 and 12.3 summarize the performance of the different models on the synthetic dataset. Table 12.2 shows that class conditional RF performs better in the case of cubic class, which requires prediction of only one parameter a. However, when multiple labels need to be predicted, as in trigonal and tetragonal classes, the class conditional Deep Regressor model performs better. The CAENN integrated models outperformed both the RF and Multitask networks. The CAENN and Multitask models were trained with 500 epochs each. A longer training of the models has the potential to further improve the results.

12.5.3   Experimental Data

Experimental neutron powder diffraction data of barium titanate as a function of temperature was collected on the NOMAD instrument housed in the Spallation Neutron Source at Oak Ridge National Laboratory. In all cases, "traditional" structure analysis was carried

TABLE 12.2
MSE: Class Conditional Models – Synthetic Test Set. Transfer Learning-Based Models C_2 and C_3 Outperform RF for Multilabel Scenarios.

| Symmetry | RF (C_1) | Model MSE | |
		Transfer (C_2) Learning	Deep (C_3) Regressor
Cubic	$\mathbf{1.20 \times 10^{-6}}$	4.71×10^{-4}	1.00×10^{-5}
Trigonal	8.14×10^{-4}	1.01×10^{-2}	$\mathbf{1.40 \times 10^{-5}}$
Tetragonal	5.84×10^{-6}	5.18×10^{-4}	$\mathbf{2.60 \times 10^{-5}}$

TABLE 12.3
MSE: Integrated Models – Synthetic Test Set. Integrated Models Perform Better Than Class Conditional Models

Model	MSE
RF (I_1)	1.48×10^{-4}
Multitask(I_3)	1.90×10^{-5}
CAENN (I_2)	$\mathbf{5.96 \times 10^{-6}}$

out to obtain the structural parameters. The crystallographic class and the lattice parameter set $\{a, c, \alpha\}$ were used as labels and the ML models were evaluated against this ground truth set. A total of 15 experimental diffraction patterns were evaluated – one belonging to the trigonal symmetry class and the remaining fourteen belonging to the tetragonal class.

12.5.3.1 Science Guided Pre-Processing

As mentioned in Section 12.1, experimental signals contain detector-specific background noise. Background signals in neutron detectors originate from a variety of sources (diffuse scattering, air scattering, detector readout noise and others) and need to be subtracted out to improve the signal-to-noise ratio. A second-order Chebyschev polynomial of the first kind is used to model a NOMAD-specific background signal for each experimentally observed diffraction pattern independently. A signal threshold in the experimental Bragg profile is adjusted such that the area under the profile closely matches (differs by less than 10^{-4}) with that under the Chebyschev polynomial. This polynomial is then subtracted out from the original experimental signal. Preliminary results indicate that this method is more robust to experimental conditions than previous quantitative measures used. In addition to the background corrections, the x-axis (ToF) also needs to be adjusted for better consistency between the simulated and experimentally collected Bragg profiles. For this, each $(x, I(x))$ pair in the experimental diffraction pattern is matched with the closest TOF from the simulated ToF (which is the same for all the GSAS-II generated diffraction patterns). Finally, the intensities, $I(x)$, for the experimental and Bragg profiles are clipped to the $[0,1]$ range. Examples of the pre-processing of experimental data, including the background estimation and the processed experimental diffraction pattern, are included in Figure 12.6.

12.5.3.2 Model Performance

Tables 12.4 and 12.5 summarize the performance on the experimental data. Figure 12.7 (center and bottom rows) shows the comparison of the three first experimental data samples with the diffraction patterns generated from the predicted unit cell parameters.

The main outcome of these experiments is that optimizing the combination of cross entropy and MSE losses is more effective than using integer class labels and optimizing

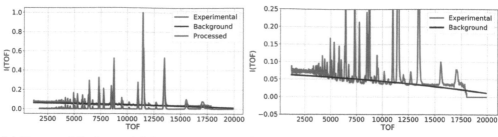

(a) Tetragonal Background Subtraction

(b) Tetragonal Background Subtraction-zoom

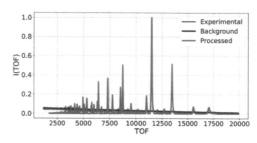

(c) Trigonal Background Substraction

FIGURE 12.6

Experimental data with background noise. Since the inverse model is built without the noise, the experimental data with the noise will result in wrong prediction of cell length and angle. (a): show the zoomed view of presence of background noise for a tetragonal symmetric class and the corresponding processed data to remove this noise is shown in (b). (c): shows the experimental data of trigonal symmetric class with detector specific background noise and our proposed way of removing this noise.

TABLE 12.4

MSE: Class Conditional – Experimental Data

	Model MSE		
Symmetry	**RF (C_1)**	**Transfer (C_2)**	**Deep (C_3)**
Trigonal	6.30×10^{-2}	1.91×10^{-1}	6.75×10^{-2}
Tetragonal	1.08×10^{-2}	3.08×10^{-2}	3.08×10^{-4}

TABLE 12.5

MSE: Integrated Models – Experimental. Deep Learning Based Models Predict Experimental Parameters with More Accuracy Than RF

Model	MSE
RF (I_1)	1.17×10^{-1}
Multitask (I_2)	$\mathbf{1.23 \times 10^{-3}}$
CAENN (I_3)	2.00×10^{-3}

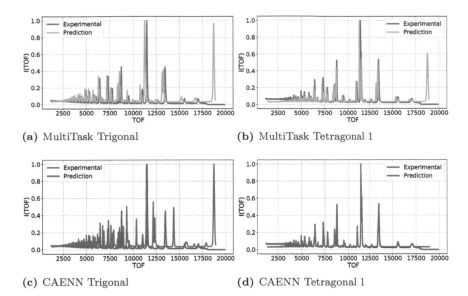

FIGURE 12.7

Examples of integrated model predictions for experimental data. Comparison of experimental measurements and diffraction patterns generated from predicted unit cell parameters using Multitask and CAENN. The ground truths for trigonal are $a = 3.9968$ and $\alpha = 89.84°$, and tetragonal are $a = 3.9857$ and $c = 4.0277$. (a): Multitask (MT) trigonal prediction for $a = 3.9272$ and $\alpha = 89.3611$; (b) MT tetragonal predicted $a = 3.9318, c = 4.0414$. (c): CAENN trigonal prediction $a = 4.0094$ and $\alpha = 97.61°$; (d) CAENN tetragonal prediction $a = 3.9851$ and $c = 4.0358$.

the MSE loss. This is mainly due to the fact that the minimization of the cross entropy effectively maximizes the likelihood of the classes predicted by the model, which is not guaranteed for the minimization of the MSE loss over integer labels.

12.6 Conclusions

This chapter demonstrates the viability of a data-driven approach to the long-standing problem of determining material structure from neutron scattering data. Existing methods are extremely time-consuming and rely on the fidelity of physics-driven forward models for accuracy. The alternative presented here is fast, data-driven and less reliant on the fidelity of the underlying physics. Using perovskite as an example material sample, the chapter reports an extensive comparative study of the efficacies of multiple deep learning ML models (and combinations thereof) in predicting its structural parameters. The overall structure prediction task involves the classification task of predicting the crystallographic class that the sample belongs to and the regression task of predicting the unit cell lengths/angles corresponding to that class.

In this context, we presented the performance results of two types of ML models – class-conditional and integrated. Class-conditional models learn the class followed by the corresponding cell parameters in a sequence of two learning tasks while the integrated models learn them both in a single learning task. Multiple variants of these two broad categories were trained using synthetically generated data. These trained models were validated against experimental data and good prediction accuracies were obtained. Overall, we note that deep learning models benefit more from the multi-task approach than RF models. For the integrated models, we found that optimizing the combination of cross entropy and MSE losses is more effective than using integer class labels and optimizing the MSE loss, mainly due to the fact that minimization of the cross entropy effectively maximizes the likelihood of the classes predicted by the model, which is not guaranteed for the minimization of the MSE loss over integer labels. In future, multi-task networks that can predict the crystallographic classes not studied in this report will be trained in addition to exploring more sophisticated transfer learning models capable of accurate predictions on experimental diffraction patterns gathered from a wider range of diffractometers.

Bibliography

[1] Scikit-learn: Machine Learning in Python, 2020.

[2] Leo Breiman. Random forests. *Machine Learning*, 45(1):5–32, October 2001.

[3] Cristina Garcia-Cardona, Ramakrishnan Kannan, Travis Johnston, Thomas Proffen, Katharine Page, and Sudip K. Seal. Learning to predict material structure from neutron scattering data. In *2019 IEEE International Conference on Big Data (Big Data)*, Los Angeles, CA, USA, December 9-12, 2019, pages 4490–4497, 2019.

[4] Aurélien Géron. *Hands-On Machine Learning with Scikit-Learn & TensorFlow*. O'Reilly, 1 edition, 2017.

[5] G. E. Hinton, A. Krizhevsky, and S. D. Wang. Transforming auto-encoders. In Timo Honkela, Włodzisław Duch, Mark Girolami, and Samuel Kaski, editors, *Artificial Neural Networks and Machine Learning – ICANN 2011*, pages 44–51, 2011.

[6] Borui Hou and Ruqiang Yan. Convolutional auto-encoder based deep feature learning for finger-vein verification. In *2018 IEEE International Symposium on Medical Measurements and Applications (MeMeA)*. IEEE, 2018.

[7] Diederik P. Kingma and Jimmy Lei Ba. ADAM: a method for stochastic optimization. In *International Conference on Learning Representations*, pages 1–13, 2015.

[8] Charles Kittel. *Introduction to Solid State Physics*. Wiley, 8th edition, 2004.

[9] Y. LeCun, Y. Bengio, and G. E. Hinton. Deep learning. *Nature*, 521:436–444, 2015.

[10] Deyu Lu, Matthew Carbone, Mehmet Topsakal, and Shinjae Yoo. Using machine learning to predict local chemical environments from x-ray absorption spectra. In *APS March Meeting Abstracts*, vol. 2019, pp. A18-005, 2019.

[11] Oak Ridge National Laboratory. *NOMAD*.

[12] Anjana M. Samarakoon, Kipton Barros, Ying Wai Li, Markus Eisenbach, Qiang Zhang, Feng Ye, V. Sharma, Z. L. Dun, Haidong Zhou, Santiago A. Grigera, Cristian D. Batista, and D. Alan Tennant. Machine-learning-assisted insight into spin ice dy2ti2o7. *Nature Communications*, 11(1):892, 2020.

[13] B. H. Toby and R. B. Von Dreele. GSAS-II: the genesis of a modern open-source all purpose crystallography software package. *Journal of Applied Crystallography*, 46(2):544–549, 2013.

[14] Sam Jackson Tony Hey, Keith Butler, and Jeyarajan Thiyagalingam. Machine learning and big scientific data. *Philosophical Transactions of the Royal Society A: Mathematical, Physical and Engineering Sciences*, 378(2166), 2020.

[15] Robert Twyman, Stuart Gibson, James Molony, and Jorge Quintanilla. A machine-learning approach to magnetic neutron scattering. In *APS March Meeting Abstracts*, vol. 2019, pp. A18-010, 2019.

[16] Jordan Venderley, Michael Matty, and Eun-Ah Kim. Unsupervised machine learning of single crystal x-ray diffraction data. In APS March Meeting Abstracts, vol. 2019, pp. A18-001, 2019.

[17] Pascal Vincent , Hugo Larochelle, Isabelle Lajoie, Yoshua Bengio, Pierre-Antoine Manzagol, and Léon Bottou. "Stacked denoising autoencoders: Learning useful representations in a deep network with a local denoising criterion." *Journal of machine learning research*, 11, 12, 2010.

13

Physics-Infused Learning: A DNN and GAN Approach

Zhibo Zhang, Ryan Nguyen, Souma Chowdhury, and Rahul Rai

CONTENTS

13.1   Introduction

Modeling the behavior of complex physical systems is imperative to many science and engineering applications. A predictive modeler is often faced with the following (some very limiting) conditions including (1) the unavailability of a complete system model leading to an abstraction of the real system, (2) the overall physical system is described primarily by an interconnection of physical components, (3) the constitutive physics equations of the

DOI: 10.1201/9781003143376-13

system components being known for only a subset of the components, (4) the lack of the parameters of the system components, (5) a highly nonlinear multi-physics system having multiple operating modes, and (6) sparse observations of the system behavior available through a limited number of sensors. The two main approaches commonly used to model physical systems include: using *data-driven* algorithms resulting in a black-box type of models and using *physics-based models*.

Traditionally, physics-based modeling is based on existing knowledge of the world, e.g., derived from first principles and observing the system behavior [25]. However, physics-based methods often either fail to fully capture the complex characteristics of system behavior due to the modeling abstractions resulting in low fidelity and reduced-order models, or are computationally prohibitive for usage in time-sensitive (e.g., controls) and iterative (e.g., design and diagnosis problem) settings due to the high computational cost associated with high-fidelity simulations.

Purely data-driven based methods have found widespread success in domains such as image processing, natural language understanding, and Big Data analytics [14,27]. However, data-driven approaches are found to be poor at generalizing and extrapolating beyond their initial set of training data, especially when dealing with complex nonlinear systems. Their black-box nature can be a double-edged sword as they can be undesirably physics agnostic. Failure to respect physics principles raise reliability concerns for their usage in modeling real-life cyber-physical system applications. Additionally, highly accurate data-driven models such as Deep Learning based data-driven approaches are "data-hungry". In many engineering applications, the data set is often limited or sparse due to the significant cost of collecting data via expensive simulations or physical experiments [9,11,33].

To overcome the aforementioned limitations of both the approaches, it is prudent if not imperative to combine physics equation based models (if and when available) with data-driven models. In this vein, we propose two novel hybrid architectures termed PI-DNN (Physics-Infused DNN) and PI-GAN (Physics-Infused GAN), which are amalgamations of computationally inexpensive physics-based models and data-driven models. Specifically, the *central contribution* of the current work lies in: **(1)** *Proposing two different data-driven based hybrid architectures PI-DNN and PI-GAN* **(2)** *identifying the performance trade-offs of integrating the (low-fidelity) physics output into characteristically different layers of the DNN*, and **(3)** *demonstrating the benefits (in terms of performance and robustness metrics) of our hybrid architectures over purely data-driven architectures across wide range of hyper-parameter settings for two different dynamic system problems*. We show that the hybrid models provide noticeably better performance when compared with purely data-driven models on several metrics and these differences are relatively independent of DNN's hyperparameter choices.

Our model is inspired by previous work where physics is integrated with data-driven models in order to enhance the predictive capabilities of the overall hybrid model [6,11,13, 26,38]. Most of the existing work clearly shows that the physics of the system is pivotal in guiding the data-driven predictions and set a precedent for the outlined work. However, we innovate on several fronts. First, we outline several ways of infusing information with DNNs to create simple hybrid architectures. Second, we explore using similar infusions to a more complex GAN-based hybrid architecture. Third, several metrics and a couple of new example problems specifically suited to hybrid modeling domain have been outlined. Fourth, it is shown that when it comes to hybrid models all physics-based models are not created equal. In other words, the performance of the hybrid models is dependent on the quality of physics models available.

The remainder of this paper is organized as follows. Some related works are shown in Section 13.2. Section 13.3 outlines our proposed new hybrid architectures. Section 13.4 describes the two test problems and the metrics used for testing and comparing the performance of each architecture. The training and testing results are discussed in Section 13.5. Section 13.6 ends with concluding remarks and future work.

13.2 Related Work

In this section, we briefly review the related work.

13.2.1 Hybrid Modeling

Currently, with the rapid emergence of different powerful data-driven models, the hybrid model has returned to our vision. It becomes possible for us to explore a wiser way to combine the physics-based model and data-driven model. In recent years, existing modeling frameworks derived from this hybrid modeling concept can be divided into three categories based on how they use the physics model [2, 39]. (1) **Combination Approaches**: In this category, the output of the physics-based model is directly combined with the data-driven model either as an extra input (parallel combination) or as the only input to the data-driven model (sequential combination) [3, 9, 11, 26]. This synergy is relatively straightforward and requires minimal changes to the manner in which the data-driven model is trained. However, in this approach, since the Physics model outcomes are merely an input to the data-driven model, while accuracy (or faster training) benefits might be realizable, there's hardly any theoretical guarantees that this will improve generalizability or extrapolability. (2) **Constraint Approaches**: Researchers employ physical information as constraints to the learning process, by manipulating the loss function [11, 22, 32]. Considering the physical information as constraints is an insightful way to utilize physical information. A non-standard loss function allows the model to pay specific attention to different variables. Nonetheless, the existing works only propose simple constraints such as monotonicity and bounds [22]. Complex constraints invoke difficulties in the training procedure. (3) **Embedding Approaches**: In this class of approaches, the data-driven model is used to replace the computationally expensive component in the physics-based model in order to speed up or enhance the physics-based solver [12, 16, 17, 19]. Although these methods facilitate improved accuracy when the computational component is easy to split, the application domain of these methods is limited. Commonly, the physics models are complex and highly coupled, so these methods are difficult to apply widely. Our proposed methods come from combination approaches. To advance the hybrid model's performance, a simplified physics model, partial physics model, is derived. The partial physics model shares the same input and output with the ground truth model (experiment or high-fidelity simulation). However, the partial physics model owns the lower computational complexity.

13.2.2 GAN

In this subsection, existing work related to GANs is discussed. GANs have many uses ranging from improving image resolution [4, 15] to creating music [20]. Due to their range of application and modularity, they are widely studied. In the vein of hybrid modeling, there are two classes of fusing physics and data driven models: adding physics-derived constraints to the data driven model and sequential data transfer between models. Authors of [24, 36] and [37] discuss methods of adding physics-derived constraints while [34] adopts a sequential data transfer approach. Authors of [24] introduce PhysicsGAN, which implements a physics constraint on the training process. PhysicsGAN uses a GAN to improve the capabilities of deblurring images. The GAN is constrained by a physics model for the degradation process to guarantee the GAN is producing images that are consistent with the observed inputs. Authors of [36] and [37] take similar approaches to constraining the GAN architecture and they both refer to their architecture as: PI-GAN. Authors of [36] use their architecture to solve forward, inverse and mixed stochastic problems based on a limited number of sparse measurements. They encoded the governing physical laws in the form of stochastic differential equations (SDEs) into the architecture of GANs. The authors demonstrate that this method is effective in solving SDEs for up to 30 dimensions, but mention that it can be extrapolated to higher dimensions in theory. Authors of [37] similarly constrains the prediction using partial differential equations (PDE), but is used to propagate uncertainty through complex physical systems. These physics-informed constraints provide a regularization mechanism for effectively training deep probabilistic models for modeling physical systems. Pivoting focus, we draw attention to a sequential data transfer approach: 3D-PhysNet, introduced by [34], 3D-PhysNet is a deep variational encoder with a discriminator that is trained using the data from a finite element simulator for discovering the behavior of deformable objects under external forces. The data first enters the finite element simulator model, which is the physics model, and then the output of the physics model is provided to GAN, the data driven model.

Most GANs suffer from a lack of stability; a small change in hyperparameters generates drastically different results; this makes it challenging to train GANs. One example of a GAN modification to improve stability is the Wasserstein GAN (WGAN). WGAN [1] is similar to the regular GAN with minor differences that improve the overall performance. One key difference is that the discriminator does not have a sigmoid function as the output activation function, so the output of the WGAN's discriminator is not constrained to be in the range $[-1, 1]$. Another related approach is the least-squares GAN. LSGAN [18] differs from the regular GAN by modifying the log loss with an L2 loss function. Therefore, the LSGAN penalizes samples that are far away from the decision boundary. A common challenge that GANs face is the vanishing gradient; this is where the discriminator starts to overpower the generator, and the gradient diminishes until there is a negligible change, and the generator stops learning. By penalizing outliers in the sample set, more gradients can be generated when updating the generator. Outlier penalization helps with the vanishing gradient problem and stabilizes the learning process [18].

As previously mentioned, our current work is focused on using the physics model's output as input to the data-driven model as opposed to using *features* derived from a class of data-driven techniques into a different class of data-driven technique. We plan to extend the literature in hybrid models that focuses on sequential data transfer – opposed to constraining the data-driven model. Our model combines a partial physics model with a data-driven model. We leverage modern GAN stability techniques to achieve optimal results.

13.3   Methodology

Details pertaining to PI-DNN and PI-GAN architectures are outlined next.

13.3.1   PI-DNN

In complex dynamical system, a set $R = \{(x^{(i)}, y^{(i)})\}_{i=1}^{n}$ is generated by high fidelity physics model, where $x^{(i)} \in X$ represents the observed state and control input at time zero and $y^{(i)} \in Y_r$ represents the corresponding state predicted at a future time. X and Y_r serves as the ground truth. A purely data-driven model form another set $M = \{(x^{(i)}, \hat{y}^{(i)})\}_{i=1}^{n}$, where $\hat{y}^{(i)} \in \hat{Y}$ is the output of data-driven model that seeks to approximate Y_r. On the other hand, using the same input set, $x^{(i)}$, a partial physics model generates $y_p^{(i)} \in Y_p$.

The goal of the hybrid model is to exploit the information from the partial physics model to aid the data-driven model for a better approximation of the ground truth. Our choice of the data-driven model, DNN, is expected to act as a universal approximator that lacks an intrinsic ability to conform to physics. The partial physics predictions could potentially address this gap. Thus, our hypothesis is to use the output of the physics model Y_p as an additional input to the DNN model to better approximate the ground truth. We outline three different hybrid DNN architectures that have different locations where the partial physics model information is infused (Figures 13.1–13.3). Infusing physics information in multi-location could play the same role as the skip connection in ResNet [7], which is beneficial for the model convergence, especially for complex problems.

The three configurations resulting from different locations in the DNN network where the partial physics model input is amalgamated are: *front infused hybrid architecture, back infused architecture*, and *mixed infused architecture*.

In front infused hybrid architecture (as shown in Figure 13.1), the first layer serves as a port of confluence for the output of the partial physics model Y_p, along with the standard input X. The goal is to trace a function $h(t)$, where $Y_r \approx h(X, Y_p)$ for each training example. To find a function $h(t)$ we must decide on its representation. In this architecture, the function $h(t)$ is described by Equation (13.1).

$$h^{(i)} = \begin{cases} g^{(1)}(W^{(1)^T}(X, Y_p) + b^{(1)}) & i = 1 \\ g^{(i)}(W^{(i)^T}h^{(i-1)} + b^{(i)}) & i = 2 \ to \ L \end{cases} \quad (13.1)$$

where g is the activation function, L is the total number of layers, W is the vector of hidden layer weights, b is the array of hidden layer bias and $h^{(L)}$ is the final prediction [5].

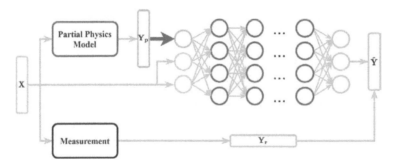

FIGURE 13.1
Front infused model.

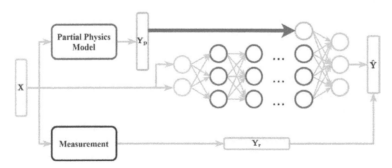

FIGURE 13.2
Back infused model.

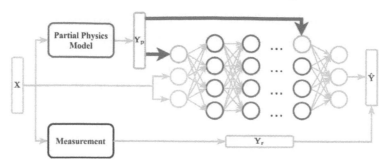

FIGURE 13.3
Mixed infused model.

As shown in Figure 13.2, the back infused hybrid architecture intakes the output of partial physics model Y_p in the output layer. Function $h(t)$, as discussed before, is given by Equation (13.2).

$$h^{(i)} = \begin{cases} g^{(i)}(W^{(i)^T}X + b^{(i)}) & i = 1 \; to \; L-1 \\ g^{(L)}(W^{(L)^T}(h^{(L-1)}, Y_p) + b^{(L)}) & i = L \end{cases} \tag{13.2}$$

For mixed infused hybrid architecture (Figure 13.3), the output of partial physics (Y_p) is used as input in both the first and last layers of the neural network. This architecture is a combination of first and second architectures. Thus, function $h(t)$ is given by Equation (13.3).

$$h^{(i)} = \begin{cases} g^{(1)}(W^{(1)^T}(X, Y_p) + b^{(1)}) & i = 1 \\ g^{(i)}(W^{(i)^T}X + b^{(i)}) & i = 2 \; to \; L-1 \\ g^{(L)}(W^{(L)^T}(h^{(L-1)}, Y_p) + b^{(L)}) & i = L \end{cases} \tag{13.3}$$

where m is the intermediate layer infused with Y_p. In the next step, our task is to find a choice of W and b such that $h_{W,b}(y_p^{(i)})$ best approximates $y_r^{(i)}$ [5]. In other words, we search for a choice of W and b that minimizes Equation (13.4):

$$J(W, b) = MSE(h_{W,b}(X, Y_p, Y_r)) = \frac{1}{N}\sum_{i=1}^{N}\|g(W^T(X, Y_p) + b) - Y_r\| \tag{13.4}$$

We use gradient decent optimization approaches to minimize the objective function J.

13.3.2   PI-GAN

The GAN has two main components illustrated in Figure 13.4: the generator and the discriminator. The GAN architecture presents a unique environment where two neural networks compete against one another in a minimax game [8] or a zero-sum non-cooperative game. The adversaries' key intent is to maximize their action impact and minimize the impact of the opponent's action. The GAN converges when the discriminator and the generator reach a Nash equilibrium [8].

For the Physics Infused GAN (PI-GAN) hybrid model (Figure 13.4), the generator takes y_p as the input from the physics-based model, and outputs $\hat{y}$ via function $g(y_p, W^{(g)})$ in which $W^{(g)}$ is the vector of hidden layer weights in the generator architecture. This is inherently different than using noise as input, which is traditionally used by generators in

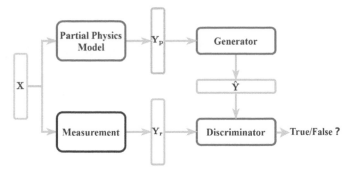

FIGURE 13.4
Flow chart for PI-GANs model.

the GAN framework. The innovation is more visible through the lens of residual modeling. This approach fixes the residuals to a desirable location, y_p, and that fixed location should reduce the difficulty of the mapping to $\hat{y}$.

Its adversary discriminator gives probability $d(\hat{y}, y_r, W^{(d)})$ based on $\hat{y}$ and the real output y_r, in which $W^{(d)}$ is the vector of hidden layer weights in the discriminator architecture. Furthermore, function $v(W^{(g)}, W^{(d)})$ specifies the rewards for the discriminator. The generator receives $-v(W^{(g)}, W^{(d)})$ as its reward. Both generator and discriminator maximize their rewards in zero-sum game. Finally, according to Equation 13.5, the function converges at:

$$g^* = argmin_g(max_d(v(g, d)))$$ (13.5)

Here, we particularly exploit Least Squares GAN (LSGAN). LSGAN is a modification of a GAN that uses L2 loss instead of log loss to determine the performance of each network (Equations 13.6 and 13.7):

$$D_{L2_{loss}} = \frac{1}{2}E_{x \sim p_{data}}(x)[(D(x) - 1)^2] + \frac{1}{2}E_{z \sim p_z}(z)[(D(G(z))^2]$$ (13.6)

$$G_{L2_{loss}} = \frac{1}{2}E_{z \sim p_z}(z)[(D(G(z)) - 1)^2]$$ (13.7)

LSGAN uses an Adam Optimizer to minimize the loss after each iteration.

13.4 Numerical Experiment

Two numerical dynamic problems are used to illustrate the efficacy of the proposed PI-DNN and PI-GAN models. These numerical problems are related to inverted pendulum and cancer cell growth.

13.4.1 Inverted Pendulum

The inverted-pendulum system (IP) is one of the most popular examples of an unstable dynamical system used for testing reinforcement learning or control techniques. In the IP

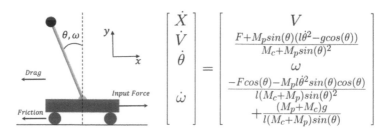

FIGURE 13.5
Inverted pendulum problem.

problem, the angle and angular velocity of a pendulum are controlled by moving the cart (Figure 13.5). The position of the cart and the force applied to it are bounded.

Two types of *modified IP* partial physics models are considered while formulating the problem statement. In both models, the average wind speed is considered, which differs from the real wind speed. The only difference between these two models is the coefficient of friction involved. The fusion of two levels of partial physics models with our network yields two types of hybrid models, namely Hybrid 1 and Hybrid 2. A later section of this paper shows that the quality of the partial physics model or its abstraction ability significantly impacts the prediction accuracy of the overall hybrid model. The hybrid model aims to determine the state of the IP with respect to different spatial and temporal inputs.

The state vector includes X, V, θ, ω, which are the position, the velocity of the cart, the angle, and the angular velocity of the pendulum, respectively. The state-space equations used for both the partial and the complete physics models are given in Equation in Figure 13.5, M_c, M_P, l, g represent the mass of the cart, the mass of the pole, the length of the pole and the gravitational acceleration, respectively.

We denote the applied force by F. To make the model more realistic, this term is modified considering *air drag* and *friction* (Equation (13.8), (13.9), (13.10)):

$$\tilde{F} = F - F_D - F_f \tag{13.8}$$

$$F_D = \frac{\rho_{Air} C_D A_C (V + V_{wind} cos(\phi_{wind}))^2}{2} \tag{13.9}$$

$$F_f = \mu(M_c + M_P)g \tag{13.10}$$

where F_D and F_f denote the air drag and friction forces, respectively. The two additional forces, change the force $\tilde{F}$ applied to the cart and are considered for both partial and complete physics models. The partial physics model uses constant values for both the wind speed and friction, as expressed in Equation (13.11), while in the complete physics, a different friction coefficient is used, and a deterministically varying wind (which is not directly observable) is considered, as expressed in Equation (13.12). This added complexity is beyond the simple IP problem typically used as a Reinforcement Learning or controls domain benchmark.

$$\begin{bmatrix} V_w(t) \\ \mu(t) \end{bmatrix}_{partial} = \begin{bmatrix} V_{w,0} \\ \mu_0 \end{bmatrix} \tag{13.11}$$

$$\begin{bmatrix} V_w(t) \\ \mu(t) \end{bmatrix}_{complete} = \begin{bmatrix} V_{w,0} + \sum_{i=1}^{4} A_{w,i} \sin(\omega_{w,i} + \phi_{w,i}) \\ \mu_1 \end{bmatrix} \tag{13.12}$$

The input to our hybrid model contains the initial state (at time zero), the input force,

TABLE 13.1
Inverted Pendulum Problem: High-Fidelity (Ground Truth) and Partial Physics Models

Model	Wind Speed	Friction
Complete Model	$V_{wind}(t) = 4 + 0.4\sin(2.4t) + 0.32\sin(5.4t) +$ $1.6\sin(0.2t + 0.2) + 0.4\sin(176t - 0.04)$	$\mu_k = 0.3$
Partial Model - I	$V_{wind}(t) = 4$	$\mu_k = 0.3$
Partial Model - II	$V_{wind}(t) = 4$	$\mu_k = 0.03$

and time elapsed, along with the output state (at the time elapsed) of the physics model, making the total number of inputs equal to 10. The outputs to be predicted by the hybrid model are the four state variables, representing the state of the system at the time elapsed (Equation (13.13)).

$$
f\left(\begin{bmatrix} X_0 \\ V_0 \\ \theta_0 \\ \omega_0 \end{bmatrix}, F, t_f \right) = \begin{bmatrix} X_f \\ V_f \\ \theta_f \\ \omega_f \end{bmatrix} \tag{13.13}
$$

Table 13.1 lists the parameter values used for different models of the Inverted Pendulum problem.

13.4.2 Cancer Cell Growth

Cancer cells exhibit uncontrolled growth and no longer respond to neural signals that control cell growth inside the body. Cancer cells originate within the tissues and keep on dividing. In the later stages, these cells metastasize, meaning they will break through tissues and spread to nearby tissues and other organs. Our objective is to model the growth of cancer cells, i.e., to estimate the tumor's size based on its initial size and growth rate of cells.

The physics models characterizing tumor growth can be classified into two classes: (i) closed-form differential equation models [23, 29–31] and (ii) discrete cellular automata-type [21, 28] and agent-based models [35]. Discrete models are often closer to reality when compared to differential equation models but are computationally expensive. We used discrete models to generate training data. As a partial physics-based model, we use one based on a system of ordinary differential equations (ODEs). Systems of ODEs based partial physics model can estimate tumor growth, based on differential equations, but with less accuracy.

We use the cellular automata model [21, 28] as a high-fidelity model that classifies the cells into three categories: Stem cells, semi-differentiated cells, and fully differentiated cells. Their cellular differentiation mechanism is depicted in Figure 13.6. Only the stem cell has the ability to continue dividing, while the other two types have limited divisibility. Stem cells can divide symmetrically to produce new stem cells known as daughter cells, and hence can increase the tumor size. Through asymmetric division, they can produce differentiated cells, which can only divide to a certain extent. Semi-differentiated cells can divide up to some extent, while the fully differentiated ones cannot divide at all. The probability of dividing for each cell, p_d, and the probability of having symmetric or asymmetric division, p_{as} are considered as parameters for the model. Differentiated cells die due to factors such as lack of glucose or attack from immune cells. Thus, in the cellular automata model, the rate of cell death α is one of the important parameters. In this model, the overall running time is also one of the input parameters.

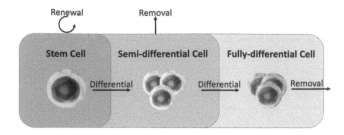

FIGURE 13.6
Cancer cell differentiation model.

Our physics model for the cancer cell growth problem is based on a model proposed by [10]. In this model, a non-linear ODE is used to model tumor growth and stability criterion for the system. This model is generalized by considering 12 state variables. Two of the variables are the numbers of stem and fully-differentiated cells. Semi-differentiated cells can have 10 divisions before acquiring fully-differentiated state. The rest of the ten state variables are characterized by the number of cells corresponding to each of these 10 divisible cellular conditions. Evolution of these states are governed by Equations (13.14)–(13.18).

$$X = [N_s, N_{d,10}, N_{d,9}, ..., N_{d,1}, N_{d,0}]^T \tag{13.14}$$

$$\frac{dN_s}{dt} = r_s N_s \tag{13.15}$$

$$\frac{dN_{d,10}}{dt} = r_{as} N_s - \alpha N_{d,10} - r_d N_{d,10} \tag{13.16}$$

$$\frac{dN_{d,i}}{dt} = 2r_d N_{d,i+1} - \alpha N_{d,i} - r_d N_{d,i}, 1 \leq i \leq 9 \tag{13.17}$$

$$\frac{dN_{d,0}}{dt} = 2r_d N_{d,1} - \alpha N_{d,0} \tag{13.18}$$

where, X represents the state vector, N_s is the number of stem cells, $N_{d,i}$ is the number of differentiated cells with i remaining divisions, $N_{d,0}$ is the number of fully differentiated cells, and α is the removal rate for differentiated cells and r_d is the division rate of these cells. Each division generates two cells. For stem cell, the rates of symmetric and asymmetric division are r_s and r_{as}, respectively.

Both observing and estimating the number of cells at different levels of divisibility potential are challenging. Therefore, another alternate (simplified) partial physics model is proposed. This alternate model, instead of calculating each cell type, considers the total population of cells. Equation (13.19) explains this new partial physics model used as input.

$$N = N_s + \sum_{i=0}^{10} N_{d,i} \tag{13.19}$$

The total number of inputs in this problem is five, the total cell population N being one of the inputs while the remaining four inputs are the parameters p_d, p_{as}, α, and the time difference Δt. The physics-based model used in our hybrid model has one output, i.e., the total cell population after time Δt. In the hybrid model, the neural network takes a total of six inputs, the first five being the same as those of the physics-based model and the last one is the partial physics model's output.

13.4.3   Evaluation Protocol

The different measures of performance used for testing and comparing the hybrid architectures with each other and with the purely data-driven model are outlined here.

13.4.3.1   Generalizability

The generalizability refers to the ability of a learned model to fit unseen instances. Generalization error is a measure of how accurately an algorithm is able to predict outcome values for unseen test points inside the training input domain (i.e., input space spanned by the training set). The generalization error expectation is defined by mean squared error (MSE), which measures the average squared difference between the prediction value and ground truth value. The MSE can be expressed by Equation (13.20):

$$MSE = \frac{\sum_{i=1}^{n} (\hat{y}_i - y_i)^2}{n} \tag{13.20}$$

where $\hat{y}$ is the predicted value, y is the ground truth value, and n is the sample size.

13.4.3.2   Extrapolability

Extrapolability is a measure of how accurately an algorithm is able to predict outcome values for unseen test points outside of the training domain. Similar to generalizability, extrapolability also evaluates the model's performance on a new data set. MSE is again used to quantify this metric, but the computations are carried out for predicted values outside of the input space spanned by the training data set.

13.4.3.3   Model Complexity

The model complexity metric provides a measure of the computational complexity of the given model. It is based on the number of floating point operations (flops) required by the architecture for generating the output. Memory is calculated by estimating the storage required for various model attributes like weights. Metrics encapsulating computational time and memory requirement regulates trade-offs between performance and computational speed.

13.4.3.4   Robustness to Noisy Input

This metric is used to capture the stability of models in the presence of noisy data. Higher robustness of a model indicates its capability to perform well, even when accurate measurements are not available, causing the measured readings to deviate from their real values. A robust model is useful in real-world modeling systems where noisy measurements are the norm.

13.4.3.5   Sensitivity to Data Set Size

We use data-sets of different sizes to train both the data-driven and hybrid models. Observations are made to demonstrate the change in generalization accuracy with varying data sizes. For comparison purposes, network and training process hyperparameters such as learning rate, initial state, etc. are kept constant. The sensitivity is quantified using generalizability. Here also, MSE is used as a metric for evaluation.

13.5   Results and Analysis

The results of the performance of PI-DNN and PI-GAN models are discussed next.

13.5.1   Data Generation

In each of the example problems, we generate a data set R of 5000 data points from the black-box model. This includes the real input X, and the ground truth output Y_r. For inverted pendulum and cancer cell growth problems, this black box model comes from the high fidelity physics model. We also generate data sets M from each of the partial physics models (low fidelity models), which contains 5000 data points corresponding to input X. The 5000 data points are divided into two parts, 4000 for training, 1000 for testing. After getting the datasets above, we apply the data pre-processing step. The data is normalized and zero-centralized based on Equation (13.21).

$$[Data - \mathbf{Mean}(Data)]/\mathbf{Std}(Data) \tag{13.21}$$

13.5.2   Training Detail

The experiments are conducted on a server with Intel Xeon 6130 processor (32×2.10GHz), Linux Centos 7.5.x operating system, 128GB RAM, and double NVIDIA Volta Tesla V100 PCIe GPUs.

13.5.2.1   PI-DNN

In the hyper-parameter tuning process, we consider the epoch number, the learning rate of the optimizer, and different architecture parameters that include the number of layers and the number of nodes in each layer. The range of the hyper-parameters and training data size are presented in Table 13.2 (FC in the figure represents *fully connected hidden layer*). The combination of different hyper-parameters and training data size generates different results. All the example problems have the same tuning procedure to allow a fair comparison. We use LeakyRelu (Leaky version of a Rectified Linear Unit) as our activation function for all the hidden layers. The dropout technique is then used in each fully-connected layer to avoid over-fitting. The dropout rate is prescribed depending on the problem.

In the beginning, we need to compare three different architectures. For the sake of brevity, the results of all three hybrid architecture variations are presented only for one training size case of the inverted pendulum problem. We use the front infused hybrid architecture for all other case studies and the tumor growth problem and compare it with the classic DNN architecture.

First, a set of hyper-parameters is tuned w.r.t. the pure DNN model. Next, using this hyper-parameter set as constant, we train four proposed hybrid models. To find the contribution of the physics model, each model's training MSE loss has been shown individually. The results are shown in Figure 13.7. We can observe from Figure 13.7 that all three hybrid models have smaller training MSE loss than the pure DNN model. The difference is most noticeable in case of the velocity V. Time series analysis showed that V exhibits the most non-linear variation among the three state variables. Therefore, our physics model has a significant contribution to improving the highly non-linear variable of the model.

Among the different hybrid models, the front infused model has the shortest convergence time (which might be an artifact of the specific backpropagation technique used), although

TABLE 13.2

Hyper-parameter Range for PI-DNN

Hyper-Parameter	Value
Epoch number	[50, 100, 200, 400]
Learning rate	[0.05, 0.01, 0.005, 0.001, 0.0005]
Architectures	FC1(200)-FC2(150)-FC3(100)-FC4(50) FC1(150)-FC2(100)-FC3(50)-FC4(50) FC1(100)-FC2(50)-FC3(20) FC1(100)-FC2(50)
Training Size	**Value**
Data set size	[50, 100, 500, 1000, 2000]

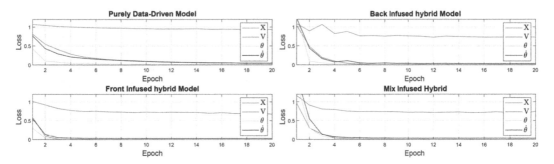

FIGURE 13.7

Architecture performance comparison, inverted pendulum problem, 5000 sample points (4000 training, 1000 validation), hidden layer: FC(100)-FC(60)-FC(60), FC is fully connected layer), y-axis is training loss.

the overall convergence outcomes are very similar. The complexity comparison of different architectures, presented in Table 13.3, provides a significant differentiation of their quality. The complexity of the front and mixed infused model are the same. While the back infused model is observed to provide a significant reduction in the complexity of the model. The decrease in complexity can be attributed to the number of variations coming from the physics model Y_p. If the computational resource or memory space constraints, these three models may be a preferred choice.

TABLE 13.3

Complexity of Different Architectures for PI-DNN

Model	Front	Back	Mixed
Flops	26992	25832	26992
Memory	13354	12638	13354

TABLE 13.4

Hyper-parameters for PI-GAN

Hyper-Parameter	Value
Epoch number	1000
Learning rate	0.001
Generator Architecture	FC1(300)-FC2(150)-FC3(75)-FC4(75)-FC5(75)-FC6(75)-FC7(75)-FC8(Output Size)
Discriminator Architecture	FC1(200)-FC2(100)-FC3(75)-FC4(75)-FC5(50)-FC6(50)-FC7(1)
Training Size	**Value**
Data set size	[100, 200, 500, 1000, 2000]

13.5.2.2   PI-GAN

For the inverted pendulum and the cancer cell growth problems, the PI-GAN hybrid model consists of seven fully-connected layers in the generator and six fully connected layers in the discriminator. The activation for the hidden layers is an exponential linear unit (ELU), and the output layer has a linear activation function for both the generator and discriminator. Network details are outlined in Table 13.4.

After training, the output of the generator $\hat{y}$ aims to be close to the output of the real model y_r. After the training is complete, the discriminator component is discarded, and the final output of the generator is used to predict the output values.

13.5.3   Results: Inverted Pendulum

- **Hyper-parameter tuning for PI-DNN**

  We analyze the sensitivity of the hybrid and DNN models to hyper-parameter choices to elicit whether they prefer significantly different hyper-parameter combinations (derived from combining the setting stated in Table 13.2) to produce the most accurate testing outcomes. The comparative results have been shown in Figure 13.8. The x-axis represents different combinations of hyper-parameters, and the y-axis is the testing MSE loss. Each of the first five sub-figures represents a different training size case, with the testing MSE results shown for the pure DNN and the Hybrid Levels 1 and 2 models. We sort the hyper-parameter combinations (see Table 13.2) in accordance with increasing MSE values obtained by the hybrid 1 model (blue line). The bottom right-most sub-figure in Figure 13.8 depicts only the testing MSE loss for hybrid 1 model, trained with different sized data sets. The hyper-parameter combinations in this sub-figure are sorted according to the increasing MSE for the 2000-sized training data set case. Figure 13.8 highlights: Overall, the hybrid 1 model has the best performance. We can conclude that for some cases (where the hybrid model performs poorer than the pure DNN), using physics models will not assist in getting better results; instead, it may be counterproductive. From the first five figures, we can observe that the trend of the hybrid model and purely data-driven model is close in terms of response to the hyper-parameter setting. This is indeed an important outcome when put in the context of using pure DNNs that have been tediously trained over the years in various domains. Specifically, we observe that the hybrid model allows the re-usability of existing hyper-parameter-tuned neural networks. Furthermore, we observe that the difference in the performance of

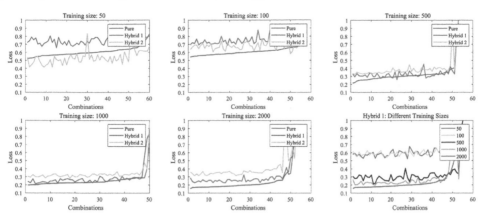

FIGURE 13.8

Hyper-parameter comparison for inverted pendulum problem, y-axis is testing loss on 500 samples.

purely data-driven and hybrid models is amplified at lower sample sizes, almost independent of hyper-parameter choices. For the hybrid model, a small training set can result in an acceptable level of accuracy. These results highlight the contribution and utility of the partial physics model in hybrid architectures. Finally, the last sub-figure in Figure 13.8 shows that similar hyper-parameter combinations work well with the hybrid architectures across varying training sample sizes, thus allowing greater portability.

- **Hyper-parameter tuning for PI-GAN**

Stable GAN training is an open research problem. There is no standard method for tuning. Most applications use architectures that have been proven to improve stability in GANs such as Wasserstein GAN (WGAN) or LSGAN. An issue with using WGAN or LSGAN in our applications is the architectures are designed for classification problems, not regression problems. So we modified the generator and discriminator of LSGAN to perform regression by using a DNN in both networks. We chose LSGAN over WGAN because it has shown a more significant improvement on stability than WGAN. Due to the hypersensitivity to hyper-parameters, a global optimum is not easily found, so we settled with the first stable network we could produce. The hyper-parameters are outlined in Table 13.4.

- **Generalizability**

From the earlier described analysis, we identify the best model for each dataset and train the model 100 times to generate violin plots (Figure 13.9(a)) for robustness analysis. From the violin plot, we observe that hybrid models show better performance on generalizability compared to the pure DNN, and this difference is again most pronounced at sparse sample sets.

Similarly, for the hybrid GAN (Figures 13.9(d)), one of the hybrid models is performing better than the pure GAN for this metric–the hybrid 1 GAN. The hybrid 2 model is actually making the performance much worse.

- **Extrapolability**

Error on test samples outside of the training range is also important to evaluate our models. We randomly pick 500 testing samples, which are outside of the training range and evaluate them on our existing trained models. The result is shown in Figure 13.9(b).

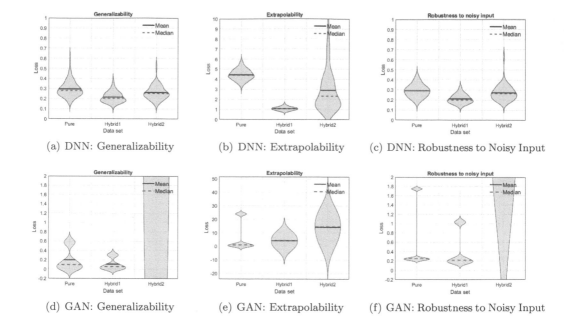

(a) DNN: Generalizability   (b) DNN: Extrapolability   (c) DNN: Robustness to Noisy Input

(d) GAN: Generalizability   (e) GAN: Extrapolability   (f) GAN: Robustness to Noisy Input

FIGURE 13.9
Violin Plots: Inverted pendulum (generalizability, extrapolability, and robustness to noisy input).

The violin plot shows the hybrid 1 model again delivers the best performance; however, the performance is poorer than estimated for generalizability. More importantly, the hybrid 1 model's superiority over the classic DNN is established here.

However, the performance of the GAN model shown in Figure 13.9(e) illustrates that all of the models perform significantly worse for this metric. It fair to note that although it is performing poorly, the pure model is performing best, and the hybrid 2 model is, expectedly, performing the worst.

- **Complexity**

We use Flops and memory to evaluate the complexity of models. The result is shown in Table 13.5. It is evident that the hybrid model does not compromise much on computational efficiency and memory with performance. Also, it can be observed that although hybrid 1 and hybrid 2 models have the similar complexity, but due to better quality physics involved, hybrid 1 has a better performance to cost ratio than hybrid 2.

TABLE 13.5
Complexity of DNN and GAN

		IP			CC	
		Pure	**Hybrid 1**	**Hybrid 2**	**Pure**	**Hybrid**
DNN	**Flops**	12872	109522	109522	103608	104009
	Memory	6354	52704	54554	51551	51751
GAN	**Flops**	246341	248745	248745	245740	246341
	Memory	122455	246341	346341	122155	122455

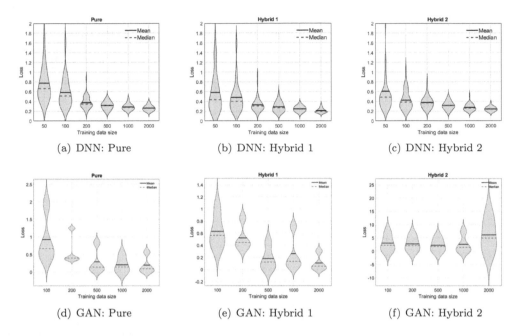

FIGURE 13.10

Violin plots: Inverted pendulum (sensitivity to data set size).

- **Robustness to noisy data**

  We used data with noise to explore robustness to noisy data. The result is shown as a violin plot in Figure 13.9(c). All three models provide reasonable performance for this metric.

  The first two models are performing well for this metric, and the hybrid 1 GAN is performing the best (as shown in Figure 13.9(f)). Therefore, the physics model is improving the network's ability to handle noise.

- **Sensitivity to the number of samples**

  We train the three models (two hybrid and the pure DNN) on different data sizes – sets of 50, 100, 200, 500, 1000, and 2000 samples – and compare the results. Each model is run 50 times to account for variability. The results are shown in Figure 13.10, (a) pure DNN model, (b) hybrid 1 model, and (c) hybrid 2 model. It can be observed from the results that the pure DNN model is more sensitive to training data size compared to the hybrid model. However, the variance in performance across various training data sizes remains unremarkable for the hybrid and pure DNN models.

  As depicted from Figure 13.10(d)–(f), the first two models, pure and hybrid 1, are showing differences in the sensitivity to training dataset size, but similar to DNN, the differences are unremarkable, and it is inconclusive, which is performing better for this metric.

13.5.4 Results: Cancer Cell Growth

- **Generalizability**

  As presented in the Table 13.6, the pure DNN, pure GAN, and hybrid models provide

TABLE 13.6

MSE Loss Median Values for Different Metrics (Cancer Cell Problem)

		Generalizability	Extrapolability	Robustness to noise
DNN	Pure	0.0714	0.3716	0.1215
	Hybrid	0.0205	0.1201	0.0962
GAN	Pure	0.251	0.933	0.211
	Hybrid	0.157	0.383	0.101

reasonable generalizability, with the hybrid model offering approximately two times improvement in both cases.

- **Extrapolability**

  The result is shown in Table 13.6. Again, the hybrid models provide significantly better extrapolability compared to the pure models.

- **Complexity**

  The result is shown in Table 13.5. Although the purely data-driven and hybrid model has a similar neural network structure, they involve different complexity (e.g., the hybrid model has a higher number of effective connecting edges), since the hybrid model needs to incorporate the partial physics information.

- **Robustness to the noisy data**

  As evident from the results of DNN in Table 13.6, the hybrid model only performs slightly better in terms robustness to noisy data. However, as depicted from the results of GAN in Table 13.6, the hybrid model is showing more than two times the improvement.

- **Sensitivity to the number of samples**

  In the results of DNN, for the training size of 50, 100, 200, 500, 1000, 2000, the median MSE loss of purely data-driven model are: 0.41, 0.19, 0.13, 0.09, 0.07, 0.06 and the median MSE loss of hybrid model are: 0.25, 0.13, 0.08, 0.05, 0.02, 0.01. As shown in the results, the hybrid model has markedly smaller errors compared to the pure DNN model across different training sample sizes. The superiority of the hybrid model here (as in the previous problem) is most significant for the sparse sample set of 50.

  For the GAN model we used training sizes of 100, 200, 500, 1000, and 2000. The median MSE loss of the purely data-driven model are: 0.97, 0.68, 0.44, 0.36, 0.25 and the median MSE loss of hybrid model are: 0.71, 0.53, 0.27, 0.19, 0.15. Exactly as shown by DNN, the hybrid model has markedly smaller error compared to the pure GAN model across different training sample sizes. The superiority of the hybrid model here (as in the previous problem) is most significant for the sparse sample set of 100.

13.6 Conclusion and Future Work

In this paper, two-hybrid architectures (PI-DNN, PI-GAN) that utilize a physics-based model for guiding the data-driven model are outlined. The outlined hybrid models demonstrate the feasibility of integrating a physics-based model with data-driven models to more accurately predict a physical system's dynamics. As evident from empirically derived results, the performance of hybrid models when compared to purely data-driven model is better for both the inverted pendulum and cancer cell growth problems.

From the results, it is empirically evident that the quality of the available physics model also plays a significant role in determining the performance of the hybrid models. Due to the better quality of physics involved, the level 1 hybrid architecture delivers the best performance. On the other hand due to the involvement of comparatively lower quality physics, the level 2 hybrid architecture lags behind both the level 1 hybrid model and data-driven model in terms of performance. Thus, it can be emphasized that along with the efficiency of involved data-driven architectures, the quality of the physics-based models also affects the accuracy of the overall hybrid model.

In addition, we proposed a set of different metrics to standardize the way we evaluate the comprehensive performance of hybrid models. This is more exhaustive than just comparing the prediction accuracy.

Compared to the results of PI-DNN, PI-GAN's results are non-satisfactory. However, as the first exploration of infusing physics with generative networks, PI-GAN shows promising potential to be more potent. GANs are difficult to train due to their instability and high sensitivity to hyper-parameter tuning, so this reveals an avenue for future work.

Other avenues of work include: developing a benchmark problem to become the baseline metric for hybrid modeling and exploring new ways to infuse physical information into the deep learning models. The prior will allow us to properly gauge the performance of each network that is developed in this domain; this should be a more practical problem as these networks plan to be implemented in modern systems. The former will force us to be exhaustive in exploring physics infusions in deep learning models. An exhaustive approach will most likely lead to an optimal method to develop a standard for future infusions.

Bibliography

[1] Martin Arjovsky, Soumith Chintala, and Léon Bottou. Wasserstein gan. *arXiv preprint arXiv:1701.07875*, 2017.

[2] Yunhao Ba, Guangyuan Zhao, and Achuta Kadambi. Blending diverse physical priors with neural networks. *arXiv preprint arXiv:1910.00201*, 2019.

[3] Amir Behjat, Chen Zeng, Rahul Rai, Ion Matei, David Doermann, and Souma Chowdhury. A physics-aware learning architecture with input transfer networks for predictive modeling. *Applied Soft Computing*, 96:106665, 2020.

[4] Andrew Brock, Theodore Lim, James M Ritchie, and Nick Weston. Neural photo editing with introspective adversarial networks. *arXiv preprint arXiv:1609.07093*, 2016.

[5] Ian Goodfellow, Yoshua Bengio, Aaron Courville, and Yoshua Bengio. *Deep Learning*, volume 1. MIT Press, Cambridge, 2016.

[6] H. Hanachi, W. Yu, I.Y. Kim, and C.K. Mechefske. Hybrid physics-based and data-driven phm. 2017.

[7] Kaiming He, Xiangyu Zhang, Shaoqing Ren, and Jian Sun. Deep residual learning for image recognition. In *Proceedings of the IEEE Conference on Computer Vision and Pattern Recognition*, pages 770–778, 2016.

[8] Briland Hitaj, Giuseppe Ateniese, and Fernando Perez-Cruz. Deep models under the gan: information leakage from collaborative deep learning. In *Proceedings of the 2017 ACM SIGSAC Conference on Computer and Communications Security*, pages 603–618. ACM, 2017.

[9] Xiaowei Jia, Anuj Karpatne, Jared Willard, Michael Steinbach, Jordan Read, Paul C Hanson, Hilary A Dugan, and Vipin Kumar. Physics guided recurrent neural networks for modeling dynamical systems: Application to monitoring water temperature and quality in lakes. *arXiv preprint arXiv:1810.02880*, 2018.

[10] Matthew D Johnston, Carina M Edwards, Walter F Bodmer, Philip K Maini, and S Jonathan Chapman. Mathematical modeling of cell population dynamics in the colonic crypt and in colorectal cancer. *Proceedings of the National Academy of Sciences*, 104(10):4008–4013, 2007.

[11] Anuj Karpatne, William Watkins, Jordan Read, and Vipin Kumar. Physics-guided neural networks (pgnn): An application in lake temperature modeling. *arXiv preprint arXiv:1710.11431*, 2017.

[12] Byungsoo Kim, Vinicius C Azevedo, Nils Thuerey, Theodore Kim, Markus Gross, and Barbara Solenthaler. Deep fluids: A generative network for parameterized fluid simulations. In *Computer Graphics Forum*, volume 38, pages 59–70. Wiley Online Library, 2019.

[13] Werner Kristjanpoller, Anton Fadic, and Marcel C Minutolo. Volatility forecast using hybrid neural network models. *Expert Systems with Applications*, 41(5):2437–2442, 2014.

[14] Ankit Kumar, Ozan Irsoy, Peter Ondruska, Mohit Iyyer, James Bradbury, Ishaan Gulrajani, Victor Zhong, Romain Paulus, and Richard Socher. Ask me anything: Dynamic memory networks for natural language processing. In *International Conference on Machine Learning*, pages 1378–1387, 2016.

[15] Christian Ledig, Lucas Theis, Ferenc Huszár, Jose Caballero, Andrew Cunningham, Alejandro Acosta, Andrew Aitken, Alykhan Tejani, Johannes Totz, Zehan Wang, et al. Photo-realistic single image super-resolution using a generative adversarial network. *arXiv preprint*, 2017.

[16] Beibei Liu, Gemma Mason, Julian Hodgson, Yiying Tong, and Mathieu Desbrun. Model-reduced variational fluid simulation. *ACM Transactions on Graphics (TOG)*, 34(6):244, 2015.

[17] Yun Long, Xueyuan She, and Saibal Mukhopadhyay. Hybridnet: integrating model-based and data-driven learning to predict evolution of dynamical systems. *arXiv preprint arXiv:1806.07439*, 2018.

[18] Xudong Mao, Qing Li, Haoran Xie, Raymond Yiu Keung Lau, Zhen Wang, and Stephen Paul Smolley. On the effectiveness of least squares generative adversarial networks. *IEEE Transactions on Pattern Analysis and Machine Intelligence*, 2018.

[19] Ion Matei, Chen Zeng, Souma Chowdhury, Rahul Rai, and Johan de Kleer. Controlling draft interactions between quadcopter unmanned aerial vehicles with physics-aware modeling. *Journal of Intelligent & Robotic Systems*, 101(1):1–21, 2021.

[20] Olof Mogren. C-rnn-gan: Continuous recurrent neural networks with adversarial training. *arXiv preprint arXiv:1611.09904*, 2016.

[21] Joana Moreira and Andreas Deutsch. Cellular automaton models of tumor development: a critical review. *Advances in Complex Systems*, 5(02n03):247–267, 2002.

[22] Nikhil Muralidhar, Mohammad Raihanul Islam, Manish Marwah, Anuj Karpatne, and Naren Ramakrishnan. Incorporating prior domain knowledge into deep neural networks. In *2018 IEEE International Conference on Big Data (Big Data)*, pages 36–45. IEEE, 2018.

[23] Hope Murphy, Hana Jaafari, and Hana M Dobrovolny. Differences in predictions of ode models of tumor growth: a cautionary example. *BMC Cancer*, 16(1):163, 2016.

[24] Jinshan Pan, Jiangxin Dong, Yang Liu, Jiawei Zhang, Jimmy Ren, Jinhui Tang, Yu-Wing Tai, and Ming-Hsuan Yang. Physics-based generative adversarial models for image restoration and beyond. *arXiv preprint arXiv:1808.00605*, 2018.

[25] Alexander G Parlos, Omar T Rais, and Amir F Atiya. Multi-step-ahead prediction using dynamic recurrent neural networks. *Neural Networks*, 13(7):765–786, 2000.

[26] Prashanth Pillai, Anshul Kaushik, Shivanand Bhavikatti, Arjun Roy, and Virendra Kumar. A hybrid approach for fusing physics and data for failure prediction. *International Journal of Prognostics and Health Management*, 7(025):1–12, 2016.

[27] Pedro O Pinheiro, Ronan Collobert, and Piotr Dollár. Learning to segment object candidates. In *Advances in Neural Information Processing Systems*, pages 1990–1998, 2015.

[28] Jan Poleszczuk and Heiko Enderling. A high-performance cellular automaton model of tumor growth with dynamically growing domains. *Applied Mathematics*, 5(1):144, 2014.

[29] B Ribba, Nick H Holford, P Magni, I Trocóniz, I Gueorguieva, P Girard, C Sarr, M Elishmereni, C Kloft, and Lena E Friberg. A review of mixed-effects models of tumor growth and effects of anticancer drug treatment used in population analysis. *CPT: Pharmacometrics & Systems Pharmacology*, 3(5):1–10, 2014.

[30] Tiina Roose, S Jonathan Chapman, and Philip K Maini. Mathematical models of avascular tumor growth. *SIAM Review*, 49(2):179–208, 2007.

[31] RK Sachs, LR Hlatky, and P Hahnfeldt. Simple ode models of tumor growth and anti-angiogenic or radiation treatment. *Mathematical and Computer Modelling*, 33(12-13):1297–1305, 2001.

[32] Russell Stewart and Stefano Ermon. Label-free supervision of neural networks with physics and domain knowledge. In *Thirty-First AAAI Conference on Artificial Intelligence*, 2017.

[33] Natarajan Viswanathan and CC-N Chu. Fastplace: efficient analytical placement using cell shifting, iterative local refinement, and a hybrid net model. *IEEE Transactions on Computer-Aided Design of Integrated Circuits and Systems*, 24(5):722–733, 2005.

[34] Zhihua Wang, Stefano Rosa, Bo Yang, Sen Wang, Niki Trigoni, and Andrew Markham. 3d-physnet: Learning the intuitive physics of non-rigid object deformations. *arXiv preprint arXiv:1805.00328*, 2018.

[35] Zhihui Wang, Joseph D Butner, Romica Kerketta, Vittorio Cristini, and Thomas S Deisboeck. Simulating cancer growth with multiscale agent-based modeling. In *Seminars in Cancer Biology*, volume 30, pages 70–78. Elsevier, 2015.

[36] Liu Yang, Dongkun Zhang, and George Em Karniadakis. Physics-informed generative adversarial networks for stochastic differential equations. *arXiv preprint arXiv:1811.02033*, 2018.

[37] Yibo Yang and Paris Perdikaris. Physics-informed deep generative models. *arXiv preprint arXiv:1812.03511*, 2018.

[38] Chih-Chieh Young, Wen-Cheng Liu, and Ming-Chang Wu. A physically based and machine learning hybrid approach for accurate rainfall-runoff modeling during extreme typhoon events. *Applied Soft Computing*, 53:205–216, 2017.

[39] Zhibo Zhang, Rahul Rai, Souma Chowdhury, and David Doermann. Midphynet: Memorized infusion of decomposed physics in neural networks to model dynamic systems. *Neurocomputing*, 428:116–129, 2021.

14

Combining System Modeling and Machine Learning into Hybrid Ecosystem Modeling

Markus Reichstein, Bernhard Ahrens, Basil Kraft, Gustau Camps-Valls,
Nuno Carvalhais, Fabian Gans, Pierre Gentine, and Alexander J. Winkler

CONTENTS

14.1   Introduction

Process understanding and modeling is at the core of scientific reasoning. Principled, yet typically *parametric*, mechanistic modeling has dominated science and engineering until recently with the advent of machine learning (ML). Despite great success in many areas, ML algorithms in the Earth sciences face the problem of interpretability and consistency, as often they do not respect the most elementary laws of physics like energy or mass conservation, or scientific laws of other disciplines such as chemistry, biology or ecology. Physical – or more generally: mechanistic – modeling and ML have often been considered as completely different, and even irreconcilable, fields in Earth sciences and many other disciplines. Yet, these approaches are indeed complementary: mechanistic approaches are interpretable and allow extrapolation beyond the observation space by construction, where data-driven approaches are highly flexible and adaptive to data. Their synergy has gained attention and momentum lately in many fields of science.

Physicists and environmental scientists attempt to model systems in a principled way through analytic descriptions that encode prior beliefs of the underlying processes. Conservation laws, physical principles or phenomenological behaviors are generally formalized

DOI: 10.1201/9781003143376-14

using mechanistic models and differential equations. This mechanistic paradigm has been, and still is, the main framework for modeling complex natural phenomena like e.g., those involved in the Earth system. With the availability of large data sets captured with different sensory systems, the mechanistic modeling paradigm is being challenged (and in many cases replaced) by the statistical ML paradigm, which offers a prior-agnostic approach (Reichstein et al., Halevy, Norvig, and Pereira, de Bézenac, Pajot, and Gallinari).

ML models can fit observations very well, but predictions may be physically inconsistent or even implausible, e.g., owing to extrapolation or observational biases. This has been perhaps the most important criticism to ML algorithms, and a relevant reason why, historically, mechanistic modeling and ML have often been treated as two different fields under very different scientific paradigms (theory-driven versus data-driven).

Likewise, there is an on-going debate about the limitations of traditional methodological frameworks: both about their scientific insight and discovery limits in general science (Halevy, Norvig, and Pereira 2009), in hydrology (Karpatne, Atluri, et al. 2017) and in remote sensing (Camps-Valls et al. 2018). Recently, however, integrating domain knowledge and achieving physical consistency by teaching ML models about the governing physical rules of the Earth system has been proposed as a principled way to provide strong theoretical constraints in addition to observational ones (Reichstein et al. 2019). The synergy between the two approaches has been gaining attention, by either redesigning models' architecture, augmenting the training data set with simulations, or by including physical constraints in the cost function to minimize (Raissi and Karniadakis 2018; Karpatne, Watkins, et al. 2017; Camps-Valls et al. 2018; Svendsen et al. 2018; Reichstein and Carvalhais 2019).

In this chapter, we will first give an overview and a typology of the hybrid modeling approach, followed by three illustrative case studies addressing major hybrid modeling types and a discussion where we address opportunities and challenges with such hybrid modeling approaches. A summary of notations and acronyms used in this chapter is provided later in Table 14.3.

14.2 Hybrid Modeling Approaches

Science-based modeling and ML interact in a wide diversity of ways (Reichstein et al. 2019). A sub-field of such interplay is *hybrid modeling*, which can be generally defined as a modeling approach where ML (black box) and mechanistic modeling (glass box) are combined in one integrated modeling system. Such a modeling system can come in different flavors, with each type having specific challenges. To distinguish these types, we start with a simplified, abstract representation of a system modeling approach (Figure 14.1). Therein we have a sub-model 1, which processes some system-external forcing into an output, which is the input to another sub-model 2, which in turn produces some output, which is the entity of interest and can be compared, e.g., to observations. If the output is feeding back into sub-model 1, then we have a coupled or feedback system (e.g., two coupled differential equations). Both sub-models can have parameters, which in turn can be derived using other models ("meta"-model in Figure 14.1). In a hybrid model, one of the sub-models is replaced by an ML approach that maps the same input to the (structurally) same output, yet without explicit, directly interpretable parameters.

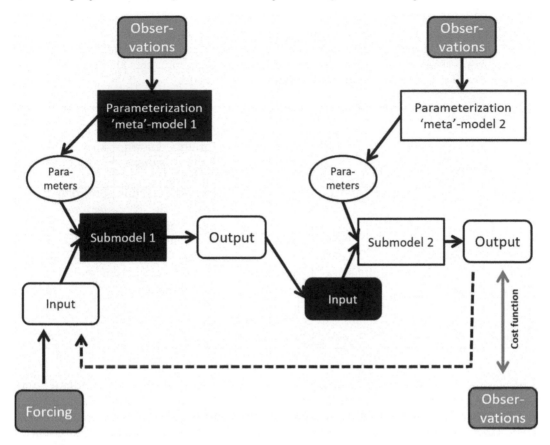

FIGURE 14.1
Simplified representation of a system model as a basis for discussing hybrid modeling types (adapted from Reichstein et al. 2019).

14.2.1 Parametric versus Non-Parametric Models

For discussing hybrid modeling types, it is helpful to analyze which parts of the model are either fully known, structurally known or fully unknown ("structurally known" means that the model can be expressed in a parametric way and only some parameters are unknown). This classification is attempted in Table 14.1, where two sub-models f and g are considered, and where g is an inner function of f. If the structure of f and g is known (lower right corner Table 14.1), we are in the parametric description known from pure mechanistic or semi-empirical modeling, including inverse parameter estimation. If neither the structure of g and f are known, we are in the pure machine-learning domain (upper left, black corner Table 14.1).

A hybrid model emerges, when exactly only one sub-model, i.e. either the inner function g or the outer function f is at least structurally known (grey cells Table 14.1). If the inner function g is fully known, the situation resembles the classical approach of pre-computing features. If the outer function f is fully known, ML generates the mechanistically interpretable input to function f. Examples of this approach include the work by de Bezenac et al. (2019), who machine-learned a motion field and applied the motion field with the physical dynamic model to update the field of states, or by Kraft et al. (2020), who machine-learned eco-hydrological parameters and water fluxes and fed them into a global

TABLE 14.1

Classification of modeling approaches based on whether parameters or structure of the sub-models have to be learned. The sub-models here are expressed as inner and outer functions g and f, respectively. $\theta_{f,g}$, $X_{f,g}$ are matrices containing the parameters and input variables, respectively. If the model is completely unknown, θ is empty.

		Sub-Model 1: $g(\theta_g, X_g)$		
		Completely unknown: *learn all*	(Only) structurally *known: learn parameters*	Completely known: *nothing to learn*
Sub-Model 2: $f(\theta_f, X_f, g)$	Completely unknown: *learn all*	Pure ML	Hybrid, semi-parametric modeling	pre-computing features
	(Only) structurally known: *learn parameters*	Hybrid, semi-parametric modeling	Pure mechanistic modeling (including classical inverse parameter estimation and data-assimilation)	
	Completely known: *nothing to learn*	Hybrid inference of latent variables		

hydrological mass-conserving modeling approach. In both approaches intermediate latent variables are computed by the ML model, resembling classical data assimilation schemes.

The most challenging situation arises when the inner function g is completely unknown while the parameters for the outer function f have to be estimated (or *vice versa*). This is the semi-parametric case, where parametric and non-parametric estimation are combined, strongly related to varying-coefficient models, a subclass of semi-parametric statistical models (Hastie and Tibshirani 1993, Park et al. 2015). There have also been scattered examples of this approach in the chemical engineering literature since the late 1990s, but, interestingly, no broad proliferation (von Stosch et al. 2014; Bhutani, Rangaiah, and Ray 2006; Molga and Cherbański 1999).

The notion of an inner and outer function is a simplification for clarity. In a system of coupled equations (e.g. differential equations), there is of course no inner and outer function. This case either characterizes semi-parametric modeling or inference of latent variables (Table 14.1).

In this chapter, we give a couple of case studies on the semi-parametric case with a simple but ecologically very relevant yet uncertain equation, using neural networks (NN) for the non-parametric part and a differentiable programming approach to estimate neural network weights and the mechanistic parameters simultaneously. The major challenge arises from the risk that the estimation of the neural network weights and the mechanistic parameters are dependent on each other leading to equifinality in the modeling of the process of interest and thus weak identifiability of the mechanistic parameters. Please refer to Section 14.2, where we discuss the concept of equifinality and its challenges in more detail.

14.2.2 Stateless versus Stateful Models

A complementary way to characterize hybrid models is based on the question whether they contain (dynamic) states, i.e., stateless versus stateful models, in both the mechanistic part and the ML part. Most mechanistic models describe the change of a state over time or space

TABLE 14.2

Classification of hybrid modeling approaches based on whether the mechanistic modeling (MM) part is stateful (differential equations) or stateless (algebraic equations), and whether the ML part is stateless (feedforward neural networks, FNN) or stateful (recurrent neural networks, RNN). $R(t)$ is an algebraic equation that describes a flux changing over time t. dC/dt describes the change in a state over time as a differential equation. $X(t)$ describes how external forcing changes with time. θ describes the parameters of the process-based modeling branch, while W describes the parameters of the ML branch.

MM \ ML	Stateless (Feedforward Neural Network)	Stateful (Recurrent Neural Network)
Stateless (Algebraic Equation)	$R(t) =$ $f\left(X\left(t\right),\theta,FNN\left(X\left(t\right),W\right)\right)$	$R(t) =$ $f\left(X\left(t\right),\theta,RNN\left(X\left(t\right),W\right)\right)$
Stateful (Differential Equation)	**Universal differential equations** $\frac{dC}{dt} =$ $f(C,X(t),\theta,\ FNN(C,X(t),W))$ **PINNs** $\frac{dC}{dt} = f\left(C,X\left(t\right),\theta\right)$ $FNN = FNN\left(t,W\right) \approx C\left(t\right)$ $L =$ $\sum\left(\frac{dFNN}{dt} - f\left(FNN,X\left(t\right),\theta\right)\right)+$ L_{Data}	As lower left but with RNN instead of FNN

and are thereby stateful models. In the simple example in Figure 14.1, an ML model (sub-model 1) could be embedded as the input to differential equations (sub-model 2). This would be the rather simple case of an ML model and a system of differential equations in series. If, however, the terms of the differential equations are not well described by our process knowledge or first principles, ML approaches can be embedded directly into the system of differential equations. This approach of embedding universal function approximators (like neural networks) into differential equations has been recently termed "universal differential equations" (Rackauckas et al. 2020).

For universal differential equations, differential equations are hybridized by embedding neural networks into them (Table 14.2). One can also make the ML part of a universal differential equation stateful by embedding recurrent neural networks such as LSTMs into the differential equations (Kraft et al. 2020). For universal differential equations, one can further distinguish between types where 1) the state of the process-based model is feeding back into the neural network or 2) universal differential equations where the ML part is purely driven by external forcing. The study by Kraft et al. (2020) is an example for a universal differential equation where states from the mechanistic model are fed into an ML model (Kraft et al. 2020), and the states of the mechanistic part of the hybrid model are even fed into a stateful ML model. This setup creates a feedback system between the mechanistic and ML model. It remains to be evaluated if universal differential equations only need the inherent statefulness of differential equations and the statefulness of recurrent neural networks, or also the feedback between both to represent "memory" in the studied system.

Physics-informed neural networks (PINNs) offer an alternative approach for stateful hybrid models (Raissi and Karniadakis 2018; Raissi, Yazdani, and Karniadakis 2020; Yazdani et al. 2020). With PINNs, neural networkss are hybridized by embedding the solving of the differential equation into the loss function (Table 14.2). Thereby, one ensures that the neural network obeys physical laws while being able to formulate the task as a pure ML problem. PINNS arise as a computationally efficient complement to universal differential equations that represent the statefulness of natural systems and offer the possibility to combine data streams of states and fluxes. PINNs achieve this by minimizing the residuals between the left-hand side and the right-hand side of differential equations, in addition to minimizing the loss function (Table 14.2). This essentially offers the possibility to learn the solution of differential equations alongside to providing insights from data.

Finally, another approach to integrate statefulness into hybrid models consists of introducing stateful ML approaches such as recurrent neural network architectures (RNN) into mechanistically motivated but otherwise stateless algebraic equations (Table 14.2).

14.3   Case Studies: Overview

After these relatively general considerations, we will give illustrative example case studies, which all revolve around carbon cycle processes within ecosystems. In the following, a short introduction to the underlying domain science is given. Simplified, CO_2 is taken up by ecosystems via plant photosynthesis, which also is called gross primary production (GPP), while CO_2 is mainly released by various respiratory processes (R_{eco}) from soil microbes, fungi, and animals and below- and above-ground plant tissue (Bonan 2015). Relevant for case study II, the net CO_2 exchange (NEE) is the difference between respiration losses (R_{eco}) and carbon uptake (GPP) (positive when the ecosystem releases carbon, $R_{eco} > GPP$) and is measured at ecosystem level with a non-destructive micrometeorological method, called eddy-covariance method (Moncrieff et al. 1997).

A very minimal conceptual model of the temporal variation at one point in space (ecosystem) can be constructed by the following equations:

$$GPP(t) = RUE(t) \cdot APAR(t) \tag{14.1}$$

$$\frac{dC_B}{dt} = \eta \cdot GPP(t) - k_B(t)\, C_B - L(t) \tag{14.2}$$

$$\frac{dC_s}{dt} = L(t) - k_S(t)\, C_S \tag{14.3}$$

where RUE is the radiation use efficiency, with which the absorbed radiation ($APAR$) is converted into chemical energy, C_B is the vegetation biomass carbon, η is the efficiency with which the assimilated carbon is converted to biomass, k_B indicates the fraction of C_B lost by maintenance respiration, and L is litterfall input into the soil, adding to the soil carbon stock (C_S), which in turn is decomposed at the rate k_S. All the quantities with (t) depend on time, via dependencies on weather and soil conditions. The respiration of the system then follows as:

$$R_{eco}(t) = (1 - \eta) \cdot GPP(t) + k_B(t)\, C_B + k_S(t)\, C_S, \tag{14.4}$$

hence varying in time with the time-dependent conditions, and the states C_B and C_S.

With climate change and global warming, it is of particular interest how respiration responds to temperature. Thus, often a further simplified semi-empirical model

$$R_{eco}(t) = R_b(t) * Q_{10}^{\left(\frac{T(t) - T_{ref}}{10}\right)} \tag{14.5}$$

is employed. There, all the respiration components of Equation 14.4 are lumped into a "base respiration" R_b, which is independent of temperature. The temperature dependence of R is described as a parametric function of temperature T, defined by the temperature sensitivity Q_{10}. At reference temperature T_{ref}, R_{eco} equals R_b. R_b is hard to model from first principles since it depends on many biotic and abiotic factors (like root and soil animal activity, soil moisture) in a very heterogeneous setting (Davidson et al. 2012 , Reichstein and Beer 2008, Migliavacca et al. 2011). In the semi-parametric hybrid model setting (cf. Table 14.1), the goal is to estimate both $R_b(t)$ and Q_{10}, given the time series of R_{eco}, T and other variables (e.g. radiation, soil moisture), which have an unknown influence on R_b. This setting is being addressed in case studies I and II below. In those, $R_b(t)$ will be estimated with a feedforward (stateless) neural network (upper-left cell in Table 14.2), but of course, the estimation also is possible with a stateful (e.g., recurrent) neural network (cf. Kraft et al. 2020). If the Q_{10} was known, and R_b to be estimated, we would be in the lower left cell of Table 14.1, where $R_b = g(t, \mathbf{X})$, where g is fully unknown and $\mathbf{X}$ denotes the input matrix. Since in this simple example, the inference would be trivial by analytically inverting Equation 14.5 for R_b, we do not further treat this in the case studies.

Case studies I and II are based on the simplified regression described in Equation 14.5, which assumes that all respired CO_2 immediately leaves the soil and can be measured as soil respiration. Yet, in fact, a diffusion process is involved, which can be modeled as

$$\frac{\partial CO_2(t, z)}{\partial t} = R_b \cdot Q_{10}^{0.1 \cdot (T(t) - T_{ref})} - \frac{\partial}{\partial z}\left(-D_S \frac{\partial CO_2(t, z)}{\partial z}\right), \tag{14.6}$$

where the left-hand side of the differential equation describes the change of CO_2 concentration over time t in soil depth z. $R_b \cdot Q_{10}^{0.1 \cdot (T(t) - T_{ref})}$ is a simple Q_{10} function to describe the CO_2 evolution in depth z and the spatial derivative describes the CO_2 diffusion across different soil layers z. This stateful system with the CO_2 concentration as state variable will be considered in case study III.

14.3.1 Case Study I: Ecosystem Respiration

In the first case study, we demonstrate a simple hybrid toy model using synthetic (simulated) data of ecosystem respiration. We use Equation 14.5 and assume that the ecosystem respiration (R_{eco}) and temperature (T) are observed, while R_b and Q_{10} are to be estimated. For the experiment, data was simulated with $Q_{10} = 1.5$ and time-varying $R_b(t)$, dependent on daily potential solar (shortwave) radiation, $I_{SW}(t)$, and its time-derivative, $dI_{SW}(t)$, which simply introduces a seasonal cycle of R_b, co-varying with T.

To demonstrate the potential but also key challenges of hybrid modeling, two different setups were tested. In both experiments, $R_b(t)$ is modeled using a two-layer feedforward network (N_F) with a hidden size of 16 nodes each, with $I_{SW}(t)$ and $dI_{SW}(t)$ as inputs. In both settings, Q_{10} is a free but time-constant parameter, estimated jointly with the neural network parameters. Under these conditions, it should be easy to get a perfect prediction, as all inputs are available. While in the first setup, the temperature is not an input to the neural network (setup 1), the second setup uses T as an additional input to introduce equifinality (setup 2): T is used to estimate the R_b term in Equation 14.5 but also appears in the Q_{10} exponent.

$$\textbf{\textit{Setup 1:}} \ \ R_{eco}(t) = N_F(I_{SW}(t), \ dI_{SW}(t)) \cdot Q_{10}^{\left(\frac{T(t) - T_{ref}}{10}\right)} \tag{14.7}$$

$$\textbf{\textit{Setup 2:}} \ \ R_{eco}(t) = N_F(I_{SW}(t), \ dI_{SW}(t), \ T(t)) \cdot Q_{10}^{\left(\frac{T(t) - T_{ref}}{10}\right)} \tag{14.8}$$

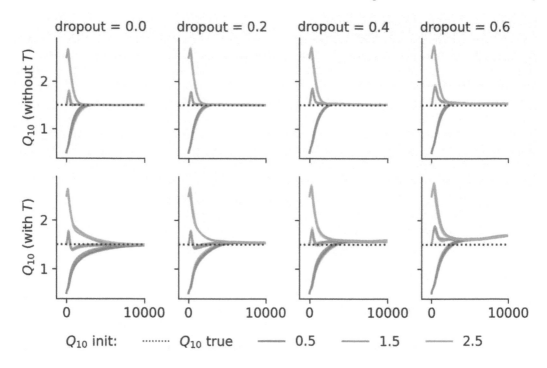

FIGURE 14.2
Model-based estimation of Q_{10} without (top row) and with (bottom row) using temperature as predictor. The lines represent repeated runs with different random seeds and different Q_{10} initial values (colors). The columns represent different dropout values.

To investigate the robustness of the simulations and to test potential interactions with the model setup, we used different initial values of $Q_{10} = \{0.5, 1.5, 2.5\}$ and dropout $= \{0.0, 0.2, 0.4, 0.6\}$, and for each combination, we initialize the neural network parameters with a different random seed. Dropout was applied on the activations of the two hidden layers but not on the inputs and was deactivated during validation.

The parameter Q_{10} was estimated robustly and accurately in the first setup, where the temperature was not used as input to the neural network (Figure 14.2, top). The initial value had no apparent impact on the final estimation, and also dropout only marginally impacted the results. When the temperature was used as input to the neural network (the second setup), the Q_{10} estimation was still robust, but we observed a stronger interaction with the dropout (Figure 14.2, bottom).

Interestingly, the Q_{10} simulations were relatively robust even if the temperature was used as an additional input (Figure 14.3). This indicates that in our experiment, random initialization of the neural network parameters and altering the initial Q_{10} is not sufficient to diagnose equifinality, which we know to be present in the second setup. Instead of large variations of Q_{10}, we observed strong interaction of the loss, Q_{10}, and dropout. This finding is intriguing, as it shows that we do not just potentially face equifinality, but also biases in the simulations depending on the model setup.

In this experiment, we may choose to not use dropout and conclude that we are able to estimate Q_{10} robustly. In real-world applications, however, we may need to introduce dropout or regularization to improve mode convergence and generalizability, which, as demonstrated here, could introduce biases in the simulations. Furthermore, we usually do not have a

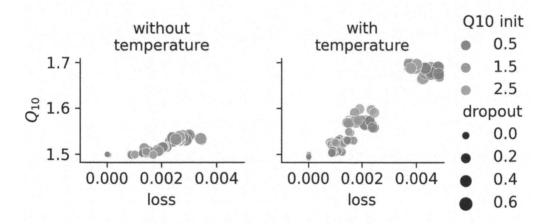

FIGURE 14.3
Performance versus estimated Q_{10} in interaction with dropout and the initial Q_{10} for the model without (left) and the one with (right) temperature as input.

ground truth for the latent variables, which renders detection of biases and equifinality difficult or even impossible. The fact that we face unforeseen issues in such a simplistic toy example highlights the need for a better understanding and methodological framework for hybrid modeling.

The code and data for this case study are available here: https://github.com/bask0/q10hybrid

14.3.2 Case Study II: Net Ecosystem Exchange

Following up on the first example, we introduce a bit more complexity and address a real-world problem in ecosystem science. The starting point is the net ecosystem exchange (NEE), the difference between respiration (R_{eco}) and carbon uptake (GPP) as described above in Section 14.3. An important task is to infer the individual CO_2 fluxes (photosynthesis, respiration) from the time series of NEE and the meteorological conditions influencing GPP and R_{eco}. This technique is called "flux partitioning". This flux partitioning has long relied on assumptions how photosynthesis and respiration depend on environmental factors. Recently, it was shown that this task can also be achieved with minimal assumptions via a varying coefficient model implemented with artificial neural network (Tramontana et al. 2020):

$$NEE = a \cdot PAR + b, \tag{14.9}$$

where PAR is the incoming photosynthetically active radiation, a and b are the varying coefficients to be estimated by a non-parametric model and represent the apparent radiation-use efficiency and respiration, respectively. The first term of the sum ($a \cdot PAR$) in Equation 14.9 represents the gross primary productivity (GPP).

In addition, it is of interest to estimate the temperature sensitivity of respiration, e.g., expressed as Q_{10} (Equation 14.5). This can be done by replacing b in Equation 14.9 by the right-hand side of Equation 14.5. The hybrid modeling task then is – given the time series of NEE and environmental conditions – to estimate the (time-varying) radiation-use efficiency and base respiration as well as the temperature sensitivity of respiration, as illustrated in Figure 14.4.

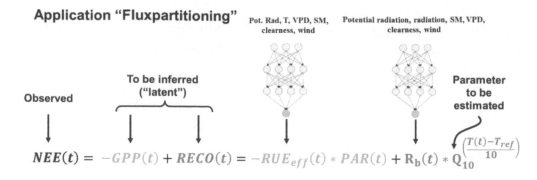

FIGURE 14.4
Illustration of the task and approach to estimate carbon flux quantities from the time-series of net ecosystem exchange. See text for details.

In the real-world, neither RUE nor R_b are directly observable – thus, we test the ability of the hybrid approach to retrieve the quantities with a synthetic test data set, which we create as follows. We take a data set from the collection of FLUXNET sites (Pastorello et al. 2020), the Neustift site (AT-Neu), where meteorological quantities and net ecosystem exchange of CO_2 are measured (available at www.fluxdata.org). Then, according to the equation in Figure 14.5, the respective quantities are modeled:

$$R_{b,syn} = SW_{POT_{sm}} * 0.01 - SW_{POT_{sm,diff}} * 0.005$$
$$RUE_{syn} = 0.5 * exp\left(-(0.1 * (T - 20))^2\right) * \min\left(1, exp\left(-0.1 * (VPD - 10)\right)\right)$$
$$GPP_{syn} = RUE_{syn} * SW_{IN}$$
$$RECO_{syn} = Rb_{syn} * Q_{10}^{0.1*(T-15.0)}$$
$$NEE_{syn} = (RECO_{syn} - GPP_{syn}) * (1 + \epsilon)$$

$$\epsilon \sim N(0, \sigma^2) \tag{14.10}$$

The suffix "_syn" means synthetic. Essentially, R_b is modeled with a smooth seasonal cycle of the incoming potential radiation (SW_POT_sm). Figure 14.6 shows the variation of all the synthetic variables in so-called "fingerprints". Most variables vary seasonally and diurnally, but Rb_syn only has a seasonal variation. The observational noise of NEE is modeled as relative (heteroscedastic) noise.

Figure 14.7 illustrates the challenge of estimating the Q_{10} from the time-series of R_{eco} and temperature. Often such Q_{10} is estimated by fitting an exponential curve to the bivariate scatter, which, however, does not yield the real, "intrinsic" or "true" Q_{10}, but only a confounded, "apparent Q_{10}", because the R_b coefficient correlates positively with temperature in this example. The challenge is to estimate the time-series of R_b and the intrinsic Q_{10} parameter simultaneously. Here the estimation is performed with a hybrid model according to Figure 14.4. For simplicity, the neural network was a simple one-layer feedforward neural network with 16 hidden nodes, without temperature as a predictor (see above, case study I), but any architecture including recurrent ones can be used.

The hybrid modeling is able to infer the between experiment variation of Q_{10} across four different noise levels with r^2 between 0.88 and 1.0 (Figure 14.7). As expected, the uncertainty with the Q_{10} estimation scales with the level of noise introduced. The retrieval is not unbiased with slopes modeled versus observed slightly above 1, but still is much closer to the real value than the confounded estimate (Figure 14.7, red dots). It is noted that given

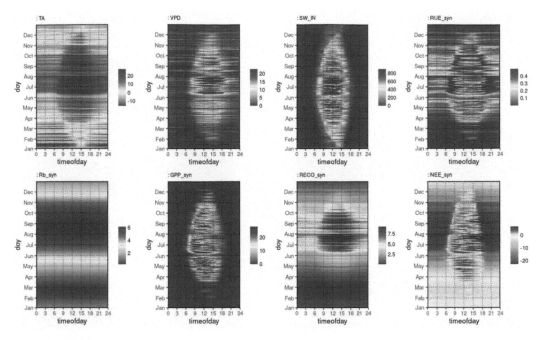

FIGURE 14.5

Isopleth diagrams ("fingerprints") of the different variables in the synthetic experiment. In those diagrams, x- and y-axis denote the hour of the day and day of the year, respectively, and colors code the value of the variable during the hour and day of the year. TA = air temperature [°C], VPD = Vapor pressure deficit [hPa], SW_IN = incoming short-wave radiation [W m^{-2}], RUE = synthetic radiation-use efficiency, Rb = base respiration, GPP = gross primary production, Reco = Ecosystem respiration, NEE = Net ecosystem exchange; all in [μmol m^{-2} s^{-1}].

the fact that both R_b, R_{eco} and *GPP*, *RUE* are estimated from the net flux only, there are more effects of confounding possible than in the pure respiration example of case study I, where photosynthesis processes do not need to be estimated simultaneously.

The time-varying latent variables (*GPP*, R_{eco}, R_b, *RUE*) are retrieved with high determination ($r^2 > 0.95$) as well (Figure 14.8), although biases are apparent at high R_{eco} estimates. These may be related to the overestimation of the Q_{10} even though also the R_b is slightly overestimated at the high end.

The synthetic example serves as a proof-of-concept for the hybrid model estimation approach. In the real world, the crux is that the variables *GPP*, R_{eco}, R_b, and *RUE* are not independently observed. Hence, an ultimate validation of the retrieval of these variables is not possible. Yet, at least we can rely on established, more heuristic flux-partitioning approaches to estimate *GPP* and R_{eco} and as a validation or plausibility check. For this we analyzed a Mediterranean evergreen oak site (Puéchabon, France, FR-Pue) with the same setup as in the synthetic example. The hybrid partitioning of *NEE* into *GPP* and R_{eco} yielded similar monthly mean diurnal courses as the established methods (Figure 14.9), including the asymmetric diurnal courses from May to September even though the estimates of *GPP* and R_{eco} were underestimated and overestimated in June and August, respectively. It is not possible to tell which method is right or wrong, but the classical methods allow the estimation of R_b independently for 4-day windows, while the hybrid approach here trains a neural net to the entire data set. Thus, the hybrid approach may not be flexible enough

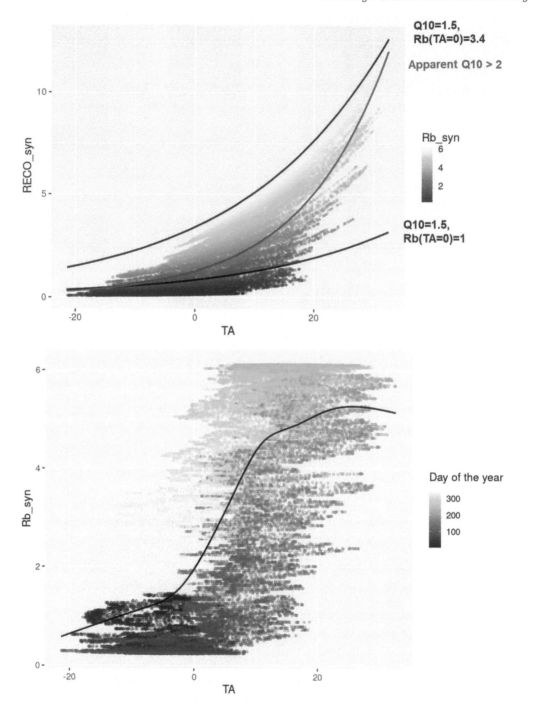

FIGURE 14.6
Upper panel, bivariate scatter plot of ecosystem respiration versus temperature, colored by the base respiration. The Q_{10} was set to 1.5. The exponential response is modulated by the changing R_b, yielding a higher apparent temperature sensitivity (red regression line), because of the confounding R_b variation with temperature, which is shown in the lower panel.

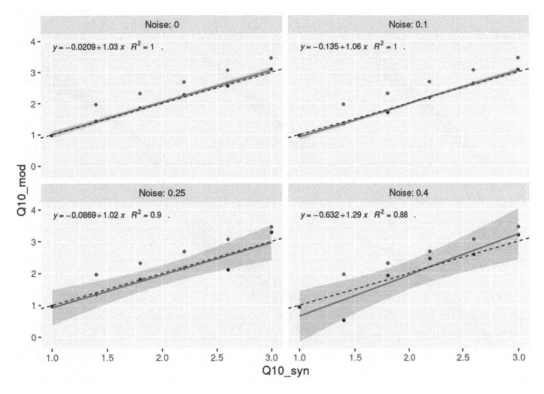

FIGURE 14.7
Retrieval of the Q_{10} via the hybrid modeling approach in a factorial experiment where the synthetic data was generated with different Q_{10} values (1 to 3 with steps of 0.4) and different (multiplicative) noise levels indicated multiples of standard deviations in the facets. Red dots indicate the confounded estimate from a simple bivariate regression as in Figure 14.6.

to account for drought effects or re-wetting events. Tramontana et al. (2020) performed a hybrid flux-partitioning (but without R_b estimation) within sub-seasonal time windows but still found differences between the hybrid and the established approaches. In addition, the neural network chosen here to predict RUE and R_b were feedforward neural nets and thus did not account for any memory effects, which could cause instance hysteresis in environment-flux relations. Of course, adding a different architecture for the neural net is simple (e.g., recurrent) and should be tried out in future work. Nevertheless, the overall flux partitioning appears to be consistent with the classical methods (Figure 14.10). In fact, at a half-hourly scale, the hybrid partitioning is more similar to the Lasslop-2010 partitioning (left panel) than the two established partitioning methods are with each other (right panel). Thus, we assume that we can infer all except very subtle patterns with the simple hybrid approach. In addition to the flux-partitioning itself, the hybrid approach allows inference of more variables and thus insight into how the ecosystem reacts to environmental drivers. As an example, we show how the inferred RUE and R_b covary with environmental drivers (Figure 14.11). Inferred RUE decreases with increasing vapor pressure deficit (VPD) and soil water deficit (left panel, deficit expressed as negative values). Yet, with low VPD the RUE does not drop below 0.03, while RUE gets close to zero when VPD and soil water deficit are both high, indicating a strong interaction effect. In contrast, R_b sharply drops

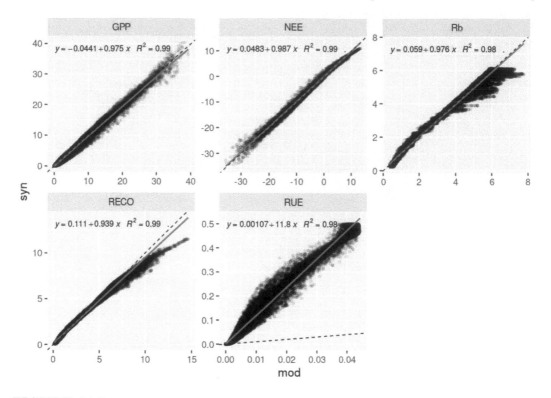

FIGURE 14.8
Observed variables versus inferred variables by the hybrid modeling estimation for the experiment when $Q_{10} = 1.5$, relative noise $= 0.1$.

at soil water deficits >50 mm (right panel). These results indicate that respiration strongly depends on the soil moisture in the top-soil (at a deficit of 50 mm the first 20–30 cm of soil are essentially dry in this site with 70% stone content) while vegetation still has access to deeper soil layers, keeping its activity even at water deficits as high as 100 mm. When water is not limiting, a dependence on *GPP* is seen, indicating that respiration is co-limited by the carbon supply. The decrease of R_b at very high *GPP* needs further attention, but it could be due to the fact that respiration tends to lag behind *GPP* (because the assimilated carbon first needs to be transported to the microbial sites in the soil).

The hybrid modeling approach thus offers promises to infer ecosystem processes, states, and functional properties (Reichstein et al. 2014) more generally. For instance, starting from the equation in Figure 14.5, further equations or terms could be added, e.g., by integrating water cycle (i.e., evapotranspiration) observations and relating them to *GPP* via water-use efficiency (Nelson et al. 2020).

14.3.3   Case Study III: Universal Differential Equations

Case studies I and II were examples where neural network were embedded into algebraic equations to model the CO_2 flux from the soil to the atmosphere. More mechanistic models are generally formulated as differential equations, and thereby they cannot only model fluxes but also states. Ordinary Differential Equations (ODE), in which certain terms of a differential equation or even the complete right-hand side of a differential equation are

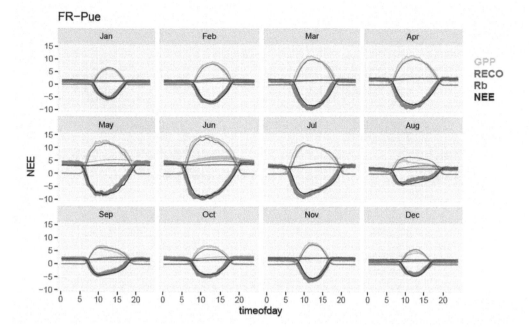

FR-Pue

FIGURE 14.9

Observed and modeled diurnal courses of the carbon flux quantities for the Puéchabon site. The solid lines indicate the estimates from the hybrid modeling system, while the transparent bands indicate the range of estimates of *GPP* and R_{eco} with Reichstein et al. (2005) and Lasslop et al. (2010) methods.

formulated as a neural network have been termed universal differential equations by Rackauckas et al. (2020). The ability to estimate the parameters of these neural network embedded within the differential equations while at the same time estimating the mechanistic parameters relies on gradient calculation through the ODE solver (Rackauckas et al. 2020).

In mechanistic models, one can generally distinguish between pools of an entity with a particular state and fluxes of that entity that connect different pools or describe the process of entering or leaving the system of pools. In the Q_{10} hybrid respiration example from above, we modeled a flux that instantaneously depended on temperature $Q_{10}^{\left(\frac{T(t)-T_{ref}}{10}\right)}$. However, the CO_2 efflux from heterotrophic and root respiration is not produced directly at the soil-atmosphere interface but is produced throughout the soil and must diffuse to the soil surface as a function of soil temperature and soil moisture (Maier et al. 2020). Building on the previous synthetic experiments data set, we show how neural nets can be embedded in differential equations to represent unknown relationships with environmental drivers while being stateful.

We consider the following simplified model for representing CO_2 diffusion:

$$\frac{\partial CO_2(t,z)}{\partial t} = R_b \cdot Q_{10}^{0.1 \cdot (T(t)-T_{ref})} - \frac{\partial}{\partial z}\left(-D_S \frac{\partial CO_2(t,z)}{\partial z}\right), \tag{14.11}$$

where the left-hand side of the differential equation describes the change of CO_2 concentration over time t in soil depth z. $R_b \cdot Q_{10}^{0.1 \cdot (T(t)-T_{ref})}$ is a simple Q_{10} function to describe the CO_2 evolution in depth z and the spatial derivative describes the CO_2 diffusion across

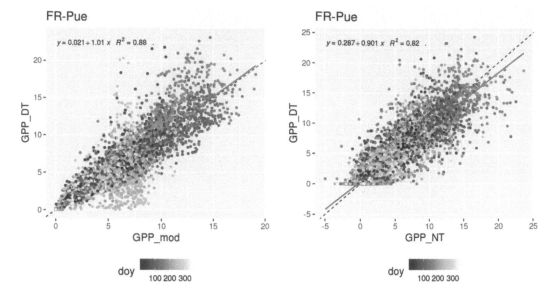

FIGURE 14.10
Evaluation scatter plot for the inference of *GPP* at the Puéchabon site. Left: Classical method by Lasslop et al. (2010) versus hybrid inferred GPP; right: Classical methods against each other (Lasslop [2010] versus Reichstein et al. [2005]).

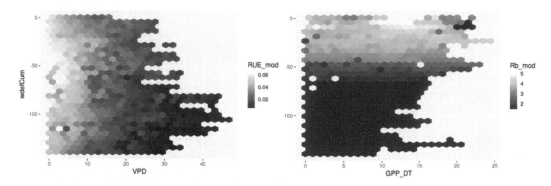

FIGURE 14.11
Inferred co-variability of the *RUE* with soil water deficit and vapor pressure deficit (left) and of R_b with soil water deficit and *GPP* (right).

different soil layers z. For the sake of simplicity and illustration purposes, we assume here that R_b is a constant parameter as well as Q_{10}. The diffusion coefficient, D_S, varies with time as a function of temperature and soil moisture. The temperature influence (and air pressure influence – which we also assume here to be constant) on D_S is well-known from first principles. The influence of water content or tortuosity on D_S is described throughout the scientific literature by different approaches (Roland et al. 2015):

$$D_S = D_a \cdot \xi, \qquad (14.12)$$

where D_a describes the CO_2 diffusion coefficient in free air $D_a = D_{a0} \cdot \left(\frac{P}{P_0}\right) \cdot \left(\frac{T}{T_0}\right)^{1.75}$

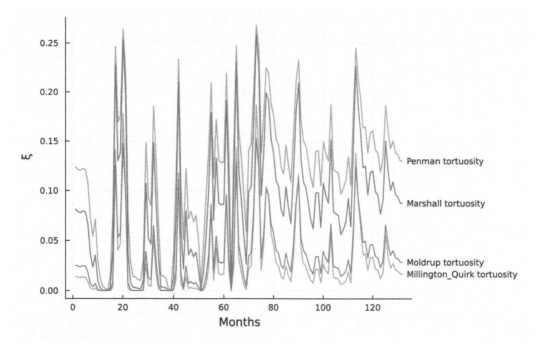

FIGURE 14.12
Overview of the effect of monthly soil moisture on tortuosity functions at the Neustift site.

with D_{a0} the standard diffusion coefficient of $1.47 \cdot 10^{-5}$ m^2 s^{-1} at T_0 of 293.15 K and P_0 of 1013 hPa (Roland et al., Maier and Schack-Kirchner). The parameter ξ is the so-called tortuosity factor and describes the effect of pore architecture and water content on diffusivity. This relationship is often derived experimentally or by geometric consideration about pore architecture. Figure 14.12 gives an overview of how different the formulations of the tortuosity factor can be:

This synthetic experiment shows that the tortuosity function can also be derived from field measurements of CO_2 efflux and CO_2 concentrations within the soil profile.

Hence, we formulate the following universal differential equation where the tortuosity function is learned from data by a neural net that receives soil water content (SWC) as input while simultaneously estimating Q_{10} and R_b:

$$\frac{\partial CO_2(t,z)}{\partial t} = R_b \cdot Q_{10}^{0.1 \cdot (T(t) - T_{ref})} - \frac{\partial}{\partial z} \left(-D_a \cdot NN \left(SWC\left(t\right)\right) \frac{\partial CO_2(t,z)}{\partial z} \right).$$

Due to the stiffness of the problem, we use the BFGS algorithm to estimate the parameters of the neural net and the mechanistic parameters Q_{10} and R_b. We created artificial data using mean monthly air temperature and soil moisture measurements from the Neustift site and employing the Moldrup tortuosity function (Figure 14.12). Figure 14.13 shows the effect of CO_2 diffusion on soil CO_2 efflux compared to an algebraic Q_{10} model, which is stateless and instantaneous. Figure 14.14 shows the hybrid model's predictions of CO_2 build-up using a neural net initialized with random parameters, while Figure 14.14 shows the hybrid model's predictions after the neural net has been trained for 68 iterations with the BFGS algorithm. The differential equations for this case study have been formulated using the Julia package DifferentialEquations.jl (Rackauckas and Nie 2017), parameters were optimized using the Julia package Optim.jl (Mogensen and Riseth 2018), neural network have been formulated with the Julia package Flux.jl (Innes 2018) and the

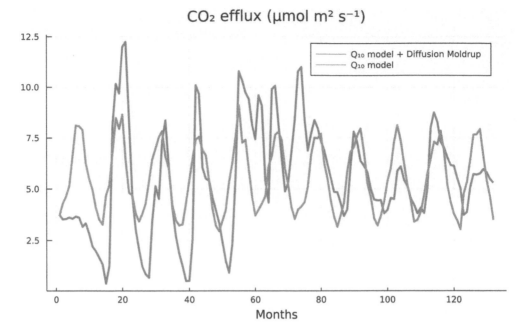

FIGURE 14.13
Effect of CO_2 diffusion (Q_{10} model + Diffusion Moldrup) compared to a stateless Q_{10} model with the same R_b and Q_{10} parameters.

universal differential equation capabilities of the Julia package DiffEqFlux.jl (Rackauckas et al. 2020).

The synthetic experiment also shows that there are two ways to represent stateful system behavior for a stateful system. Due to the diffusion, the CO_2 efflux is not instantaneous to temperature and moisture anymore. A hybrid modeling approach that does not simulate diffusion but represents the stateful system in an ML setting is also conceivable. One could, for example, try to represent the statefulness by using a stateful ML model such as an RNN in the form of an LSTM:

$$R(t) = NN_{Rb,LSTM}\left(SWC, T\right) \cdot Q_{10}^{0.1 \cdot (T(t) - T_{ref})}$$

The universal differential equation approach, however, can encode prior knowledge more easily than the 'universal algebraic equations' approach. At the same time, universal differential equations could use the additional data streams of (synthetic) CO_2 concentrations in various soil depths, thereby increasing the overall information content that can be exploited in this exercise.

For hybrid models, reconciling observations of fluxes and pools into a consistent framework that can extract scientific insights is currently a challenge. For universal differential equations, mostly differential equations without exogenous forcing have been explored (Rackauckas et al. 2020). Here, we have shown an example of a universal differential equation with exogenous forcing (temperature and moisture). It became evident that efficient automatic differentiation can become a computational bottleneck. Decomposing or "denoising" the exogenous forcing into a combination of automatically differentiable functions (sines and cosines) with Fourier transform could be a path worthwhile exploring for universal differential equations. This approach might also be helpful to prevent spectral bias in learning neural network, which generally learn slow frequencies quicker (Rahaman et al. 2019).

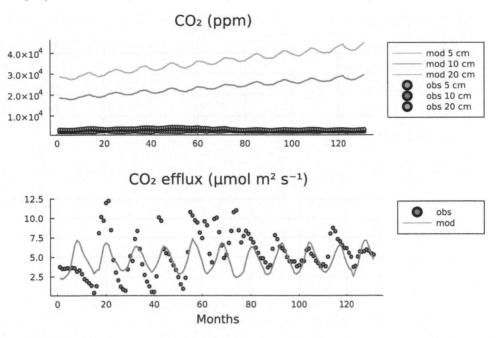

FIGURE 14.14
Hybrid partial differential equation of CO_2 build-up through respiration and diffusion to the soil surface with random parameters from the initialization of the neural net. State variables in the top panel (CO_2 in ppm) and CO_2 efflux in the bottom panel.

14.4 Discussion

14.4.1 Hybrid Modeling as a Regularizer

From a physical modeling perspective, any parameter has a physical meaning, which makes it conceptually unacceptable to cross known or inferred boundaries, even if by doing so would fit the data better. The fact that a parameter has a physical interpretation does not mean though that it has been measured, or that it is even a measurable quantity, but the ability to determine the ones that have been measured confer robustness and support using these models for attribution and causal experiments. Notwithstanding, the determination of a meaningful parameter, or parameter set, embeds the challenge of avoiding local minima, via global optimization approaches, and being resistant to equifinality. Often, regularization is used as an approach that has taken many forms by including constraints on multiple output variables, as well as priors on parameters (e.g., Bayesian approaches), or by associating specific parameters to particular observations.

Notationally, a standard purely data-driven (ML) approach would try to fit Y from X using a flexible model $g(X;W)$ parametrized by W. In order to control the capacity of the model family class, and one typically regularizes the problem by adding a penalty term on the function, $\Omega(g)$, e.g., imposing smoothness $\Omega(g) = ||g||_2$ or sparsity $\Omega(g) = ||g||_1$. In a hybrid ML approach, however, the regularization is more explicit as the domain knowledge is incorporated in the definition of the function g itself, as now it becomes a chain of two models: a physics-prescribed one f that operates on a data-driven one $h(.)$, that is

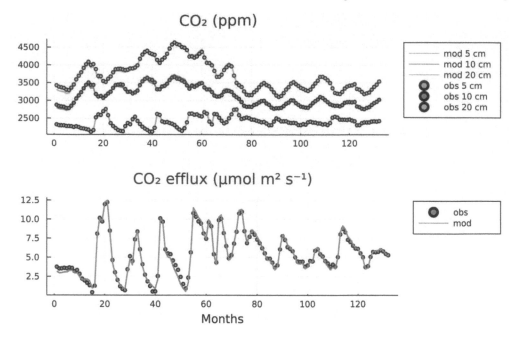

FIGURE 14.15

Hybrid partial differential equations of CO_2 build-up through respiration and diffusion to the soil surface after 68 iterations with the BFGS algorithm. State variables in the top panel (CO_2 in ppm) and CO_2 efflux in the bottom panel.

$f(X,h(X;W);\theta)$ which is parametrized by θ. Even if theoretically one could define a regularizer $\Omega(g)$ that recovers the exact same solution of the composition, $g = f * h$, the rationale to learn the full chain of functions -and not the regularizer-offers important benefits: (1) improved interpretability (since the θ parameters are learned and have a physical meaning) and (2) implicit complexity control (since imposing conditions in f will translate into the overall model class).

Actually, the integration of theory and mechanistic knowledge in ML models may not only achieve improved performance and generalization but, more importantly, may lead to improved consistency and credibility of the ML models. Actually, the hybridization may have an interesting regularization effect, given that the physics limits the parameter space to search and thus (if done properly) may discard implausible models. Therefore, physics-aware ML models combat overfitting better, become typically simpler (sparser), and require less amount of training data to achieve similar performance (Stewart and Ermon 2016). Physics-aware ML thus may lead to enhanced computational efficiency and constitute a stepping stone towards achieving more interpretable and robust ML models (Samek et al. 2019).

14.4.2 Equifinality as a Major Potential Challenge

A relevant problem in ML in general and in hybrid ML, in particular, is the above-mentioned equifinality, that is, one can achieve the same result or state description by many potential solutions and model parametrizations. Equifinality has been traditionally cast as a *curse* in many areas where not just accurate fitting but identification of meaningful parameters is the main objective, like in hydrology, but instead as a blessing for doing inference (Savenije 2001).

Equifinality is tightly linked to the broad concept of *identifiability* (or better a lack of) in statistics, by which two models (or parametrizations) are observationally equivalent or indistinguishable. Identifiability has been largely treated in signal processing, control theory, ML theory and causal inference (Ljung and Glad 1994, Walter , Robins and Greenland 2014, Grewal and Glover 1976). Dealing with equifinality/identifiability issues is equivalent to dealing with uncertainty in model parameterization and is still an unresolved problem in statistics. Even for simple linear parametric models, it is complicated to tell whether a coefficient is significant or not after model selection.

When splitting the function into a mechanistic plus a fully non-parametric part, the effect could be catastrophic in cases of model misspecification, as the model solution would be confined to a solution subspace with little expressive power and even implausible solutions. Allowing for more flexibility in the definition of the model class f along with even including an extra regularizer for f is advisable, e.g., via constrained optimization that includes bounds on θ. Another common case may arise when physical predictors are incorporated in the ML counterpart of the hybrid model to ideally improve its capacity; in such cases, collinearity issues, interactions, and compensatory effects may arise between the two model components. Removing potentially explanatory (physical) variables from the h model may not be a good solution. Alternatives exist in the literature by forcing correlation or dependence of the prediction function with ancillary data and models. The concept of algorithmic fairness has recently been adapted to geoscience problems by defining dependence-regularizers and could be adapted to enforce independence between functions f and h while still using all available covariates $\mathbf{X}$ possible in both models (Pérez-Suay et al. 2017). In all these problems, regularization appears as the key concept that links prior/domain knowledge for inference, and in the case of hybrid ML, physics knowledge can be cast as a powerful regularizer, but the exact "How?" will keep research busy in the coming years.

14.4.3 Outlook: Promising Ecosystem Ecological and Earth System Applications

In this chapter, we only addressed a small part of ecosystem ecological and Earth system relevant applications, related to photosynthesis and respiration at ecosystem scale. Processes and latent states which are strongly controlled and eco-physiological and biological dynamics and thus not derived from first principles were approximated via the hybrid modeling approach (i.e., the base respiration, and radiation-use efficiency, as well as the temperature sensitivity). Other processes worthwhile describing include transpiration, vegetation phenology, allocation and mortality as well as turnover and carbon stabilization in the soil and disturbance processes such as fire (Figure 14.16). A challenge here is to integrate different time-scales (or treat them separately) and very diverse observational constraints (rounded boxes Figure 14.16). Yet, once successful, this approach may lead to a new generation of Earth system models, which may be exhibit more data-driven and thus more realistic land-carbon and water-cycle feedbacks and at least complements classical purely mechanistic Earth system modeling approaches. A summary of notations and acronyms used in this chapter is provided in Table 14.3.

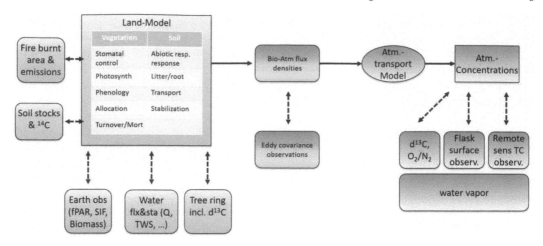

FIGURE 14.16

Processes in vegetation and soil worthwhile describing (Box Land-Model) with a hybrid modeling approach and respective observational constraints. Outputs from the land-model can be directly constrained with observations on fire, soil carbon stocks and apparent age (^{14}C), Earth Observation variables, water fluxes and states and tree rings. When the land model is coupled with an atmospheric transport model, further observations such as atmospheric observations are accessible as additional constraints. Similar schemes are certainly possible with ocean carbon cycle modeling.

TABLE 14.3

Overview of notations and acronyms used in this chapter.

RUE	Radiation use efficiency
NEE	Net ecosystem exchange
Q_{10}	Respiration sensitivity to temperature
GPP	Gross primary production
PAR	Photosynthetic active radiation
$APAR$	Absorbed photosynthetic active radiation
T_a	Air temperature
R_{eco}	Ecosystem respiration
R_b	Base respiration
N_F/FNN	Feedforward neural network
N_R/RNN	Recurrent neural networks
$PINN$	Physics-informed neural network
VPD	Vapor pressure deficit
SWC	Soil water content
I_{SW}/SW	Incoming solar/shortwave radiation

Bibliography

[1] Bhutani, N., G. P. Rangaiah, and A. K. Ray. 2006. "First-Principles, Data-Based, and Hybrid Modeling and Optimization of an Industrial Hydrocracking Unit." *Industrial & Engineering Chemistry Research* 45 (23):7807-7816. doi: 10.1021/ie060247q.

[2] Bonan, G. 2015. *Ecological climatology: concepts and applications*: Cambridge University Press.

[3] Camps-Valls, G., et al. 2018. "Physics-aware Gaussian processes in remote sensing." *Applied Soft Computing* 68:69-82. doi: 10.1016/j.asoc.2018.03.021.

[4] Davidson, E. A., S. Samanta, S. S. Caramori, and K. Savage. 2012. "The D ual A rrhenius and M ichaelis–M enten kinetics model for decomposition of soil organic matter at hourly to seasonal time scales." *Global Change Biology* 18 (1):371-384.

[5] de Bézenac, E., A. Pajot, and P. Gallinari. 2019. "Deep learning for physical processes: incorporating prior scientific knowledge." *Journal of Statistical Mechanics: Theory and Experiment* 2019 (12):124009. doi: 10.1088/1742-5468/ab3195.

[6] Grewal, M., and K. Glover. 1976. "Identifiability of linear and nonlinear dynamical systems." *IEEE Transactions on Automatic Control* 21 (6):833-837. doi: 10.1109/tac.1976.1101375.

[7] Halevy, A., P. Norvig, and F. Pereira. 2009. "The Unreasonable Effectiveness of Data." *IEEE Intelligent Systems* 24 (2):8-12. doi: 10.1109/mis.2009.36.

[8] Hastie, T., and R. Tibshirani. 1993. "Varying-coefficient models." *Journal of the Royal Statistical Society: Series B (Methodological)* 55 (4):757-779.

[9] Innes, M. 2018. "Flux: Elegant machine learning with Julia." *Journal of Open Source Software* 3 (25):602.

[10] Karpatne, A., et al. 2017. "Theory-guided Data Science: A New Paradigm for Scientific Discovery from Data." *IEEE Transactions on Knowledge and Data Engineering* PP (99):1-1. doi: 10.1109/TKDE.2017.2720168.

[11] Karpatne, A., W. Watkins, J. Read, and V. Kumar. 2017. "Physics-guided Neural Networks (PGNN): An Application in Lake Temperature Modeling." *arXiv preprint arXiv:1710.11431.*

[12] Kraft, B., M. Jung, M. Körner, and M. Reichstein. 2020. "Hybrid modeling: Fusion of a deep approach and physics-based model for global hydrological modeling." *The International Archives of Photogrammetry, Remote Sensing and Spatial Information Sciences* XLIII-B2-2020:1537-1544. doi: 10.5194/isprs-archives-XLIII-B2-2020-1537-2020.

[13] Lasslop, G., et al. 2010. "Separation of net ecosystem exchange into assimilation and respiration using a light response curve approach: critical issues and global evaluation." *Global Change Biology* 16 (1):187-208. doi: 10.1111/j.1365-2486.2009.02041.x.

[14] Ljung, L., and T. Glad. 1994. "On global identifiability for arbitrary model parametrizations." *Automatica* 30 (2):265-276. doi: 10.1016/0005-1098(94)90029-9.

[15] Maier, M., V. Gartiser, A. Schengel, and V. Lang. 2020. "Long Term Soil Gas Monitoring as Tool to Understand Soil Processes." *Applied Sciences* 10 (23):8653. doi: 10.3390/app10238653.

[16] Maier, M., and H. Schack-Kirchner. 2014. "Using the gradient method to determine soil gas flux: A review." *Agricultural and Forest Meteorology* 192-193:78-95. doi: 10.1016/j.agrformet.2014.03.006.

[17] Migliavacca, M., et al. 2011. "Semiempirical modeling of abiotic and biotic factors controlling ecosystem respiration across eddy covariance sites." *Global Change Biology* 17 (1):390-409. doi: 10.1111/j.1365-2486.2010.02243.x.

[18] Mogensen, P. K., and A. N. Riseth. 2018. "Optim: A mathematical optimization package for Julia." *Journal of Open Source Software* 3 (24).

[19] Molga, E., and R. Cherbański. 1999. "Hybrid first-principle–neural-network approach to modelling of the liquid–liquid reacting system." *Chemical Engineering Science* 54 (13-14):2467-2473. doi: 10.1016/s0009-2509(98)00506-5.

[20] Moncrieff, J., R. Valentini, S. Greco, G. Seufert, and P. Ciccioli. 1997. "Trace gas exchange over terrestrial ecosystems: methods and perspectives in micrometeorology." *Journal of Experimental Botany* 48 (310):1133-1142. doi: 10.1093/jxb/48.5.1133.

[21] Nelson, J. A., et al. 2020. "Ecosystem transpiration and evaporation: Insights from three water flux partitioning methods across FLUXNET sites." *Global Change Biology.* doi: 10.1111/gcb.15314.

[22] Park, B. U., E. Mammen, Y. K. Lee, and E. R. Lee. 2015. "Varying coefficient regression models: a review and new developments." *International Statistical Review* 83 (1):36-64. doi: 10.1111/insr.12029.

[23] Pastorello, G., et al. 2020. "The FLUXNET2015 dataset and the ONEFlux processing pipeline for eddy covariance data." *Scientific Data* 7 (1):225. doi: 10.1038/s41597-020-0534-3.

[24] Pérez-Suay, A., et al. 2017. "Fair kernel learning." In *Joint European Conference on Machine Learning and Knowledge Discovery in Databases. ECML PKDD 2017*, edited by M. Ceci, J. Hollmén, L. Todorovski, C. Vens and S. Džeroski, 339-355. Springer.

[25] Rackauckas, C., et al. 2020. "Universal Differential Equations for Scientific Machine Learning." *PREPRINT (Version 1) available at Research Square.* doi: 10.21203/rs.3.rs-55125/v1.

[26] Rackauckas, C., and Q. Nie. 2017. "Differentialequations. jl–a performant and feature-rich ecosystem for solving differential equations in julia." *Journal of Open Research Software* 5 (1):15. doi: 10.5334/jors.151.

[27] Rahaman, N., et al. 2019. "On the spectral bias of neural networks." International Conference on Machine Learning.

[28] Raissi, M., and G. E. Karniadakis. 2018. "Hidden physics models: Machine learning of nonlinear partial differential equations." *Journal of Computational Physics* 357:125-141. doi: 10.1016/j.jcp.2017.11.039.

[29] Raissi, M., A. Yazdani, and G. E. Karniadakis. 2020. "Hidden fluid mechanics: learning velocity and pressure fields from flow visualizations." *Science* 367 (6481):1026-1030. doi: 10.1126/science.aaw4741.

[30] Reichstein, M., and C. Beer. 2008. "Soil respiration across scales: The importance of a model-data integration framework for data interpretation." *Journal of Plant Nutrition and Soil Science* 171 (3):344-354. doi: 10.1002/jpln.200700075.

[31] Reichstein, M., et al. 2019. "Deep learning and process understanding for data-driven Earth system science." *Nature* 566 (7743):195-204. doi: 10.1038/s41586-019-0912-1.

[32] Reichstein, M., and N. Carvalhais. 2019. "Aspects of Forest Biomass in the Earth System: Its Role and Major Unknowns." *Surveys in Geophysics* 40 (4):693-707. doi: 10.1007/s10712-019-09551-x.

[33] Reichstein, M., et al. 2005. "On the separation of net ecosystem exchange into assimilation and ecosystem respiration: review and improved algorithm." *Global Change Biology* 11:1424-1439.

[34] Reichstein, M., A. D. Richardson, M. Migliavacca, and N. Carvalhais. 2014. "Plant–Environment Interactions Across Multiple Scales." In *Ecology and the Environment*, edited by R. K. Monson, 1-23. New York: Springer.

[35] Robins, J. M., and S. Greenland. 1992. "Identifiability and exchangeability for direct and indirect effects." *Epidemiology* 3 (2):143-155. doi: 10.1097/00001648-199203000-00013.

[36] Roland, M., et al. 2015. "Importance of nondiffusive transport for soil CO_2 efflux in a temperate mountain grassland." *Journal of Geophysical Research: Biogeosciences* 120 (3):502-512. doi: 10.1002/2014JG002788.

[37] Samek, W., G. Montavon, A. Vedaldi, L. K. Hansen, and K.-R. Müller, eds. 2019. *Explainable AI: Interpreting, Explaining and Visualizing Deep Learning*. Vol. 11700, *Lecture Notes in Computer Science*. Cham: Springer.

[38] Savenije, H. H. G. 2001. "Equifinality, a blessing in disguise?" *Hydrological Processes* 15 (14):2835-2838. doi: 10.1002/hyp.494.

[39] Stewart, R., and S. Ermon. 2016. "Label-Free Supervision of Neural Networks with Physics and Domain Knowledge." *arXiv preprint*.

[40] Svendsen, D. H., L. Martino, M. Campos-Taberner, F. J. García-Haro, and G. Camps-Valls. 2018. "Joint Gaussian Processes for Biophysical Parameter Retrieval." *IEEE Transactions on Geoscience and Remote Sensing* 56 (3):1718-1727. doi: 10.1109/TGRS.2017.2767205.

[41] Tramontana, G., et al. 2020. "Partitioning net carbon dioxide fluxes into photosynthesis and respiration using neural networks." *Global Change Biology*. doi: 10.1111/gcb.15203.

[42] von Stosch, M., R. Oliveira, J. Peres, and S. Feyo de Azevedo. 2014. "Hybrid semi-parametric modeling in process systems engineering: Past, present and future." *Computers & Chemical Engineering* 60:86-101. doi: 10.1016/j.compchemeng.2013.08.008.

[43] Walter, E. 2014. *Identifiability of Parametric Models*. Burlington: Elsevier Science.

[44] Yazdani, A., L. Lu, M. Raissi, and G. E. Karniadakis. 2020. "Systems biology informed deep learning for inferring parameters and hidden dynamics." *PLoS computational biology* 16 (11):e1007575. doi: 10.1371/journal.pcbi.1007575.

Physics-Guided Neural Networks (PGNN): An Application in Lake Temperature Modeling

Arka Daw, Anuj Karpatne, William D. Watkins, Jordan S. Read, and Vipin Kumar

CONTENTS

This chapter introduces a framework for combining scientific knowledge of physics-based models with neural networks to advance scientific discovery. This framework, termed physics-guided neural networks (PGNN), leverages the output of physics-based model simulations along with observational features in a hybrid modeling setup to generate predictions using a neural network architecture. Further, this framework uses physics-based loss functions in the learning objective of neural networks to ensure that the model predictions not only show lower errors on the training set but are also scientifically consistent with the known physics on the unlabeled set. We illustrate the effectiveness of PGNN for the problem of lake temperature modeling, where physical relationships between the temperature, density, and depth of water are used to design a physics-based loss function. By using scientific knowledge to guide the construction and learning of neural networks, we are able to show that the proposed framework ensures better generalizability as well

DOI: 10.1201/9781003143376-15

as scientific consistency of results. All the code and datasets used in this study have been made available on this link `https://github.com/arkadaw9/PGNN`.

15.1   Introduction

Data science has become an indispensable tool for knowledge discovery in the era of big data, as the volume of data continues to explode in practically every research domain. Recent advances in data science such as deep learning have been immensely successful in transforming the state-of-the-art in a number of commercial and industrial applications such as natural language translation and image classification, using billions or even trillions of data samples. In light of these advancements, there is a growing anticipation in the scientific community to unlock the power of data science methods for accelerating scientific discovery [1, 5, 9, 22].

However, a major limitation in using "black-box" data science models, that are agnostic to the underlying scientific principles driving real-world phenomena, is their sole dependence on the available labeled data, which is often limited in a number of scientific problems. In particular, a black-box data science model for a supervised learning problem can only be as good as the representative quality of the labeled data trained on. When the size of both the training and test sets are small, it is easy to learn spurious relationships that look deceptively good on both training and test sets (even after using standard methods for model evaluation such as cross-validation), but do not generalize well outside the available labeled data. A more serious concern with black-box applications of data science models is the lack of consistency of its predictions with respect to the known laws of physics (demonstrated in Section 15.4). Hence, even if a black-box model achieves somewhat more accurate performance but lacks the ability to adhere to mechanistic understandings of the underlying physical processes, it cannot be used as a basis for subsequent scientific developments.

On the other end of the spectrum, physics-based models, which are founded on core scientific principles, strive to advance our understanding of the physical world by learning explainable relationships between input and output variables. These models have been the cornerstone of knowledge discovery in a wide range of scientific and engineering disciplines. There are two basic forms in which physical knowledge is generally available: (a) as physics-based rules or equations that dictate relationships between physical variables, and (b) in the form of numerical models of complex physical systems, e.g., simulations of dynamical systems that are heavily used in computational chemistry, fluid dynamics, climate science, and particle physics. While these models have significantly advanced our understanding of the physical universe, they are limited in their ability to extract knowledge directly from data and are mostly reliant only on the available physics. For example, many physics-based models use parameterized forms of approximations for representing complex physical processes that are either not fully understood or cannot be solved using computationally tractable methods. Calibrating the parameters in physics-based models is a challenging task because of the combinatorial nature of the search space. In particular, this can result in the learning of over-complex models that lead to incorrect insights even if they appear interpretable at a first glance. For example, these and other challenges in modeling hydrological processes using state-of-the-art physics-based models were the subject of a series of debate papers in the *Journal of Water Resources Research* (WRR) [6, 10, 13]. One perspective [6] argues that many physics-based models are excessively constrained by their *a priori* parameterizations. The dichotomy between physics-based models and black-box neural network models is schematically depicted in Figure 15.1, where they both occupy

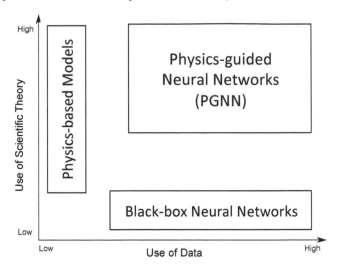

FIGURE 15.1
A schematic representation of physics-guided neural networks in the context of other knowledge discovery approaches that either use physics or data. The X-axis measures the use of data while the Y-axis measures the use of scientific knowledge.

the two extreme ends of knowledge discovery, either relying only on the data (black-box neural networks) or only on scientific knowledge (physics-based models).

In this chapter, we introduce a framework of knowledge discovery in scientific problems that combines the power of neural networks with physics-based models, termed physics-guided neural networks (PGNN). There are two primary contributions of this work. First, we present an approach to create hybrid combinations of physics-based models and neural network architectures to make full use of both physics and data. Second, we present a novel framework for training neural network architectures using the knowledge contained in physics-based equations, to ensure the learning of physically consistent solutions. To demonstrate the framework of PGNN, we consider the illustrative problem of modeling the temperature of water in a lake at varying depths and times, using input drivers as well as physics-based model simulations. For this problem, we exploit a key physical relationship between the temperature, density, and depth of water in the form of physics-based loss function.

The remainder of this chapter is organized as follows. Section 15.2 presents the generic framework of physics-guided neural networks that can be applied in any domain with some availability of scientific knowledge. Section 15.3 presents the specific PGNN formulation for the illustrative problem of lake temperature modeling. Section 15.4 describes the evaluation procedure and presents experimental results. Section 15.5 presents some discussion on the approach used for hybrid modeling, while Section 15.6 provides concluding remarks.

15.2 Physics-Guided Neural Networks

The generic framework of PGNN involves two key steps: (a) creating hybrid combinations of physics-based models and neural networks, termed hybrid-physics-data (HPD) models, and (b) using scientific knowledge as physics-based loss functions in the learning objective of neural networks, as described in the following.

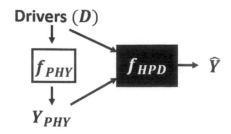

FIGURE 15.2
A schematic illustration of a basic hybrid-physics-data (HPD) model, where the output Y_{PHY} of a physics-based model f_{PHY} is used as another feature in the data science model f_{HPD} along with the drivers D to produce the final outputs $\hat{Y}$. In this schematic, white boxes represent physics-based models while black boxes represent ML models.

15.2.1 Constructing Hybrid-Physics-Data Models

Consider a predictive learning problem where we are given a set of input drivers, $\mathbf{D}$, that are physically related to a target variable of interest, Y. A standard approach is to train a data science model, e.g., a neural network, $f_{NN} : \mathbf{D} \rightarrow Y$, over a set of training instances, which can then be used to produce estimates of the target variable, $\hat{Y}$. Alternatively, we can also use a physics-based numerical model, $f_{PHY} : \mathbf{D} \rightarrow Y$, to simulate the value of the target variable, Y_{PHY}, given its physical relationships with the input drivers. Analogous to the process of training, physics-based models often require "calibrating" their model parameters using observational data – a process that is both time-consuming and label-expensive. Furthermore, Y_{PHY} may provide an incomplete representation of the target variable due to simplified or missing physics in f_{PHY}, thus resulting in model discrepancies with respect to observations. Hence, the basic goal of HPD modeling is to combine f_{PHY} and f_{NN} so as to overcome their complementary deficiencies and leverage information in both physics and data.

One simple way for combining f_{PHY} and f_{NN} is to use the simulated outputs of the physics-based model, Y_{PHY}, as another input in the data science model (neural network) along with the drivers, $\mathbf{D}$. This results in the following basic HPD model:

$$f_{HPD} : \mathbf{X} = [\mathbf{D}, \, Y_{PHY}] \rightarrow Y,$$

which is schematically illustrated in Figure 15.2. In this setup, notice that if the physics-based model is accurate and Y_{PHY} perfectly matches with observations of Y, then the HPD model can learn to predict $\hat{Y} = Y_{PHY}$. However, if there are systematic discrepancies (biases) in Y_{PHY}, then f_{HPD} can learn to complement them by extracting complex features from the space of input drivers and thus reducing our knowledge gaps.

15.2.2 Using Physics-Based Loss Functions

A standard approach for training the HPD model described in Figure 15.2 is to minimize the empirical loss of its model predictions, $\hat{Y}$, on the training set, while maintaining low model complexity as follows:

$$\arg\min_{f} \quad Loss(\hat{Y}, Y) + \lambda \, R(f), \tag{15.1}$$

where $R(.)$ measures the complexity of a model and λ is a trade-off hyper-parameter. However, the effectiveness of any such training procedure is limited by the size of the labeled training set, which is often small in many scientific problems. In particular, there is no guarantee that model trained by minimizing Equation 15.1 will produce results that are *consistent* with our knowledge of physics. Hence, we introduce physics-based loss functions to guide the learning of data science models to physically consistent solutions as follows.

Let us denote the physical relationships between the target variable, Y, and other physical variables, $\mathbf{Z}$ using the following equations:

$$\begin{aligned}
\mathcal{G}(Y, \mathbf{Z}) &= 0, \\
\mathcal{H}(Y, \mathbf{Z}) &\leq 0.
\end{aligned} \qquad (15.2)$$

Note that $\mathcal{G}$ and $\mathcal{H}$ are generic forms of physics-based equations that can either involve algebraic manipulations of Y and $\mathbf{Z}$ (e.g., in the laws of kinematics), or their partial differentials (e.g., in the Navier–Stokes equation for studying fluid dynamics or in the Schrödinger equation for studying computational chemistry). These physics-based equations must meet the same criteria as other loss function terms (i.e., continuous and differentiable). One way to measure if these physics-based equations are being violated in the model predictions, $\hat{Y}$, is to evaluate the following physics-based loss function:

$$Loss.PHY(\hat{Y}) = \|\mathcal{G}(\hat{Y}, \mathbf{Z})\|^2 + \text{ReLU}\,(\mathcal{H}(\hat{Y}, \mathbf{Z})), \qquad (15.3)$$

where ReLU(.) denotes the rectified linear unit function. Since *Loss.PHY* does not require actual observations of the target variable, Y, it can be evaluated even on unlabeled data instances, in contrast to traditional loss functions. The complete learning objective of PGNN involving *Loss.PHY* can then be stated as:

$$\underset{f}{\arg\min} \quad \underbrace{Loss(\hat{Y}, Y)}_{\text{Empirical Error}} \quad + \quad \underbrace{\lambda\,R(f)}_{\text{Structural Error}} \quad + \quad \underbrace{\lambda_{PHY}\,Loss.PHY(\hat{Y})}_{\text{Physical Inconsistency}}, \qquad (15.4)$$

where λ_{PHY} is the hyper-parameter that decides the relative importance of minimizing physical inconsistency compared to the empirical loss and the model complexity. Since the known laws of physics are assumed to hold equally well for any unseen data instance, ensuring physical consistency of model outputs as a learning objective in PGNN can help in achieving better generalization performance even when the training data is small and not fully representative. Additionally, the output of a PGNN model can also be interpreted by a domain expert and ingested in scientific workflows, thus leading to scientific advancements.

There are several optimization algorithms that can be used for minimizing Equation 15.4, e.g., the stochastic gradient descent (SGD) algorithm and its variants that have found great success in training deep neural networks. In particular, the gradients of *Loss.PHY* w.r.t model parameters can be easily computed using the automatic differentiation procedures available in standard deep learning packages. This makes neural networks a particularly suited choice for incorporating physics-based loss functions in the learning objective of data science models.

15.3   PGNN for Lake Temperature Modeling

In this section, we describe our PGNN formulation for the illustrative problem of modeling the temperature of water in lakes. In the following, we first provide some background information motivating the problem of lake temperature modeling, and then describe our PGNN approach.

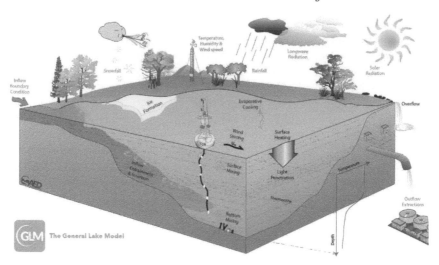

FIGURE 15.3
A pictorial description of the physical processes governing the dynamics of temperature in a lake. Figure courtesy: [8].

15.3.1   Background: Lake Temperature Modeling

The temperature of water in a lake is known to be an ecological "master factor" [11] that controls the growth, survival, and reproduction of fish (e.g., [19]). Warming water temperatures can increase the occurrence of aquatic invasive species [16, 18], which may displace fish and native aquatic organisms, and result in more harmful algal blooms (HABs) [7, 14]. Understanding temperature change and the resulting biotic "winners and losers" is timely science that can also be directly applied to inform priority action for natural resources. Accurate water temperatures (observed or modeled) are critical to understanding contemporary change, and for predicting future thermal habitat of economically valuable fish.

Since observational data of water temperature at broad spatial scales is incomplete (or non-existent in some regions) high-quality temperature modeling is necessary. Of particular interest is the problem of modeling the temperature of water at a given depth[1], d, and on a certain time, t. This problem is referred to as 1D-modeling of temperature (depth being the single dimension). A number of physics-based models have been developed for studying lake temperature, e.g., the state-of-the-art general lake model (GLM) [8]. This model captures a variety of physical processes governing the dynamics of temperature in a lake, e.g., the heating of the water surface due to incoming shortwave radiation from the sun, the attenuation of radiation beneath the surface and the mixing of layers with varying energies at different depths, and the dissipation of heat from the surface of the lake via evaporation or longwave radiation, shown pictorially in Figure 15.3. We use GLM as our preferred choice of physics-based model for lake temperature modeling.

The GLM has a number of parameters (e.g., parameters related to vertical mixing, wind energy inputs, and water clarity) that needs to be custom-calibrated for each lake if some training data is available. The basic idea behind these calibration steps is to run the model for each possible combination of parameter values and select the one that has maximum agreement with the observations. Because this step of custom-calibrating is both labor- and computation-intensive, there is a trade-off between increasing the accuracy of the model and expanding the feasability of study to a large number of lakes.

15.3.2 Proposed PGNN Formulation

We consider the physical variables governing the dynamics of lake temperature at every depth and time-step as the set of input drivers, $\mathbf{D}$. This includes meteorological recordings at the surface of water such as the amount of solar radiation at different wavelengths, wind speed, and air temperature, as well as the value of depth and the day of the year. To construct an HPD model of the type shown in Figure 15.2, we use simulations of lake temperature from the GLM, Y_{PHY}, along with the input drivers $\mathbf{D}$ at every depth and time-step to obtain the augmented set of features,

$$\mathbf{X} = [\mathbf{D},\ Y_{PHY}].$$

We adopt a basic multi-layer perceptron architecture to regress the temperature, Y, on any given depth and time, using $\mathbf{X}$. For a fully-connected network with L hidden layers, this amounts to the following modeling equations relating the input features, $\mathbf{x}$, to its target prediction, $\hat{y}$:

$$\mathbf{z}_1 = \mathbf{W}_1^T \mathbf{x} + \mathbf{b}_1 \tag{15.5}$$

$$\mathbf{z}_i = \mathbf{W}_i^T \mathbf{a}_{i-1} + \mathbf{b}_i \quad \forall\, i = 2 \text{ to } L \tag{15.6}$$

$$\mathbf{a}_i = f(\mathbf{z}_i) \quad \forall\, i = 1 \text{ to } L \tag{15.7}$$

$$\hat{y} = \mathbf{w}_{L+1}^T \mathbf{a}_L + b_{L+1} \tag{15.8}$$

where $(\mathbf{W}, \mathbf{b}) = \{(\mathbf{W}_i, \mathbf{b}_i)\}_1^{L+1}$ represents the set of weight and bias parameters across all hidden and output layers, and f is the activation function used at the hidden layers. We use the mean squared error as our choice of loss function and L_1 and L_2 norms of network weights, $\mathbf{W}$ as regularization terms in Equation 15.1 as follows:

$$Loss(\hat{Y}, Y) = \frac{1}{n} \sum_{i=1}^{n} (y_i - \hat{y}_i)^2, \tag{15.9}$$

$$\lambda\, R(\mathbf{W}) = \lambda_1 ||\mathbf{W}||_1 + +\lambda_2 ||\mathbf{W}||_2, \tag{15.10}$$

where $\{\mathbf{x}, y\}_1^n$ is the set of training instances.

To incorporate the knowledge of physics as a loss function in the training of neural networks, we employ a key physical relationship between the temperature, density, and depth of water as our physics-based equation (Equation 15.2). In the following, we introduce the two key components of this physical relationship and describe our approach for using it to ensure the learning of physically consistent results.

15.3.2.1 Temperature–Density Relationship

The temperature, Y, and density, ρ, of water are non-linearly related to each other according to the following known physical equation [12]:

$$\rho = 1000 \times \left(1 - \frac{(Y + 288.9414) \times (Y - 3.9863)^2}{508929.2 \times (Y + 68.12963)}\right) \tag{15.11}$$

Figure 15.4(a) shows a plot of this relationship between temperature and density, where we can see that water is maximally dense at 4°C (due to the hydrogen bonding between water molecules)[2]. Given the temperature predictions of a model, $\hat{Y}[d, t]$, at depth, d, and time-step, t, we can use Equation 15.11 to compute the corresponding density prediction, $\hat{\rho}[d, t]$.

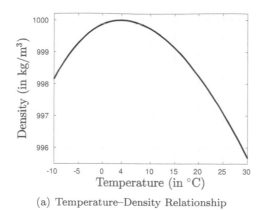

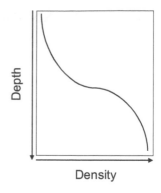

(a) Temperature–Density Relationship   (b) Density–Depth Relationship

FIGURE 15.4

Plots of physical relationships between temperature, density, and depth of water that serve as the basis for introducing physical consistency in PGNN.

15.3.2.2   Density–Depth Relationship

The density of water monotonically increases with depth as shown in the example plot of Figure 15.4(b), since denser water is heavier and goes down to the bottom of the lake. Formally, the density of water at two different depths, d_1 and d_2, on the same time-step, t, are related to each other in the following manner:

$$\rho[d_1, t] - \rho[d_2, t] \leq 0 \quad \text{if } d_1 < d_2. \tag{15.12}$$

To ensure that this physics-based equation is upheld in the temperature predictions of a physics-based model, $\hat{Y}$, we can construct a physics-based loss function as follows. Let us consider an unlabeled data set of input features on a regular grid of n_d depth values and n_t time-steps. On any pair of consecutive depth values, d_i and d_{i+1} $(d_i < d_{i+1})$, we can compute the difference in the density estimates of a model on time-step t as

$$\Delta[i, t] = \hat{\rho}[d_i, t] - \hat{\rho}[d_{i+1}, t] \tag{15.13}$$

A positive value of $\Delta[i, t]$ can be viewed as a violation of the physics-based Equation 15.12 on depth d_i and time t. This can be evaluated as a non-zero occurrence of $\text{ReLU}(\Delta[d_i, t])$. Hence, we can consider the mean of all physical violations across every consecutive depth-pair and time-step as our physics-based loss function:

$$PHY.Loss(\hat{Y}) = \frac{1}{n_t(n_d - 1)} \sum_{t=1}^{n_t} \sum_{i=1}^{n_d-1} \text{ReLU}(\Delta[i, t]). \tag{15.14}$$

Using this physics-based loss (Equation 15.14) along with the empirical loss (Equation 15.9) and regularization terms (Equation 15.10) in the learning objective (Equation 15.4), we obtain our complete PGNN formulation. Note that in our particular problem of lake temperature modeling, even though the neural network is being trained to improve its accuracy on the task of predicting water temperatures, the use of physics-based loss function ensures that the temperature predictions also translate to consistent relationships between other physical variables, namely density and depth, thus resulting in a wholesome solution to the physical problem.

15.4   Evaluation

In this section, we first describe the data collected over two lakes for evaluation along with the experimental design, choice of baselines, evaluation metrics, and experimental results.

15.4.1   Data

We consider two example lakes to demonstrate the effectiveness of our PGNN framework for lake temperature modeling, Mille Lacs Lake in Minnesota, USA, and Lake Mendota in Wisconsin, USA. Both these lakes are reasonably large (536 km^2 and 40 km^2 in area, respectively), have extensive observation records relative to other similar lakes, and show sufficient dynamics in the temperature profiles across depth over time to make them interesting test cases for analyses. Observations of lake temperature were collated from a variety of sources including Minnesota Department of Natural Resources and a web resource that collates data from federal and state agencies, academic monitoring campaigns, and citizen data [17]. These temperature observations vary in their distribution across depths and time, with some years and seasons being heavily sampled, while other time periods having little to no observations.

The overall data for Mille Lacs Lake consisted of 7,072 temperature observations from 17 June 1981 to 01 Jan 2016, and the overall data for Lake Mendota consisted of 13,543 temperature observations from 30 April 1980 to 02 Nov 2015. For each observation, we used a set of 11 meteorological drivers as input variables, listed in Table 15.1. While many of these drivers were directly measured, we also used some domain-recommended ways of constructing derived features such as Growing Degree Days [15]. We used the GLM [8] as the physics-based approach for modeling lake temperature in our experimental studies. The GLM uses the drivers listed in Table 15.1 as input parameters and balances the energy and water budget of lakes or reservoirs on a daily or sub-daily timestep. It performs a 1D modeling (along depth) of a variety of lake variables (including water temperature) using a vertical Lagrangian layer scheme.

Apart from the labeled set of data instances where we have observations of temperature, we also considered a large set of unlabeled instances (where we do not have temperature observations) on a regular grid of depth values at discrete steps of 0.5m, and on a daily time-scale from 02 April 1980 to 01 Jan 2016 (amounting to 13,058 dates). We ran the GLM model on the unlabeled instances to produce Y_{PHY} along with the input drivers $\mathbf{D}$ at every unlabeled instance. Ignoring instances with missing values, this amounted to a total of 299,796 unlabeled instances in Mille Lacs Lake and 662,781 unlabeled instances in Lake Mendota.

15.4.2   Experimental Design

We considered contiguous windows of time to partition the labeled data set into training and test splits, to ensure that the test set is indeed independent of the training set and the two data sets are not temporally auto-correlated. In particular, we chose the center portion of the overall time duration for testing, while the remainder time periods on both ends were used for training. For example, to construct a training set of n instances, we chose the median date in the overall data and kept on adding dates on both sides of this date for testing, till the number of observations in the remainder time periods became less than or equal to n. Using this protocol, we constructed training sets of size $n = 3000$ for both Mille Lacs Lake and Lake Mendota, which were used for calibrating the physics-based

TABLE 15.1

Input Drivers for Lake Temperature Modeling.

	Input Drivers
1	Day of Year (1–366)
2	Depth (in m)
3	Short-wave Radiation (in W/m^2)
4	Long-wave Radiation (in W/m^2)
5	Air Temperature (in °C)
6	Relative Humidity (0–100 %)
7	Wind Speed (in m/s)
8	Rain (in cm)
9	Growing Degree Days [15]
10	Is Freezing (True or False)
11	Is Snowing (True or False)

model, PHY, on both lakes. We used the entire set of unlabeled instances for evaluating the physics-based loss function on every lake.

All neural network models used in this chapter were implemented using the Keras package [2] using Tensorflow backend. We used the AdaDelta algorithm [25] for performing SGD on the model parameters of the neural network. We used a batch size of 1000 with maximum number of epochs equal to 10,000. To avoid over-fitting, we employed an early stopping procedure using 10% of the training data for validation, where the value of patience was kept equal to 500. We also performed gradient clipping (for gradients with L_2 norm greater than 1) to avoid the problem of exploding gradients common in regression problems (since the value of Y is unbounded). We standardized each dimension of the input attributes to have 0 mean and 1 standard deviation, and applied the same transformation on the test set. The fully-connected neural network architecture comprised of 3 hidden layers, each with 12 hidden nodes. The value of hyper-parameters λ_1 and λ_2 (corresponding to the L_1 and L_2 norms of network weights, respectively) were kept equal to 1 in all experiments conducted in the chapter, to demonstrate that no special tuning of hyper-parameters was performed for any specific problem. The value of the hyper-parameter λ_{PHY} corresponding to the physics-based loss function was kept equal to $std(Y^2)/std(\rho)$, to factor in the differences in the scales of the physics-based loss function and the mean squared error loss function. We used uniformly random initialization of neural network weights from 0 to 1. Hence, in all our experiments, we report the mean and standard deviation of evaluation metrics of every neural network method over 50 runs, each run involving a different random initialization.

15.4.3 Baseline Methods and Evaluation Metrics

We compared the results of PGNN with the following baseline methods:

- **PHY**: The GLM models calibrated on the training sets of size $n = 3000$ for both lakes were used as the physics-based models, PHY.

- **Black-box Models**: In order to demonstrate the value in incorporating the knoweldge of physics with data science models, we consider three standard non-linear regression models: support vector machine (**SVM**) with radial basis function (RBF) kernel, least squares boosted regression trees (**LSBoost**), and the neural network (**NN**) model. All of these models were trained to predict temperature using the same set of input drivers as PGNN, but without using any knowledge of physics (either in the form of model simulations or as physics-based loss functions).

- **PGNN0**: In order to understand the contribution of the physics-based loss function in PGNN, we consider an intermediate product of our framework, PGNN0, as another baseline, which uses the HPD modeling setup described in Figure 15.2, but does not use the physics-based loss function in its learning objective (Equation 15.1). Hence, PGNN0 differs from black-box models in its use of physics-based model simulations as input attributes, and differs from PGNN in its use of a purely data-driven learning objective.

We considered the following evaluation metrics for comparing the performance of different algorithms:

- **RMSE**: We use the root mean squared error (RMSE) of a model on the test set as an estimate of its generalization performance. The units of this metric are in °C.

- **Physical Inconsistency**: Apart from ensuring generalizability, a key contribution of PGNN is to ensure the learning of physically consistent model predictions. Hence, apart from computing the RMSE of the model on the test set, we also compute the fraction of time-steps where the model makes physically inconsistent predictions (i.e., the density-depth relationship stated in Equation 15.12 is violated). We report this fraction as the physical inconsistency measure in Figures 15.5, 15.6(b), and 15.7(a). Note that this measure does not require actual observations, and hence, we compute this measure over the plentifully large unlabeled data set.

15.4.4 Results

Figure 15.5 provides a summary of the performance of different methods for modeling lake temperature on the two example lakes, Mille Lacs Lake and Lake Mendota. The X-axis in these plots represents the physical inconsistency of a model, while the Y-axis represents the RMSE of the model predictions w.r.t. observations on the test set. We also show the standard deviation around the evaluation metrics of neural network-based methods (i.e.,

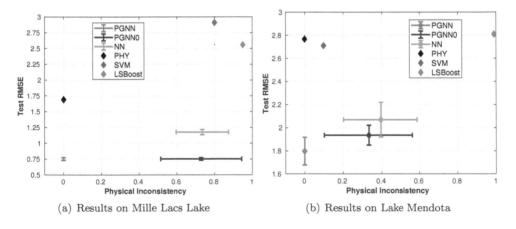

(a) Results on Mille Lacs Lake   (b) Results on Lake Mendota

FIGURE 15.5
Scatter plots showing test RMSE values (Y-axis) and physical inconsistency (X-axis) of comparative methods. Points and error bars respectively represent the mean and +/- one standard deviation from the mean of results from all 50 random weight initializations.

PGNN, PGNN0, and NN), since we used random initialization of network weights for every one of the 50 runs.

For Mille Lacs Lake, we can see from Figure 15.5(a) that the test RMSE of the physics-based model, PHY, is 1.69. If we use black-box data science models such as SVM and LSBoost, that try to learn non-linear relationships between drivers and temperature directly without using physics, we would end up with a test RMSE that is even higher than that of PHY. Further, they also show high physical inconsistency in their model predictions (greater than 0.8). If we instead use a black-box NN model that learns non-linear compositions of features from the space of input drivers, we can achieve a test RMSE of 1.18 that is significantly lower than that of PHY. This provides evidence of the information contained in the driver data, which if used effectively, can help in closing the knowledge gaps of PHY. However, this improvement in RMSE comes at the cost of a large value of physical inconsistency in the model predictions of NN (almost 73% of the time-steps have inconsistent density-depth relationships in its predictions). This makes NN unfit for use in the process of scientific discovery, because although it is able to somewhat improve the predictions of the target variable (i.e., temperature), it is incurring large errors in capturing the physical relationships of temperature with other variables, leading to non-meaningful results.

If we use the output of the physics-based model along with the drivers as inputs in the PGNN0 model, we can achieve an even lower value of test RMSE than that of NN. This is because the output of PHY (although with a high RMSE) contains vital physical information about the dynamics of lake temperature, which when coupled with powerful data science frameworks such as neural networks, can result in major improvements in RMSE. However, the results of PGNN0 are still physically inconsistent for roughly 72% of the time. In contrast, it is only by the use of physics-based loss functions in PGNN that we can not only achieve an RMSE of 0.73, but also substantially lower value of physical inconsistency (close to 0). To appreciate the significance of a drop in RMSE of 0.96°C, note that a lake-specific calibration approach that produced a median RMSE of 1.47°C over 28 lakes is considered to be the state-of-the-art in the field [3]. By being accurate as well as physically consistent, PGNN provides an opportunity to produce physically meaningful analyses of lake temperature dynamics that can be used in subsequent scientific studies.

A similar summary of results can also be obtained from Figure 15.5(b) for Lake Mendota. We can see that the test RMSE of the physics-based model in this lake is 2.77, which is considerably higher than that of Mille Lacs Lake. This shows the relatively complex nature of temperature dynamics in Lake Mendota compared to Mille Lacs Lake, which are more difficult for any model to approximate. Mille Lacs Lake is generally well-mixed (i.e., bottom temperature is similar to the surface temperature) while Lake Mendota is more stratified. The average test RMSE scores of NN and PGNN0 for Lake Mendota are 2.07 and 1.93, respectively. On the other hand, PGNN is able to achieve an average RMSE of 1.79, while being physically consistent. This is a demonstration of the added value of using physical consistency in the learning objective of data science models for improving generalization performance.

15.4.4.1   Effect of Varying Training Size

We next demonstrate the effect of varying the size of the training set on the performance of PGNN, in comparison with other baseline methods. Figure 15.6 shows the variations in the test RMSE and physical inconsistency of different methods on Mille Lacs Lake, as we vary the training size from 3000 to 800. We can see from Figure 15.6(a) that the test RMSE values of all data science methods increase as we reduce the training size. For example, the test RMSE of the black-box model, NN, can be seen to over-shoot the test RMSE of the physics-based model for training sizes smaller than 1500. On the other hand, both

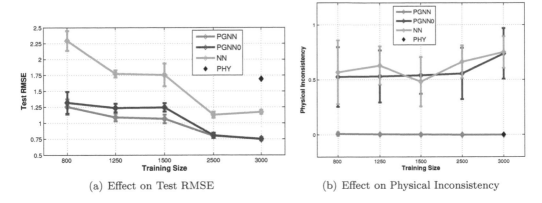

(a) Effect on Test RMSE   (b) Effect on Physical Inconsistency

FIGURE 15.6
Effect of varying training size on the performance of different methods on Mille Lacs Lake. Points and error bars respectively represent the mean and +/- one standard deviation from the mean of results from all 50 random weight initializations.

PGNN and PGNN0 show a more gradual increase in their test RMSE values on reducing training size. In fact, the PGNN can be seen to provide smaller RMSE values than all baseline methods, especially at training sizes of 1250 and 1500. This is because the use of physics-based loss function ensures that the learned PGNN model is consistent with our knowledge of physics and thus is not spurious. Such a model thus stands a better chance at capturing generalizable patterns and avoiding the phenomena of over-fitting, even after being trained with limited number of training samples. If we further reduce the training size to 800, the results of PGNN and PGNN0 become similar because there is not much information left in the data that can provide improvements in RMSE.

While the lower RMSE values of PGNN is promising, the biggest gains in using PGNN arise from its drastically lower values of physical inconsistency as compared to other data science methods, as shown in Figure 15.6(b), even when the training sizes are small. Note that the results of PGNN are physically consistent across all time-steps, while PGNN0 and NN violate the density-depth relationship more than 50% of time-steps on an average. We can also see that PHY has an almost zero value of physical inconsistency, since it is inherently designed to be physically consistent.

15.4.4.2 Sensitivity to Hyperparameter λ_{PHY}

To understand how the choice of the trade-off hyperparameter λ_{PHY} affects the model results, we analyse the physical inconsistency and the Test RMSE while varying λ_{PHY} (see Figure 15.7). With the increase in the value of λ_{PHY}, we impose a more stringent physics-constraint on the model which ultimately leads to the generation of more and more physically consistent predictions (Figure 15.7(a)). Simultaneously, it can be observed that the change in λ_{PHY} does not significantly affect the Test RMSE of the learned model, which is also desirable (Figure 15.7(b)). Ideally, with the introduction of the physics-based loss during training, we would want the model to generate more physically consistent predictions while not degrading its predictive performance.

15.4.4.3 Analysis of Results

To provide a deeper insight into the results produced by competing methods, we analyze the predictions of lake temperature produced by a model as follows. As described previously,

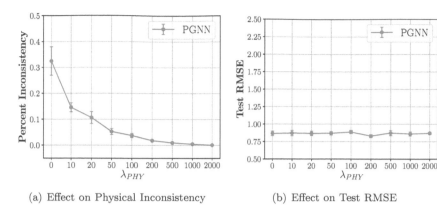

(a) Effect on Physical Inconsistency   (b) Effect on Test RMSE

FIGURE 15.7

Sensitivity to hyperparameter λ_{PHY} on Mille Lacs Lake. Points and error bars respectively represent the mean and $+/-$ one standard deviations from the mean of results from all 50 random weight initializations.

any estimate of temperature can be converted to its corresponding density estimate using the physical relationship between temperature and density represented in Equation 15.11. Hence, on any given time-step, we can produce a profile of density estimates at varying values of depth for every model, and match it with the density estimates of observed temperature on test instances. Visualizing such density profiles can help us understand the variations in model predictions across depth, in relationship to test observations. Some examples of density profiles on different dates in Mille Lacs Lake and Lake Mendota are provided in Figure 15.8, where the X-axis represents estimated density, and the Y-axis represents depth.

In the density profiles of different algorithms on Mille Lacs Lake in Figure 15.8(a), we can see that the density estimates of PHY are removed from the actual observations by a certain amount, indicating a bias in the physics-based model. All three data science methods, NN, PGNN0, and PGNN, attempt to compensate for this bias by shifting their density profiles closer to the actual observations. On the three depth values where we have observations, we can see that both PGNN and PGNN0 show lower discrepancy with observations as compared to PHY. In fact, the density profile of PGNN matches almost perfectly with the observations, thus demonstrating the value in using physics-based loss function for better generalizability. However, the most striking insight from Figure 15.8(a) is that although the density estimate of PGNN0 is reasonably close to the three observations (thus indicating a low value of test RMSE), the density estimates soon start showing physically inconsistent patterns as we move lower in depth beyond the observations. In particular, the density estimates of PGNN0 start decreasing as we increase the depth beyond 6m. This is a violation of the monotonic relationship between density and depth as illustrated in Figure 15.4(b). The presence of such physical inconsistencies reduces the usefulness of a model's predictions in scientific analyses, even if the model shows low test RMSE. In contrast, the predictions of PGNN, while being closer to the actual observations, are always consistent with the monotonic relationship between density and depth.

Figure 15.8(b) shows another example of density profiles on a different date in Lake Mendota. We can see that PGNN is again able to improve upon PHY and produce density estimates that are closest to the observations. On the other hand, both PGNN0 and NN shows large discrepancies with respect to the actual observations. This is because of the complex nature of relationships between the drivers and the temperature in Lake Mendota that are difficult to be captured without the use of physical relationships in the learning of

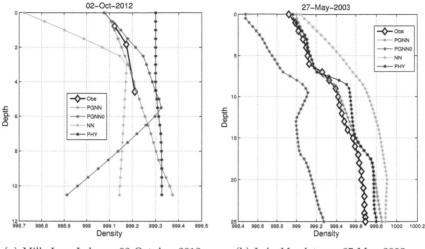

(a) Mille Lacs Lake on 02-October-2012   (b) Lake Mendota on 27-May-2003

FIGURE 15.8
Density profiles of varying algorithms on different dates in Mille Lacs Lake (a) and Lake Mendota (b).

neural networks. Additionally, the model predictions of PGNN0 can be seen to violate the physical relationship between density and depth (density estimates of PGNN0 decrease as we increase the depth from 10m to 12m), thus further reducing our confidence in PGNN0 representing physically meaningful results.

15.5   Discussion on Alternate HPD Model Designs

So far, we have demonstrated the value of HPD modeling using a simple HPD design as illustrated in Figure 15.2, where the outputs of the physics-based model are fed into the neural network model as additional features, along with the input drivers. In this section, we discuss its relevance in the context of two alternate HPD model designs based on residual modeling techniques (see Figure 15.9), which are commonly used in the scientific literature to correct residuals of physics-based models using data-driven methods. The first HPD design (Figure 15.9(a)), termed the "Residual Model," uses a simple ML model f_{Res} to fix the residuals of physics-based model outputs Y_{PHY} as additive correction terms. Specifically, instead of building an ML model to directly predict the target variable Y from the input drivers D, we adopt a residual modeling strategy to predict $Y_{Res}(= Y - Y_{PHY})$, which when added to Y_{PHY} provides corrected estimates of the target variable. Note that residual modeling is one of the simplest and most commonly used strategies for HPD modeling [4, 23, 20, 21, 24]. The primary motivation for building a residual model is to solve the simpler problem of estimating the residuals of a physics-based model, which are indicative of the systematic biases or equivalently the uncaptured variability of the physics-based model, instead of estimating the complete functional mapping from D to Y. The final prediction of the target variable Y is obtained by simply adding the predicted residual Y_{Res} with the output of the physics model Y_{PHY}. In other words, a residual model can be thought of as a rectifying unit which aims to correct the predictions of the physics-based model.

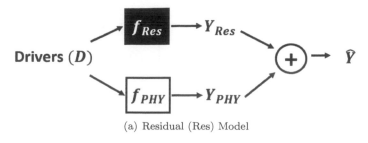

(a) Residual (Res) Model

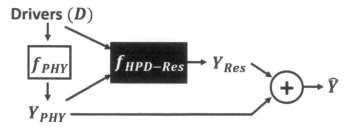

(b) Hybrid-Physics-Data-Residual (HPD-Res) Model

FIGURE 15.9
Alternate HPD model designs, where white boxes represent physics-based models while black boxes represent ML models.

Another innovation in HPD design is illustrated in Figure 15.9(b), where the idea of residual modeling is combined with the idea of the basic HPD model described in Figure 15.2. In this alternate HPD design, termed the "Hybrid-Physics-Data-Residual (HPD-Res) Model," the ML model uses both the input drivers D as well as the output of the physics-based models Y_{PHY} to predict the residuals of the physics-based model Y_{Res}. The predicted residuals are then added to Y_{PHY} to obtain the final predictions of the target variable Y. Note that HPD-Res shares some similarity with the basic residual (Res) model, as both of them predict the residual of the physics-based model instead of directly predicting the target variable. However, the difference in HPD-Res is that it uses Y_{PHY} as additional inputs in the ML architecture, which simplifies the task of learning the residuals (note that in some cases, it may be easier to identify patterns of systematic biases in the physics-based model by observing D and Y_{PHY} together). HPD-Res is also similar to the basic HPD model as both of them use D and Y_{PHY} as inputs in the ML model. However, the difference is that HPD-Res only predicts the residual Y_{Res} to be added to Y_{PHY} for deriving final predictions of the target variable Y. Hence, HPD-Res can be viewed as a "fusion" of the basic HPD and the basic Res models.

To empirically understand the differences between the three HPD designs: basic HPD, basic Res, and HPD-Res, we compare their performances on Lake Mendota and Mille Lacs Lake at varying training sizes in Figure 15.10. Note that in these experiments, we did not include the physics-based loss function in the learning objective to solely evaluate the effect of HPD designs on generalization performance (as a result, the performance of the basic HPD model here corresponds to the PGNN0 baseline). We can see that across both lakes, the *HPD-Res* performs slightly better than the basic HPD and the basic Residual formulations. In Lake Mendota, HPD-Res has a considerable difference in performance from HPD across all training sizes, and from Res at larger training sizes. On the other hand, in Mille Lacs Lake, the Res model performs the worst out of the three while HPD performs almost equivalently as HPD-Res. These results provide new insights on the differences between

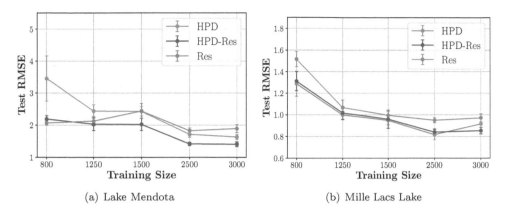

(a) Lake Mendota   (b) Mille Lacs Lake

FIGURE 15.10
Comparing the performance of different HPD model designs on Mille Lacs Lake and Lake Mendota at varying training sizes. Points and error bars respectively represent the mean and +/- one standard deviations from the mean of results from all 50 random weight initializations. The HPD model here corresponds to PGNN0 in Figure 15.5. Note that mean and standard deviations also vary from Figure 15.5 due to different random weight initializations, and different versions of the Keras library used.

HPD model designs and suggests that further research on the choice of constructing HPD models is necessary. For example, one potential reason behind HPD-Res performing better than the basic HPD and the basic Res models is that HPD-Res combines the strengths of both these models; it uses the input drivers as well as Y_{PHY} as inputs in the ML model, and the ML output is further added to Y_{PHY} to correct its biases. Further research is needed to evaluate the validity of such claims regarding HPD model designs in different scientific problems involving a combination of physics knowledge and data.

15.6   Conclusions and Potential Future Work

This chapter presented a novel framework for learning PGNN, by using the outputs of physics-based model simulations as well as by leveraging physics-based loss functions to guide the learning of neural networks to physically consistent solutions. By anchoring neural network methods with scientific knowledge, we are able to show that the proposed framework not only shows better generalizability, but also produces physically meaningful results in comparison to black-box data science methods.

This chapter serves as a stepping stone in the broader theme of research on using physics-based learning objectives in the training of data science models. While the specific formulation of PGNN explored in this chapter was developed for the example problem of modeling lake temperature, similar developments could be explored in a number of other scientific and engineering disciplines where known forms of physical relationships can be exploited as physics-based loss functions. This chapter paves the way towards learning neural networks by not only improving their ability to solve a given task, but also being cognizant of the physical relationships of the model outputs with other tasks, thus producing a more holistic view of the physical problem.

There are a number of directions of future research that can be explored as a continuation of this work. First, for the specific problem of lake temperature modeling, given the spatial and temporal nature of the problem domain, a natural extension would be to exploit the spatial and temporal dependencies in the test instances, e.g., by using recurrent neural network-based architectures. Second, the analysis of the physically consistent model predictions produced by PGNN could be used to investigate the modeling deficiencies of the baseline physics-based model in detail. Third, while this chapter presented a simple way of constructing HPD models where Y_{PHY} was ingested as an input in the data science model, more complex ways of constructing HPD models where the physics-based and data science components are tightly coupled need to be explored. Fourth, theoretical analyses studying the impact of introducing physics-based loss functions on the sample complexity or convergence guarantees need to be investigated. Fifth, the research direction of PGNN can be complemented with other related efforts on producing interpretable data science results. In particular, the use of physics-based equations for interpreting the results of data science methods needs to be explored. Finally, while this chapter explored the use of physical relationships between temperature, density, and depth of water in the learning of multi-layer perceptrons, other forms of physical relationships in different neural network models can be explored as future work. Of particular value would be to develop generative models that are trained to not only capture the structure in the unlabeled data, but are also guided by physics-based models to discover and emulate the known laws of physics. The paradigm of PGNN, if effectively utilized, could help in combining the strengths of physics-based and data science models, and opening a novel era of scientific discovery based on both physics and data.

Disclaimer: Any use of trade, firm, or product names is for descriptive purposes only and does not imply endorsement by the US Government.

Notes

[1] Depth is measured in the direction from the surface of the water to the lake bottom.

[2] This simple fact is responsible for the sustenance of all forms of aquatic life on our planet, as water at 4°C moves down to the bottom and stops the freezing of lakes and oceans.

Bibliography

[1] Tim Appenzeller. The scientists' apprentice. *Science*, 357(6346):16–17, 2017.

[2] François Chollet. keras. `https://github.com/fchollet/keras`, 2015.

[3] Xing Fang, Shoeb R Alam, Heinz G Stefan, Liping Jiang, Peter C Jacobson, and Donald L Pereira. Simulations of water quality and oxythermal cisco habitat in minnesota lakes under past and future climate scenarios. *Water Quality Research Journal*, 47(3-4):375–388, 2012.

[4] Urban Forssell and Peter Lindskog. Combining semi-physical and neural network modeling: An example ofits usefulness. *IFAC Proceedings Volumes*, 30(11):767–770, 1997.

[5] D Graham-Rowe, D Goldston, C Doctorow, M Waldrop, C Lynch, F Frankel, R Reid, S Nelson, D Howe, SY Rhee, et al. Big data: science in the petabyte era. *Nature*, 455(7209):8–9, 2008.

[6] Hoshin V Gupta and Grey S Nearing. Debates—the future of hydrological sciences: A (common) path forward? using models and data to learn: A systems theoretic perspective on the future of hydrological science. *Water Resources Research*, 50(6):5351–5359, 2014.

[7] Ted D Harris and Jennifer L Graham. Predicting cyanobacterial abundance, microcystin, and geosmin in a eutrophic drinking-water reservoir using a 14-year dataset. *Lake and Reservoir Management*, 33(1):32–48, 2017.

[8] MR Hipsey, LC Bruce, and DP Hamilton. Glm—general lake model: Model overview and user information. *Perth (Australia): University of Western Australia Technical Manual*, 2014.

[9] TO Jonathan, AM Gerald, et al. Special issue: dealing with data. *Science*, 331(6018):639–806, 2011.

[10] Upmanu Lall. Debates—the future of hydrological sciences: A (common) path forward? one water. one world. many climes. many souls. *Water Resources Research*, 50(6):5335–5341, 2014.

[11] John J Magnuson, Larry B Crowder, and Patricia A Medvick. Temperature as an ecological resource. *American Zoologist*, 19(1):331–343, 1979.

[12] James L Martin and Steven C McCutcheon. *Hydrodynamics and Transport for Water Quality Modeling*. CRC Press, 1998.

[13] Jeffrey J McDonnell and Keith Beven. Debates—the future of hydrological sciences: A (common) path forward? a call to action aimed at understanding velocities, celerities and residence time distributions of the headwater hydrograph. *Water Resources Research*, 50(6):5342–5350, 2014.

[14] Hans W Paerl and Jef Huisman. Blooms like it hot. *Science*, 320(5872):57–58, 2008.

[15] I Colin Prentice, Wolfgang Cramer, Sandy P Harrison, Rik Leemans, Robert A Monserud, and Allen M Solomon. Special paper: a global biome model based on plant physiology and dominance, soil properties and climate. *Journal of Biogeography*, pages 117–134, 1992.

[16] Frank J Rahel and Julian D Olden. Assessing the effects of climate change on aquatic invasive species. *Conservation Biology*, 22(3):521–533, 2008.

[17] Emily K Read, Lindsay Carr, Laura De Cicco, Hilary A Dugan, Paul C Hanson, Julia A Hart, James Kreft, Jordan S Read, and Luke A Winslow. Water quality data for national-scale aquatic research: The water quality portal. *Water Resources Research*, 53(2):1735–1745, 2017.

[18] James J Roberts, Kurt D Fausch, Mevin B Hooten, and Douglas P Peterson. Nonnative trout invasions combined with climate change threaten persistence of isolated cutthroat trout populations in the southern rocky mountains. *North American Journal of Fisheries Management*, 37(2):314–325, 2017.

[19] James J Roberts, Kurt D Fausch, Douglas P Peterson, and Mevin B Hooten. Fragmentation and thermal risks from climate change interact to affect persistence of native trout in the colorado river basin. *Global Change Biology*, 19(5):1383–1398, 2013.

[20] Omer San and Romit Maulik. Machine learning closures for model order reduction of thermal fluids. *Applied Mathematical Modelling*, 60:681–710, 2018.

[21] Omer San and Romit Maulik. Neural network closures for nonlinear model order reduction. *Advances in Computational Mathematics*, 44(6):1717–1750, 2018.

[22] Terrence J Sejnowski, Patricia S Churchland, and J Anthony Movshon. Putting big data to good use in neuroscience. *Nature Neuroscience*, 17(11):1440–1441, 2014.

[23] Michael L Thompson and Mark A Kramer. Modeling chemical processes using prior knowledge and neural networks. *AIChE Journal*, 40(8):1328–1340, 1994.

[24] Zhong Yi Wan, Pantelis Vlachas, Petros Koumoutsakos, and Themistoklis Sapsis. Data-assisted reduced-order modeling of extreme events in complex dynamical systems. *PloS One*, 13(5):e0197704, 2018.

[25] Matthew D Zeiler. Adadelta: an adaptive learning rate method. *arXiv preprint arXiv:1212.5701*, 2012.

16

Physics-Guided Recurrent Neural Networks for Predicting Lake Water Temperature

Xiaowei Jia, Jared D. Willard, Anuj Karpatne, Jordan S. Read, Jacob A. Zwart, Michael Steinbach, and Vipin Kumar

CONTENTS

In this chapter, we present a physics-guided recurrent neural network model (PGRNN) for predicting water temperature in lake systems. Standard machine learning (ML) methods, especially deep learning models, often require a large amount of labeled training samples, which are often not available in scientific problems due to the substantial human labor and material costs associated with data collection. Moreover, ML methods are focused on discovering statistical relationships from training data but may not be able to fully capture underlying physical processes that drive complex data dynamics. This makes standard ML approaches less generalizable to unseen scenarios. To overcome these challenges, we propose to integrate the physical knowledge embedded in physics-based models into ML to improve predictions. In particular, The PGRNN has the flexibility to incorporate fundamental physical laws such as energy conservation into the model architecture and the training process. We further enhance this approach by using a pre-training method that leverages simulated data from a physics-based model to address the scarcity of observed data. We show that a PGRNN can improve prediction accuracy over existing physics-based models and ML models, generate physically-consistent outputs, and better generalize to out-of-sample scenarios[1]. Although this methodology is developed and evaluated in the context of modeling the dynamics of temperature in lakes, it is applicable more widely to a range of scientific and engineering disciplines where physics-based (also known as mechanistic) models are used.

16.1   Introduction

Machine learning (ML) models have found tremendous success in several commercial applications, e.g., computer vision and natural language processing. Hence, there is a surge of interest in the use of ML models to advance scientific discovery in many disciplines. For example, state-of-the-art ML models such as long-short term memory (LSTM) and convolutional neural networks (CNN) have shown promising results on several isolated scientific problems [10, 9]. The power of these models come from their ability to automatically learn complex spatial and temporal relationships from data. These approaches are especially promising for modeling physical systems when the underlying processes are prohibitively complex, challenging to observe or parameterize, or are not fully understood.

However, the direct application of black-box ML models to environmental prediction problems are often met with several major challenges. First, state-of-the-art ML models are not designed for explicitly representing the complex physical processes that interact on multiple spatiotemporal scales, and thus additional complexity (e.g., network layers and hidden units) and large training data are often needed to adequately resolve these processes with a model. As a result, ML models can learn spurious relationships that look deceptively good on training data but do not generalize well to out-of-sample scenarios. For example, a learned relationship between water temperature and weather conditions will generate poor predictions if applied to different seasons or geographies. Second, environmental prediction problems commonly involve a large number of relevant variables but limited amounts of observations. This makes it challenging to train ML models and especially difficult for deep learning models. Third, an appropriately designed model optimization process likely needs to consider additional factors beyond predictive accuracy. The known relationships between physical variables and any associated constraints (such as conservation of mass and energy) provide critical guidance for model training that can encourage maintaining physical realism of predictions. As such, an ML model grounded by scientific theory stands a better chance of safeguarding against learning spurious patterns from the data that lead to non-generalizable performance. Fourth, the input data can be highly uncertain given a variety of noise factors related observation errors or precision of reporting, which poses a challenge for standard ML models to learn robust representations. Finally, traditional ML research often aims to develop actionable black-box models, while the advancement of scientific knowledge occurs when learned patterns and relationships can help better understand the underlying processes (e.g., by identifying limitations of existing physical representation). Hence, even if a black-box model achieves more accurate performance but produces physically inconsistent results (and thus lacks the ability to deliver a mechanistic understanding of the underlying processes), it should not be used as a basis for subsequent scientific developments. All these challenges prevent ML models from reaching the same level of success that has been achieved in language translation and computer vision.

On the other hand, physics-based models have been widely used in scientific disciplines [15, 1]. These models are built based on known physical laws that govern relationships between input and output variables. For example, existing physics-based lake models simulate water temperature change by balancing energy gains or losses as the lake interacts with the atmosphere and other forcings, and simulates differences in temperature at various depths (i.e., the phenomena of thermal stratification) based on accounting for various sources of turbulence that interact with the temperature-density relationship and various sources of depth-specific heating and cooling. However, these models have well-known limitations because they are necessarily approximations and parameterizations of reality due to the excessive complexity and the incomplete knowledge of complex environmental systems. In addition, these models often contain a large number of parameters whose values must be estimated with the help of limited observed data or prior studies that may not be generalizable to new applications. A standard approach for calibrating these parameters is to exhaustively search the space of parameters and choose values that result in the best performance on training data. Besides its computational cost, this approach can also result in sub-optimal parameters given a large number of combinations of these parameters and the dynamics of parameters due to heterogeneity in the underlying processes in both space and time. These limitations of physics-based models have been widely studied in scientific disciplines; e.g., see a series of debate papers in hydrology [28, 12, 34].

Hence, neither an ML-only nor a scientific knowledge-only approach can be considered sufficient for knowledge discovery in complex scientific and engineering applications. There is a tremendous opportunity to systematically advance modeling in scientific domains by leveraging the complementary strength of ML methods and physics-based models. Effective representation of physical processes in such systems will require development of novel abstractions, architectures, and learning strategies. In addition, the optimization process to produce an ML model will have to consider not just accuracy (i.e., how well the output matches the observations) but also its ability to provide physically consistent results.

In this chapter, we present Physics-Guided Recurrent Neural Networks (PGRNN) as a general framework for modeling physical processes in engineering and environmental systems. As an alternative to physics-based and empirical models, PGRNN is a hybrid modeling approach. PGRNN is built upon the LSTM model, which uses the internal memory structure to preserve long-term temporal dependencies that last over several months or years (e.g., seasonal cycles). However, standard LSTM models may not capture underlying physical processes, e.g., the energy transfer process leading to degraded performance when the LSTM is directly applied to sparse data or used to make out-of-sample predictions. To counteract these limitations, we introduce a customized recurrent structure to capture the energy exchanges that drive water temperature dynamics.

The proposed PGRNN explicitly incorporates physical laws such as energy conservation or mass conservation. This is done by leveraging additional physical variables introduced in the recurrent structure to keep track of physical states (e.g., lake thermal energy budget), which are then used to check for consistency with physical laws. In addition, we generalize the loss function to include a penalty for violating such physical laws. Thus, the overall training loss becomes a combination of standard supervised loss and the physics-based loss, as $\mathcal{L} = $ supervised loss(Y_{pred}, Y_{true}) + physics-based penalty, where the first term on the right-hand side represents the supervised difference between the predicted outputs Y_{pred} and the observed outputs Y_{true} (e.g., RMSE in regression or cross-entropy in classification), and the second term represents the penalty for physical inconsistency. Another major side-benefit of including physics-based penalty in the loss function is that it can be applied even to instances for which output (observed) data is not available since the computation of physics-based penalty only requires input (driver) data. This results in a more robust training, especially in situations where observed output is available on only a small number of time steps. Note that in absence of physics-based penalty, training loss can be computed only on those time steps where observed output is available.

Moreover, PGRNN leverages the rich domain knowledge encoded by physics-based/mechanistic models, which goes well beyond what can be captured as constraints such conservation laws. In particular, "synthetic" observation data can be generated at no- or low-cost by driving physics-based models with a variety input drivers and parameters, and used to pre-train the ML model. Training from synthetic data generated by a physical model (even an imperfect model) can allow the ML model to get close enough to the target solution so that only a small amount of observed data (ground truth labels) are needed to further refine the model. In addition, the synthetic data is guaranteed to be physically consistent due to the nature of the process model being founded on physical principles.

In this work, we evaluate the proposed PGRNN model in the context of predicting lake water temperatures at different depths and dates. The temperature of water in a lake is known to be an ecological "master factor" [33] that controls the growth, survival, and reproduction of fish [45]. Warming water temperatures can increase the occurrence of aquatic invasive species [41, 46], which may displace fish and native aquatic organisms, result in more harmful algal blooms (HABs) [14, 36]. The prediction of lake water temperature also is critical for understanding the impact of changing climate on aquatic ecosystems and assisting in aquatic resource management decisions. Given the importance of accurate temperature prediction, the aquatic science community has developed numerous physics-based models for the simulation of temperature, including the general lake model (GLM) [15], which simulates the physical processes (e.g., vertical mixing, and the warming or cooling of water via energy lost or gained from fluxes such as solar radiation and evaporation, etc.). As is typical for any such model, GLM is only an approximation of the physical reality, and has a number of parameters (e.g., water clarity, mixing efficiency, and wind sheltering) that often need to be calibrated using observations. We will discuss how we transfer known physical relationships embodied in existing physics-based aquatic models to the design of a new ML model.

We have tested the proposed PGRNN method in a real-world system, Lake Mendota (Wisconsin), which is one of the most extensively studied lakes in the world. This lake was chosen because it is large and deep enough to present challenges for modeling temperature dynamics (40 m^2 lake surface and 25 m depth) and has plenty of observation data that can be used to evaluate the performance of new approaches. In particular, we conducted evaluations on multiple aspects. First, we measured the performance of physics-based models, ML-based models, and the proposed method by varying the amount of observations used for training. This helps test the effectiveness of each method in data-scarce scenarios, which is important since most real-world lakes have very few observations or are not observed at all (they usually have less than 1% of observations that are available for Lake Mendota). Second, we showed that the PGRNN model can indeed preserve consistency to physical laws such as energy conservation. Third, we verified the generalizability of the proposed method to scenarios that differ greatly from training data. Fourth, we further studied the effectiveness of pre-training in the training process. Finally, Lake Mendota is large and deep enough such that it shows a variety of temperature patterns (e.g., stratified temperature patterns in warmer seasons and well-mixed patterns in colder seasons) and we provided some insights about the improvement produced by PGRNN over the existing physics-based model in capturing such complex temperature patterns.

The proposed method has general applicability to many scientific applications. In fact, its effectiveness has already been shown in two different applications in aquatic science [43, 13]. This idea is further extended to estimate temperatures in many U.S. lakes [55]. As discussed in [54], the overall approach is applicable to a wide range of domains such as hydrology, computational fluid dynamics (CFD), and crop modeling.

The organization of this chapter is as follows: Section 16.2 describes related existing work. Section 16.3 presents discussion of the proposed PGRNN model. In Section 16.4, we extensively evaluate the proposed method in a real-world dataset collected from Lake Mendota. We then conclude our work in Section 16.5.

16.2 Related Work

This paper focuses on improving the predictive performance of ML in scientific applications. The idea of integrating physics into ML has been explored in the context of multiple objectives (as discussed in our recent survey [54]). In particular, researchers started pursing this direction by using residual modeling, where an ML model is learned to predict the errors, or residuals, made by a physics-based model [8, 56, 53]. The key concept is to learn biases of the physics-based models (relative to observations) and use predictions of biases to make corrections to the physical model's predictions. Karpatne et al. further extended residual modeling to a hybrid modeling approach which combines model outputs from physics-based models and ML models [24, 57, 40]. This hybrid model learns to use the output of the physics model as the final output for the input drivers for which physics-based model performs well, and make corrections where it makes mistakes. These approaches still run physics-based models and ML models separately without fully leveraging their complementary strengths. Besides, they mostly use simple data-driven methods (plain regression models or standard neural network models) and also cannot incorporate general physical constraints that are based on internal states of the physical system (e.g., energy or mass conservation). Hence, they are limited in their ability to capture complex patterns of physical processes that are evolving and interacting over space and time. In addition, most of these approaches still require a lot of training data, and thus cannot address the data scarcity challenge.

Recently, new research has shown a great potential for using physical knowledge to guide the design and training of ML models, which includes use of a physics-guided loss function [20, 7, 24, 43, 50], model initialization by transferring physics [21, 43, 17, 52], and physics-guided model architecture [5, 35, 31, 59, 48]. The key objective here is to develop new ML methods that combine elements of physics-based modeling to better capture the dynamics of scientific systems. These new ML methods are expected to provide better prediction accuracy even with a much smaller number of training samples as well as exhibit generalizability in out-of-sample scenarios. In the following, we discuss the related literature for each of these topics.

16.2.1 Physics-Guided Loss Function

One of the most common techniques to make ML models consistent with physical laws is to incorporate physical constraints into the loss function of ML models. Incorporating physical constraints into the loss function enables regularizing learned ML models to be consistent with domain-specific knowledge. In addition to favoring solutions that are physically consistent, this also allows training in absence of labels, since physics-based loss can be computed even in absence of class labels. Recently, several papers have considered the use of constraints, specifically based on physical knowledge, on the output of a machine learning model so that these models can be trained even with unlabeled data by relying on physical principles or important physical properties [44, 50]. In image restoration particularly, physics-infused models have shown recent success. In [37], physical models for image blurring and hazing are used to guide the generative adversarial networks for image restoration tasks. This technique was taken further by focusing specifically on the interaction between atmospheric light and heavy rain in images in order to remove the blur due to the rain [30]. Moreover, the blending of physics-based principles of dynamical systems and regression models has been explored in [18], where principles of energy conservation were embedded into the nonlinear multilevel regression terms to prevent finite-time blow-up of solutions in statistical-dynamical problems. Some recent applications of this approach to combining physical knowledge in ML can also be found in computer vision [51, 49], natural language processing [27], object tracking [50], and pose estimation [44].

16.2.2   Physics-Guided Model Initialization

Advanced ML models, especially deep learning models, often require a large amount of training data for tuning model parameters. Moreover, the training process is sensitive to the initial choice of model parameters before training. Poor initialization can cause models to anchor in local minimum, which is especially true for deep neural networks. In contrast, a better initialization informed by physics can potentially reduce the need for large training data and also converge faster to the target solution.

Researchers have explored different ways to physically inform a model starting state. One way to inform the model initialization is to use transfer learning. In transfer learning, a model can be pre-trained on a related task prior to being fine-tuned with limited training data to fit the desired task. The pre-trained model serves as an informed initial state that ideally is closer to the desired parameters for the desired task than random initialization. For example, researchers in computer vision have used large-scale datasets such as ImageNet to pre-train network models with the aim to learn useful feature extractors before having them fine-tuned with target dataset [16]. Similarly, in scientific problems, one way to harness physical knowledge is to use the physics-based model's simulated data to pre-train the ML model, which also alleviates data paucity issues. Here the availability of simulation data is not a limitation which makes it possible to train even highly complex ML models. However, the simulation data may be inaccurate due to approximations and parameterizations used in physics-based models. The pre-trained model is generally expected to do only as well as the physics-based model used for generating the simulation data. Depending on the bias of the physics-based model, varying amounts of true observations may be needed to fine-tune the pre-trained model to a quality model.

16.2.3   Physics-Guided Model Architecture

A recent research direction has been to construct new ML architectures that can make use of the specific characteristics of the problem being solved. For example, in neural networks, one way to embed known physical principles into the model architecture design is to ascribe physical meaning for certain neurons. It is also possible to declare physically relevant variables explicitly. In lake temperature modeling, Daw et al. [5] incorporated an intermediate physical variable as part of a monotonicity-preserving structure in the LSTM architecture. This model produced physically consistent predictions in addition to appending a dropout layer for uncertainty quantification. In Muralidlar et al. [35], a similar approach was taken to insert physics-constrained variables as the intermediate variables in the CNN architecture, resulting in significant improvement over state-of-the-art physics-based models on the problem of predicting drag force on particle suspensions in moving fluids.

Moreover, new network architectures have been built to capture interactions amongst physical processes. Jia et al. developed a Process Guided Recurrent Graph Neural Network (PGRGrN) to model the temperature and flow of the segments of a river network [22]. This model explicitly captured the spatial interactions among multiple hydrologic processes as well as their temporal dynamics. They further used simulated intermediate physical variables to add supervision on graph embeddings so as to enforce the physical processes of energy and mass advection from upstream to downstream segments.

An additional benefit of adding physically relevant intermediate variables in an ML architecture is that they can help extract physically meaningful hidden representation that can be interpreted by domain scientists. This is particularly valuable, as standard deep learning models are limited in their interpretability since they can only extract abstract hidden variables from highly complex connected structures.

16.3 Incorporating Physics into Machine Learning

In this section, we will discuss the PGRNN model in detail. The PGRNN model is developed in the context of simulating water temperature in lake systems. Here our goal is to simulate the temperature of water in the lake at each depth d, and on each date t, given physical conditions (e.g., weather) that control the dynamics of lake temperature. This problem is referred to as 1D-modeling of temperature (depth being the single dimension). Specifically, we consider input physical variables for each specific date t, which include meteorological recordings or estimates at the surface of the water, such as the amount of solar radiation (in W/m^2, for short-wave and long-wave), wind speed (in m/s), air temperature (in °C), relative humidity (0–100%), rain (in mm/day), snow indicator (True or False), as well as the value of depth (in m) and day of year (1–366). These chosen features are known to be the primary drivers of lake thermodynamics [15, 47]. Given these input meteorological drivers and a depth d below the surface, we aim to predict water temperature $\{y_{d,t}\}_{t=1}^{T}$ at each depth d over the entire study period (with a total of T dates). In this chapter, we use $x_{t,d}$ represent the combination of meteorological drivers on date t and a specific depth value d.

In this work, we aim to build a global ML model for all the depth layers of Lake Mendota, i.e., the model parameters are shared across all the depth values d. For simplicity, we use x_t and y_t to represent $x_{t,d}$ and $y_{t,d}$ in the method discussion when it causes no ambiguity. In the following, we first describe the architecture of PGRNN. Then we discuss how to incorporate the energy conservation law in the loss function. Finally, we introduce a pre-training method to improve the learning performance even with limited training data.

16.3.1 Physics-Guided Recurrent Neural Network

State-of-the-art deep learning models have the power to automatically extract temporal data dependencies from multi-variate time series data. As one of the most popular temporal deep learning models, recurrent neural network (RNN) models have shown success in a broad range of applications, such as machine translation [32], weather prediction [58], and remote sensing [19]. The power of the RNN model lies in its ability to combine the input data at the current and previous time steps to extract an informative hidden representation. In this part, we will start with describing the RNN and LSTM models, and then extend them to the proposed PGRNN architecture.

16.3.1.1   Recurrent Neural Networks and Long-Short Term Memory

In an RNN, the hidden representation h_t is generated using the following equation:

$$h_t = \tanh(W_h h_{t-1} + W_x x_t + b),\qquad(16.1)$$

where W_h and W_x represent the weight parameters that connect h_{t-1} and x_t, respectively, and b represents the bias term. According to Eq. 16.1, the hidden representation h_t is computed recursively using both the input at time t and the hidden representation at the previous time step h_{t-1}. Hence, the hidden representation encodes the temporal data patterns prior to time t.

While the standard RNN can model transitions across consecutive time steps, they gradually lose the connections to long histories due to the vanishing gradient problem in the optimization process [2]. Therefore, the standard RNN model may fail to grasp important long-term patterns in scientific applications. For example, the seasonal patterns and yearly patterns that commonly exist in environmental systems can last for many time steps if we use data at a daily scale. The standard RNN fails to memorize long-term temporal patterns because it does not explicitly preserve a long-term memory to store previous information but only captures the transition patterns between consecutive time steps. It is well-known [4, 38] that such issue of memory is a major difficulty in the study of dynamical system.

As an extended version of the RNN, LSTM is better in modeling long-term dependencies where each time step needs more contextual information from the past [11]. LSTM differs from the standard RNN in the generation of hidden representation h_t. In essence, the LSTM model defines a transition relationship for the hidden representation h_t through an LSTM cell. Each LSTM cell contains a cell state c_t, which serves as a memory and forces the hidden variables h_t to preserve information from the past. Then the transition of cell state over time forms a memory flow, which enables the modeling of long-term dependencies.

We now describe the recurrent process of generating the cell state x_t and hidden representation h_t from the previous time step. The LSTM first generates a candidate cell state $\tilde{c}_t$ by combining input x_t and h_{t-1} into the $\tanh(\cdot)$ function, as follows:

$$\tilde{c}_t = \tanh(W_h^c h_{t-1} + W_x^c x_t + b^c),\qquad(16.2)$$

where $\{W_h^c, W_x^c, b^c\}$ are model parameters used to generate candidate cell state.

Then the LSTM generates a forget gate f_t, an input gate g_t, and an output gate o_t via the sigmoid function $\sigma(\cdot)$, as follows:

$$\begin{aligned}
f_t &= \sigma(W_h^f h_{t-1} + W_x^f x_t + b^f),\\
g_t &= \sigma(W_h^g h_{t-1} + W_x^g x_t + b^g),\\
o_t &= \sigma(W_h^o h_{t-1} + W_x^o x_t + b^o),
\end{aligned}\qquad(16.3)$$

where $\{W_h^f, W_x^f, W_h^g, W_x^g, W_h^o, W_x^o, b^f, b^g, b^o\}$ denote model parameters for generating these gating variables. The value of sigmoid function outputs ranges in [0,1]. Hence, these gating variables can be used to filter the information from different sources. In particular, the forget gate f_t is used to filter the information inherited from c^{t-1}, and the input gate g_t is used to filter the candidate cell state at t. Then, we aggregate the information from the current time and the previous time into the new cell state. We also generate the hidden representation by filtering the cell state with the output gate. This can be expressed as follows:

$$\begin{aligned}
c_t &= f_t \otimes c_{t-1} + g_t \otimes \tilde{c}_t,\\
h_t &= o_t \otimes \tanh(c_t),
\end{aligned}\qquad(16.4)$$

where $\otimes$ denotes the entry-wise product.

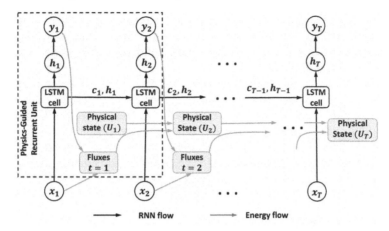

FIGURE 16.1
The flow of the PGRNN model [20]. The model includes the standard RNN flow and the energy flow in the recurrent process.

The hidden representation h_t summarizes both the current status and the temporal context, which provides sufficient information to predict target values. We generate the predicted temperature $\hat{y}_t$ at each time step t via a linear combination of hidden units. Here we use $\hat{y}_t$ to represent the predicted label (to differentiate with the provided label y_t). This transformation is as follows:

$$\hat{y}_t = W^y h_t + b^y, \tag{16.5}$$

where W^y and b^y are model parameters to transform hidden representation into target variables.

16.3.1.2 Extension to Physics-Guided Recurrent Neural Networks

In Figure 16.1, we show the flow of the proposed PGRNN model, which integrates the flow of energy transfer into the recurrent process. While the recurrent flow in the standard RNN can capture data dependencies across time, the modeling of energy flow ensures that the change of lake environment and predicted temperature conforms to the law of energy conservation. Here we describe the energy transfer process which drives the temperature dynamics.

The design of the energy flow is inspired by the general framework of physics-based energy budget models which simulate a set of intermediate states and fluxes. The state variables are updated in response to flux variables, and finally state variables and flux variables jointly determine the target variables. In the lake modeling problem, we consider the lake thermal energy budget U_t as the state variable which balances incoming and outgoing energy fluxes as the lake interacts with the atmosphere and other forcings. The lake energy U_t at each time is updated by multiple types of incoming and outgoing heat fluxes [47]. For example, the lake thermal energy increases if there is more incoming heat fluxes $\mathcal{F}_{in}$ than outgoing fluxes $\mathcal{F}_{out}$. This process can be expressed as follows:

$$\Delta U_t = \mathcal{F}_{in} - \mathcal{F}_{out}, \tag{16.6}$$

where $\Delta U_t = U_{t+1} - U_t$. Here, $\mathcal{F}_{in}$ and $\mathcal{F}_{out}$ consists of multiple types of heat fluxes. In particular, the incoming heat fluxes include terrestrial long-wave radiation and incoming short-wave radiation. The lake loses heat mainly through the outward fluxes of back radiation (R_{LWout}), sensible heat fluxes (H), and latent evaporative heat fluxes (E). Here the latent heat fluxes are related to changes in phase between liquids, gases, and solids while the sensible heat fluxes are related to changes in temperature with no change in phase [3]. These fluxes can be estimated from climate drivers and predicted surface temperature, as discussed in our previous work [20].

The energy flow in PGRNN explicitly captures the energy transfer process that leads to temperature change in dynamical systems – the heat energy fluxes that are transferred from one time to the next. By following such general physical process, PGRNN has a better chance at learning patterns that are generalizable to unseen scenarios [43]. In the energy flow, the physical state, i.e., the lake thermal energy U_t, is computed by combining the physical state at the previous time step and heat fluxes at the current time. This conforms to the underlying governing equation (Eq. 16.6).

16.3.2 Physics-Based Loss Function

ML models need to be optimized by minimizing a pre-defined loss function given observation data. Once we have the loss function defined, the model can be trained efficiently using the standard back-propagation algorithm. We now describe the loss function used in the standard RNN model in the context of lake modeling and how the loss function is generalized in PGRNN.

16.3.2.1 Loss Function of Recurrent Neural Networks in Lake Modeling

In real-world scientific problems, one major issue for training ML models is to handle the sparse training data. The collected labeled data may be only available at certain locations and on certain dates due to the high cost associated with deploying sensors or other measuring instruments. The loss function defined for training ML models needs to account for such data sparsity so that prediction errors can be back-propagated properly from reference data points.

We consider a global RNN model for all the depths in a lake system. Specifically, we apply the RNN model (or its variant such as LSTM) for each depth separately to generate predictions $\hat{y}_{d,t}$ for every depth $d \in [1, N_d]$ and for every date $t \in [1, T]$. Then given the true observation $y_{d,t}$ for the dates and depths where the sparse observation data are available, i.e., $\mathcal{S} = \{(d, t) : y_{d,t} \text{ exists}\}$, our training loss is defined as the mean squared loss over $\mathcal{S}$:

$$\mathcal{L}_{\text{RNN}} = \frac{1}{|\mathcal{S}|} \sum_{(d,t) \in \mathcal{S}} (y_{d,t} - \hat{y}_{d,t})^2. \tag{16.7}$$

It is noteworthy that even if the training loss is only defined on the depths and time steps where observations are available, the transition modeling (Eqs. 16.2–16.4) can be applied to all the time steps. Hence, the time steps without observation data can still contribute to learning temporal patterns by feeding their input drivers into the sequential model.

16.3.2.2 Loss Function of Physics-Guided Recurrent Neural Networks

To further regularize the ML model, we extend the loss function of RNN to enforce the law of energy conservation. The law of energy conservation states that the change of lake thermal energy U_t of a lake system over time is equivalent to the net gain of heat energy fluxes, which is the difference between incoming energy fluxes and any energy losses from the lake. The explicit modeling of energy conservation is critical for capturing temperature dynamics since a mismatch in losses and gains results in a temperature change, i.e., more incoming heat fluxes than outgoing heat fluxes will warm the lake, and more outgoing heat fluxes than incoming heat fluxes will cool the lake. Any violation to the energy conservation may result in predicted water temperature to be inconsistent with the net gain of energy.

Hence, we propose a physics-based loss function to measure the inconsistency between the lake thermal energy obtained from the energy flow and the predicted water temperature. In particular, the total thermal energy of the lake and water temperature (at multiple depths) have the following relation:

$$U_t = c_w \sum_d a_d y_{d,t} \rho_{d,t} \partial z_d, \tag{16.8}$$

where $y_{d,t}$ is the temperature at depth d at time t, c_w the specific heat of water (4186 J kg^{-1}°C^{-1}), a_d the cross-sectional area of the water column (m^2) at depth d, $\rho_{d,t}$ the water density (kg/m^3) at depth d at time t, and ∂z_d the thickness (m) of the layer at depth d. In this work, we simulate water temperature for every 0.5 m and thus we set $\partial z_d = 0.5$. The computation of U_t requires the output of temperature $y_{d,t}$ through a feed-forward process (Eqs. 16.1–16.5) for all the depths, as well as the cross-sectional area a_d, which is available in the training process.

The physics-based loss function for energy conservation can be defined in two ways ($\mathcal{L}_{\text{EC}}^1$ and $\mathcal{L}_{\text{EC}}^2$ below), as follows:

$$\mathcal{L}_{\text{EC}}^1 = \frac{1}{T_{\text{ice-free}}} \sum_{t \in \text{ice-free}} \text{ReLU}(|\Delta U_t^{\text{pred}} - \Delta U_t^{\text{flow}}| - \tau_{\text{EC}})$$

$$= \frac{1}{T_{\text{ice-free}}} \sum_{t \in \text{ice-free}} \text{ReLU}(|\Delta U_t^{\text{pred}} - (\mathcal{F}_{in} - \mathcal{F}_{out})| - \tau_{\text{EC}}), \tag{16.9}$$

$$\mathcal{L}_{\text{EC}}^2 = \frac{1}{T_{\text{ice-free}}} \sum_{t \in \text{ice-free}} \text{ReLU}(|U_t^{\text{pred}} - U_t^{\text{flow}}| - \tau_{\text{EC}}),$$

where U_t^{pred} denotes the thermal energy at t estimated using the predicted water temperature (Eq. 16.8), U_t^{flow} denotes the thermal energy obtained from the energy flow, $T_{\text{ice-free}}$ represents the length of the ice-free period. Here we consider the energy conservation only for ice-free periods since the lake exhibits drastically different reflectance and energy loss dynamics when covered in ice and snow, and the modeling of ice and snow was considered out of scope for this study. For both $\mathcal{L}_{\text{EC}}^1$ and $\mathcal{L}_{\text{EC}}^2$, we aim to penalize the inconsistency between the thermal energy obtained from the energy flow and from the predicted water temperature. $\mathcal{L}_{\text{EC}}^2$ directly measures the inconsistency on the value of thermal energy while $\mathcal{L}_{\text{EC}}^1$ considers the discrepancy over the change of lake thermal energy across time. The results shown in Section 16.4 will follow the use of $\mathcal{L}_{\text{EC}}^2$.

The value τ_{EC} is a threshold for the loss of energy conservation. This threshold is introduced because physical processes can be affected by unknown less important factors, which are not included in the model, or by observation errors in the metereological data. The function ReLU($\cdot$) is adopted such that only the difference larger than the threshold is counted towards the penalty. In our implementation of $\mathcal{L}_{\text{EC}}^2$, the threshold is set as the largest value of $|\Delta U_t - (\mathcal{F}_{in} - \mathcal{F}_{out})|$ in the physics-based model (General Lake Model [15]) model for daily averages.

We then combine this physics-based loss with the training objective of standard LSTM model in the following equation:

$$\mathcal{L} = \mathcal{L}_{\text{RNN}} + \lambda \mathcal{L}_{\text{EC}}, \tag{16.10}$$

where λ is a hyper-parameter that controls the balance between the RNN loss and the physics-based loss. The hyper-parameter λ_{EC} controls the balance between the loss of the standard RNN and the energy conservation loss. The model with this loss function can be updated using the back-propagation with the ADAM optimizer [26].

16.3.3   Model Pre-Training Using Physics-Based Simulations

Observations can be scarce in real-world environmental systems due to the high cost associated with deployment of sensors and measuring instruments. For example, collecting water temperature data commonly requires highly trained scientists to travel to sampling locations and deploy sensors within a lake or stream. Amongst the lakes being studied by U.S. Geological Survey (USGS), less than 1% of lakes have 100 or more days of temperature observations and less than 5% of lakes have 10 or more days of temperature observations [42].

Given the complexity of RNN-based models, e.g., the large number of model parameters used in the LSTM cell, the model trained with limited observed data can lead to poor performance. Specifically, ML models may focus on statistical data patterns that overfit limited training data but cannot generalize to scenarios that look different from training data. In addition, ML models often require an initial choice of model parameters before training. Poor initialization can cause models to anchor in local minimum, which is especially true for deep neural networks. If physical knowledge can be used to help inform the initialization of the weights, model training can accelerated (i.e., require fewer epochs for training) and also need fewer training samples to achieve good performance.

To address these issues, we propose to pre-train the PGRNN model using the simulation data produced by a generic physics-based model GLM, also referred to as uncalibrated GLM, which uses lake-specific values for physical parameters such as mixing rates, wind-sheltering, and water clarity (see [43]). The intuition is that RNN-based models after being pre-trained using simulation data are more likely to extract hidden representations that represent underlying physical relationships, and thus the ML model only requires a small amount of labeled training data to adjust itself to match true observations. This idea is similar to transfer learning [39] and self-supervised learning [23] where ML models can be significantly improved by transferring knowledge from related datasets (e.g., ImageNet [6]) or proxy tasks (e.g., colorization [29] and in-painting [25]). By pre-training RNN to predict simulated water temperature, we anticipate the model to be able to capture the spatial and temporal relationships enforced by physical processes and also transfer knowledge from the physics-based model.

In particular, given the input drivers, we run the generic GLM to predict temperature at every depth and at every day. Such temperature profiles are simulated based on the energy transfer process given heat fluxes and the penetration of solar radiation to deeper waters. These simulated temperature data from the generic GLM are imperfect but they provide a synthetic realization of physical responses of a lake to a given set of meteorological drivers. Hence, pre-training a neural network using simulations from the generic GLM allows the network to emulate a synthetic but physically realistic phenomena. When applying the pre-trained model to a real lake system, we fine-tune the model using true observations.

Our pre-training strategy is directly conducted by using simulated target variables, i.e., water temperature. This method can be further extended to pre-train ML models using simulated intermediate physical variables [21]. For example, when modeling water temperature dynamics a specific stream segment, one can build a more generalizable model by incorporating the information of physical variables (streamflow and temperature of upstream rivers, groundwater discharge, etc.) that have direct impact on the target stream segment. Another extension of this method is to pre-train the ML model while also addressing the imperfection of simulation data due to the uncertainty in parameterization. One solution is to pre-train the ML model using multiple runs of simulations generated using different parameterizations in an ensemble learning fashion.

16.4 Results in Predicting Lake Water Temperature

The proposed method has been evaluated using real data collected from Lake Mendota in Wisconsin, US. This lake system is reasonably large ($\sim$40 km^2 in area and 25 m in depth) and exhibits large changes in water temperatures in response to seasonal and sub-seasonal weather patterns. For example, the surface temperature ranges from 0 to 30°C and the lake bottom temperature ranges from 0 to 16°C over different seasons, and the water temperatures also vary within each season across different years. Observations of lake temperature were collected from North Temperate Lakes Long-Term Ecological Research Program.

We will discuss results on multiple aspects. First, we show the improved model performance for modeling dynamics of water temperature over multiple baselines when we are provided with limited training data. Second, we demonstrate the effectiveness in maintaining physical consistency by incorporating the energy transfer process. Third, we wish to confirm the model can generalize to scenarios that are different with training data, e.g., data from different years or different seasons. Fourth, we discuss how pre-training helps initialize ML models by transferring physical knowledge in the physics-based model. We also consider some special situations in which the model is pre-trained using simulation data produced under different parameterizations of the process-based lake model (i.e., purposefully modifying the lake's original measurements for hypsography and clarity). Finally, we further analyze the predicted temperature profiles and provide some insights about limitations of existing methods.

16.4.1 Training with Limited Samples

Here we compare the performance of multiple methods, including the physics-based GLM model, the RNN model (with the LSTM cell), and two versions of our proposed method, RNN^{EC} – combining the RNN with the energy flow and the physics-based loss function to preserve energy conservation, and RNN^{EC,pre} – pre-training the RNN^{EC} using simulation data and then fine-tuning the model using true observations. We use the dataset collected from April 02, 1980 to December 30, 2014 for this test (see [43] for data access and description). In particular, we use the data from April 02, 1980 to October 31, 1991 and the data from June 01, 2003 to December 30, 2014 (in total 8,037 observations) for training each model. Then we apply the trained model to predict the temperature at different depths for the period from November 01, 1991 to May 31, 2003 (in total 5,121 observations) and measure the root mean squared error (RMSE) in the testing period.

To test the performance of each model when trained with limited data, we randomly select a smaller proportion of data from the training period. Specifically, we randomly select 0.2%, 2% and 20% data from the training period and use them to train each model. We repeat this process for each iteration of training data 10 times. For each data level (0.2%, 2%, 20%), we repeat the test 10 times by randomly selecting different data samples (but maintain the same amount of selected data samples) and report the mean RMSE in the test period in Figure 16.2. It is noteworthy that the physics-based GLM model can also be fine-tuned to fit observations in a specific lake by optimizing the parameter set to minimize model error [3], which is also referred to as model calibration. For calibrated GLM simulations in this study, we optimized parameter values of cd (bulk aerodynamic transfer coefficient for momentum), sw_factor (scaling factor for shortwave radiation), and coef_mix_hyp (mixing efficiency of hypolimnetic turbulence [15]).

According to this figure, we can see that the performance of the calibrated physics-based GLM model improves, but not substantially when provided additional data ($\geq$20%).

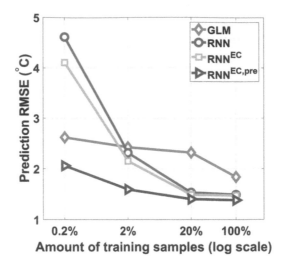

FIGURE 16.2

The performance (measured in terms of prediction RMSE) for different models trained with varying amounts of data.

This is because the GLM model has inherent bias due to the imperfect perameterization and approximations. Even when adjusting model parameters to reduce errors between the model and observations (i.e., the calibration routine), the model still has to follow the rigid form of mathematical equations used to build the physics-based model. Compared to the GLM model, we can see that RNN and RNN^{EC} models have much better performance when they are trained with more than 20% training data. This shows the capacity of ML models to automatically extract complex and useful patterns from data. However, when provided with limited data, e.g., 0.2% training data, the performance of RNN and RNN^{EC} becomes much worse because ML models are more likely to overfit the limited data. In contrast, the GLM model still have reasonable performance because it follows some general physical relationships. The uncalibrated GLM model, i.e., the GLM model using lake-specific parameters and trained with 0% data, achieves an RMSE of 2.950 in the test period.

When comparing RNN^{EC} and RNN, it can be seen that RNN^{EC} consistently outperforms RNN. The gap is larger when using smaller subsets of observed data (e.g., 0.2% or 2% data). Furthermore, the pre-training using physical simulations can greatly boost the model performance given limited data when we compare $\text{RNN}^{EC,\text{pre}}$ against RNN^{EC} and RNN. Especially, $\text{RNN}^{EC,\text{pre}}$ fine-tuned with 2% data can already achieve comparable performance with with RNN and RNN^{EC} trained with 100% data. This shows that the model gets a much better initialized state after being pre-trained using a large amount of simulations. However, given plenty of observed data, we notice that RNN, RNN^{EC}, and $\text{RNN}^{EC,\text{pre}}$ can achieve similar performance because the data is sufficient for ML models to capture dynamic patterns of water temperature.

16.4.2   Conservation of Energy over Time

Here we validate that RNN^{EC} after incorporating the energy conservation law contributes to a physically consistent solution. In particular, we aim to verify that the change in lake thermal energy is consistent to the net gain of heat fluxes. Here, the lake thermal energy is estimated using predicted water temperature at different depth layers following Eq. 16.8

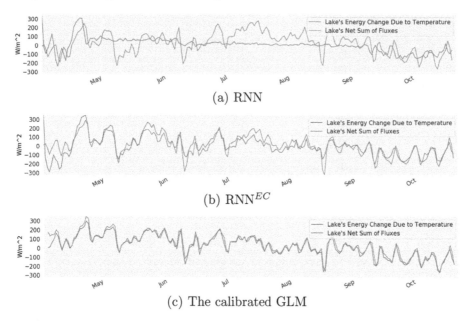

(a) RNN

(b) RNN^{EC}

(c) The calibrated GLM

FIGURE 16.3
The sum of heat fluxes and the lake energy change generated by (a) RNN, (b) RNN^{EC}, and (c) the calibrated GLM, from April 02, 1980 to October 22, 1980.

while the heat fluxes are estimated using climate drivers and the predicted surface temperature.

By comparing RNN^{EC} and RNN in Figure 16.3, we can observe that RNN^{EC} produces a better match between energy fluxes and lake energy change while RNN leads to a large energy inconsistency. This confirms that the inclusion of energy conservation in the loss function and model architecture for RNN^{EC} results in a model that helps preserve energy conservation in the test data. Also, from Figure 16.2, we can see that RNN^{EC}, which optimizes on both the training RMSE and the energy conservation, has lower RMSE than RNN, which focuses only on reducing RMSE during the training phase. This shows that a more physically realistic model can also be more generalizable.

When compared with the calibrated GLM, RNN^{EC} still has a larger energy inconsistency between the lake's energy change and the net sum of fluxes. This is because we have only applied the energy conservation as a soft constraint with its weight controlled by λ (Eq. 16.10). It is possible for RNN^{EC} to obtain a smaller energy inconsistency by simply using a larger value of λ during the training phase. However, in practice we can only capture a subset of major physical processes when estimating $\mathcal{F}_{in}$ and $\mathcal{F}_{out}$ in Eq. 16.9 and ignore certain minor processes that can be challenging to precisely model [43]. Hence, strict compliance to the simplified energy conservation term used in the loss function of RNN^{EC} can reduce the prediction accuracy in unseen data.

In Figure 16.4, we show the change of model prediction performance as we change the value of λ. The prediction performance improves when we increase the weight of energy conservation loss (λ) from 0 to 0.02. As we keep increasing the value of λ, the performance becomes worse, as indicated by increased RMSE. This shows the negative impact caused by strictly conforming to the simplified energy conservation while reducing the weight on the standard supervised training loss.

During the training process, the value of λ needs to be determined without the access to testing data. One popular solution is to manually try different values of λ and select the one

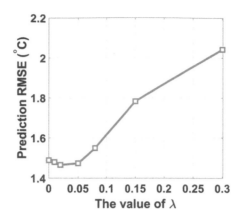

FIGURE 16.4
The performance of RNN^{EC} given different weights of energy conservation in the loss function, i.e., the value of λ.

that leads to the best performance in a separate validation dataset. Such a validation set can be created by separating a subset of the original training data. An extension of this method is to use to idea of meta-learning in automatically tuning the value of λ. In this approach, we consider two levels of parameters - model parameters (e.g., weight parameters in neural networks) and hyper-parameters (e.g., λ). One can define a validation loss based on the performance on the validation set using the model parameters updated from the training data. Then the optimal value of λ can be estimated by minimizing the validation loss.

16.4.3 Generalizability to Unseen Scenarios

One novel aspect of PGRNN is that it can track the general energy transfer processes that drive water temperature dynamics. This makes PGRNN more likely to generalize to different scenarios. To validate the generalizability of PGRNN, we measure the performance of physics-based GLM, ML-based RNN, and our proposed PGRNN in three tests using data from Lake Mendota: 1) We randomly select temperature profiles from 500 dates in 2009–2017 for training and test in the remaining data of this 9-year period. This test serves as a baseline in which the model is trained and tested using data from a similar distribution. 2) We take six colder years from 2009 to 2017 for training and test in the remaining three warmer years. 3) We train each model using data from spring and fall water temperatures and then test in summer. For all these three tests, we pre-trained the PGRNN model using physical simulations from 1980 to 2009. The result is presented in Figure 16.5.

The RNN model, when tested across years, becomes less accurate compared to the RNN trained using randomly selected data. The performance of RNN becomes much worse when trained using data only from colder seasons. This is because warmer seasons commonly exhibit a stronger stratification and/or rapid changes in stratification. The influence of stratification on model performance in the colder seasons is weaker. Hence, the data patterns learned by the RNN model from colder seasons cannot generalize to the summer.

The predictions of the physics-based GLM model also become less accurate from the baseline test (using similar data for training and testing) to the test across seasons. Since the GLM model mostly relies on general physical processes, it is able to provide reasonable predictions when tested in different seasons that have not been used for training, and the performance is much better than the ML-based RNN model in this scenario.

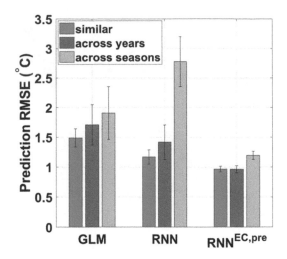

FIGURE 16.5
Performance of GLM, RNN, RNN^{EC,pre} when (1) trained and tested using similar data, (2) trained using data from colder years and tested in warmer years, and (3) trained from colder seasons and tested in summer.

As observed from the performance of RNN^{EC,pre}, combining ML and physical knowledge can significantly improve the generalizability of the model. The RNN^{EC,pre} is better than the GLM model because RNN^{EC,pre} does not need to strictly follow rigid mathematical forms defined in the physics-based model while also leveraging the power of ML in learning arbitrary relationships directly from data. The RNN^{EC,pre} also performs much better than the standard RNN model, especially when tested across seasons. This is because the RNN^{EC,pre} captures the general energy transfer process that occurs in different seasons. Also the model has been pre-trained using historical simulations over multiple years and thus it is more likely to extract general temperature patterns that hold in different time periods.

16.4.4   Analysis about Model Pre-Training

Pre-training using physical simulations has been shown to significantly improve the model performance according to previous results. We now wish to better understand how pre-training helps in model training by providing more analysis on this. In particular, we first compare the pre-trained model and fine-tuned model and analyze what information is captured by each model. Then we further validate the robustness of this pre-training method when we are provided with imperfect simulations.

16.4.4.1   Comparison between Pre-Trained and Fine-Tuned Models

The basic intuition of the pre-training strategy is that GLM simulations can provide a synthetic realization of physical responses of the lake energy budget and water temperature to a given set of meteorological drivers. Hence, the pre-training process allows the RNN^{EC} model to emulate a synthetic realization of the physical phenomena. We hypothesize that such a pre-trained model requires fewer labeled samples to achieve good generalization performance, even if the GLM simulations do not match with the observations.

In Figure 16.6, we show the predictions made by the uncalibrated GLM model (i.e., generic physical simulations), the pre-trained RNN^{EC} model without being fine-tuned using

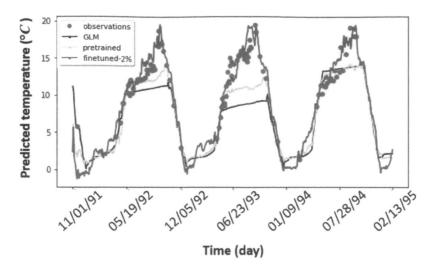

FIGURE 16.6
Predictions made by uncalibrated GLM, pre-trained RNN^{EC}, and fine-tuned RNN^{EC} using 2% training data, at 13 min depth.

observations, and the pre-trained RNN^{EC} model and fine-tuned using 2% data from the same training period as described in Section 16.4.1. Here we show the predictions at 13 m depth. The GLM simulations have been created using a GLM model with generic parameter values that are not calibrated for Lake Mendota, resulting in large errors in modeled temperature profiles with respect to the real observations at this depth for Lake Mendota. We can also see the predictions made by the pre-trained model stay close to GLM simulations while the fine-tuned model matches true observations much better.

Here the GLM performs poorly because it strictly follows the physics-based mathematical equations and parameter values used to build the model and thus likely suffers from parameter errors and an over-simplified representation of the true underlying physical processes. In particular, GLM tracks temperature at various depth layers that grow and shrink, split, or combine based on prevailing conditions. As adjacent layers split or combine, prediction artifacts that are not representative of the real-world lake system are introduced, which can result in additional variability of predicted temperatures at lower depths. In this case, the resulting temperature variability can increase GLM error for Lake Mendota.

Despite the inherent errors of a default parameterization, GLM can still capture general temperature dynamics (e.g., seasonal patterns and temperature responses to short-term cold fronts). As a result, the ML model pre-trained using these simulation data is also more likely to reflect such patterns. Once pre-trained, the ML model can be fine-tuned using a small amount of observations (e.g., 2% data) to more closely reflect the patterns of the true underlying processes.

16.4.4.2   Pre-Training Using Imperfect Simulations

The ML model can get a better initialized state if it is pre-trained using highly accurate simulations. However, in practice, the physics-based model may not have access to true values of parameters (e.g., the depth-area shape of the lake and water clarity), and therefore can only generate simulations based on default and inaccurate values for parameters that influence lake temperature dynamics. One key parameter in GLM is lake hypsography, which is not defined for most lakes. In Figure 16.7, we consider pre-training the RNN^{EC} model

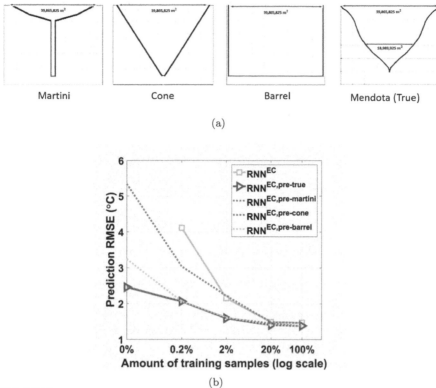

FIGURE 16.7

(a) Different hypsography structures that are used to generate simulations (martini, cone, barrel), and the true hypsography of Lake Mendota. (b) Predictions made by the RNN^{EC} model and the RNN^{EC} model pre-trained using the simulations generated under the true hypsography and other selected hypsography structures.

using simulations under different hypsography structures: martini, cone, and barrel, which represent the simplified shapes used to construct the depth-area relationships of these lake hypsography scenarios. Martini has most of the volume of the lake in the shallow depths, with a small portion of the lake extending deeper, the cone shape is a linear decline of surface area as the lake gets deeper, and barrel has a uniform depth-area relationship for all depths.

The cone shape is closer to the true hypsography of Lake Mendota while both barrel and martini are substantial variations from the lake's true hypsography. When comparing the performance of different pre-trained hypsography structures, we notice that the model pre-trained with the martini shape has a much larger error than the other two hypsography shapes and the cone shape has the smallest error. This result agrees with the assumption that the cone shape is closer to the true hypsography of Lake Mendota.

However, these errors can be significantly reduced after fine-tuning with small amounts of observation data. The reason is that GLM simulations still represent physical responses that strictly follow known physical laws. Hence, each of the pre-trained model variants is able to capture complex physical relationships and reach a initialized state that is physically-consistent with the parameter modifications in each GLM simulation. As seen in Figure 16.7, pre-training with a flawed set of lake parameters that are very different from the actual properties of the target lake can still significantly reduce the amount of observations required to train a quality model.

TABLE 16.1

Predictive RMSE (°C) for GLM and RNN^{EC,pre} across Seasons and Depths.

Season/Depth	0m	6m	12m	18m	24m
Spring - GLM	1.77	1.03	0.93	0.92	1.16
Spring - RNN^{EC,pre}	1.36	0.87	0.80	0.81	1.05
Summer - GLM	1.55	1.32	1.61	1.98	1.68
Summer - RNN^{EC,pre}	1.76	1.26	1.33	0.96	1.13
Fall - GLM	0.83	0.67	1.56	2.26	2.46
Fall - RNN^{EC,pre}	1.29	0.88	1.26	1.08	0.56
Winter - GLM	0.92	0.74	0.72	0.62	0.78
Winter - RNN^{EC,pre}	1.36	1.14	1.12	1.40	0.90

16.4.5   Further Analysis of Predictions over Space and Time

To better understand the difference between our proposed method and GLM predictions for different seasons, we separately measure the predictive RMSE at different lake depths for different seasons (see Table 16.1). The predictive performance of GLM becomes worse in summer and fall for lower depths (below 12 m depth). This stems from the difficulty in modeling stratification in addition to the increased range of temperatures in warmer seasons. Summer and fall typically include periods of strong stratification and also rapid changes in stratification. The influence of stratification on model performance in the spring and winter periods is weaker compared to summer and fall.

We can observe that in spring RNN^{EC,pre} and calibrated GLM (calibration with 100% of training data) have similar errors, while the difference between RNN^{EC,pre} and GLM becomes greatest in summer and fall. The RNN^{EC,pre} performs better in warmer seasons since it can extract complex relationship directly from observations while not strictly following the rigid mathematical equations defined in GLM. In contrast, the calibrated GLM offers improvement over RNN^{EC,pre} during the winter season. This shows the limitation of ML models in capturing non-stationary relationships. Since the temperature dynamics become different in winter when the lake is frozen, the model trained using all the data from multiple seasons may not perform well on specific seasons, especially when the training data from winter is much less compared to warmer seasons.

16.5   Conclusion

The proposed PGRNN provides a powerful framework for modeling spatial and temporal physical processes. It uses a new architecture to capture and track energy transfer processes, and also incorporates a penalty for deviation from energy conservation via the loss function. Furthermore, after being pre-trained using the simulated data from a generic physics-based model, PGRNN obtains higher prediction performance when a small number of observations are used for refinement when compared to a parameterized physics-based model calibrated using a greater number of observations. Thus, PGRNN can leverage the strengths of physics-based models while filling in knowledge gaps by employing state-of-the-art predictive frameworks that learn from data.

The PGRNN framework can also be viewed as a transfer learning method that transfers the knowledge from physical processes to ML models. Future research needs to determine the types of dynamical system models for which such an approach will be effective. It is entirely possible that new architectural enhancements will need to be made to the traditional LSTM framework to incorporate different types of physical laws and to model underlying physical processes that may be interacting at different spatial and temporal scales. Hence, the proposed framework can be applied to a variety of scientific problems such as nutrient exchange in lake systems and analysis of crop field production, as well as engineering problems such as auto-vehicle refueling design. Some future directions could include the estimation of uncertainty of model predictions and physical parameters (e.g., water clarity and salinity) over space and time, which could help better understand the limitation of physics-based and ML models. Moreover, one could further improve the calculation of heat transfer using sub-daily information to capture finer-grained temperature dynamics and enforce more accurate estimation of energy conservation. We anticipate this work as an important stepping-stone towards applications of ML to problems traditionally solved by physics-based models.

Note

[1]Any use of trade, firm, or product names is for descriptive purposes only and does not imply endorsement by the U.S. Government.

Bibliography

[1] Jeffrey G Arnold, Daniel N Moriasi, Philip W Gassman, Karim C Abbaspour, Michael J White, Raghavan Srinivasan, Chinnasamy Santhi, RD Harmel, Ann Van Griensven, Michael W Van Liew, et al. Swat: Model use, calibration, and validation. *Transactions of the ASABE*, 55(4):1491–1508, 2012.

[2] Yoshua Bengio, Patrice Simard, and Paolo Frasconi. Learning long-term dependencies with gradient descent is difficult. *IEEE transactions on Neural Networks*, 5(2):157–166, 1994.

[3] Louise C Bruce, Marieke A Frassl, George B Arhonditsis, Gideon Gal, David P Hamilton, Paul C Hanson, Amy L Hetherington, John M Melack, Jordan S Read, Karsten Rinke, et al. A multi-lake comparative analysis of the general lake model (glm): Stress-testing across a global observatory network. *Environmental Modelling & Software*, 102:274–291, 2018.

[4] S Chen and S A Billings. Neural networks for nonlinear dynamic system modelling and identification. *International Journal of Control*, 56(2):319–346, 1992.

[5] A Daw, RQ Thomas, CC Carey, JS Read, AP Appling, and A Karpatne. Physics-guided architecture (pga) of neural networks for quantifying uncertainty in lake temperature modeling. *arXiv:1911.02682*, 2019.

[6] Jia Deng, Wei Dong, Richard Socher, Li-Jia Li, Kai Li, and Li Fei-Fei. Imagenet: A large-scale hierarchical image database. In *2009 IEEE Conference on Computer Vision and Pattern Recognition*, pages 248–255. Ieee, 2009.

[7] Ferdinando Fioretto, Terrence WK Mak, and Pascal Van Hentenryck. Predicting ac optimal power flows: Combining deep learning and lagrangian dual methods. In *Proceedings of the AAAI Conference on Artificial Intelligence*, volume 34, pages 630–637, 2020.

[8] Urban Forssell and Peter Lindskog. Combining semi-physical and neural network modeling: An example of its usefulness. *IFAC Proceedings Volumes*, 1997.

[9] Garrett B Goh, Nathan O Hodas, and Abhinav Vishnu. Deep learning for computational chemistry. *Journal of Computational Chemistry*, 38(16):1291–1307, 2017.

[10] D Graham-Rowe, D Goldston, C Doctorow, M Waldrop, C Lynch, F Frankel, R Reid, S Nelson, D Howe, SY Rhee, et al. Big data: science in the petabyte era. *Nature*, 455(7209):8–9, 2008.

[11] Alex Graves. Long short-term memory. In *Supervised Sequence Labelling with Recurrent Neural Networks*, pages 37–45. Springer, 2012.

[12] Hoshin V Gupta et al. Debates—the future of hydrological sciences: A (common) path forward? using models and data to learn: A systems theoretic perspective on the future of hydrological science. *WRR*, 2014.

[13] Paul C Hanson, Aviah B Stillman, Xiaowei Jia, Anuj Karpatne, Hilary A Dugan, Cayelan C Carey, Joseph Stachelek, Nicole K Ward, Yu Zhang, Jordan S Read, et al. Predicting lake surface water phosphorus dynamics using process-guided machine learning. *Ecological Modelling*, 430:109136, 2020.

[14] Ted D Harris and Jennifer L Graham. Predicting cyanobacterial abundance, microcystin, and geosmin in a eutrophic drinking-water reservoir using a 14-year dataset. *Lake and Reservoir Management*, 2017.

[15] Matthew R Hipsey, Louise C Bruce, Casper Boon, Brendan Busch, Cayelan C Carey, David P Hamilton, Paul C Hanson, Jordan S Read, Eduardo De Sousa, Michael Weber, et al. A general lake model (glm 3.0) for linking with high-frequency sensor data from the global lake ecological observatory network (gleon). 2019.

[16] Fan Hu et al. Transferring deep convolutional neural networks for the scene classification of high-resolution remote sensing imagery. *Remote Sensing*, 2015.

[17] David Menéndez Hurtado, Karolis Uziela, and Arne Elofsson. Deep transfer learning in the assessment of the quality of protein models. *arXiv preprint arXiv:1804.06281*, 2018.

[18] Andrew J Majda and John Harlim. Physics constrained nonlinear regression models for time series. *Nonlinearity*, 26:201, 11 2012.

[19] Xiaowei Jia, Ankush Khandelwal, Guruprasad Nayak, James Gerber, Kimberly Carlson, Paul West, and Vipin Kumar. Incremental dual-memory lstm in land cover prediction. In *SIGKDD*. ACM, 2017.

[20] Xiaowei Jia, Jared Willard, Anuj Karpatne, Jordan Read, Jacob Zwart, Michael Steinbach, and Vipin Kumar. Physics guided rnns for modeling dynamical systems: A case study in simulating lake temperature profiles. In *Proceedings of the 2019 SIAM International Conference on Data Mining*, pages 558–566. SIAM, 2019.

[21] Xiaowei Jia, Jacob Zwart, Jeffery Sadler, Alison Appling, Samantha Oliver, Steven Markstrom, Jared Willard, Shaoming Xu, Michael Steinbach, Jordan Read, et al. Physics-guided recurrent graph networks for predicting flow and temperature in river networks. *arXiv preprint arXiv:2009.12575*, 2020.

[22] Xiaowei Jia, Jacob Zwart, Jeffrey Sadler, Alison Appling, Samantha Oliver, Steven Markstrom, Jared Willard, Shaoming Xu, Michael Steinbach, Jordan Read, et al. Physics-guided recurrent graph model for predicting flow and temperature in river networks. In *Proceedings of the 2021 SIAM International Conference on Data Mining (SDM)*, pages 612–620. SIAM, 2021.

[23] Longlong Jing and Yingli Tian. Self-supervised visual feature learning with deep neural networks: A survey. *IEEE Transactions on Pattern Analysis and Machine Intelligence*, 2020.

[24] Anuj Karpatne, William Watkins, Jordan Read, and Vipin Kumar. Physics-guided neural networks (pgnn): An application in lake temperature modeling. *arXiv preprint arXiv:1710.11431*, 2017.

[25] Isinsu Katircioglu, Helge Rhodin, Victor Constantin, Jörg Spörri, Mathieu Salzmann, and Pascal Fua. Self-supervised segmentation via background inpainting. *arXiv preprint arXiv:2011.05626*, 2020.

[26] Diederik P Kingma and Jimmy Ba. Adam: A method for stochastic optimization. *arXiv preprint arXiv:1412.6980*, 2014.

[27] Dimitrios Kotzias, Misha Denil, Nando De Freitas, and Padhraic Smyth. From group to individual labels using deep features. In *Proceedings of the 21th ACM SIGKDD International Conference on Knowledge Discovery and Data Mining*, pages 597–606. ACM, 2015.

[28] Upmanu Lall. Debates—the future of hydrological sciences: A (common) path forward? one water. one world. many climes. many souls. *WRR*, 2014.

[29] Gustav Larsson, Michael Maire, and Gregory Shakhnarovich. Colorization as a proxy task for visual understanding. In *Proceedings of the IEEE Conference on Computer Vision and Pattern Recognition*, pages 6874–6883, 2017.

[30] Ruotent Li, Loong Fah Cheong, and Robby T Tan. Heavy rain image restoration: Integrating physics model and conditional adversarial learning. *arXiv preprint arXiv:1904.05050*, 2019.

[31] J Ling, A Kurzawski, and J Templeton. Reynolds averaged turbulence modelling using deep neural networks with embedded invariance. *Journal of Fluid Mechanics*, 2016.

[32] Shujie Liu, Nan Yang, Mu Li, and Ming Zhou. A recursive recurrent neural network for statistical machine translation. 2014.

[33] John J Magnuson et al. Temperature as an ecological resource. *American Zoologist*, 19(1):331–343, 1979.

[34] Jeffrey J McDonnell and Keith Beven. Debates—the future of hydrological sciences: A (common) path forward? a call to action aimed at understanding velocities, celerities and residence time distributions of the headwater hydrograph. *WRR*, 2014.

[35] Nikhil Muralidhar, Jie Bu, Ze Cao, Long He, Naren Ramakrishnan, Danesh Tafti, and Anuj Karpatne. Phynet: Physics guided neural networks for particle drag force prediction in assembly. In *Proceedings of the 2020 SIAM International Conference on Data Mining*, pages 559–567. SIAM, 2020.

[36] Hans W Paerl and Jef Huisman. Blooms like it hot. *Science*, 320(5872):57–58, 2008.

[37] Jinshan Pan, Yang Liu, Jiangxin Dong, Jiawei Zhang, Jimmy Ren, Jinhui Tang, Yu-Wing Tai, and Ming-Hsuan Yang. Physics-based generative adversarial models for image restoration and beyond. *arXiv e-prints*, page arXiv:1808.00605, Aug 2018.

[38] Shaowu Pan and Karthik Duraisamy. Long-time predictive modeling of nonlinear dynamical systems using neural networks. *Complexity*, 2018:1–26, 12 2018.

[39] Sinno Jialin Pan and Qiang Yang. A survey on transfer learning. *IEEE Transactions on Knowledge and Data Engineering*, 22(10):1345–1359, 2009.

[40] Roberto Paolucci, Filippo Gatti, Maria Infantino, Chiara Smerzini, Ali Güney Özcebe, and Marco Stupazzini. Broadband ground motions from 3d physics-based numerical simulations using artificial neural networksbroadband ground motions from 3d pbss using anns. *Bulletin of the Seismological Society of America*, 108(3A):1272–1286, 2018.

[41] Frank J Rahel and Julian D Olden. Assessing the effects of climate change on aquatic invasive species. *Conservation Biology*, 22(3):521–533, 2008.

[42] Emily K Read et al. Water quality data for national-scale aquatic research: The water quality portal. *Water Resources Research*, 2017.

[43] Jordan S Read, Xiaowei Jia, Jared Willard, Alison P Appling, Jacob A Zwart, Samantha K Oliver, Anuj Karpatne, Gretchen JA Hansen, Paul C Hanson, William Watkins, et al. Process-guided deep learning predictions of lake water temperature. *Water Resources Research*, 2019.

[44] Hongyu Ren et al. Learning with weak supervision from physics and data-driven constraints. *AI Magazine*, 2018.

[45] James J Roberts et al. Fragmentation and thermal risks from climate change interact to affect persistence of native trout in the colorado river basin. *Global Change Biology*, 2013.

[46] James J Roberts et al. Nonnative trout invasions combined with climate change threaten persistence of isolated cutthroat trout populations in the southern rocky mountains. *North American Journal of Fisheries Management*, 2017.

[47] Martin Schmid and Jordan Read. Heat budget of lakes. In *Reference Module in Earth Systems and Environmental Sciences*. Elsevier, 2021.

[48] Kristof Schütt, Pieter-Jan Kindermans, Huziel Enoc Sauceda Felix, Stefan Chmiela, Alexandre Tkatchenko, and Klaus-Robert Müller. Schnet: A continuous-filter convolutional neural network for modeling quantum interactions. In *Advances in Neural Information Processing Systems*, pages 991–1001, 2017.

[49] Abhinav Shrivastava, Saurabh Singh, and Abhinav Gupta. Constrained semi-supervised learning using attributes and comparative attributes. In *Proceedings of the 12th European Conference on Computer Vision - Volume Part III*, ECCV'12, pages 369–383, Berlin, Heidelberg, 2012. Springer-Verlag.

[50] Russell Stewart and Stefano Ermon. Label-free supervision of neural networks with physics and domain knowledge. In *AAAI*, volume 1, pages 1–7, 2017.

[51] Pascal Sturmfels, Saige Rutherford, Mike Angstadt, Mark Peterson, Chandra Sripada, and Jenna Wiens. A domain guided cnn architecture for predicting age from structural brain images. *arXiv preprint arXiv:1808.04362*, 2018.

[52] Mohammad M Sultan, Hannah K Wayment-Steele, and Vijay S Pande. Transferable neural networks for enhanced sampling of protein dynamics. *Journal of Chemical Theory and Computation*, 14(4):1887–1894, 2018.

[53] Zhong Yi Wan, Pantelis Vlachas, Petros Koumoutsakos, and Themistoklis Sapsis. Data-assisted reduced-order modeling of extreme events in complex dynamical systems. *PloS One*, 13(5):e0197704, 2018.

[54] Jared Willard, Xiaowei Jia, Shaoming Xu, Michael Steinbach, and Vipin Kumar. Integrating Scientific Knowledge with machine learning for Earth and Environmental Systems: A survey. *ACM Computing Survey*, 2022.

[55] Jared D Willard, Jordan S Read, Alison P Appling, Samantha K Oliver, Xiaowei Jia, and Vipin Kumar. Predicting water temperature dynamics of unmonitored lakes with meta transfer learning. *Water Resources Research*, page e2021WR029579, 2021.

[56] Tianfang Xu and Albert J Valocchi. Data-driven methods to improve baseflow prediction of a regional groundwater model. *Computers & Geosciences*, 2015.

[57] Kun Yao, John E Herr, David W Toth, Ryker Mckintyre, and John Parkhill. The tensormol-0.1 model chemistry: a neural network augmented with long-range physics. *Chemical Science*, 9(8):2261–2269, 2018.

[58] Mohamed Akram Zaytar and Chaker El Amrani. Sequence to sequence weather forecasting with long short-term memory recurrent neural networks. *International Journal of Computer Applications*, 143(11):7–11, 2016.

[59] Linfeng Zhang, Jiequn Han, Han Wang, Wissam Saidi, Roberto Car, and E Weinan. End-to-end symmetry preserving inter-atomic potential energy model for finite and extended systems. In *Advances in Neural Information Processing Systems*, pages 4436–4446, 2018.

17

Physics-Guided Architecture (PGA) of LSTM Models for Uncertainty Quantification in Lake Temperature Modeling

Arka Daw, R. Quinn Thomas, Cayelan C. Carey, Jordan S. Read,
Alison P. Appling, and Anuj Karpatne

CONTENTS

This chapter focuses on meeting the need to produce neural network outputs that are physically consistent and also express uncertainties, a rare combination to date. To address both these goals, this chapter introduces a novel physics-guided architecture (PGA) of long-short-term-memory (LSTM) models in the context of lake temperature modeling where the physical constraints are hard coded in the LSTM architecture. PGA-LSTM is easy to integrate with state-of-the-art uncertainty estimation approaches such as Monte Carlo (MC) Dropout without sacrificing the physical consistency of our results. We demonstrate the effectiveness of PGA-LSTM in achieving better generalizability and physical consistency over data collected from Lake Mendota in Wisconsin and Falling Creek Reservoir in Virginia,

DOI: 10.1201/9781003143376-17

even with limited training data. We further show that the distribution of our MC estimates match the distribution of ground-truth observations better than baseline methods, thus resulting in physically grounded uncertainty quantification. All the code and datasets used in this study have been made available on this link `https://github.com/arkadaw9/PGA_LSTM`. The datasets used in this study are also available on `https://zenodo.org/record/5193687#.YRXK2IhKhPY`.

17.1   Introduction

Deep learning models have proven to be incredibly successful across commercial domains such as computer vision, speech, and natural language processing. Recently, this success has motivated the scientific community to unlock the hidden potential of deep learning methods for advancing scientific discovery [2, 10, 14, 27]. The emergence of advanced deep learning frameworks such as Conv Nets [17] and long short term memory (LSTM) models [12] that can handle complex data structures common in many scientific applications is one of the primary ingredients fueling the rising interest within the scientific community for deep learning. In addition to using deep learning to generate point estimates, there are a number of scientific problems that require precise estimation of the uncertainty bounds, e.g., in climate change applications [24]. Algorithmic innovations such as using the Monte Carlo (MC) Dropout method [9] have been crucial in bridging the gap between deep learning and uncertainty quantification.

Regardless of these dramatic advances in many commercial fields, a large number of deep learning methods have witnessed limited success in scientific applications (e.g., [4, 18, 22]), sometimes even leading to major failures (e.g., [18]). These failures can be primarily attributed to the so-called *black-box* nature of conventional deep learning frameworks, which entirely rely on the training data and are unaware of the underlying scientific principles driving complex real-world phenomena. The emerging field of research that combines scientific knowledge (or theories) with data science methods, termed *theory-guided data science* [15], is often considered the first step towards moving beyond these black-box models. This can be achieved by guiding the learning of the neural network models using *physics-based loss functions* [13, 16, 30], that measure the physical inconsistency in model predictions. We refer to this paradigm as physics-guided learning (PGL) of neural networks.

Even though PGL formulations result in improvements in the generalization performance and lead to ML predictions that are more physically consistent, simply adding the physics-based loss function in the learning objective does not overcome the black-box nature of neural network architectures, which often involve arbitrary design choices (e.g., number of layers and nodes per layer). This leaves the black-box models susceptible to generating physically inconsistent predictions even with slight perturbations in the network's weights, in spite of being trained with physics-based loss functions. This limitation poses a major concern while using methods such as MC dropout to estimate the uncertainty bounds of ML predictions, as the connections or weights in the neural networks are dropped with a small probability in the inference stage to generate a distribution of the sample predictions for every test instance. In this chapter, we demonstrate that the randomness injected by MC dropout in the network's weights easily breaks the ability of the PGL paradigm to preserve physical consistency in the sample predictions, leading to physically non-meaningful uncertainty estimates.

To overcome issues combining PGL with MC dropout for uncertainty estimation, we present innovations in the emerging field of *theory-guided data science*, where the physical principles are fused directly into the neural network design as opposed to black-box

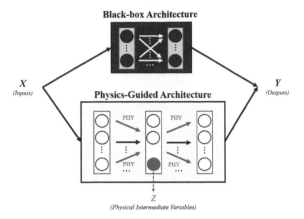

FIGURE 17.1
A visual illustration of the Physics-guided Architecture (PGA) paradigm of neural networks that aims to introduce physics in neural network designs through *physics-informed connections* among neurons and through *physical intermediate variables*, shown in red.

architectures trained with physics-driven loss functions. We refer to this paradigm as physics-guided architecture (PGA) of neural networks. More specifically, in this chapter we cover two key innovations in the PGA paradigm for the illustrative problem of lake temperature modeling as illustrated in Figure 17.1. The first innovation is the design of a neural network model with *physics-informed connections* between neurons to capture the physics-based relationships of lake temperature. Second, we associate physical meaning to some of the neurons in the network by computing physical intermediate variables Z in the neural pathway from inputs to outputs. By embedding the physics into the model architecture, our proposed PGA approach is able to guarantee physical consistency of its predictions regardless of small perturbations in the network weights, e.g., due to MC dropout. We use two lakes, Lake Mendota in Wisconsin, USA, and Falling Creek Reservoir in Virginia, USA as two benchmark lakes to compare the efficacy of our proposed approach. The two lakes differ in their physical characteristics and climatic regimes.

The remainder of the chapter is organized as follows. Section 17.2 provides a brief background of the problem of lake temperature modeling and relevant related work. Section 17.3 describes our proposed PGA-LSTM framework. Section 17.4 discusses our evaluation procedure while Section 17.5 presents results. Section 17.6 provides concluding remarks and directions for future research.

17.2 Background and Related Work

In this section, we first provide some background of the problem of lake temperature modeling and then present related work in the area of physics-guided machine learning and uncertainty quantification.

17.2.1 Lake Temperature Modeling

The temperature of water in a lake is a fundamental driver of lake biogeochemical processes, and it controls the growth, survival, and reproduction of fishes in the lake [21, 26] Hence, precise modeling of the water temperature in a lake is of paramount interest from both

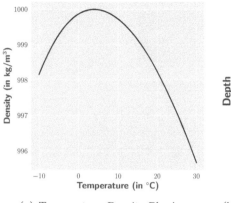
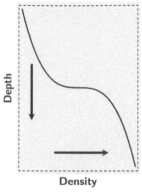

(a) Temperature–Density Physics   (b) Density–Depth Physics

FIGURE 17.2
We consider two key physical relationships in the application domain of lake temperature modeling: (a) temperature-density physics and (b) density-depth physics.

economic and ecological standpoints. Physics-based models of lake hydrodynamic processes such as the general lake model (GLM) [11] are commonly used for studying 1-dimensional variations in lake temperature across varying depth values[1] at the center or deepest part of the lake, at varying time points. We adopt the same formulation in this work to model the temperature of water in a lake, $Y_{d,t}$, at depth d and time t. The two key physical relationships that must be considered while modeling the water temperature are: (1) there exists a one-to-one non-linear mapping between the temperature and the density of the water as shown in the Figure 17.2(a) (note that the density of water is maximum at 4°C rather than 0°C), (2) density of the water monotonically increases with depth (see Figure 17.2(b)), hence, denser water gradually sinks to the bottom of the lake, residing at greater depths. These two fundamental physical factors serve as the basis of the PGA innovations proposed later in the chapter.

17.2.2 Physics-Guided Machine Learning

One of the promising lines of research in *theory-guided data science* is referred to as the Physics-guided Learning (PGL) paradigm [13, 16, 30], where the training objective of the neural network includes the standard prediction loss in the target space Y along with an additional *physics-based loss* to measure the violations of physical principles in the model outputs $\widehat{Y}$. The overall learning objective of the PGL framework is as follows:

$$\arg\min\ Loss(Y, \widehat{Y}) + \lambda_{PHY}\ PHY.Loss(\widehat{Y}), \tag{17.1}$$

where λ_{PHY} is a trade-off hyper-parameter that decides the relative importance of minimizing the physical inconsistency compared to the empirical loss and the model complexity. During training, the physics-based loss term influences the output space of the neural network to be physically consistent, thereby improving the generalizability in novel testing scenarios. In previous works, Karpatne et al. [16] developed a PGL framework in the context of lake temperature modeling to measure violations of the two physical relationships introduced in Section 17.2.1. This was extended by Jia et al. [13] to work with time-varying deep learning architectures such as LSTM models and minimized an additional physics-based loss function to enforce energy conservation. Other recent works like Xu et al. [31] integrated probabilistic logic with neural networks using semantic loss for classification tasks.

Pathak et al. [25] used linear constraints as loss functions for the task of weakly supervised segmentation. Marquez et al. [23] also developed constrained optimization formulations of neural networks to impose hard constraints on neural network outputs.

While the PGL paradigm provides an easy-to-use framework for integrating physics knowledge in neural network training, the *black-box* nature of the neural network architecture itself still remains as one of the persisting and critical limitations of PGL formulations. Note that minimizing the physics-based loss term during training only ensures that the weights of the neural network are learned in a way that would produce physically consistent predictions on the training set. However, without any architectural constraints present in the neural network, there is no guarantee that the model predictions would obey the physics constraints during the time of inference on unseen test data.

Research efforts focused on building physics-guided architecture (PGA) of neural networks have also gained traction. For example, network connections that incorporate the Hebbian rule of learning in neuroscience for view-tolerant facial detection have been proposed by Leibo et al. [19]. Anderson et al. [1] and Ling et al. [20] have explored ways of embedding various forms of invariance in neural networks for problems in molecular dynamics and turbulence modeling, respectively. Even though these works are able to incorporate the physical knowledge directly into the network architectures, none of these developments are directly applicable to our problem of temperature prediction. Our problem requires encoding the physics available in the form of monotonic relationships and presence of intermediate variables.

17.2.3 Uncertainty Quantification (UQ)

Expressing the uncertainty in model predictions is an important end-goal in a number of scientific applications, where ensuring trust in model predictions for end-users such as scientists is often critical. For example, in the context of lake modeling, by quantifying the level of confidence in our temperature estimates, we can better understand the range of uncertainty in its impact on the population of fish species and other ecological variables. In such scenarios, we are interested in generating a distribution of the target variable for every input instance, as opposed to only predicting point estimates of the target variable. A standard approach for uncertainty quantification (UQ) in the context of deep learning is to use dropout [28] on the trained neural networks during inference to produce multiple Monte Carlo samples of the target variable. This method is commonly referred to as Monte Carlo (MC) Dropout [9]. Another approach for estimating uncertainty in deep learning models is to use methods in Bayesian deep learning, where the posterior probability of the target variable is estimated by assuming Gaussian priors on every weight of the neural network [8]. This approach is generally slower than MC dropout as it involves training a network with twice the number of parameters (the mean and standard deviation of the Gaussian priors of every weight in the neural network). In our proposed PGA framework, we utilize the MC Dropout approach to generate uncertainty estimates, although our proposed innovations are generic and can be easily integrated with other UQ methods in deep learning.

17.3 Proposed Framework

A high-level overview of our proposed physics-guided architecture of LSTM (PGA-LSTM) [7] for lake temperature modeling is presented in Figure 17.3. It is composed of three basic modules: (1) an LSTM based auto-encoder framework that extracts temporal features $\widehat{V}_t$

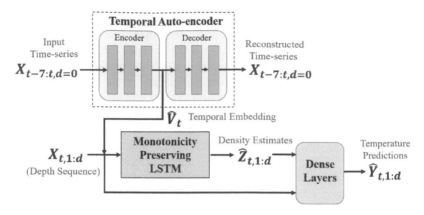

FIGURE 17.3
Proposed **PGA**-LSTM framework [7].

from the data at a given time t, (2) a *monotonicity-preserving* LSTM which utilizes both the temporal features $\widehat{V}_t$ and spatial (in this case, depth-varying) features $X_{t,1:d}$ to predict an intermediate physical quantity: density $\widehat{Z}_{t,d}$ such that $\widehat{Z}_{t,d} \geq \widehat{Z}_{t,d-1}$, and (3) a multi-layered neural network model which utilizes the intermediate density predictions $\widehat{Z}_{t,d}$ along with the input drivers $X_{t,d}$ to estimate the final water temperatures $\widehat{Y}_{t,d}$. In the following, we describe each of these three components in detail and present an end-to-end learning procedure for the complete **PGA**-LSTM framework.

17.3.1 Temporal Feature Extraction

The problem of lake temperature modeling involves both a temporal and a spatial (along the depth of the lake) dimension . Here, we describe a simple yet effective design to extract temporal features from data, which can then be used to model the variations in lake temperature across the spatial dimension. Our autoencoder architecture for extracting temporal features from input driver data comprises LSTM models in the encoder and decoder modules, as shown in Figure 17.4. The input to our encoder module is a time series of input driver features observed over the last 7 days of a target date at the surface of the lake (i.e., at depth $d = 0$). The encoder takes this input, $X_{t-7:t,d=0}$, and generates a hidden embedding $\widehat{V}_t$ for the target date. The decoder decodes this hidden representation by reconstructing the input time series. In order to do so, the representation must retain information about the sequential nature of the input data corresponding to the last 7 days. This design of auto-encoder is inspired by an earlier work of Srivastava et al. [29]. $\widehat{V}_t$ is then fed into the module for predicting variations in temperature across depth at time t.

17.3.2 Monotonicity-Preserving LSTM

We develop a variant of the LSTM model [12] for predicting the vertical 1D-sequence of lake temperature at a given time t, $Y_{t,1:d}$, given the 1D-sequence of input drivers at the same time, $X_{t,1:d}$, and the temporal features, $\widehat{V}_t$, extracted by the autoencoder model. The LSTM is a special type of recurrent neural network (RNN) architecture that is designed to capture both long-term and short-term dependencies while predicting a target sequence $Z_{1:d}$ from an input sequence $X_{1:d}$. The key idea that allows LSTMs to remember information or patterns from arbitrarily long intervals is to maintain a memory cell state C_d and hidden

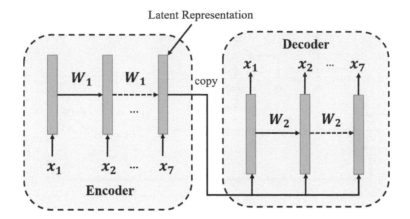

FIGURE 17.4
Proposed architecture of autoencoder model for temporal feature extraction.

state H_d that are updated at every index of the sequence, using neural network modules commonly referred to as gate operations. Two of the gates that are generally used to update the cell state and hidden state are the *input* gate and *forget* gate. These gates control the amount of information which will be added or deleted, respectively from the cell state at the previous index and are learnable functions of the features at the current index, X_d, and the hidden state at the previous index, H_{d-1}. An additional learnable *output* gate controls the information flow between the cell state and the hidden state. Finally, a stack of fully-connected layers are used to map the hidden state H_d to the estimates of the target variable $\widehat{Z}_d$. In our formulation, we consider the spatial sequence of depth values from 1 to d as indexes in the LSTM architecture.

Eventhough LSTM captures recurrence relationships between the hidden states of consecutive depths, H_d and H_{d-1}, the choice of these recurrence forms are quite arbitrary and not informed by physics. In contrast, our proposed **PGA**-LSTM formulation estimates a physically meaningful intermediate quantity: density of water $\widehat{Z}_{1:d}$. As we know from Section 17.2.1, the density of water can only increase or remain constant with increase in depth d. We embed this physical constraint into our LSTM framework by introducing novel *physics-informed* connections in LSTM to have a monotonic recurrence relationship between Z_d and Z_{d-1}. Figure 17.5 provides the schematic of our proposed monotonicity-preserving LSTM architecture.

The primary innovation in **PGA**-LSTM (shown as red in Figure 17.5) is to keep track of the physical intermediate variable, Z_d, along with H_d and C_d, and using the physical constraint that Z_d only increases with d. Specifically, we predict the positive increment in density δ_d, as a function of H_d, which when added to Z_{d-1} yields Z_d. This is achieved by applying a stack of k fully connected layers on the H_d predicted by a basic LSTM architecture, followed by a ReLU activation function to predict positive differentials of density δ_d. The set of governing equations for the forward pass of our proposed monotonicity-preserving LSTM is given by:

$$I_d = \sigma(W_i[X_d, H_{d-1}, \mathbf{Z_{d-1}}] + b_i),$$
$$F_d = \sigma(W_f[X_d, H_{d-1}, \mathbf{Z_{d-1}}] + b_f),$$
$$C_d = F_d \circ C_{d-1} + I_d \circ \tanh(W_c[X_d, H_{d-1}, \mathbf{Z_{d-1}}] + b_c),$$
$$O_d = \sigma(W_o[X_d, H_{d-1}, \mathbf{Z_{d-1}}] + b_o),$$
$$H_d = O_d \circ \tanh(C_d),$$

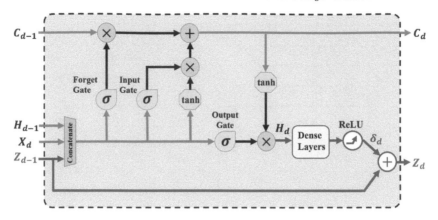

FIGURE 17.5

Visual schematic of the proposed monotonicity-preserving LSTM Architecture. Components in red represent the physics-informed innovations introduced in the basic LSTM.

$$\mathbf{L_d^1} = \text{Activation}(\mathbf{W_1 H_d} + \mathbf{b_1}),$$
$$\mathbf{L_d^i} = \text{Activation}(\mathbf{W_i L_d^{i-1}} + \mathbf{b_i}), \text{ where } i = 2,...,\text{k.},$$
$$\delta_\mathbf{d} = \mathbf{ReLU}(W_\delta L_d^k + b_\delta),$$
$$\mathbf{Z_d} = \mathbf{Z_{d-1}} + \delta_\mathbf{d}.$$

Note that $\sigma(.)$ denotes the sigmoid activation, $\circ$ denotes the Hadamard product, $[a, b]$ denotes the concatenation of a and b, and $(W, b)_q$ denotes learnable weight and bias terms for all values of q. Note that the density-depth physics serves as the key motivation behind the physics-informed innovations introduced in our **PGA**-LSTM framework. However, the idea of preserving monotonicity in LSTM outputs is useful in many other scientific applications. In general, our **PGA**-*monotonicity-preserving* LSTM framework can be used in applications where the target variable obeys monotonic constraints.

17.3.3 Mapping Density to Temperature

The final component in our **PGA**-LSTM framework is mapping the computed density estimates $\widehat{Z}_d$ at depth d to their corresponding estimates of temperature $\widehat{Y}_d$ at depth d. The temperature-density physics introduced in Section 17.2.1 can be utilized to infer the density from the temperature estimates. However, the inverse mapping from density to temperature is one-to-many and thus non-unique (see Figure 17.2(a)). In particular, a given value of density Z can be mapped to two possible values of temperature Y, one corresponding to the freezing phase ($Y < 4°$ C) and the other corresponding to the warming phase ($Y > 4°$ C). To circumvent this one-to-many mapping, we utilize the input drivers X_d along with the density estimates $\widehat{Z}_d$ to predict $\widehat{Y}_d$ by training a fully connected neural network. As $\widehat{Z}_d$ is already a strong physical predictor of Y_d, we do not require a deep architecture to map density to temperature and thus a small number of hidden layers is sufficient.

17.3.4 End-to-End Learning Procedure

Our proposed **PGA**-LSTM framework can predict the target variable: temperature, $\widehat{Y}$, along with the physical intermediate variable: density, $\widehat{Z}$, as ancillary outputs. The ground-truth observations of temperature, Y, can be converted into ground-truth estimates of density, Z, from the physical principles introduced in Section 17.2.1. This allows us to train the **PGA**-LSTM model in an end-to-end fashion by minimizing the empirical loss over both Y and Z in the following learning objective:

$$\arg\min_{(W,b)} \quad \text{Loss}(Y, \widehat{Y}) + \lambda_Z \, \text{Loss}(Z, \widehat{Z}) + \lambda_R \, \text{R}(W),$$

$$\text{where, } \text{R}(W) = ||W||_2. \tag{17.2}$$

Here, $Y_{d,t}$ and $Z_{d,t}$ are observations of temperature and density values, respectively, at depth d and time t, N is the total number of observations, (W, b) is the combined set of weights and bias terms across all components of **PGA**-LSTM, and λ_Z and λ_R are the trade-off parameters for the density prediction loss and regularization loss, respectively.

17.4 Evaluation Setup

In this section, we describe the data and experiment design, evaluation metrics, and baselines used in the empirical analyses of this chapter.

17.4.1 Data and Experiment Design

We chose Lake Mendota in Wisconsin, USA and Falling Creek Reservoir in Virginia, USA as two benchmark lakes to conduct our study on. These lakes differ in depth, size, and demonstrate a wide variation in climatic conditions, thus serving as ideal benchmarks. Lake Mendota is approximately 40 km^2 in surface area with a maximum depth of approximately 25 m. Lake Mendota is a dimictic lake with seasonal variation in water temperatures from 0° in the winter to nearly 30° in the summer. The overall data for lake Mendota consisted of 35,213 observations. Falling Creek Reservoir on the other hand is much smaller as compared to lake Mendota with approximately 0.119 km^2 in surface area with a maximum depth of 9.3 m [5]. Similar to Mendota, FCR is also dimictic and has seasonal variation in water temperatures from 0° in the winter to nearly 30° in the summer. The overall data for FCR consisted of 7588 observations [6].

The input drivers for both lakes comprised of the following features: day of year, depth, air temperature, shortwave radiation, longwave radiation, relative humidity, wind speed, rain, growing degree days, if the lake was frozen, and if it was snowing. With the exception of depth, all these variables were measured on the surface of the lake or calculated from meteorological datasets, and thus remained constant for a particular time t across all depths. The input features were also concatenated with simulated water temperature output generated by a physics-based model (GLM). The training and the test data were taken from two disjoint contiguous time windows such that there is no temporal auto-correlation between the training and test sets. Specifically, the first 4 years were used for training for both the lakes and the remainder were used for testing. The input X and density outputs Z were normalized to zero mean unity standard deviation; however, temperature output Y was not normalized. See [7] for detailed description of the data and model specifications [2]. To obtain uncertainty estimates, we used MC Dropout with a dropout probability of 0.2. Specifically, for each input we randomly created 100 different dropout networks to get a distribution on the model outputs.

17.4.2   Evaluation Metrics

We used the root mean square error (RMSE) of a model to measure its efficacy in predicting the lake water temperature accurately. To evaluate its physical consistency, we defined Physical Inconsistency as the fraction of times the MC sample predictions at consecutive depths are physically inconsistent, i.e., they violate the density-depth physics. We used a tolerance value of 10^{-5} kg/m^3 to determine if a difference in density across consecutive depths is physically inconsistent. Note that smaller values for both Test RMSE and Physical Inconsistency are preferred.

17.4.3   Baselines

To evaluate the efficacy of our model, we considered the following baselines: (1) *black-box* LSTM, and (2) PGL-LSTM, which utilizes an additional physics-guided loss term along with the standard empirical loss during the training phase. The physics-loss is computed by evaluating the physical inconsistency between every consecutive pair of depth output values. The architecture of all the LSTM models including our proposed **PGA**-LSTM were kept similar w.r.t. the number of layers and parameters in the network. In particular, all LSTM models had 8 memory units, which were followed by four fully connected layers with 5 neurons each, and finally an output layer.

17.5   Results

Figure 17.6 compares the performance of **PGA**-LSTM with baseline methods on Lake Mendota and FCR, using 40% data for training on both lakes. Our evaluation metrics of interest are the Test RMSE and Physical Inconsistency of the predicted temperature profiles. Both of these metrics can be evaluated either on the individual MC samples (referred to as *Per Sample*) or on the mean of the MC samples (referred to as *Mean*). (Note that we are interested in *Per Sample* evaluation as we want every MC sample to be accurate and physically consistent for the results to make sense in scientific applications.) From Figure 17.6(a), we can observe that for Lake Mendota the *black-box* LSTM has higher *Per Sample* Test RMSE, which indicates the limitations of black-box models in achieving good generalizability. Further, the *Per Sample* Physical inconsistency of LSTM is 0.32, which indicates that the MC samples generated from LSTM are physically inconsistent 32% of the time. Furthermore, defying the high expectations for PGL, PGL-LSTM shows little to no improvement over LSTM in either Test RMSE or Physical Inconsistency. By using MC Dropout during inference, a different dropout network is generated every time, which is a slightly perturbed version of the originally trained network. Ideally, we would want every dropout network to generate physically consistent predictions so that the final UQ analysis is meaningful. However, even after employing the PGL paradigm, the black-box nature of the PGL-LSTM model architecture is unaltered, and the perturbed networks generated by MC Dropout produce physically inconsistent predictions at a similar rate to *black-box* LSTM. This is because the dropout procedure injects a small amount of randomness in the neural network weights, which may be sufficient to *unlearn* the physical consistency introduced during training by the PGL paradigm. In contrast, the **PGA**-LSTM model shows the smallest *Per Sample* Test RMSE while ensuring that the predictions are always physically consistent even after applying MC dropout. Figure 17.6(b), demonstrates that if we compare the mean of the MC samples generated from each model, we can get lower

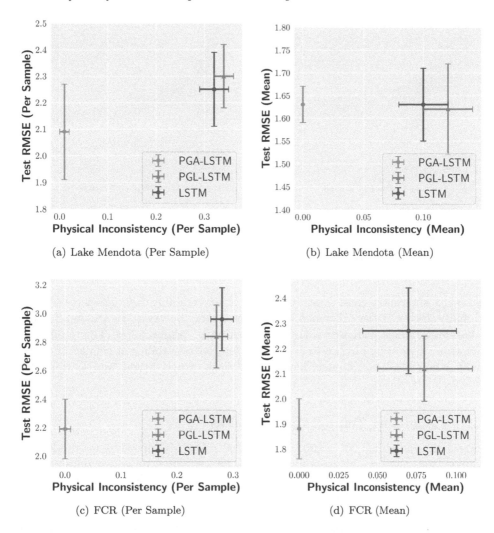

FIGURE 17.6
Comparing Test RMSE and Physical Inconsistency of baseline methods on Lake Mendota and FCR.

Mean Test RMSE, due to the cancellation of noise through aggregation. However, the *Mean* Physical Inconsistency of both LSTM and PGL-LSTM are still significantly high. Figures 17.6(c) and 17.6(d) show similar trends in the results of **PGA**-LSTM w.r.t. baseline methods on FCR.

17.5.1 Effect of Varying Training Size

Figure 17.7 shows the *Per Sample* Test RMSE of different methods on varying training fractions. We can observe that the test RMSE of all the methods increases as fewer training data-points are available for both Lake Mendota and FCR. Although Lake Mendota and FCR represent heavily studied water bodies, most of the lakes in the USA (and the world) have either very scarce observations or none at all. Hence, the goal of this analysis is to study the behavior of these models in low-data regimes, which are intended to simulate the real-world scenarios on other unseen lakes where temperature models have to be deployed.

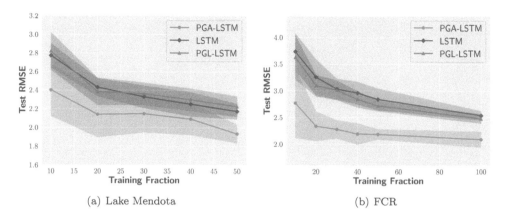

(a) Lake Mendota   (b) FCR

FIGURE 17.7
Test RMSE (*per sample*) on varying training sizes.

PGA-LSTM shows the least Test RMSE for every training fraction across both lakes. Additionally, for FCR the difference in the test RMSE between the **PGA**-LSTM and all other baseline models increases with the reduction in training size. This emphasises the benefits of incorporating physics to achieve better generalizability at smaller training sizes, especially when black-box models have higher risks of over-fitting and learning spurious patterns from the data.

17.5.2   Visualizing Temperature Profiles

To analyze the individual MC samples generated using MC dropout, we randomly select 15 samples from the pool of dropout MC samples generated on a test date across all 10 random runs of training. Figures 17.8(a), 17.8(b), and 17.8(c) show plots of the 15 sample temperature profiles generated by comparative models on a representative test date of October 15, 2013 in Lake Mendota, when trained on 40% data. It can be easily seen that each one of the individual sample profiles of LSTM and PGL-LSTM suffers from a number of physical inconsistencies, i.e., the profiles do not obey the monotonicity constraint with depth. Hence, even if the RMSE values are on par with other models, a lake scientist would be skeptical while using such predicted profiles in subsequent scientific analyses. On the other hand, **PGA**-LSTM is able to generate sample profiles that are always physically consistent, and hence are scientifically meaningful from the perspective of a domain expert.

Figures 17.8(d), 17.8(e), and 17.8(f) show the mean and variance of comparative models for the complete pool of dropout samples generated on this test date across all 10 random runs of training. The error bars in these plots represent two standard deviations around the mean (or equivalently the empirical coverage of the 95% Confidence Intervals). It can be observed that the mean profiles of the LSTM and PGL-LSTM closely follow the ground-truth profile and the error bars engulf the ground-truth predictions in the shallower portion of the lake (depth < 10 m). However, in deeper portions of the lake (depth > 10 m), the error bars of both LSTM and PGL-LSTM fail to contain the ground-truth predictions and the quality of the predictions deteriorate. On the contrary, the distribution of samples generated using **PGA**-LSTM accurately envelops the ground-truth observations at every portion of the lake irrespective of depth.[3]

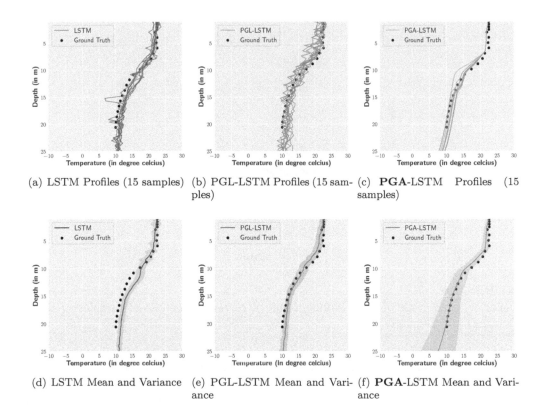

(a) LSTM Profiles (15 samples)

(b) PGL-LSTM Profiles (15 samples)

(c) **PGA**-LSTM Profiles (15 samples)

(d) LSTM Mean and Variance

(e) PGL-LSTM Mean and Variance

(f) **PGA**-LSTM Mean and Variance

FIGURE 17.8

Temperature profiles of comparative models on the same date for Lake Mendota.

17.5.3 Assessing Uncertainty Estimates

Although Figure 17.8(f) shows that the ground-truth observations lie in the 95% confidence intervals of the predictions of **PGA**-LSTM for a particular date in Lake Mendota, it fails to quantitatively validate our uncertainty estimates when compared to other baseline methods across all dates. In the ideal case, the uncertainty estimates of the predictions of a model should match the distribution of ground-truth observations on test points. In other words, if we look at the kth percentile of samples generated by an ideal model, then we should expect to observe $k\%$ of ground-truth test points to fall within it [3]. To capture this idea, we first fit a Gaussian distribution on the complete pool of samples generated by a model on a test point, and then estimate the two-tailed percentile of the ground-truth observed at that point. Figure 17.9 plots the cumulative percentage of ground-truth observations (Y-axis) that fall within a certain percentile of samples generated by comparative models (X-axis). Under the Gaussian assumption, the ideal model can be represented by the diagonal line $y = x$, where the percentage of ground-truth points within a percentile is equal to the percentile value. In general, models that tend to be over-confident would lie below the diagonal as they would have fewer ground truth estimates within a certain percentile. On the other hand, models that tend to be under-confident would lie above the $y = x$ diagonal. From Figure 17.9, it can be seen that both LSTM and PGL-LSTM lie slightly below the diagonal and hence would tend to produce slightly over-confident uncertainty estimates, i.e., the distribution of ground-truth points sometimes falls outside the distribution of MC samples. On the other hand, **PGA**-LSTM resides mostly above the diagonal and hence

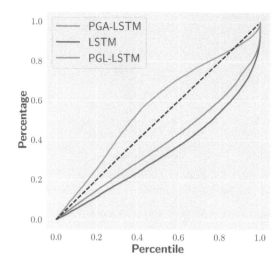

FIGURE 17.9
Cumulative percentage of observations within a certain percentile of samples of baseline models on Lake Mendota [3].

produces slightly larger uncertainty estimates than what is ideally expected. It is generally desirable to be slightly under-confident and produce wider uncertainty bounds than to be over-confident with narrower bounds when we have no prior knowledge about the ground-truth distribution of the test set. Further, in spite of having larger uncertainty bounds the **PGA**-LSTM produces lower *Per Sample* Test RMSE than all other baseline methods while always being physically consistent. This demonstrates that the uncertainty estimates are not only physically meaningful but also more accurate than the alternatives.

17.6   Conclusions and Future Work

This chapter explored a promising direction of research in the area of *theory-guided data science* that aims to move beyond traditional black-box neural network architectures. We presented a PGA of neural networks that is not only informed by physics but is also more robust and generalizable. We specifically developed a **PGA**-LSTM model for the problem of lake temperature modeling, comprising a *monotonicity-preserving* LSTM module that always produces physically consistent density estimates. We compared our **PGA**-LSTM model with baseline methods to demonstrate its ability to produce generalizable and physically consistent solutions, even after making minor perturbations in the network weights by the MC dropout method for uncertainty quantification.

In the future we aim to explore other applications of the proposed **PGA**-LSTM which show monotonic recurrence relationships. Other future works can also include studying the effect of other state-of-the-art uncertainty quantification methods with **PGA**-LSTM. We also intend to develop more generic PGA frameworks that can capture more complex forms of physical relationships in space and time. Future work can also study the impact of **PGA**-LSTM on physical interpretability of neural networks, since the features extracted at the hidden layers of the network should correspond to physically meaningful concepts.

Acknowledgment

We thank NSF DEB-1753639, DBI-1933016 and DBI-1933102 in support for the data collection at the Falling Creek Reservoir site. Any use of trade, firm, or product names is for descriptive purposes only and does not imply endorsement by the US Government.

Notes

[1]Depth is measured in the direction from lake surface to lake bottom.

[2]The codes for **PGA**-LSTM are available at Github: https://github.com/arkadaw9/ PGA_LSTM. The data used in this study are available at `https://zenodo.org/record/ 5193687#.YRXK2IhKhPY`.

[3]While Figure 17.8 provides results over a single test date in Lake Mendota, videos of the results for both lakes for all test dates are available at the following link : `https://drive. google.com/drive/folders/1IoPYhEhsO6134HvryUDoD-CCRE7hk3dy?usp=sharing`

Bibliography

[1] Brandon Anderson, Truong-Son Hy, and Risi Kondor. Cormorant: Covariant molecular neural networks. *arXiv preprint arXiv:1906.04015*, 2019.

[2] Tim Appenzeller. The scientists' apprentice. *Science*, 357(6346):16–17, 2017.

[3] Jochen Bröcker and Leonard A Smith. Increasing the reliability of reliability diagrams. *Weather and Forecasting*, 22(3):651–661, 2007.

[4] Peter M Caldwell, Christopher S Bretherton, Mark D Zelinka, Stephen A Klein, Benjamin D Santer, and Benjamin M Sanderson. Statistical significance of climate sensitivity predictors obtained by data mining. *Geophysical Research Letters*, 41(5):1803–1808, 2014.

[5] CC Carey, JP Doubek, RP McClure, and PC Hanson. Oxygen dynamics control the burial of organic carbon in a eutrophic reservoir. *Limnology and Oceanography-Letters*, 3:293–301, 2018.

[6] CC Carey, RP McClure, AB Gerling, JP Doubek, S Chen, ME Lofton, and KD Hamre. Time series of high-frequency profiles of depth, temperature, dissolved oxygen, conductivity, specific conductivity, chlorophyll a, turbidity, ph, and oxidation-reduction potential for beaverdam reservoir, carvins cove reservoir, falling creek reservoir, gatewood reservoir, and spring hollow reservoir in southwestern Virginia, USA, 2013–2018. *Environmental Data Initiative, link to dataset*, 2019.

[7] Arka Daw, R Quinn Thomas, Cayelan C Carey, Jordan S Read, Alison P Appling, and Anuj Karpatne. Physics-guided architecture (pga) of neural networks for quantifying uncertainty in lake temperature modeling. In *Proceedings of the 2020 Siam International Conference on Data Mining*, pages 532–540. SIAM, 2020.

[8] Meire Fortunato, Charles Blundell, and Oriol Vinyals. Bayesian recurrent neural networks. *arXiv:1704.02798*, 2017.

[9] Yarin Gal and Zoubin Ghahramani. Dropout as a bayesian approximation: Representing model uncertainty in deep learning. In *ICML*, pages 1050–1059, 2016.

[10] D Graham-Rowe, D Goldston, C Doctorow, M Waldrop, C Lynch, F Frankel, R Reid, S Nelson, D Howe, SY Rhee, et al. Big data: science in the petabyte era. *Nature*, 455(7209):8–9, 2008.

[11] Matthew R Hipsey, Louise C Bruce, Casper Boon, Brendan Busch, Cayelan C Carey, David P Hamilton, Paul C Hanson, Jordan S Read, Eduardo de Sousa, Michael Weber, et al. A general lake model (glm 3.0) for linking with high-frequency sensor data from the global lake ecological observatory network (gleon). *Geoscientific Model Development*, 12(1):473–523, 2019.

[12] Sepp Hochreiter and Jürgen Schmidhuber. Long short-term memory. *Neural Computation*, 9(8):1735–1780, 1997.

[13] Xiaowei Jia, Jared Willard, Anuj Karpatne, Jordan Read, Jacob Zwart, Michael Steinbach, and Vipin Kumar. Physics guided rnns for modeling dynamical systems: A case study in simulating lake temperature profiles. In *SDM*, pages 558–566. SIAM, 2019.

[14] TO Jonathan, AM Gerald, et al. Special issue: dealing with data. *Science*, 331(6018):639–806, 2011.

[15] Anuj Karpatne, Gowtham Atluri, James H Faghmous, Michael Steinbach, Arindam Banerjee, Auroop Ganguly, Shashi Shekhar, Nagiza Samatova, and Vipin Kumar. Theory-guided data science: A new paradigm for scientific discovery from data. *IEEE Transactions on Knowledge and Data Engineering*, 29(10):2318–2331, 2017.

[16] Anuj Karpatne, William Watkins, Jordan Read, and Vipin Kumar. Physics-guided neural networks (pgnn): An application in lake temperature modeling. *arXiv preprint arXiv:1710.11431*, 2017.

[17] Alex Krizhevsky, Ilya Sutskever, and Geoffrey E Hinton. Imagenet classification with deep convolutional neural networks. In *NIPS*, pages 1097–1105, 2012.

[18] David Lazer, Ryan Kennedy, Gary King, and Alessandro Vespignani. The parable of google flu: Traps in big data analysis. *Science (New York, N.Y.)*, 343(6176):1203–1205, 2014.

[19] Joel Z Leibo, Qianli Liao, Fabio Anselmi, Winrich A Freiwald, and Tomaso Poggio. View-tolerant face recognition and hebbian learning imply mirror-symmetric neural tuning to head orientation. *Current Biology*, 27(1):62–67, 2017.

[20] Julia Ling, Andrew Kurzawski, and Jeremy Templeton. Reynolds averaged turbulence modelling using deep neural networks with embedded invariance. *Journal of Fluid Mechanics*, 807:155–166, 2016.

[21] John J Magnuson, Larry B Crowder, and Patricia A Medvick. Temperature as an ecological resource. *American Zoologist*, 19(1):331–343, 1979.

[22] Gary Marcus and Ernest Davis. Eight (no, nine!) problems with big data. *The New York Times*, 6(04):2014, 2014.

[23] Pablo Márquez-Neila, Mathieu Salzmann, and Pascal Fua. Imposing hard constraints on deep networks: Promises and limitations. *arXiv:1706.02025*, 2017.

[24] James M Murphy, David MH Sexton, David N Barnett, Gareth S Jones, Mark J Webb, Matthew Collins, and David A Stainforth. Quantification of modelling uncertainties in a large ensemble of climate change simulations. *Nature*, 430(7001):768, 2004.

[25] Deepak Pathak, Philipp Krahenbuhl, and Trevor Darrell. Constrained convolutional neural networks for weakly supervised segmentation. In *ICCV*, pages 1796–1804, 2015.

[26] James J Roberts, Kurt D Fausch, Douglas P Peterson, and Mevin B Hooten. Fragmentation and thermal risks from climate change interact to affect persistence of native trout in the colorado river basin. *Global Change Biology*, 19(5):1383–1398, 2013.

[27] Terrence J Sejnowski, Patricia S Churchland, and J Anthony Movshon. Putting big data to good use in neuroscience. *Nature Neuroscience*, 17(11):1440–1441, 2014.

[28] Nitish Srivastava, Geoffrey Hinton, Alex Krizhevsky, Ilya Sutskever, and Ruslan Salakhutdinov. Dropout: a simple way to prevent neural networks from overfitting. *JMLR*, 15(1):1929–1958, 2014.

[29] Nitish Srivastava, Elman Mansimov, and Ruslan Salakhutdinov. Unsupervised learning of video representations using LSTMs. In *ICML*, ICML'15, pages 843–852. JMLR.org, 2015.

[30] Russell Stewart and Stefano Ermon. Label-free supervision of neural networks with physics and domain knowledge. In *AAAI*, 2017.

[31] Jingyi Xu, Zilu Zhang, Tal Friedman, Yitao Liang, and Guy Van den Broeck. A semantic loss function for deep learning with symbolic knowledge. *arXiv preprint arXiv:1711.11157*, 2017.

Index

Note: Page numbers in italics refer to figures and in bold refer to tables.